iPhone iOS 6 Development Essentials

iPhone iOS 6 Development Essentials – First Edition

ISBN-13: 978-1479211418

© 2012 Neil Smyth. All Rights Reserved.

This book is provided for personal use only. Unauthorized use, reproduction and/or distribution strictly prohibited. All rights reserved.

The content of this book is provided for informational purposes only. Neither the publisher nor the author offers any warranties or representation, express or implied, with regard to the accuracy of information contained in this book, nor do they accept any liability for any loss or damage arising from any errors or omissions.

This book contains trademarked terms that are used solely for editorial purposes and to the benefit of the respective trademark owner. The terms used within this book are not intended as infringement of any trademarks.

Rev 1.0h

Table of Contents

1. **Start Here** 1
   1.1 For New iOS Developers 1
   1.2 For iOS 5 Developers 2
   1.3 Source Code Download 3
   1.4 Feedback 3
   1.5 Errata 3

2. **Joining the Apple iOS Developer Program** 5
   2.1 Registered Apple Developer 5
   2.2 Downloading Xcode and the iOS 6 SDK 5
   2.3 iOS Developer Program 5
   2.4 When to Enroll in the iOS Developer Program? 6
   2.5 Enrolling in the iOS Developer Program 6
   2.6 Summary 8

3. **Installing Xcode 4 and the iOS 6 SDK** 9
   3.1 Identifying if you have an Intel or PowerPC based Mac 9
   3.2 Installing Xcode 4 and the iOS 6 SDK 10
   3.3 Starting Xcode 10

4. **Creating a Simple iPhone iOS 6 App** 13
   4.1 Starting Xcode 4 13
   4.2 Creating the iOS App User Interface 18
   4.3 Changing Component Properties 20
   4.4 Adding Objects to the User Interface 20
   4.5 Building and Running an iOS App in Xcode 4 21
   4.6 Dealing with Build Errors 22
   4.7 Testing Different Screen Sizes 22

5. **iOS 6 Architecture and SDK Frameworks** 25
   5.1 iPhone OS becomes iOS 25
   5.2 An Overview of the iOS 6 Architecture 25
   5.3 The Cocoa Touch Layer 26
     5.3.1 UIKit Framework (UIKit.framework) 27
     5.3.2 Map Kit Framework (MapKit.framework) 28
     5.3.3 Push Notification Service 28
     5.3.4 Message UI Framework (MessageUI.framework) 28
     5.3.5 Address Book UI Framework (AddressUI.framework) 28
     5.3.6 Game Kit Framework (GameKit.framework) 28

5.3.7 iAd Framework (iAd.framework) 29
5.3.8 Event Kit UI Framework (EventKit.framework) 29
5.3.9 Accounts Framework (Accounts.framework) 29
5.3.10 Social Framework (Social.framework) 29
5.4 The iOS Media Layer 29
5.4.1 Core Video Framework (CoreVideo.framework) 29
5.4.2 Core Text Framework (CoreText.framework) 29
5.4.3 Image I/O Framework (ImageIO.framework) 29
5.4.4 Assets Library Framework (AssetsLibrary.framework) 30
5.4.5 Core Graphics Framework (CoreGraphics.framework) 30
5.4.6 Core Image Framework (CoreImage.framework) 30
5.4.7 Quartz Core Framework (QuartzCore.framework) 30
5.4.8 OpenGL ES framework (OpenGLES.framework) 30
5.4.9 GLKit Framework (GLKit.framework) 31
5.4.10 NewsstandKit Framework (NewsstandKit.framework) 31
5.4.11 iOS Audio Support 31
5.4.12 AV Foundation framework (AVFoundation.framework) 31
5.4.13 Core Audio Frameworks (CoreAudio.framework, AudioToolbox.framework and AudioUnit.framework) 31
5.4.14 Open Audio Library (OpenAL) 31
5.4.15 Media Player Framework (MediaPlayer.framework) 31
5.4.16 Core Midi Framework (CoreMIDI.framework) 31
5.5 The iOS Core Services Layer 32
5.5.1 Address Book Framework (AddressBook.framework) 32
5.5.2 CFNetwork Framework (CFNetwork.framework) 32
5.5.3 Core Data Framework (CoreData.framework) 32
5.5.4 Core Foundation Framework (CoreFoundation.framework) 32
5.5.5 Core Media Framework (CoreMedia.framework) 32
5.5.6 Core Telephony Framework (CoreTelephony.framework) 32
5.5.7 EventKit Framework (EventKit.framework) 33
5.6 Foundation Framework (Foundation.framework) 33
5.6.1 Core Location Framework (CoreLocation.framework) 33
5.6.2 Mobile Core Services Framework (MobileCoreServices.framework) 33
5.6.3 Store Kit Framework (StoreKit.framework) 33
5.6.4 SQLite library 33
5.6.5 System Configuration Framework (SystemConfiguration.framework) 34
5.6.6 Quick Look Framework (QuickLook.framework) 34
5.7 The iOS Core OS Layer 34
5.7.1 Accelerate Framework (Accelerate.framework) 34
5.7.2 External Accessory Framework (ExternalAccessory.framework) 34
5.7.3 Security Framework (Security.framework) 34

5.7.4 System (LibSystem) 34

6. Testing iOS 6 Apps on the iPhone – Developer Certificates and Provisioning Profiles 37

6.1 Creating an iOS Development Certificate Signing Request 37
6.2 Submitting the iOS Development Certificate Signing Request 40
6.3 Installing an iOS Development Certificate 41
6.4 Assigning Devices 42
6.5 Creating an App ID 43
6.6 Creating an iOS Development Provisioning Profile 44
6.7 Enabling an iPhone Device for Development 45
6.8 Associating an App ID with an App 45
6.9 iOS and SDK Version Compatibility 46
6.10 Installing an App onto a Device 47
6.11 Summary 47

7. The Basics of Objective-C Programming 49

7.1 Objective-C Data Types and Variables 49
7.2 Objective-C Expressions 50
7.3 Objective-C Flow Control with if and else 53
7.4 Looping with the for Statement 55
7.5 Objective-C Looping with do and while 55
7.6 Objective-C do ... while loops 56

8. The Basics of Object Oriented Programming in Objective-C 57

8.1 What is an Object? 57
8.2 What is a Class? 57
8.3 Declaring an Objective-C Class Interface 57
8.4 Adding Instance Variables to a Class 58
8.5 Define Class Methods 59
8.6 Declaring an Objective-C Class Implementation 60
8.7 Declaring and Initializing a Class Instance 61
8.8 Automatic Reference Counting (ARC) 61
8.9 Calling Methods and Accessing Instance Data 62
8.10 Objective-C and Dot Notation 62
8.11 How Variables are Stored 63
8.12 An Overview of Indirection 64
8.13 Indirection and Objects 66
8.14 Indirection and Object Copying 66
8.15 Creating the Program Section 67
8.16 Bringing it all Together 68
8.17 Structuring Object-Oriented Objective-C Code 70

v

9. The Basics of Modern Objective-C ... 73
9.1 Default Property Synthesis ... 73
9.2 Method Ordering ... 75
9.3 NSNumber Literals ... 75
9.4 Array Literals ... 76
9.5 Dictionary Literals ... 77
9.6 Summary ... 77

10. An Overview of the iPhone iOS 6 Application Development Architecture ... 79
10.1 Model View Controller (MVC) ... 79
10.2 The Target-Action pattern, IBOutlets and IBActions ... 80
10.3 Subclassing ... 81
10.4 Delegation ... 81
10.5 Summary ... 82

11. Creating an Interactive iOS 6 iPhone App ... 83
11.1 Creating the New Project ... 83
11.2 Creating the User Interface ... 83
11.3 Building and Running the Sample Application ... 86
11.4 Adding Actions and Outlets ... 86
11.5 Connecting the Actions and Outlets to the User Interface ... 89
11.6 Building and Running the Finished Application ... 93
11.7 Summary ... 94

12. Writing iOS 6 Code to Hide the iPhone Keyboard ... 95
12.1 Creating the Example App ... 95
12.2 Hiding the Keyboard when the User Touches the Return Key ... 96
12.3 Hiding the Keyboard when the User Taps the Background ... 97
12.4 Summary ... 99

13. Establishing Outlets and Actions using the Xcode Assistant Editor ... 101
13.1 Displaying the Assistant Editor ... 101
13.2 Using the Assistant Editor ... 103
13.3 Adding an Outlet using the Assistant Editor ... 103
13.4 Adding an Action using the Assistant Editor ... 105
13.5 Summary ... 106

14. Understanding iPhone iOS 6 Views, Windows and the View Hierarchy ... 107
14.1 An Overview of Views ... 107
14.2 The UIWindow Class ... 107
14.3 The View Hierarchy ... 108

14.4 View Types 110
   14.4.1 The Window 110
   14.4.2 Container Views 111
   14.4.3 Controls 111
   14.4.4 Display Views 111
   14.4.5 Text and Web Views 111
   14.4.6 Navigation Views and Tab Bars 111
   14.4.7 Alert Views and Action Sheets 111
14.5 Summary 111

15. An Introduction to Auto Layout in iOS 6 113

15.1 An Overview of Auto Layout 113
15.2 Alignment Rects 115
15.3 Intrinsic Content Size 115
15.4 Content Hugging and Compression Resistance Priorities 115
15.5 Three Ways to Create Constraints 115
15.6 Constraints in more Detail 116
15.7 Summary 117

16. Working with iOS 6 Auto Layout Constraints in Interface Builder 119

16.1 A Simple Example of Auto Layout in Action 119
16.2 Enabling and Disabling Auto Layout in Interface Builder 119
16.3 The Auto Layout Features of Interface Builder 123
   16.3.1 Automatic Constraints 123
   16.3.2 Visual Cues 124
   16.3.3 Viewing and Editing Constraints Details 125
16.4 Creating New Constraints in Interface Builder 127
16.5 Summary 128

17. An iPhone iOS 6 Auto Layout Example 129

17.1 Preparing the Project 129
17.2 Designing the User Interface 129
17.3 Adjusting Constraint Priorities 131
17.4 Alignment and Width Equality 135
17.5 Testing the Application 137
17.6 Summary 137

18. Implementing iOS 6 Auto Layout Constraints in Code 139

18.1 Creating Constraints in Code 139
18.2 Adding a Constraint to a View 141
18.3 Turning off Auto Resizing Translation 142
18.4 An Example Application 142

vii

18.5 Creating the Views 142
18.6 Creating and Adding the Constraints 143
18.7 Removing Constraints 145
18.8 Summary 145

19. Implementing Cross-Hierarchy Auto Layout Constraints in iOS 6 147

19.1 The Example Application 147
19.2 Establishing Outlets 148
19.3 Writing the Code to Remove the Old Constraint 149
19.4 Adding the Cross Hierarchy Constraint 150
19.5 Testing the Application 150
19.6 Summary 150

20. Understanding the iOS 6 Auto Layout Visual Format Language 153

20.1 Introducing the Visual Format Language 153
20.2 Visual Language Format Examples 153
20.3 Using the constraintsWithVisualFormat: Method 155
20.4 Summary 156

21. Using Xcode Storyboarding 157

21.1 Creating the Storyboard Example Project 157
21.2 Accessing the Storyboard 157
21.3 Adding Scenes to the Storyboard 159
21.4 Configuring Storyboard Segues 161
21.5 Configuring Storyboard Transitions 161
21.6 Associating a View Controller with a Scene 162
21.7 Passing Data Between Scenes 164
21.8 Unwinding Storyboard Segues 165
21.9 Triggering a Storyboard Segue Programmatically 166
21.10 Summary 167

22. Using Xcode Storyboards to Create an iOS 6 iPhone Tab Bar Application 169

22.1 An Overview of the Tab Bar 169
22.2 Understanding View Controllers in a Multiview Application 169
22.3 Setting up the Tab Bar Example Application 170
22.4 Reviewing the Project Files 170
22.5 Renaming the Initial View Controller 171
22.6 Adding the View Controller for the Second Content View 171
22.7 Adding the Tab Bar Controller to the Storyboard 171
22.8 Adding a Second View Controller to the Storyboard 173
22.9 Designing the View Controller User interfaces 174
22.10 Configuring the Tab Bar Items 175

22.11 Building and Running the Application 176
22.12 Summary 177

23. An Overview of iOS 6 Table Views and Xcode Storyboards 179

23.1 An Overview of the Table View 179
23.2 Static vs. Dynamic Table Views... 179
23.3 The Table View Delegate and dataSource 180
23.4 Table View Styles... 180
23.5 Table View Cell Styles 181
23.6 Table View Cell Reuse... 181
23.7 Summary 183

24. Using Xcode Storyboards to Build Dynamic TableViews with Prototype Table View Cells 185

24.1 Creating the Example Project 185
24.2 Adding the TableView Controller to the Storyboard 186
24.3 Creating the UITableViewController and UITableViewCell Subclasses 187
24.4 Declaring the Cell Reuse Identifier 188
24.5 Designing a Storyboard UITableView Prototype Cell 188
24.6 Modifying the CarTableViewCell Class 189
24.7 Creating the Table View Datasource 190
24.8 Downloading and Adding the Image Files 194
24.9 Compiling and Running the Application 194
24.10 Summary 195

25. Implementing TableView Navigation using Xcode Storyboards... 197

25.1 Understanding the Navigation Controller 197
25.2 Adding the New Scene to the Storyboard 198
25.3 Adding a Navigation Controller 199
25.4 Establishing the Storyboard Segue 199
25.5 Modifying the CarDetailViewController Class 200
25.6 Using prepareForSegue: to Pass Data between Storyboard Scenes 202
25.7 Testing the Application... 203
25.8 Summary 204

26. Using an Xcode Storyboard to Create a Static Table View 205

26.1 An Overview of the Static Table Project... 205
26.2 Creating the Project.. 205
26.3 Adding a Table View Controller 206
26.4 Changing the Table View Content Type 206
26.5 Designing the Static Table 207
26.6 Adding Items to the Table Cells.. 208
26.7 Modifying the StaticTableViewController Class 211

26.8 Building and Running the Application 211
26.9 Summary 212

27. Implementing a Page based iOS 6 iPhone Application using UIPageViewController 213

27.1 The UIPageViewController Class 213
27.2 The UIPageViewController DataSource 213
27.3 Navigation Orientation 214
27.4 Spine Location 214
27.5 The UIPageViewController Delegate Protocol 215
27.6 Summary 215

28. An Example iOS 6 iPhone UIPageViewController Application 217

28.1 The Xcode Page-based Application Template 217
28.2 Creating the Project 217
28.3 Adding the Content View Controller 218
28.4 Creating the Data Model 220
28.5 Initializing the UIPageViewController 224
28.6 Running the UIPageViewController Application 226
28.7 Summary 227

29. Using the UIPickerView and UIDatePicker Components 229

29.1 The DatePicker and PickerView Components 229
29.2 A DatePicker Example 230
29.3 Designing the User Interface 230
29.4 Coding the Date Picker Example Functionality 231
29.5 Building and Running the iPhone Date Picker Application 232

30. An iOS 6 iPhone UIPickerView Example 233

30.1 Creating the iOS 6 PickerView Project 233
30.2 UIPickerView Delegate and DataSource 233
30.3 The PickerViewController.h File 234
30.4 Designing the User Interface 234
30.5 Initializing the Arrays 236
30.6 Implementing the DataSource Protocol 236
30.7 Implementing the Delegate Protocol 237
30.8 Hiding the Keyboard 238
30.9 Testing the Application 238

31. Working with Directories on iOS 6 239

31.1 The Application Documents Directory 239
31.2 The Objective-C NSFileManager, NSFileHandle and NSData Classes 240
31.3 Understanding Pathnames in Objective-C 240

31.4 Obtaining a Reference to the Default NSFileManager Object 240
31.5 Identifying the Current Working Directory 241
31.6 Identifying the Documents Directory 241
31.7 Identifying the Temporary Directory 242
31.8 Changing Directory 242
31.9 Creating a New Directory 243
31.10 Deleting a Directory 244
31.11 Listing the Contents of a Directory 245
31.12 Getting the Attributes of a File or Directory 245

32. Working with iPhone Files on iOS 6 247

32.1 Creating an NSFileManager Instance 247
32.2 Checking for the Existence of a File 247
32.3 Comparing the Contents of Two Files 248
32.4 Checking if a File is Readable/Writable/Executable/Deletable 248
32.5 Moving/Renaming a File 249
32.6 Copying a File 249
32.7 Removing a File 249
32.8 Creating a Symbolic Link 250
32.9 Reading and Writing Files with NSFileManager 250
32.10 Working with Files using the NSFileHandle Class 251
32.11 Creating an NSFileHandle Object 251
32.12 NSFileHandle File Offsets and Seeking 251
32.13 Reading Data from a File 252
32.14 Writing Data to a File 253
32.15 Truncating a File 253
32.16 Summary 254

33. iOS 6 iPhone Directory Handling and File I/O – A Worked Example 255

33.1 The Example iPhone Application 255
33.2 Setting up the Application project 255
33.3 Designing the User Interface 255
33.4 Checking the Data File on Application Startup 256
33.5 Implementing the Action Method 258
33.6 Building and Running the Example 258

34. Preparing an iOS 6 App to use iCloud Storage 261

34.1 What is iCloud? 261
34.2 iCloud Data Storage Services 261
34.3 Preparing an Application to Use iCloud Storage 262
34.4 Creating an iOS 6 iCloud enabled App ID 262

xi

34.5 Creating and Installing an iCloud Enabled Provisioning Profile 263
34.6 Creating an iCloud Entitlements File 264
34.7 Manually Creating the Entitlements File 265
34.8 Accessing Multiple Ubiquity Containers 266
34.9 Ubiquity Container URLs 267
34.10 Summary 267

35. Managing Files using the iOS 6 UIDocument Class 269

35.1 An Overview of the UIDocument Class 269
35.2 Subclassing the UIDocument Class 269
35.3 Conflict Resolution and Document States 270
35.4 The UIDocument Example Application 270
35.5 Creating a UIDocument Subclass 271
35.6 Designing the User Interface 271
35.7 Implementing the Application Data Structure 272
35.8 Implementing the contentsForType Method 272
35.9 Implementing the loadFromContents Method 273
35.10 Loading the Document at App Launch 273
35.11 Saving Content to the Document 277
35.12 Testing the Application 277
35.13 Summary 277

36. Using iCloud Storage in an iOS 6 iPhone Application 279

36.1 iCloud Usage Guidelines 279
36.2 Preparing the iCloudStore Application for iCloud Access 280
36.3 Configuring the View Controller 280
36.4 Implementing the viewDidLoad Method 281
36.5 Implementing the metadataQueryDidFinishGathering: Method 284
36.6 Implementing the saveDocument Method 287
36.7 Enabling iCloud Document and Data Storage on an iPhone 287
36.8 Running the iCloud Application 288
36.9 Reviewing and Deleting iCloud Based Documents 288
36.10 Making a Local File Ubiquitous 289
36.11 Summary 290

37. Synchronizing iPhone iOS 6 Key-Value Data using iCloud 291

37.1 An Overview of iCloud Key-Value Data Storage 291
37.2 Sharing Data Between Applications 292
37.3 Data Storage Restrictions 292
37.4 Conflict Resolution 292
37.5 Receiving Notification of Key-Value Changes 293

37.6 An iCloud Key-Value Data Storage Example 293
37.7 Enabling the Application for iCloud Key Value Data Storage 293
37.8 Designing the User Interface 294
37.9 Implementing the View Controller 295
37.10 Modifying the viewDidLoad Method 295
37.11 Implementing the Notification Method 296
37.12 Implementing the saveData Method 296
37.13 Testing the Application 297

38. iOS 6 iPhone Data Persistence using Archiving 299

38.1 An Overview of Archiving 299
38.2 The Archiving Example Application 300
38.3 Designing the User Interface 300
38.4 Checking for the Existence of the Archive File on Startup 302
38.5 Archiving Object Data in the Action Method 303
38.6 Testing the Application 304
38.7 Summary 305

39. iOS 6 iPhone Database Implementation using SQLite 307

39.1 What is SQLite? 307
39.2 Structured Query Language (SQL) 308
39.3 Trying SQLite on MacOS X 308
39.4 Preparing an iPhone Application Project for SQLite Integration 309
39.5 Key SQLite Functions 310
39.6 Declaring a SQLite Database 311
39.7 Opening or Creating a Database 311
39.8 Preparing and Executing a SQL Statement 312
39.9 Creating a Database Table 312
39.10 Extracting Data from a Database Table 313
39.11 Closing a SQLite Database 314
39.12 Summary 314

40. An Example SQLite based iOS 6 iPhone Application 315

40.1 About the Example SQLite iPhone Application 315
40.2 Creating and Preparing the SQLite Application Project 315
40.3 Importing sqlite3.h and declaring the Database Reference 316
40.4 Designing the User Interface 316
40.5 Creating the Database and Table 317
40.6 Implementing the Code to Save Data to the SQLite Database 319
40.7 Implementing Code to Extract Data from the SQLite Database 320
40.8 Building and Running the Application 321

xiii

40.9 Summary 322

41. Working with iOS 6 iPhone Databases using Core Data 323

41.1 The Core Data Stack 323
41.2 Managed Objects 324
41.3 Managed Object Context 324
41.4 Managed Object Model 325
41.5 Persistent Store Coordinator 325
41.6 Persistent Object Store 325
41.7 Defining an Entity Description 326
41.8 Obtaining the Managed Object Context 327
41.9 Getting an Entity Description 327
41.10 Creating a Managed Object 328
41.11 Getting and Setting the Attributes of a Managed Object 328
41.12 Fetching Managed Objects 328
41.13 Retrieving Managed Objects based on Criteria 329
41.14 Summary 329

42. An iOS 6 iPhone Core Data Tutorial 331

42.1 The iPhone Core Data Example Application 331
42.2 Creating a Core Data based iPhone Application 331
42.3 Creating the Entity Description 331
42.4 Adding a View Controller 333
42.5 Designing the User Interface 334
42.6 Saving Data to the Persistent Store using Core Data 335
42.7 Retrieving Data from the Persistent Store using Core Data 336
42.8 Building and Running the Example Application 337
42.9 Summary 338

43. An Overview of iOS 6 iPhone Multitouch, Taps and Gestures 339

43.1 The Responder Chain 339
43.2 Forwarding an Event to the Next Responder 340
43.3 Gestures 340
43.4 Taps 340
43.5 Touches 340
43.6 Touch Notification Methods 340
    43.6.1 touchesBegan method *341*
    43.6.2 touchesMoved method *341*
    43.6.3 touchesEnded method *341*
    43.6.4 touchesCancelled method *341*
43.7 Summary 341

44. An Example iOS 6 iPhone Touch, Multitouch and Tap Application 343
44.1 The Example iOS 6 iPhone Tap and Touch Application 343
44.2 Creating the Example iOS Touch Project 343
44.3 Designing the User Interface 343
44.4 Enabling Multitouch on the View 344
44.5 Implementing the touchesBegan Method 345
44.6 Implementing the touchesMoved Method 345
44.7 Implementing the touchesEnded Method 346
44.8 Getting the Coordinates of a Touch 346
44.9 Building and Running the Touch Example Application 347

45. Detecting iOS 6 iPhone Touch Screen Gesture Motions 349
45.1 The Example iOS 6 iPhone Gesture Application 349
45.2 Creating the Example Project 349
45.3 Designing the Application User Interface 349
45.4 Implementing the touchesBegan Method 351
45.5 Implementing the touchesMoved Method 351
45.6 Implementing the touchesEnded Method 351
45.7 Building and Running the Gesture Example 352
45.8 Summary 352

46. Identifying iPhone Gestures using iOS 6 Gesture Recognizers 353
46.1 The UIGestureRecognizer Class 353
46.2 Recognizer Action Messages 354
46.3 Discrete and Continuous Gestures 354
46.4 Obtaining Data from a Gesture 354
46.5 Recognizing Tap Gestures 354
46.6 Recognizing Pinch Gestures 355
46.7 Detecting Rotation Gestures 355
46.8 Recognizing Pan and Dragging Gestures 355
46.9 Recognizing Swipe Gestures 356
46.10 Recognizing Long Touch (Touch and Hold) Gestures 356
46.11 Summary 357

47. An iPhone iOS 6 Gesture Recognition Tutorial 359
47.1 Creating the Gesture Recognition Project 359
47.2 Designing the User Interface 359
47.3 Implementing the Action Methods 361
47.4 Testing the Gesture Recognition Application 362

48. An Overview of iOS 6 Collection View and Flow Layout 363

48.1 An Overview of Collection Views 363
48.2 The UICollectionView Class 366
48.3 The UICollectionViewCell Class 366
48.4 The UICollectionReusableView Class 367
48.5 The UICollectionViewFlowLayout Class 367
48.6 The UICollectionViewLayoutAttributes Class 367
48.7 The UICollectionViewDataSource Protocol 368
48.8 The UICollectionViewDelegate Protocol 369
48.9 The UICollectionViewDelegateFlowLayout Protocol 369
48.10 Cell and View Reuse 370
48.11 Summary 372

49. An iPhone iOS 6 Storyboard-based Collection View Tutorial 373

49.1 Creating the Collection View Example Project 373
49.2 Removing the Template View Controller 373
49.3 Adding a Collection View Controller to the Storyboard 374
49.4 Adding the Collection View Cell Class to the Project 375
49.5 Designing the Cell Prototype 376
49.6 Implementing the Data Model 377
49.7 Implementing the Data Source 378
49.8 Testing the Application 380
49.9 Setting Sizes for Cell Items 381
49.10 Changing Scroll Direction 382
49.11 Implementing a Supplementary View 383
49.12 Implementing the Supplementary View Protocol Methods 385
49.13 Deleting Collection View Items 387
49.14 Summary 388

50. Subclassing and Extending the iOS 6 Collection View Flow Layout 389

50.1 About the Example Layout Class 389
50.2 Subclassing the UICollectionViewFlowLayout Class 389
50.3 Extending the New Layout Class 390
50.4 Implementing the layoutAttributesForItemAtIndexPath: Method 390
50.5 Implementing the layoutAttributesForElementsInRect: Method 392
50.6 Implementing the modifyLayoutAttributes: Method 392
50.7 Adding the New Layout and Pinch Gesture Recognizer 393
50.8 Implementing the Pinch Recognizer 394
50.9 Avoiding Image Clipping 397
50.10 Adding the QuartzCore Framework to the Project 397
50.11 Testing the Application 397
50.12 Summary 398

51. Drawing iOS 6 iPhone 2D Graphics with Quartz 399
51.1 Introducing Core Graphics and Quartz 2D... 399
51.2 The drawRect Method.. 399
51.3 Points, Coordinates and Pixels 400
51.4 The Graphics Context 400
51.5 Working with Colors in Quartz 2D.. 400
51.6 Summary 402

52. An iOS 6 iPhone Graphics Tutorial using Quartz 2D and Core Image 403
52.1 The iOS iPhone Drawing Example Application 403
52.2 Creating the New Project 403
52.3 Creating the UIView Subclass 403
52.4 Locating the drawRect Method in the UIView Subclass.. 404
52.5 Drawing a Line 405
52.6 Drawing Paths 407
52.7 Drawing a Rectangle... 408
52.8 Drawing an Ellipse or Circle 409
52.9 Filling a Path with a Color 410
52.10 Drawing an Arc 412
52.11 Drawing a Cubic Bézier Curve 413
52.12 Drawing a Quadratic Bézier Curve.. 414
52.13 Dashed Line Drawing.. 415
52.14 Drawing an Image into a Graphics Context 416
52.15 Image Filtering with the Core Image Framework.. 418
52.16 Summary 419

53. Basic iOS 6 iPhone Animation using Core Animation 421
53.1 UIView Core Animation Blocks 421
53.2 Understanding Animation Curves 422
53.3 Receiving Notification of Animation Completion 422
53.4 Performing Affine Transformations... 423
53.5 Combining Transformations 423
53.6 Creating the Animation Example Application 424
53.7 Implementing the Interface File 424
53.8 Drawing in the UIView... 424
53.9 Detecting Screen Touches and Performing the Animation 425
53.10 Building and Running the Animation Application 426
53.11 Summary 427

54. Integrating iAds into an iOS 6 iPhone App 429
54.1 iOS iPhone Advertising Options.. 429

54.2 iAds Advertisement Formats 430
54.3 Basic Rules for the Display of iAds 430
54.4 Creating an Example iAds iPhone Application 431
54.5 Adding the iAds Framework to the Xcode Project 431
54.6 Configuring the View Controller 431
54.7 Designing the User Interface 432
54.8 Creating the Banner Ad 433
54.9 Displaying the Ad 433
54.10 Implementing the Delegate Methods 435
    54.10.1 bannerViewActionShouldBegin 435
    54.10.2 bannerViewActionDidFinish 436
    54.10.3 bannerView:didFailToReceiveAdWithError 436
    54.10.4 bannerViewWillLoadAd 436
54.11 Summary 436

55. An Overview of iOS 6 iPhone Multitasking 437

55.1 Understanding iOS Application States 437
55.2 A Brief Overview of the Multitasking Application Lifecycle 438
55.3 Disabling Multitasking for an iOS Application 439
55.4 Checking for Multitasking Support 440
55.5 Supported Forms of Background Execution 440
55.6 The Rules of Background Execution 442
55.7 Scheduling Local Notifications 442

56. Scheduling iOS 6 iPhone Local Notifications 443

56.1 Creating the Local Notification iPhone App Project 443
56.2 Locating the Application Delegate Method 443
56.3 Adding a Sound File to the Project 444
56.4 Scheduling the Local Notification 444
56.5 Testing the Application 445
56.6 Cancelling Scheduled Notifications 446
56.7 Immediate Triggering of a Local Notification 446
56.8 Summary 446

57. An Overview of iOS 6 Application State Preservation and Restoration 447

57.1 The Preservation and Restoration Process 447
57.2 Opting In to Preservation and Restoration 448
57.3 Assigning Restoration Identifiers 449
57.4 Default Preservation Features of UIKit 450
57.5 Saving and Restoring Additional State Information 450
57.6 Understanding the Restoration Process 451

57.7 Saving General Application State 452

57.8 Summary 453

58. An iOS 6 iPhone State Preservation and Restoration Tutorial 455

58.1 Creating the Example Application 455

58.2 Trying the Application without State Preservation 455

58.3 Opting-in to State Preservation 456

58.4 Setting Restoration Identifiers 456

58.5 Encoding and Decoding View Controller State 457

58.6 Adding a Navigation Controller to the Storyboard 459

58.7 Adding the Third View Controller 461

58.8 Creating the Restoration Class 463

58.9 Summary 464

59. Integrating Maps into iPhone iOS 6 Applications using MKMapItem 465

59.1 MKMapItem and MKPlacemark Classes 465

59.2 An Introduction to Forward and Reverse Geocoding 466

59.3 Creating MKPlacemark Instances 468

59.4 Working with MKMapItem 469

59.5 MKMapItem Options and Enabling Turn-by-Turn Directions 470

59.6 Adding Item Details to an MKMapItem 471

59.7 Summary 473

60. An Example iOS 6 iPhone MKMapItem Application 475

60.1 Creating the MapItem Project 475

60.2 Designing the User Interface 475

60.3 Converting the Destination using Forward Geocoding 477

60.4 Launching the Map 478

60.5 Adding Build Libraries 479

60.6 Building and Running the Application 479

60.7 Summary 480

61. Getting iPhone Location Information using the iOS 6 Core Location Framework 481

61.1 The Basics of Core Location 481

61.2 Configuring the Desired Location Accuracy 482

61.3 Configuring the Distance Filter 482

61.4 The Location Manager Delegate 482

61.5 Obtaining Location Information from CLLocation Objects 483

61.5.1 Longitude and Latitude 483

61.5.2 Accuracy 483

61.5.3 Altitude 484

61.6 Calculating Distances 484

xix

61.7 Location Information and Multitasking 484
61.8 Summary 484

62. An Example iOS 6 iPhone Location Application 485

62.1 Creating the Example iOS 6 iPhone Location Project 485
62.2 Adding the Core Location Framework to the Project 485
62.3 Designing the User Interface 485
62.4 Creating the CLLocationManager Object 487
62.5 Implementing the Action Method 488
62.6 Implementing the Application Delegate Methods 488
62.7 Building and Running the iPhone Location Application 490

63. Working with Maps on the iPhone with MapKit and the MKMapView Class 493

63.1 About the MapKit Framework 493
63.2 Understanding Map Regions 493
63.3 About the iPhone MKMapView Tutorial 494
63.4 Creating the iPhone Map Tutorial 494
63.5 Adding the MapKit Framework to the Xcode Project 494
63.6 Creating the MKMapView Instance and Toolbar 494
63.7 Configuring the Map View 496
63.8 Changing the MapView Region 497
63.9 Changing the Map Type 497
63.10 Testing the iPhone MapView Application 498
63.11 Updating the Map View based on User Movement 498
63.12 Adding Basic Annotations to a Map View 499

64. Using iOS 6 Event Kit to Create Date and Location Based Reminders 501

64.1 An Overview of the Event Kit Framework 501
64.2 The EKEventStore Class 502
64.3 Accessing Calendars in the Database 504
64.4 Accessing Current Reminders 504
64.5 Creating Reminders 505
64.6 Creating Alarms 506
64.7 Creating the Example Project 506
64.8 Designing the User Interface for the Date/Time Based Reminder Screen 506
64.9 Implementing the Reminder Code 508
64.10 Hiding the Keyboard 510
64.11 Designing Location-based Reminder Screen 510
64.12 Creating a Location-based Reminder 511
64.13 Adding the Core Location and Event Kit Frameworks 515
64.14 Testing the Application 515

  64.15 Summary 516

65. Accessing the iPhone Camera and Photo Library 517

  65.1 The iOS 6 UIImagePickerController Class 517
  65.2 Creating and Configuring a UIImagePickerController Instance 517
  65.3 Configuring the UIImagePickerController Delegate 518
  65.4 Detecting Device Capabilities 520
  65.5 Saving Movies and Images 520
  65.6 Summary 521

66. An Example iOS 6 iPhone Camera Application 523

  66.1 An Overview of the Application 523
  66.2 Creating the Camera Project 523
  66.3 Adding Framework Support 523
  66.4 Designing the User Interface 523
  66.5 Implementing the Action Methods 525
  66.6 Writing the Delegate Methods 526
  66.7 Building and Running the Application 528

67. Video Playback from within an iOS 6 iPhone Application 531

  67.1 An Overview of the MPMoviePlayerController Class 531
  67.2 Supported Video Formats 531
  67.3 The iPhone Movie Player Example Application 532
  67.4 Adding the MediaPlayer Framework to the Project 532
  67.5 Designing the User Interface 532
  67.6 Declaring the MoviePlayer Instance 532
  67.7 Implementing the Action Method 533
  67.8 The Target-Action Notification Method 533
  67.9 Build and Run the Application 534

68. Playing Audio on an iPhone using AVAudioPlayer 535

  68.1 Supported Audio Formats 535
  68.2 Receiving Playback Notifications 536
  68.3 Controlling and Monitoring Playback 536
  68.4 Creating the iPhone Audio Example Application 536
  68.5 Adding the AVFoundation Framework 537
  68.6 Adding an Audio File to the Project Resources 537
  68.7 Designing the User Interface 537
  68.8 Implementing the Action Methods 539
  68.9 Creating and Initializing the AVAudioPlayer Object 539
  68.10 Implementing the AVAudioPlayerDelegate Protocol Methods 540
  68.11 Building and Running the Application 541

69. Recording Audio on an iPhone with AVAudioRecorder 543

69.1 An Overview of the iPhone AVAudioRecorder Tutorial 543
69.2 Creating the Recorder Project 543
69.3 Designing the User Interface 544
69.4 Creating the AVAudioRecorder Instance 545
69.5 Implementing the Action Methods 546
69.6 Implementing the Delegate Methods 548
69.7 Testing the Application 548

70. Integrating Twitter and Facebook into iPhone iOS 6 Applications 549

70.1 The iOS 6 UIActivityViewController class 549
70.2 The Social Framework 549
70.3 iOS 6 Accounts Framework 550
70.4 Using the UIActivityViewController Class 551
70.5 Using the SLComposeViewController Class 554
70.6 Summary 555

71. An iPhone iOS 6 Facebook Integration Tutorial using UIActivityViewController 557

71.1 Creating the Facebook Social App 557
71.2 Designing the User Interface 557
71.3 Creating Outlets and Actions 558
71.4 Implementing the selectImage and Delegate Methods 559
71.5 Hiding the Keyboard 560
71.6 Posting the Message to Facebook 561
71.7 Adding the Social Framework to the Build Phases 561
71.8 Running the Social Application 562
71.9 Summary 563

72. iPhone iOS 6 Facebook and Twitter Integration using SLRequest 565

72.1 Using SLRequest and the Account Framework 565
72.2 Twitter Integration using SLRequest 566
72.3 Facebook Integration using SLRequest 569
72.4 Summary 571

73. An iOS 6 iPhone Twitter Integration Tutorial using SLRequest 573

73.1 Creating the TwitterApp Project 573
73.2 Designing the User Interface 573
73.3 Modifying the Interface File 575
73.4 Accessing the Twitter API 575
73.5 Calling the getTimeLine Method 578
73.6 The Table View Delegate Methods 578

73.7 Adding the Account and Social Frameworks to the Build Phases 579
73.8 Building and Running the Application 579
73.9 Summary 580

74. Making Store Purchases with the SKStoreProductViewController Class 581

74.1 The SKStoreProductViewController Class 581
74.2 Creating the Example Project 582
74.3 Creating the User Interface 582
74.4 Displaying the Store Kit Product View Controller 583
74.5 Implementing the Delegate Method 585
74.6 Adding the Store Kit Framework to the Build Phases 585
74.7 Testing the Application 585
74.8 Summary 587

75. Building In-App Purchasing into iPhone iOS 6 Applications 589

75.1 In-App Purchase Options 589
75.2 Uploading App Store Hosted Content 590
75.3 Configuring In-App Purchase Items 590
75.4 Sending a Product Request 590
75.5 Accessing the Payment Queue 592
75.6 The Transaction Observer Object 592
75.7 Initiating the Purchase 592
75.8 The Transaction Process 593
75.9 Transaction Restoration Process 595
75.10 Testing In-App Purchases 595
75.11 Summary 595

76. Preparing an iOS 6 Application for In-App Purchases 597

76.1 About the Example Application 597
76.2 Creating the App ID 597
76.3 Creating the Provisioning Profile 598
76.4 Creating the Xcode Project 599
76.5 Installing the Provisioning Profile 599
76.6 Configuring Code Signing 600
76.7 Configuring the Application in iTunes Connect 600
76.8 Creating an In-App Purchase Item 601
76.9 Summary 603

77. An iPhone iOS 6 In-App Purchase Tutorial 605

77.1 The Application User Interface 605
77.2 Designing the Storyboard 606
77.3 Creating the Purchase View Controller 607

xxiii

77.4 Completing the InAppDemoViewController Class 608
77.5 Completing the PurchaseViewController Class 610
77.6 Adding the StoreKit Framework to the Build 613
77.7 Testing the Application 613
77.8 Troubleshooting 614
77.9 Summary 615

78. Configuring and Creating App Store Hosted Content for iOS 6 In-App Purchases 617

78.1 Configuring an Application for In-App Purchase Hosted Content 617
78.2 The Anatomy of an In-App Purchase Hosted Content Package 618
78.3 Creating an In-App Purchase Hosted Content Package 618
78.4 Archiving the Hosted Content Package 619
78.5 Validating the Hosted Content Package 620
78.6 Uploading the Hosted Content Package 621
78.7 Summary 621

79. Preparing and Submitting an Application to the App Store 623

79.1 Generating an iOS Distribution Certificate Signing Request 623
79.2 Submitting the Certificate Signing Request 623
79.3 Installing the Distribution Certificate 624
79.4 Generating an App Store Distribution Provisioning Profile 624
79.5 Adding an Icon to the Application 624
79.6 Archiving the Application for Distribution 625
79.7 Configuring the Application in iTunes Connect 627
79.8 Validating and Submitting the Application 628

Index 631

Chapter 1

1. Start Here

When details of iOS 6 were first announced at the Apple World Wide Development Conference in June, 2012 it seemed, on the surface at least, that the iOS 5 edition of this book would not need to be significantly updated for iOS 6. After gaining access to the pre-release versions of the iOS 6 SDK and working with the new features, however, it quickly became clear that whilst there are areas that have not changed since iOS 5, there is much more to the new features of iOS 6 than it had at first appeared. In actual fact, 23 new chapters had to be written to cover the new features of iOS 6 and every code example updated to reflect the changes made to Objective-C.

How you make use of this book will depend to a large extent on whether you are new to iOS development, or have worked with iOS 5 and need to get up to speed on the features of iOS 6. Rest assured, however, that the book is intended to address both category of reader.

1.1 For New iOS Developers

If you are entirely new to iOS development then the entire contents of the book will be relevant to you.

Beginning with the basics, this book provides an outline of the steps necessary to set up an iOS development environment. An introduction to the architecture of iOS 6 and programming in Objective-C is provided, followed by an in-depth look at the design of iPhone applications and user interfaces. More advanced topics such as file handling, database management, in-app purchases, graphics drawing and animation are also covered, as are touch screen handling, gesture recognition, multitasking, iAds integration, location management, local notifications, camera access and video and audio playback support. New iOS 6 specific features are also covered including Auto Layout, Twitter and Facebook integration, event reminders, App Store hosted in-app purchase content, collection views and much more.

The aim of this book, therefore, is to teach you the skills necessary to build your own apps for the iPhone. Assuming you are ready to download the iOS 6 SDK and Xcode, have an Intel-based Mac and some ideas for some apps to develop, you are ready to get started.

Start Here

1.2 For iOS 5 Developers

If you have already read iPhone iOS 5 Development Essentials, or have experience with the iOS 5 SDK then you might prefer to go directly to the new chapters in this iOS 6 edition of the book. As previously mentioned, if you have already read iPhone iOS 5 Development Essentials, you will find no fewer than 23 new chapters in this latest edition.

Chapters included in this edition that were not contained in the previous edition are as follows:

- The Basics of Modern Objective-C
- An Introduction to Auto Layout in iOS 6
- Working with iOS 6 Auto Layout Constraints in Interface Builder
- An iPhone iOS 6 Auto Layout Example
- Implementing iOS 6 Auto Layout Constraints in Code
- Implementing Cross-Hierarchy Auto Layout Constraints in iOS 6
- Understanding the iOS 6 Auto Layout Visual Format Language
- An Overview of iOS 6 Collection View and Flow Layout
- An iPhone iOS 6 Storyboard-based Collection View Tutorial
- Subclassing and Extending the iOS 6 Collection View Flow Layout
- An Overview of iOS 6 Application State Preservation and Restoration
- An iOS 6 iPhone State Preservation and Restoration Tutorial
- Integrating Maps into iPhone iOS 6 Applications using MKMapItem
- An Example iOS 6 iPhone MKMapItem Application
- Using iOS 6 Event Kit to Create Date and Location Based Reminders
- Integrating Twitter and Facebook into iPhone iOS 6 Applications
- An iPhone iOS 6 Facebook Integration Tutorial using UIActivityViewController
- iPhone iOS 6 Facebook and Twitter Integration using SLRequest
- Making Store Purchases with the SKStoreProductViewController Class
- Building In-App Purchasing into iPhone iOS 6 Applications
- Preparing an iOS 6 Application for In-App Purchases
- An iPhone iOS 6 In-App Purchase Tutorial
- Configuring and Creating App Store Hosted Content for iOS 6 In-App Purchases

In addition, the chapter entitled *Using Xcode Storyboarding* has been updated to include coverage of the new segue unwinding feature of iOS 6 and *An Overview of iOS 6 Table Views and Xcode Storyboards* has been modified to introduce the new iOS 6 model for reusing Table View cells.

Finally, all the code examples have been updated to reflect the changes to Objective-C including the removal of the *viewDidUnload*: method, literal syntax for number, array and dictionaries and default property synthesis.

1.3 Source Code Download

The source code and Xcode project files for the examples contained in this book are available for download at *http://www.ebookfrenzy.com/code/iphoneios6.zip*.

1.4 Feedback

We want you to be satisfied with your purchase of this book. If you find any errors in the book, or have any comments, questions or concerns please contact us at *feedback@ebookfrenzy.com*.

1.5 Errata

Whilst we make every effort to ensure the accuracy of the content of this book, it is inevitable that a book covering a subject area of this size and complexity may include some errors and oversights. Any known issues with the book will be outlined, together with solutions at the following URL:

http://www.ebookfrenzy.com/errata/iphone_ios6.html

In the event that you find an error not listed in the errata, please let us know by emailing our technical support team at *feedback@ebookfrenzy.com*.

Chapter 2

2. Joining the Apple iOS Developer Program

The first step in the process of learning to develop iOS 6 based iPhone applications involves gaining an understanding of the differences between *Registered Apple Developers* and *iOS Developer Program Members*. Having gained such an understanding, the next choice is to decide the point at which it makes sense for you to pay to join the iOS Developer Program. With these goals in mind, this chapter will cover the differences between the two categories of developer, outline the costs and benefits of joining the developer program and, finally, walk through the steps involved in obtaining each membership level.

2.1 Registered Apple Developer

There is no fee associated with becoming a registered Apple developer. Simply visit the following web page to begin the registration process:

http://developer.apple.com/programs/register/

An existing Apple ID (used for making iTunes or Apple Store purchases) is usually adequate to complete the registration process.

Once the registration process is complete, access is provided to developer resources such as online documentation and tutorials. Registered developers are also able to download older versions of the iOS SDK and Xcode development environment.

2.2 Downloading Xcode and the iOS 6 SDK

The latest versions of both the iOS SDK and Xcode can be downloaded free of charge from the Mac App Store. Since the tools are free, this raises the question of whether to upgrade to the iOS Developer Program, or to remain as a Registered Apple Developer. It is important, therefore, to understand the key benefits of the iOS Developer Program.

2.3 iOS Developer Program

Membership in the iOS Developer Program currently costs $99 per year. As previously mentioned, membership includes access to the latest versions of the iOS SDK and Xcode development environment. The benefits of membership, however, go far beyond those offered at the Registered Apple Developer level.

Joining the Apple iOS Developer Program

One of the key advantages of the developer program is that it permits the creation of certificates and provisioning profiles to test applications on physical devices. Although Xcode includes device simulators which allow for a significant amount of testing to be performed, there are certain areas of functionality, such as location tracking and device motion, which can only fully be tested on a physical device. Of particular significance is the fact that iCloud access, Reminders and In-App Purchasing can only be tested when applications are running on physical devices.

Of further significance is the fact that iOS Developer Program members have unrestricted access to the full range of guides and tutorials relating to the latest iOS SDK and, more importantly, have access to technical support from Apple's iOS technical support engineers (though the annual fee covers the submission of only two support incident reports).

By far the most important aspect of the iOS Developer Program is that membership is a mandatory requirement in order to publish an application for sale or download in the App Store.

Clearly, developer program membership is going to be required at some point before your application reaches the App Store. The only question remaining is when exactly to sign up.

2.4 When to Enroll in the iOS Developer Program?

Clearly, there are many benefits to iOS Developer Program membership and, eventually, membership will be necessary to begin selling applications. As to whether or not to pay the enrollment fee now or later will depend on individual circumstances. If you are still in the early stages of learning to develop iOS applications or have yet to come up with a compelling idea for an application to develop then much of what you need is provided in the Registered Apple Developer package. As your skill level increases and your ideas for applications to develop take shape you can, after all, always enroll in the developer program at a later date.

If, on the other hand, you are confident that you will reach the stage of having an application ready to publish or know that you will need to test the functionality of the application on a physical device as opposed to a simulator then it is worth joining the developer program sooner rather than later.

2.5 Enrolling in the iOS Developer Program

If your goal is to develop iPhone applications for your employer then it is first worth checking whether the company already has membership. That being the case, contact the program administrator in your company and ask them to send you an invitation from within the iOS Developer Program Member Center to join the team. Once they have done so, Apple will send you an email entitled *You Have Been Invited to Join an Apple Developer Program* containing a link to activate your membership. If you or your company is not already a program member, you can enroll online at:

http://developer.apple.com/programs/ios/

Apple provides enrollment options for businesses and individuals. To enroll as an individual you will need to provide credit card information in order to verify your identity. To enroll as a company you

Joining the Apple iOS Developer Program

must have legal signature authority (or access to someone who does) and be able to provide documentation such as Articles of Incorporation and a Business License.

Acceptance into the developer program as an individual member typically takes less than 24 hours with notification arriving in the form of an activation email from Apple. Enrollment as a company can take considerably longer (sometimes weeks or even months) due to the burden of the additional verification requirements.

Whilst awaiting activation you may log into the Member Center with restricted access using your Apple ID and password at the following URL:

http://developer.apple.com/membercenter

Once logged in, clicking on the *Your Account* tab at the top of the page will display the prevailing status of your application to join the developer program as *Enrollment Pending*:

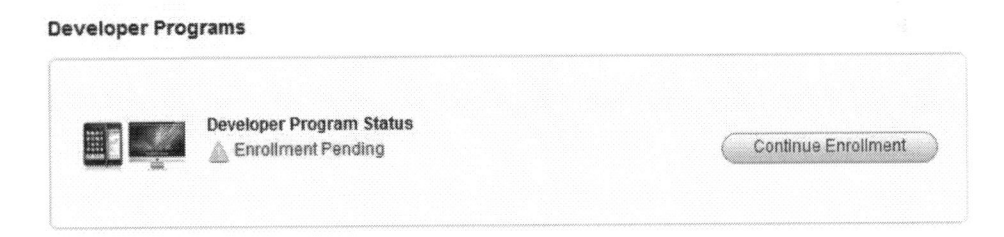

Figure 2-1

Once the activation email has arrived, log into the Member Center again and note that access is now available to a wide range of options and resources as illustrated in Figure 2-2:

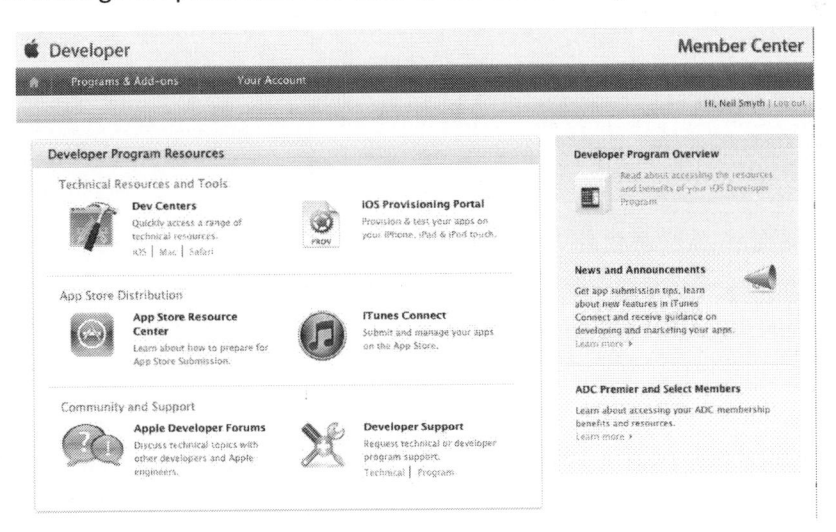

Figure 2-2

2.6 Summary

An important early step in iPhone iOS 6 application development process involves registering as an Apple Developer and identifying the best time to upgrade to iOS Developer Program membership. This chapter has outlined the differences between the two programs, provided some guidance to keep in mind when considering developer program membership and walked briefly through the enrollment process. The next step is to download and install the iOS 6 SDK and Xcode development environment.

Chapter 3

3. Installing Xcode 4 and the iOS 6 SDK

iPhone apps are developed using the iOS SDK in conjunction with Apple's Xcode 4.x development environment. The iOS SDK contains the development frameworks that will be outlined in *iOS 6 Architecture and Frameworks*. Xcode 4.x is an integrated development environment (IDE) within which you will code, compile, test and debug your iOS iPhone applications. The Xcode 4.x environment also includes a feature called Interface Builder which enables you to graphically design the user interface of your application using the components provided by the UIKit framework.

In this chapter we will cover the steps involved in installing both Xcode and the iOS 6 SDK on Mac OS X.

3.1 Identifying if you have an Intel or PowerPC based Mac

Only Intel based Mac OS X systems can be used to develop applications for iOS. If you have an older, PowerPC based Mac then you will need to purchase a new system before you can begin your iPhone app development project. If you are unsure of the processor type inside your Mac, you can find this information by clicking on the Apple menu in the top left hand corner of the screen and selecting the *About This Mac* option from the menu. In the resulting dialog check the *Processor* line. Figure 3-1 illustrates the results obtained on an Intel based system.

If the dialog on your Mac does not reflect the presence of an Intel based processor then your current system is, sadly, unsuitable as a platform for iPhone iOS app development.

In addition, the iOS 6 SDK with Xcode 4.5 environment requires that the version of Mac OS X running on the system be version 10.7.4 or later. If the "About This Mac" dialog does not indicate that Mac OS X 10.7.4 or later is running, click on the *Software Update...* button to download and install the appropriate operating system upgrades.

Installing Xcode 4 and the iOS 6 SDK

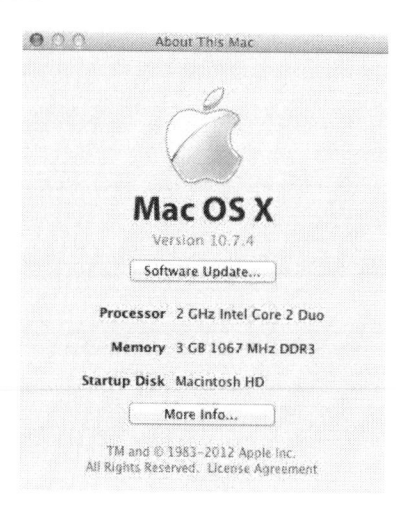

Figure 3-1

3.2 Installing Xcode 4 and the iOS 6 SDK

The best way to obtain the latest versions of Xcode 4 and the iOS SDK is to download them from the Apple iOS Dev Center web site at:

https://developer.apple.com/xcode/

The download is over 1.6GB in size and may take a number of hours to complete depending on the speed of your internet connection.

3.3 Starting Xcode

Having successfully installed the SDK and Xcode, the next step is to launch it so that we can write and then create a sample iPhone application. To start up Xcode, open the Finder and search for *Xcode*. Since you will be making frequent use of this tool take this opportunity to drag and drop it into your dock for easier access in the future. Click on the Xcode icon in the dock to launch the tool.

Once Xcode has loaded, and assuming this is the first time you have used Xcode on this system, you will be presented with the *Welcome* screen from which you are ready to proceed:

Installing Xcode 4 and the iOS 6 SDK

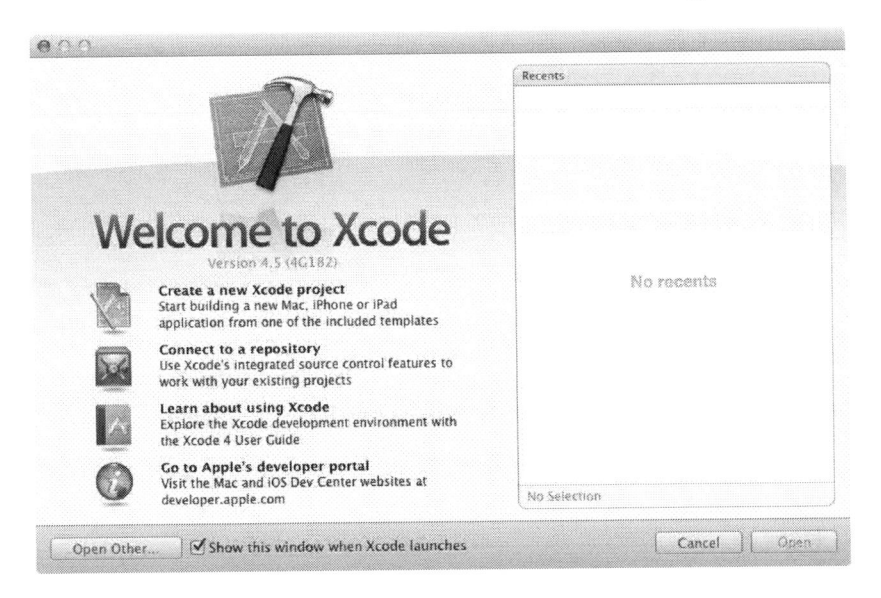

Figure 3-2

Having installed the iOS 6 SDK and successfully launched Xcode 4 we can now look at *Creating a Simple iPhone iOS 6 App*.

Chapter 4

4. Creating a Simple iPhone iOS 6 App

It is traditional in books covering programming topics to provide a very simple example early on. This practice, though still common, has been maligned by some authors of recent books. Those authors, however, are missing the point of the simple example. One key purpose of such an exercise is to provide a very simple way to verify that your development environment is correctly installed and fully operational before moving on to more complex tasks. A secondary objective is to give the reader a quick success very early in the learning curve to inspire an initial level of confidence. There is very little to be gained by plunging into complex examples that confuse the reader before having taken time to explain the underlying concepts of the technology.

With this in mind, *iPhone iOS 6 Development Essentials* will remain true to tradition and provide a very simple example with which to get started. In doing so, we will also be honoring another time honored tradition by providing this example in the form of a simple "Hello World" program. The "Hello World" example was first used in a book called the C Programming Language written by the creators of C, Brian Kernighan and Dennis Richie. Given that the origins of Objective-C can be traced back to the C programming language it is only fitting that we use this example for iOS 6 and the iPhone.

4.1 Starting Xcode 4

As with all iOS examples in this book, the development of our example will take place within the Xcode 4 development environment. If you have not already installed this tool together with the latest iOS SDK refer first to the *Installing Xcode 4 and the iOS 6 SDK* chapter of this book. Assuming that the installation is complete, launch Xcode either by clicking on the icon on the dock (assuming you created one) or use the Finder to locate the Xcode binary.

When launched for the first time, and until you turn off the *Show this window when Xcode launches* toggle, the screen illustrated in Figure 4-1 will appear by default:

Creating a Simple iPhone iOS 6 App

Figure 4-1

If you do not see this window, simply select the *Window -> Welcome to Xcode* menu option to display it. From within this window click on the option to *Create a new Xcode project*. This will display the main Xcode 4 project window together with the *New Project* panel where we are able to select a template matching the type of project we want to develop:

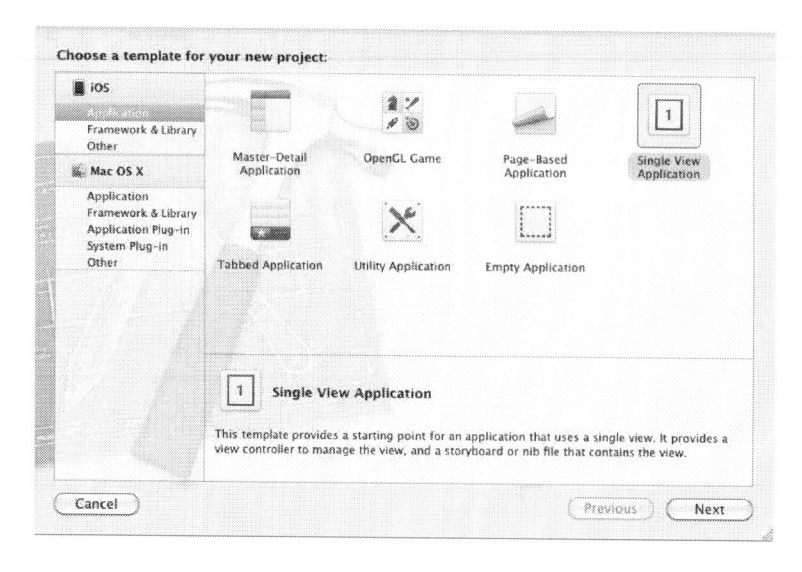

Figure 4-2

The panel located on the left hand side of the window allows for the selection of the target platform, providing options to develop an application either for an iOS based device or Mac OS X.

Begin by making sure that the *Application* option located beneath *iOS* is selected. The main panel contains a list of templates available to use as the basis for an application. The options available are as follows:

14

- **Master-Detail Application** – Used to create a list based application. Selecting an item from a master list displays a detail view corresponding to the selection. The template then provides a *Back* button to return to the list. You may have seen a similar technique used for news based applications, whereby selecting an item from a list of headlines displays the content of the corresponding news article. When used for an iPad based application this template implements a basic split-view configuration.
- **OpenGL Game** – The OpenGL ES framework provides an API for developing advanced graphics drawing and animation capabilities. The OpenGL ES Game template creates a basic application containing an OpenGL ES view upon which to draw and manipulate graphics, and a timer object.
- **Page-based Application** – Creates a template project using the page view controller designed to allow views to be transitioned by turning pages on the screen.
- **Tabbed Application** – Creates a template application with a tab bar. The tab bar typically appears across the bottom of the device display and can be programmed to contain items that, when selected, change the main display to different views. The iPhone's built-in *Phone* user interface, for example, uses a tab bar to allow the user to move between favorites, contacts, keypad and voicemail.
- **Utility Application** – Creates a template consisting of a two sided view. For an example of a utility application in action, load up the standard iPhone weather application. Pressing the blue info button flips the view to the configuration page. Selecting *Done* rotates the view back to the main screen.
- **Single View Application** – Creates a basic template for an application containing a single view and corresponding view controller.
- **Empty Application** – This most basic of templates creates only a window and a delegate. If none of the above templates match your requirements then this is the option to take.

For the purposes of our simple example, we are going to use the *Single View Application* template so select this option from the new project window and click *Next* to configure some project options:

Creating a Simple iPhone iOS 6 App

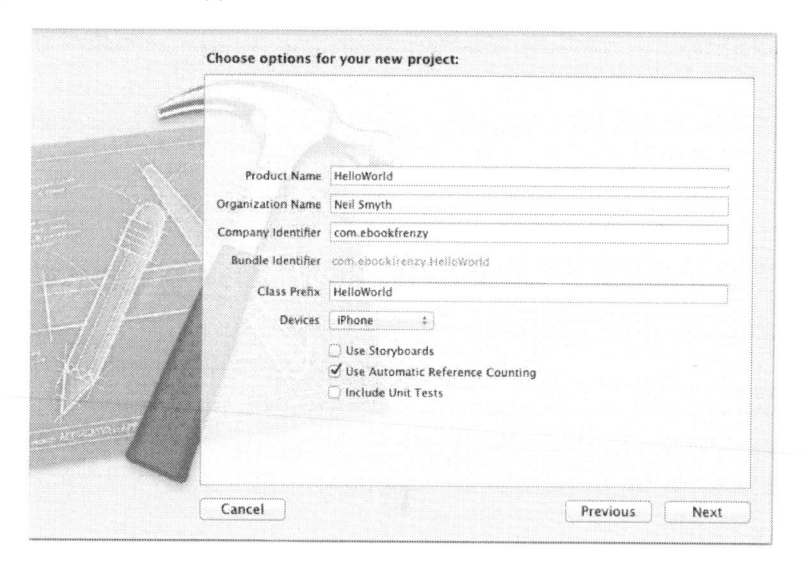

Figure 4-3

On this screen, enter a Product name for the application that is going to be created, in this case "HelloWorld" and make sure that the class prefix matches this name. The company identifier is typically the reversed URL of your company's website, for example "com.mycompany". This will be used when creating provisioning profiles and certificates to enable applications to be tested on a physical iPhone device (covered in more detail in *Testing iOS 6 Apps on the iPhone – Developer Certificates and Provisioning Profiles*). Enter the *Class Prefix* value of "HelloWorld" which will be used to prefix any classes created for us by Xcode when the template project is created.

Make sure that *iPhone* is currently selected from the *Devices* menu and that neither the *Use Storyboard* nor the *Include Unit Tests* options are currently selected.

Automatic Reference Counting is a feature included with the Objective-C compiler which removes much of the responsibility from the developer for releasing objects when they are no longer needed. This is an extremely useful new feature and, as such, the option should be selected before clicking the *Next* button to proceed. On the final screen, choose a location on the file system for the new project to be created and click on *Create*.

Once the new project has been created, the main Xcode window will appear as illustrated in Figure 4-4:

16

Creating a Simple iPhone iOS 6 App

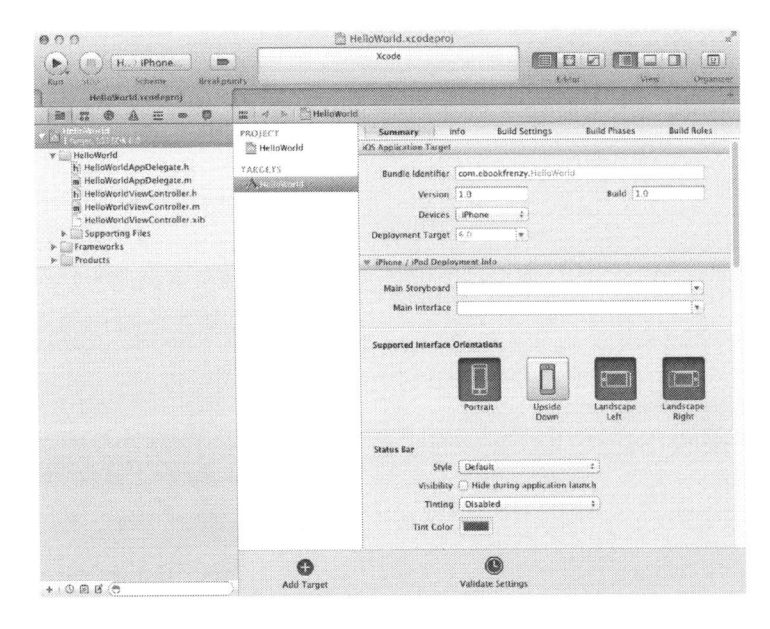

Figure 4-4

Before proceeding we should take some time to look at what Xcode has done for us. Firstly it has created a group of files that we will need to create our application. Some of these are Objective-C source code files (with a .m extension) where we will enter the code to make our application work, others are header or interface files (.h) that are included by the source files and are where we will also need to put our own declarations and definitions. In addition, the .xib file is the save file used by the Interface Builder tool to hold the user interface design we will create. Older versions of Interface Builder saved designs in files with a .nib extension so these files, even today, are called NIB files. Also present will be one or more files with a .plist file extension. These are *Property List* files which contain key/value pair information. For example, the *HelloWorld-info.plist* file contains resource settings relating to items such as the language, icon file, executable name and app identifier. The list of files is displayed in the *Project Navigator* located in the left hand panel of the main Xcode project window. A toolbar at the top of this panel contains options to display other information such as build and run history, breakpoints and compilation errors.

By default, the center panel of the window shows a summary of the settings for the application. This includes the identifier specified during the project creation process and the target device. Options are also provided to configure the orientations of the device that are to be supported by the application together with options to upload an icon (the small image the user selects on the device screen to launch the application) and splash screen image (displayed to the user while the application loads) for the application.

In addition to the Summary screen, tabs are provided to view and modify additional settings consisting of Info, Build Settings, Build Phases and Build Rules. As we progress through subsequent chapters of this book we will explore some of these other configuration options in greater detail. To return to the Summary panel at any future point in time, make sure the *Project Navigator* is selected in the left hand panel and select the top item (the application name) in the navigator list.

Creating a Simple iPhone iOS 6 App

When a source file is selected from the list in the navigator panel, the contents of that file will appear in the center panel where it may then be edited. To open the file in a separate editing window, simply double click on the file in the list.

4.2 Creating the iOS App User Interface

Simply by the very nature of the environment in which they run, iPhone apps are typically visually oriented. As such, a key component of just about any app involves a user interface through which the user will interact with the application and, in turn, receive feedback. Whilst it is possible to develop user interfaces by writing code to create and position items on the screen, this is a complex and error prone process. In recognition of this, Apple provides a tool called Interface Builder which allows a user interface to be visually constructed by dragging and dropping components onto a canvas and setting properties to configure the appearance and behavior of those components. Interface Builder was originally developed some time ago for creating Mac OS X applications, but has now been updated to allow for the design of iOS app user interfaces.

As mentioned in the preceding section, Xcode pre-created a number of files for our project, one of which has a .xib filename extension. This is an Interface Builder save file (remember that they are called NIB files, not XIB files). The file we are interested in for our HelloWorld project is called *HelloWorldViewController.xib*. To load this file into Interface Builder simply select the file name in the list in the left hand panel. Interface Builder will subsequently appear in the center panel as shown in Figure 4-5:

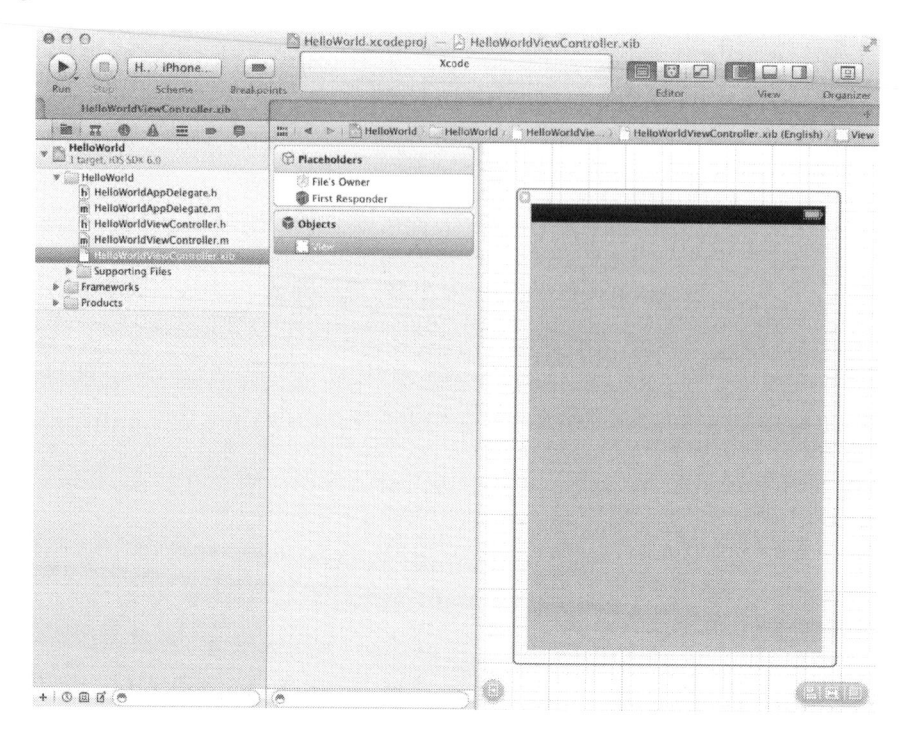

Figure 4-5

Creating a Simple iPhone iOS 6 App

In the center panel a visual representation of the user interface of the application is displayed. Initially this consists solely of the UIView object. This *UIView* object was added to our design by Xcode when we selected the Single View Application option during the project creation phase. We will construct the user interface for our HelloWorld app by dragging and dropping user interface objects onto this UIView object. Designing a user interface consists primarily of dragging and dropping visual components onto the canvas and setting a range of properties and settings. In order to access objects and property settings it is necessary to display the Xcode right hand panel. This is achieved by selecting the right hand button in the *View* section of the Xcode toolbar:

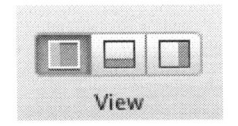

Figure 4-6

The right hand panel, once displayed, will appear as illustrated in Figure 4-7:

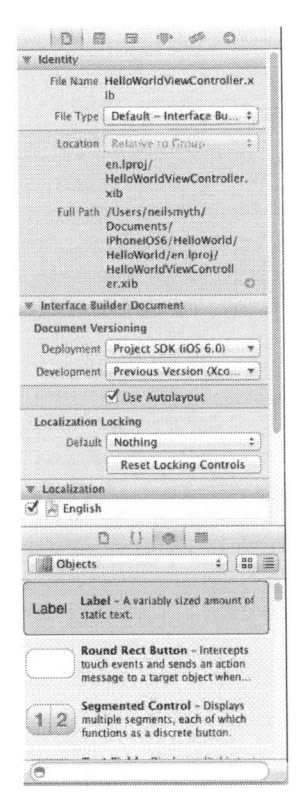

Figure 4-7

Along the top edge of the panel is a row of buttons which change the settings displayed in the upper half of the panel. By default the *File Inspector* is displayed. Options are also provided to display quick help, the *Identity Inspector*, *Attributes Inspector*, *Size Inspector* and *Connections Inspector*. Before proceeding, take some time to review each of these selections to gain some familiarity with the

19

configuration options each provides. Throughout the remainder of this book extensive use of these inspectors will be made.

The lower section of the panel defaults to displaying the file template library. Above this panel is another toolbar containing buttons to display other categories. Options include frequently used code snippets to save on typing when writing code, the object library and the media library. For the purposes of this tutorial we need to display the object library so click in the appropriate toolbar button (the three dimensional cube). This will display the UI components that can be used to construct our user interface. Move the cursor to the line above the lower toolbar and click and drag to increase the amount of space available for the library if required. In addition, the objects are categorized into groups which may be selected using the menu beneath the toolbar. The layout buttons may also be used to switch from a single column of objects with descriptions to multiple columns without descriptions.

4.3 Changing Component Properties

With the property panel for the View selected in the main panel, we will begin our design work by changing the background color of this view. Begin by making sure the View is selected and that the Attribute Inspector (*View -> Utilities -> Show Attribute Inspector*) is displayed in the right hand panel. Click on the gray rectangle next to the *Background* label to invoke the *Colors* dialog. Using the color selection tool, choose a visually pleasing color and close the dialog. You will now notice that the view window has changed from gray to the new color selection.

4.4 Adding Objects to the User Interface

The next step is to add a Label object to our view. To achieve this, select *Cocoa Touch -> Controls* from the library panel menu, click on the *Label* object and drag it to the center of the view. Once it is in position release the mouse button to drop it at that location:

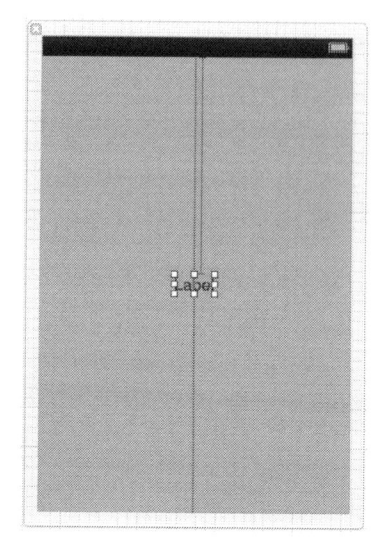

Figure 4-8

Creating a Simple iPhone iOS 6 App

Using the resize markers surrounding the label border, stretch first the left and then right side of the label out to the edge of the view until the vertical blue dotted lines marking the recommended border of the view appear. With the Label still selected, click on the centered alignment button in the *Layout* attribute section of the Attribute Inspector (*View -> Utilities -> Show Attribute Inspector*) to center the text in the middle of the screen. Click on the current font attribute setting to choose a larger font setting, for example a Georgia bold typeface with a size of 24.

Finally, double click on the text in the label that currently reads "Label" and type in "Hello World". At this point, your View window will hopefully appear as outlined in Figure 4-9 (allowing, of course, for differences in your color and font choices).

Having created our simple user interface design we now need to save it. To achieve this, select *File -> Save* or use the Command+S keyboard shortcut.

Figure 4-9

4.5 Building and Running an iOS App in Xcode 4

Before an app can be run it must first be compiled. Once successfully compiled it may be run either within a simulator or on a physical iPhone, iPad or iPod Touch device. The process for testing an app on a physical device requires some additional steps to be performed involving developer certificates and provisioning profiles and will be covered in detail in *Testing iOS 6 Apps on the iPhone – Developer Certificates and Provisioning Profiles*. For the purposes of this chapter, however, it is sufficient to run the app in the simulator.

Within the main Xcode 4 project window, make sure that the menu located in the top left hand corner of the window (to the right of the Stop button) has the *iPhone 6.0 Simulator* option selected and then click on the *Run* toolbar button to compile the code and run the app in the simulator. The

21

small iTunes style window in the center of the Xcode toolbar will report the progress of the build process together with any problems or errors that cause the build process to fail. Once the app is built, the simulator will start and the HelloWorld app will run:

Figure 4-10

4.6 Dealing with Build Errors

As we have not actually written or modified any code in this chapter it is unlikely that any errors will be detected during the build and run process. In the unlikely event that something did get inadvertently changed thereby causing the build to fail it is worth taking a few minutes to talk about build errors within the context of the Xcode environment.

If for any reason a build fails, the status window in the Xcode 4 toolbar will report that an error has been detected by displaying "Build" together with the number of errors detected and any warnings. In addition, the left hand panel of the Xcode window will update with a list of the errors. Selecting an error from this list will take you to the location in the code where corrective action needs to be taken.

4.7 Testing Different Screen Sizes

With the introduction of the iPhone 5, applications now need to work on three different screens, consisting of the standard resolution original iPhone screen, the 3.5 inch retina screen of the iPhone 4 and the new 4 inch retina display of the iPhone 5.

In order to test the appearance of an application on these different displays, simply launch the application in the iOS Simulator and switch between the different displays using the *Hardware -> Device* menu options.

Chapter 5

5. iOS 6 Architecture and SDK Frameworks

By just about any measure, the iPhone is an impressive achievement in the fields of industrial design and hardware engineering. When we develop apps for the iPhone, however, Apple does not allow us direct access to any of this hardware. In fact, all hardware interaction takes place exclusively through a number of different layers of software which act as intermediaries between the application code and device hardware. These layers make up what is known as an *operating system*. In the case of the iPhone, this operating system is known as iOS.

In order to gain a better understanding of the iPhone development environment, this chapter will look in detail at the different layers that comprise the iOS operating system and the frameworks that allow us, as developers, to write iPhone applications.

5.1 iPhone OS becomes iOS

Prior to the release of the iPad in 2010, the operating system running on the iPhone was generally referred to as *iPhone OS*. Given that the operating system used for the iPad is essentially the same as that on the iPhone it didn't make much sense to name it *iPad OS*. Instead, Apple decided to adopt a more generic and non-device specific name for the operating system. Given Apple's predilection for names prefixed with the letter 'i' (iTunes, iBookstore, iMac etc) the logical choice was, of course, *iOS*. Unfortunately, iOS is also the name used by Cisco for the operating system on its routers (Apple, it seems, also has a predilection for ignoring trademarks). When performing an internet search for iOS, therefore, be prepared to see large numbers of results for Cisco's iOS which have absolutely nothing to do with Apple's iOS.

5.2 An Overview of the iOS 6 Architecture

As previously mentioned, iOS consists of a number of different software layers, each of which provides programming frameworks for the development of applications that run on top of the underlying hardware.

These operating system layers can be presented diagrammatically as illustrated in Figure 5-1:

iOS 6 Architecture and SDK Frameworks

```
┌─────────────────────┐
│    Cocoa Touch      │
├─────────────────────┤
│   Media Services    │
├─────────────────────┤
│   Core Services     │
├─────────────────────┤
│     Core OS         │
└─────────────────────┘
        ⬆    ⬇
┌─────────────────────┐
│   iPhone Hardware   │
└─────────────────────┘
```

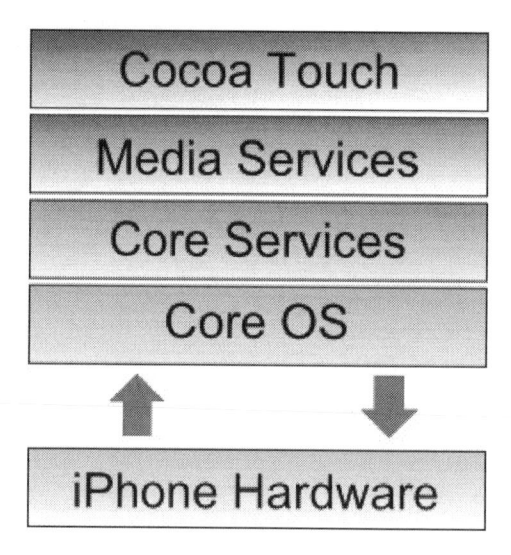

Figure 5-1

Some diagrams designed to graphically depict the iOS software stack show an additional box positioned above the Cocoa Touch layer to indicate the applications running on the device. In the above diagram we have not done so since this would suggest that the only interface available to the app is Cocoa Touch. In practice, an app can directly call down any of the layers of the stack to perform tasks on the physical device.

That said, however, each operating system layer provides an increasing level of abstraction away from the complexity of working with the hardware. As an iOS developer you should, therefore, always look for solutions to your programming goals in the frameworks located in the higher level iOS layers before resorting to writing code that reaches down to the lower level layers. In general, the higher level of layer you program to, the less effort and fewer lines of code you will have to write to achieve your objective. And as any veteran programmer will tell you, the less code you have to write the less opportunity you have to introduce bugs.

Now that we have identified the various layers that comprise iOS 6 we can now look in more detail at the services provided by each layer and the corresponding frameworks that make those services available to us as application developers.

5.3 The Cocoa Touch Layer

The Cocoa Touch layer sits at the top of the iOS stack and contains the frameworks that are most commonly used by iPhone application developers. Cocoa Touch is primarily written in Objective-C, is based on the standard Mac OS X Cocoa API (as found on Apple desktop and laptop computers) and has been extended and modified to meet the needs of the iPhone hardware.

The Cocoa Touch layer provides the following frameworks for iPhone app development:

5.3.1 UIKit Framework (UIKit.framework)

The UIKit framework is a vast and feature rich Objective-C based programming interface. It is, without question, the framework with which you will spend most of your time working. Entire books could, and probably will, be written about the UIKit framework alone. Some of the key features of UIKit are as follows:

- User interface creation and management (text fields, buttons, labels, colors, fonts etc)
- Application lifecycle management
- Application event handling (e.g. touch screen user interaction)
- Multitasking
- Wireless Printing
- Data protection via encryption
- Cut, copy, and paste functionality
- Web and text content presentation and management
- Data handling
- Inter-application integration
- Push notification in conjunction with Push Notification Service
- Local notifications (a mechanism whereby an application running in the background can gain the user's attention)
- Accessibility
- Accelerometer, battery, proximity sensor, camera and photo library interaction
- Touch screen gesture recognition
- File sharing (the ability to make application files stored on the device available via iTunes)
- Blue tooth based peer to peer connectivity between devices
- Connection to external displays

To get a feel for the richness of this framework it is worth spending some time browsing Apple's UIKit reference material which is available online at:

http://developer.apple.com/library/ios/#documentation/UIKit/Reference/UIKit_Framework/index.html

5.3.2 Map Kit Framework (MapKit.framework)

If you have spent any appreciable time with an iPhone then the chances are you have needed to use the Maps application more than once, either to get a map of a specific area or to generate driving directions to get you to your intended destination. The Map Kit framework provides a programming interface which enables you to build map based capabilities into your own applications. This allows you to, amongst other things, display scrollable maps for any location, display the map corresponding to the current geographical location of the device and annotate the map in a variety of ways.

5.3.3 Push Notification Service

The Push Notification Service allows applications to notify users of an event even when the application is not currently running on the device. Since the introduction of this service it has most commonly been used by news based applications. Typically when there is breaking news the service will generate a message on the device with the news headline and provide the user the option to load the corresponding news app to read more details. This alert is typically accompanied by an audio alert and vibration of the device. This feature should be used sparingly to avoid annoying the user with frequent interruptions.

5.3.4 Message UI Framework (MessageUI.framework)

The Message UI framework provides everything you need to allow users to compose and send email messages from within your application. In fact, the framework even provides the user interface elements through which the user enters the email addressing information and message content. Alternatively, this information may be pre-defined within your application and then displayed for the user to edit and approve prior to sending.

5.3.5 Address Book UI Framework (AddressUI.framework)

Given that a key function of the iPhone is as a communications device and digital assistant it should not come as too much of a surprise that an entire framework is dedicated to the integration of the address book data into your own applications. The primary purpose of the framework is to enable you to access, display, edit and enter contact information from the iPhone address book from within your own application.

5.3.6 Game Kit Framework (GameKit.framework)

The Game Kit framework provides peer-to-peer connectivity and voice communication between multiple devices and users allowing those running the same app to interact. When this feature was first introduced it was anticipated by Apple that it would primarily be used in multi-player games (hence the choice of name) but the possible applications for this feature clearly extend far beyond games development.

5.3.7 iAd Framework (iAd.framework)

The purpose of the iAd Framework is to allow developers to include banner advertising within their applications. All advertisements are served by Apple's own ad service.

5.3.8 Event Kit UI Framework (EventKit.framework)

The Event Kit UI framework was introduced in iOS 4 and is provided to allow the calendar and reminder events to be accessed and edited from within an application.

5.3.9 Accounts Framework (Accounts.framework)

iOS 5 introduced the concept of system accounts. These essentially allow the account information for other services to be stored on the iOS device and accessed from within application code. Currently system accounts are limited to Twitter accounts, though other services such as Facebook will likely appear in future iOS releases. The purpose of the Accounts Framework is to provide an API allowing applications to access and manage these system accounts.

5.3.10 Social Framework (Social.framework)

The Social Framework allows Twitter, Facebook and Sina Weibo integration to be added to applications. The framework operates in conjunction the Accounts Framework to gain access to the user's social network account information.

5.4 The iOS Media Layer

The role of the Media layer is to provide iOS with audio, video, animation and graphics capabilities. As with the other layers comprising the iOS stack, the Media layer comprises a number of frameworks which may be utilized when developing iPhone apps. In this section we will look at each one in turn.

5.4.1 Core Video Framework (CoreVideo.framework)

The Core Video Framework provides buffering support for the Core Media framework. Whilst this may be utilized by application developers it is typically not necessary to use this framework.

5.4.2 Core Text Framework (CoreText.framework)

The iOS Core Text framework is a C-based API designed to ease the handling of advanced text layout and font rendering requirements.

5.4.3 Image I/O Framework (ImageIO.framework)

The Image I/O framework, the purpose of which is to facilitate the importing and exporting of image data and image metadata, was introduced in iOS 4. The framework supports a wide range of image formats including PNG, JPEG, TIFF and GIF.

5.4.4 Assets Library Framework (AssetsLibrary.framework)

The Assets Library provides a mechanism for locating and retrieving video and photo files located on the iPhone device. In addition to accessing existing images and videos, this framework also allows new photos and videos to be saved to the standard device photo album.

5.4.5 Core Graphics Framework (CoreGraphics.framework)

The iOS Core Graphics Framework (otherwise known as the Quartz 2D API) provides a lightweight two dimensional rendering engine. Features of this framework include PDF document creation and presentation, vector based drawing, transparent layers, path based drawing, anti-aliased rendering, color manipulation and management, image rendering and gradients. Those familiar with the Quartz 2D API running on MacOS X will be pleased to learn that the implementation of this API is the same on iOS.

5.4.6 Core Image Framework (CoreImage.framework)

A new framework introduced with iOS 5 providing a set of video and image filtering and manipulation capabilities for application developers.

5.4.7 Quartz Core Framework (QuartzCore.framework)

The purpose of the Quartz Core framework is to provide animation capabilities on the iPhone. It provides the foundation for the majority of the visual effects and animation used by the UIKit framework and provides an Objective-C based programming interface for creation of specialized animation within iPhone apps.

5.4.8 OpenGL ES framework (OpenGLES.framework)

For many years the industry standard for high performance 2D and 3D graphics drawing has been OpenGL. Originally developed by the now defunct Silicon Graphics, Inc (SGI) during the 1990s in the form of GL, the open version of this technology (OpenGL) is now under the care of a non-profit consortium comprising a number of major companies including Apple, Inc., Intel, Motorola and ARM Holdings.

OpenGL for Embedded Systems (ES) is a lightweight version of the full OpenGL specification designed specifically for smaller devices such as the iPhone.

iOS 3 or later supports both OpenGL ES 1.1 and 2.0 on certain iPhone models (such as the iPhone 3GS and iPhone 4). Earlier versions of iOS and older device models support only OpenGL ES version 1.1.

5.4.9 GLKit Framework (GLKit.framework)

The GLKit framework is an Objective-C based API designed to ease the task of creating OpenGL ES based applications.

5.4.10 NewsstandKit Framework (NewsstandKit.framework)

The Newsstand application is a new feature of iOS 5 and is intended as a central location for users to gain access to newspapers and magazines. The NewsstandKit framework allows for the development of applications that utilize this new service.

5.4.11 iOS Audio Support

iOS is capable of supporting audio in AAC, Apple Lossless (ALAC), A-law, IMA/ADPCM, Linear PCM, µ-law, DVI/Intel IMA ADPCM, Microsoft GSM 6.10 and AES3-2003 formats through the support provided by the following frameworks.

5.4.12 AV Foundation framework (AVFoundation.framework)

An Objective-C based framework designed to allow the playback, recording and management of audio content.

5.4.13 Core Audio Frameworks (CoreAudio.framework, AudioToolbox.framework and AudioUnit.framework)

The frameworks that comprise Core Audio for iOS define supported audio types, playback and recording of audio files and streams and also provide access to the device's built-in audio processing units.

5.4.14 Open Audio Library (OpenAL)

OpenAL is a cross platform technology used to provide high-quality, 3D audio effects (also referred to as positional audio). Positional audio may be used in a variety of applications though is typically used to provide sound effects in games.

5.4.15 Media Player Framework (MediaPlayer.framework)

The iOS Media Player framework is able to play video in .mov, .mp4, .m4v, and .3gp formats at a variety of compression standards, resolutions and frame rates.

5.4.16 Core Midi Framework (CoreMIDI.framework)

Introduced in iOS 4, the Core MIDI framework provides an API for applications to interact with MIDI compliant devices such as synthesizers and keyboards via the iPhone's dock connector.

5.5 The iOS Core Services Layer

The iOS Core Services layer provides much of the foundation on which the previously referenced layers are built and consists of the following frameworks.

5.5.1 Address Book Framework (AddressBook.framework)

The Address Book framework provides programmatic access to the iPhone Address Book contact database allowing applications to retrieve and modify contact entries.

5.5.2 CFNetwork Framework (CFNetwork.framework)

The CFNetwork framework provides a C-based interface to the TCP/IP networking protocol stack and low level access to BSD sockets. This enables application code to be written that works with HTTP, FTP and Domain Name servers and to establish secure and encrypted connections using Secure Sockets Layer (SSL) or Transport Layer Security (TLS).

5.5.3 Core Data Framework (CoreData.framework)

This framework is provided to ease the creation of data modeling and storage in Model-View-Controller (MVC) based applications. Use of the Core Data framework significantly reduces the amount of code that needs to be written to perform common tasks when working with structured data within an application.

5.5.4 Core Foundation Framework (CoreFoundation.framework)

The Core Foundation framework is a C-based Framework which provides basic functionality such as data types, string manipulation, raw block data management, URL manipulation, threads and run loops, date and times, basic XML manipulation and port and socket communication. Additional XML capabilities beyond those included with this framework are provided via the libXML2 library. Though this is a C-based interface, most of the capabilities of the Core Foundation framework are also available with Objective-C wrappers via the Foundation Framework.

5.5.5 Core Media Framework (CoreMedia.framework)

The Core Media framework is the lower level foundation upon which the AV Foundation layer is built. Whilst most audio and video tasks can, and indeed should, be performed using the higher level AV Foundation framework, access is also provided for situations where lower level control is required by the iOS application developer.

5.5.6 Core Telephony Framework (CoreTelephony.framework)

The iOS Core Telephony framework is provided to allow applications to interrogate the device for information about the current cell phone service provider and to receive notification of telephony related events.

5.5.7 EventKit Framework (EventKit.framework)

An API designed to provide applications with access to the calendar, reminders and alarms on the device.

5.6 Foundation Framework (Foundation.framework)

The Foundation framework is the standard Objective-C framework that will be familiar to those who have programmed in Objective-C on other platforms (most likely Mac OS X). Essentially, this consists of Objective-C wrappers around much of the C-based Core Foundation Framework.

5.6.1 Core Location Framework (CoreLocation.framework)

The Core Location framework allows you to obtain the current geographical location of the device (latitude, longitude and altitude) and compass readings from with your own applications. The method used by the device to provide coordinates will depend on the data available at the time the information is requested and the hardware support provided by the particular iPhone model on which the app is running (GPS and compass are only featured on recent models). This will either be based on GPS readings, Wi-Fi network data or cell tower triangulation (or some combination of the three).

5.6.2 Mobile Core Services Framework (MobileCoreServices.framework)

The iOS Mobile Core Services framework provides the foundation for Apple's Uniform Type Identifiers (UTI) mechanism, a system for specifying and identifying data types. A vast range of predefined identifiers have been defined by Apple including such diverse data types as text, RTF, HTML, JavaScript, PowerPoint .ppt files, PhotoShop images and MP3 files.

5.6.3 Store Kit Framework (StoreKit.framework)

The purpose of the Store Kit framework is to facilitate commerce transactions between your application and the Apple App Store. Prior to version 3.0 of iOS, it was only possible to charge a customer for an app at the point that they purchased it from the App Store. iOS 3.0 introduced the concept of the "in app purchase" whereby the user can be given the option to make additional payments from within the application. This might, for example, involve implementing a subscription model for an application, purchasing additional functionality or even buying a faster car for you to drive in a racing game. With the introduction of iOS 6, content associated with an in-app purchase can now be hosted on, and downloaded from, Apple's servers.

5.6.4 SQLite library

Allows for a lightweight, SQL based database to be created and manipulated from within your iPhone application.

5.6.5 System Configuration Framework (SystemConfiguration.framework)

The System Configuration framework allows applications to access the network configuration settings of the device to establish information about the "reachability" of the device (for example whether Wi-Fi or cell connectivity is active and whether and how traffic can be routed to a server).

5.6.6 Quick Look Framework (QuickLook.framework)

The Quick Look framework provides a useful mechanism for displaying previews of the contents of file types loaded onto the device (typically via an internet or network connection) for which the application does not already provide support. File format types supported by this framework include iWork, Microsoft Office document, Rich Text Format, Adobe PDF, Image files, public.text files and comma separated (CSV).

5.7 **The iOS Core OS Layer**

The Core OS Layer occupies the bottom position of the iOS stack and, as such, sits directly on top of the device hardware. The layer provides a variety of services including low level networking, access to external accessories and the usual fundamental operating system services such as memory management, file system handling and threads.

5.7.1 Accelerate Framework (Accelerate.framework)

The Accelerate Framework provides a hardware optimized C-based API for performing complex and large number math, vector, digital signal processing (DSP) and image processing tasks and calculations.

5.7.2 External Accessory Framework (ExternalAccessory.framework)

Provides the ability to interrogate and communicate with external accessories connected physically to the iPhone via the 30-pin dock connector or wirelessly via Bluetooth.

5.7.3 Security Framework (Security.framework)

The iOS Security framework provides all the security interfaces you would expect to find on a device that can connect to external networks including certificates, public and private keys, trust policies, keychains, encryption, digests and Hash-based Message Authentication Code (HMAC).

5.7.4 System (LibSystem)

As we have previously mentioned, iOS is built upon a UNIX-like foundation. The System component of the Core OS Layer provides much the same functionality as any other UNIX like operating system. This layer includes the operating system kernel (based on the Mach kernel developed by Carnegie Mellon University) and device drivers. The kernel is the foundation on which the entire iOS platform is built and provides the low level interface to the underlying hardware. Amongst other things, the kernel is responsible for memory allocation, process lifecycle management, input/output, inter-process communication, thread management, low level networking, file system access and thread management.

As an app developer your access to the System interfaces is restricted for security and stability reasons. Those interfaces that are available to you are contained in a C-based library called LibSystem. As with all other layers of the iOS stack, these interfaces should be used only when you are absolutely certain there is no way to achieve the same objective using a framework located in a higher iOS layer.

Chapter 6

6. Testing iOS 6 Apps on the iPhone – Developer Certificates and Provisioning Profiles

In the chapter entitled *Creating a Simple iPhone iOS 6 App* we were able to run an application in the iOS Simulator environment bundled with the iOS 6 SDK. Whilst this is fine for most cases, in practice there are a number of areas that cannot be comprehensively tested in the simulator. For example, no matter how hard you shake your computer (not something we actually recommend) or where in the world you move it to, neither the accelerometer nor GPS features will provide real world results within the simulator (though the simulator does have the option to perform a basic virtual shake gesture and to simulate location data). If we really want to test an iOS application thoroughly in the real world, therefore, we need to install the app onto a physical iPhone device.

In order to achieve this a number of steps are required. These include generating and installing a developer certificate, creating an App ID and provisioning profile for your application, and registering the devices onto which you wish to directly install your apps for testing purposes. In the remainder of this chapter we will cover these steps in detail.

Note that the provisioning of physical devices requires membership in the iOS Developer Program, a topic covered in some detail in the chapter entitled *Joining the Apple iOS Developer Program*.

6.1 Creating an iOS Development Certificate Signing Request

Any apps that are to be installed on a physical iPhone device must first be signed using an iOS Development Certificate. In order to generate a certificate the first step is to generate a Certificate Signing Request (CSR). Begin this process by opening the Keychain Access tool on your Mac system. This tool is located in the *Applications -> Utilities* folder. Once launched, the Keychain Access main window will appear as illustrated in Figure 6-1:

Testing iOS 6 Apps on the iPhone – Developer Certificates and Provisioning Profiles

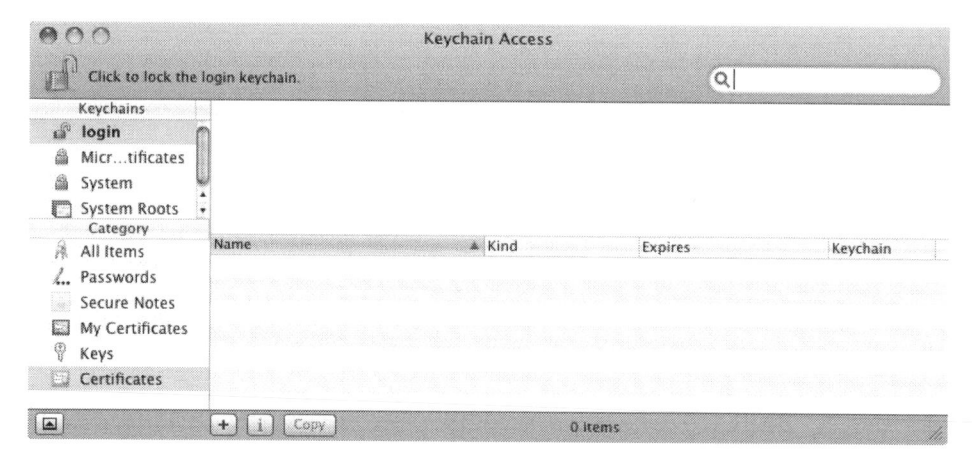

Figure 6-1

Within the Keychain Access utility, perform the following steps:

1. Select the *Keychain Access -> Preferences* menu and select *Certificates* in the resulting dialog:

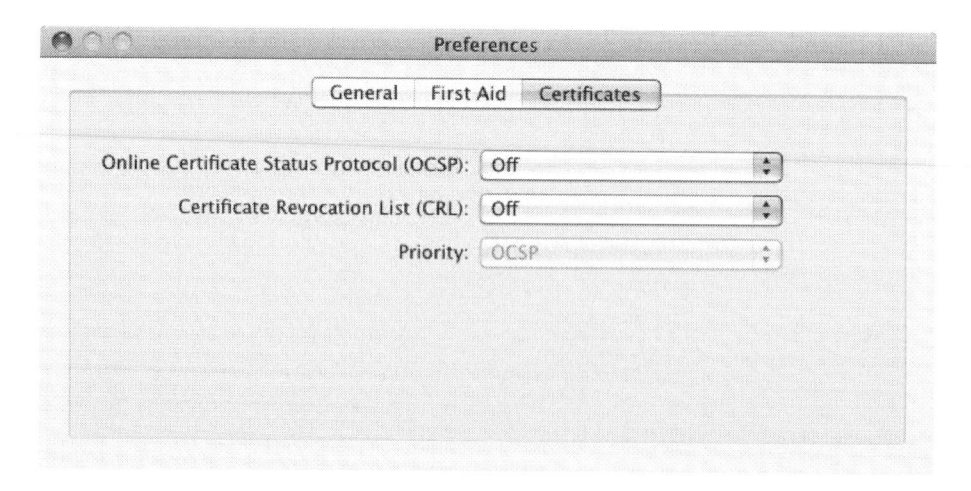

Figure 6-2

2. Within the Preferences dialog make sure that the Online Certificate Status Protocol (OCPS) and Certificate Revocation List (CRL) settings are both set to *Off*, then close the dialog.

3. Select the *Keychain Access -> Certificate Assistant -> Request a Certificate from a Certificate Authority...* menu option and enter your email and name exactly as registered with the iOS Developer Program. Leave the *CA Email Address* field blank and select the *Saved to Disk* and *Let me specify key pair information* options:

Testing iOS 6 Apps on the iPhone – Developer Certificates and Provisioning Profiles

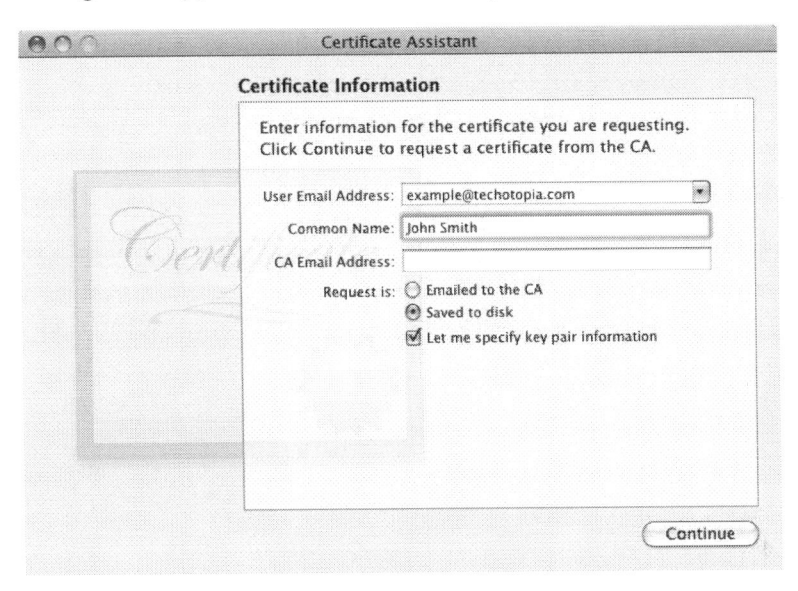

Figure 6-3

4. Clicking the *Continue* button will prompt for a file and location into which the CSR is to be saved. Either accept the default settings, or enter alternative information as desired at which point the *Key Pair Information* screen will appear as illustrated in Figure 6-4:

Figure 6-4

5. Verify that the 2048 bits key size and RSA algorithm options are selected before clicking on the *Continue* button. The certificate request will be created in the file previously specified and the *Conclusion* screen displayed. Click *Done* to dismiss the *Certificate Assistant* window.

6.2 Submitting the iOS Development Certificate Signing Request

Having created the Certificate Signing Request (CSR) the next step is to submit it for approval. This is performed within the iOS Provisioning Portal that is accessed from the Member Center of the Apple developer web site. Under *Developer Program Resources* on the main member center home page select *iOS Provisioning Portal*. Within the portal, select the *Certificates* link located in the left hand panel to display the Certificates page:

Figure 6-5

Click on the *Request Certificate* button, scroll down to the bottom of the text under the heading *Create an iOS Development Certificate* and click on the *Choose File* button. In the resulting file selection panel, navigate to the certificate signing request file created in the previous section and click on *Choose*. Once your file selection is displayed next to the *Choose File* button, click on the *Submit* button located in the bottom right hand corner of the web page. At this point you will be returned to the main Certificates page where your certificate will be listed as *Pending Issuance*.

Click on the link to download the *WWDR intermediate certificate* and, once downloaded, double click on it to install it into the keychain. This certificate is used by Xcode to verify that your certificates are both valid and issued by Apple.

If you are not the Team Administrator, you will need to wait until that person approves your request. If, on the other hand, you are the administrator for the iOS Developer Program membership you may approve your own certificate request by clicking on the *Approve* button located in the *Action* column of the *Current Certificates* table. If no approval button is present simply refresh the web page and the certificate should automatically appear listed as *Issued*. Your certificate is now active and the table will have refreshed to include a button to *Download* the certificate:

Figure 6-6

6.3 Installing an iOS Development Certificate

Once a certificate has been requested and issued it must be installed on the development system so that Xcode can access it and use it to sign any applications you develop. The first step in this process is to download the certificate from the iOS Provisioning Portal by clicking on the *Download* button located on the Certificates page outlined in the previous section. Once the file has downloaded, double click on it to load it into the Keychain Access tool. The certificate will then be listed together with a status (hopefully one that reads *This certificate is valid*):

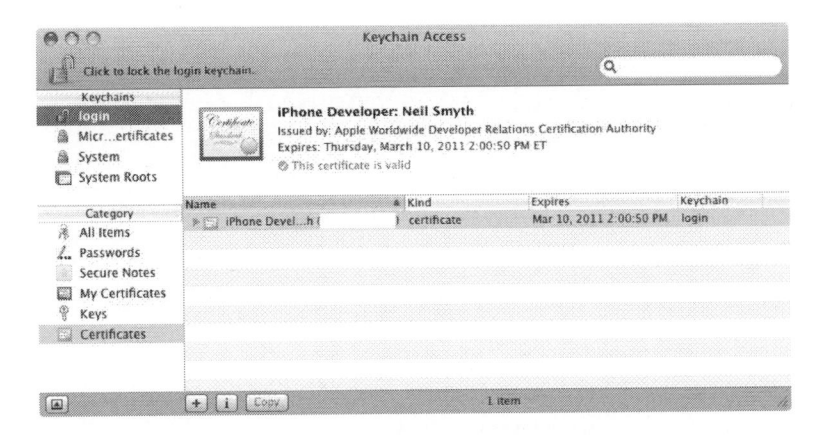

Figure 6-7

Your certificate is now installed into your Keychain and you are ready to move on to the next step.

41

6.4 Assigning Devices

Once you have a development certificate installed, the next step is to specify which devices are to be used to test the iOS apps you are developing. This is achieved by entering the Unique Device Identifier (UDID) for each device into the Provisioning Portal. Note that Apple restricts developers to 100 provisioned devices per year.

A new device may be added to the list of supported test devices either from within the Xcode Organizer window, or by logging into the iOS Developer Portal and manually adding the device. To add a device to the portal from within Organizer, simply connect the device, open the Organizer window in Xcode using the *Organizer* toolbar button, select the attached device from the left hand panel and click on the *Add to Portal* button. The Organizer will prompt for the developer portal login and password before connecting and enabling the device for testing.

Manually adding a device, on the other hand, requires the use of the iPhone's UDID. This may be obtained either via Xcode or iTunes. Begin by connecting the device to your computer using the docking connector. Once Xcode has launched the Organizer window will appear displaying summary information about the device (or may be opened by selecting the *Organizer* button in the Xcode toolbar). The UDID is listed next to the *Identifier* label as illustrated in Figure 6-8:

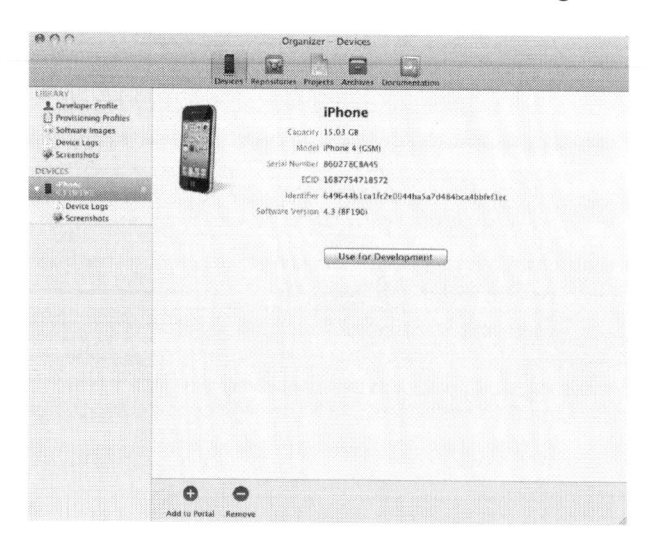

Figure 6-8

Alternatively, launch iTunes, select the device in the left hand pane and review the Summary information page. One of the fields on this page will be labeled as *Serial Number*. Click with the mouse on this number and it will change to display the UDID.

Testing iOS 6 Apps on the iPhone – Developer Certificates and Provisioning Profiles

Having identified the UDIDs of any devices you plan to use for app testing, select the *Devices* link located in the left hand panel of the iOS Provisioning Portal, and click on *Add Devices* in the resulting page. On the *Add Devices* page enter a descriptive name for the device and the 40 character UDID:

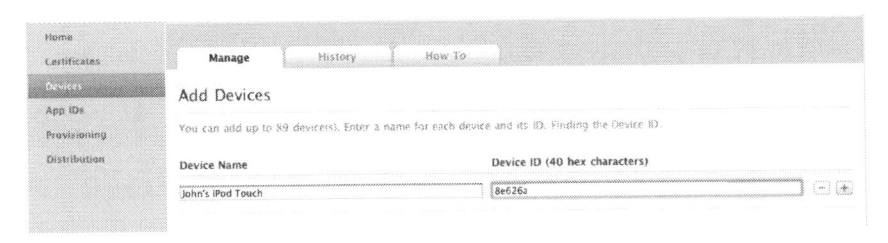

Figure 6-9

In order to add more than one device at a time simply click on the "+" button to create more input fields. Once you have finished adding devices click on the *Submit* button. The newly added devices will now appear on the main Devices page of the portal.

6.5 Creating an App ID

The next step in the process is to create an App ID for each app that you create. This ID allows your app to be uniquely identified within the context of the Apple iOS ecosystem. To create an App ID, select the *App IDs* link in the provisioning portal and click on the *New App ID* button to display the *Create App ID* screen as illustrated in Figure 6-10:

Figure 6-10

43

Enter a suitably descriptive name into the Description field and then make a Bundle Seed ID selection. If you have not created any previous Seed IDs then leave the default *Generate New* selection unchanged. If you have created a previous App ID and would like to use this for your new app, click on the menu and select the desired ID from the drop down list. Finally enter the Bundle Identifier. This is typically set to the reversed domain name of your company followed by the name of the app. For example, if you are developing an app called *MyApp,* and the URL for your company is *www.mycompany.com* then your Bundle identifier would be entered as:

```
com.mycompany.MyApp
```

If you would like to create an App ID that can be used for multiple apps then the wildcard character (*) can be substituted for the app name. For example:

```
com.mycompany.*
```

Having entered the required information, click on the *Submit* button to return to the main App ID page where the new ID will be listed.

6.6 Creating an iOS Development Provisioning Profile

The Provisioning Profile is where much of what we have created so far in the chapter is pulled together. The provisioning profile defines which developer certificates are allowed to install an application on a device, which devices can be used and which applications can be installed. Once created, the provisioning profile must be installed on each device on which the designated application is to be installed.

To create a provisioning profile, select the *Provisioning* link in the Provisioning Portal and click on the *New profile* button. In the resulting *Create iPhone Provisioning Profile* screen, perform the following tasks:

1. In the *Profile Name* field enter a suitably descriptive name for the profile you are creating.
2. Set the check box next to each certificate to specify which developers are permitted to use this particular profile.
3. Select an App ID from the menu.
4. Select the devices onto which the app is permitted to be installed.
5. Click on the *Submit* button.

Initially the profile will be listed as *Pending.* Refresh the page to see the status change to *Active.*

Now that the provisioning profile has been created, the next step is to download and install it. To do so, click on the *Download* button next to your new profile and save it to your local system (note that the file will have a *.mobileprovision* file name extension). Once saved, either drag and drop the file onto the Xcode icon in the dock or onto the *Provisioning Profiles* item located under *Library* in the

Xcode Organizer window. Once the provisioning profile is installed, it should appear in the Organizer window (Figure 6-11):

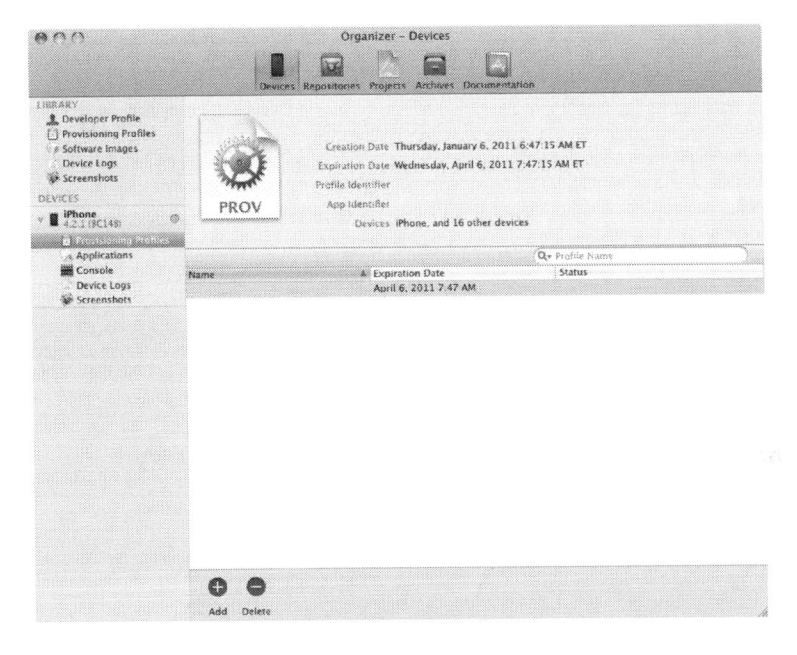

Figure 6-11

6.7 Enabling an iPhone Device for Development

With the provisioning profile installed select the target device in the left hand panel of the Organizer window and click on the *Use for Development* button. The Organizer will then prompt you for your Apple developer login and password.

Once a valid login and password have been entered, the Organizer will perform the steps necessary to install the provisioning profile on the device and enable it for application testing.

6.8 Associating an App ID with an App

Before we can install our own app directly onto a device, we must first embed the App ID created in the iOS Provisioning Portal and referenced in the provisioning profile into the app itself. To achieve this:

1. In the left hand panel of the main Xcode window, select the project navigator toolbar button and select the top item (the application name) from the resulting list.

2. Select the *Info* tab from in the center panel:

45

Testing iOS 6 Apps on the iPhone – Developer Certificates and Provisioning Profiles

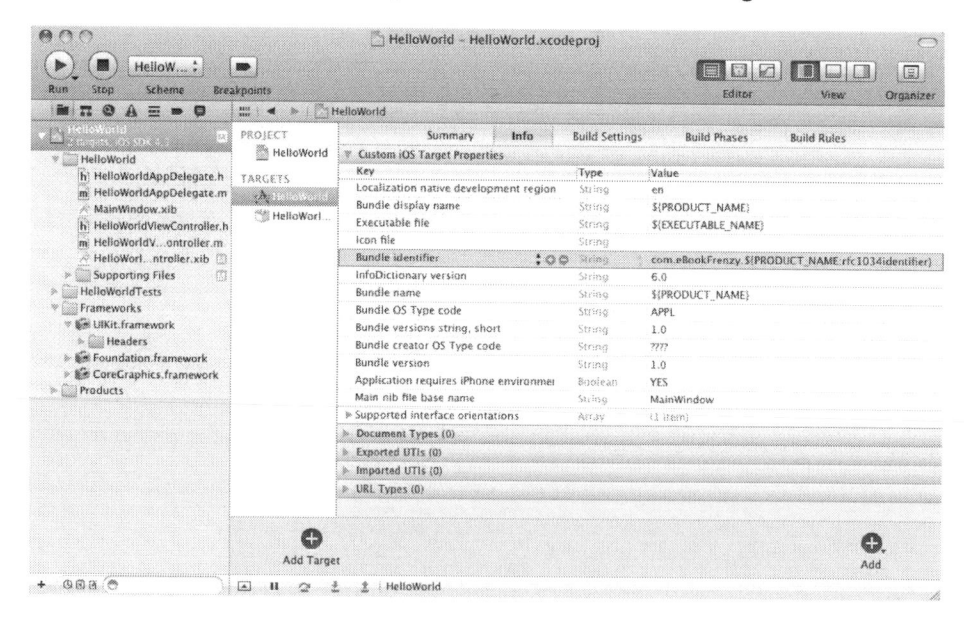

Figure 6-12

In the *Bundle Identifier* field enter the App ID you created in the iOS Provisioning Portal. This can either be in the form of your reverse URL and app name (for example *com.mycompany.HelloWorld*) or you can have the product name substituted for you by entering *com.mycompany.${PRODUCT_NAME:rfc1034indentifer}* as illustrated in Figure 6-12.

Once the App ID has been configured the next step is to build the application and install it onto the iPhone or iPod Touch device.

6.9 iOS and SDK Version Compatibility

Before attempting to install and run an application on a physical iPhone device it is important to be aware of issues relating to version compatibility between the SDK used for the development and the operating system running on the target device. For example, if the application was developed using version 4.3 of the iOS SDK then it is important that the iPhone on which the app is to be installed is running iOS version 4.3 or later. An attempt to run the app on an iPhone with an older version of iOS will result in an error reported by Xcode that reads "Xcode cannot run using the selected device. No Provisioned iOS devices are available. Connect an iOS device or choose an iOS simulator as the destination".

The absence in this message of any indication that the connected device simply has the wrong version of iOS installed on it may lead the developer to assume that a problem exists either with the connection or with the certification or provisioning profile. If you encounter this error message, therefore, it is worth checking version compatibility before investing what typically turns into many hours of effort trying to resolve non-existent connectivity and provisioning problems.

6.10 Installing an App onto a Device

Located in the top left hand corner of the main Xcode window is drop down menu which, when clicked, provides a menu of options to control the target run environment for the current app.

If either the iPhone or iPad simulator option is selected then the app will run within the corresponding simulated environment when it is built. To instruct Xcode to install and run the app on the device itself, simply change this menu to the setting corresponding to the connected device. Assuming the device is connected, click on the *Run* button and watch the status updates as Xcode compiles and links the source code. Once the code is built, Xcode will need to sign the application binary using your developer certificate. If prompted with a message that reads "codesign wants to sign using key "<key name>" in your keychain", select either *Allow* or *Always Allow* (if you do not wish to be prompted during future builds). Once signing is complete the status will change to "Installing <appname>.app on iPhone...". After a few seconds the app will be installed and will automatically start running on the device where it may be tested in a real world environment.

6.11 Summary

Without question, the iOS Simulator included with the iOS 6 SDK is an invaluable tool for application development. There are, however, a number of situations where it is necessary to test an application on a physical iPhone device. In this chapter we have covered the steps involved in provisioning applications for installation on an iPhone device.

Chapter 7

7. The Basics of Objective-C Programming

In order to develop iOS apps for the iPhone it is necessary to use a programming language called Objective-C. A comprehensive guide to programming in Objective-C is beyond the scope of this book. In fact, if you are unfamiliar with Objective-C programming we strongly recommend that you read a copy of a book called *Objective-C 2.0 Essentials*. This is the companion book to *iPhone iOS 6 Development Essentials* and will teach you everything you need to know about programming in Objective-C.

In the next two chapters we will take some time to go over the fundamentals of Objective-C programming with the goal of providing enough information to get you started.

7.1 Objective-C Data Types and Variables

One of the fundamentals of any program involves data, and programming languages such as Objective-C define a set of *data types* that allow us to work with data in a format we understand when writing a computer program. For example, if we want to store a number in an Objective-C program we could do so with syntax similar to the following:

```
int mynumber = 10;
```

In the above example, we have created a variable named *mynumber* of data type *integer* by using the keyword *int*. We then assigned the value of 10 to this variable.

Objective-C supports a variety of data types including int, char, float, double, boolean (BOOL) and a special general purpose data type named *id*.

Data type qualifiers are also supported in the form of long, long long, short, unsigned and signed. For example if we want to be able to store an extremely large number in our *mynumber* declaration we can qualify it as follows:

```
long long int mynumber =  345730489;
```

A variable may be declared as constant (i.e. the value assigned to the variable cannot be changed subsequent to the initial assignment) through the use of the *const* qualifier:

```
const char myconst = 'c';
```

7.2 Objective-C Expressions

Now that we have looked at variables and data types we need to look at how we work with this data in an application. The primary method for working with data is in the form of *expressions*.

The most basic expression consists of an *operator*, two *operands* and an *assignment*. The following is an example of an expression:

```
int myresult = 1 + 2;
```

In the above example the (+) operator is used to add two operands (1 and 2) together. The *assignment operator* (=) subsequently assigns the result of the addition to an integer variable named *myresult*. The operands could just have easily been variables (or a mixture of constants and variables) instead of the actual numerical values used in the example.

In the above example we looked at the addition operator. Objective-C also supports the following arithmetic operators:

Operator	Description
-(unary)	Negates the value of a variable or expression
*	Multiplication
/	Division
+	Addition
-	Subtraction
%	Modulo

Another useful type of operator is the compound assignment operator. This allows an operation and assignment to be performed with a single operator. For example one might write an expression as follows:

```
x = x + y;
```

The above expression adds the value contained in variable x to the value contained in variable y and stores the result in variable x. This can be simplified using the addition compound assignment operator:

```
x += y
```

Objective-C supports the following compound assignment operators:

The Basics of Objective-C Programming

Operator	Description
x += y	Add x to y and place result in x
x -= y	Subtract y from x and place result in x
x *= y	Multiply x by y and place result in x
x /= y	Divide x by y and place result in x
x %= y	Perform Modulo on x and y and place result in x
x &= y	Assign to x the result of logical AND operation on x and y
x |= y	Assign to x the result of logical OR operation on x and y
x ^= y	Assign to x the result of logical Exclusive OR on x and y

Another useful shortcut can be achieved using the Objective-C increment and decrement operators (also referred to as *unary operators* because they operate on a single operand). As with the compound assignment operators described in the previous section, consider the following Objective-C code fragment:

```
x = x + 1; // Increase value of variable x by 1
x = x - 1; // Decrease value of variable x by 1
```

These expressions increment and decrement the value of x by 1. Instead of using this approach it is quicker to use the ++ and -- operators. The following examples perform exactly the same tasks as the examples above:

```
x++; Increment x by 1
x--; Decrement x by 1
```

These operators can be placed either before or after the variable name. If the operator is placed before the variable name the increment or decrement is performed before any other operations are performed on the variable.

In addition to mathematical and assignment operators, Objective-C also includes a set of logical operators useful for performing comparisons. These operators all return a Boolean (*BOOL*) *true* (1) or *false* (0) result depending on the result of the comparison. These operators are *binary operators* in that they work with two operands.

Comparison operators are most frequently used in constructing program flow control logic. For example an *if* statement may be constructed based on whether one value matches another:

```
if (x == y)
      // Perform task
```

The result of a comparison may also be stored in a *BOOL* variable. For example, the following code will result in a *true* (1) value being stored in the variable result:

The Basics of Objective-C Programming

```
BOOL result;
int x = 10;
int y = 20;

result = x < y;
```

Clearly 10 is less than 20, resulting in a *true* evaluation of the *x < y* expression. The following table lists the full set of Objective-C comparison operators:

Operator	Description
x == y	Returns true if x is equal to y
x > y	Returns true if x is greater than y
x >= y	Returns true if x is greater than or equal to y
x < y	Returns true if x is less than y
x <= y	Returns true if x is less than or equal to y
x != y	Returns true if x is not equal to y

Objective-C also provides a set of so called logical operators designed to return boolean *true* and *false*. In practice *true* equates to 1 and *false* equates to 0. These operators both return boolean results and take boolean values as operands. The key operators are NOT (!), AND (&&), OR (||) and XOR (^).

The NOT (!) operator simply inverts the current value of a boolean variable, or the result of an expression. For example, if a variable named *flag* is currently 1 (true), prefixing the variable with a '!' character will invert the value to 0 (false):

```
bool flag = true; //variable is true
bool secondFlag;
secondFlag = !flag; // secondFlag set to false
```

The OR (||) operator returns 1 if one of its two operands evaluates to *true*, otherwise it returns 0. For example, the following example evaluates to true because at least one of the expressions either side of the OR operator is true:

```
if ((10 < 20) || (20 < 10))
       NSLog (@"Expression is true");
```

The AND (&&) operator returns 1 only if both operands evaluate to be true. The following example will return 0 because only one of the two operand expressions evaluates to *true*:

```
if ((10 < 20) && (20 < 10))
       NSLog (@"Expression is true");
```

The Basics of Objective-C Programming

The XOR (^) operator returns 1 if one and only one of the two operands evaluates to true. For example, the following example will return 1 since only one operator evaluates to be true:

```
if ((10 < 20) ^ (20 < 10))
     NSLog("Expression is true");
```

If both operands evaluated to true or both were false the expression would return false.

Objective-C uses something called a *ternary operator* to provide a shortcut way of making decisions. The syntax of the ternary operator (also known as the conditional operator) is as follows:

```
[condition] ? [true expression] : [false expression]
```

The way this works is that *[condition]* is replaced with an expression that will return either *true* (1) or *false* (0). If the result is true then the expression that replaces the *[true expression]* is evaluated. Conversely, if the result was *false* then the *[false expression]* is evaluated. Let's see this in action:

```
int x = 10;
int y = 20;
NSLog(@"Largest number is %i", x > y ? x : y );
```

The above code example will evaluate whether x is greater than y. Clearly this will evaluate to false resulting in y being returned to the NSLog call for display to the user:

```
2009-10-07 11:14:06.756 t[5724] Largest number is 20
```

7.3 Objective-C Flow Control with *if* and *else*

Since programming is largely an exercise in applying logic, much of the art of programming involves writing code that makes decisions based on one or more criteria. Such decisions define which code gets executed and, conversely, which code gets by-passed when the program is executing. This is often referred to as *flow control* since it controls the *flow* of program execution.

The *if* statement is perhaps the most basic of flow control options available to the Objective-C programmer.

The basic syntax of the Objective-C *if* statement is as follows:

```
if (boolean expression) {
// Objective-C code to be performed when expression evaluates to true
}
```

Note that the braces ({}) are only required if more than one line of code is executed after the *if* expression. If only one line of code is listed under the *if* the braces are optional. For example, the following is valid code:

The Basics of Objective-C Programming

```
int x = 10;
if (x > 10)
        x = 10;
```

The next variation of the *if* statement allows us to also specify some code to perform if the expression in the *if* statement evaluates to *false*. The syntax for this construct is as follows:

```
if (boolean expression) {
// Code to be executed if expression is true
} else {
// Code to be executed if expression is false
}
```

Using the above syntax, we can now extend our previous example to display a different message if the comparison expression evaluates to be *false*:

```
int x = 10;
if ( x > 9 )
{
        NSLog (@"x is greater than 9!");
} else {
        NSLog (@"x is less than 9!");
}
```

In this case, the second NSLog statement would execute if the value of x was less than 9.

So far we have looked at *if* statements which make decisions based on the result of a single logical expression. Sometimes it becomes necessary to make decisions based on a number of different criteria. For this purpose we can use the *if ... else if ...* construct, the syntax for which is as follows:

```
int x = 9;
if (x == 10)
{
        NSLog (@"x is 10");
}
else if (x == 9)
{
        NSLog (@"x is 9");
}
else if (x == 8)
{
        NSLog (@"x is 8");
}
```

7.4 Looping with the *for* Statement

The syntax of an Objective-C *for loop* is as follows:

```
for ( ''initializer''; ''conditional expression''; ''loop expression'' )
{
     // statements to be executed
}
```

The *initializer* typically initializes a counter variable. Traditionally the variable name *i* is used for this purpose, though any valid variable name will do. For example:

```
i = 0;
```

This sets the counter to be the variable *i* and sets it to zero. Note that the current widely used Objective-C standard (c89) requires that this variable be declared prior to its use in the *for* loop. For example:

```
int i=0;
for (i = 0; i < 100; i++)
{
     // Statements here
}
```

The next standard (c99) allows the variable to be declared and initialized in the *for* loop as follows:

```
for (int i=0; i<100; i++)
{
     //Statements here
}
```

It is possible to break out of a *for* loop before the designated number of iterations have been completed using the *break;* statement.

7.5 Objective-C Looping with *do* and *while*

The Objective-C *for* loop described previously works well when you know in advance how many times a particular task needs to be repeated in a program. There will, however, be instances where code needs to be repeated until a certain condition is met, with no way of knowing in advance how many repetitions are going to be needed to meet that criteria. To address this need, Objective-C provides the *while* loop.

The *while* loop syntax is defined follows:

```
while (''condition'')
{
        // Objective-C statements go here
}
```

7.6 Objective-C *do ... while* loops

It is often helpful to think of the *do ... while* loop as an inverted *while* loop. The *while* loop evaluates an expression before executing the code contained in the body of the loop. If the expression evaluates to *false* on the first check then the code is not executed. The *do ... while* loop, on the other hand, is provided for situations where you know that the code contained in the body of the loop will *always* need to be executed at least once.

The syntax of the *do ... while* loop is as follows:

```
do
{
        // Objective-C statements here
} while (''conditional expression'')
```

Chapter 8

8. The Basics of Object Oriented Programming in Objective-C

Objective-C provides extensive support for developing object-oriented iOS iPhone applications. The subject area of object oriented programming is, however, large. It is not an exaggeration to state that entire books have been dedicated to the subject. As such, a detailed overview of object oriented software development is beyond the scope of this book. Instead, we will introduce the basic concepts involved in object oriented programming and then move on to explaining the concept as it relates to Objective-C application development. Once again, whilst we strive to provide the basic information you need in this chapter, we recommend reading a copy of *Objective-C 2.0 Essentials* if you are unfamiliar with Objective-C programming.

8.1 What is an Object?

Objects are self-contained modules of functionality that can be easily used, and re-used as the building blocks for a software application.

Objects consist of data variables and functions (called *methods*) that can be accessed and called on the object to perform tasks. These are collectively referred to as *members*.

8.2 What is a Class?

Much as a blueprint or architect's drawing defines what an item or a building will look like once it has been constructed, a class defines what an object will look like when it is created. It defines, for example, what the *methods* will do and what the *member* variables will be.

8.3 Declaring an Objective-C Class Interface

Before an object can be instantiated we first need to define the class 'blueprint' for the object. In this chapter we will create a Bank Account class to demonstrate the basic concepts of Objective-C object oriented programming.

An Objective-C class is defined in terms of an *interface* and an *implementation*. In the interface section of the definition we specify the base class from which the new class is derived and also

The Basics of Object Oriented Programming in Objective-C

define the members and methods that the class will contain. The syntax for the interface section of a class is as follows:

```
@interface NewClassName: ParentClass {
    ClassMembers;
}
ClassMethods;
@end
```

The *ClassMembers* section of the interface defines the variables that are to be contained within the class (also referred to as *instance variables*). These variables are declared in the same way that any other variable would be declared in Objective-C.

The *ClassMethods* section defines the methods that are available to be called on the class. These are essentially functions specific to the class that perform a particular operation when called upon.

To create an example outline interface section for our BankAccount class, we would use the following:

```
@interface BankAccount: NSObject
{
}
@end
```

The parent class chosen above is the *NSObject* class. This is a standard base class provided with the Objective-C Foundation framework and is the class from which most new classes are derived. By deriving BankAccount from this parent class we inherit a range of additional methods used in creating, managing and destroying instances that we would otherwise have to write ourselves.

Now that we have the outline syntax for our class, the next step is to add some instance variables to it.

8.4 Adding Instance Variables to a Class

A key goal of object oriented programming is a concept referred to as *data encapsulation*. The idea behind data encapsulation is that data should be stored within classes and accessed only through methods defined in that class. Data encapsulated in a class are referred to as *instance variables*.

Instances of our BankAccount class will be required to store some data, specifically a bank account number and the balance currently held by the account. Instance variables are declared in the same way any other variables are declared in Objective-C. We can, therefore, add these variables as follows:

```
@interface BankAccount: NSObject
```

```
{
        double accountBalance;
        long accountNumber;
}
@end
```

Having defined our instance variables, we can now move on to defining the methods of the class that will allow us to work with our instance variables while staying true to the data encapsulation model.

8.5 Define Class Methods

The methods of a class are essentially code routines that can be called upon to perform specific tasks within the context of an instance of that class.

Methods come in two different forms, *class methods* and *instance methods*. Class methods operate at the level of the class, such as creating a new instance of a class. Instance methods, on the other hand, operate only on the instance of a class (for example performing an arithmetic operation on two instance variables and returning the result). *Class methods* are preceded by a plus (+) sign in the declaration and instance methods are preceded by a minus (-) sign. If the method returns a result, the name of method must be preceded by the data type returned enclosed in parentheses. If a method does not return a result, then the method must be declared as *void*. If data needs to be passed through to the method (referred to as *arguments*), the method name is followed by a colon, the data type in parentheses and a name for the argument. For example, the declaration of a method to set the account number in our example might read as follows:

```
-(void) setAccountNumber: (long) y;
```

The method is an *instance method* so it is preceded by the minus sign. It does not return a result so it is declared as *(void)*. It takes an argument (the account number) of type *long* so we follow the *accountNumber* name with a colon (:) specify the argument type *(long)* and give the argument a name (in this case we simply use *y*).

The following method is intended to return the current value of the account number instance variable (which is of type *long*):

```
-(long) getAccountNumber;
```

Methods may also be defined to accept more than one argument. For example to define a method that accepts both the account number and account balance we could declare it as follows:

```
-(void) setAccount: (long) y andBalance: (double) x;
```

Now that we have an understanding of the structure of method declarations within the context of the class *interface* definition, we can extend our BankAccount class accordingly:

The Basics of Object Oriented Programming in Objective-C

```objectivec
@interface BankAccount: NSObject
{
        double accountBalance;
        long accountNumber;
}
-(void) setAccount: (long) y andBalance: (double) x;
-(void) setAccountBalance: (double) x;
-(double) getAccountBalance;
-(void) setAccountNumber: (long) y;
-(long) getAccountNumber;
-(void) displayAccountInfo;
@end
```

Having defined the interface, we can now move on to defining the *implementation* of our class.

8.6 Declaring an Objective-C Class Implementation

The next step in creating a new class in Objective-C is to write the code for the methods we have already declared. This is performed in the *@implementation* section of the class definition. An outline implementation is structured as follows:

```objectivec
@implementation NewClassName
      ClassMethods
@end
```

In order to implement the methods we declared in the *@interface* section, therefore, we need to write the following code:

```objectivec
@implementation BankAccount

-(void) setAccount: (long) y andBalance: (double) x;
{
        accountBalance = x;
        accountNumber = y;
}
-(void) setAccountBalance: (double) x
{
        accountBalance = x;
}
-(double) getAccountBalance
{
        return accountBalance;
}
-(void) setAccountNumber: (long) y
{
```

```
        accountNumber = y;
}
-(long) getAccountNumber
{
        return accountNumber;
}
-(void) displayAccountInfo
{
        NSLog (@"Account Number %i has a balance of %f", accountNumber,
accountBalance);
}
@end
```

We are now at the point where we can write some code to work with our new BankAccount class.

8.7 Declaring and Initializing a Class Instance

So far all we have done is define the blueprint for our class. In order to do anything with this class, we need to create instances of it. The first step in this process is to declare a variable to store a pointer to the instance when it is created. We do this as follows:

```
BankAccount *account1;
```

Having created a variable to store a reference to the class instance, we can now allocate memory in preparation for initializing the class:

```
account1 = [BankAccount alloc];
```

In the above statement we are calling the *alloc* method of the BankAccount class (note that *alloc* is a *class method* inherited from the parent *NSObject* class, as opposed to an *instance method* created by us in the BankAccount class).

Having allocated memory for the class instance, the next step is to initialize the instance by calling the *init* instance method:

```
account1 = [account1 init];
```

For the sake of economy of typing, the above three statements are frequently rolled into a single line of code as follows:

```
BankAccount *account1 = [[BankAccount alloc] init];
```

8.8 Automatic Reference Counting (ARC)

In the first step of the previous section we allocated memory for the creation of the class instance. In releases of the iOS SDK prior to iOS 5, good programming convention would have dictated that memory allocated to a class instance be released when the instance is no longer required. Failure to do so, in fact, would have resulted in memory leaks with the result that the application would continue to use up system memory until it was terminated by the operating system. Those familiar with Java will be used to relying on the *garbage collector* to free up unused memory automatically. Historically, Objective-C has provided similar functionality on other platforms but not for iOS. That has now changed with the introduction of automatic reference counting in the iOS 5 SDK and it is not necessary to call the release method of an object when it is no longer used in an application.

When creating a new project, Xcode now provides the option to implement automatic reference counting in the application code. If this option is selected, the code should not make calls to *release*, *retain*, *autorelease* or *dealloc* methods. Management of objects at this level is now handled for you by ARC.

8.9 Calling Methods and Accessing Instance Data

Given the length of this chapter, now is probably a good time to recap what we have done so far. We have now created a new class called *BankAccount*. Within this new class we declared some instance variables to contain the bank account number and current balance together with some instance methods used to set, get and display these values. In the preceding section we covered the steps necessary to create and initialize an instance of our new class. The next step is to learn how to call the instance methods we built into our class.

The syntax for invoking methods is to place the object pointer variable name and method to be called in square brackets ([]). For example, to call the *displayAccountInfo* method on the instance of the class we created previously we would use the following syntax:

```
[account1 displayAccountInfo];
```

When the method accepts a single argument, the method name is followed by a colon (:) followed by the value to be passed to the method. For example, to set the account number:

```
[account1 setAccountNumber: 34543212];
```

In the case of methods taking multiple arguments (as is the case with our *setAccount* method) syntax similar to the following is employed:

```
[account1 setAccount: 4543455 andBalance: 3010.10];
```

8.10 Objective-C and Dot Notation

Those familiar with object oriented programming in Java, C++ or C# are probably reeling a little from the syntax used in Objective-C. They are probably thinking life was much easier when they could just

use something called *dot notation* to set and get the values of instance variables. The good n
that one of the features introduced into version 2.0 of Objective-C is support for dot notation.

Dot notation involves accessing an instance variable by specifying a class instance followed by a dot followed in turn by the name of the instance variable or property to be accessed:

```
classinstance.property
```

For example, to the get current value of our *accountBalance* instance variable:

```
double balance1 = account1.accountBalance;
```

Dot notation can also be used to set values of instance properties:

```
account1.accountBalance = 6789.98;
```

A key point to understand about dot notation is that it only works for instance variables for which synthesized accessor methods have been declared. If you attempt to use dot notation to access an instance variable for which no synthesized accessor is available the code will fail to compile with an error similar to:

```
error: request for member 'accountBalance' in something not a structure or union
```

8.11 How Variables are Stored

When we declare a variable in Objective-C and assign a value to it we are essentially allocating a location in memory where that value is stored. Take, for example, the following variable declaration:

```
int myvar = 10;
```

When the above code is executed, a block of memory large enough to hold an integer value is reserved in memory and the value of 10 is placed at that location. Whenever we reference this variable in code, we are actually using the variable value. For example, the following code adds the value of *myvar* (i.e. 10) to the constant value 20 to arrive at a result of 30.

```
int result = 20 + myvar;
```

Similarly, when we pass a variable through as an argument to a method or function we are actually passing the *value* of the variable, not the variable itself. To better understand this concept, consider the following sample program:

```
#import <Foundation/Foundation.h>

void myFunction (int i)
{
```

63

```
        i = i + 10;
}

int main (int argc, const char * argv[])
{
    @autoreleasepool {

        int myvar = 10;

        NSLog (@"Before call to function myvar = %i", myvar);
        myFunction (myvar);
        NSLog (@"After call to function myvar = %i", myvar);
    }
    return 0;
}
```

The above program consists of a main function that declares our *myvar* variable and displays the current value. It then calls the function *myFunction* passing through the value of the *myvar* variable. The *myFunction* function adds 10 to the value it was passed as an argument and then returns to the main function where the value of *myvar* is once again displayed. When compiled and executed the following output is displayed:

```
Before call to function myvar = 10
After call to function myvar = 10
```

Clearly, even though the value passed through to *myFunction* was increased by 20 the value of *myvar* remained unchanged. This is because what was passed through as an argument to *myFunction* was the *value* of *myvar*, not the *myvar* variable itself. Therefore, in *myFunction* we were simply working on a constant value of 10 that had absolutely no connection to the original *myvar* variable.

In order to be able to work on the actual variable in the function we need to use something called indirection.

8.12 An Overview of Indirection

Indirection involves working with pointers to the location of variables and objects rather than the contents of those items. In other words, instead of working with the *value* stored in a variable, we work with a *pointer* to the *memory address* where the variable is located.

Pointers are declared by prefixing the name with an asterisk (*) character. For example to declare a pointer to our *myvar* variable we would write the following code:

```
int myvar = 10;
```

```
int *myptr;
```

In the above example we have declared our *myvar* variable and then declared a variable named *myptr* as being of type *pointer to an integer*. Having declared both our variable and our pointer we now need to assign the *address* of our variable to the pointer. The address of a variable is referenced by prefixing it with the ampersand (&) character. We can, therefore, extend our example to assign the address of the *myvar* variable to the *myptr* variable:

```
int myvar = 10;
int *myptr;

myptr = &myvar;
```

We now have now implemented a level of indirection by creating a *pointer* to our variable. As such, we can now pass this pointer through as an argument to our function such that we will be able to work on the actual variable, rather than just the value (10) of the variable. In order to access the value of a variable using a pointer to that variable, we prefix the pointer variable name with an asterisk (*). When we do this we are telling the compiler we want to work with the contents of the variable or object at the memory address contained within the pointer:

```
int myvar = 10;
int *myptr;

myptr = &myvar;

*myptr = *myptr + 15;
```

Similarly, we can modify our function to accept a pointer to an integer and perform the addition on that variable. As such, we can now modify our previous program as follows:

```
#import <Foundation/Foundation.h>

void myFunction (int *i)
{
        *i = *i + 10;
}

int main (int argc, const char * argv[])
{
     @autoreleasepool {

            int myvar = 10;
            int *myptr;
```

```
            myptr = &myvar;
            NSLog (@"Before call to function myvar = %i", myvar);
            myFunction (myptr);
            NSLog (@"After call to function myvar = %i", myvar);
    }
    return 0;
}
```

Now because we are passing through a pointer to *myvar* when we call the function and have modified the function to work with the contents of the variable, the output clearly indicates that the function changed the value of *myvar* when it was called. We have, therefore, just used indirection.

```
Before call to function myvar = 10
After call to function myvar = 20
```

8.13 Indirection and Objects

So far in this chapter we have used indirection with a variable. The same concept applies for objects. In previous chapters we worked with our BankAccount class. When doing so we wrote statements similar to the following:

```
BankAccount *account1;
```

```
BankAccount *account1 = [[BankAccount alloc] init];
```

The first line of code (BankAccount *account1;) is actually declaring that the variable named *account1* is a *pointer to an object of type BankAccount*. We are, therefore, using indirection to provide a handle to our object. The calls to the *alloc* and *init* methods subsequently create the object in memory and the assign the address of that object to the *account1* pointer variable. We are, therefore, using indirection once again.

One key point to note is that we do not need to prefix the object pointer with a * when perform operations such as calling methods. For example, we can call a method on our *account1* object without using an asterisk:

```
[account1 displayAccountInfo];
```

8.14 Indirection and Object Copying

Due to the fact that references to objects utilize indirection it is important to understand that when we use the assignment operator (=) to assign one object to another we are not actually creating a copy of the object. Instead, we are creating a copy of the pointer to the object. Consider, therefore, the following code:

```
BankAccount *account1;
BankAccount *account2;

BankAccount *account1 = [[BankAccount alloc] init];

account2 = account1;
```

In the above example, we will end up with two pointers (*account1* and *account2*) that point to the same location in memory.

8.15 Creating the Program Section

The last stage in this exercise is to bring together all the components we have created so that we can actually see the concept working. The last section we need to look at is called the *program section*. This is where we write the code to create the class instance and call the instance methods. Most Objective-C programs have a *main()* routine which is the start point for the application. The following sample main routine creates an instance of our class and calls the methods we created:

```
int main (int argc, const char * argv[])
{
  @autoreleasepool {

        // Create a variable to point to our class instance
        BankAccount *account1;

        // Allocate memory for class instance
        account1 = [BankAccount alloc];

        // Initialize the instance
        account1 = [account1 init];

        // Set the account balance
        [account1 setAccountBalance: 1500.53];

        // Set the account number
        [account1 setAccountNumber: 34543212];

        // Call the method to display the values of
        // the instance variables
        [account1 displayAccountInfo];

        // Set both account number and balance
        [account1 setAccount: 4543455 andBalance: 3010.10];
```

67

```objectivec
        // Output values using the getter methods
        NSLog(@"Number = %i, Balance = %f",
        [account1 getAccountNumber],
        [account1 getAccountBalance]);
    }
    return 0;

}
```

8.16 Bringing it all Together

Our example is now complete so let's bring all the components together:

```objectivec
#import <Foundation/Foundation.h>

// Interface Section Starts Here

@interface BankAccount: NSObject
{
        double accountBalance;
        long accountNumber;
}
-(void) setAccount: (long) y andBalance: (double) x;
-(double) getAccountBalance;
-(long) getAccountNumber;
-(void) setAccountBalance: (double) x;
-(void) setAccountNumber: (long) y;
-(void) displayAccountInfo;
@end


// Implementation Section Starts Here

@implementation BankAccount

-(void) setAccount: (long) y andBalance: (double) x;
{
        accountBalance = x;
        accountNumber = y;
}
-(void) setAccountBalance: (double) x
{
        accountBalance = x;
}
-(double) getAccountBalance
```

```
{
        return accountBalance;
}
-(void) setAccountNumber: (long) y
{
        accountNumber = y;
}
-(long) getAccountNumber
{
        return accountNumber;
}
-(void) displayAccountInfo
{
        NSLog (@"Account Number %i has a balance of %f",
            accountNumber, accountBalance);
}
@end

// Program Section Starts Here

int main (int argc, const char * argv[])
{
   @autoreleasepool {
     BankAccount *account1;
     account1 = [BankAccount alloc];
     account1 = [account1 init];
     [account1 setAccountBalance: 1500.53];
     [account1 setAccountNumber: 34543212];
     [account1 displayAccountInfo];
     [account1 setAccount: 4543455 andBalance: 3010.10];
     NSLog(@"Number = %i, Balance = %f",
        [account1 getAccountNumber], [account1 getAccountBalance]);
    }
   return 0;
}
```

When the above code is saved, compiled and executed we should expect to see the following output:

```
2009-10-14 14:44:06.634 t[4287:10b] Account Number 34543212 has a balance of 1500.530000
2009-10-14 14:44:06.635 t[4287:10b] Number = 4543455, Balance = 3010.100000
```

The Basics of Object Oriented Programming in Objective-C

8.17 Structuring Object-Oriented Objective-C Code

Our example is currently contained within a single source file. In practice, the convention is to place the interface and implementation in their own include files that are then *included* in the program source file. Generally the interface section is contained within a file called *ClassName.h* where *ClassName* is the name of the class. In our case, we would create a file called *BankAccount.h* containing the following:

```
#import <Foundation/Foundation.h>

@interface BankAccount: NSObject
{
        double accountBalance;
        long accountNumber;
}
-(void) setAccount: (long) y andBalance: (double) x;
-(double) getAccountBalance;
-(long) getAccountNumber;
-(void) setAccountBalance: (double) x;
-(void) setAccountNumber: (long) y;
-(void) displayAccountInfo;
@end
```

Next, the implementation section goes in a file traditionally named *ClassName.m* where *ClassName* once again is refers to the name of the class. For example, *BankAccount.m* will contain the following (note that it is necessary to import the *BankAccount.h* file into this file):

```
#import "BankAccount.h"

@implementation BankAccount

-(void) setAccount: (long) y andBalance: (double) x;
{
        accountBalance = x;
        accountNumber = y;
}
-(void) setAccountBalance: (double) x
{
        accountBalance = x;
}
-(double) getAccountBalance
{
        return accountBalance;
}
```

```
-(void) setAccountNumber: (long) y
{
        accountNumber = y;
}
-(long) getAccountNumber
{
        return accountNumber;
}
-(void) displayAccountInfo
{
        NSLog (@"Account Number %i has a balance of %f",
           accountNumber, accountBalance);
}
@end
```

Finally, we will create our program file and call it *bank.m* (though any suitable name will do as long as it has a *.m* filename extension). This file also needs to import our interface file (*BankAccount.h*):

```
#import "BankAccount.h"

int main (int argc, const char * argv[])
{
  @autoreleasepool {

      BankAccount *account1;
      account1 = [BankAccount alloc];
      account1 = [account1 init];
      [account1 setAccountBalance: 1500.53];
      [account1 setAccountNumber: 34543212];
      [account1 displayAccountInfo];
      [account1 setAccount: 4543455 andBalance: 3010.10];
      NSLog(@"Number = %i, Balance = %f",
         [account1 getAccountNumber], [account1 getAccountBalance]);
  }
  return 0;
}
```

Chapter 9

9. The Basics of Modern Objective-C

The preceding two chapters have provided an introduction to Objective-C for readers encountering the language for the first time. This chapter, however, is intended for those programmers familiar with Objective-C 2.0 who would like to get a quick overview of some of the new features added to the language to coincide with the release of the iOS 6 SDK. These changes have combined to create what, for want of a better description, has come to be referred to as "Modern Objective-C"

Whilst an in-depth analysis of all the changes in Modern Objective-C is beyond the scope of this book, it is intended that this chapter will cover some key features that will make your life easier as an iOS developer.

9.1 Default Property Synthesis

Experienced iOS developers will be intimately familiar with the concept of declaring a property in an interface file and then having to synthesize that property within the implementation file. Consider, for example, the following typical interface file for a class in an iOS application:

```
@interface AudioViewController : UIViewController
    <AVAudioPlayerDelegate>

@property (strong, nonatomic) AVAudioPlayer *audioPlayer;
@property (strong, nonatomic) IBOutlet UISlider *volumeControl;
@end
```

Prior to the changes in Modern Objective-C, the above properties would have required matching @synthesize directives in the corresponding implementation file in order to be accessible from within the implementation code:

```
#import "AudioViewController.h"

@interface AudioViewController ()

@end
```

73

The Basics of Modern Objective-C

```
@implementation AudioViewController
@synthesize audioPlayer = _audioPlayer;
@synthesize volumeControl = _volumeControl;
    .
    .
    .
@end
```

In the case of Modern Objective-C, however, the synthesis takes place by default, making the use of @synthesize declarations unnecessary:

```
#import "AudioViewController.h"

@interface AudioViewController ()

@end

@implementation AudioViewController
    .
    .
    .
@end
```

When using default property synthesis, instance variable properties are accessible from within code using the property name prefixed with an underscore. For example, the following code accesses the previously declared *volumeControl* property:

```
#import "AudioViewController.h"

@interface AudioViewController ()

@end

@implementation AudioViewController
    .
    .
    .
- (void)enableVolume {
    _volumeControl.enable = YES;
}
@end
```

9.2 Method Ordering

Method ordering refers to the positions in which methods are declared relative to each other within an Objective-C source file. In previous versions of the language, a method had to be declared above any points in the code file from which it was called. Placing a method after a location where it was called resulted in a compilation error.

Historically, the following code would result in a compilation error stating that the method named *flushBuffer* could not be found:

```
@implementation DatabaseHandler

- (void)closeDatabaseFile {
    [self flushBuffer];
}

- (void)flushBuffer {
    // Code here to flush buffer
}
```

With Modern Objective-C the ordering of methods is no longer an issue and the above code will compile without any errors.

9.3 NSNumber Literals

Up until the introduction of Modern Objective-C, the initialization of NSNumber objects required calling class methods and, consequently, a considerable amount of typing for what was really a very basic coding task. For the sake of an example, consider the code to initialize an NSNumber object with an integer value:

```
NSNumber *number = [NSNumber numberWithInt:512];
```

With Modern Objective-C, the same result can be achieved with the following, much simpler, line of code:

```
NSNumber *number = @512;
```

Similarly, consider the code to initialize an NSNumber instance with a floating point number:

```
NSNumber *number = [NSNumber numberWithFloat:512.123f];
```

The above code can now be replaced with the following:

```
NSNumber *number = @512.123f;
```

The Basics of Modern Objective-C

In fact, all the *numberWith<type>* methods of the NSNumber class can now be replaced with literals when using Modern Objective-C:

```
NSNumber *number;

number = @'A'; // Character
number = @YES; // Boolean
number = @43231ul // Unsigned Long
number = @12343111 // Long Long
number = @1254.23 // Float
number = @123 // Integer
number = @123.432 // Double
```

9.4 Array Literals

Modern Objective-C also considerably simplifies the task of working with NSArray objects. With array literals, the initialization of an NSArray now involves considerably less typing and finished code that is easier to read.

The following code fragment demonstrates the old way of initializing an NSArray object:

```
NSArray *carMakes;

carMakes = [[NSArray alloc]
                initWithObjects:@"Chevy",
                @"BMW",
                @"Toyota",
                @"Volvo",
                @"Smart", nil];
```

Using array literals, the above code can now be replaced with the following simpler syntax:

```
NSArray *carMakes;

carMakes = @[@"Chevy", @"BMW", @"Toyota", @"Volvo", @"Smart"];
```

Similarly, accessing array elements now requires less typing. For example, the following code used to be required to access element 0 of an array:

```
NSString *firstCar = [carMakes objectAtIndex:0];
```

With Modern Objective-C, this can be shortened to the following syntax:

```
NSString *firstCar = carMakes[0];
```

This new syntax uses a programming construct referred to as *index subscripting* and will be familiar to those who have used other programming languages such as Java, C, C++ or C#.

Similarly, the same index subscripting syntax can be used when setting array elements. For example, the following line of code assigns a new string to the second element of the array:

```
carMakes[1] = @"VW Jetta";
```

Note that the literal syntax creates immutable arrays by default. If a mutable array is required when using this syntax, the *mutableCopy* method of the object must be called. For example:

```
NSMutableArray *carMakes = [@[@"Chevy", @"BMW", @"Toyota", @"Volvo",
@"Smart"] mutableCopy];
```

9.5 Dictionary Literals

Modern Objective-C brings a similar approach to managing NSDictionary objects. Using classic Objective-C syntax, an NSDictionary object would typically be initialized with multiple key-value pairs using the following syntax:

```
NSDictionary *bookListing = [NSDictionary dictionaryWithObjectsAndKeys:
object1, key1, object2, key2, object3, key3, nil];
```

With Modern Objective-C, however, this same code can be simplified using the following, easier to read syntax:

```
NSDictionary *bookListing = @{key1 : object1, key2 : object2, key3 :
object3};
```

As with arrays, subscripting may be used when referencing dictionary items. The following code, for example, extracts the object for "key1" from the bookListing dictionary using *keyed subscripting*:

```
bookObject = bookListing[key1];
```

Similarly, the following code replaces the object associated with "key2" in the dictionary with the object referenced by newBookObject:

```
bookListing[key2] = newBookObject;
```

As is the case with arrays, dictionary objects created using this literal syntax are immutable by default.

9.6 Summary

The Objective-C compiler version that accompanies the iOS 6 SDK includes a number of improvements designed to make code easier to read and to minimize the amount of typing required

The Basics of Modern Objective-C

by the programmer. This chapter has covered some of the key features added to what is referred to as Modern Objective-C. Where appropriate, the code examples in the remainder of this book will use Modern Objective-C syntax.

Chapter 10

10. An Overview of the iPhone iOS 6 Application Development Architecture

So far we have covered a considerable amount of ground intended to provide a sound foundation of knowledge on which to begin building iPhone iOS 6 based apps. Before plunging into writing your first app, however, it is vital that you have a basic understanding of some key methodologies associated with the overall architecture of an iOS application.

These methodologies, also referred to as *design patterns,* clearly define how your applications should be designed and implemented in terms of code structure. The patterns we will explore in this chapter are *Model View Controller (MVC), Subclassing, Delegation* and *Target-Action*.

If you are new to these concepts this can seem a little confusing to begin with. Much of this will become clearer, however, once we start working on some examples in subsequent chapters.

10.1 Model View Controller (MVC)

In the days before object-oriented programming (and even for a time after object-oriented programming became popular) there was a tendency to develop applications where the code for the user interface was tied tightly to the code containing the application logic and data handling. This coupling made application code difficult to maintain and locked the application to a single user interface. If, for example, an application written for Microsoft Windows needed to be migrated to Mac OS, all the code written specifically for the Windows UI toolkits had to be ripped out from amongst the data and logic code and replaced with the Mac OS equivalent. If the application then needed to be turned into a web based solution, the process would have to be repeated again. Attempts to achieve this feat were usually found to be prohibitively expensive and ultimately ended up with the applications being completely re-written each time a new platform needed to be targeted.

The goal of the MVC design pattern is to divorce the logic and data handling code of an application from the presentation code. In this concept, the Model encapsulates the data for the application, the View presents and manages the user interface and the Controller provides the basic logic for the application and acts as the go-between, providing instructions to the Model based on user interactions with the View and updating the View to reflect responses from the Model. The true value of this approach is that the Model knows absolutely nothing about the presentation of the application. It just knows how to store and handle data and perform certain tasks when called upon by the Controller. Similarly, the View knows nothing about the data and logic model of the application.

Within the context of an object-oriented programming environment such as the iOS 6 SDK and Objective-C, the Model, View and Controller components are objects. It is also worth pointing out that applications are not restricted to a single model, view and controller. In fact, an app can consist of multiple view objects, controller objects and model objects.

The way that a view controller object interacts with a Model is through the methods and properties exposed by that model object. This, in fact, is no different from the way one object interacts with another in any object-oriented programming environment.

In terms of the view controller's interactions with the view, however, things get a little more complicated. In practice, this is achieved using the *Target-Action pattern*, together with *Outlets* and *Actions*.

10.2 The Target-Action pattern, IBOutlets and IBActions

When you create an iOS 6 iPhone app you will typically design the user interface (the view) using the Interface Builder tool and write the view controller and model code in Objective-C using the Xcode code editor. The previous section looked briefly at how the view controller interacts with the model. In this section we will look at how the view created in Interface Builder and our view controller code interact with each other.

When a user interacts with objects in the view, for example touching and releasing a button control, an *event* is triggered (in this case the event is called a *Touch Up Inside* event). The purpose of the *Target-Action* pattern is to allow you to specify what happens when such events are triggered. In other words, this is how you connect the objects in the user interface you have designed in the Interface Builder tool to the back end Objective-C code you have written in the Xcode environment. Specifically, this allows you to define which method of which controller object gets called when a user interacts in a certain way with a view object.

The process of wiring up a view object to call a specific method on a view controller object is achieved using something called an *Action*. An action is a method defined within a view controller object that is designed to be called when an event is triggered in a view object. This allows us to connect a view object created within a nib file using Interface Builder to the code that we have written in the view controller class. This is one of the ways that we bridge the separation between the *View* and the *Controller* in our MVC design pattern. As we will see in *Creating an Interactive iOS 6 iPhone App*, action methods are declared using the *IBAction* keyword.

The opposite of an *Action* is the *Outlet*. As previously described, an Action allows a view object to call a method on a controller object. An Outlet, on the other hand, allows a view controller object method to directly access the properties of a view object. A view controller might, for example, need to set the text on a UILabel object. In order to do so an Outlet must first have been defined using the *IBOutlet* keyword. In programming terms, an *IBOutlet* is simply an instance variable that references the view object to which access is required.

10.3 Subclassing

Subclassing is an important feature of any object-oriented programming environment and the iOS SDK is no exception to this rule. Subclassing allows us to create a new class by deriving from an existing class and then extending the functionality. In so doing we get all the functionality of the parent class combined with the ability to extend the new class with additional methods and properties.

Subclassing is typically used where a pre-existing class does most, but not all, of what you need. By subclassing we get all that existing functionality without having to duplicate it and simply add on the functionality that was missing.

We will see an example of subclassing in the context of iOS 6 development when we start to work with view controllers. The UIKit framework contains a class called the UIViewController. This is a generic view controller from which we will create a subclass so that we can add our own methods and properties.

10.4 Delegation

Delegation allows an object to pass the responsibility for performing one or more tasks on to another object. This allows the behavior of an object to be modified without having to go through the process of subclassing it.

A prime example of delegation can be seen in the case of the UIApplication class. The UIApplication class, of which every iOS iPhone application must have one (and only one) instance, is responsible for the control and operation of the application within the iOS environment. Much of what the UIApplication object does happens in the background. There are, however, instances where it gives us the opportunity to include our own functionality into the mix. UIApplication allows us to do this by delegating some methods to us. As an example, UIApplication delegates the *didFinishLaunchingWithOptions*: method to us so that we can write code to perform specific tasks when the app first loads (for example taking the user back to the point they were at when they last exited). If you still have a copy of the Hello World project created earlier in this book you will see the template for this method in the *HelloWorldAppDelegate.m* file.

10.5 Summary

In this chapter we have provided an overview of a number of design patterns and discussed the importance of these patterns in terms of structuring iOS 6 applications to run on the iPhone. Whilst these patterns may seem unclear to some, the relevance and implementation of such concepts will become clearer as we progress through the examples included in subsequent chapters of this book.

Chapter 11

11. Creating an Interactive iOS 6 iPhone App

In the previous chapter we looked at the design patterns that we will need to learn and use regularly in the course of developing iOS 6 based iPhone applications. In this chapter we will work through a detailed example intended to demonstrate the View-Controller relationship together with the implementation of the Target-Action pattern to create an example interactive iOS 6 based iPhone application.

11.1 Creating the New Project

The purpose of the application we are going to create is to perform unit conversions from Fahrenheit to Centigrade. Obviously the first step is to create a new Xcode project to contain our application. Start Xcode and on the Welcome screen select *Create a new Xcode project.* On the template screen choose the *Application* option located under *iOS* in the left hand panel and select *Single View Application.* Click *Next,* set the product name and class prefix to *UnitConverter,* enter your company identifier, make sure that the *Devices* menu is set to *iPhone* and that the storyboard and unit test options are switched off. On the final screen, choose a location in which to store the project files and click on *Create* to proceed to the main Xcode project window.

11.2 Creating the User Interface

Before we begin developing the logic for our interactive application we are going to start by designing the user interface. When we created the new project, Xcode generated an Interface Builder NIB file for us and named it *UnitConverterViewController.xib.* It is within this file that we will create our user interface, so select this file from the project navigator in the left hand panel to load it into Interface Builder. Once Interface Builder has loaded the file, select the far right of the three *View* buttons in the Xcode toolbar to display the right hand panel. In the lower panel, select the *Show the Object library* toolbar button (the black 3D cube) to display the UI components. Alternatively, simply select the *View -> Utilities -> Show Object Library* menu option:

Creating an Interactive iOS 6 iPhone App

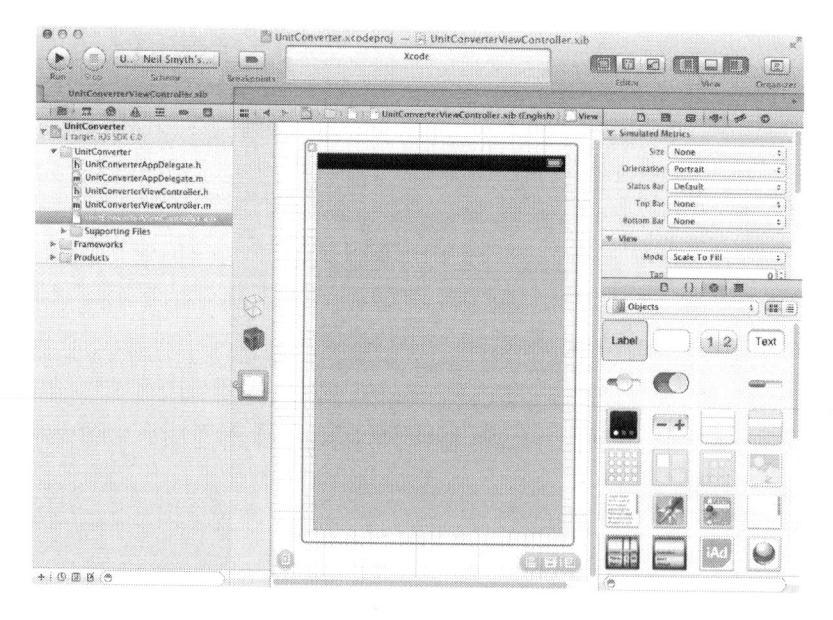

Figure 11-1

From the Object Library panel, drag a Text Field object onto the View design area. Resize the object and position it so that it appears as outlined in Figure 11-2.

Within the Attribute Inspector panel (*View -> Utilities -> Show Attribute Inspector*), type the words *Enter temperature* into the *Placeholder* text field. This text will then appear in a light gray color in the text field as a visual cue to the user.

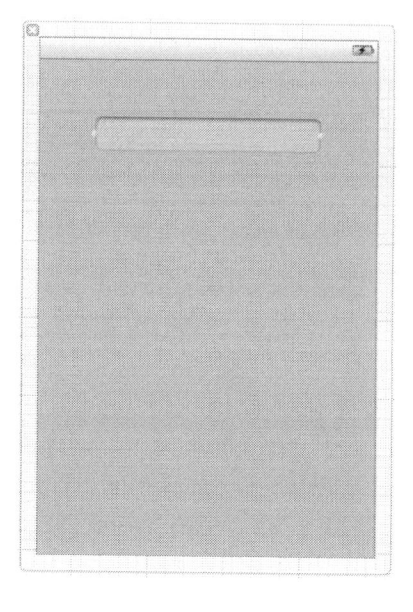

Figure 11-2

84

Creating an Interactive iOS 6 iPhone App

Now that we have created the text field into which the user will enter a temperature value, the next step is to add a Button object which may be pressed to initiate the conversion. To achieve this drag and drop a *Rounded Rect Button* object from the Library to the View. Double click the button object so that it changes to text edit mode and type the word *Convert* onto the button. Finally, select the button and drag it beneath the text field until the blue dotted line appears indicating it is centered vertically in relation to the text field before releasing the mouse button.

The last user interface object we need to add is a label where the result of the conversion will be displayed. Add this by dragging a Label object from the Library window to the View and position it beneath the button. Stretch the width of the label so that it is approximately a third of the overall width of the view and reposition it using the blue guidelines to ensure it is centered in relation to the button.

Double click on the label to highlight the text and press the backspace key to clear it (we will set the text from within a method of our View Controller class when the conversion calculation has been performed). Though the label is now no longer visible it is still present in the view. If you click where it is located it will be highlighted with the resize dots visible.

At this point the user interface design phase of our project is complete and the view should appear as illustrated in Figure 11-3. We now are ready to try out a test build and run.

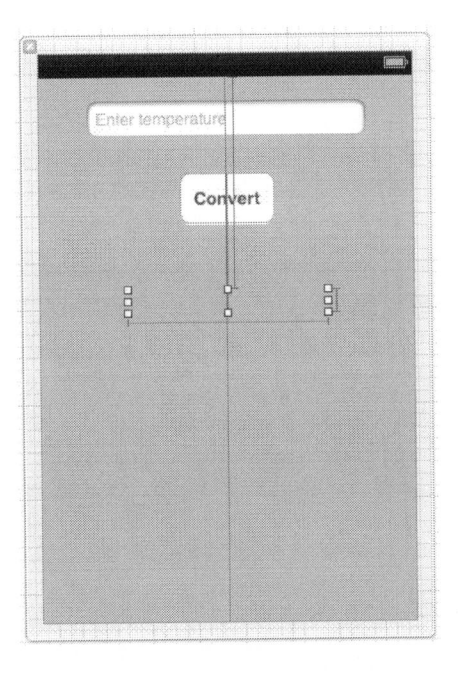

Figure 11-3

85

Creating an Interactive iOS 6 iPhone App

11.3 Building and Running the Sample Application

Before we move on to implementing the controller code for our application and then connecting it to the user interface we have designed we should first perform a test build and run of the application so far. Click on the *Run* button located in the toolbar to compile the application and run it in the simulator. If you are not happy with the way your interface looks feel free to reload it into Interface Builder and make improvements. Assuming the user interface appears to your satisfaction in the simulator we are ready to start writing some Objective-C code to add some logic to our controller. Exit from the simulator before proceeding to the next step by selecting the *iOS Simulator -> Quit iOS Simulator* menu option.

11.4 Adding Actions and Outlets

When the user enters a temperature value into the text field and touches the convert button we need to trigger an action which will perform a calculation to convert the temperature. The result of that calculation will then be presented to the user via the label object. The *Action* will be in the form of a method which we will declare and implement in our View Controller class. Access to the text field and label objects from the view controller method will be implemented through the use of *Outlets*.

Before we begin, now is a good time to highlight an example of the use of subclassing as previously described in *An Overview of the iPhone iOS 6 Application Development Architecture*. The UIKit framework contains a class called UIViewController which provides the basic foundation for adding view controllers to an application. In order to create a functional application, however, we inevitably need to add functionality specific to our application to this generic view controller class. This is achieved by subclassing the UIViewController class and extending it with the additional functionality we need.

When we created our new project, Xcode anticipated our needs and automatically created a subclass of UIViewController and named it UnitConverterViewController (using the class prefix entered when the project was initially created). In so doing, Xcode also created two source files; a header file named *UnitConverterViewController.h* and a source code file named *UnitConverterViewController.m*.

Selecting the *UnitConverterViewController.h* file in the Xcode project navigator panel will display the contents of the file in the editing pane:

```
#import <UIKit/UIKit.h>

@interface UnitConverterViewController : UIViewController
@end
```

Creating an Interactive iOS 6 iPhone App

As we can see from the above code, a new class called UnitConverterViewController has been created that is a subclass of the UIViewController class belonging to the UIKit framework.

The next step is to extend the subclass to include the two outlets and our action method. We will begin by adding outlets for our text field and label objects by declaring variables and using the IBOutlet keyword:

```
#import <UIKit/UIKit.h>

@interface UnitConverterViewController : UIViewController

@property (strong, nonatomic) IBOutlet UILabel *resultLabel;
@property (strong, nonatomic) IBOutlet UITextField *tempText;
@end
```

Next we need to declare the action that will be called when the user touches the Convert button in our user interface. This is declared using the IBAction keyword:

```
#import <UIKit/UIKit.h>

@interface UnitConverterViewController : UIViewController

@property (strong, nonatomic) IBOutlet UILabel *resultLabel;
@property (strong, nonatomic) IBOutlet UITextField *tempText;
- (IBAction)convertTemp:(id)sender;
@end
```

We have now declared that our View Controller class contains a method called *convertTemp:*. Having made that declaration, we need to implement the method in the implementation source file. To do so, select the *UnitConverterViewController.m* file so that the contents appear in the editing pane.

```
#import "UnitConverterViewController.h"

@interface UnitConverterViewController ()

@end

@implementation UnitConverterViewController

- (void)viewDidLoad
{
    [super viewDidLoad];
    // Do any additional setup after loading the view, typically from a nib.
```

87

Creating an Interactive iOS 6 iPhone App

```objc
}

- (void)didReceiveMemoryWarning
{
    [super didReceiveMemoryWarning];
    // Dispose of any resources that can be recreated.
}

@end
```

At the bottom of the file, and before the @end marker, add the new *convertTemp:* method as follows:

```objc
#import "UnitConverterViewController.h"

@implementation UnitConverterViewController
  .
  .
  .
- (IBAction) convertTemp: (id) sender {
    double fahrenheit = [_tempText.text doubleValue];
    double celsius = (fahrenheit - 32) / 1.8;

    NSString *resultString = [[NSString alloc]
            initWithFormat: @"Celsius %f", celsius];
    _resultLabel.text = resultString;
}
@end
```

Before we proceed it is probably a good idea to pause and explain what is happening in the above code. Those already familiar with Objective-C, however, may skip the next few paragraphs.

In this file we are implementing the *convertTemp:* method originally declared in the .h file. This method takes as a single argument a reference to the *sender*. The sender is the object that triggered the call to the method (in this case our Button object). Whilst we won't be using this object in the current example, this can be used to create a general purpose method in which the behavior of the method changes depending on how (i.e. via which object) it was called. We could, for example, create two buttons labeled *Convert to Fahrenheit* and *Convert to Celsius* respectively, each of which calls the same *convertTemp:* method. The method would then access the *sender* object to identify which button triggered the event and perform the corresponding type of unit conversion.

Next, the code declares a variable of type double in order to handle the fact that the user may have entered a floating point value. We then use dot notation to access the *text* property (which holds the text displayed in the text field) of the UITextField object. By convention this object is referenced using the property name declared for the outlet prefixed with an underscore character (in this case *_tempText*). This property is itself an object of type NSString. The NSString class has an instance method named *doubleValue* that converts the string value to a double. We therefore call this method on the text property and assign the result to our Fahrenheit variable.

Having extracted the text entered by the user and converted it to a number, we then perform the conversion to Celsius and store the result in another variable named celsius. Next, we create a new NSString object and initialize it with text comprising the word Celsius and the result of our conversion. In doing so, we declare a pointer to this new object and call it resultText.

Finally, we use dot notation to assign the new string to the text property of our UILabel object so that it is displayed to the user.

Before proceeding to the next section of this chapter, now is a good time to perform a build and run to make sure that no errors exist in the code. Click on the *Run* button in the toolbar and correct any reported syntax errors or warnings.

11.5 Connecting the Actions and Outlets to the User Interface

The final step in developing our application is to connect the actions and outlets we have declared in the view controller class to the actual objects in the user interface view. Fortunately, this can all be done visually from within the Interface Builder tool.

With this in mind, select the *UnitConverterViewController.xib* file to load the user interface into Interface Builder. We will begin by connecting the IBOutlet instance variables we created in our view controller class to the label and text field objects respectively. Located in the narrow panel to the left of the graphical view of the user interface are three icons. Clicking on the grey circle containing a white arrow at the bottom of this panel will expand the panel to provide more detail if it is not already expanded:

Creating an Interactive iOS 6 iPhone App

Figure 11-4

The top icon is the *File's Owner*. This icon represents the file containing the class that invokes the user interface contained in the NIB file when the application runs. In this instance it is the UnitConverterViewController class, where we declared our actions and outlets.

To connect the resultLabel IBOutlet variable to the label object, hold down the Control key on the keyboard, click on the *File's Owner* icon and drag the mouse to the location of the label object in the user interface design. A blue line will extend from the icon to the object as illustrated in Figure 11-5:

Creating an Interactive iOS 6 iPhone App

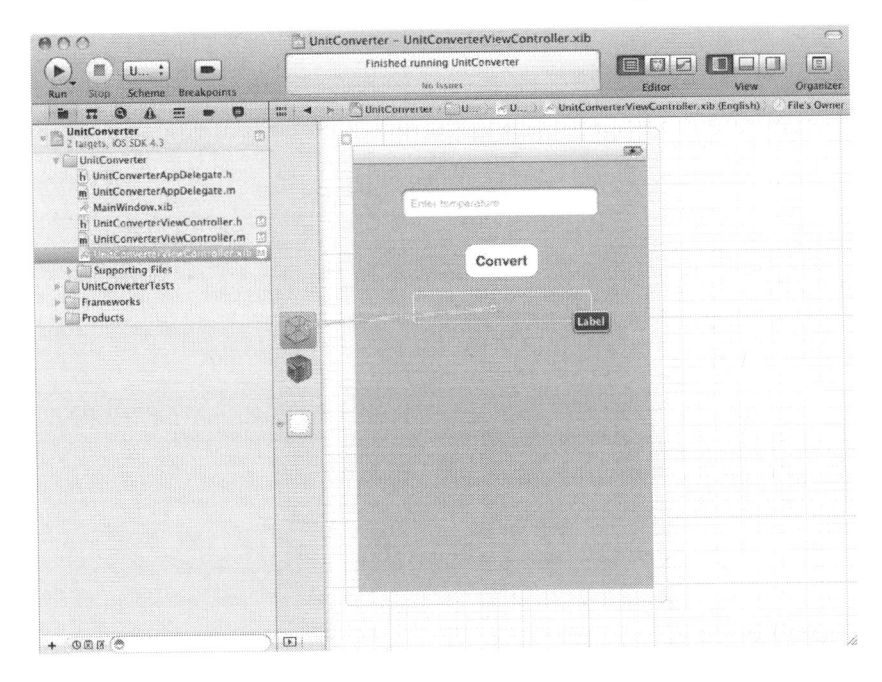

Figure 11-5

Upon releasing the mouse button, Interface Builder will display a list of IBOutlet variables matching the type of the object selected:

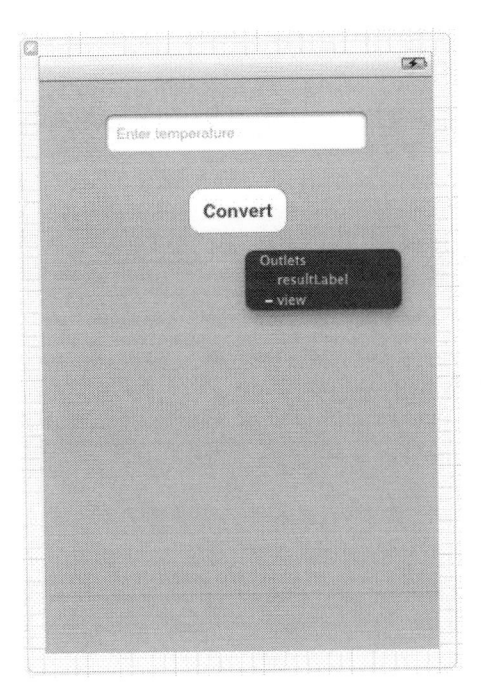

Figure 11-6

91

Select *resultLabel* from the menu to complete the connection. Repeat these steps to connect the *tempText* outlet to the text field object. In order to view the connections you have created, display the Connections Inspector by selecting the far right hand toolbar option in the *top* section of the right hand panel or selecting *View -> Utilities -> Show Connections Inspector*. For example, Figure 11-7 shows the connection information for our label object listed under *Referencing Outlets*:

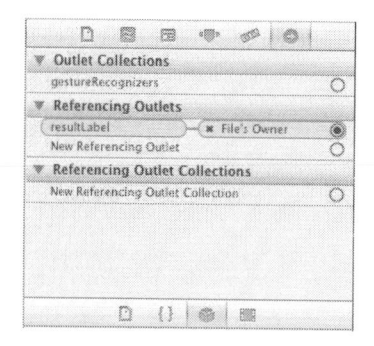

Figure 11-7

The final step is to connect the button object to our *convertTemp* action method. Cocoa Touch objects typically have a wide range of events that may be triggered by the user. To obtain a full listing of the events available on a particular object, display the *Connections Inspector* and select the button object in the view window. Listed under *Sent Events* in the connections panel is a list of the events that may be triggered by the button object. In this instance, we are interested in the *Touch Up Inside* event. This event is triggered when a user touches and then releases the button without first sliding it outside the boundaries of the button. When this action is performed we want our *convertTemp* method to be called. To make this connection, move the mouse pointer to the small circle next to the *Touch Up Inside* event in the connections panel, click the mouse button and drag to the *File's Owner* icon as illustrated in Figure 11-8.

Releasing the mouse button over the *File's Owner* object will display a menu with a list of methods available in the view controller class. In our case the only method is *convertTemp* so select that method to initiate the connection. The event listing in the Connections panel will subsequently update to reflect the new connection.

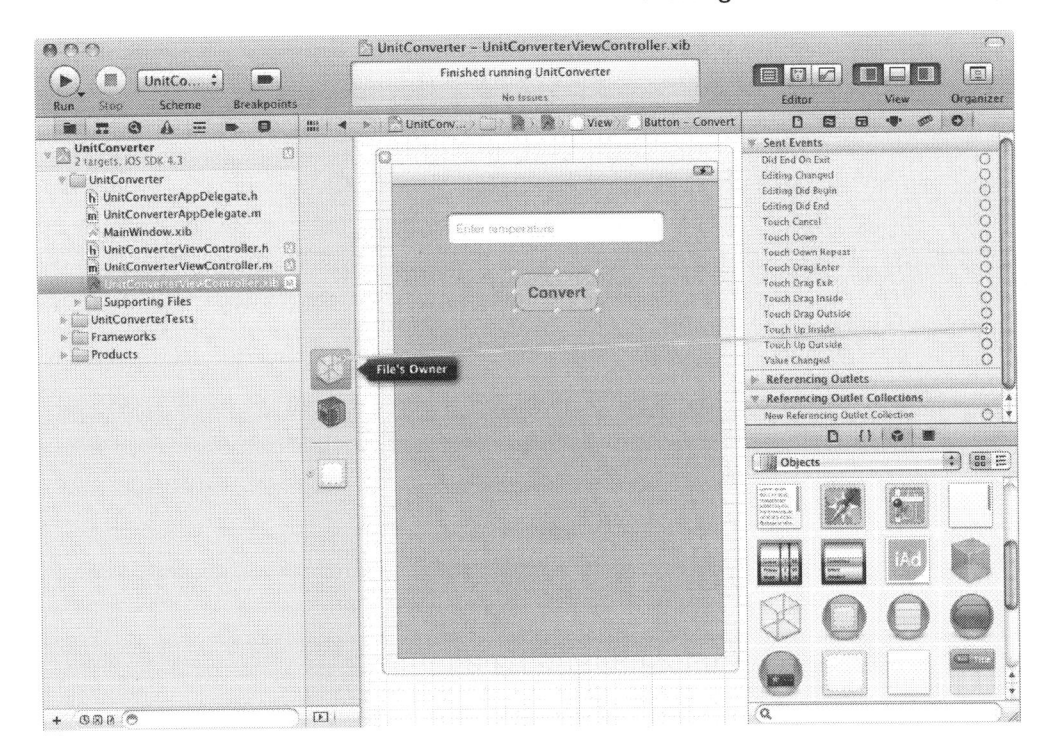

Figure 11-8

11.6 Building and Running the Finished Application

From within the Xcode project window click on *Run* to compile the application and run it in the simulator. Once the application is running, click inside the text field and enter a Fahrenheit temperature. Next, click on the Convert button to display the equivalent temperature in Celsius. Assuming all went to plan your application should appear as outlined in the following figure (note that if the keyboard obscures the result label you will need to reload the user interface design into Interface Builder and move the label, button and text field objects so that they are all positioned in the top half of the view):

Figure 11-9

11.7 Summary

In this chapter we have put into practice some of the theory covered in previous chapters, in particular the separation of the view from the controller, the use of subclassing and the implementation of the Target-Action pattern through the use of actions and outlets.

You may have noticed whilst testing your application that once the keyboard is displayed it doesn't then go away even when you touch the *Return* key or any other area on the screen. In order to make the keyboard disappear we need to write some code. The next chapter, entitled *Writing iOS 6 Code to Hide the iPhone Keyboard* provides a tutorial on how to hide the keyboard when either the keyboard Return key or the background view are touched by the user.

Chapter 12

12. Writing iOS 6 Code to Hide the iPhone Keyboard

When the user of an iPhone iOS 6 app is required to enter data (typically as a result of touching a text input view such as a text field) the keyboard automatically appears on the screen. As illustrated in the preceding chapter, however, the keyboard does not automatically go away when the user has finished typing.

If you have experience of using other iPhone apps you will have noticed that pressing the Return key on the keyboard or tapping anywhere on the background of the user interface usually causes the keyboard to recede from view. In actual fact, the developers of these applications had to write some code specifically to implement this functionality. In this chapter we will cover the steps necessary to implement this behavior in your own iOS 6 apps.

12.1 Creating the Example App

If you are reading this book sequentially you can perform the steps outlined in this chapter using the example application outlined in the previous chapter. For those who are dipping into this book as a reference source and would like to try out a simple example it will first be necessary to create a sample application.

Begin by launching Xcode and creating a new Single View based iPhone iOS application product named *HideKeyboard* with a matching class prefix. From within the main Xcode window select the *HideKeyboardViewController.xib* file to edit the user interface. Within the Interface Builder panel drag a Text Field object from the *Object Library* panel (*View -> Utilities -> Show Object Library*) onto the *View* area.

Now that we have the user interface designed, we need to create an *outlet* so that we can reference our text field from our view controller code. Within the main Xcode window select the *HideKeyboardViewController.h* file and edit it so that it appears as follows:

```
#import <UIKit/UIKit.h>

@interface HideKeyboardViewController : UIViewController

@property (strong, nonatomic) IBOutlet UITextField *textField;
```

Writing iOS 6 Code to Hide the iPhone Keyboard

@end

Select the *HideKeyboardViewController.xib* file once again and connect the text field to the view controller outlet by holding down the Ctrl key while clicking and dragging with the mouse from the *File's Owner* icon to the text field object in the View. From the resulting menu select the *textField* outlet.

12.2 Hiding the Keyboard when the User Touches the Return Key

The next step is to wire up our application so that the keyboard is dismissed when the user touches the keyboard *Return* key. To do so, we need to write a method that will *resign* the *first responder* on the text field (in other words hide the keyboard) when the return key is pressed.

Begin by editing the *HideKeyboardViewController.h* interface file to declare the method which we will name *textFieldReturn*:

```
#import <UIKit/UIKit.h>

@interface HideKeyboardViewController : UIViewController

@property (strong, nonatomic) IBOutlet UITextField *textField;
-(IBAction)textFieldReturn:(id)sender;
@end
```

Having declared the method we now need to implement it in the *HideKeyboardViewController.m* implementation file:

```
#import "HideKeyboardViewController.h"

@interface HideKeyboardViewController ()

@end

@implementation HideKeyboardViewController

-(IBAction)textFieldReturn:(id)sender
{
    [sender resignFirstResponder];
}
.
.
.
@end
```

In the above method we are making a call to the *resignFirstResponder* method of the object that triggered the event. The *first responder* is the object with which the user is currently interacting (in this instance, the virtual keyboard displayed on the iPhone screen).

Having written the code for our method we now need to wire up our user interface so that it gets called at the appropriate time. We will perform this task in Interface Builder, so select *HideKeyboardViewController.xib* once more.

Select the text field in the view and display the Connections Inspector (*View -> Utilities -> Connections Inspector*) in the right hand panel. Click on the circle to the right of the *Did End on Exit* event, drag the line to the *File's Owner* icon and select *textFieldReturn* from the list of available methods.

Click on the *Run* button in the Xcode toolbar. When the application appears in the iOS Simulator, select the text field so that the keyboard appears and then touch the *Return* key. The keyboard should subsequently disappear from view.

12.3 Hiding the Keyboard when the User Taps the Background

The second mechanism for hiding the keyboard involves wiring up an event to be called when the user touches the background view of the screen. We will begin the process by writing the action method to perform this task. From within Xcode select the *HideKeyboardViewController.h* file and add a declaration for our new *backgroundTouched* action method:

```
#import <UIKit/UIKit.h>

@interface HideKeyboardViewController : UIViewController

@property (nonatomic, strong) IBOutlet UITextField *textField;
- (IBAction)textFieldReturn:(id)sender;
- (IBAction)backgroundTouched:(id)sender;
@end
```

Select the *HideKeyboardViewController.m* file and implement the action by calling the *resignFirstResponder* method of our textField object:

```
#import "HideKeyboardViewController.h"

@interface HideKeyboardViewController ()

@end

@implementation HideKeyboardViewController
```

97

```objc
-(IBAction)textFieldReturn:(id)sender
{
    [sender resignFirstResponder];
}

-(IBAction)backgroundTouched:(id)sender
{
    [_textField resignFirstResponder];
}
    .
    .
    .
@end
```

Having written the code for our action method we now need to make sure it gets called when the user touches the background view. This involves some work in Interface Builder, so select the *HideKeyboardViewController.xib* file.

In order to make the keyboard disappear we need to configure our user interface so that the action method gets called when the background view is touched by the user. By default, Interface Builder has given us an instance of the UIView class as the background to our interface. Unfortunately UIView instances are unable to respond to events so there is no way, given the current configuration, that we can trigger our action method. We must, therefore, change the class of the view to be an instance of the UIControl class. In the center panel beneath the *File's Owner* and *First Responder* icons is a *View*. This represents the main view of our interface. Select this icon and display the Identity Inspector from the right hand panel and within the inspector pane change the *Class* setting from UIView to UIControl:

Writing iOS 6 Code to Hide the iPhone Keyboard

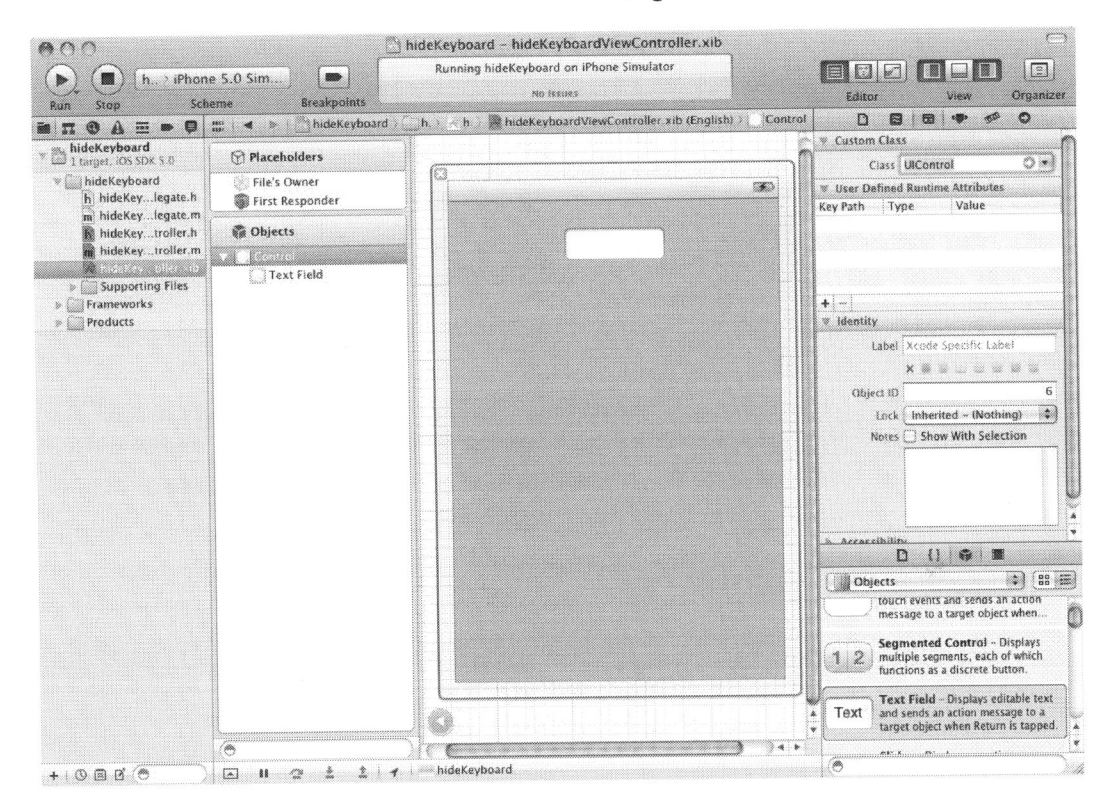

Figure 12-1

Now that we have changed the class of the background view to UIControl (which is itself a subclass of UIView) we will be able to set up a connection to our *backgroundTouched* action method. Select the background of the user interface design and display the Connections Inspector panel (*View -> Utilities -> Show Connections Inspector*). Click on the circle to the right of the *Touch Down* event and drag the connection line to the *File's Owner* icon. Release the mouse button and select the *backgroundTouched* method from the resulting menu. Save the design and then build and run the application. When the iOS Simulator starts up, select the text field so that the keyboard appears. Touching any area of the background should cause the keyboard to disappear.

12.4 Summary

Whilst the iPhone onscreen keyboard appears automatically when the user is required to input information, the subsequent removal of the keyboard is left at the discretion of the application. Convention dictates that the keyboard be dismissed when the user touches the keyboard Return key (unless multi-line input is required) or when the background of the user interface is tapped. In this chapter we have explored and detailed the steps and code necessary to implement both of these functions.

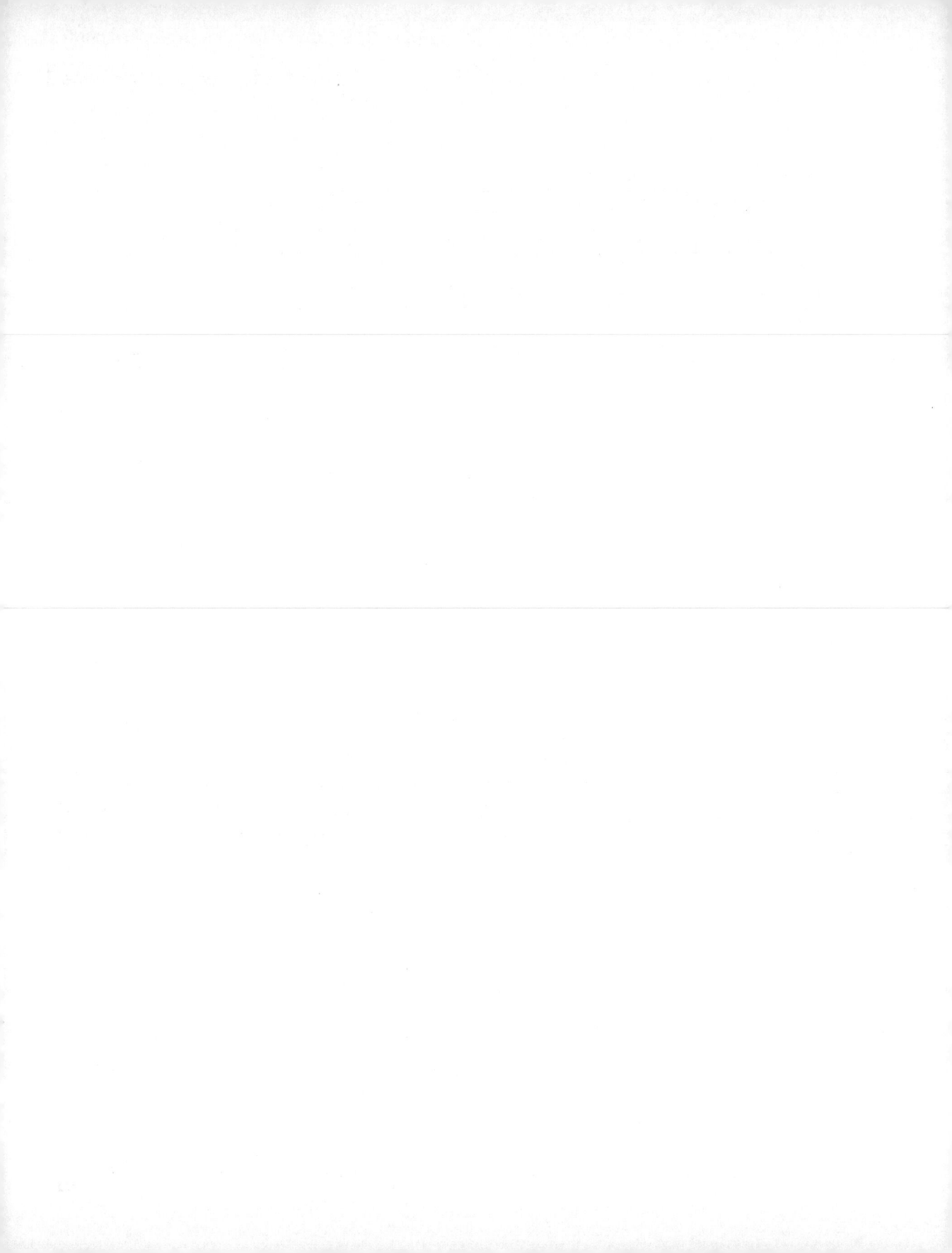

Chapter 13

13. Establishing Outlets and Actions using the Xcode Assistant Editor

In the preceding few chapters we have looked at the concepts of actions and outlets and subsequently worked through a simple example application intended to put this theory into practice. Within the example project outlined in the chapter entitled *Creating an Interactive iOS 6 iPhone App*, we manually entered the declarations for both the outlets and actions contained within the application code. In practice, however, Xcode provides a second mechanism for implementing actions and outlets via a feature of Xcode known as the *Assistant Editor.*

The goal of this chapter is to outline how the Xcode Assistant Editor can be used to implement actions and outlets within an application project.

Having covered this topic, the choice of whether to create those actions and outlets manually or using the Assistant Editor will be left to the discretion and preference of the individual reader for a number of reasons.

Firstly, some developers still prefer to manually implement actions and outlets. Secondly, the Assistant Editor approach to action and outlet declaration makes the assumption that the user interface will always be the first part of an application to be developed. In practice, it is often the case that the back end logic of an application will be developed before the user interface is implemented. In fact, in many software development teams the user interface will be implemented by a human interface specialist or graphic designer while the code is written by the developer, with the two elements being combined in a later stage of the development process. That said, for the average developer the Assistant Editor can save considerable amounts of effort when implementing actions and outlets. For this reason, most tutorials in the remainder of this book will use the Assistant Editor when establishing outlet and action connections.

13.1 Displaying the Assistant Editor

The Assistant Editor is not displayed by default when Xcode is initially started. It may, however, be displayed on demand by selecting the *View -> Assistant Editor -> Show Assistant Editor* menu option. Alternatively, it may also be displayed by selecting the center button (the one containing an image of

Establishing Outlets and Actions using the Xcode Assistant Editor

a bow tie and tuxedo) of the row of Editor toolbar buttons in the top right hand corner of the main Xcode window as illustrated in the following figure:

Figure 13-1

In the event that multiple Assistant Editor panels are required, additional tiles may be added using the *View -> Assistant Editor -> Add Assistant Editor* menu option.

By default, the editor panel will appear to the right of the main editing panel in the Xcode window. For example, in Figure 13-2 the panel to the immediate right of the Interface Builder panel is the Assistant Editor:

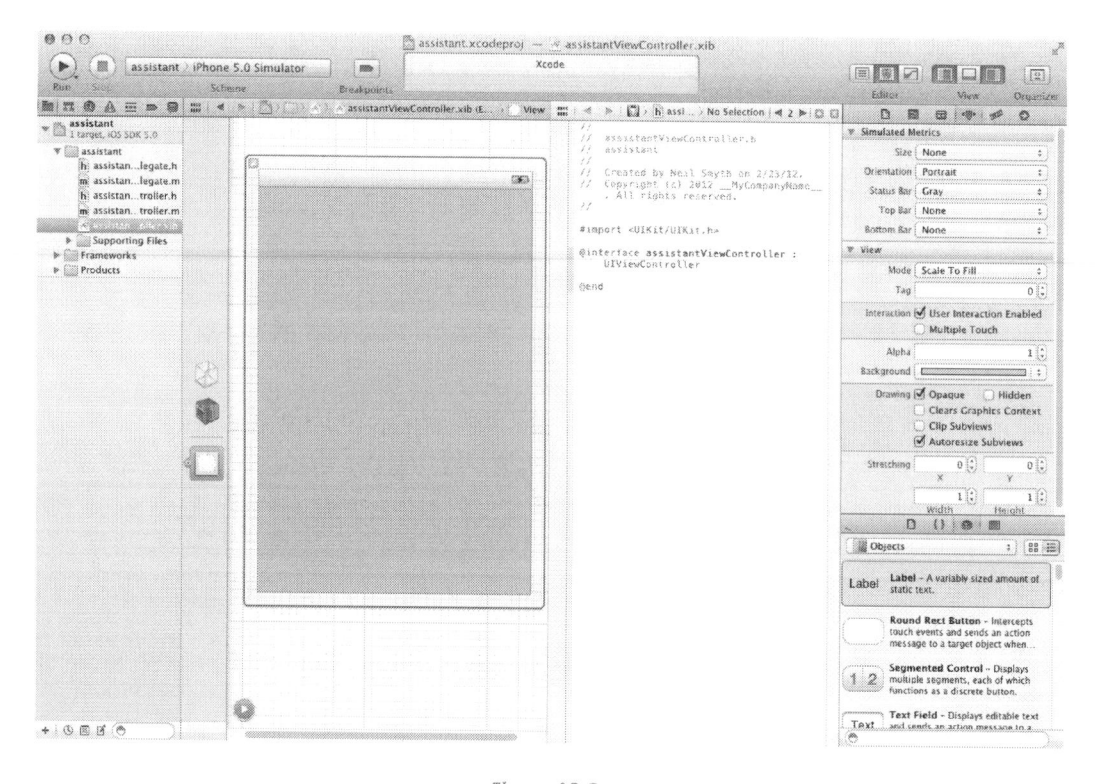

Figure 13-2

By default, the Assistant Editor will be in *Automatic* mode, whereby it automatically attempts to display the correct source file based on the currently selected item in Interface Builder. If the correct file is not displayed, use the toolbar along the top of the editor panel to select the correct file. The small instance of the tuxedo icon in this toolbar can be used to switch to *Manual* mode allowing the file to be selected from a pull-right menu containing all the source files in the project

13.2 Using the Assistant Editor

In the remainder of this chapter we will create a simple project and use it to demonstrate the ease with which outlets and actions may be declared using the Assistant Editor. For the purposes of this example, create a new Xcode iPhone project named *Assistant* using the *Single View Application* template. Once the project has been created, select the *AssistantViewController.xib* file so that the Interface Builder panel appears, and then drag and drop a button and label onto the view canvas:

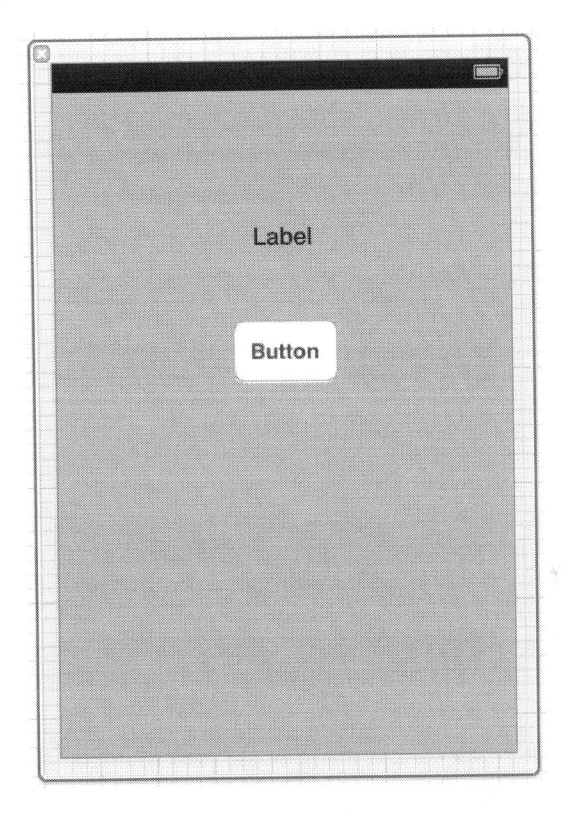

Figure 13-3

The ultimate goal of the application is to display a message on the label when the button is touched. In order to achieve this it will be necessary to implement an action method for the button to call and an outlet to provide access to the text property of the label. As outlined in the chapter entitled *Creating an Interactive iOS 6 iPhone App*, this can be achieved by manually adding the appropriate declarations to the interface and implementation files of the view controller. This time, however, the Assistant Editor is going to do the work for us.

13.3 Adding an Outlet using the Assistant Editor

Assuming that the Interface Builder panel is still visible, select the label object in the view canvas and display the Assistant Editor panel as outlined earlier in the chapter, verifying that the panel is

103

Establishing Outlets and Actions using the Xcode Assistant Editor

displaying the contents of *the AssistantViewController*.h file. In order to establish an outlet for the label object, simply Ctrl-click on the label object in the view and drag the resulting line to the area immediately beneath the @interface directive in the Assistant Editor panel as illustrated in Figure 13-4:

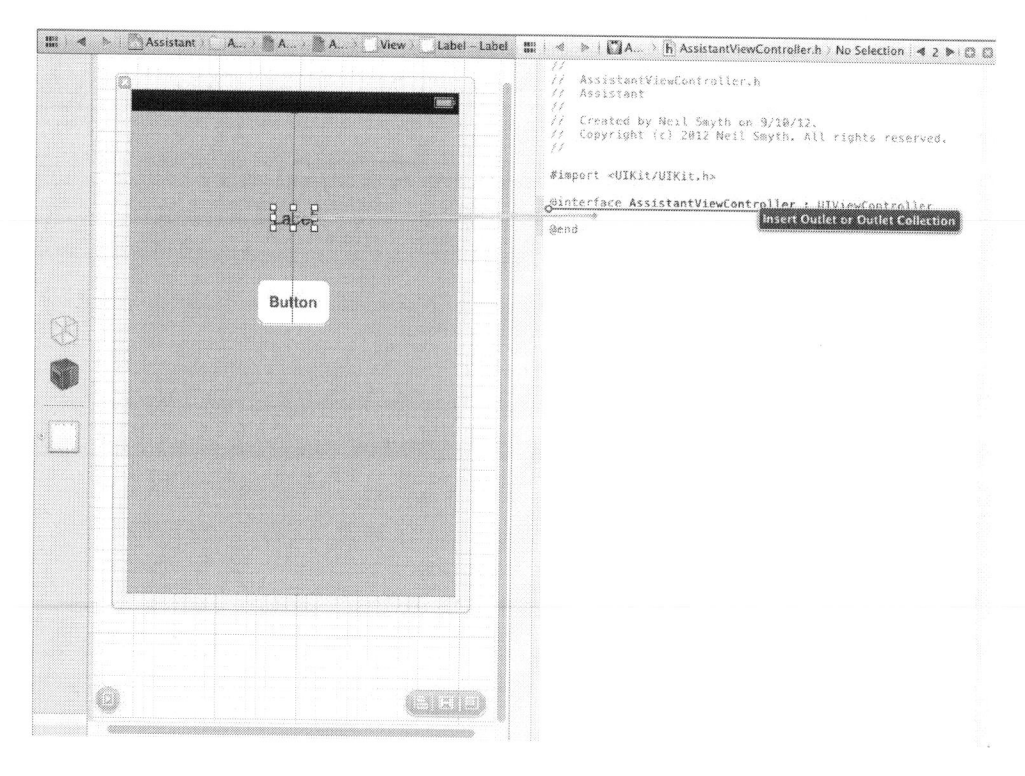

Figure 13-4

Upon releasing the line, the configuration panel illustrated in Figure 13-5 will appear requesting details about the outlet to be defined.

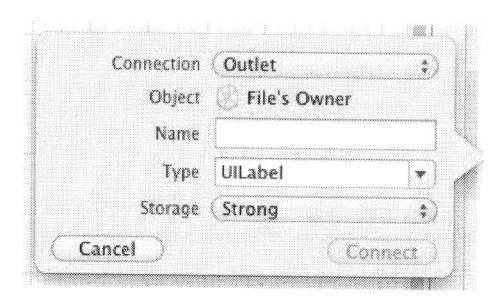

Figure 13-5

Establishing Outlets and Actions using the Xcode Assistant Editor

Since this is an outlet the *Connection* menu should be left as *Outlet*. The type and storage values are also correct for this type of outlet. The only task that remains is to enter a name for the outlet, so in the *Name* field enter *statusLabel* before clicking on the *Connect* button.

Once the connection has been established, select the *AssistantViewController.h* file and note that the outlet property has been declared for us by the assistant:

```
#import <UIKit/UIKit.h>

@interface AssistantViewController : UIViewController
@property (strong, nonatomic) IBOutlet UILabel *statusLabel;

@end
```

Clearly, this saves a considerable amount of effort when declaring outlets. The same is also true of actions.

13.4 Adding an Action using the Assistant Editor

The steps to declare an action using the Assistant Editor are essentially the same as those for an outlet. Once again, select the *AssistantViewController.xib* file, but this time Ctrl-click on the button object. Drag the resulting line to the area beneath the @interface line in the Assistant Editor panel before releasing it. The connection box will once again appear. Since we are creating an action rather than an outlet, change the *Connection* menu to *Action*. Name the action *buttonTouched* and make sure the *Event* type is set to *Touch Up Inside*. Since we will not need access to the button object within our action method change the *Arguments* menu to *None*:

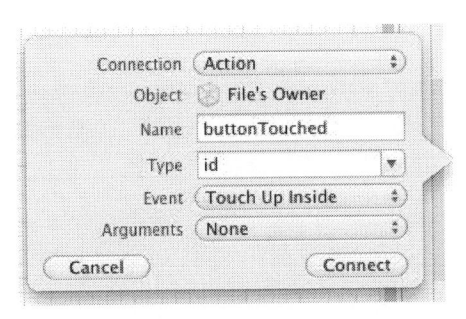

Figure 13-6

Click on the *Connect* button to create the action.

Select the *AssistantViewController.h* file and note that the action has now been declared for us by the assistant:

```
#import <UIKit/UIKit.h>
```

105

Establishing Outlets and Actions using the Xcode Assistant Editor

```
@interface AssistantViewController : UIViewController
- (IBAction)buttonTouched;
@property (strong, nonatomic) IBOutlet UILabel *statusLabel;

@end
```

Next, select the *AssistantViewController.m* file and note that a stub method for the action has also been added automatically:

```
- (IBAction)buttonTouched {
}
```

All that remains, therefore, is to implement the code in the action method to display some text on the label via the *statusLabel* outlet:

```
- (IBAction)buttonTouched {
    _statusLabel.text = @"Hello";
}
```

Compile and run the application and touch the button to display the "Hello" text on the label.

13.5 Summary

The task of implementing actions and outlets can be significantly eased by making use of the Xcode Assistant Editor. This chapter has worked through the use of the Assistant Editor to establish both outlet and action connections. Since both this method and hand coding are valid options for implementing actions and outlets, feel free to use the mechanism with which you are most comfortable in the remainder of this book.

Chapter 14

14. Understanding iPhone iOS 6 Views, Windows and the View Hierarchy

In the preceding chapters we have created a number of user interfaces in the course of building our example iOS 6 iPhone applications. In doing so, we have been using *views* and *windows* without actually providing much in the way of explanation. Before moving on to other topics, however, it is important to have a clear understanding of the concepts behind the way that iPhone iOS user interfaces are constructed and managed. In this chapter we will cover the concepts of *views, windows* and *view hierarchies*.

14.1 An Overview of Views

Views are visual objects that are assembled to create the user interface of an iOS application. They essentially define what happens within a specified rectangular area of the screen, both visually and terms of user interaction. All views are subclasses of the UIKit UIView class and include items such the label (UILabel) and image view (UIImageView) and controls such as the button (UIButton) and text field (UITextField).

Another type of view that is of considerable importance is the UIWindow class.

14.2 The UIWindow Class

If you have developed (or even used) applications for desktop systems such as Windows or Mac OS X you will be familiar with the concept of windows. A typical desktop application will have multiple windows, each of which has a title bar of some sort containing controls that allow you to minimize, maximize or close the window. Windows in this context essentially provide a surface area on the screen onto which the application can present information and controls to the user.

The UIWindow class provides a similar function for iOS based applications in that it also provides the surface on which the view components are displayed. There are, however, some differences in that an iOS app typically only has one window, the window must fill the entire screen and it lacks the title bar we've come to expect on desktop applications.

107

Understanding iPhone iOS 6 Views, Windows and the View Hierarchy

As with the views described previously, UIWindow is also a subclass of the UIView class and sits at the root of the view hierarchy which we will discuss in the next section. The user does not see or interact directly with the UIWindow object. These windows may be created programmatically, but are typically created automatically by Interface Builder when you design your user interface.

14.3 The View Hierarchy

iPhone iOS 6 user interfaces are constructed using a hierarchical approach whereby different views are related through a parent/child relationship. At the top of this hierarchy sits the UIWindow object. Other views are then added to the hierarchy. If we take the example from the chapter entitled *Creating an Interactive iOS 6 iPhone App*, we have a design that consists of a window, a view, a text field, a button and a label. The view hierarchy for this user interface would be drawn as illustrated in Figure 14-1:

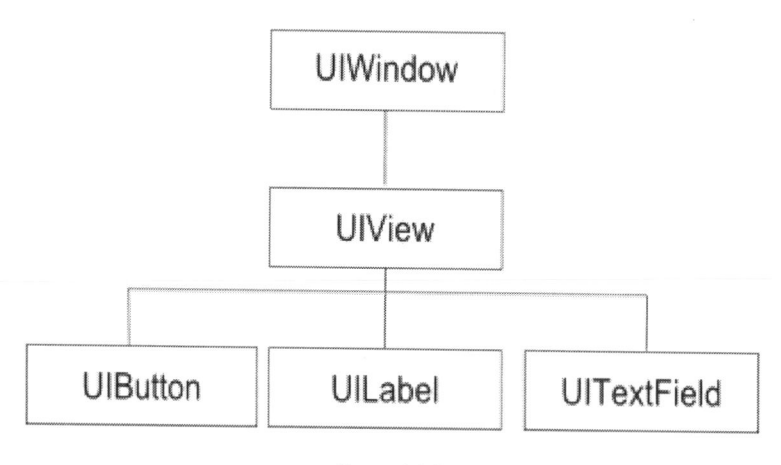

Figure 14-1

In this example, the UIWindow object is the parent or *superview* of the UIView instance and the UIView is the child, or *subview* of the UIWindow. Similarly, the text, label and button objects are all *subviews* of the UIView. A subview can only have one direct parent. As shown in the above example, however, a superview may have multiple subviews.

In addition, view hierarchies can be nested to any level of depth. Consider, for example, the following hierarchy diagram:

Understanding iPhone iOS 6 Views, Windows and the View Hierarchy

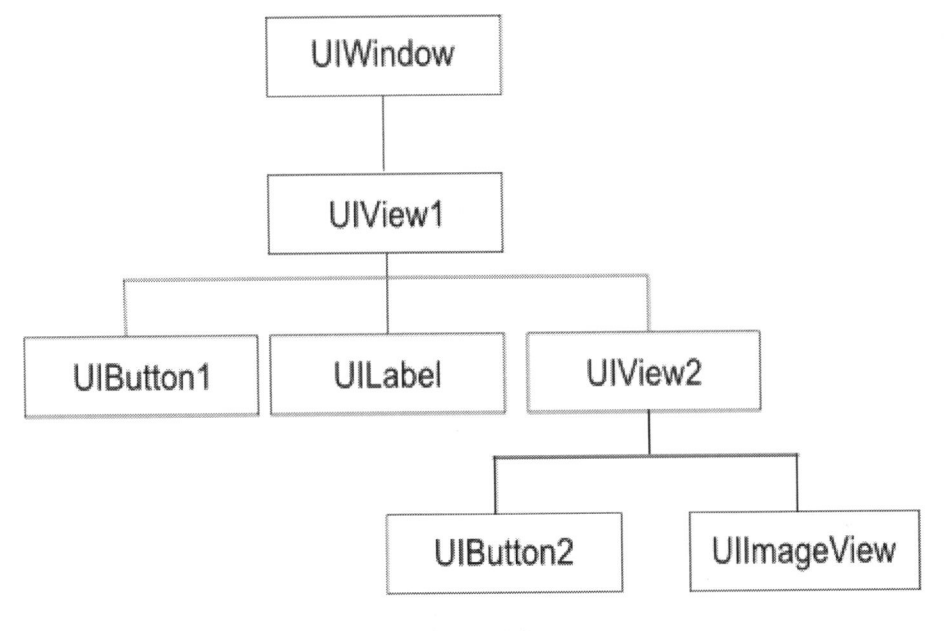

```
                    UIWindow
                        |
                     UIView1
         _____ ____|____ _____
        |                |                |
     UIButton1        UILabel          UIView2
                                          |
                                   _____|_____
                                  |               |
                              UIButton2      UIImageView
```

Figure 14-2

The hierarchical structure of a user interface has significant implications for how the views appear and behave. Visually, subviews always appear on top of and within the visual frame of their corresponding parent. The button in the above example, therefore, appears on top of the parent view in the running application. Furthermore, the resizing behavior of subviews (in other words the way in which the views change size when the device is rotated) is defined in relation to the parent view. Superviews also have the ability to modify the positioning and size of their subviews.

If we were to design the above nested view hierarchy in Interface Builder it might appear as illustrated in Figure 14-3.

In this example, the UIWindow instance is not visible because it is fully obscured by the UIView1 instance. Displayed on top of, and within the frame of, UIView1 are the UIButton1, UILabel and UIView2 subviews. Displayed on top of, and within the frame of, UIView2 are its respective subviews, namely UIButton2 and UIImageView.

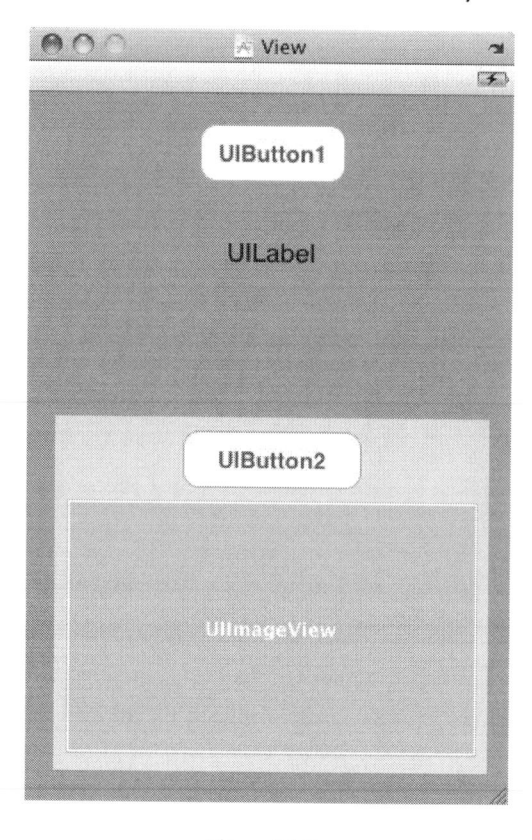

Figure 14-3

The view hierarchy also defines how events are handled when a user interacts with the interface, essentially defining something called the *responder chain*. If, for example, a subview receives an event that it cannot handle, that event is passed up to the immediate superview. If that superview is also unable to handle the event it is passed up to the next parent and so on until it reaches a level within the responder chain where it can be dealt with.

14.4 View Types

Apple groups the various views included in the UIKit framework into a number of different categories:

14.4.1 The Window

The UIWindow is the root view of the view hierarchy and provides the surface on which all subviews draw their content.

14.4.2 Container Views

Container views enhance the functionality of other view objects. The UIScrollView class, for example, provides scrollbars and scrolling functionality for the UITableView and UITextView classes. Another example is the UIToolbar view which serves to group together multiple controls in a single view.

14.4.3 Controls

The controls category encompasses views that both present information and respond to user interaction. Control views inherit from the UIControl class (itself a subclass of UIView) and include items such as buttons, sliders and text fields.

14.4.4 Display Views

Display views are similar to *controls* in that they provide visual feedback to the user, the difference being that they do not respond to user interaction. Examples of views in this category include the UILabel and UIImageView classes.

14.4.5 Text and Web Views

The UITextView and UIWebView classes both fall into this category and are designed to provide a mechanism for displaying formatted text to the user. The UIWebView class, for example, is designed to display HTML content formatted so that it appears as it would if loaded into a web browser.

14.4.6 Navigation Views and Tab Bars

Navigation views and tab bars provide mechanisms for navigating through an application user interface. They work in conjunction with the view controller and are typically created from within Interface Builder.

14.4.7 Alert Views and Action Sheets

Views in this category are designed specifically for prompting the user with urgent or important information together with optional buttons to call the user to action. The UIAlertView class displays a blue popup box on the screen and the UIActionSheet causes a panel to slide up from the bottom of the screen.

14.5 Summary

In this chapter we have explored the concepts of using views in terms of constructing an iPhone application user interface and also how these views relate to each other within the context of a view hierarchy. We have also discussed how the view hierarchy dictates issues such as the positioning and resize behavior of subviews and defines the response chain for the user interface.

Chapter 15

15. An Introduction to Auto Layout in iOS 6

Arguably one of the most important parts of designing the user interface for an application involves getting the layout correct. In an ideal world, designing a layout would simply consist of dragging view objects to the desired location on the screen and fixing them at these positions using absolute X and Y screen coordinates. In reality, the world of iOS devices is more complex than that and a layout must be able to adapt to variables such the device rotating between portrait and landscape modes, dynamic changes to content and differences in screen resolution and size.

Prior to the release of iOS 6, layout handling involved use of a concept referred to as *autosizing*. Autosizing involves the use of a series of "springs" and "struts" to define, on a view by view basis, how a subview will be resized and positioned relative to the superview in which it is contained. Limitations of autosizing, however, typically meant that considerable amounts of coding was required to augment the autosizing in response to orientation or other changes.

Perhaps one of the most significant new features in iOS 6 is the introduction of Auto Layout. Auto Layout is an extremely large subject area allowing layouts of just about any level of flexibility and complexity to be created once the necessary skills have been learned.

The goal of this and subsequent chapters will be to introduce the basic concepts of Auto Layout, work through some demonstrative examples and provide a basis on which to continue learning about Auto Layout as your application design needs evolve. Auto layout introduces a lot of new concepts and can, initially, seem a little overwhelming. By the end of this sequence of chapters, however, it should be clearer how the pieces fit together to provide a powerful and flexible layout management system for iOS based user interfaces.

15.1 An Overview of Auto Layout

Though Auto Layout is new to iOS, it was actually first introduced in the Mac OS X Lion release. The purpose of Auto Layout is to allow the developer to describe the behavior that is required from the views in a layout independent of the device screen size and orientation. This behavior is implemented through the creation of *constraints* on the views that comprise a user interface screen.

A button view, for example, might have a constraint that tells the system that it is to be positioned in the horizontal center of its superview. A second constraint might also declare that the bottom edge of the button should be positioned a fixed distance from the bottom edge of the superview. Having set these constraints, no matter what happens to the superview, the button will always be centered horizontally and a fixed distance from the bottom edge.

Unlike autosizing, auto layout allows constraints to be declared not just between a subview and superview, but between subviews. Auto layout, for example, would allow a constraint to be configured such that two button views are always positioned a specific distance apart from each other regardless of changes in size and orientation of the superview. Constraints can also be configured to cross superview boundaries to allow, for example, two views with different superviews (though in the same screen) to be aligned. This is a concept referred to as *cross-view hierarchy constraints*.

Constraints can also be explicit or variable (otherwise referred to in auto layout terminology as *equal* or *unequal*). Take for example, a width constraint on a label object. An explicit constraint could be declared to fix the width of the label at 70. This might be represented as a constraint equation that reads as follows:

```
myLabel.width = 70
```

This explicit width setting might, however, become problematic if the label is required to display dynamic content. An attempt to display text on the label that requires a greater width will result in the content being clipped.

Constraints can, however, also be declared using *less-than or equal to* or *greater than or equal to* controls. For example the width of a label could be constrained to any width as long as it is less than or equal to 800:

```
myLabel.width <= 800
```

The label is now permitted to grow in width up to the specified limit, allowing longer content to be displayed without clipping.

Auto layout constraints are by nature interdependent and, as such, situations can arise where a constraint on one view competes with a constraint on another view to which it is connected. In such situations it may be necessary to make one constraint *stronger* and the other *weaker* in order to provide the system with a way of arriving at a layout solution. This is achieved by assigning *priorities* to constraints.

Priorities are assigned on a scale of 0 to 1000 with 1000 representing a *required constraint* and lower numbers equating to *optional constraints*. When faced with a decision between the needs of a required constraint and an optional constraint, the system will meet the needs of the required constraint exactly while attempting to get as close as possible to those of the optional constraint. In the case of two optional constraints, the needs of the constraint with the higher priority will be addressed before those of the lower.

15.2 Alignment Rects

When working with constraints it is important to be aware that constraints operate on the content of a view, not the frame in which a view is displayed. This content is referred to as the *alignment rect* of the view. Alignment constraints such as those that cause the center of one view to align with that of another will do so based on the alignment rects of the views, disregarding any padding that may have been configured for the frame of the view.

15.3 Intrinsic Content Size

Some views also have what is known as an *intrinsic content size*. This is the preferred size that a view itself believes it needs to be to display its content to the user. A Button view, for example, will have an intrinsic content size in terms of height and width that is based primarily on the text or image it is required to display and internal rules on the margins that should be placed around that content. When a view has an intrinsic content size, auto layout will automatically assign two constraints for each dimension for which the view has indicated an intrinsic content size preference (i.e. height and/or width). One constraint is intended to prevent the size of the view becoming larger than the size of the content (otherwise known as the *content hugging* constraint). The other constraint is intended to prevent the view from being sized smaller than the content (referred to as the *compression resistance* constraint).

15.4 Content Hugging and Compression Resistance Priorities

The resize behavior of a view with an intrinsic content size can be controlled by specifying compression resistance and content hugging priorities. A view with a high compression resistance priority and a low content hugging priority will be allowed to grow but will resist shrinking in the corresponding dimension. Similarly, a high compression resistance priority in conjunction with a high content hugging priority will cause the view to resist any form of resizing, keeping the view as close as possible to its intrinsic content size.

15.5 Three Ways to Create Constraints

There are three ways in which constraints in a user interface layout can be created:

- **Interface Builder** – The latest release of Interface Builder has been modified extensively to provide support for the visual implementation of auto layout constraints in user interface

designs. Examples of using this approach are covered in the *Working with iOS 6 Auto Layout Constraints in Interface Builder* and *An iPhone iOS 6 Auto Layout Example* chapters of this book.
- **Visual Format Language** – The visual format language defines a syntax that allows constraints to be declared using a sequence of ASCII characters that visually approximate the nature of the constraint being created with the objective of making constraints in code both easier to write and understand. Use of the visual format language is documented in the chapter entitled *Understanding the iOS 6 Auto Layout Visual Format Language*.
- **Writing API code** – This approach involves directly writing code to create constraints using the standard programming API calls, the topic of this is covered in *Implementing iOS 6 Auto Layout Constraints in Code*.

Wherever possible, Interface Builder is the recommended approach to creating constraints. When creating constraints in code, the visual format language is generally recommended over the API based approach.

15.6 Constraints in more Detail

A constraint is created as an instance of the NSLayoutConstraint class which, having been created, is then added to a view. The rules for a constraint can generally be represented as an equation, the most complex form of which can be described as follows:

```
view1.attribute = multiplier * view.attribute2 + constant
```

In the above equation, a constraint relationship is being established between two views named view1 and view2 respectively. In each case an attribute is being targeted by the constraint. Attributes are represented by NSLayoutAttribute<*name*> constants where <*name*> is one of either Left, Right, Top, Bottom, Leading, Trailing, Width, Height, CenterX, CenterY or Baseline (i.e. NSLayoutAttributeWidth). The multiplier and constant elements are floating point values used to modify the constraint.

A simple constraint that dictates that view1 and view2 should, for example, be the same width would be represented using the following equation:

```
view1.width = view2.width
```

Similarly, the equation for a constraint to align the horizontal center of view1 and with the horizontal center of view 2 would read as follows:

```
view1.centerX = view2.centerX
```

A slightly more complex constraint to position view1 so that its bottom edge is positioned a distance of 20 points above the bottom edge of view2 would be expressed as follows:

```
view1.bottom = view2.bottom - 20
```

The following constraint equation specifies that view1 is to be twice the width of view2 minus a width of 30 points:

```
view1.width = view2.width * 2 - 30
```

So far the examples have focused on equality. As previously discussed, constraints also support inequality in the form of <= and >= operators. For example:

```
view1.width >= 100
```

A constraint based on the above equation would limit the width of view1 to any value greater than or equal to 100.

The reason for representing constraints in the form of equations is less obvious when working with constraints within Interface Builder but will become invaluable when setting constraints in code either using the API or the visual format language.

15.7 Summary

iOS 6 introduces the concept of Auto Layout in application user interface development. Auto layout involves the use of constraints to descriptively express the geometric properties, behavior and relationships of views in a user interface.

Constraints can be created using Interface Builder, or in code using either the new visual format language or the standard SDK API calls of the new NSLayoutConstraint class.

Constraints are typically expressed using a linear equation, an understanding of which will be particularly beneficial when working with constraints in code.

Having covered the basic concepts of auto layout, the next chapter will introduce the creation and management of constraints within Interface Builder.

Chapter 16

16. Working with iOS 6 Auto Layout Constraints in Interface Builder

By far the most productive and intuitive way to work with constraints is to do so using the auto layout features of Interface Builder. Not only does this avoid the necessity to write time consuming code (though for complex layout requirements some code will be inevitable) but it also provides instant visual feedback on constraints as they are configured.

Within this chapter, a simple example will be used to demonstrate the effectiveness of auto layout together with an in-depth look at the auto layout features of Interface Builder. The chapter will then move on to demonstrate the concepts of content hugging and constraint priorities.

16.1 A Simple Example of Auto Layout in Action

Before digging deeper into the auto layout features of Interface Builder, the first step in this chapter will be to quickly demonstrate the basic concept of auto layout. Begin, therefore, by creating new Xcode project for the iPhone using the *Single View Application* template. Enter *AutoLayout* as the product name and class prefix, making sure that the storyboard and automatic reference counting options are both selected.

16.2 Enabling and Disabling Auto Layout in Interface Builder

By default, Auto Layout is switched on for user interface design files, both for storyboard and individual NIB files. Begin by selecting the *MainStoryboard.storyboard* file from the project navigator panel and then display the File Inspector panel (*View -> Utilities-> Show File Inspector*). Located within this inspector is an option labeled *Use Autolayout* as illustrated in Figure 16-1:

Working with iOS 6 Auto Layout Constraints in Interface Builder

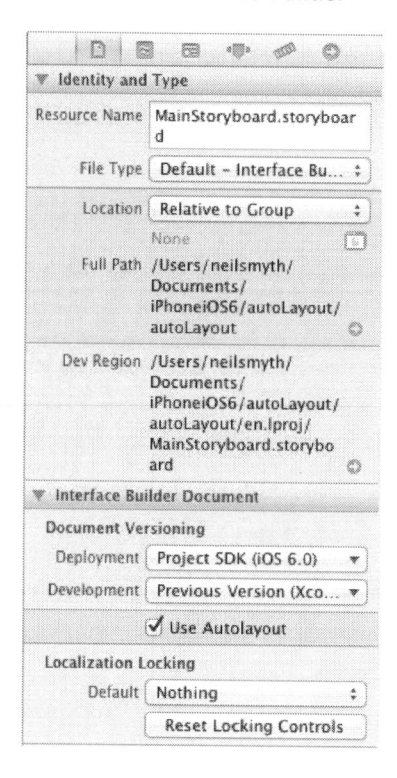

Figure 16-1

Within the File Inspector panel, turn off the *Use Autolayout* option so that we can demonstrate the effect of not using Auto Layout.

With auto layout turned off, drag a label view from the Object Library and position it towards the bottom of the view in the horizontal center of the view canvas so the vertical blue guideline appears indicating that it is centered before dropping the view into place. In actual fact, the location of the view has just been defined using hard coded absolute x and y coordinates on the screen. As far as the view is concerned, the label is positioned perfectly as long as the device remains in portrait orientation:

Working with iOS 6 Auto Layout Constraints in Interface Builder

Figure 16-2

A problem arises, however, when the device rotates to landscape orientation. This can be demonstrated by compiling and running the application on a physical iPhone device or iOS Simulator in the usual way. Alternatively, the effect of an orientation change can be tested within the Interface Builder environment using a feature known as *simulated metrics*. Within the Document Outline panel (located to the left of the storyboard canvas panel), select the *Auto Layout View Controller* entry in the *Auto Layout View Controller Scene* box and, with the entry selected, display the Attributes Inspector in the Utilities panel on the far right. Under the *Simulated Metrics* heading, locate the *Orientation* option and change the menu setting from *Portrait* to *Landscape* as outlined in Figure 16-4. Similarly, the layout behavior of the user interface on different screens may be tested using the *Size* setting. For example, the appearance on the 4 inch iPhone 5 screen can be tested by setting the *Size* menu to *Retina 4 Full Screen*. The device form factor setting can also be toggled by using the button in the bottom right hand corner of the storyboard canvas (the control on the far left of the array of controls illustrated in Figure 16-3:

Figure 16-3

Whilst this is a useful and quick way to check that the layout is working as intended, it is important to note Interface Builder does not output any diagnostic information in the event that constraints are invalid or conflict with each other. If the layout is not behaving as intended in Interface Builder, build

121

Working with iOS 6 Auto Layout Constraints in Interface Builder

and run the application either on a physical device or the simulator and check the console log for warnings about unsatisfiable or conflicting constraints.

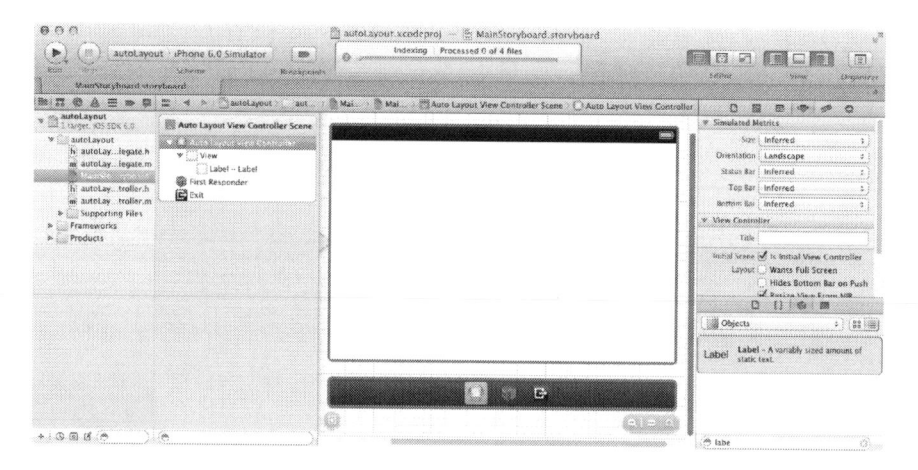

Figure 16-4

As illustrated in the above figure, the label is no longer visible. This is because it remains positioned at the same geographical coordinates in relation to the parent view, which in landscape orientation, is outside the visible bounds of the parent view.

In previous versions of iOS, options to address this would have either involved using springs and struts or writing code to detect the rotation of the device and to move the label to the new location on the screen. In iOS 6, however, the problem can be solved using auto layout.

Begin by returning the view to portrait orientation in the simulated metrics panel so that the label is once again visible. Display the File Inspector in the Utilities panel and turn on the *Use Autolayout* option. Pick up the label and move it away from the current location before dragging it back so that Interface Builder knows to implement constraints for the view. By default, Interface Builder will create constraints that it believes provide the desired layout behavior. These can, of course, be viewed and modified, but at this stage the defaults will suffice to demonstrate auto layout in action.

Having switched to auto layout, rotate the orientation once again, noting this time that the label is visible and positioned sensibly:

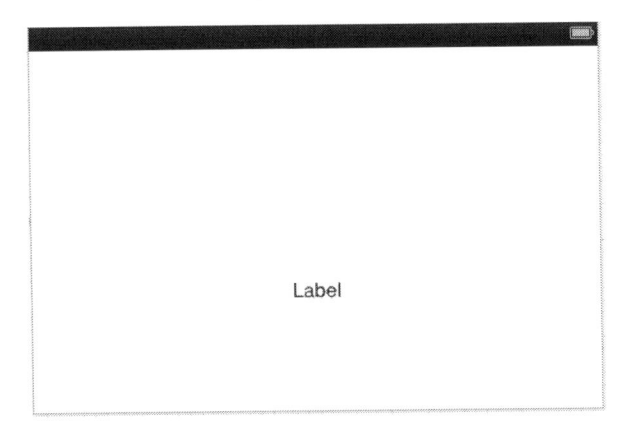

Figure 16-5

Clearly, Interface Builder has anticipated the layout needs for the user interface. This will not, however, always be the case. In recognition of this fact, Interface Builder provides a wide range of options and visual cues that are designed to ease the task of creating auto layout constraints.

16.3 The Auto Layout Features of Interface Builder

A number of features have been added to Interface Builder in order to assist in the implementation of auto layout based constraints. This section will present a guided tour of these features.

16.3.1 Automatic Constraints

As is evident from the previous example, Interface Builder will automatically set constraints on views as they are added to a layout and will continue to add and remove constraints as necessary as changes are made to the layout during the design process. It is important to understand that there is a distinction between constraints added automatically by Interface Builder and those added manually by the developer. In fact, constraints added manually are referred to as *user constraints*. As will be demonstrated later in this chapter, constraints added by Interface Builder may be removed by first promoting them to be user constraints. User constraints may also be configured for standard spacing as will be demonstrated later in this chapter.

The way that a view is positioned on the layout will also dictate how an Interface Builder constraint is configured. Moving the view to the center of the parent view will cause center guidelines to appear. Dropping the view at that point will result in a center constraint being created. Moving a view close to the edge of the window view will result in a margin guideline appearing as illustrated in Figure 16-6. If placed at that location, Interface Builder will implement a constraint that fixes the corresponding edge of the view from the edge of the display using the Apple recommended *standard spacing* distance.

Figure 16-6

The same standard setting will also be implemented if one view is moved close to the edge of another view as indicated by the vertical guide that appears on the edge of the view approaching the second view. This guide is visible on the right hand edge of the Save button in Figure 16-7 as it is moved close to the Cancel button:

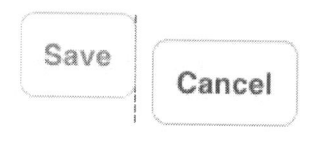

Figure 16-7

16.3.2 Visual Cues

Interface Builder includes a number of visual cues in the layout canvas to highlight the constraints currently configured on a view. When a view is selected within the Interface Builder layout canvas, the constraints that reference that view will be represented visually. Consider, for example, the label view created in our *AutoLayout* example application. When selected in the canvas, a number of additional lines appear as shown in Figure 16-8:

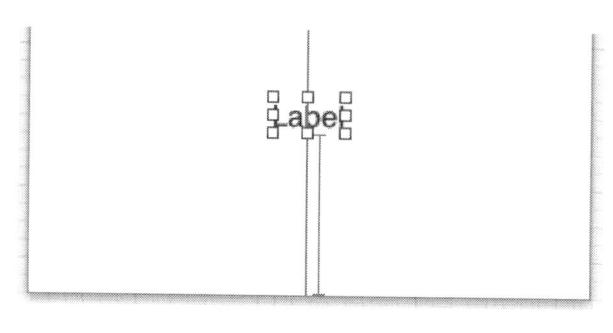

Figure 16-8

The vertical line that runs through the center of the label indicates the presence of a constraint that positions the label in the horizontal center of the parent view (analogous to the NSLayoutAttributeCenterX attribute). If expressed as an equation, therefore, this would read as:

```
label.NSLayoutAttributeCenterX = superview.NSLayoutAttributeCenterX
```

The I-beam line running from the bottom edge of the label view to the bottom edge of the parent view indicates that a vertical space constraint is in place between the two views. The absence of any additional visual information on the line indicates that this is an *equality* constraint. Figure 16-9 shows an example of a "greater than or equal to" horizontal constraint between two button views:

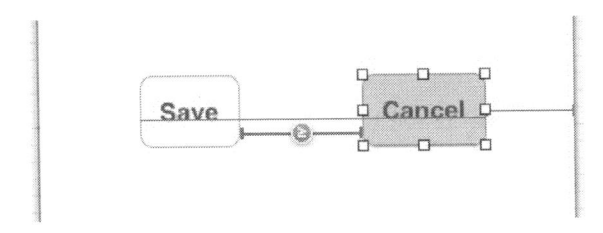

Figure 16-9

The horizontal line running beneath the Button label text indicates that constraints are in place to horizontally align the content baseline (represented by NSLayoutAttributeBaseline) of the two buttons. It should also be noted that the horizontal space constraint line is drawn thicker and bolder than the horizontal alignment line. The heavier line indicates that this is a *user constraint* whilst the narrow line indicates a constraint added automatically by Interface Builder.

Width constraints are indicated by an I-beam line running parallel to the edge of the view in the corresponding dimension. The text view object in Figure 16-10, for example, has a "greater than or equal to" width constraint configured:

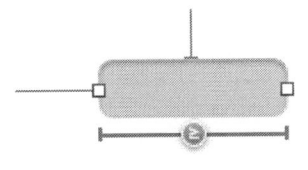

Figure 16-10

16.3.3 Viewing and Editing Constraints Details

All of the constraints currently set on the views of a user interface may be viewed at any time from within the Document Outline panel that is positioned to the left of the Interface Builder canvas area. Within this outline, a category listed as *Constraints* will be present which, when unfolded, will list all of the constraints currently configured for the layout. Note that when more than one container view is present in the view hierarchy there will be a separate constraints list for each one. Figure 16-11, for example, lists the constraints for the user interface represented in Figure 16-9 above:

Working with iOS 6 Auto Layout Constraints in Interface Builder

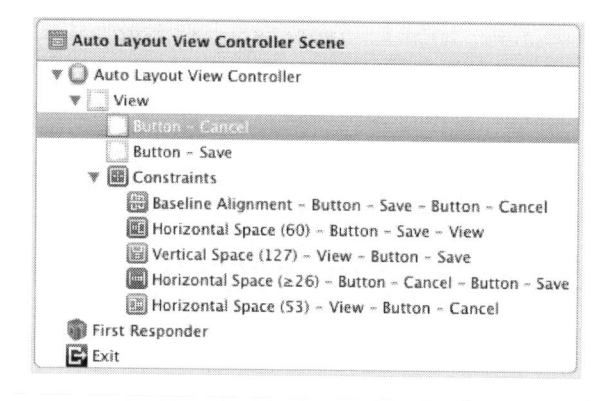

Figure 16-11

As each constraint is selected from the outline list, the corresponding visual cue element will highlight within the layout canvas.

The details of a particular constraint may be viewed and edited at any time using a variety of methods. One method is to select the constraint either from within the layout canvas or in the Document Outline panel. Once selected, display the Size Inspector in the Utilities panel (*View -> Utilities -> Attributes Inspector*) to view and edit the properties of the constraint. Figure 16-12 illustrates the settings for an equality spacing constraint. The exact settings displayed will depend of the nature of the constraint selected. Note, however, that in this instance it is possible to change the relation, constant, direction and priority of the constraint. To set the constant to a value that reflects the recommended standard spacing, simply select the *Standard* checkbox:

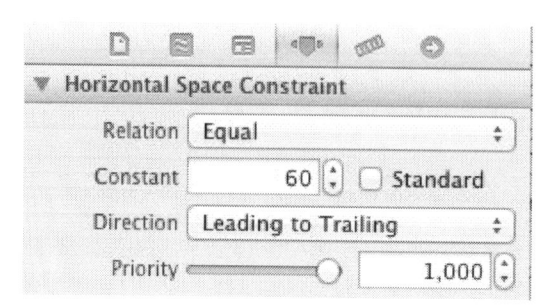

Figure 16-12

A listing of the constraints that reference a specific view can be obtained by selecting that view in the layout canvas and displaying the Size Inspector in the Utilities panel. Figure 16-13, for example, lists the four constraints that reference the currently selected view. Clicking on the settings cog icon on any constraint will provide options to edit or delete the constraint. In the event that the constraint is not a user constraint, the *Promote to User Constraint* option must first be selected before the Delete option will become accessible. In addition to the constraints, note also that this is where the Content

126

Hugging and Content Compression Resistance Priority values outlined in *An Introduction to Auto Layout in iOS 6* are set.

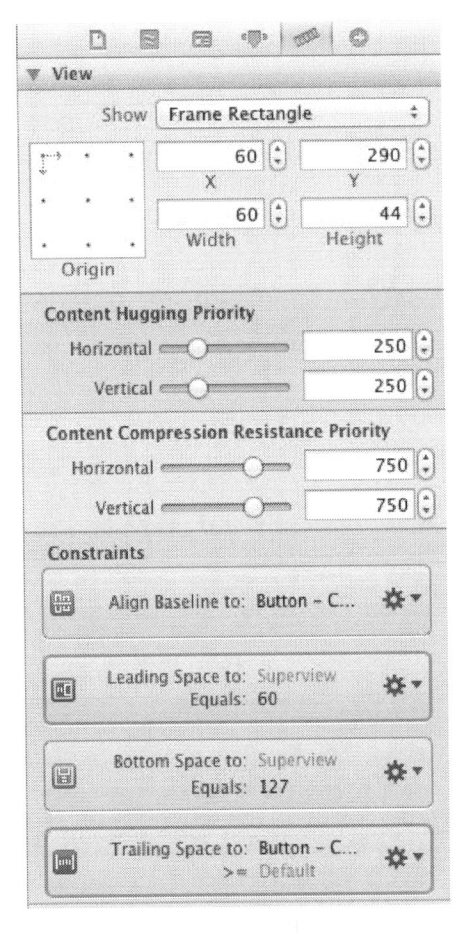

Figure 16-13

16.4 Creating New Constraints in Interface Builder

New user constraints can be created in Interface Builder using a variety of approaches, keeping in mind that constraints can relate to more than one view at a time.

One way to add a constraint to a single view (for example a width constraint) is to select the view in the layout canvas and then select the Xcode *Edit -> Pin* menu. The Pin menu will then provide a list of available constraints that may be applied to the selected view (such as width, height and the connection of all edges to the superview).

The Editor menu may also be used to set constraints that impact more than one view. Select all the required views by holding down the keyboard Shift key whilst clicking on each view and then use the *Editor -> Pin* menu to once again set constraints. In this case, however, the constraint selections will

127

apply to all selected views. When multiple views are selected, the *Editor -> Align* menu may also be used to align the selected views using a variety of criteria options (left edges, right edges, baseline etc).

As an alternative to using the Editor menu, it may be quicker to use the mini toolbar bar located in the bottom right hand corner of the Interface Builder main canvas next to the zoom in and out buttons as highlighted in Figure 16-14.

Figure 16-14

16.5 Summary

Within this chapter we have looked at a very simplistic example of the benefits of using Auto Layout in iOS 6 user interface design. The remainder of the chapter has been dedicated to providing an overview of the Auto Layout features that have been added to the latest release of Interface Builder.

Chapter 17

17. An iPhone iOS 6 Auto Layout Example

Having covered the basics of auto layout and the auto layout features of Interface Builder in the preceding chapters, this chapter will work through an example user interface design intended to demonstrate the use of Interface Builder to create auto layout constraints. This example will also include a demonstration of constraint priorities.

17.1 Preparing the Project

Using the *Single View Application* template, create a new Xcode iPhone application project using *AutoLayoutExample* as both the project name and class prefix with both the Automatic Reference Counting and Storyboard options enabled.

17.2 Designing the User Interface

Initially, the user interface will simply require two Label views and a second View. Begin, however, by selecting the *MainStoryboard.storyboard* file and selecting the background view canvas. Display the Attribute Inspector in the Utilities panel and change the color to light gray.

Drag a Label view from the Object Library and position it so that it is centered horizontally and on the top margin guideline as indicated in Figure 17-1.

Drag a second Label view and position it to the left of the first label, moving it close enough that an automatic constraint is set to the standard spacing distance as outlined in *Working with iOS 6 Auto Layout Constraints in Interface Builder*.

An iPhone iOS 6 Auto Layout Example

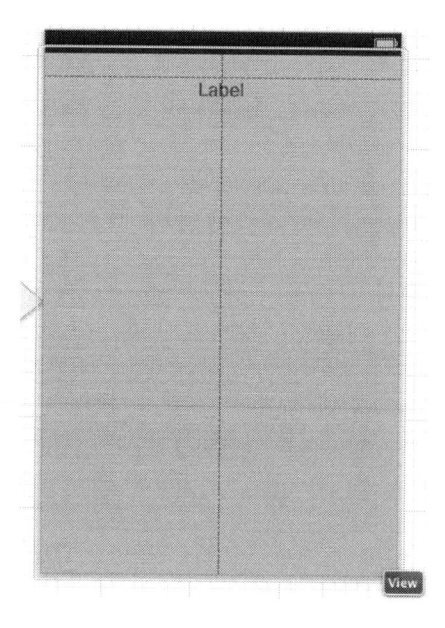

Figure 17-1

Finally locate the View object in the Object Library. As a shortcut, simply type the word "view" into the search bar located immediately beneath the Object Library panel (Figure 17-2) to narrow the search down and then scroll to find the View object.

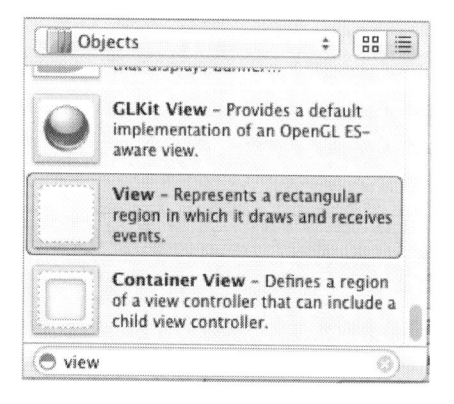

Figure 17-2

Drag and drop the view onto the layout and resize it to fill the space below the two labels with appropriate margins from the outer edges of the screen:

Figure 17-3

Verify that Interface Builder has automatically set up sensible constraints by rotating the display into landscape mode. To achieve this, select the *Auto Layout Example View Controller* item from the Document Outline panel located to the left of the Interface Builder canvas. Display the Attribute Inspector in the Utilities panel and change the *Orientation* value under *Simulated Metrics* to *Landscape.* The view should appear correctly in the new orientation as outlined in Figure 17-4.

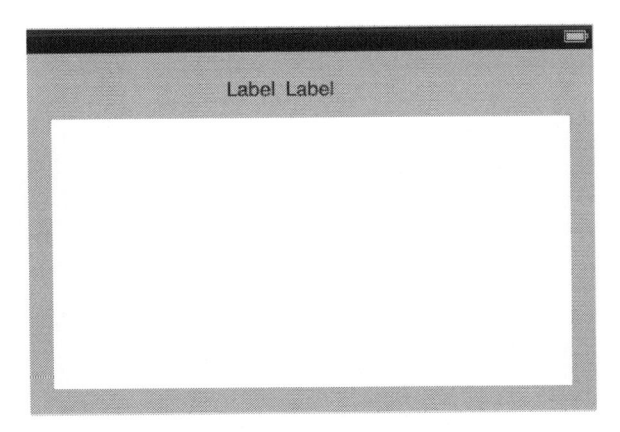

Figure 17-4

17.3 Adjusting Constraint Priorities

Up until this point, the layout is behaving correctly using the Interface Builder default constraints. We are now, however, going to introduce some problems that cannot be handled adequately by the constraints as they currently stand. With the view still in landscape mode, double click on the left hand label and change the text so that it reads *Customer Record:*.

With the view in landscape mode the label appears correctly positioned. Rotate the view to portrait orientation, however, and the label is clearly being clipped by the left hand edge of the parent view:

Figure 17-5

Clearly there is some work to be done to make the user interface appear correctly in both orientations. The first step is to consider the constraints that are currently set on the label views. The right hand label has a constraint that forces it to be centered horizontally in the parent view. The left hand label, on the other hand, has a constraint that connects its trailing edge to the leading edge of the second label using the standard default spacing. The absence of a constraint on the left hand edge of the Customer Record label is resulting in the label being pushed off the screen in portrait mode.

One possible solution to this problem is to create a new constraint on the Customer Record label that puts some space between the left hand edge of the customer record label and the left hand edge of the parent view. To add this constraint, rotate the view back to landscape so that the label is fully visible, select the Customer Record label and select the *Editor -> Pin -> Leading Space to Superview* menu option. Select the new constraint in the layout and change the spacing to *Standard*. Now rotate to Portrait mode and note that the label is, unfortunately, now compressed.

Figure 17-6

The reason for this problem is that the right hand label contains a constraint which forces it to be centered horizontally within the super view with a priority of 1000. Similarly, the customer record label has constraints that dictate that the leading and trailing edges of the label must be the standard width from the superview and right hand label respectively. Since these also have a priority of 1000, the system has no choice but to compress the label in order to satisfy the constraints. In order for the label to be fully visible, one of these priorities needs to be reduced.

We already know from experience that without the constraint on the leading edge of the customer record label, the left hand edge will be clipped by the superview window when the device is in portrait orientation. Another option is to lower the priority on the space constraint between the two labels. With this in mind, select the constraint and in the Attribute Inspector slowly move the Priority slider to the left. Note that as the slider moves, a panel appears (Figure 17-7) that describes the implication of the currently selected priority value. When seeking specific layout behavior it is important to make sure that the correct priority is selected.

An iPhone iOS 6 Auto Layout Example

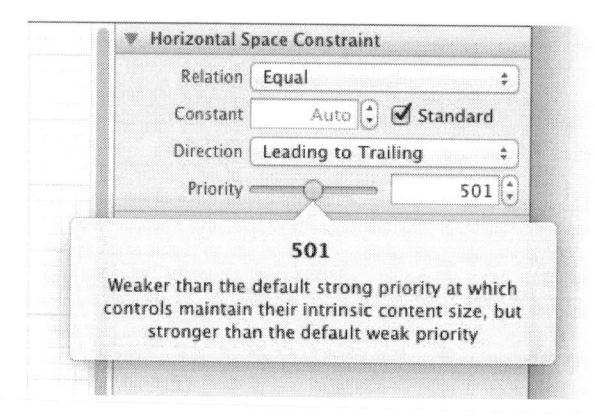

Figure 17-7

Using the slider, select a priority value close to 500. Check the labels in the view in portrait orientation and note that they are now overlapping. Clearly the space between the labels needs to be a required constraint to prevent overlap. Select the constraint once again, therefore, and return the priority value to 1000.

The only remaining constraint to experiment with is the horizontal center constraint on the right hand label. Select the label and display the Size Inspector in the Utilities panel. Under the *Constraints* section, select the option to *Select and Edit* the *Align Center X to: superview* constraint (depending on how the layout was created, this may read *Align Center X to: view*) and, in the resulting attribute inspector, reduce the priority to 500.

As a result of this setting, the label will only be centered when another constraint with a higher priority does not require that the label be moved. As such, the label will be centered when the device is in landscape mode but will be pushed off center when the space is needed by the Customer Record label in portrait orientation.

Figure 17-8

17.4 Alignment and Width Equality

The last change that will be made to the layout in this chapter involves the use of constraints to implement alignment and width equality.

Modify the user interface by dragging an Image View and a Button onto the layout and resize, configure and move the objects so that the layout resembles that of Figure 17-9.

An iPhone iOS 6 Auto Layout Example

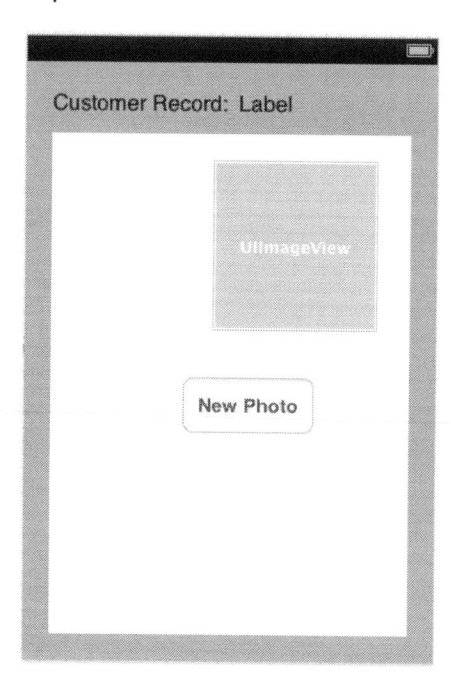

Figure 17-9

The first step is to use constraints to make the button and image view the same width. Hold down the Shift key on the keyboard and click on the button and image view to select both items. Using either the *Editor -> Pin* menu or the toolbar in the bottom right of the Interface Builder canvas, select the option to configure *Widths Equally*.

Next, select both views once again and use the *Editor -> Align* menu option (or the corresponding menu in the canvas menu) to add a constraint to align the *Horizontal Centers* of the two views. With both views selected, add a vertical space between the bottom of the image view and the top of the button configured to use standard spacing, then drag both selected items to the horizontal center of the superview. Once the changes are complete, the user interface should appear as illustrated in Figure 17-10:

Figure 17-10

17.5 Testing the Application

Throughout this tutorial, the behavior of the user interface layout in response to orientation changes has been performed using simulated metrics within Interface Builder. As a full test of the layout, build and run the application either on a physical iPhone device or the iOS Simulator and check that the layout handles device rotation. This involves both a visual check that the views appear as intended and a review of the console to ensure no errors are reported with relation to the auto layout constraints.

17.6 Summary

Within this chapter, a sequence of steps have been outlined demonstrating the creation of an application that uses auto layout constraints to design a user interface that responds sensibly to orientation changes of the device. The example introduced practical examples of the importance of constraint priorities and the application of constraints to implement width matching and view alignment.

Now that the implementation of auto layout constraints in Interface Builder has been covered, the next chapter will begin to explore the creation of constraints in code.

Chapter 18

18. Implementing iOS 6 Auto Layout Constraints in Code

In addition to using Interface Builder, it is also possible to create auto layout constraints directly within the code of an application. These approaches, however, are not necessarily mutually exclusive. There are, for example, situations where a layout will be constructed using a combination of Interface Builder and manual coding. Furthermore, some types of constraint cannot yet be implemented in Interface Builder, constraints that cross view hierarchies being a prime example. Interface Builder is also of limited use when user interfaces are created dynamically at run time.

Given these facts, an understanding of how to create auto layout constraints in code is an important skill, and is the focus of this chapter.

18.1 Creating Constraints in Code

Implementing constraints in code is a two step process which involves first creating the constraint, and then adding the constraint to a view.

In order to create a constraint, an instance of the NSLayoutConstraint class must be created and initialized with the appropriate settings for the auto layout behavior it is to implement. This is achieved by calling the *constraintWithItem:* method and passing through a set of arguments for the constraint.

When considering this syntax, it is helpful to recall to the way in which constraints can be represented using linear equations (as outlined in *An Introduction to Auto Layout in iOS 6*) because the elements of the equation match the arguments used to create an NSLayoutConstraint instance.

Consider, for example, the following constraint expressed as an equation:

```
view1.bottom = view2.bottom - 20
```

The objective of this constraint is to position view1 so that its bottom edge is positioned a distance of 20 points above the bottom edge view2. This same equation can be represented in code as follows:

Implementing iOS 6 Auto Layout Constraints in Code

```
NSLayoutConstraint *myConstraint =[NSLayoutConstraint
                constraintWithItem:view1
                attribute:NSLayoutAttributeBottom
                relatedBy:NSLayoutRelationEqual
                toItem:view2
                attribute:NSLayoutAttributeBottom
                multiplier:1.0
                constant:-20];
```

As we can see, the arguments to the method exactly match those of the equation (with the exception of the multiplier which is absent from the equation and therefore equates to 1 in the method call).

The following equation sets the width of a Button view named *myButton* to be 5 times the width of a Label view named *mylabel*:

```
NSLayoutConstraint *myConstraint =[NSLayoutConstraint
                constraintWithItem:mybutton
                attribute:NSLayoutAttributeWidth
                relatedBy:NSLayoutRelationEqual
                toItem:mylabel
                attribute:NSLayoutAttributeWidth
                multiplier:5
                constant:0];
```

So far the examples shown in this chapter have been *equality* based constraints and, as such, the *relatedBy:* argument has been set to NSLayoutRelationEqual. The following equation uses a greater than or equal to operator:

```
mybutton.width >= 200;
```

Translated into code, this reads as follows:

```
NSLayoutConstraint *myConstraint =[NSLayoutConstraint
                constraintWithItem:mybutton
                attribute:NSLayoutAttributeWidth
                relatedBy:NSLayoutRelationGreaterThanOrEqual
                toItem:nil
                attribute:NSLayoutAttributeWidth
                multiplier:1
                constant:200];
```

Note that since this constraint is not related to another view, the *toItem:* argument is set to *nil*.

18.2 Adding a Constraint to a View

Once a constraint has been created, it needs to be assigned to a view in order to become active. This is achieved by passing it through as an argument to the *addConstraint:* method of the view instance to which it is being added. In the case of multiple constraints, each is added by a separate call to the *addConstraint:* method. This leads to the question of how to decide which view the constraint should be added to.

In the case of a constraint that references a single view, the constraint must be added to the immediate parent of the view. When a constraint references two views, the constraint must be applied to the closest ancestor of the two views. Consider, for the purposes of an example, the view hierarchy illustrated in Figure 18-1.

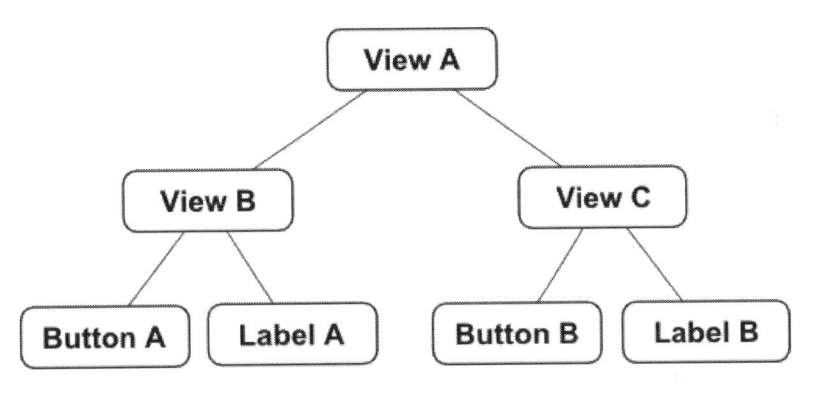

Figure 18-1

A constraint referencing only *Label A* should be added to the immediate parent, in this case *View B*. A constraint referencing *Button B* and *Label B*, on the other hand, must be added to the nearest common ancestor, which in this case is *View C*. A constraint referencing *Button A* and *Button B* must, once again, be added to the nearest common ancestor which equates to *View A*.

For the purposes of an example, the following code excerpt creates a new constraint and adds it to a view:

```
NSLayoutConstraint *myConstraint =[NSLayoutConstraint
          constraintWithItem:mybutton
          attribute:NSLayoutAttributeWidth
          relatedBy:NSLayoutRelationEqual
          toItem:mylabel
          attribute:NSLayoutAttributeWidth
          multiplier:5
          constant:0];

[superview addConstraint: myConstraint];
```

18.3 Turning off Auto Resizing Translation

When adding views to a layout in code the toolkit will, by default, attempt to convert the autosizing mask for that view to auto layout constraints. Unfortunately those auto-generated constraints will conflict with any constraints added within the application code. It is essential, therefore, that translation be turned off for views to which constraints are to be added. This is achieved by calling the *setTranslatesAutoresizingMaskIntoConstraints:* method of the target view, passing through *NO* as an argument. For example, the following code creates a new Button view, turns off translation and then adds it to the parent view:

```
UIButton *mybutton = [UIButton buttonWithType:UIButtonTypeRoundedRect];
[mybutton setTitle:@"My Button" forState:UIControlStateNormal];

[mybutton setTranslatesAutoresizingMaskIntoConstraints:NO];

[superview addSubview:mybutton];
```

18.4 An Example Application

Create a new Xcode project for the iPhone using the *Single View Application* template. Enter *AutoLayoutCode* as the product name and class prefix, making sure that the storyboard and automatic reference counting options are both selected.

18.5 Creating the Views

For the purpose of this example, the code to create the views and constraints will be added to the *viewDidLoad:* method of the *AutoLayoutCode* view controller. Select the *AutoLayoutCodeViewController.m* file, locate this method and modify it to create a button and a label and add them to the main view:

```
- (void)viewDidLoad
{
    [super viewDidLoad];
    UIView *superview = self.view;

    UILabel *mylabel = [[UILabel alloc]init];
    [mylabel setTranslatesAutoresizingMaskIntoConstraints:NO];
    mylabel.text = @"hello";

    UIButton *mybutton = [UIButton
        buttonWithType:UIButtonTypeRoundedRect];
    [mybutton setTitle:@"My Button"
        forState:UIControlStateNormal];
    [mybutton setTranslatesAutoresizingMaskIntoConstraints:NO];
```

```
    [superview addSubview:mylabel];
    [superview addSubview:mybutton];
}
```

18.6 Creating and Adding the Constraints

Constraints will be added to position the label in the horizontal and vertical center of the superview. The button will then be constrained to be positioned to the left of the label with the baselines of both views aligned. To achieve this layout, the *viewDidLoad:* method needs to be modified as follows:

```
- (void)viewDidLoad
{
    [super viewDidLoad];
    UIView *superview = self.view;

    UILabel *mylabel = [[UILabel alloc]init];
    [mylabel setTranslatesAutoresizingMaskIntoConstraints:NO];
    mylabel.text = @"MyLabel";

    UIButton *mybutton = [UIButton
            buttonWithType:UIButtonTypeRoundedRect];
    [mybutton setTitle:@"My Button"
            forState:UIControlStateNormal];
    [mybutton setTranslatesAutoresizingMaskIntoConstraints:NO];

    [superview addSubview:mylabel];
    [superview addSubview:mybutton];

    NSLayoutConstraint *myConstraint =[NSLayoutConstraint
                    constraintWithItem:mylabel
                    attribute:NSLayoutAttributeCenterY
                    relatedBy:NSLayoutRelationEqual
                    toItem:superview
                    attribute:NSLayoutAttributeCenterY
                    multiplier:1.0
                    constant:0];

    [superview addConstraint:myConstraint];

    myConstraint =[NSLayoutConstraint
                    constraintWithItem:mylabel
                    attribute:NSLayoutAttributeCenterX
```

Implementing iOS 6 Auto Layout Constraints in Code

```
                relatedBy:NSLayoutRelationEqual
                toItem:superview
                attribute:NSLayoutAttributeCenterX
                multiplier:1.0
                constant:0];

    [superview addConstraint:myConstraint];


    myConstraint =[NSLayoutConstraint constraintWithItem:mybutton
                attribute:NSLayoutAttributeTrailing
                relatedBy:NSLayoutRelationEqual
                toItem:mylabel
                attribute:NSLayoutAttributeLeading
                multiplier:1
                constant:-10];

    [superview addConstraint:myConstraint];

    myConstraint =[NSLayoutConstraint constraintWithItem:mybutton
                attribute:NSLayoutAttributeBaseline
                relatedBy:NSLayoutRelationEqual
                toItem:mylabel
                attribute:NSLayoutAttributeBaseline
                multiplier:1
                constant:0];

    [superview addConstraint:myConstraint];
}
```

When the application is compiled and run, the layout of the two views should match that illustrated in Figure 18-2.

Figure 18-2

18.7 Removing Constraints

Whilst it has not been necessary to do so in this example, it is important to be aware that it is also possible to remove constraints from a view. This can be achieved simply by calling the *removeConstraint:* method of the view to which the constraint was added, passing through as an argument the NSLayoutConstraint object matching the constraint to be removed:

```
[self.myview removeConstraint:self.myconstraint];
```

It is also worth knowing that constraints initially created in Interface Builder can be connected to outlet properties, thereby allowing them to be referenced in code. The steps involved in creating an outlet for a constraint are covered in more detail in *Implementing Cross-Hierarchy Auto Layout Constraints in iOS 6*.

18.8 Summary

Whilst Interface Builder is the recommended method for implementing auto layout constraints, there are still situations where it may be necessary to implement constraints in code. This is typically necessary when dynamically creating user interfaces, or in situations where specific layout behavior cannot be achieved using Interface Builder (a prime example of this being constraints that cross view hierarchies as outlined in the next chapter).

Implementing iOS 6 Auto Layout Constraints in Code

Constraints are created in code by instantiating instances of the NSLayoutConstraint class, configuring those instances with the appropriate constraint settings and then adding the constraints to the appropriate views in the user interface.

Chapter 19

19. Implementing Cross-Hierarchy Auto Layout Constraints in iOS 6

One of the few types of auto layout constraint that cannot be implemented within the Interface Builder environment is one that references views contained in different view hierarchies. Constraints of this type must, therefore, be implemented in code. Fortunately, however, the steps to achieve this are quite simple. The objective of this chapter is to work through an example that demonstrates the creation of a cross-view hierarchy auto layout constraint.

19.1 The Example Application

For the purposes of this example, a very simple user interface will be created consisting of two Views, a Button and a Text Field. In terms of the physical view hierarchy, the user interface will be constructed as outlined in Figure 19-1.

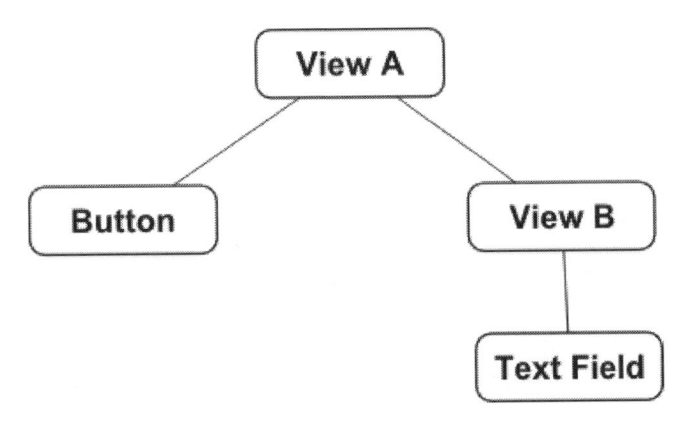

Figure 19-1

The goal will be to implement a constraint that aligns the centers of the Button and Text Field which are part of different view hierarchies - the button being part of the hierarchy contained by View A and the text field being part of the View B sub-hierarchy.

In terms of visual layout, the user interface should appear as illustrated in Figure 19-2. Key points to note are that the text field should have constraints associated with it which horizontally and vertically center it within View B and the button view should be positioned so that it is slightly off center in the horizontal axis:

Figure 19-2

Begin by launching Xcode and selecting the options to create a new iPhone iOS application based on the *Single View Application* template. Enter *CrossView* as the product name and class prefix, set the device to *iPhone* and select the *Use Storyboards* and *Use Automatic Reference Counting* options if they are not already selected.

Select the *MainStoryboard.storyboard* file from the project navigator panel and drag and drop UIView, Button and Text Field views onto the design canvas as illustrated in Figure 19-2, making sure to center the text field object horizontally and vertically within the parent view.

19.2 Establishing Outlets

In order to set a cross hierarchy constraint within code, it will be necessary to implement some outlets. Since the constraint will need to reference both the button and the text view, outlets need to be configured for these views. Select the Text Field object and display the Assistant Editor using *View -> Assistant Editor -> Show Assistant Editor* menu option or by selecting the center button (the one containing an image of a bow tie and tuxedo) of the row of Editor toolbar buttons in the top right hand corner of the main Xcode window.

Ctrl-click on the Text Field object in the view and drag the resulting line to the area immediately beneath the @interface directive in the Assistant Editor panel. Upon releasing the line, the configuration panel will appear. Configure the connection as an *Outlet* named *myTextView* and click on the *Connect* button. Repeat the above steps to add an outlet for the button object named *myButton*.

As currently constrained, the text field object is centered horizontally and vertically within the view we are referring to as View B. In place of this constraint, we need the text field to be aligned with the center of the button object. This will involve removing the CenterX constraint and replacing it with a new constraint referencing the button. This requires outlets for both the View B instance and the CenterX constraint.

Ctrl-click on the View B parent of the text field object and drag the resulting line to the area immediately beneath the @interface directive in the Assistant Editor. Release the line and configure an outlet named *viewB*. Next, with the text field selected, locate the *CenterX Alignment* constraint in the Document Outline panel (Figure 19-3) and create a new outlet for this object named *centerConstraint*.

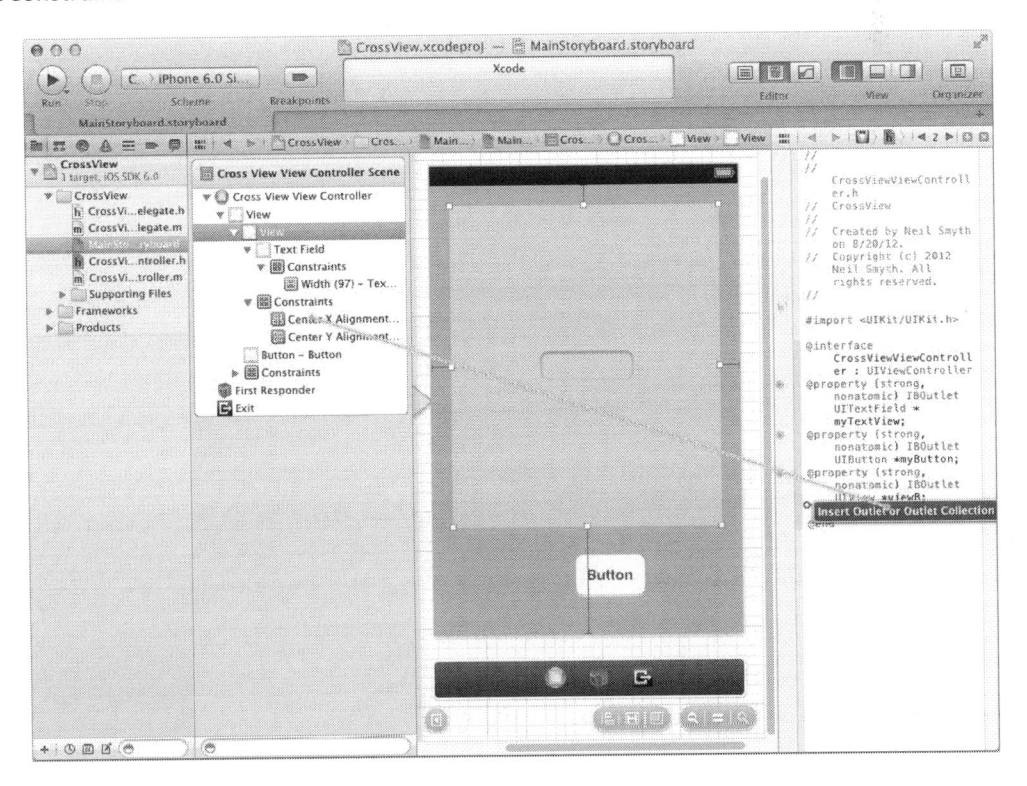

Figure 19-3

19.3 Writing the Code to Remove the Old Constraint

With the necessary outlets created, the next step is to write some code to remove the center constraint from the text field object. For the purposes of this example, all code will be added to the

Implementing Cross-Hierarchy Auto Layout Constraints in iOS 6

viewDidLoad: method of the view controller. Select the *CrossViewViewController.m* file and locate and modify the method as follows:

```
- (void)viewDidLoad
{
    [super viewDidLoad];
    [_viewB removeConstraint:_centerConstraint];
}
```

All that the code is doing is calling the *removeConstraint:* method of view B using the previously configured outlet, and passing through a reference to the CenterX constraint, once again using the previously configured outlet to that object.

19.4 Adding the Cross Hierarchy Constraint

All that remains is to add the constraint to align the centers of the text field and button. With the appropriate outlets already configured, this is simply a question of creating the NSLayoutConstraint object with the appropriate values, and adding it to the closest common ancestor:

```
- (void)viewDidLoad
{
    [super viewDidLoad];
    [self.viewB removeConstraint:self.centerConstraint];

    NSLayoutConstraint *constraint = [NSLayoutConstraint
                        constraintWithItem:_myTextView
                        attribute: NSLayoutAttributeCenterX
                        relatedBy:NSLayoutRelationEqual
                        toItem:_myButton
                        attribute:NSLayoutAttributeCenterX
                        multiplier:1.0
                        constant:0.0];
    [self.view addConstraint:constraint];
}
```

19.5 Testing the Application

Compile and run the application either on a physical iPhone device, or using the iOS Simulator. When the application is running, the text field should be aligned with the button and this alignment should be maintained when the device is rotated into landscape orientation.

19.6 Summary

The current version of Interface Builder does not provide a way to select two views that reside in different view-hierarchies and configure a constraint between them. The desired result can, as outlined in this chapter, be achieved in code. Of key importance in this process is that fact that constraints, just like any other view object in a user interface, may be connected to an outlet and accessed via code.

Chapter 20

20. Understanding the iOS 6 Auto Layout Visual Format Language

The third and final option for the creation of auto layout constraints involves a combination of code and the new visual format language. The goal of this chapter is to provide an introduction to the visual format language and to work through some code samples that demonstrate the concept in action.

20.1 Introducing the Visual Format Language

The visual format language is not a new programming language in the way that C++, Java and Objective-C are all programming languages. Instead, the visual format language defines a syntax through which auto layout constraints may be created using sequences of ASCII characters. These visual format character sequences are then turned into constraints by passing them through to the *constraintsWithVisualFormat:* method of the NSLayoutConstraint class.

What makes the language particularly appealing and intuitive is that the syntax used to define a constraint involves characters sequences that, to a large extent, visually represent the constraint that is being created.

20.2 Visual Language Format Examples

By far the easiest way to understand the concepts behind the visual format language is to look at some examples of the syntax. Take for example, visual format language syntax to describe a view object:

```
[mybutton]
```

As we can see, view objects are described in the visual format language by surrounding the view name with square brackets ([]).

Two views may be constrained to be positioned flush with each other by placing the views side by side in the visual format string:

```
[mybutton1][mybutton2]
```

Understanding the iOS 6 Auto Layout Visual Format Language

Similarly, a horizontal spacer between two view objects is represented by a hyphen:

```
[mybutton1]-[mybutton2]
```

The above example instructs the auto layout system to create a constraint using the standard spacing for views. The following construct, on the other hand, specifies a spacing distance of 30 points between the two views:

```
[mybutton1]-30-[mybutton2]
```

By default, constraints of the type outlined above are assumed to be horizontal constraints. Vertical constraints are declared using a *V:* prefix. For example, the following syntax establishes a vertical spacing constraint between two views:

```
V:[mylabel]-50-[mybutton]
```

For consistency and completeness, horizontal constraints may, optionally, be prefixed with *H:*.

The width of a view can be set specifically as follows:

```
[mybutton(100)]
```

Alternatively, inequality can be used:

```
[mybutton(<=100)]
```

Using similar syntax, the width of one view can be constrained to match that of a second view:

```
[mylabel(==mybutton2)]
```

When using the visual format language, the superview of the view for which the constraint is being described is represented by the | character. For example, the following visual format language construct declares a constraint for the mybutton1 view that attaches the leading and trailing edges of the view to the left and right edges of the containing superview with a spacing of 20 and 30 points respectively:

```
|-20-[mybutton1]-30-|
```

The language also allows priorities to be declared. The following excerpt specifies that the width of mybutton1 must be greater than, or equal to 70 points with a priority value of 500:

```
[mybutton1(>=70@500)]
```

Of particular importance, however, is the fact that the language may be used to construct multiple constraints in a single sequence, for example:

```
V:|-20-[mybutton1(>=70@500)]-[mybutton2(==mybutton1)]-30-[mybutton3]-|
```

Understanding the iOS 6 Auto Layout Visual Format Language

20.3 Using the constraintsWithVisualFormat: Method

As previously described, visual language format based constraints are created via a call to the *constraintsWithVisualFormat:* method of the NSLayoutConstraint class. There are, however a number of other arguments that the method is able to accept. The syntax the method is as follows:

```
[NSLayoutConstraint constraintsWithVisualFormat:<visual format string>
    options:<options>
    metrics:<metrics>
    views: <views dictionary>
];
```

The <visual format string> is, of course, the visual format language string that describes the constraints that are to be created. The <options> are required to be set when the constraint string references more than one view. The purpose of this is to indicate how the views are to be aligned and the value must be of type NSLayoutFormatOptions (for example NSLayoutFormatAlignAllLeft, NSLayoutFormatAlignAllRight, NSLayoutFormatAlignAllTop, NSLayoutFormatAlignAllBaselines etc).

The <metrics> argument is an optional NSDictionary object containing the corresponding values for any constants referenced in the format string.

Finally, the <views dictionary> is an NSDictionary object that contains the view objects that match the view names referenced in the format string. The iOS 6 SDK provides a convenience macro that can be used to construct this dictionary for the objects referenced in the format string, for example:

```
NSDictionary *viewsDictionary = NSDictionaryOfVariableBindings
(mybutton1, mybutton2);
```

When using a visual format string that will result in the creation of multiple constraints, the options should include an alignment directive such as NSLayoutFormatAlignAllBaseLines.

Since the method is able to create multiple constraints based on the visual format string, it returns an array of NSLayoutConstraint objects, one for each constraint, which must then be added to the appropriate view object.

Some sample code to create views and then specify multiple constraints using a visual format language string, would, therefore, read as follows:

```
// Get a reference to the superview
UIView *superview = self.view;

//Create a label
UILabel *mylabel = [[UILabel alloc]init];
```

```
[mylabel setTranslatesAutoresizingMaskIntoConstraints:NO];
mylabel.text = @"My Label";

//Create a button
UIButton *mybutton = [UIButton buttonWithType:UIButtonTypeRoundedRect];
[mybutton setTitle:@"My Button" forState:UIControlStateNormal];
[mybutton setTranslatesAutoresizingMaskIntoConstraints:NO];

//Add the button and label to the superview
[superview addSubview:mylabel];
[superview addSubview:mybutton];

// Get the views dictionary
NSDictionary *viewsDictionary =
        NSDictionaryOfVariableBindings(mylabel, mybutton);

//Create the constraints using the visual language format
NSArray *constraintsArray = [NSLayoutConstraint
        constraintsWithVisualFormat:@"|-[mybutton]-
[mylabel(==mybutton)]-|"
        options:NSLayoutFormatAlignAllBaseline metrics:nil
        views:viewsDictionary];

//Work through the array of constraints, applying each to the superview
for (int i = 0; i<constraintsArray.count; i++) {
        [superview addConstraint:constraintsArray[i]];
}
```

20.4 Summary

The visual format language allows auto layout constraints to be created using sequences of characters that have been designed to visually represent the constraint that is being described. Visual format strings are converted into constraints via a call to the *constraintsWithVisualFormat:* method of the NSLayoutConstraints class which, in turn, returns an array containing an NSLayoutConstraint object for each new constraint created as a result of parsing the visual format string.

Chapter 21

21. Using Xcode Storyboarding

Storyboarding is a feature built into Xcode that allows both the various screens that comprise an iOS application and the navigation path through those screens to be visually assembled. Using the Interface Builder component of Xcode, the developer simply drags and drops view and navigation controllers onto a canvas and designs the user interface of each view in the normal manner. The developer then drags lines to link individual trigger controls (such as a button) to the corresponding view controllers that are to be displayed when the control is selected by the user. Having designed both the screens (referred to in the context of storyboarding as *scenes*) and specified the transitions between scenes (referred to as *segues*) Xcode generates all the code necessary to implement the defined behavior in the completed application. The style of transition for each segue (page fold, cross dissolve etc) may also be defined within Interface Builder. Further, segues may also be triggered programmatically in situations where behavior cannot be defined graphically using Interface Builder.

The finished design is saved by Xcode to *a storyboard file*. Typically, an application will have a single storyboard file, though there is no restriction preventing the use of multiple storyboard files within a single application.

The remainder of this chapter will work through the creation of a simple application using storyboarding to implement multiple scenes with segues defined to allow user navigation.

21.1 Creating the Storyboard Example Project

Begin by launching Xcode and creating a new project using the *Single View Application* template. On the project options panel enter *Storyboard* as both the product name and class prefix and make sure that the *Use Storyboard* and *Use Automatic Reference Counting* options are selected before clicking *Next*. Save the project to a suitable location by clicking on the *Create* button.

21.2 Accessing the Storyboard

Upon creation of the new project, Xcode will have created what appears to be the usual collection of files for a single view application. Instead of a NIB file for the initial view controller, however, Xcode has created a storyboard file named *MainStoryboard.storyboard*. Select this file in the project navigator panel to view the storyboard canvas as illustrated in Figure 21-1:

Using Xcode Storyboarding

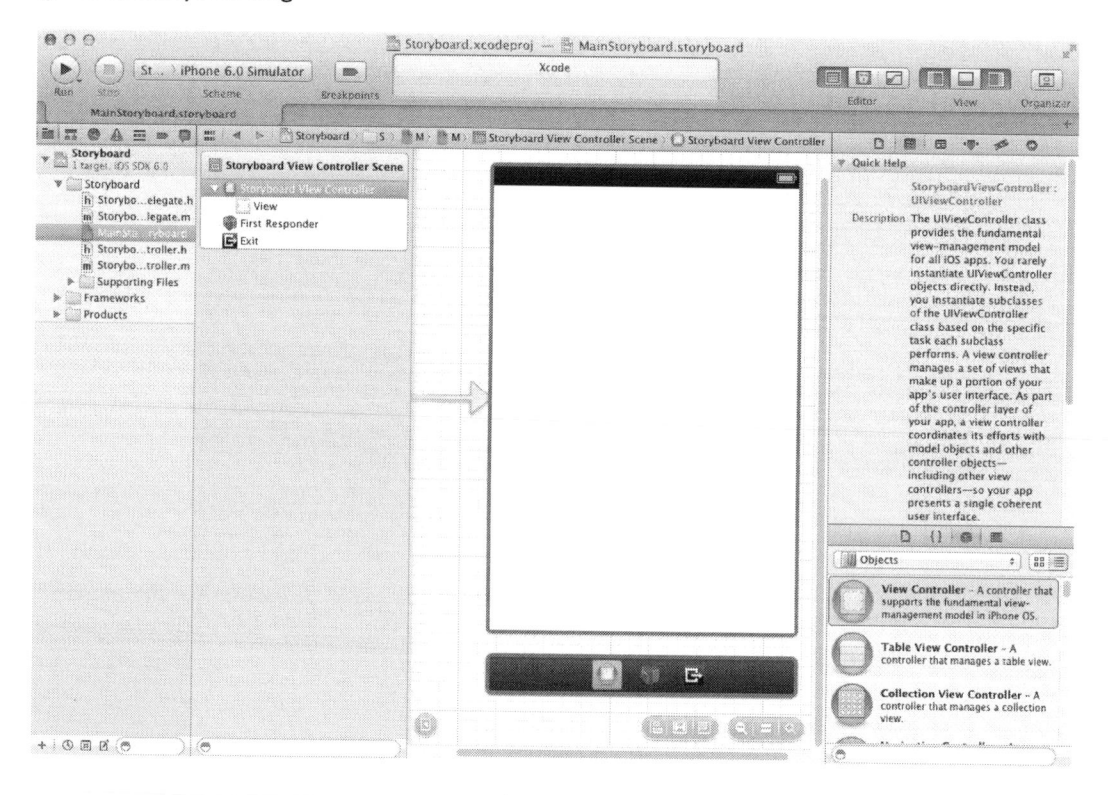

Figure 21-1

The view displayed on the canvas is the view for the *StoryboardViewController* created for us by Xcode when we selected the *Single View Application* template. The arrow pointing inwards to the left side of the view indicates that this is the initial view and will be the first view displayed when the application launches. Objects may be added to the view in the usual manner by dragging and dropping items from the Object library (*View -> Utilities -> Show Object Library*) onto the view canvas. For the purposes of this example, drag a label and a button onto the view canvas. Using the properties panel, change the label text to *Scene One* and the button text to *Go to Scene 2*:

Using Xcode Storyboarding

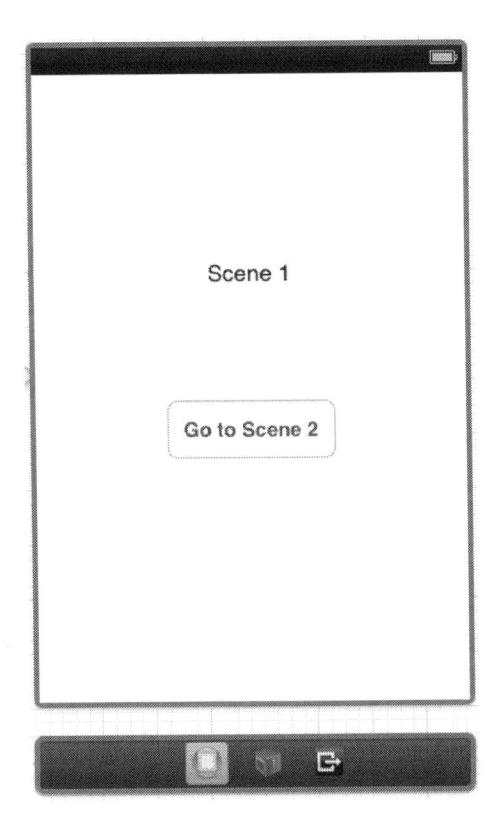

Figure 21-2

In order to manipulate text displayed on the label object from within the application code it will be necessary to first establish an outlet. Select the label in the storyboard canvas and display the Assistant Editor (*View -> Assistant Editor -> Show Assistant Editor*). Check that the Assistant Editor is showing the content of the *StoryboardViewController.h* file and then Ctrl-click on the label button and drag the resulting line to just below the @interface line in the Assistant Editor panel. In the resulting connection dialog, enter *scene1Label* as the outlet name and click on the *Connect* button. Upon completion of the connection, the *StoryboardViewController.h* file should read as follows:

```
#import <UIKit/UIKit.h>

@interface StoryboardViewController : UIViewController
@property (strong, nonatomic) IBOutlet UILabel *scene1Label;

@end
```

21.3 Adding Scenes to the Storyboard

To add a second scene to the storyboard, simply drag a view controller object from the Object Library panel onto the canvas. Figure 21-3 shows a second scene added to a storyboard:

Using Xcode Storyboarding

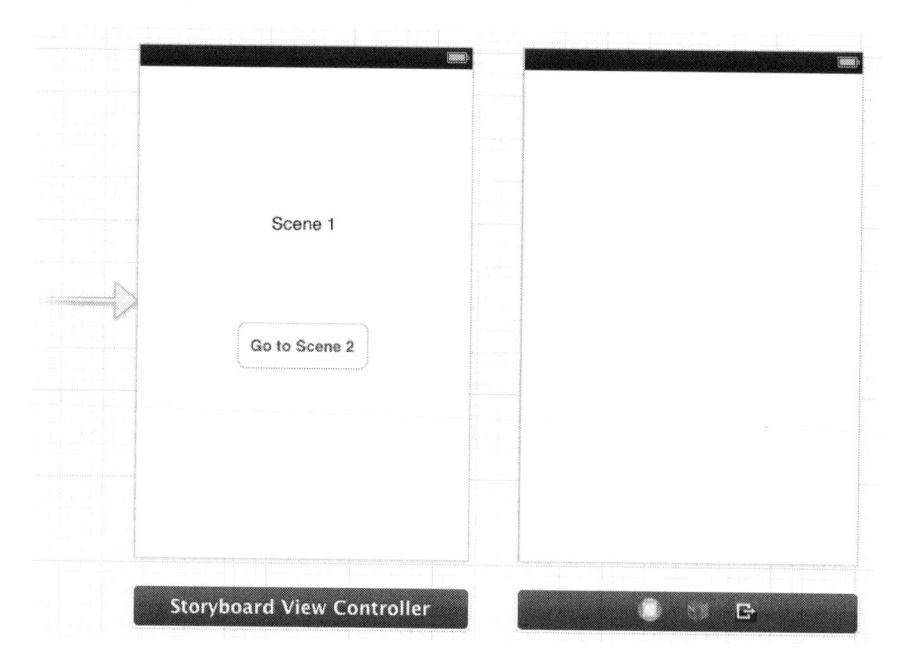

Figure 21-3

Drag and drop a label and a button into the second scene and configure the objects so that the view appears as follows:

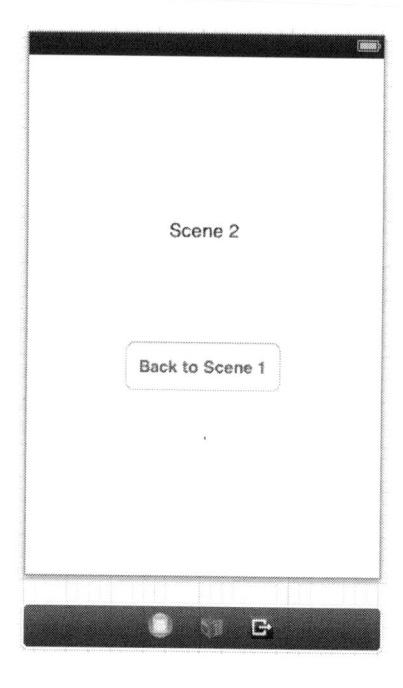

Figure 21-4

160

As many scenes as necessary may be added to the storyboard, but for the purposes of this exercise we will use just two scenes. Having implemented the scenes the next step is to configure segues between the scenes.

21.4 Configuring Storyboard Segues

As previously discussed, a segue is the transition from one scene to another within a storyboard. Within the example application, touching the *Go to Scene 2* button will segue to scene 2. Conversely, the button on scene 2 is intended to return the user to scene 1. To establish a segue, hold down the Ctrl key on the keyboard, click over a control (in this case the button on scene 1) and drag the resulting line to the scene 2 view. Upon releasing the mouse button a menu will appear. Select the *modal* menu option to establish the segue.

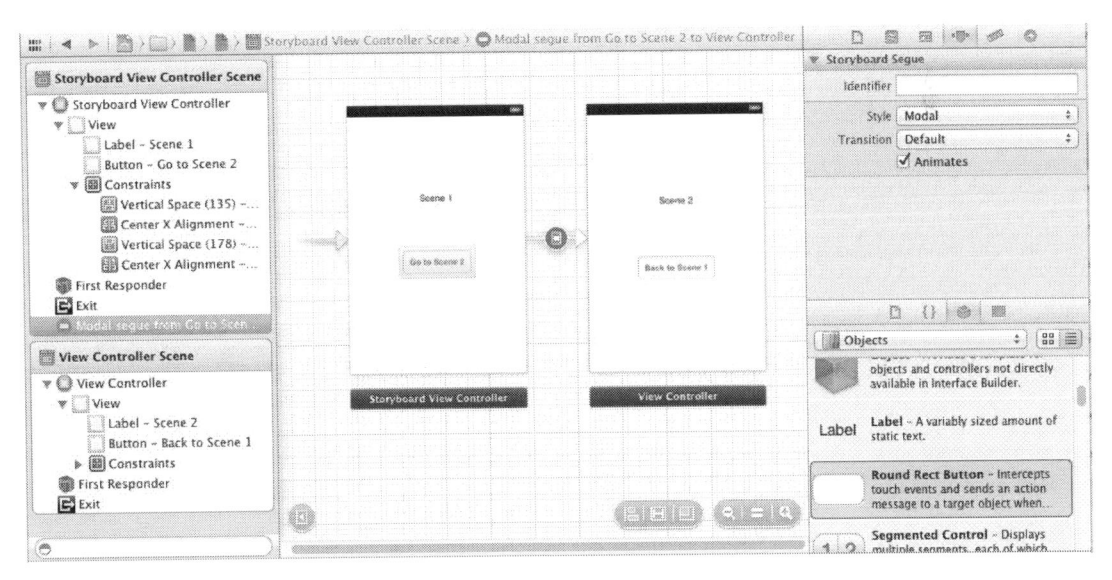

Figure 21-5

As more scenes are added to a storyboard, it becomes increasingly difficult to see more than a few scenes at one time on the canvas. To zoom out simply double click on the canvas. To zoom back in again simply double click once again on the canvas. Zoom buttons are also provided in the bottom right hand corner of the design canvas. Note that when zoomed out, it will not be possible to drag and drop items from the Object Library onto the scenes.

21.5 Configuring Storyboard Transitions

Xcode provides the option to change the visual appearance of the transition that takes place during a segue. By default a *Cover Vertical* transition is performed whereby the new scene slides vertically upwards from the bottom of the view to cover the currently displayed scene. To change the transition, select the corresponding segue line, display the attributes inspector (*View -> Utilities ->*

Show Attributes Inspector) and modify the *Transition* setting. In Figure 21-6 the transition has been changed to *Cross Dissolve*:

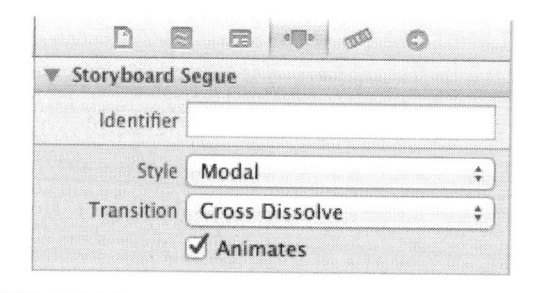

Figure 21-6

If animation is not required during the transition, turn off the *Animates* option. To delete a segue from a storyboard simply select the arrow and press the keyboard delete key.

Compile and run the application. Note that touching the "Go to Scene 2" button causes Scene 2 to appear.

21.6 Associating a View Controller with a Scene

At this point in the example we have two scenes but only one view controller (the one created by Xcode when we selected *Single View Application*). Clearly in order to be able to add any functionality behind scene 2 it too will need a view controller. The first step, therefore, is to add the files for a view controller to the project. Ctrl-click on the *Storyboard* target at the top of the project navigator panel and select *New File...* from the resulting menu. In the new file panel select *Objective-C class* and click *Next* to proceed. On the options screen verify that the *Subclass of* menu is set to *UIViewController* and that the *Targeted for iPad* and *With XIB for user interface* options are both deselected (since the view already exists in the storyboard there is no need for an NIB user interface file) and name the class *Scene2ViewContoller*.

Select the *MainStoryboard.storyboard* file in the project navigator panel and select the View Controller button located in the panel beneath the Scene 2 view as shown in Figure 21-7:

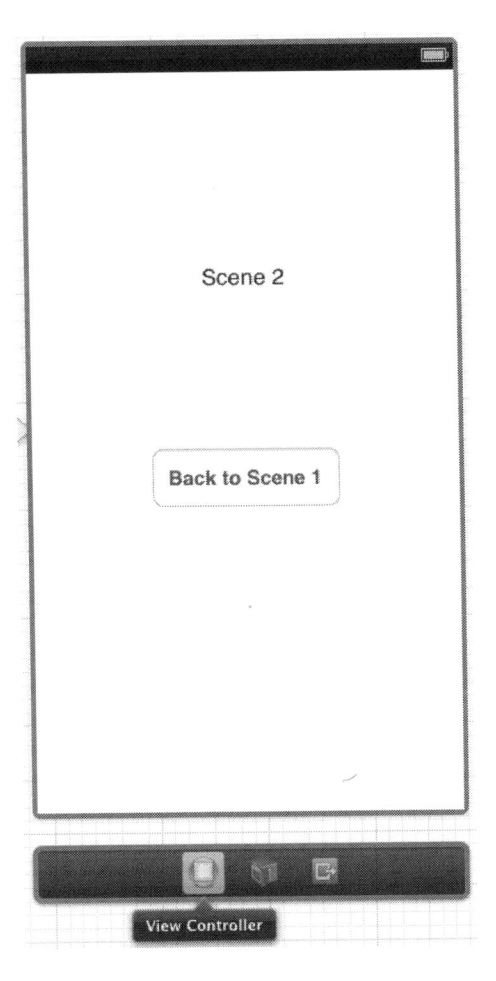

Figure 21-7

With the view controller for scene 2 selected within the storyboard canvas, display the Identity Inspector (*View -> Utilities -> Identity Inspector*) and change the *Class* from *UIViewController* to *Scene2ViewController*:

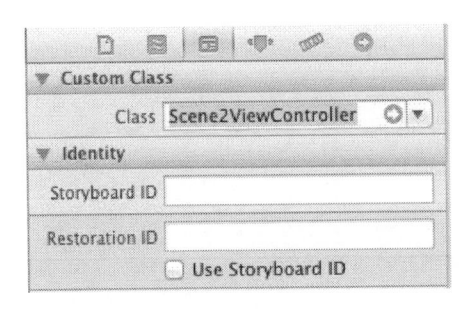

Figure 21-8

Using Xcode Storyboarding

Scene 2 now has a view controller and corresponding source files where code may be written to implement any required functionality.

Select the label object in scene 2 and display the Assistant Editor. Make sure that the *Scene2ViewController.h* file is displayed in the editor and then establish an outlet for the label named *scene2Label*.

21.7 Passing Data Between Scenes

One of the most common requirements when working with storyboards involves the transfer of data from one scene to another during a segue transition. This is achieved using the *prepareForSegue:* method.

Before a segue is performed by the storyboard runtime environment, a call is made to the *prepareForSegue:* method of the current view controller. If any tasks need to be performed prior to the segue taking place simply implement this method in the current view controller and add code to perform any necessary tasks. Passed as an argument to this method is a segue object from which a reference to the destination view controller may be obtained and subsequently used to transfer data.

To see this in action, begin by selecting *Scene2ViewController.h* and adding a new data property:

```objc
#import <UIKit/UIKit.h>

@interface Scene2ViewController : UIViewController
@property (strong, nonatomic) IBOutlet UILabel *scene2Label;
@property (strong, nonatomic) NSString *labelText;
@end
```

This property will hold the text to be displayed on the label when the storyboard transitions to this scene. As such, some code needs to be added to the *viewDidLoad:* method located in the *Scene2ViewController.m* file:

```objc
- (void)viewDidLoad
{
    [super viewDidLoad];
    _scene2Label.text = _labelText;
}
```

Next, select the *StoryboardViewController.h* file and import the header file for the Scene2ViewController class:

```objc
#import <UIKit/UIKit.h>
#import "Scene2ViewController.h"
```

```
@interface StoryboardViewController : UIViewController
@property (strong, nonatomic) IBOutlet UIButton *scene1Label;

@end
```

Finally, select the *StoryboardViewController.m* file and implement the segue methods as follows:

```
-(void)prepareForSegue:(UIStoryboardSegue *)segue sender:(id)sender
{
    Scene2ViewController *destination =
            [segue destinationViewController];

    destination.labelText = @"Arrived from Scene 1";
}
```

All this method does is obtain a reference to the destination view controller and then assigns a string to the *labelText* property of the object so that it appears on the label.

Compile and run the application once again and note that when scene 2 is displayed the new label text appears. We have, albeit using a very simple example, transferred data from one scene to the next.

21.8 Unwinding Storyboard Segues

The next step is to configure the button on scene 2 to return to scene 1. It might seem as though the obvious choice is to simply implement a segue from the button on scene 2 to scene 1. Instead of returning the original instance of scene 1, however, this would create an entirely new instance of the StoryboardViewController class. If a user were to perform this transition repeatedly, therefore, the application would continue to use more memory and would eventually be terminated by the operating system.

The application should, instead, make use of the Storyboard *unwind* feature introduced into Xcode 4.5. This involves implementing a method in the view controller of the scene to which the user is to be returned and then connecting a segue to that method from the source view controller. This enables an unwind action to be performed across multiple levels of scene.

To implement this in our example application, begin by selecting the *StoryBoardViewController.m* file and implementing a method to be called by the unwind segue named *returned*:

```
-(IBAction)returned:(UIStoryboardSegue *)segue {
    _scene1Label.text = @"Returned from Scene 2";
}
```

Using Xcode Storyboarding

All that is required of this method for this example is that it set some new text on the label object of scene 1. Once the method has been added, it is important to save the *StoryBoardViewController.m* file before continuing.

The next step is to establish the unwind segue. To achieve this, locate scene 2 within the storyboard canvas and ctrl-click and drag from the button to the "exit" icon (the green button with the white square and the right facing arrow pointing outward shown in Figure 21-9) in the panel located beneath the view. Release the line and select the *returned:* method from the resulting menu:

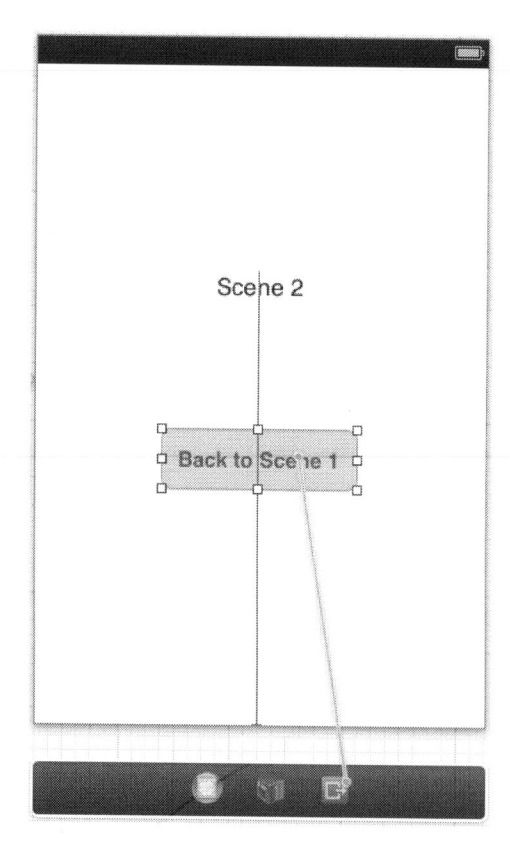

Figure 21-9

Once again, run the application and note that the button on scene 2 now returns to scene 1 and, in the process, calls the *returned:* method resulting in the label on scene 1 changing.

21.9 Triggering a Storyboard Segue Programmatically

In addition to wiring up controls in scenes to trigger a segue, it is also possible to initiate a preconfigured segue from within the application code. This can be achieved by assigning an identifier to the segue and then making a call to the *performSegueWithIdentifier:* method of the view controller from which the segue is to be triggered.

To set the identifier of a segue, select it in the storyboard canvas, display the Attribute Inspector (*View -> Utilities -> Show Attribute Inspector*) and set the value in the *Identifier* field.

Assuming a segue with the identifier of *SegueToScene1*, this could be triggered from within code as follows:

```
[self performSegueWithIdentifier: @"SegueToScene1"
           sender: self];
```

21.10 Summary

The Storyboard feature of Xcode allows for the navigational flow between the various views in an iOS application to be visually constructed without the need to write code. In this chapter we have covered the basic concepts behind storyboarding and worked through the creation of an example iPhone application using storyboards and, in doing so, also explored the new unwind feature of Xcode 4.5.

Chapter 22

22. Using Xcode Storyboards to Create an iOS 6 iPhone Tab Bar Application

Having worked through a simple Storyboard based application in the previous chapter, the goal of this chapter will be to create a slightly more complex storyboard example.

So far in this book we have worked exclusively with applications that present a single view to the user. In practice, however, it is more likely that an application will need to display a variety of different content depending on the actions of the user. This is typically achieved by creating multiple views (often referred to as content views) and then providing a mechanism for the user to navigate from one view to another. One of a number of mechanisms for achieving this involves the use of either the UINavigationBar or UITabBar components. In this chapter we will begin by using the storyboard feature of Xcode to implement a multiview application using a Tab Bar.

22.1 An Overview of the Tab Bar

The UITabBar component is typically located at the bottom of the screen and presents an array of tabs containing text and an optional icon that may be selected by the user to display a different content view. Typical examples of the tab bar in action include the iPhone's built-in Music and Phone applications. The Music application, for example, presents a tab bar with options to display playlists, artists, songs and videos. Depending on the selection made from the tab bar, a different content view is displayed to the user.

22.2 Understanding View Controllers in a Multiview Application

In preceding chapters we have talked about the model-view-controller concept in relation to each view having its own view controller (for additional information on this read the chapter entitled *An Overview of the iOS 6 iPhone Application Development Architecture*). In a multiview application, on the other hand, each content view will still have a view controller associated with it to handle user interaction and display updates. Multiview applications, however, also require an additional controller.

Multiview applications need a visual control that will be used by the user to switch from one content view to another, and this often takes the form of a tab or navigation bar. Both of these components are also *views* and as such also need to have a *view controller*. In the context of a multiview application, this is known as the *root controller* and is responsible for controlling which content view is currently displayed to the user. As an app developer you are free to create your own root controller by subclassing from the UIViewController class, but in practice it usually makes more sense to use an instance of either the UIKit UITabBarController or UINavigationController classes.

Regardless of the origins of your chosen root controller, it is the first controller that is loaded by the application when it launches. Once loaded, it is responsible for displaying the first content view to the user and then switching the various content views in and out as required based on the user's subsequent interaction with the application.

Since this chapter is dedicated to the creation of a tab bar based application we will be using an instance of the UITabBarController as our root controller.

22.3 Setting up the Tab Bar Example Application

The first step in creating our example application is to create a new Xcode project. To do so, launch Xcode and select the option to *Create a new Xcode project*.

Amongst the new project template options provided by Xcode is the *Tabbed Application* template. When selected, this template creates a pre-configured application consisting of a Tab Bar application with two content views. Whilst we could have used this template in this chapter, to do so would fail to convey a number of skills that will be essential when developing more complicated applications using storyboards. Whilst it is useful, therefore, to be aware of this template option for future reference, in the interest of providing a sound knowledge foundation we will be using the Single View Application template in this example.

On the template selection screen, select *Single View Application* and click *Next* to proceed. On the next screen enter *TabBar* as the product name and class prefix, make sure that the *Devices* menu is set to *iPhone* and that the *Use Storyboard* and *Use Automatic Reference Counting* options are switched on. Proceed to the final screen and browse to a suitable location for the project files before clicking on the *Create* button.

22.4 Reviewing the Project Files

Based on our selections during the project creation process, Xcode has pre-populated the project with a number of files. In addition to the standard application delegate files it has, for example, provided the files necessary for a single view controller based application named *TabBarViewController.m* and *TabBarViewController.h*. As a result of selecting the *Use Storyboard* option a *MainStoryboard.storyboard* file has also been created.

22.5 Renaming the Initial View Controller

The next step in creating the application involves renaming the TabBarViewController class provided by Xcode to a more descriptive name. Since this view controller presents the view that will be displayed when the user touches the first tab on the tab bar, we will name this class Tab1ViewController. To achieve this, select the *TabBarViewController.h* file and use the mouse to highlight the *TabBarViewController* class name in the editing panel. With the name highlighted select the *Edit -> Refactor -> Rename...* menu option.

In the resulting panel enter Tab1ViewController into the text box and click on *Preview*. In the preview panel select the *Save* button followed by the option to *Disable* snapshots.

22.6 Adding the View Controller for the Second Content View

The ultimate goal of this chapter is to create a tab bar based application consisting of two tabs with corresponding views. Xcode has already created the first view controller for us and we have subsequently renamed this class. The next step, therefore, is to add the view controller for the second view. To achieve this, select the *File -> New -> File...* menu option and on the resulting panel select *Objective-C class*. Click *Next* and on the next screen, name the new class *Tab2ViewController* and change the *Subclass of* menu to *UIViewController*. Ensure that the options to target iPad and create an XIB file are switched off before clicking *Next* and proceed with the creation process.

22.7 Adding the Tab Bar Controller to the Storyboard

As previously explained, the navigation between view controllers in a Tab Bar based interface is handled by a Tab Bar Controller. It will be necessary, therefore, to add one of these to our storyboard. Begin by selecting the *MainStoryboard.storyboard* file in the Xcode project navigator panel and note, as illustrated in Figure 22-1, that the storyboard currently only contains the original view controller instance added for us by Xcode when the project was created.

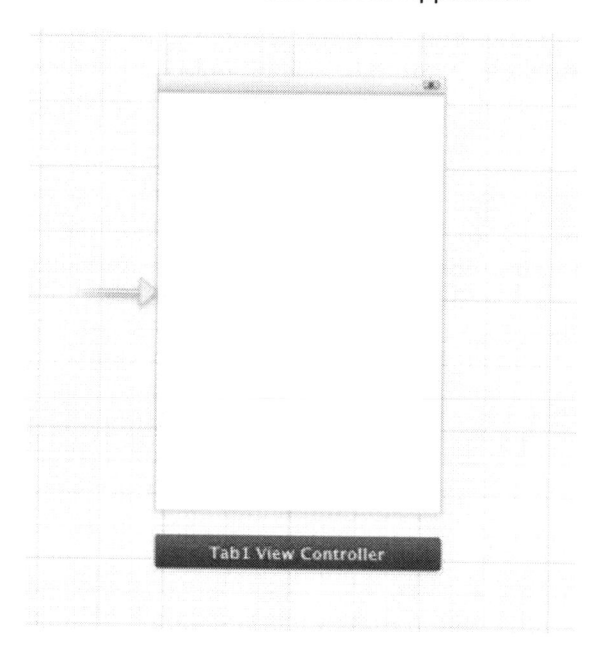

Using Xcode Storyboards to Create an iOS 6 iPhone Tab Bar Application

Figure 22-1

In order to add a Tab Bar Controller to the storyboard, select the Tab1 View Controller in the storyboard design area and select the *Editor -> Embed In -> Tab Bar Controller* menu option. The Tab Bar Controller will subsequently appear in the storyboard already connected to the Tab Bar Controller as shown in Figure 22-2:

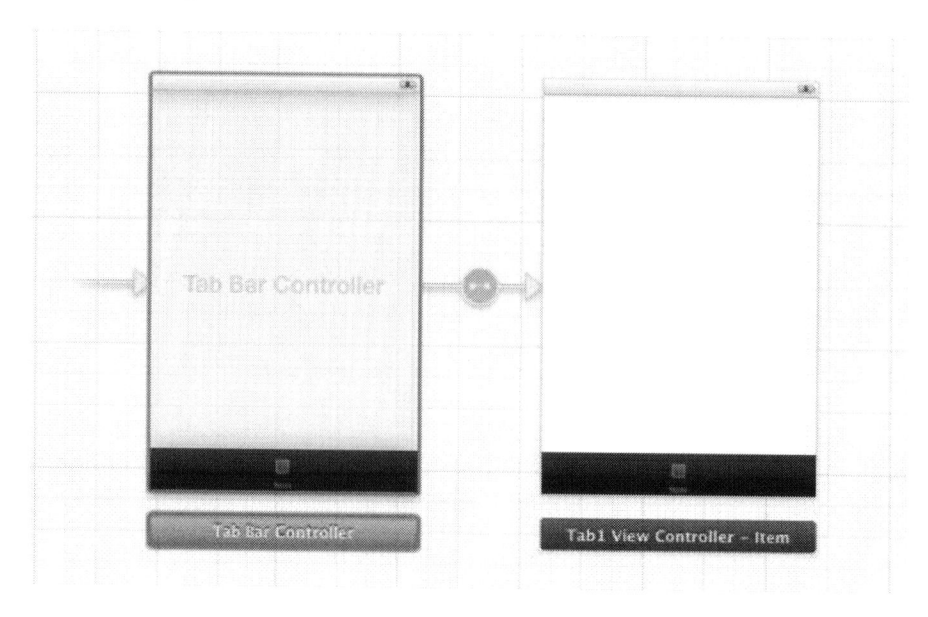

Figure 22-2

Now that the Tab Bar Controller has been added, the next task is to add a view controller to the storyboard that will correspond to the Tab2ViewController class previously added to the project.

22.8 Adding a Second View Controller to the Storyboard

The second view controller may be added to the storyboard simply by dragging and dropping one from the Object Library panel (*View -> Utilities -> Show Object Library*). Once the new view controller has been added to the storyboard canvas, select it so that it is highlighted with a blue border and then display the Identity Inspector panel (*View -> Utilities -> Show Identity Inspector*). Within the inspector panel change the *Class* setting from *UIViewController* to *Tab2ViewController*.

With the storyboard view controller mapped to our Tab2ViewController class we now need to establish a relationship between this new view controller and the Tab Bar Controller. To achieve this simply Ctrl-click on the Tab Bar Controller object in the storyboard canvas and drag the line to the Tab2ViewController. Upon releasing the line select the *viewControllers* menu option listed under *Relationship Segue* as illustrated in Figure 22-3. This will add the Tab2ViewController to the *viewControllers* property of the Tab Bar Controller object so that it will be included in the tab navigation.

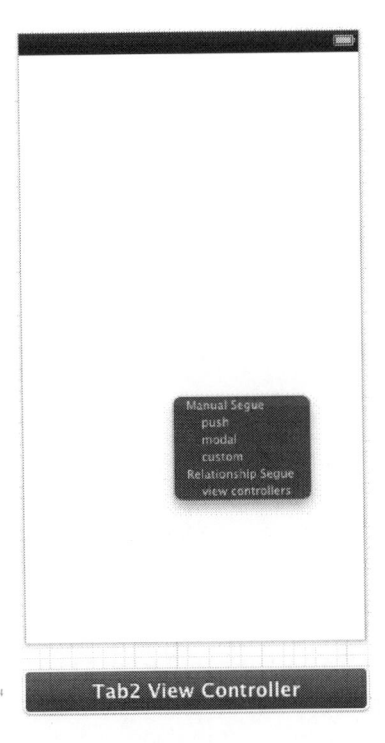

Figure 22-3

At this point in the design process the storyboard should now consist of one Tab Bar controller with relationships established with both Tab1ViewController and Tab2ViewController. Allowing for

Using Xcode Storyboards to Create an iOS 6 iPhone Tab Bar Application

differences in positioning of the storyboard elements, the canvas should now appear as shown in the following figure:

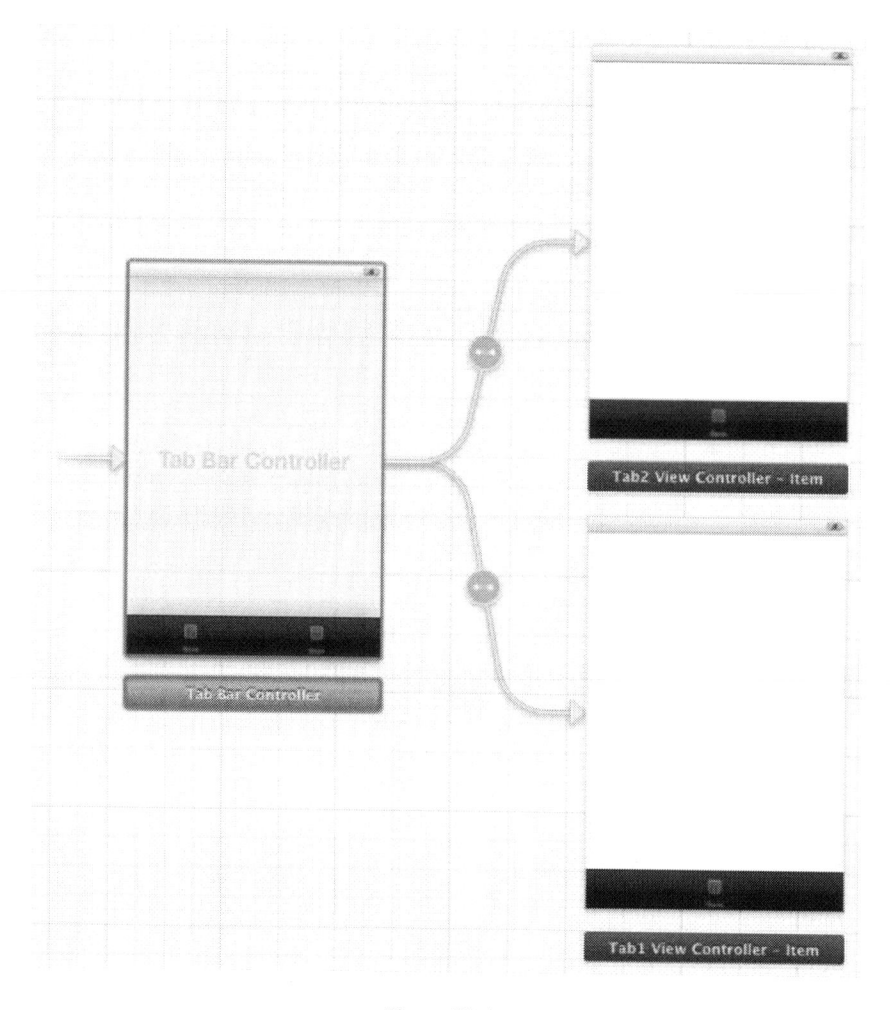

Figure 22-4

All that remains in order to complete the application is to configure the tab bar items and design rudimentary user interfaces for the two view controllers.

22.9 Designing the View Controller User interfaces

In order to visually differentiate the two view controllers we will add labels to the views and change the background colors. If you are currently zoomed out of the canvas begin by zooming in using the controls in the lower right hand corner of the storyboard canvas (if the canvas is zoomed out it will not be possible to make changes to the views). Begin by selecting the view of the Tab1ViewController object. Within the Attribute Inspector panel (*View -> Utilities -> Show Attribute Inspector*) click on the white rectangle next to the *Background* label and select a shade of red from the resulting Colors dialog. Next, drag and drop a Label object from the Object Library panel and position it in the center of the red view. Double click on the label so that it becomes editable and change the text to *Screen One*.

Once completed, the Tab1ViewController storyboard scene should appear as shown in Figure 22-5:

Figure 22-5

Repeat the above steps to change the background of the Tab2ViewController view to green and to add a label displaying text that reads *Screen Two*.

22.10 Configuring the Tab Bar Items

As is evident from the tab bars shown across the bottom of the two view controller elements, the tab items are currently configured to display text which reads "Item". In addition, the small icon containing a question mark indicates that no images have been assigned to the items. The final task prior to compiling and running the application, therefore, is to rectify these issues. Begin by double clicking on the word "Item" in the tab bar of Tab1ViewController so that the text highlights and enter *Screen One*. Repeat this step to change the text of the tab bar item for Tab2ViewController to *Screen Two*.

Using Xcode Storyboards to Create an iOS 6 iPhone Tab Bar Application

In the event that you already have some icons suitable to be displayed on the tab bar items feel free to use them for this project. Alternatively, download some example icons using the following URL and unzip them into a suitable location on your system:

http://www.ebookfrenzy.com/code/tabbaricons.zip

The icon archive contains two PNG format icon images named *first.png* and *second.png*. Locate these files (or any two other icons you have chosen to use) in a Finder window and drag and drop them onto the *Supporting Files* entry in the Xcode project navigator panel. With the icons added to the project, click on the placeholder icon in the tab bar of the Tab1ViewController and in the Attribute Inspector panel use the *Image* drop down menu to select *first.png* as the image file:

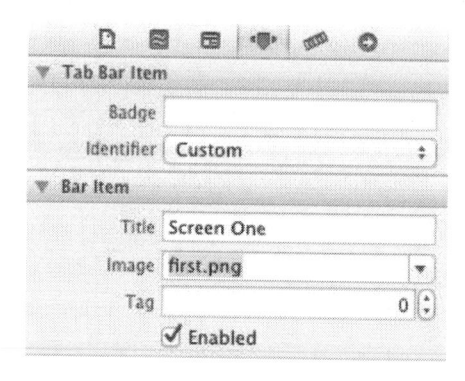

Figure 22-6

Perform the same steps to specify *second.png* as the image file for Tab2ViewController.

22.11 Building and Running the Application

The design and implementation of the example application is now complete and all that remains is to build and run it. Click on the *Run* button located in the Xcode toolbar and wait for the code to compile and the application to launch within the iOS Simulator environment. The application should appear with the Tab1ViewController active and the two tab items in the tab bar visible across the bottom of the screen. Clicking on the Screen Two tab will navigate to the Tab2ViewController view:

176

Figure 22-7

22.12 Summary

The Storyboard feature of Xcode allows Tab Bar based navigation to be quickly and easily built into applications. Perhaps the most significant point to make is that the example project created in this chapter was implemented without the need to write a single line of Objective-C code.

Chapter 23

23. An Overview of iOS 6 Table Views and Xcode Storyboards

If you have spent an appreciable amount of time using iOS on an iPhone the chances are good that you have interacted with a UIKit Table View object. Table Views are the cornerstone of the navigation system for many iOS iPhone applications. For example, both the iPhone *Mail* and *Settings* applications make extensive use of Table Views to present information to users in a list format and to enable users to drill down to more detailed information by selecting a particular list item.

Historically, table views have been one of the more complex areas of iOS user interface implementation. In recognition of this fact, Apple introduced ways to implement table views through the use of the Xcode Storyboard feature.

The goal of this chapter is to provide an overview of the concept of the UITableView class together with an introduction to the ways in which storyboards can be used to ease the table view implementation process. Once these basics have been covered a series of chapters, starting with *Using Xcode Storyboards to Build Dynamic TableViews with Prototype Table View Cells*, will work through the creation of example projects intended to demonstrate the use of storyboards in the context of table views.

23.1 An Overview of the Table View

Table Views present the user with data in a list format and are represented by the UITableView class of the UIKit framework. The data is presented in rows, whereby the content of each row is implemented in the form of a UITableViewCell object. By default, each table cell can display a text label (textLabel), a subtitle (detailedTextLabel) and an image (imageView). More complex cells can be created by either adding subviews to the cell, or subclassing UITableViewCell and adding your own custom functionality and appearance.

23.2 Static vs. Dynamic Table Views

When implementing table views using an Xcode storyboard it is important to understand the distinction between *static* and *dynamic* tables. Static tables are useful in situations when a fixed number of rows need to be displayed in a table. The settings page for an application, for example, would typically have a predetermined number of configuration options and would be an ideal candidate for a static table.

Dynamic tables (also known as *prototype-based* tables), on the other hand, are intended for use when a variable number of rows need to be displayed from a data source. Within the storyboard editor, Xcode allows you to visually design a prototype table cell which will then be replicated in the dynamic table view at runtime in order to display data to the user.

23.3 The Table View Delegate and dataSource

Each table view in an application needs to have a *delegate* and a *dataSource* associated with it (with the exception of static tables which do not have data source). The dataSource implements the UITableViewDataSource protocol, which basically consists of a number of methods that define title information, how many rows of data are to be displayed, how the data is divided into different sections and, most importantly, supplies the table view with the cell objects to be displayed. The delegate implements the UITableViewDelegate protocol and provides additional control over the appearance and functionality of the table view including detecting when a user touches a specific row, defining custom row heights and indentations and also implementation of row deletion and editing functions.

23.4 Table View Styles

Table views may be configured to use either *plain* or *grouped* style. In the grouped style, the rows are grouped together in sections represented by rounded rectangles. For example, Figure 23-1 shows a table view configured to use the grouped style:

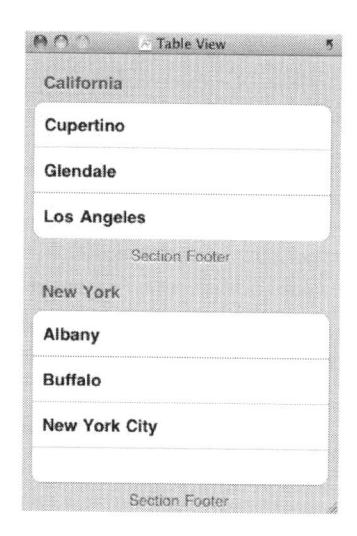

Figure 23-1

In the case of the plain style, the items are listed without separation and using the full width of the display:

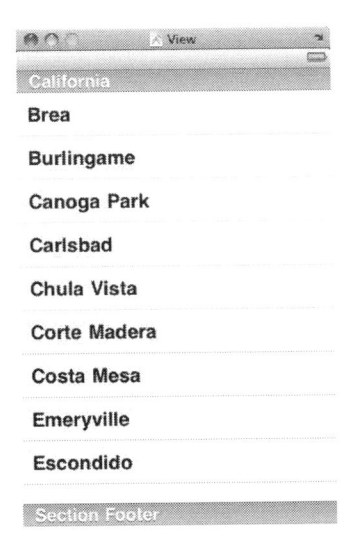

Figure 23-2

Table Views using plain style can also be *indexed*, whereby rows are organized into groups according to specified criteria, such as alphabetical or numerical sorting.

23.5 Table View Cell Styles

In addition to the style of the Table View itself, different styles may also be specified for the individual table cells (unless custom table cells are being used). The iOS 6 SDK currently supports four different cell styles:

- **UITableViewCellStyleDefault** – only the labelText in black and left aligned.
- **UITableViewCellStyleSubtitle** – labelText in black and left aligned with the detailLabeltext positioned beneath it in a smaller font using a gray foreground.
- **UITableViewCellStyleValue1** – labelText in black left aligned and the smaller detailLabelText in blue, on the same line and right aligned.
- **UITableViewCellStyleValue2** – labelText in blue on left side of cell, right aligned and detailedLabelText on right of cell, left aligned and black.

23.6 Table View Cell Reuse

A table view is, at the basic level, comprised of a UITableView object and a UITableViewCell for each row to be displayed. When developing using iOS releases prior to iOS 6, it was the responsibility of the developer to write code to create instances of the cells as required by the table view object. In iOS 6 this has changed.

181

An Overview of iOS 6 Table Views and Xcode Storyboards

The code for a typical iOS 6 application using a table view will not directly create instances of a cell. The reasoning behind this becomes evident when performance and memory requirements are taken into consideration. Consider, for example, a table view that is required to display 1000 photo images. It can be assumed with a reasonable degree of certainty that only a small percentage of cells will be visible to the user at any one time. If the application was permitted to create each of the 1000 cells in advance the device would very quickly run into memory and performance limitations.

Instead, the application begins by registering with the table view object the class to be used for cell objects, along with the *reuse identifier* previously assigned to that class. If the cell class was written in code, the registration is performed using the *registerClass:* method of UITableView object. For example:

```
[self.tableView registerClass:[CarTableViewCell class]
  forCellWithReuseIdentifier:@"carTableCell"];
```

In the event that the cell is contained within an Interface Builder NIB file, the *registerNib:* method is used instead.

Perhaps the most important point to remember from this chapter is that if the cell is created using prototypes within a storyboard it is not necessary to register the class and, in fact, doing so will prevent the cell or view from appearing when the application runs.

As the table view initializes, it calls the *cellForRowAtIndexPath:* method of the datasource class passing through the index path for which a cell object is required. This method will then call the *dequeueReusableCellWithReuseIdentifier:* method of the table view object, passing through both the index path and the reuse ID assigned to the cell class when it was registered, to find out if there is a reusable cell object in the queue that can be used for this new cell. Since this is the initialization phase and no cells have been deemed eligible for reuse, the method will create a new cell and return it. Once all the visible cells have been created, the table view will stop asking for more cells. The code for the *cellForCellAtIndexPath:* will typically read as follows (the code to customize the cell before returning it will be implementation specific):

```
- (UITableViewCell *)tableView:(UITableView *)tableView
  cellForRowAtIndexPath:(NSIndexPath *)indexPath
{
    static NSString *CellIdentifier = @"carTableCell";
    CarTableViewCell *cell = [tableView
         dequeueReusableCellWithIdentifier:CellIdentifier
         forIndexPath:indexPath];

    // Configure the cell here ...
```

```
        return cell;
}
```

Developers familiar with Table Views in iOS 5 or older will note the absence in the above delegate method of the following line of code which used to be required to create table cells:

```
// This step no longer required in iOS 6
if (cell == nil) {
        cell = [[CarTableViewCell alloc]
            initWithStyle:UITableViewCellStyleDefault
            reuseIdentifier:CellIdentifier];
}
```

As the user scrolls through the table view, some cells will move out of the visible frame. When this happens, the table view places them on the reuse queue. As cells are moving out of view, new ones are likely to be coming into view. For each cell moving into the view area, the table view will call *cellForRowAtIndexPath:*. This time, however, when a call to *dequeueReusableCellWithReuseIdentifier:* is made, it is most likely that an existing cell object will be returned from the reuse queue, thereby avoiding the necessity to create a new object.

23.7 Summary

Whilst table views provide a popular mechanism for displaying data and implementing view navigation within applications, implementation has historically been a complex process. That changed with the introduction of storyboard support in Xcode. Xcode now provides a mechanism for visually implementing a considerable amount of Table View functionality with minimal coding. Such table views can be implemented as either *static* or *dynamic* depending on the requirements of the table and the nature of the data being displayed.

Chapter 24

24. Using Xcode Storyboards to Build Dynamic TableViews with Prototype Table View Cells

Arguably one of the most powerful features of Xcode storyboards involves a new way to implement table views through the concept of prototype table cells. This allows the developer to visually design the user interface elements that will appear in a table cell (such as labels, images etc) and then replicate that prototype cell on demand within the table view of the running application. Prior to the introduction of Storyboards, this would have involved a considerable amount of coding work combined with trial and error.

The objective of this chapter is to work through a detailed example designed to demonstrate dynamic table view creation within a storyboard using table view prototype cells. Once this topic has been covered, the next chapter (entitled *Implementing TableView Navigation using Xcode Storyboards*) will explore the implementation of table view navigation and the passing of data between scenes using storyboards.

24.1 Creating the Example Project

Start Xcode and create a single view application. Name the project and class prefix *TableViewStory*.

A review of the files in the project navigator panel will reveal that, as requested, Xcode has created a view controller subclass for us named TableViewStoryViewController. In addition, this view controller is represented within the Storyboard file, the content of which may be viewed by selecting the *MainStoryboard.storyboard* file.

In order to fully understand the steps involved in creating a Storyboard based TableView application we will start with a clean slate by removing the view controller added for us by Xcode. Within the storyboard canvas, select the *Table View Story View Controller* item so that it is highlighted in blue and press the Delete key on the keyboard. Next, select and delete both the corresponding *TableViewStoryViewController.m* and *TableViewStoryViewController.h* files from the project navigator panel. In the resulting panel select the option to move the files to trash.

185

Using Xcode Storyboards to Build Dynamic TableViews with Prototype Table View Cells

At this point we have a template project consisting solely of a storyboard file and the standard app delegate code files and are ready to begin building a storyboard based iPhone application using the UITableView and UITableViewCell classes.

24.2 Adding the TableView Controller to the Storyboard

From the perspective of the user, the entry point into this application will be a table view containing a list of cars, with each table view cell containing the vehicle make, model and corresponding image. As such, we will need to add a Table View Controller instance to the storyboard file. Select the *MainStoryboard.storyboard* file so that the canvas appears in the center of the Xcode window. From within the Object Library panel (accessible via the *View -> Utilities -> Show Object Library* menu option) drag a *Table View Controller* object and drop it onto the storyboard canvas as illustrated in Figure 24-1:

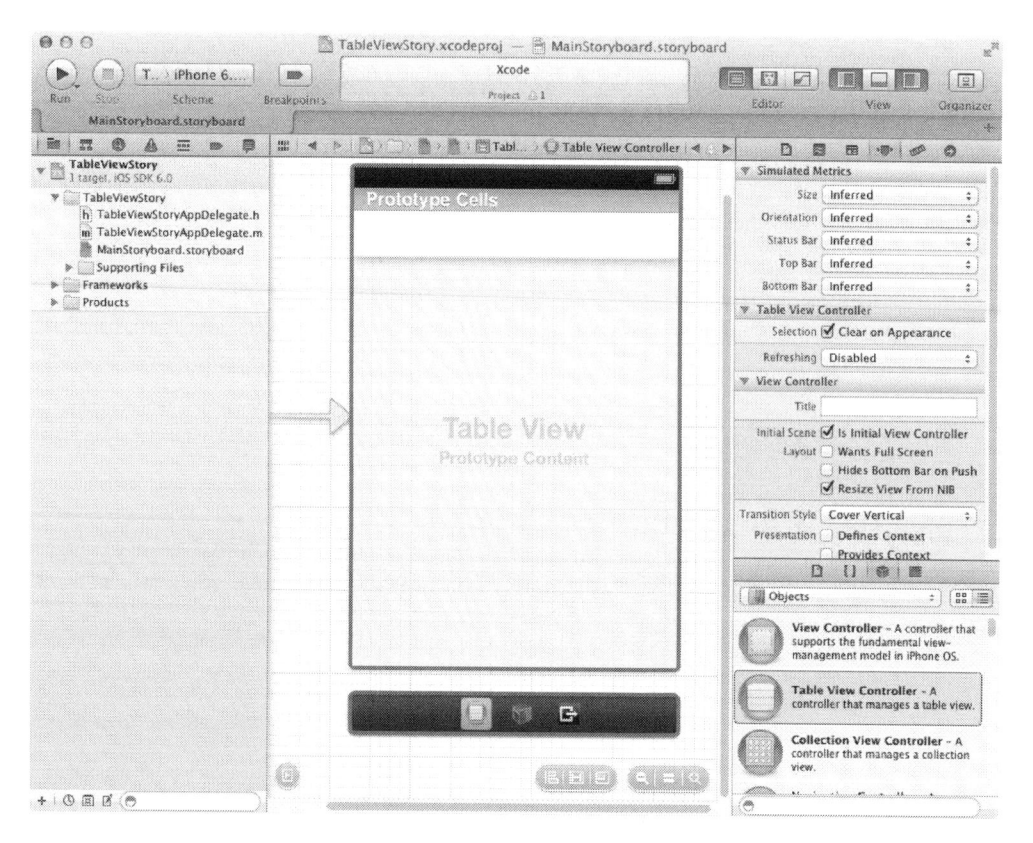

Figure 24-1

Within the storyboard we now have a table view controller instance. Within this instance is also a prototype table view cell that we will be able to configure to design the cells for our table. At the moment these are generic UITableViewCell and UITableViewController classes that do not give us much in the way of control within our application code. So that we can extend the functionality of

186

these instances we need to declare them as being subclasses of UITableViewController and UITableViewCell respectively. Before doing so, however, we need to actually create those subclasses.

24.3 Creating the UITableViewController and UITableViewCell Subclasses

We will be declaring the Table View Controller instance within our storyboard as being a subclass of UITableViewController named *CarTableViewController*. At present, this subclass does not exist within our project so clearly we need to create it before proceeding. To achieve this, select the *File -> New -> File...* menu option and in the resulting panel select the option to create a new Objective-C class. Click *Next* and on the subsequent screen, name the class *CarTableViewController* and change the *Subclass of* menu to *UITableViewController*. Make sure that the *Targeted for iPad* and *With XIB for user interface* options are both turned off and click *Next* followed by *Create*.

Within the Table View Controller added to the storyboard in the previous section, Xcode also added a prototype table cell. Later in this chapter we will add two labels and an image view object to this cell. In order to extend this class it is necessary to, once again, create a subclass. Perform this step by selecting the *File -> New -> File....* menu option. Within the new file dialog select *Objective-C class* and click *Next*. On the following screen, name the new class *CarTableViewCell*, change the *Subclass of* menu to *UITableViewCell* and proceed with the class creation.

Next, the items in the storyboard need to be configured to be instances of these subclasses. Begin by selecting the *MainStoryboard.storyboard* file and select the Table View Controller scene so that it is highlighted in blue. Within the identity inspector panel (*View -> Utilities -> Show Identity Inspector*) use the *Class* drop down menu to change the class from *UITableViewController* to *CarTableViewController* as illustrated in Figure 24-2:

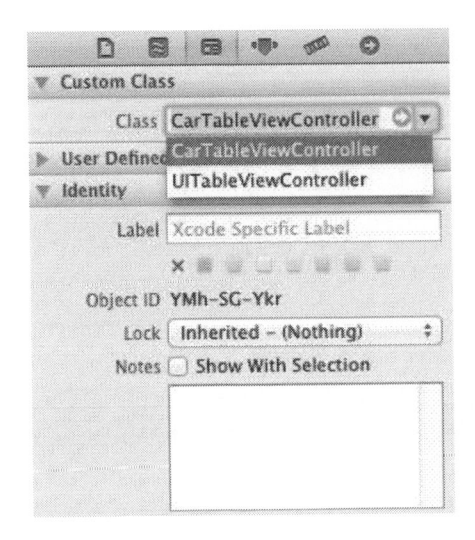

Figure 24-2

187

Similarly, select the prototype table cell within the table view controller storyboard scene and change the class from *UITableViewCell* to the new *CarTableViewCell* subclass.

With the appropriate subclasses created and associated with the objects in the storyboard, the next step is to design the prototype cell.

24.4 Declaring the Cell Reuse Identifier

Later in the chapter some code will be added to the project to replicate instances of the prototype table cell. This will require that the cell be assigned a reuse identifier. With the storyboard still visible in Xcode, select the prototype table cell and display the Attributes Inspector. Within the inspector, change the *Identifier* field to *carTableCell*:

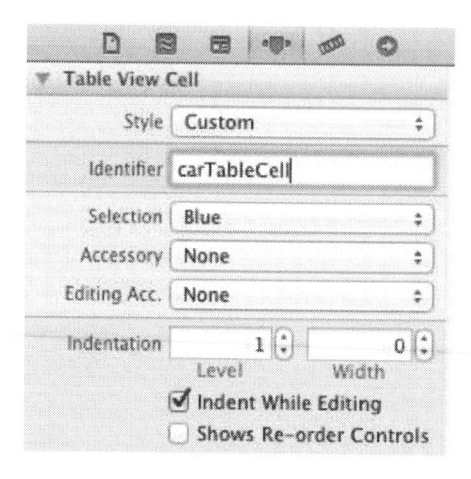

Figure 24-3

24.5 Designing a Storyboard UITableView Prototype Cell

Table Views are made up of multiple cells, each of which is actually either an instance of the UITableViewCell class or a subclass thereof. A useful feature of storyboarding allows the developer to visually construct the user interface elements that are to appear in the table cells and then replicate that cell at runtime. For the purposes of this example each table cell needs to display an image view and two labels which, in turn, will be connected to outlets that we will later declare in the *CarTableViewCell* subclass. Much like Interface Builder, components may be dragged from the Object Library panel and dropped onto a scene within the storyboard. Note, however, that this is only possible when the storyboard view is zoomed in. With this in mind, verify that the storyboard is zoomed in using the controls in the bottom right hand corner of the canvas and then drag and drop two Labels and an Image View object onto the prototype table cell. Resize and position the items so that the cell layout resembles that illustrated in Figure 24-4, making sure to stretch the label objects so that they extend toward the right hand edge of the cell.

Figure 24-4

Having configured the storyboard elements for the table view portion of the application it is time to begin modifying the table view and cell subclasses.

24.6 Modifying the CarTableViewCell Class

Within the storyboard file, two labels and an image view were added to the prototype cell which, in turn, has been declared as an instance of our new CarTableViewCell class. In order to manipulate these user interface objects from within our code we need to establish three outlets connected to the objects in the storyboard scene. Begin, therefore, by selecting the image view object, displaying the Assistant Editor and making sure that it is displaying the content of the *CarTableViewCell.h* file. If it is not, use the bar across the top of the editor panel to select this file.

Ctrl-click on the image view object in the prototype table cell and drag the resulting line to a point just below the @interface line in the Assistant Editor window. Release the line and use the connection panel to establish an outlet named *carImage*.

Using Xcode Storyboards to Build Dynamic TableViews with Prototype Table View Cells

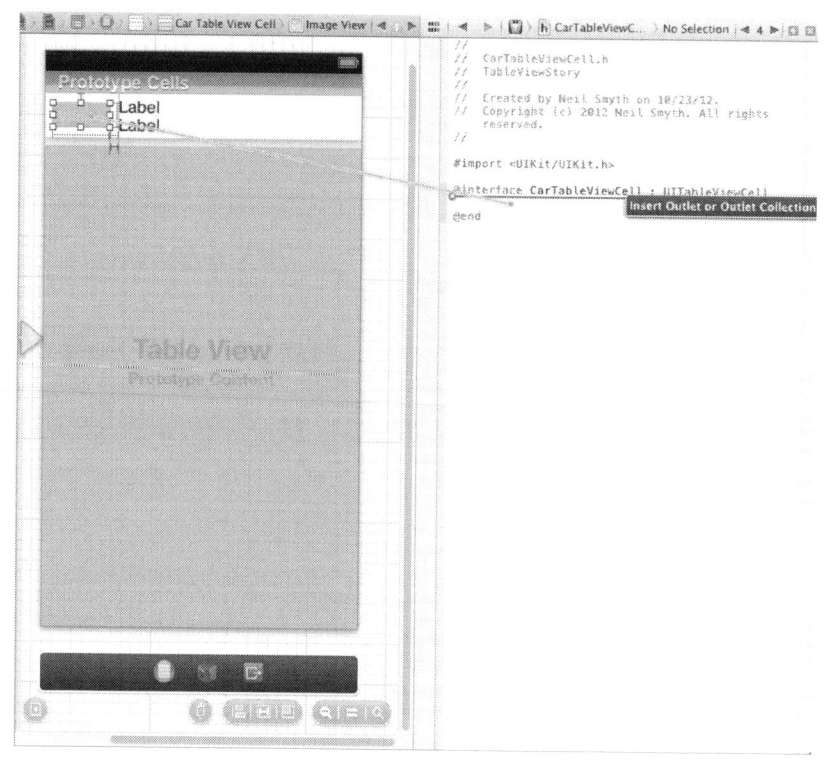

Figure 24-5

Repeat these steps to establish outlets for the two labels named *makeLabel* and *modelLabel* respectively. Once the connections are in place, the *CarTableViewCell.h* file should read as follows:

```
#import <UIKit/UIKit.h>

@interface CarTableViewCell : UITableViewCell
@property (nonatomic, strong) IBOutlet UIImageView *carImage;
@property (nonatomic, strong) IBOutlet UILabel *makeLabel;
@property (nonatomic, strong) IBOutlet UILabel *modelLabel;
@end
```

24.7 Creating the Table View Datasource

Dynamic Table Views require a *datasource* to provide the data that will be displayed to the user within the cells. By default, Xcode has designated the *CarTableViewController* class as the datasource for the table view controller in the storyboard. It is within this class, therefore, that we can build a very simple data model for our application consisting of a number of arrays. The first step is to declare these as properties in the *CarTableViewController.h* file:

```
#import <UIKit/UIKit.h>
```

190

```
@interface CarTableViewController : UITableViewController

@property (nonatomic, strong) NSArray *carImages;
@property (nonatomic, strong) NSArray *carMakes;
@property (nonatomic, strong) NSArray *carModels;
@end
```

In addition, the arrays need to be initialized with some data when the application has loaded, making the *viewDidLoad*: method an ideal location. Select the *CarTableViewController.m* file within the project navigator panel and modify it as outlined in the following code fragment. Since we will be working with CarTableViewCell instances within the code it is also necessary to import the *CarTableViewCell.h* file:

```
#import "CarTableViewController.h"
#import "CarTableViewCell.h"

@implementation CarTableViewController
.
.
.
- (void)viewDidLoad
{
    [super viewDidLoad];
    _carMakes = @[@"Chevy",
                  @"BMW",
                  @"Toyota",
                  @"Volvo",
                  @"Smart"];

    _carModels = @[@"Volt",
                   @"Mini",
                   @"Venza",
                   @"S60",
                   @"Fortwo"];

    _carImages = @[@"chevy_volt.jpg",
                   @"mini_clubman.jpg",
                   @"toyota_venza.jpg",
                   @"volvo_s60.jpg",
                   @"smart_fortwo.jpg"];
}
```

For a class to act as the datasource for a table view controller a number of methods must be implemented. These methods will be called by the table view object in order to obtain both

Using Xcode Storyboards to Build Dynamic TableViews with Prototype Table View Cells

information about the table and also the table cell objects to display. When we created the CarTableViewController class we specified that it was to be a subclass of UITableViewController. As a result, Xcode created templates of these data source methods for us within the *CarTableViewController.m* file. To locate these template datasource methods, scroll down the file until the *#pragma mark – Table view data source* marker comes into view. The first template method, named *numberOfSectionsInTableView:* needs to return the number of sections in the table. For the purposes of this example we only need one section so will simply return a value of 1 (note also that the #warning line needs to be removed):

```
- (NSInteger)numberOfSectionsInTableView:(UITableView *)tableView
{
    // Return the number of sections.
    return 1;
}
```

The next method is required to return the number of rows to be displayed in the table. This is equivalent to the number of items in our carModels array so can be modified as follows:

```
- (NSInteger)tableView:(UITableView *)tableView
numberOfRowsInSection:(NSInteger)section
{
    // Return the number of rows in the section.
    return _carModels.count;
}
```

The above code returns the *count* property of the *carModels* array object to obtain the number of items in the array and returns that value to the table view.

The final datasource method that needs to be modified is *cellForRowAtIndexPath:*. Each time the table view controller needs a new cell to display it will call this method and pass through an index value indicating the row for which a cell object is required. It is the responsibility of this method to return an instance of our *CarTableViewCell* class and extract the correct car make, model and image file name from the data arrays based on the index value passed through to the method. The code will then set those values on the appropriate outlets on the CarTableViewCell object. Begin by removing the template code from this method and then re-write the method so that it reads as follows:

```
- (UITableViewCell *)tableView:(UITableView *)tableView
cellForRowAtIndexPath:(NSIndexPath *)indexPath
{
    static NSString *CellIdentifier = @"carTableCell";
    CarTableViewCell *cell = [tableView
        dequeueReusableCellWithIdentifier:CellIdentifier
```

```
        forIndexPath:indexPath];

    // Configure the cell...

    int row = [indexPath row];

    cell.modelLabel.text = _carModels[row];
    cell.makeLabel.text = _carMakes[row];
    cell.carImage.image = [UIImage imageNamed:_carImages[row]];

    return cell;
}
```

Before proceeding with this tutorial we need to take some time to deconstruct this code to explain what is actually happening.

The code begins by creating a string that represents the reuse identifier that was assigned to the CarTableViewCell class within the storyboard (in this instance the identifier was set to *carTableCell*):

```
static NSString *CellIdentifier = @"carTableCell";
```

Next, the *dequeueReusableCellWithIdentifier:* method of the table view object is called, passing through the cell identifier and index path as arguments. If system will find out if a CarTableViewCell cell object is available for reuse, or create a new one and return it to the method:

```
CarTableViewCell *cell = [tableView
        dequeueReusableCellWithIdentifier:CellIdentifier
        forIndexPath:indexPath];
```

Having either created a new cell, or obtained an existing reusable cell the code simply uses the outlets previously added to the CarTableViewCell class to set the labels with the car make and model, using the row from the index path as an index into the data arrays. The code then creates a new UIImage object configured with the image of the current car and assigns it to the image view outlet. Finally, the method returns the modified cell object to the table view:

```
int row = [indexPath row];
cell.modelLabel.text = _carModels[row];
cell.makeLabel.text = _carMakes[row];
cell.carImage.image = [UIImage imageNamed:_carImages[row]];
return cell;
```

193

24.8 Downloading and Adding the Image Files

Before a test run of the application can be performed the image files referenced in the code need to be added to the project. An archive containing the images may be downloaded from the following URL:

http://www.ebookfrenzy.com/code/carImages.zip

Once the file has been downloaded, unzip the files and then drag and drop them from a Finder window onto the *Supporting Files* category of the Xcode project navigator panel.

24.9 Compiling and Running the Application

Now that the storyboard work and code modifications are complete the final step in this chapter is to run the application by clicking on the *Run* button located in the Xcode toolbar. Once the code has compiled the application will launch and execute within an iOS Simulator session as illustrated in Figure 24-6.

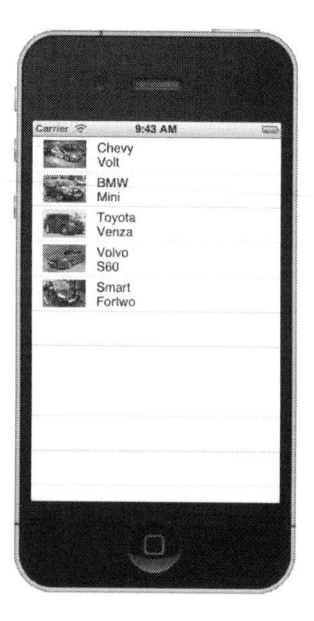

Figure 24-6

Clearly the table view has been populated with multiple instances of our prototype table view cell, each of which has been customized through outlets to display different car information and photos. The next step, which will be outlined in the next chapter entitled *Implementing TableView Navigation using Xcode Storyboards* will be to use the storyboard to add navigation capabilities to the application so that selecting a row from the table results in a detail scene appearing to the user.

24.10 Summary

The Storyboard feature of Xcode significantly eases the process of creating complex table view based interfaces within iPhone applications. Arguably the most significant feature is the ability to visually design the appearance of a table view cell and then have that cell automatically replicated at run time to display information to the user in table form.

Chapter 25

25. Implementing TableView Navigation using Xcode Storyboards

The objective of this chapter is to extend the application created in the previous chapter (entitled *Using Xcode Storyboards to Build Dynamic TableViews with Prototype Table View Cells*) and, in so doing, demonstrate the steps involved in implementing table view navigation within a storyboard. In other words, we will be modifying the car example from the previous chapter such that selecting a row from the table view displays a second scene containing additional information about the selected car. As part of this exercise we will also explore the transfer of data between different scenes in a storyboard.

25.1 Understanding the Navigation Controller

Navigation based applications present a hierarchical approach to displaying information to the user. Such applications typically take the form of a navigation bar (UINavigationBar) and a series of Table based views (UITableView). Selecting an item from the table list causes the view associated with that selection to be displayed. The navigation bar will display a title corresponding to the currently displayed view together with a button that returns the user to the previous view when selected. For an example of this concept in action, spend some time using the iPhone *Mail* or *Music* applications.

When developing a navigation-based application, the central component of the architecture is the *navigation controller*. In addition, each scene has a view and a corresponding view controller. The navigation controller maintains a stack of these view controllers. When a new view is displayed it is *pushed* onto the navigation controller's stack and becomes the currently active controller. The navigation controller automatically displays the navigation bar and the "back" button. When the user selects the button in the navigation bar to move back to the previous level, that view controller is *popped* off the stack and the view controller beneath it moved to the top becoming the currently active controller.

The view controller for the first table view that appears when the application is started is called the *root view controller*. The root view controller cannot be popped off the navigation controller stack.

25.2 Adding the New Scene to the Storyboard

For the purposes of this example we will be adding a ViewController to our storyboard to act as the second scene. With this in mind, begin by loading the *TableViewStory* project created in the previous chapter into Xcode.

Once the project has loaded we will need to add a new UIViewController subclass to our project files so select the *File -> New - > File...* menu item and choose the *Objective-C class* option. On the options screen, make sure that the *Subclass of* menu is set to UIViewController, name the new class *CarDetailViewController* and make sure that the *Targeted for iPad* and *With XIB file for user interface* options are off.

Next, select the *MainStoryboard.storyboard* file from the project navigator so that the storyboard canvas is visible. From the Object library, select a View Controller and drag and drop it to the right of the existing table view controller as outlined in Figure 25-1. With the new view controller added, select it and display the identity inspector (*View -> Utilities -> Show Identity Inspector*) and change the class setting from UIViewController to CarDetailViewController.

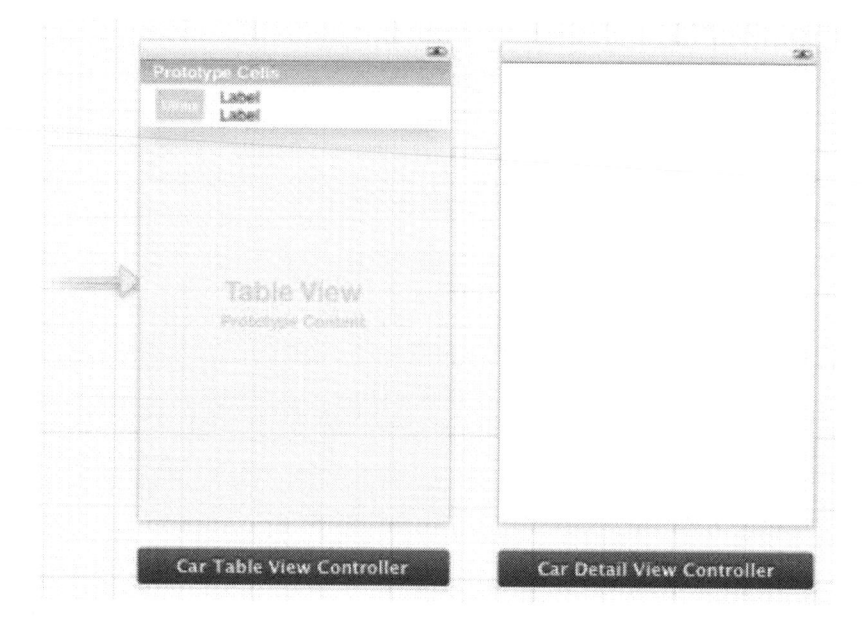

Figure 25-1

The detail scene has now been added and assigned to the newly created subclass where code can be added to bring the scene to life.

198

Implementing TableView Navigation using Xcode Storyboards

25.3 Adding a Navigation Controller

Once the application is completed, selecting a row from the Table View will trigger a segue to display the detail view controller. The detail view will contain a button which, when selected by the user, will navigate back to the table view. This functionality will be made possible by the addition of a Navigation Controller to the storyboard. This can be added by selecting the Car Table View Controller item in the storyboard so that it highlights in blue, and then selecting the Xcode *Editor -> Embed In -> Navigation Controller* menu option. Once performed, the storyboard will appear as outlined in Figure 25-2:

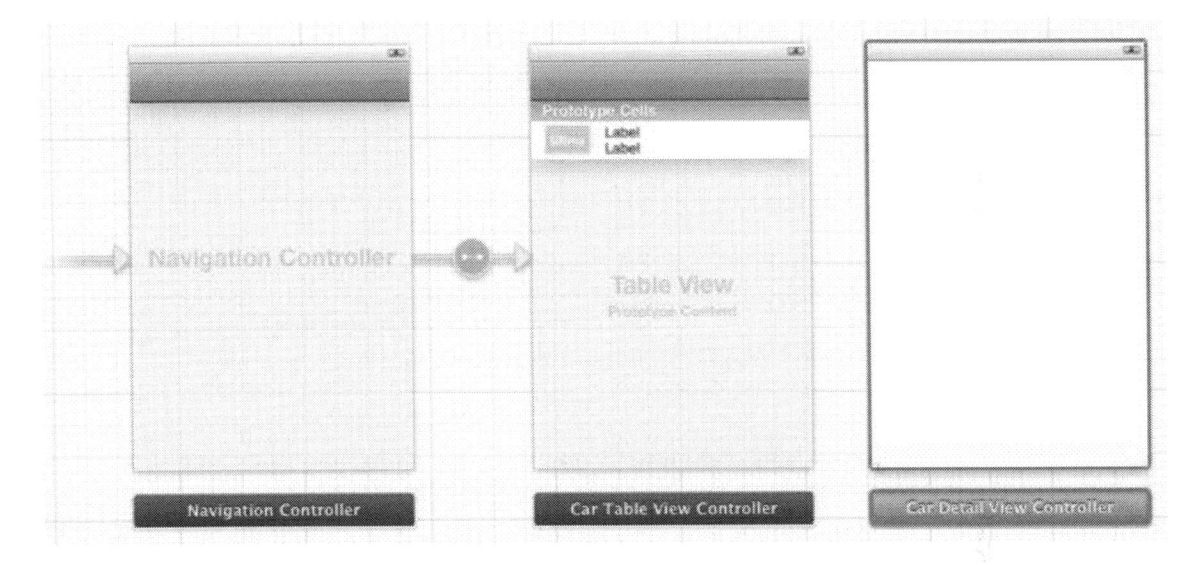

Figure 25-2

25.4 Establishing the Storyboard Segue

When the user selects a row within the table view, a segue needs to be triggered to display the car detail view controller. In order to establish this segue, Ctrl-click on the *prototype cell* located in the Car Table View Controller scene and drag the resulting line to the Car Detail View Controller scene. Upon releasing the line, select the *push* option from the resulting menu. The storyboard will update to display a segue connection between the table view cell and the view controller. In code that will be implemented later in this chapter it will be necessary to reference this specific segue. In order to do so it must, therefore, be given an identifier. Click on the segue connection between Car Table View Controller and Car Detail View Controller, display the Attributes Inspector (*View -> Utilities -> Show Attributes Inspector*) and change the Identifier value to *ShowCarDetails*.

In addition, a toolbar should have appeared in both scenes. Double click on these toolbars and change the title to "Cars" and "Car Details" respectively:

199

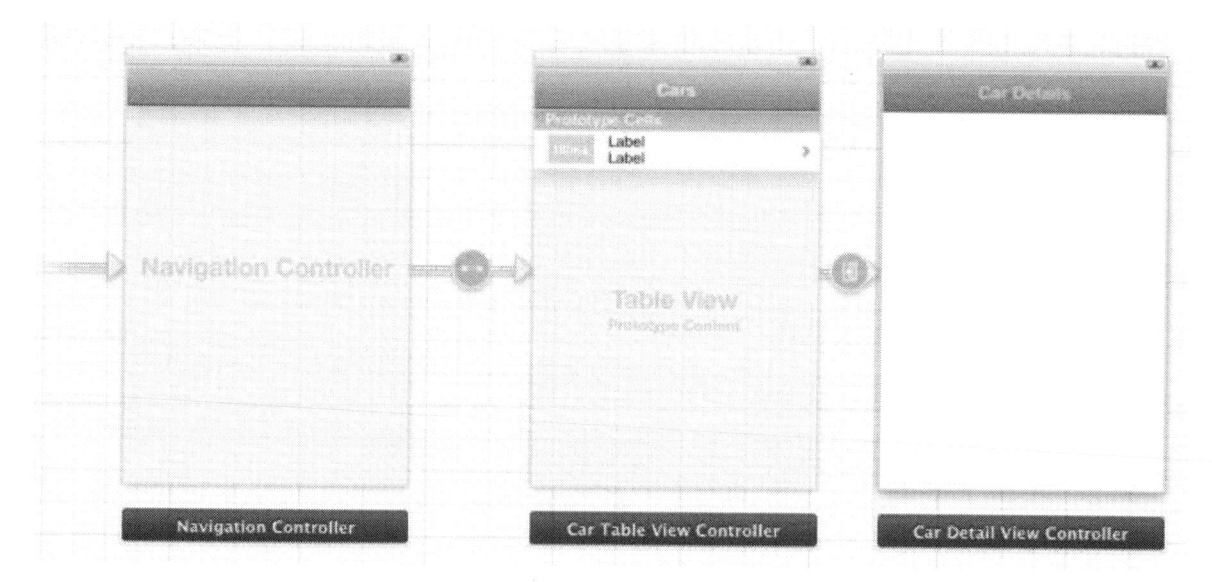

Implementing TableView Navigation using Xcode Storyboards

Figure 25-3

Build and run the application and note that selecting a row in the table view now displays the second view controller which, in turn, has a button in the toolbar to return to the table view. Clearly, we now need to do some work on the CarDetailViewController class so that details about the selected car are displayed in the view.

25.5 Modifying the CarDetailViewController Class

For the purposes of this example application, the car detail view is going to display the make and model of the selected car together with a photograph. In order to achieve this, the class is going to need outlets to two labels and a UIImageView object which will later be added to the view.

In addition to the outlets, the class is also going to need an internal data model that contains information about the car. It will be the job of the table view controller to update this model prior to the segue occurring so that it reflects data on the selected car. For the sake of simplicity, the data model will take the form of an NSArray object. Select the *CarDetailViewController.h* file and modify it as follows to declare this array:

```
#import <UIKit/UIKit.h>

@interface CarDetailViewController : UIViewController

@property (strong, nonatomic) NSArray *carDetailModel;
@end
```

The next step is to design the user interface for the detail view and connect the user interface elements to outlet properties. Select the storyboard file in the navigation controller, ensure that the view is zoomed in and drag and drop items from the object library so that the user interface appears as illustrated in Figure 25-4:

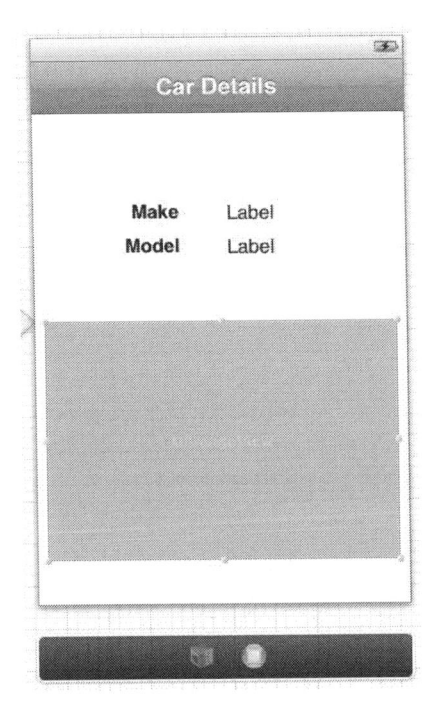

Figure 25-4

Select the label to the right of the "Make" label in the view canvas, display the Assistant Editor panel and verify that the editor is displaying the contents of the *CarDetailViewController.h* file. Ctrl-click on the label again and drag to a position just below the @interface line in the Assistant Editor. Release the line and in the resulting connection dialog establish an outlet connection named *makeLabel*. Repeat these steps to establish outlet connections for the second label (the one located to the right of the "Model" label) and the image view to properties named *modelLabel* and *imageView* respectively.

On completion of the outlet connections, the *CarDetailViewController.h* should read as follows:

```
#import <UIKit/UIKit.h>

@interface CarDetailViewController : UIViewController
@property (strong, nonatomic) IBOutlet UILabel *makeLabel;
@property (strong, nonatomic) IBOutlet UILabel *modelLabel;
@property (strong, nonatomic) IBOutlet UIImageView *imageView;
@property (strong, nonatomic) NSArray *carDetailModel;
```

When the detail view appears, the user interface objects will need to be updated with items from the data model array. This can be achieved by adding code to the *viewDidLoad:* method of the *CarDetailViewController.m* file as follows:

```
- (void)viewDidLoad
{
    [super viewDidLoad];

    _makeLabel.text = _carDetailModel[0];
    _modelLabel.text = _carDetailModel[1];
    _imageView.image = [UIImage imageNamed:_carDetailModel[2]];
}
```

25.6 Using prepareForSegue: to Pass Data between Storyboard Scenes

The last step in the implementation of this project is to add code so that the data model contained within the CarDetailViewController class is updated with details of the selected car when a table view row is touched by the user. As previously outlined in *Using Xcode Storyboarding*, the *prepareForSegue:* method on an originating scene is called prior to a segue being performed. This is the ideal place to add code to pass data between source and destination scenes. The *prepareForSegue:* method needs to be added to the *CarTableViewController.m* file as outlined in the following code fragment. Note that since the code will need to access an instance of CarDetailViewController it is also necessary to import the *CarDetailViewController.h* file:

```
#import "CarTableViewController.h"
#import "CarTableViewCell.h"
#import "CarDetailViewController.h"
.
.
.
-(void)prepareForSegue:(UIStoryboardSegue *)segue sender:(id)sender
{
    if ([[segue identifier] isEqualToString:@"ShowCarDetails"])
    {
        CarDetailViewController *detailViewController =
            [segue destinationViewController];

        NSIndexPath *myIndexPath = [self.tableView
            indexPathForSelectedRow];
```

```
        int row = [myIndexPath row];

        detailViewController.carDetailModel = @[_carMakes[row],
        _carModels[row], _carImages[row]];
    }
}
```

The first task performed by this method is to check that the triggering segue is the *ShowCarDetails* segue we added to the storyboard. Having verified that to be the case the code then obtains a reference to the view controller of the destination scene (in this case an instance of our CarDetailViewController class). The table view object is then interrogated to find out the index of the selected row which, in turn, is used to prime the data in the CarDetailViewController instance's carDataModel array property.

25.7 Testing the Application

The final step is to compile and run the application. Click on the *Run* button located in the Xcode toolbar and wait for the application to launch in the iOS Simulator. Select a car from the table and watch as the second view controller appears primed with data about the car:

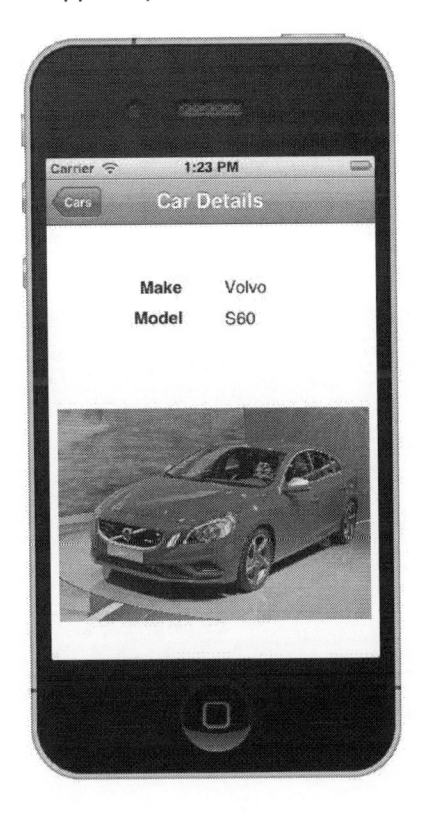

Figure 25-5

25.8 Summary

A key component of implementing table view navigation using storyboards involves the use of segues and the transfer of data between scenes. In this chapter we have used a segue to display a second scene based on table view row selections. The use of the *prepareForSeque:* method as a mechanism for passing data during a segue also been explored and demonstrated.

Chapter 26

26. Using an Xcode Storyboard to Create a Static Table View

The preceding chapters have covered in detail the steps involved in using a storyboard to implement dynamic table views in iOS 6 iPhone applications. As outlined in the chapter entitled *An Overview of iOS 6 Table Views and Xcode Storyboards*, Xcode also provides the option to create static table views.

Static table views are ideal in situations where a pre-determined number of items need to be displayed to the user. The fact that static table views do not need a data source makes them fast and easy to implement.

The goal of this chapter is to work through the creation of a simple application designed to demonstrate the use of an Xcode storyboard to implement a static table view.

26.1 An Overview of the Static Table Project

The preceding chapters worked through the implementation of an application designed to present the user with a list of cars. A dynamic table was used for this list since the number of table cells to be displayed was dependent upon the number of cars present in a data model. Selecting a car from the list triggered a segue to a second screen displaying details about the selected car. Regardless of the car selected, the detail screen always displays three items (the car's make and model together with a photograph). Whist the previous example used a generic view controller and UIView for this purpose, clearly this is an ideal candidate for a static table view.

The remainder of this chapter will work through the implementation of a simple, stand alone application designed to demonstrate the implementation of a static table view using a storyboard. The finished application will essentially implement the car detail view from the previous chapter as a static table view.

26.2 Creating the Project

As with the previous project we will take advantage of the template provided by the Single View Application without actually using the single view provided by Xcode. Begin, therefore, by launching

205

Using an Xcode Storyboard to Create a Static Table View

Xcode and creating a new single view application named *StaticTable* with a matching class prefix. Before creating the project, make sure that both the Storyboard and Automatic Reference Counting options are enabled.

As we will not be needing the provided view controller, select and delete the *StaticTableViewController.h* and *StaticTableViewController.m* files from the navigation panel. Also select the *MainStoryboard.storyboard* file and within the storyboard editor, select the *Static Table View Controller* item before pressing the keyboard delete key to remove the scene.

26.3 Adding a Table View Controller

The example application is going to consist of a single table view controller. Adding this controller is a two step process involving the addition of both a new scene to the storyboard and also the files for a new subclass of UITableViewController.

With the storyboard editor still visible, drag and drop a Table View Controller object from the Object Library panel onto the storyboard canvas. With the scene added, select the *File -> New -> File...* menu option and select the option to add an Objective-C class. Click *Next* and on the options screen, name the new class StaticTableViewController and set the *Subclass of* menu to *UITableViewController*. Make sure that both the *Targeted for iPad* and *With XIB for user interface* options are disabled before proceeding with the creation process.

Once again, select the *MainStoryboard.storyboard* file and select the Table View Controller scene so that it is highlighted in blue. Display the Identity Inspector panel (*View -> Utilities -> Show Identity Inspector*) and use the *Class* drop down menu to change the class from UITableViewController to StaticTableViewController.

26.4 Changing the Table View Content Type

By default, Xcode makes the assumption that the table view is to be dynamic. The most obvious indications of this are the presence of a Prototype Cell within the table view and the words "Prototype Content" in the view. Click within the grey area of the table view and display the Attributes Inspector panel. The Content attribute will currently be set to *Dynamic Prototypes* so use the menu to change the attribute to *Static Cells*. At this point the table view within the storyboard will change to display a static table containing three rows as illustrated in Figure 26-1:

Using an Xcode Storyboard to Create a Static Table View

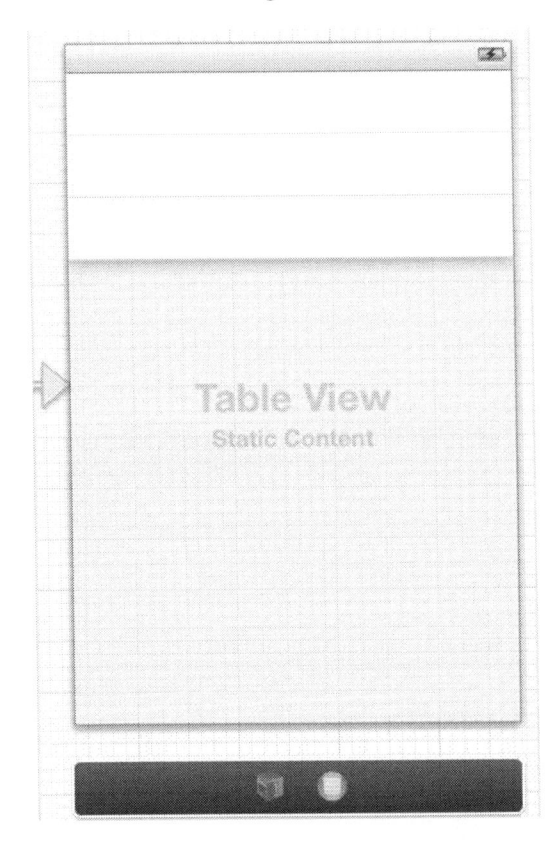

Figure 26-1

26.5 Designing the Static Table

With a static table view added to the project, the full power of Interface Builder is available to us to design the layout and content of the table and cells. The first step is to change the table view style. With the table view selected in the storyboard and the Attributes Panel displayed, change the *Style* attribute to *Grouped* and the *Sections* attribute to 2. The table view should now consist of two group sections with three rows per section. For the purposes of this example we only need two rows in the top section so click on the third row to highlight it and press the delete key on the keyboard. Note that additional rows may be added if required by selecting the corresponding table view section and changing the *Rows* property.

In the case of the bottom section, only one row is required so Command-click on the bottom two rows and delete them from the view.

Select the top section by clicking on the shaded area immediately above the cells (note that sections may also be selected by clicking on the *Table View Section* item in the toolbar strip located across the top of the storyboard editor and also from the hierarchy list located in the Document Outline panel

207

Using an Xcode Storyboard to Create a Static Table View

of the Xcode window). Within the Attributes Inspector change the *Header* property to *Car Details*. Repeat this step on the lower section to change the header to *Car Photo*.

Next, stretch the height of the single cell in the bottom section so that it fills the remainder of the table view such that the table view appears as illustrated in the following figure:

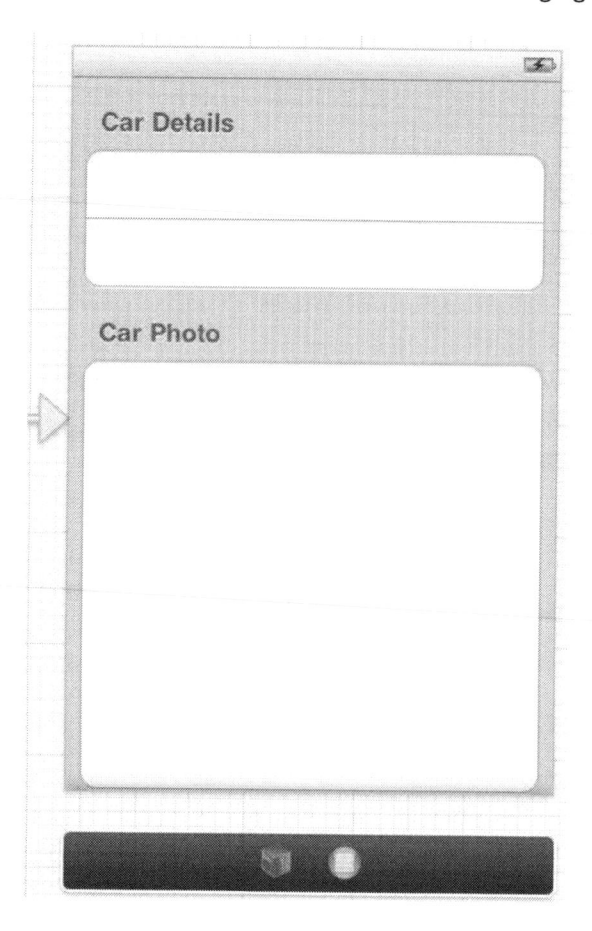

Figure 26-2

26.6 Adding Items to the Table Cells

Using the Object Library panel, drag and drop an Image View object into the cell in the bottom section and resize it to fill most of the available space. Also drag and drop labels into the two cells in the top section and set appropriate text properties so that the layout resembles that of Figure 26-3.

Using an Xcode Storyboard to Create a Static Table View

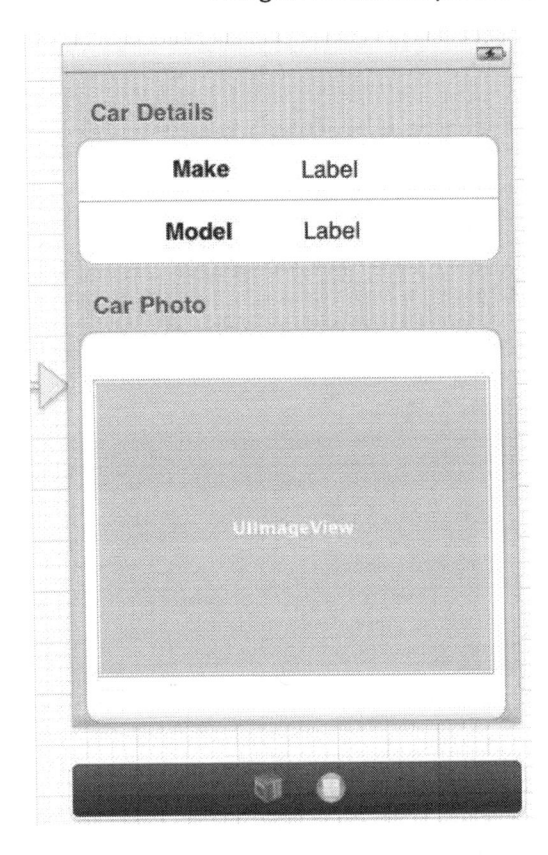

Figure 26-3

The user interface design of the table view is now complete so the next step is to create outlets to the labels and the image view. These, of course, need to be declared in the StaticTableViewController subclass.

Display the Assistant Editor either from the *View -> Assistant Editor -> Show Assistant Editor* menu option, or by selecting the middle button in the *Editor* cluster of buttons in the Xcode toolbar (the button displaying the bow tie and tuxedo image). Click on the label located to the right of the "Make" label to select it, and then Ctrl-click and drag the resulting line to the body of the @interface section in the assistant editor panel as illustrated in Figure 26-4:

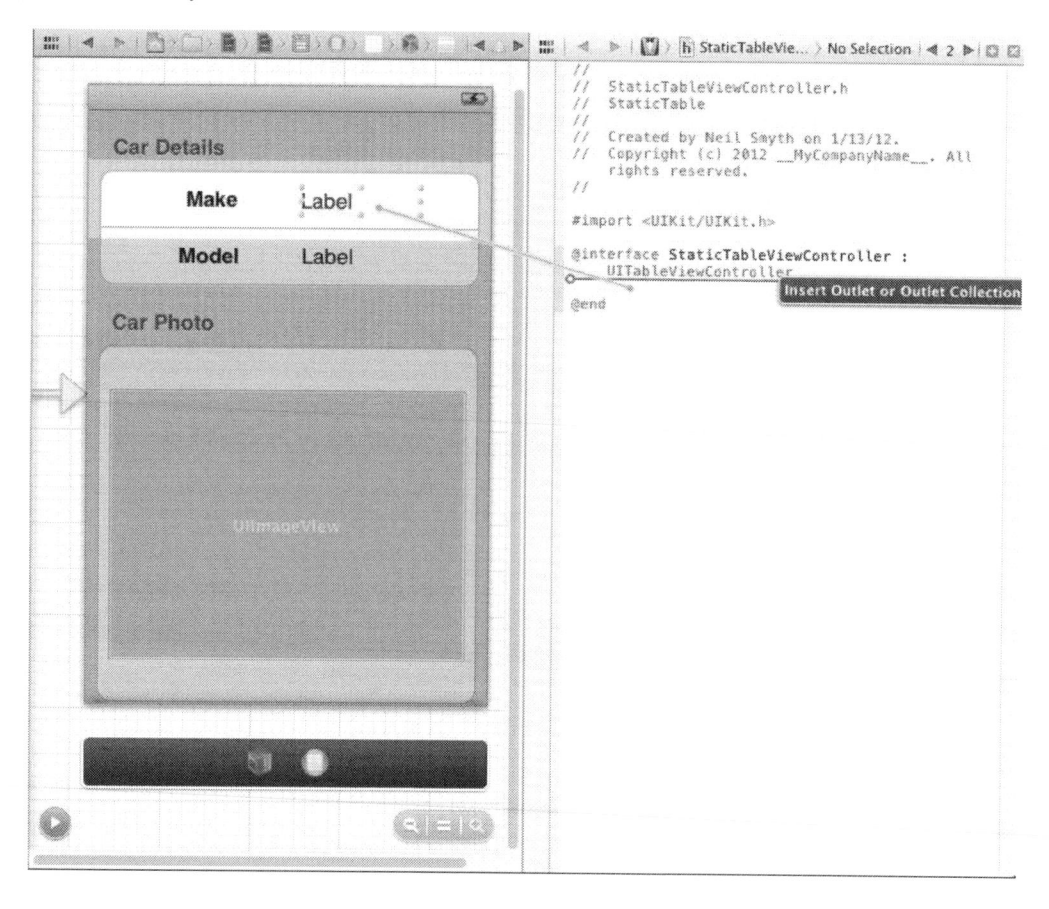

Using an Xcode Storyboard to Create a Static Table View

Figure 26-4

Upon releasing the line a dialog (Figure 26-5) will appear where information about the outlet needs to be declared. The default settings do not need to be changed so simply enter *carMakeLabel* into the *Name* field before clicking on the *Connect* button.

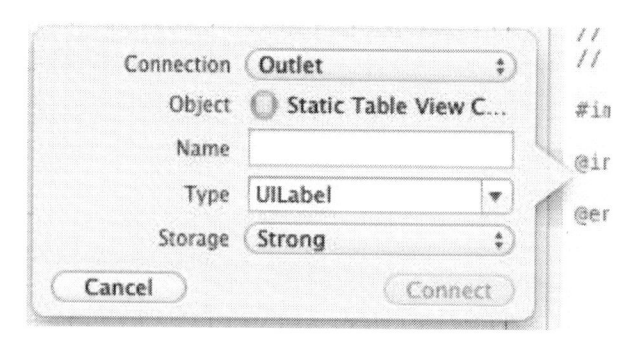

Figure 26-5

Repeat the above steps to establish connections between the second label and the image view, naming the outlets *carModelLabel* and *carImageView* respectively. Once the outlets are created and connected close the assistant window before proceeding.

26.7 Modifying the StaticTableViewController Class

When the StaticTableViewController class was created earlier in the chapter it was declared as being a subclass of UITableViewController. As a result of this selection, Xcode added a number of template methods intended to provide the basis for a data source for the table view. As previously discussed, however, static table views do not use a data source so these methods need to be removed.

Select the *StaticTableViewController.m* file and scroll down to the line that reads:

```
#pragma mark - Table view data source
```

To remove the data source from the class, delete the methods after this marker until you reach the delegate marker line:

```
#pragma mark - Table view delegate
```

All that remains to be implemented is the code to set the label and image outlets. Since this only needs to be performed once, the code may simply be added to the *viewDidLoad:* method of the class:

```
- (void)viewDidLoad
{
    [super viewDidLoad];

    _carMakeLabel.text = @"Volvo";
    _carModelLabel.text = @"S60";
    _carImageView.image = [UIImage imageNamed:@"volvo_s60.jpg"];
}
```

Finally, use a Finder window to locate the *Volvo_s60.jpg* file downloaded in the previous chapter and drag and drop it onto the *Supported Files* section of the project navigator.

26.8 Building and Running the Application

The application is now complete and ready to run. Click on the *Run* button in the Xcode toolbar and wait for the application to load into the IOS Simulator. Once loaded the static table should appear:

211

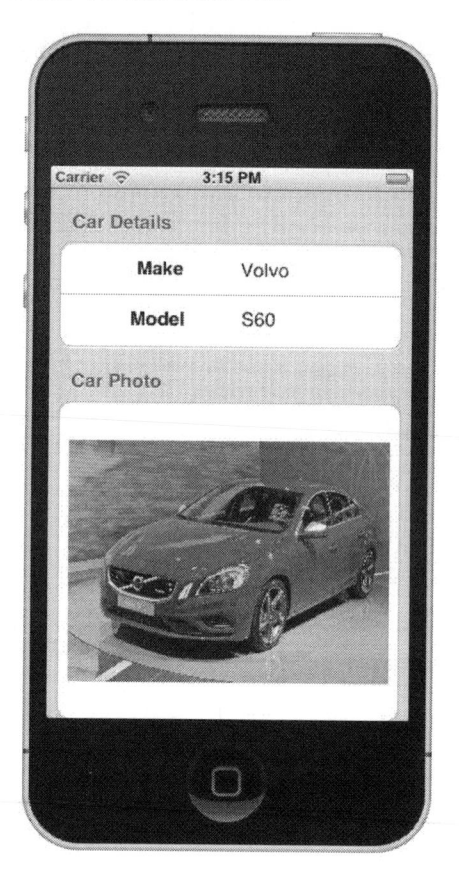

Figure 26-6

As an exercise to provide further re-enforcement of the concept of storyboards and table views, replace the standard view controller based car detail scene in the TableViewStory application from the previous chapter with a static table view similar to that outlined in this chapter.

26.9 Summary

Whilst dynamic, or prototype content, based table views are ideal for displaying data from a data source that will have a variable number of elements, static table views provide an ideal alternative when a known number of items need to be displayed. In this chapter we have worked through a simple example that demonstrates the use of storyboards to create a static table view.

Chapter 27

27. Implementing a Page based iOS 6 iPhone Application using UIPageViewController

The UIPageViewController class was introduced into the iOS 5 SDK as a mechanism to implement a page turning style of user interface in iOS applications. This chapter will provide a brief overview of the concepts behind the page view controller before working through the development of an example application in the next chapter.

27.1 The UIPageViewController Class

The UIPageViewController class highlights the distinction between a *view controller* and a *container controller*. A view controller is responsible for managing a user interface view, typically in the form of a view hierarchy contained within an Interface Builder NIB file. Creating a *Single View Application* with Xcode, for example, will create a single view controller class with a corresponding .xib Interface Builder file.

A *container controller*, on the other hand, is a class designed to contain and manage multiple *view controllers*, usually providing a mechanism for switching from one view controller to another, either programmatically or in response to user interaction.

The UIPageViewController class is a *container controller* designed to facilitate navigation through multiple views using a page curling visual transition. When implemented, this allows users to page through content using screen based gestures, much in the same way Apple's iBooks application allows a user to move backwards and forwards within the pages of an eBook using page turning gestures. Each page displayed to the user is actually a view controller created on demand for the page controller by a *data source*.

27.2 The UIPageViewController DataSource

In order to function, a UIPageViewController instance must be assigned a data source which, in turn, is responsible for providing view controller objects as required for each page. The data source takes the form of a class instance that implements the <UIPageViewControllerDataSource> protocol which, at a minimum, must implement the following two methods:

- **viewControllerAfterViewController:** - This method is passed a view controller representing the currently displayed page and is required to return the view controller corresponding to the next page in the paging sequence.
- **viewControllerBeforeViewController:** - This method is passed the view controller representing the currently displayed page and is required to return the view controller corresponding to the previous page in the paging sequence.

The mechanism used to create the requested view controllers and the content therein will generally be application specific and is at the discretion of the developer. Apple does, however, recommend that in order to ensure optimal performance and minimal resource usage, the view controllers be created on an as-needed basis rather than pre-created.

When a UIPageViewController object is initialized, a number of configuration options may be specified to configure the appearance and behavior of the contained views.

27.3 Navigation Orientation

The page controller is capable of transitioning between views using either a vertical or horizontal paradigm. In the case of horizontal navigation, page transitions take place in the same way pages are turned in a physical book by sweeping a finger on the screen either left or right.

In the case of horizontal navigation, pages are turned by making vertical gestures in much the same way the pages of a wall calendar are flipped. These options are configured using the following constants:

- UIPageViewControllerNavigationOrientationHorizontal
- UIPageViewControllerNavigationOrientationVertical

27.4 Spine Location

The UIPageViewController class allows for the location of the *spine* to be configured. The term *spine* in this context is analogous to the spine of a book and dictates the location of the axis on which each page will turn.

The behavior of the spine location settings vary depending on the navigation orientation setting. For example, the default for most configurations is UIPageViewControllerSpineLocationMin which places the spine on the left hand side or top of the screen depending on whether the navigation orientation is horizontal or vertical. Similarly, the UIPageViewControllerSpineLocationMax setting will position the spine at the right or bottom edge of the display. In order to display two pages simultaneously the UIPageViewControllerSpineLocationMid setting should be used.

The view controller may also be configured to treat pages as being double sided via the doubleSided property.

Note that when using UIPageViewControllerSpineLocationMid spine location it will be necessary to provide the page controller with two view controllers (one for the left hand page and one for the right) for each page turn. Similarly, when using either the min or max spine location together with the double sided setting, view controllers for both the front and back of the current page will be required for each page.

27.5 The UIPageViewController Delegate Protocol

In addition to a data source, instances of the UIPageViewController class may also be assigned a delegate which, in turn, may implement the following delegate methods:

- **spineLocationForInterface:** - The purpose of this delegate method is to allow the spine location to be changed in the event that the device is rotated by the user. An application might, for example, switch to UIPageViewControllerSpineLocationMid layout when the device is placed in a landscape orientation. The method is passed the new orientation and must return a corresponding spine location value. Before doing so it may, for example, also set up two view controllers if a switch is being made to a UIPageViewControllerSpineLocationMid spine location.
- **transitionComplete:** - This method is called after the user initiates a page transition via a screen based gesture. The success or otherwise of the transition may be indentified through the implementation of a completion handler.

27.6 Summary

The UIPageViewController class is categorized as a container controller in that it is responsible for containing view controllers and managing which view is displayed to the user. The main purpose of the UIPageViewController is to allow the user to navigate through different views using a page curl transition style. Implementation of this functionality requires the configuration of navigation orientation, spine location and a number of data source methods.

The theory covered in this chapter will be put into practice in the next chapter entitled *An Example iOS 6 iPhone UIPageViewController Application*.

Chapter 28

28. An Example iOS 6 iPhone UIPageViewController Application

The previous chapter entitled *Implementing a Page based iOS 6 iPhone Application using UIPageViewController* covered the theory behind implementing page curling view transitions using the UIPageViewController class. This chapter will work through the creation of an application designed to demonstrate this class in action.

28.1 The Xcode Page-based Application Template

When creating a new project within the Xcode environment, an option is provided to base the project on the *Page-based Application* template. When selected, this option generates a project containing an application designed to display a page for each month of the year. This is somewhat strange and something of an anomaly in that this is the only instance where Xcode provides a template that goes beyond providing a basic foundation on which to build and actually provides a sample application. Whilst this is useful for initial learning, unless an application with 12 pages labeled with months of the year is what you need, effort will be need to be invested removing existing functionality from the template before it can be used for other purposes.

Rather than use Xcode's Page-based Application template, this chapter will work through the implementation of page based behavior using the *Single View Application* template as a starting point. The reasons for this are two-fold. Firstly, implementing UIPageViewController functionality without recourse to the page-based template provides the reader with a better understanding of how the implementation actually works. Secondly, it will typically be quicker to implement the UIPageViewController code by hand than to attempt to repurpose the example application provided by the Page-based Application template.

28.2 Creating the Project

Begin by launching Xcode and creating a new iOS Single View Application iPhone project with a product name and class prefix of *PageApp*, making sure that the *Use Storyboard* and *Automatic Reference Counting* options are selected.

217

An Example iOS 6 iPhone UIPageViewController Application

28.3 Adding the Content View Controller

The example application will use instances of a single view controller class to display pages to the user. The view will contain a UIWebView object onto which different HTML content will be displayed depending on the currently selected page. The view controller class will also need a data object property that will be used to hold the HTML content for the view.

To add the content view controller, select the Xcode *File -> New - > File…* menu option and create a new Objective-C class. Configure the class to be a subclass of UIViewController without an XIB file and name the class *ContentViewController*. Select the *ContentViewController.h* file and add a reference to the data object:

```
#import <UIKit/UIKit.h>

@interface ContentViewController : UIViewController
@property (strong, nonatomic) id dataObject;
@end
```

Next, select the *MainStoryboard.storyboard* file and drag and drop a View Controller object from the Object Library to the storyboard canvas. Display the Identity Inspector (*View -> Utilities -> Show Identity Inspector*) and change the *Class* setting to *ContentViewController*. In the *Identity* section beneath the Class setting, specify a *Storyboard ID* of *contentView*.

Drag and drop a Web View object from the Object Library to the ContentViewController view in the storyboard canvas and size and position it so that it fills the entire view as illustrated in Figure 28-1.

Select the Web View object in the storyboard panel, display the Assistant Editor panel and verify that the editor is displaying the contents of the *ContentViewController.h* file. Ctrl-click on the web view object and drag to a position just below the @interface line in the Assistant Editor. Release the line and in the resulting connection dialog establish an outlet connection named *webView*.

Figure 28-1

With the user interface designed, select the *ContentViewController.m* file. Each time the user turns a page in the application, the data source methods for a UIPageViewController object are going to create a new instance of our ContentViewController class and set the *dataObject* property of that instance to the HTML that is to be displayed on the web view object. As such, the *viewWillAppear* method of ContentViewController needs to assign the value stored in the *dataObject* property to the web view object. To achieve this behavior, add the *viewWillAppear* method to assign the HTML to the web view:

```
#import "ContentViewController.h"

@interface ContentViewController ()

@end

@implementation ContentViewController

.
.
- (void)viewWillAppear:(BOOL)animated
{
    [super viewWillAppear:animated];
    [_webView loadHTMLString:_dataObject
```

219

```
        baseURL:[NSURL URLWithString:@""]];
}
.
.
.
@end
```

At this point work on the content view controller is complete. The next step is create the data model for the application.

28.4 Creating the Data Model

The data model for the application is going to consist of an array object containing a number of string objects, each configured to contain slightly different HTML content. For the purposes of this example, the data source for the UIPageViewController instance will be the application's *PageAppViewController* class. This class will, therefore, need references to an NSArray and a UIPageViewController object. It will also be necessary to declare this class as implementing the UIPageViewControllerDataSource protocol. Select the *PageAppViewController.h* file and add these references as follows together with an import directive for the *ContentViewController.h* file:

```
#import <UIKit/UIKit.h>
#import "ContentViewController.h"

@interface PageAppViewController : UIViewController
<UIPageViewControllerDataSource>

@property (strong, nonatomic) UIPageViewController *pageController;
@property (strong, nonatomic) NSArray *pageContent;
@end
```

The final step in creating the model is to add a method to the *PageAppViewController.m* file to add the HTML strings to the array and then call that method from *viewDidLoad:*:

```
#import "PageAppViewController.h"

@interface PageAppViewController ()

@end

@implementation PageAppViewController
.
.
.
- (void) createContentPages
{
    NSMutableArray *pageStrings = [[NSMutableArray alloc] init];
```

An Example iOS 6 iPhone UIPageViewController Application

```objc
    for (int i = 1; i < 11; i++)
    {
        NSString *contentString = [[NSString alloc]
initWithFormat:@"<html><head></head><body><h1>Chapter %d</h1><p>This is
the page %d of content displayed using UIPageViewController in iOS
6.</p></body></html>", i, i];
        [pageStrings addObject:contentString];
    }
    _pageContent = [[NSArray alloc] initWithArray:pageStrings];
}
.
.
.
- (void)viewDidLoad
{
    [super viewDidLoad];
    [self createContentPages];
}
```

The application now has a content view controller and a data model from which the content of each page will be extracted by the data source methods. The next logical step, therefore, is to implement those data source methods. As previously outlined in *Implementing a Page based iOS 6 iPhone Application using UIPageViewController*, instances of the UIPageViewController class need a data source. This takes the form of two methods, one of which is required to return the view controller to be displayed after the currently displayed view controller, and the other the view controller to be displayed before the current view controller. Since the *PageAppViewController* is going to act as the data source for the page view controller object, these two methods, together with two convenience methods (which we will borrow from the Xcode Page-based Application template) will need to be added to the *PageAppViewContoller.m* file. Begin by adding the two convenience functions:

```objc
#import "PageAppViewController.h"

@interface PageAppViewController ()

@end

@implementation PageAppViewController


- (ContentViewController *)viewControllerAtIndex:(NSUInteger)index
{
    // Return the data view controller for the given index.
    if (([self.pageContent count] == 0) ||
            (index >= [self.pageContent count])) {
```

221

```objc
        return nil;
    }

    // Create a new view controller and pass suitable data.
    /*
    ContentViewController *dataViewController =
        [[ContentViewController alloc] init];
    */

    UIStoryboard *storyboard =
            [UIStoryboard storyboardWithName:@"MainStoryboard"
                bundle:[NSBundle mainBundle]];

    ContentViewController *dataViewController =
            [storyboard
                instantiateViewControllerWithIdentifier:@"contentView"];

    dataViewController.dataObject = _pageContent[index];
    return dataViewController;
}

- (NSUInteger)indexOfViewController:(ContentViewController *)viewController
{
    return [_pageContent indexOfObject:viewController.dataObject];
}
.
.
@end
```

The *viewControllerAtIndex:* method begins by checking to see if the page being requested is outside the bounds of available pages by checking if the index reference is zero (the user cannot page back beyond the first page) or greater than the number of items in the *pageContent* array. In the event that the index value is valid, a new instance of the ContentViewController class is created and the dataObject property set to the contents of the corresponding item in the pageContent array of HTML strings.

Since the view controller is stored in the storyboard file, the following code is used to get a reference to the storyboard and to create a new ContentViewController instance:

```objc
UIStoryboard *storyboard =
        [UIStoryboard storyboardWithName:@"MainStoryboard"
            bundle:[NSBundle mainBundle]];
```

```objc
ContentViewController *dataViewController =
     [storyboard
         instantiateViewControllerWithIdentifier:@"contentView"];
```

The *indexOfViewController* method is passed a viewController object and is expected to return the index value of the controller. It does this by extracting the dataObject property of the view controller and finding the index of the matching element in the pageContent array.

All that remains to be implemented as far as the data source is concerned are the two data source protocol methods which, in turn, make use of the two convenience methods to return the view controllers before and after the current view controller:

```objc
- (UIViewController *)pageViewController:
(UIPageViewController *)pageViewController
viewControllerBeforeViewController:
(UIViewController *)viewController
{
    NSUInteger index = [self indexOfViewController:
        (ContentViewController *)viewController];
    if ((index == 0) || (index == NSNotFound)) {
        return nil;
    }

    index--;
    return [self viewControllerAtIndex:index];
}

- (UIViewController *)pageViewController:
(UIPageViewController *)pageViewController
viewControllerAfterViewController:(UIViewController *)viewController
{
    NSUInteger index = [self indexOfViewController:
        (ContentViewController *)viewController];
    if (index == NSNotFound) {
        return nil;
    }

    index++;
    if (index == [self.pageContent count]) {
        return nil;
    }
    return [self viewControllerAtIndex:index];
}
```

An Example iOS 6 iPhone UIPageViewController Application

With the data source implemented, the next step is to create and initialize an instance of the UIPageViewController class.

28.5 Initializing the UIPageViewController

All that remains is to create the UIPageViewController instance and initialize it appropriately. Since this needs to be performed only once per application invocation a suitable location for this code is the *viewDidLoad:* method of the PageAppViewController class. Select the *PageAppViewController.m* file and modify the viewDidLoad method so that it reads as follows:

```
- (void)viewDidLoad
{
    [super viewDidLoad];
    [self createContentPages];
    NSDictionary *options = [NSDictionary dictionaryWithObject:
       [NSNumber numberWithInteger:UIPageViewControllerSpineLocationMin]
       forKey: UIPageViewControllerOptionSpineLocationKey];

    _pageController = [[UIPageViewController alloc]
initWithTransitionStyle:UIPageViewControllerTransitionStylePageCurl
navigationOrientation:UIPageViewControllerNavigationOrientationHorizont
al
        options: options];

    _pageController.dataSource = self;
    [[_pageController view] setFrame:[[self view] bounds]];

    ContentViewController *initialViewController =
        [self viewControllerAtIndex:0];
    NSArray *viewControllers =
        [NSArray arrayWithObject:initialViewController];

    [_pageController setViewControllers:viewControllers
        direction:UIPageViewControllerNavigationDirectionForward
        animated:NO
        completion:nil];

    [self addChildViewController:_pageController];
    [[self view] addSubview:[_pageController view]];
    [_pageController didMoveToParentViewController:self];
}
```

An Example iOS 6 iPhone UIPageViewController Application

All the code for the application is now complete. Before compiling and running the application some time needs to taken to deconstruct and analyze the code in the *viewDidLoad:* method.

After constructing the data model with the call to the *createContentPage:* method an NSDictionary object is created to contain the options that will be applied to the page controller object. In this instance the only option used is to set the spine location to appear on the left of the screen:

```
NSDictionary *options =
    [NSDictionary dictionaryWithObject:
    [NSNumber numberWithInteger:UIPageViewControllerSpineLocationMin]
    forKey: UIPageViewControllerOptionSpineLocationKey];
```

Next, an instance of the UIPageViewController class is created using the previously created *options* object and specifying horizontal navigation orientation:

```
_pageController = [[UIPageViewController alloc]
 initWithTransitionStyle:UIPageViewControllerTransitionStylePageCurl
navigationOrientation:UIPageViewControllerNavigationOrientationHorizont
al
   options: options];
```

Since the current class is going to act as the data source for the page controller this also needs to be configured. We also want the pages to fill the entire screen, so need to set the bounds appropriately:

```
_pageController.dataSource = self;
    [[_pageController view] setFrame:[[self view] bounds]];
```

Before the first page can be displayed a view controller must first be created. This can be achieved by calling our *viewControllerAtIndex:* convenience method. Once a content view controller has been returned it needs to be assigned to an array object:

```
ContentViewController *initialViewController =
        [self viewControllerAtIndex:0];
NSArray *viewControllers =
        [NSArray arrayWithObject:initialViewController];
```

Note that only one content view controller is needed because the page controller is configured to display only one, single sided page at a time. Had the page controller been configured for two pages (with a mid location spine) or for double sided pages it would have been necessary to create content view controllers at this point and assign both to the array.

With an array containing the content view controller ready, the array needs to be assigned to the view controller with the navigation direction set to forward mode:

```
[_pageController setViewControllers:viewControllers
```

225

An Example iOS 6 iPhone UIPageViewController Application

```
        direction:UIPageViewControllerNavigationDirectionForward
        animated:NO
        completion:nil];
```

Finally, the standard steps need to be taken to add the page view controller to the current view:

```
[self addChildViewController:_pageController];
    [[self view] addSubview:[_pageController view]];
    [_pageController didMoveToParentViewController:self];
```

28.6 Running the UIPageViewController Application

Click on the *Run* button to compile and launch the application in the iOS iPhone Simulator. Once loaded the first content page should appear. A right to left gesture motion on the screen will cause the page to transition to the second page of content and reversing the gesture direction will page backwards:

Figure 28-2

28.7 Summary

The goal of this chapter has been to work through an example application designed to implement the page turning transition view provided by the UIPageViewController class.

Chapter 29

29. Using the UIPickerView and UIDatePicker Components

In terms of user interface design, there is much to be gained by presenting the user with controls that are similar to physical, "real world" controls. When, for example, a user is presented with a UIButton object in the user interface of an iPhone application they instinctively know that they are supposed to press it because that is what they know to do with a physical button.

In few instances is this real world paradigm more prevalent than in the case of the iOS 6 UIKit Picker components. Both the UIPickerView and UIDatePicker provide a user friendly approach to allowing a user to review and make selections from a wide range of options. In this chapter we will talk about pickers in general before working through a simple example designed to demonstrate the basics of using the Date Picker class. The next chapter, entitled *An iOS 6 iPhone UIPickerView Example*, will cover the UIPickerView in more detail.

29.1 The DatePicker and PickerView Components

If you have used the iPhone's built-in calendar application then the chances are very good that you have also used an instance of the UIDatePicker class. This class provides a user friendly and intuitive way for the user of an application to make date and time selections. Figure 29-1 illustrates the appearance of a typical DatePicker component implementation:

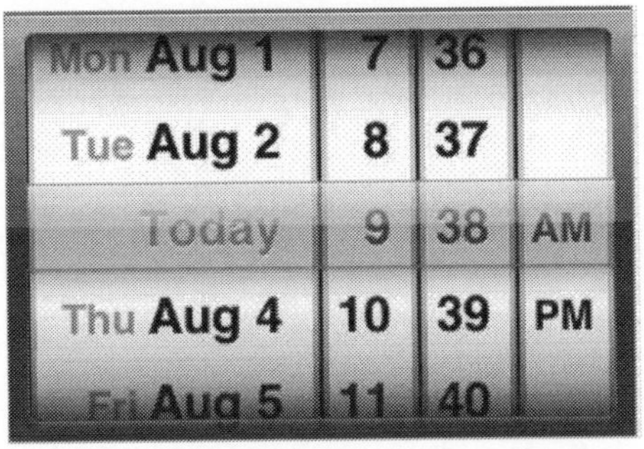

Figure 29-1

The picker is composed of multiple wheels referred to as *components* each of which spins independently of the others (at least by default since it is also possible to make components

229

Using the UIPickerView and UIDatePicker Components

dependent on each another). Each item on a wheel represents an option and is referred to as a *row*. A row in a component is deemed to be *selected* when it is positioned beneath the highlighted strip. For example, Figure 29-1 shows the *Today* row as being selected in the far left hand component.

The UIDatePicker component is a pre-configured class designed specifically for the selection of dates and times. The UIPickerView class, on the other hand, allows for the creation of custom picker controls and will explored in *An iOS 6 iPhone UIPickerView Example*.

29.2 A DatePicker Example

By way of introduction to the concept of using pickers in an iOS 6 iPhone application we will begin with a very simple example that utilizes the UIDatePicker class. The application will consist of a DatePicker, a label and a button. When the button is pressed by the user the date and time selected in the picker will be displayed on the label component.

Begin by creating a new iOS iPhone project using the *Single View Application* template with Storyboard and Automatic Reference Counting support and enter *DatePicker* for both the product name and class prefix.

29.3 Designing the User Interface

Select the *MainStoryboard.storyboard* file and drag and drop the Date Picker, Label and Button components from the Object Library panel (*View -> Utilities -> Show Object Library*) onto the view and modify and position the layout so that the view resembles Figure 29-2:

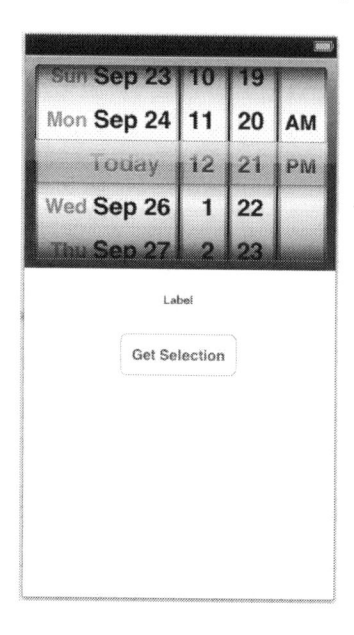

Figure 29-2

Using the UIPickerView and UIDatePicker Components

Note that the text of the label is centered, assigned a 12 point font and that it has been stretched to the outer margins of the containing view. The configuration of the Date Picker object (such as date format etc) may be changed if desired via a variety of properties accessed by selecting the object in the view and displaying the Attributes Inspector (*View -> Utilities -> Show Attribute Inspector*).

Select the Date Picker object in the view canvas, display the Assistant Editor panel and verify that the editor is displaying the contents of the *DatePickerViewController.h* file. Ctrl-click on the Date Picker object and drag to a position just below the @interface line in the Assistant Editor. Release the line and in the resulting connection dialog establish an outlet connection named *datePicker*. Repeat this step to connect the Label object to an outlet property named *dateLabel*.

Finally, Ctrl-click on the Button object, drag the line to the Assistant Editor panel and configure an *Action* connection on the *Touch Up Inside* event to a method named *getSelection*.

29.4 Coding the Date Picker Example Functionality

Now that the outlets and user interface have been implemented it is time to write the functional code that will make the application work. In actual fact, the only method that needs to be implemented for this simple example is the *getSelection* action method that is called when the user touches the button. The following code fragment outlines the required changes to the *DatePickerViewController.m* file:

```
#import "DatePickerViewController.h"

@interface DatePickerViewController ()

@end

@implementation DatePickerViewController

-(void)getSelection:(id)sender
{
    NSLocale *usLocale = [[NSLocale alloc]
        initWithLocaleIdentifier:@"en_US"];

    NSDate *pickerDate = [_datePicker date];
    NSString *selectionString = [[NSString alloc]
        initWithFormat:@"%@",
        [pickerDate descriptionWithLocale:usLocale]];
    _dateLabel.text = selectionString;
}
```

@end

The first task performed by the *getLocation* method involves the creation of an NSLocale object that will be used to configure the format of the date and time values when they are prepared for display. In this instance the US English (en_US) locale is selected, though this can be changed to match your particular regional locale. Next, the *date* method of the *datePicker* object is called to obtain the date and time selected by the user and the result assigned to *pickerDate*. A string object is then created consisting of the date description string adjusted for the specified locale. This, in turn, is displayed on the label associated with the *dateLabel* outlet via the object's *text* property.

29.5 Building and Running the iPhone Date Picker Application

Once the application project work is complete, click on the *Run* button located in the toolbar of the Xcode main project window. Once the application appears inside the iOS Simulator, select a date and time using the picker and then touch the *Get Selection* button. The label will update to reflect the selected date and time as shown in Figure 29-3.

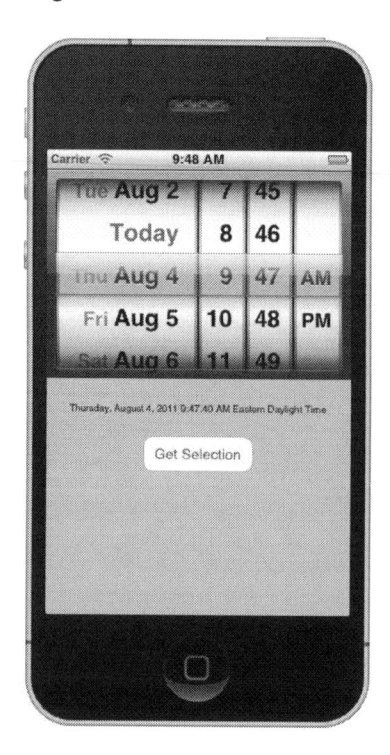

Figure 29-3

Chapter 30

30. An iOS 6 iPhone UIPickerView Example

Unlike the UIDatePicker class, which is pre-configured by Apple specifically for date and time selection, the UIPickerView class is intended to be configured to meet the specific requirements of the iPhone application developer. Having provided a basic overview of pickers and an example of the use of the DatePicker in *Using the UIPickerView and UIDatePicker Components in iOS 6 iPhone Applications*, the objective of this chapter is to provide a worked example of the UIPickerView class in action.

30.1 Creating the iOS 6 PickerView Project

The example application in this chapter is a rudimentary currency conversion tool. The user will enter a US Dollar amount into a text field and then make a currency selection from a PickerView object, at which point the equivalent amount in the chosen currency will be displayed on a label.

Begin by creating a new iOS iPhone Xcode project named *Picker* with a corresponding class prefix using the *Single View Application* template with Storyboard and Automatic Reference Counting support enabled.

30.2 UIPickerView Delegate and DataSource

Before starting on the project it is worth taking some time to talk about the delegate and datasource of the UIPickerView class. In order to obtain the options to be displayed to the user, the PickerView needs a *data source*. This data source takes the form of a protocol that defines the methods that must be implemented in order to provide the Picker with data information. At a minimum the class designated as the data source must implement the following methods:

- **numberOfComponentsInPickerView:** - Called by the PickerView to identify the number of components (i.e. selection wheels) that are to be displayed to the user.
- **numberOfRowsInComponent:** - Informs the PickerView of the number of rows (in other words the selection options) that are present in a specified component.
- **titleForRow:** - Called by the PickerView to identify the string that is to be displayed for a specified row in a specific component.

233

An iOS 6 iPhone UIPickerView Example

In addition to a data source, the PickerView also needs a mechanism for notifying the application code when a selection has been made by the user. It achieves this by calling the *didSelectRow* method of the class declared as the PickerView's delegate.

In order to fully implement a PickerView, therefore, it is necessary for the object to be assigned a data source and delegate. Typically the view controller responsible for the PickerView is the best place to implement these two protocols.

30.3 The PickerViewController.h File

The first step is to implement the declarations in the *PickerViewController.h* file. Since we plan to make our view controller both the delegate and data source for the UIPickerView instance, the view controller must be declared as implementing both the UIPickerViewDelegate and UIPickerViewDataSource protocols.

In addition, two arrays are needed to store the country names and corresponding exchange rates:

```
#import <UIKit/UIKit.h>

@interface PickerViewController : UIViewController
        <UIPickerViewDelegate, UIPickerViewDataSource>

@property (strong, nonatomic) NSArray *countryNames;
@property (strong, nonatomic) NSArray *exchangeRates;
@end
```

30.4 Designing the User Interface

To design the user interface, begin by selecting the *MainStoryboard.storyboard* file to load it into Interface Builder. Drag and drop a UIPickerView from the Object library (*View -> Utilities -> Show Object Library*) onto the view and position it at the bottom of the view. Also add a label and text field. Stretch the right and left hand edges of the label until the dotted blue margin line appears. Using the Attribute Inspector (*View -> Utilities -> Show Attribute Inspector*), configure centered alignment on the label.

Select the text field and change the *Placeholder* setting in the Attribute Inspector to *US Dollars (USD)*. Once completed, the view should appear as illustrated in the following figure:

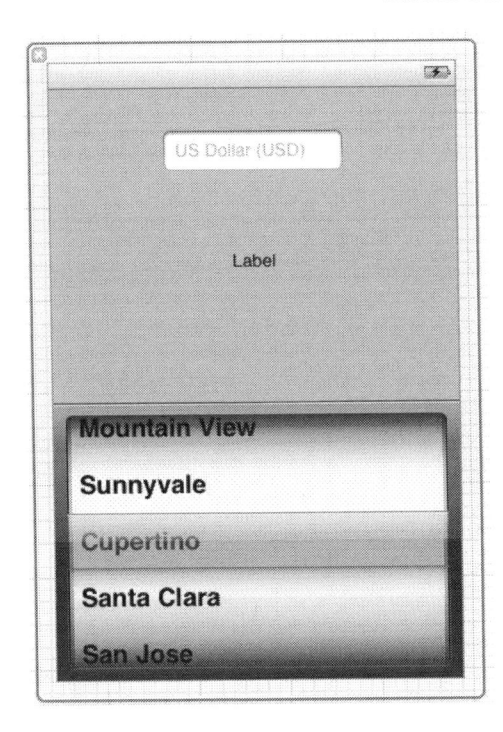

Figure 30-1

Select the Picker View object in the view canvas, display the Assistant Editor panel and verify that the editor is displaying the contents of the *PickerViewController.h* file. Ctrl-click on the Picker View object and drag to a position just below the @interface line in the Assistant Editor. Release the line and in the resulting connection dialog establish an outlet connection named *picker*. Repeat these steps to establish outlet connections from the Text Field and Label to properties named *dollarText* and *resultLabel* respectively.

Next, select the PickerView component in the View window and display the Connections Inspector (*View -> Utilities -> Show Connections Inspector*). Click in the round circle to the right of the *dataSource* outlet in the inspector window and drag the line to the *Picker View Controller* object in the document outline panel located to the left of the storyboard canvas. Repeat this task for the *delegate* outlet.

Finally, Ctrl-click on the text field object and drag the line to the area immediately beneath the newly created outlets in the Assistant Editor panel. Release the line and, within the connection dialog, establish an Action method on the *Did End On Exit* event configured to call a method named *textFieldReturn*.

The user interface is now designed and the outlets and action connected.

235

An iOS 6 iPhone UIPickerView Example

30.5 Initializing the Arrays

The data that will be used in our application is stored in two arrays, one for the country name and the other for the corresponding exchange rate. In the real world, the application would likely obtain up-to-date exchange rate information from an external source, but for the purposes of this example we will hard code the prevailing rates at the time of writing. These arrays need to be initialized when the application loads, so the necessary code should be added to the *viewDidLoad* method of the *PickerViewController.m* file:

```objc
#import "PickerViewController.h"

@interface PickerViewController ()

@end

@implementation PickerViewController

- (void)viewDidLoad {
    [super viewDidLoad];
    _countryNames = @[@"Australia (AUD)", @"China (CNY)",
        @"France (EUR)", @"Great Britain (GBP)", @"Japan (JPY)"];

    _exchangeRates = @[ @0.9922f, @6.5938f, @0.7270f,
        @0.6206f, @81.57f];
}
```

30.6 Implementing the DataSource Protocol

The next step is to implement the methods that comprise the UIPickerViewDataSource protocol. Since we have declared the pickerViewController class as the data source we need to implement the methods in the *pickerViewController.m* file:

```objc
#pragma mark -
#pragma mark PickerView DataSource

- (NSInteger)numberOfComponentsInPickerView:
(UIPickerView *)pickerView
{
    return 1;
}

- (NSInteger)pickerView:(UIPickerView *)pickerView
    numberOfRowsInComponent:(NSInteger)component
```

```
{
         return _countryNames.count;
}

- (NSString *)pickerView:(UIPickerView *)pickerView
titleForRow:(NSInteger)row
forComponent:(NSInteger)component
{
    return _countryNames[row];
}
```

The first method simply returns a value of 1 since our picker only has one component. The second method returns the number of rows in the component by counting the number of elements in the country name array. Finally, the *titleForRow* method returns the corresponding country name for the requested row by using the row number as a reference into the country names array.

30.7 Implementing the Delegate Protocol

For the purposes of this example, the only delegate method we need to implement is the one that gets called when the user makes a selection from the PickerView component. The code for this method also belongs in the *pickerViewController.m* file and should be implemented as follows:

```
#pragma mark -
#pragma mark PickerView Delegate
-(void)pickerView:(UIPickerView *)pickerView
didSelectRow:(NSInteger)row
inComponent:(NSInteger)component
{
        float rate = [_exchangeRates[row] floatValue];
        float dollars = [_dollarText.text floatValue];
        float result = dollars * rate;

        NSString *resultString = [[NSString alloc] initWithFormat:
                @"%.2f USD = %.2f %@", dollars, result,
                _countryNames[row]];
        _resultLabel.text = resultString;
}
```

This method takes the selected row number argument and uses it as an index to obtain the exchange rate from the *exchangeRates* array. Next, the dollar amount entered by the user is converted from a string to a floating point number and multiplied by the US Dollar amount to arrive at a conversion value.

An iOS 6 iPhone UIPickerView Example

Finally, a string is constructed from the dollar amount, the converted amount and the country name. This string is then displayed on the label and the string released.

30.8 Hiding the Keyboard

Since the keyboard will obscure the picker when displayed, the last task before testing the application is to make sure the keyboard is hidden when the user touches the Return key. Still within the *pickerViewController.m* file, therefore, implement the *textFieldReturn* action method as follows:

```
-(IBAction)textFieldReturn:(id)sender
{
    [sender resignFirstResponder];
}
```

30.9 Testing the Application

Once the code changes have been made and the corresponding files saved, click on the *Run* button located in the Xcode project window toolbar. The application should load into the iOS Simulator where a dollar amount may be entered and countries selected to obtain currency conversion values:

Figure 30-2

238

Chapter 31

31. Working with Directories on iOS 6

It is sometimes easy to forget that iOS is an operating system much like that running on many other computers today. Given this fact, it should come as no surprise that iOS has a file system much like any other operating system allowing applications to store persistent data on behalf of the user. Much like other platforms, the iOS file system provides a directory based structure into which files can be created and organized.

Since the introduction of iOS 5 the iPhone app developer has had two options in terms of storing data. Files and data may now be stored on the file system of the local device or remotely using Apple's iCloud service. In practice, however, it is most likely that an application will utilize iCloud storage to augment, rather than replace, the use of the local file system so familiarity with both concepts is still a necessity.

The topic of iCloud based storage will be covered in detail beginning with the chapter entitled *Preparing an iOS 6 App to use iCloud Storage*. The goal of this chapter, however, is provide an overview of how to work with local file system directories from within an iOS 6 iPhone application. Topics covered include identifying the application's document and temporary directories, finding the current working directory, creating, removing and renaming directories and obtaining listings of a directory's content. Once the topic of directory management has been covered, we will move on to handling files in *Working with Files on iOS 6*.

31.1 The Application Documents Directory

An iPhone user can install multiple applications on a single device. The iOS platform is responsible for ensuring that these applications cannot interfere with each other, both in terms of memory usage and data storage. As such, each application is restricted in terms of where it can store data on the file system of the device. iOS achieves this by allowing applications to read and write only to their own *Documents* and *tmp* directories. Within these two directories the corresponding application can create files and also sub-directories to any required level of depth. This area constitutes the application's *sandbox* and the application cannot create or modify files or directories outside of these directories.

239

31.2 The Objective-C NSFileManager, NSFileHandle and NSData Classes

The Foundation Framework provides three classes that are indispensable when it comes to working with files and directories:

- **NSFileManager** - The *NSFileManager* class can be used to perform basic file and directory operations such as creating, moving, reading and writing files and reading and setting file attributes. In addition, this class provides methods for, amongst other tasks, identifying the current working directory, changing to a new directory, creating directories and listing the contents of a directory.
- **NSFileHandle** - The *NSFileHandle* class is provided for performing lower level operations on files, such as seeking to a specific position in a file and reading and writing a file's contents by a specified number of byte chunks and appending data to an existing file. This class will be used extensively in the chapter entitled *Working with Files on iOS 6*.
- **NSData** - The *NSData* class provides a useful storage buffer into which the contents of a file may be read, or from which dynamically stored data may be written to a file.

31.3 Understanding Pathnames in Objective-C

As with Mac OS X, iOS defines pathnames using the standard UNIX convention. As such each component of a path is separated by a forward slash (/). When an application starts, the current working directory is the file system's *root directory* represented by single /. From this location, the application must navigate to its own *Documents* and *tmp* directories in order to be able to write files to the file system. Path names that begin with a / are said to be *absolute path names* in that they specify a file system location relative to the root directory. For example, */var/mobile* is an absolute path name.

Paths that do not begin with a slash are interpreted to be *relative* to a current working directory. For example, if the current working directory is */User/demo* and the path name is *mapdata/local.xml* then the file is considered to have an equivalent full, absolute pathname of */User/demo/mapdata/local.xml*.

31.4 Obtaining a Reference to the Default NSFileManager Object

The NSFileManager class contains a class method named *defaultManager* that is used to obtain a reference to the application's default file manager instance:

```
NSFileManager *filemgr;
filemgr = [NSFileManager defaultManager];
```

In the above example we have declared a variable named *filemgr* to point to an object of type NSFileManager, and then requested a pointer to the application's file manager and assigned it to the variable. Having obtained the object reference we can begin to use it to work with files and directories.

31.5 Identifying the Current Working Directory

As previously mentioned, when an application first loads, its current working directory is the application's root directory, represented by a / character. The current working directory may be identified at any time through a call to the *currentDirectoryPath* method of the file manager object. For example, the following code fragment identifies the current working directory:

```
NSFileManager *filemgr;
NSString *currentPath;

filemgr =[NSFileManager defaultManager];
currentPath = [filemgr currentDirectoryPath];
```

In this code we declare a new object named *filemgr* that is an instance of the NSFileManager class and also an NSString object named *currentPath* to contain the current working directory path. Having created a file manager instance we then call the *currentDirectoryPath* method of that instance and assign the resulting string to *currentPath*.

31.6 Identifying the Documents Directory

As previously discussed, each iPhone iOS application on a device has its own private *Documents* and *tmp* directories into which it is permitted to read and write data. Because the location of these directories is different for each application the only way to find the correct path is to ask iOS. In fact, the exact location will also differ depending on whether the application is running on a physical iPhone device or in the iOS Simulator. The *Documents* directory for an application may be identified by making a call to a C function named *NSSearchPathForDirectoriesInDomains*, passing through an argument (in this case NSDocumentDirectory) indicating that we require the path to the Documents directory. Since this is a C function, as opposed to a method of an Objective-C class, there is no need for us to establish an instance of a Foundation class such as NSFileManager before making the call. That said, the function does return an object in the form of an NSArray containing the results of the request. We can, therefore, obtain the path to the current application's Documents directory as follows:

```
NSArray *dirPaths;
NSString *docsDir;
dirPaths = NSSearchPathForDirectoriesInDomains(NSDocumentDirectory,
            NSUserDomainMask, YES);
docsDir = dirPaths[0];
```

When executed, the above code will assign the path to the *Documents* directory to the docsDir string.

When executed within the iOS Simulator environment, the path returned will take the form of:

```
/Users/<user name>/Library/Application Support
/iPhone Simulator/<sdk version>/Applications/<app id>/Documents
```

Where *<user name>* is the name of the user currently logged into the Mac OS X system on which the simulator is running, *<sdk version>* is the version of the iOS SDK used to compile the application and *<app id>* is the unique ID of the app, for example:

```
06A3AEBA-8C34-476E-937F-A27BDD2E450A
```

Clearly this references a path on your Mac OS X system so feel free to open up a Finder window and explore the file system sandbox areas for your iOS iPhone applications.

When executed on a physical iPhone device, the path returned by the function call will take the following form:

```
/var/mobile/Applications/<app id>/Documents
```

31.7 Identifying the Temporary Directory

In addition to the *Documents* directory, iOS iPhone applications are also provided with a *tmp* directory for the storage of temporary files. The path to the current application's temporary directory may be ascertained with a call to the *NSTemporaryDirectory* C function as follows:

```
NSString *tmpDir = NSTemporaryDirectory();
```

Once executed, the string object referenced by tmpDir will contain the path to the temporary directory for the application.

31.8 Changing Directory

Having identified the path to the application's document or temporary directory the chances are good that you will need to make that directory the current working directory. The current working directory of a running iPhone application can be changed with a call to the *changeCurrentDirectoryPath* method of an NSFileManager instance. The destination directory path is passed as an argument to the instance method in the form of an NSString object. Note that this method returns a boolean *YES* or *NO* result to indicate if the requested directory change was successful or not. A failure result typically indicates either that the specified directory does not exist, or that the application lacks the appropriate access permissions:

```
NSFileManager *filemgr;
```

```
NSArray *dirPaths;
NSString *docsDir;

filemgr =[NSFileManager defaultManager];

dirPaths = NSSearchPathForDirectoriesInDomains(NSDocumentDirectory,
NSUserDomainMask, YES);
docsDir = dirPaths[0];

if ([filemgr changeCurrentDirectoryPath: docsDir] == NO)
{
        // Directory does not exist - take appropriate action
}
```

In the above example, the path to the *Documents* directory is identified and then used as an argument to the *changeCurrentDirectoryPath* method of the file manager object to change the current working directory to that location.

31.9 Creating a New Directory

A new directory on an iOS device is created using the *createDirectoryAtPath* instance method of the NSFileManager class, once again passing through the pathname of the new directory as an argument and returning a boolean success or failure result. The second argument to this method defines whether any intermediate directory levels should be created automatically. For example, if we wanted to create a directory with the path */var/mobile/Applications/<app id>/Documents/mydata/maps* and the *mydata* subdirectory does not yet exist, setting the *withIntermediateDirectories* argument to *YES* will cause this directory to be created automatically before then creating the *maps* sub-directory within it. If this argument is set to *NO,* then the attempt to create the directory will fail because *mydata* does not already exist and we have not given permission for it to be created on our behalf.

This method also takes additional arguments in the form of a set of attributes for the new directory. Specifying *nil* will use the default attributes.

The final argument provides the option to reference an NSError object to contain error information in the event of a failure. If this is not required, NULL may be specified for this argument.

The following code fragment identifies the documents directory and creates a new sub-directory named *data* in that directory:

```
NSFileManager *filemgr;
NSArray *dirPaths;
NSString *docsDir;
```

Working with Directories on iOS 6

```
NSString *newDir;

filemgr =[NSFileManager defaultManager];

dirPaths = NSSearchPathForDirectoriesInDomains(NSDocumentDirectory,
            NSUserDomainMask, YES);

docsDir = dirPaths[0];
newDir = [docsDir stringByAppendingPathComponent:@"data"];

if ([filemgr createDirectoryAtPath:newDir
withIntermediateDirectories:YES
    attributes:nil error: NULL] == NO)
{
    // Failed to create directory
}
```

31.10 Deleting a Directory

An existing directory may be removed from the file system using the *removeItemAtPath* method, passing through the path of the directory to be removed as an argument. For example, to remove the data directory created in the preceding example we might write the following code:

```
NSFileManager *filemgr;
NSArray *dirPaths;
NSString *docsDir;
NSString *newDir;

filemgr =[NSFileManager defaultManager];

dirPaths = NSSearchPathForDirectoriesInDomains(NSDocumentDirectory,
        NSUserDomainMask, YES);

docsDir = dirPaths[0];

newDir = [docsDir stringByAppendingPathComponent:@"data"];

if ([filemgr removeItemAtPath: newDir error: nil] == NO)
{
    // Directory removal failed.
}
```

31.11 Listing the Contents of a Directory

A listing of the files contained within a specified directory can be obtained using the *directoryContentsAtPath* method. This method takes the directory pathname as an argument and returns an NSArray object containing the names of the files and sub-directories in that directory. The following example obtains a listing of the contents of the root directory (/) and displays each item in the Xcode console panel during execution:

```
NSFileManager *filemgr;
NSArray *filelist;
int count;
int i;

filemgr =[NSFileManager defaultManager];
filelist = [filemgr contentsOfDirectoryAtPath:@"/" error:NULL];
count = [filelist count];

for (i = 0; i < count; i++)
    NSLog(@"%@", filelist[i]);
```

31.12 Getting the Attributes of a File or Directory

The attributes of a file or directory may be obtained using the *attributesOfItemAtPath* method. This takes as arguments the path of the directory and an optional NSError object into which information about any errors will be placed (may be specified as NULL if this information is not required). The results are returned in the form of an NSDictionary dictionary object. The keys for this dictionary are as follows:

NSFileType

NSFileTypeDirectory

NSFileTypeRegular

NSFileTypeSymbolicLink

NSFileTypeSocket

NSFileTypeCharacterSpecial

NSFileTypeBlockSpecial

NSFileTypeUnknown

NSFileSize

NSFileModificationDate

NSFileReferenceCount

Working with Directories on iOS 6

```
NSFileDeviceIdentifier
NSFileOwnerAccountName
NSFileGroupOwnerAccountName
NSFilePosixPermissions
NSFileSystemNumber
NSFileSystemFileNumber
NSFileExtensionHidden
NSFileHFSCreatorCode
NSFileHFSTypeCode
NSFileImmutable
NSFileAppendOnly
NSFileCreationDate
NSFileOwnerAccountID
NSFileGroupOwnerAccountID
```

For example, we can extract the file type and POSIX permissions for the */Applications* directory using the following code excerpt:

```
NSFileManager *filemgr;
NSDictionary *attribs;

filemgr = [NSFileManager defaultManager];

attribs = [filemgr attributesOfItemAtPath:
        @"/Applications" error: NULL];

NSLog (@"File type %@", [attribs objectForKey: NSFileType]);
NSLog (@"POSIX Permissions %@", [attribs objectForKey:
NSFilePosixPermissions]);
```

When executed, results similar to the following output will appear in the Xcode console:

```
File type NSFileTypeDirectory
POSIX Permissions 509
```

Chapter 32

32. Working with iPhone Files on iOS 6

In the chapter entitled *Working with Directories on iOS 6* we looked at the NSFileManager, NSFileHandle and NSData Foundation Framework classes and discussed how the NSFileManager class in particular enables us to work with directories when developing iPhone iOS 6 based applications. We also spent some time covering the file system structure used by iOS and, in particular, looked at the temporary and *Documents* directories assigned to each application and how the location of those directories can be identified from within the application code.

In this chapter we move on from working with directories to covering the details of working with files within the iOS 6 SDK. Once we have covered file handling topics in this chapter, the next chapter will work through an application example that puts theory into practice.

32.1 Creating an NSFileManager Instance

Before proceeding, first we need to recap the steps necessary to obtain a reference to the application's NSFileManager instance. As discussed in the previous chapter, the NSFileManager class contains a class method named *defaultManager* that is used to obtain a reference. For example:

```
NSFileManager *filemgr;
filemgr = [NSFileManager defaultManager];
```

Once the file manager object has been created it can be used to perform some basic file handling tasks.

32.2 Checking for the Existence of a File

The NSFileManager class contains an instance method named *fileExistsAtPath* which checks whether a specified file already exists. The method takes as an argument an NSString object containing the path to the file in question and returns a boolean YES or NO value indicating the presence or otherwise of the specified file:

```
NSFileManager *filemgr;
filemgr = [NSFileManager defaultManager];

if ([filemgr fileExistsAtPath: @"<your file path>"] == YES)
        NSLog (@"File exists");
```

247

```
else
        NSLog (@"File not found");
```

32.3 Comparing the Contents of Two Files

The contents of two files may be compared for equality using the *contentsEqualAtPath* method. This method takes as arguments the paths to the two files to be compared and returns a boolean YES or NO to indicate whether the file contents match:

```
NSFileManager *filemgr;

filemgr = [NSFileManager defaultManager];

if ([filemgr contentsEqualAtPath:
        @"<file path 1>" andPath:
        @"<file path 2"] == YES)
        NSLog (@"File contents match");
else
        NSLog (@"File contents do not match");
```

32.4 Checking if a File is Readable/Writable/Executable/Deletable

Most operating systems provide some level of file access control. These typically take the form of attributes designed to control the level of access to a file for each user or user group. As such, it is not a certainty that your program will have read or write access to a particular file, or the appropriate permissions to delete or rename it. The quickest way to find out if your program has a particular access permission is to use the *isReadableFileAtPath*, *isWritableFileAtPath*, *isExecutableFileAtPath* and *isDeletableFileAtPath* methods. Each method takes a single argument in the form of the path to the file to be checked and returns a boolean YES or NO result. For example, the following code excerpt checks to find out if a file is writable:

```
NSFileManager *filemgr;

filemgr = [NSFileManager defaultManager];

if ([filemgr isWritableFileAtPath: @"<your file path>"]  == YES)
        NSLog (@"File is writable");
else
        NSLog (@"File is read only");
```

To check for other access permissions simply substitute the corresponding method name in place of *isWritableFileAtPath* in the above example.

32.5 Moving/Renaming a File

A file may be renamed (assuming adequate permissions) using the *moveItemAtPath* method. This method returns a boolean YES or NO result and takes as arguments the pathname for the file to be moved, the destination path and an optional NSError object into which information describing any errors encountered during the operation will be placed. If no error description information is required, this argument may be set to NULL. Note that if the destination file path already exists this operation will fail.

```
NSFileManager *filemgr;

filemgr = [NSFileManager defaultManager];

if ([filemgr moveItemAtPath:
  @"<from file path>" toPath:
  @"<to file path>" error: NULL]   == YES)
        NSLog (@"Move successful");
else
        NSLog (@"Move failed");
```

32.6 Copying a File

File copying can be achieved using the *copyItemAtPath* method. As with the *move* method, this takes as arguments the source and destination pathnames and an optional NSError object. Success of the operation is indicated by the returned boolean value:

```
if ([filemgr copyItemAtPath: @"<from file path>"" toPath: @"<to file path>" error: NULL]   == YES)
        NSLog (@"Copy successful");
else
        NSLog (@"Copy failed");
```

32.7 Removing a File

The *removeItemAtPath* method removes the specified file from the file system. The method takes as arguments the pathname of the file to be removed and an optional NSError object. The success of the operation is, as usual, reported in the form of a boolean YES or NO return value:

```
NSFileManager *filemgr;

filemgr = [NSFileManager defaultManager];

if ([filemgr removeItemAtPath:
        @"<your file path>" error: NULL]   == YES)
```

```
            NSLog (@"Remove successful");
else
            NSLog (@"Remove failed");
```

32.8 Creating a Symbolic Link

A symbolic link to a particular file may be created using the *createSymbolicLinkAtPath* method. This takes as arguments the path of the symbolic link, the path to the file to which the link is to refer and an optional NSError object. For example, the following code creates a symbolic link from */Users/demo/file1.txt* that links to the pre-existing file */tmp/myfile.txt*:

```
NSFileManager *filemgr;

filemgr = [NSFileManager defaultManager];

if ([filemgr createSymbolicLinkAtPath:
      @"<your file path>"
      withDestinationPath: @"<your file path>" error: NULL] == YES)
         NSLog (@"Remove successful");
else
         NSLog (@"Remove failed");
```

32.9 Reading and Writing Files with NSFileManager

The NSFileManager class includes some basic file reading and writing capabilities. These capabilities are somewhat limited when compared to the options provided by the NSFileHandle class, but can be useful nonetheless.

Firstly, the contents of a file may be read and stored in an NSData object through the use of the *contentsAtPath* method:

```
NSFileManager *filemgr;
NSData *databuffer;

filemgr = [NSFileManager defaultManager];

databuffer = [filemgr contentsAtPath: @"<your file path>" ];
```

Having stored the contents of a file in an NSData object that data may subsequently be written out to a new file using the *createFileAtPath* method:

```
databuffer = [filemgr contentsAtPath: @"<your file path>" ];

[filemgr createFileAtPath: @"<your file path>"
contents: databuffer attributes: nil];
```

In the above example we have essentially copied the contents from an existing file to a new file. This, however, gives us no control over how much data is to be read or written and does not allow us to append data to the end of an existing file. If the file */tmp/newfile.txt* in the above example had already existed it, and any data it contained, would have been overwritten by the contents of the source file. Clearly some more flexible mechanism is required. This is provided by the Foundation Framework in the form of the NSFileHandle class.

32.10 Working with Files using the NSFileHandle Class

The NSFileHandle class provides a range of methods designed to provide a more advanced mechanism for working with files. In addition to files, this class can also be used for working with devices and network sockets. In the following sections we will look at some of the more common uses for this class.

32.11 Creating an NSFileHandle Object

An NSFileHandle object can be created when opening a file for reading, writing or updating (in other words both reading and writing). This is achieved using the *fileHandleForReadingAtPath*, *fileHandleForWritingAtPath* and *fileHandleForUpdatingAtPath* methods respectively. Having opened a file, it must subsequently be closed when we have finished working with it using the *closeFile* method. If an attempt to open a file fails, for example because an attempt is made to open a non-existent file for reading, these methods return *nil*.

For example, the following code excerpt opens a file for reading and writing and then closes it without actually doing anything to the file:

```
NSFileHandle *file;

file = [NSFileHandle fileHandleForWritingAtPath:
    @"<your file path>"];
if (file == nil)
        NSLog(@"Failed to open file");
[file closeFile];
```

32.12 NSFileHandle File Offsets and Seeking

NSFileHandle objects maintain a pointer to the current position in a file. This is referred to as the *offset*. When a file is first opened the offset is set to 0 (the beginning of the file). This means that any read or write operations performed using the NSFileHandle instance methods will take place at offset 0 in the file. To perform operations at different locations in a file (for example to append data to the end of the file) it is first necessary to *seek* to the required offset. For example to move the current offset to the end of the file, use the *seekToEndOfFile* method. Alternatively, *seekToFileOffset* allows you to specify the precise location in the file to which the offset is to be positioned. Finally, the current offset may be identified using the *offsetInFile* method. In order to accommodate large files, the offset is stored in the form of an unsigned long long.

The following example opens a file for reading and then performs a number of method calls to move the offset to different positions, outputting the current offset after each move:

```
NSFileHandle *file;

file = [NSFileHandle fileHandleForUpdatingAtPath:
    @"<your file path>"];

if (file == nil)
        NSLog(@"Failed to open file");

NSLog (@"Offset = %llu", [file offsetInFile]);
[file seekToEndOfFile];
NSLog (@"Offset = %llu", [file offsetInFile]);
[file seekToFileOffset: 30];
NSLog (@"Offset = %llu", [file offsetInFile]);
[file closeFile];
```

File offsets are a key aspect of working with files using the NSFileHandle class so it is worth taking extra time to make sure you understand the concept. Without knowing where the current offset is in a file it is impossible to know the location in the file where data will be read or written.

32.13 Reading Data from a File

Once a file has been opened and assigned a file handle, the contents of that file may be read from the current offset position. The *readDataOfLength* method reads a specified number of bytes of data from the file starting at the current offset. For example, the following code reads 5 bytes of data from offset 10 in a file. The data read is returned encapsulated in an NSData object:

```
NSData *databuffer;
NSFileHandle *file;

file = [NSFileHandle fileHandleForReadingAtPath:
    @"<your file path>"];
if (file == nil)
        NSLog(@"Failed to open file");

[file seekToFileOffset: 10];
databuffer = [file readDataOfLength: 5];
[file closeFile];
```

Alternatively, the *readDataToEndOfFile* method will read all the data in the file starting at the current offset and ending at the end of the file.

32.14 Writing Data to a File

The *writeData* method writes the data contained in an NSData object to the file starting at the location of the offset. Note that this does not insert data but rather overwrites any existing data in the file at the corresponding location.

To see this in action, let's assume the existence of a file named *quickfox.txt* containing the following text:

```
The quick brown fox jumped over the lazy dog
```

Next, we will write code that opens the file for updating, seeks to position 10 and then writes some data at that location:

```
NSFileHandle *file;
NSMutableData *data;

const char *bytestring = "black dog";

data = [NSMutableData dataWithBytes:bytestring
    length:strlen(bytestring)];

file = [NSFileHandle fileHandleForUpdatingAtPath:
    @"<your file path>"];

if (file == nil)
    NSLog(@"Failed to open file");

[file seekToFileOffset: 10];
[file writeData: data];
[file closeFile];
```

When the above program is compiled and executed the contents of the *quickfox.txt* file will have changed to:

```
The quick black dog jumped over the lazy dog
```

32.15 Truncating a File

A file may be truncated at the specified offset using the *truncateFileAtOffset* method. To delete the entire contents of a file, specify an offset of 0 when calling this method:

253

```
NSFileHandle *file;

file = [NSFileHandle fileHandleForUpdatingAtPath:
    @"<your file path>"];

if (file == nil)
    NSLog(@"Failed to open file");
[file truncateFileAtOffset: 0];
[file closeFile];
```

32.16 Summary

Much like other operating systems, iOS provides a file system for the purposes of locally storing user and application files and data. In this and the preceding chapter, details of file and directory handling have been covered in some detail. The next chapter, entitled *iOS 6 iPhone Directory Handling and File I/O – A Worked Example* will work through the creation of an example designed specifically to demonstrate iOS file and directory handling on the iPhone.

Chapter 33

33. iOS 6 iPhone Directory Handling and File I/O – A Worked Example

In the *Working with Directories on iOS 6* and *Working with iPhone Files on iOS 6* chapters of this book we discussed in some detail the steps involved in working with the iOS 6 file system in terms of both file and directory handling from within iPhone applications. The goal of this chapter is to put theory into practice by working through the creation of a simple application that demonstrates some of the key concepts outlined in the preceding chapters.

33.1 The Example iPhone Application

The steps in this chapter walk through the creation of a simple iOS 6 iPhone application consisting of a text field and a button. When the user touches the button after entering text into the text field, that text is saved to a file. The next time the application is launched the content of the file is read by the application and pre-loaded into the text field.

33.2 Setting up the Application project

The first step in creating the application is to set up a new project. To do so, start the Xcode environment and select the option to create a new project (or select the *File -> New -> Project* menu option if Xcode is already running or the welcome screen does not appear by default).

Select the *Single View Application* template, ensure that *iPhone* is selected from the *Devices*, that the Storyboard option is on, Automatic Reference Counting is enabled and name the product and class prefix *FileExample*.

33.3 Designing the User Interface

The example application is going to consist of a button and a text field. To begin the user interface design process, select the *MainStoryboard.storyboard* file to load it into the Interface Builder environment. Drag a Button and then a Text Field from the Object library panel (*View -> Utilities -> Show Object Library*) onto the view. Double click on the button and change the text to *Save*. Position the components and resize the width of the text field so that the layout appears as illustrated Figure 33-1:

Figure 33-1

Select the Text Field object in the view canvas, display the Assistant Editor panel and verify that the editor is displaying the contents of the *FileExampleViewController.h* file. Ctrl-click on the text field object and drag to a position just below the @interface line in the Assistant Editor. Release the line and in the resulting connection dialog establish an outlet connection named *textBox*.

Ctrl-click on the button object and drag the line to the area immediately beneath the newly created outlet in the Assistant Editor panel. Release the line and, within the resulting connection dialog, establish an Action method on the *Touch Up Inside* event configured to call a method named *saveText*.

33.4 Checking the Data File on Application Startup

Each time the application is launched by the user it will need to check to see if the data file already exists (if the user has not previously saved any text, the file will not have been created). If the file does exist, the contents need to be read by the application and displayed within the text field. A good place to put initialization code of this nature is in the *viewDidLoad* method of the view controller. With this in mind, select the *FileExampleViewController.m* file, scroll down to the *viewDidLoad* method and edit it as follows:

```objc
- (void)viewDidLoad {
    [super viewDidLoad];
    NSFileManager *filemgr;
    NSString *dataFile;
    NSString *docsDir;
    NSArray *dirPaths;

    filemgr = [NSFileManager defaultManager];

    // Identify the documents directory
    dirPaths = NSSearchPathForDirectoriesInDomains(
        NSDocumentDirectory, NSUserDomainMask, YES);

    docsDir = dirPaths[0];

    // Build the path to the data file
    dataFile = [docsDir stringByAppendingPathComponent:
        @"datafile.dat"];

    // Check if the file already exists
    if ([filemgr fileExistsAtPath: dataFile])
    {
        // Read file contents and display in textBox
        NSData *databuffer;
        databuffer = [filemgr contentsAtPath: dataFile];

        NSString *datastring = [[NSString alloc]
            initWithData: databuffer
            encoding:NSASCIIStringEncoding];

        _textBox.text = datastring;
    }
}
```

Before proceeding we need to take some time to talk about what the above code is doing. First, we declare some variables that will be used in the method and then create an instance of the NSFileManager class. Because each iOS application on an iPhone device has its own *Documents* directory, we next make the appropriate calls to identify the path to that directory and assign the result to the *docsDir*. Once we know where the documents directory is located we construct the full path to our file (which is named *datafile.dat*) before checking whether the file already exists. If it exists, we read the contents of the file and assign it to the *text* property of our text field object so that it is visible to the user. Finally, we release the file manager object.

iOS 6 iPhone Directory Handling and File I/O – A Worked Example

Now that we have the initialization code implemented, we need to write the code for our action method.

33.5 Implementing the Action Method

When the user enters text into our text field component and touches the save button, the text needs to be saved to the *datafile.dat* file located in the application's *Documents* directory. In order to make this happen we need, therefore, to implement the code in our *saveText* action method. Select the *FileExampleViewController.m* file if it is not already open and modify the template *saveText* method we created previously so that it reads as follows:

```
- (void)saveText:(id)sender
{
    NSFileManager *filemgr;
    NSData *databuffer;
    NSString *dataFile;
    NSString *docsDir;
    NSArray *dirPaths;

    filemgr = [NSFileManager defaultManager];

    dirPaths = NSSearchPathForDirectoriesInDomains(
        NSDocumentDirectory, NSUserDomainMask, YES);

    docsDir = dirPaths[0];
    dataFile = [docsDir
       stringByAppendingPathComponent: @"datafile.dat"];
    databuffer = [_textBox.text
       dataUsingEncoding: NSASCIIStringEncoding];
    [filemgr createFileAtPath: dataFile
       contents: databuffer attributes:nil];
}
```

This code creates a file manager instance, identifies the documents directory and constructs the full path to our data file. It then converts the text contained in the text field object and assigns it to an NSData object, the contents of which are written to the data file by calling the *createFileAtPath* method of the file manager object.

33.6 Building and Running the Example

Once the appropriate code changes have been made, test the application by clicking on the *Run* button located in the toolbar of the main Xcode project window. Assuming no compilation errors are encountered, the application should run within the iOS Simulator.

When the application has loaded, enter some text into the text field and click on the *Save* button. Next, stop the app by clicking on the stop button in the Xcode toolbar and then restart the app by clicking *Run* again. On loading for a second time the text field will be primed with the text saved during the previous session:

Figure 33-2

Chapter 34

34. Preparing an iOS 6 App to use iCloud Storage

In 2007 Catawba County in western North Carolina used tax incentives to persuade Apple, Inc. to build a data center in the town of Maiden (current population 3269) where Apple subsequently spent $1 billion building a 500,000 sq. foot data center. During construction of the center much speculation circulated in the media as to the purpose of the building. At Apple's 2011 World Wide Developer Conference in San Francisco all speculation was laid to rest when the iCloud service was announced to the public.

This chapter is intended to provide an overview of iCloud and to walk through steps involved in preparing an iOS 6 iPhone application to utilize the services of iCloud.

34.1 What is iCloud?

From the perspective of the average iPhone or iPad owner, iCloud represents a vast remote storage service onto which device based data may be backed up and music stored for subsequent streaming to multiple iCloud supported platforms and devices. By default each registered user account gets 5GB of storage space for free and the option to purchase more as needed (stored music does not count towards the storage count).

From the perspective of the iOS application developer, on the other hand, iCloud represents a set of programming interfaces and SDK classes that facilitate the storage of files and data on iCloud servers hosted at Apple's data centers (of which the Maiden, NC facility is now just one of many) from within an iPhone or iPad application.

34.2 iCloud Data Storage Services

The current version of the iOS SDK provides support for two types of iCloud based storage, namely *iCloud Document Storage* and *iCloud Key-Value Data Storage*.

iCloud document storage allows data files and documents on the user's device to be stored on iCloud. Once stored, these files may be subsequently retrieved from iCloud storage via any supported device or platform using the owner's iCloud account details.

Preparing an iOS 6 App to use iCloud Storage

The iCloud key-value storage service allows small amounts of data packaged in key/value format to be stored in the cloud. This service is intended to provide a way for the same application to synchronize user settings and status when installed on multiple devices. A user might, for example, have the same game application installed on both an iPhone and an iPad. The game application would use iCloud key-value storage to synchronize the player's current position in the game and the prevailing score, thereby allowing the user to switch between devices and resume the game from the same state.

34.3 Preparing an Application to Use iCloud Storage

Implementing iCloud based storage within an iOS 6 application is not simply a case of making appropriate calls to the SDK iCloud APIs. In order to access iCloud services the application must be associated with an application ID and a corresponding provisioning profile configured to enable iCloud access. In addition, the application itself must also be configured with specific entitlements to enable one or both of the two iCloud storage methods outlined in the preceding section of this chapter.

Finally, it is also important to note that it is not possible to test iCloud functionality in the iOS Simulator. The application must, therefore, be installed on a physical iOS device.

Clearly, iPhone developers who are not yet members of the iOS Developer Program will need to enroll before implementing any iCloud functionality. Details on enrolling in this program are outlined in the *Joining the Apple iOS Developer Program* chapter of this book.

The remainder of this chapter will cover the steps necessary to create an iCloud enabled provisioning profile and to configure the necessary entitlements for both document and key/value based storage.

34.4 Creating an iOS 6 iCloud enabled App ID

In order to create an iCloud enabled App ID the first step is to log into the iOS Developer Program Member Center. Once logged in, select the link to the *iOS Provisioning Portal* and click on the *App IDs* link. Create a new App ID by clicking on the *New App ID* button.

In the resulting screen, name the App ID, leave the *Bundle Seed* menu set to *Generate New* and provide a bundle identifier formatted as follows:

```
com.yourdomain.yourappname
```

In the above example *com.yourdomain* will need to be replaced by the reverse URL of your domain name. Click on *Submit* and note that the new app ID is now listed on the main App ID screen:

262

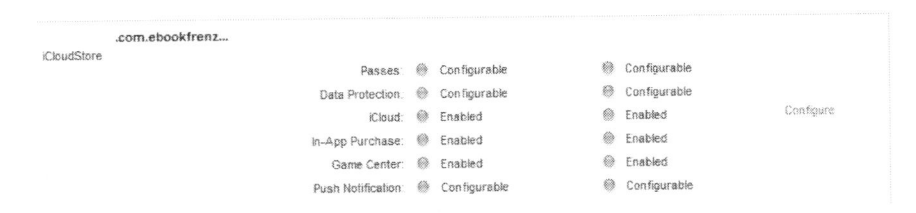

Figure 34-1

Note from the *iCloud* row of the table that this functionality is currently enabled. This is the default setting. In the event that iCloud support was not enabled by default, or to disable the option, click on the *Configure* link to display the *Configure App ID* screen. Select the check box next to *Enable for iCloud* and click *Done* to commit the configuration change:

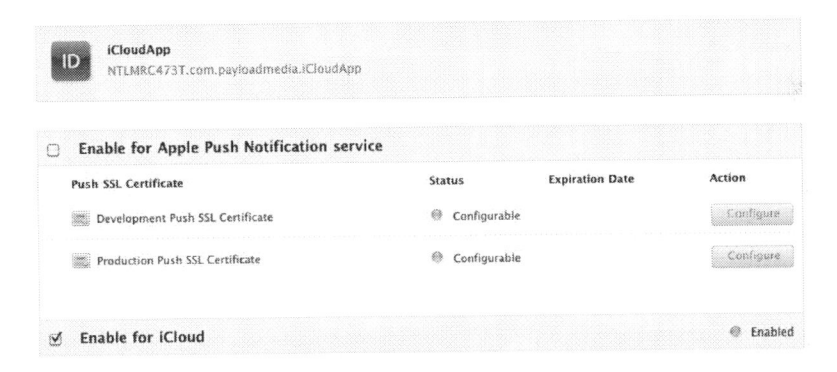

Figure 34-2

34.5 Creating and Installing an iCloud Enabled Provisioning Profile

Having creating an iCloud enabled App ID, the next step is to incorporate that ID into a provisioning profile. Remaining in the *iOS Provisioning Portal*, click on the *Provisioning* link and, in the resulting screen, click on the *New Profile* button. Within the *Create iOS Development Provisioning Profile* screen, name the new profile and select the development certificate to be used for the profile. Using the *App ID* menu, select the App ID created in the previous section followed by the devices on which the app is to be permitted to run before clicking on the *Submit* button.

If the new profile is listed as *Pending* in the main *Provisioning* screen, simply use the browser reload button to refresh the page. Once the profile is listed as active, click on the *Download* button to save the *.mobileprovision* file to your local system. Once downloaded, drag and drop the file onto the Xcode icon in the desktop dock to install it into the provisioning profiles library. At this point the Xcode Organizer window should appear. Connect your iPhone to the system so that it is listed under *DEVICES* in the left hand panel of the Organizer window. Select *Provisioning Profiles* from beneath the *LIBRARY* heading and drag and drop the new profile onto the *Provisioning Profiles* entry located beneath the iPhone device under the *DEVICES* heading.

Preparing an iOS 6 App to use iCloud Storage

Once completed, the provisioning profile is installed and ready to be used when developing an application.

34.6 Creating an iCloud Entitlements File

Any applications that intend to use iCloud storage in any way must obtain entitlements appropriate to the iCloud features to be used. These entitlements are placed into an *entitlements file* that is included in the Xcode project and built into the application at compile time.

If the application is intended to make use of iCloud document storage then the entitlements file must include a request for the *com.apple.developer.ubiquity-container-identifiers* entitlement. Similarly, if the key-value store is to be used then the *com.apple.developer.ubiquity-kvstore-identifier* entitlement must be included. Applications that require both forms of iCloud storage must include both entitlements.

The entitlements file is an XML file in which the requests are stored in a key-value format. The keys are the entitlement identifiers outlined above and the values are represented by one or more *container identifiers* comprised of the developer's ID and a custom string that uniquely identifies the application (the corresponding application's App ID is generally recommended, though not mandatory, for this value).

The entitlements file may be created either manually or automatically from within the Xcode environment.

To create the entitlements from within Xcode, select the application target from the top of the project navigator and scroll down the resulting Summary panel until the *Entitlements* section comes into view. To enable iCloud access set the *Entitlements* and *Enable iCloud* checkboxes as illustrated in Figure 34-3:

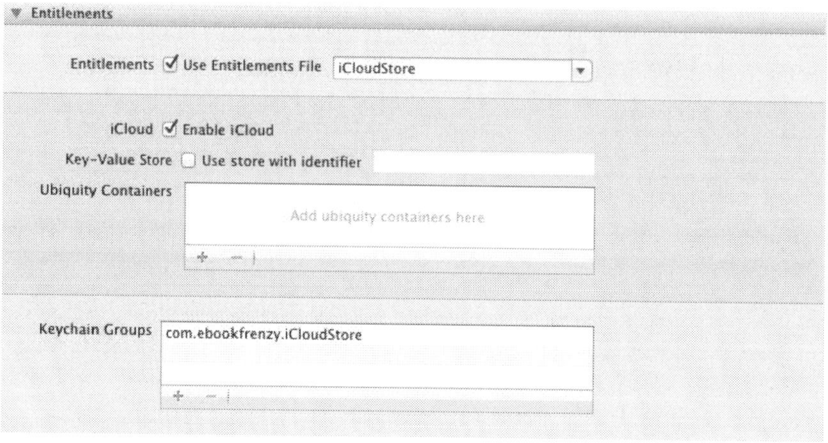

Figure 34-3

Once enabled, the entitlements file will appear in the project navigator panel. Note that by default, Xcode only enables iCloud container storage. If key-value storage is also required make sure that the *iCloud Key-Value Store* option is also selected. Having enabled container storage, the next task is to add an iCloud container into which files can be stored. To do so, simply click on the '+' button located beneath the *iCloud Containers* list box. The following figure illustrates both container and key-value entitlements enabled together with a single iCloud container:

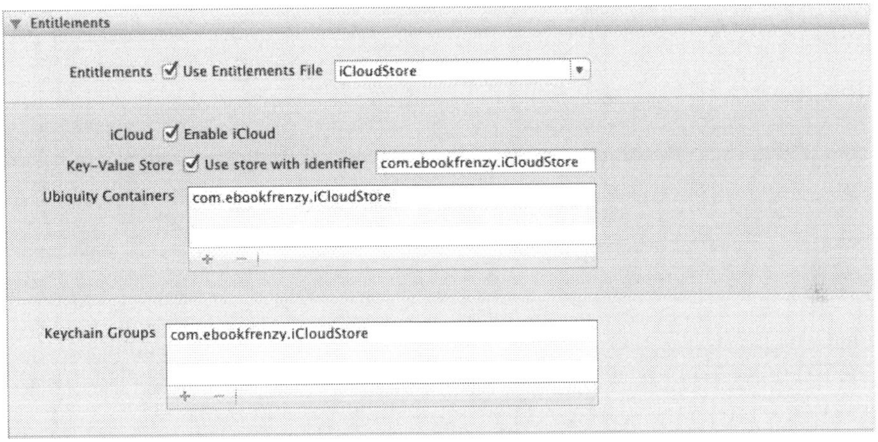

Figure 34-4

34.7 Manually Creating the Entitlements File

As an alternative to using the Xcode entitlements interface it is also possible to manually create the entitlements file. An example entitlements file containing entitlements to both document and key-value storage with a single iCloud container would read as follows:

```
<?xml version="1.0" encoding="UTF-8"?>
<!DOCTYPE plist PUBLIC "-//Apple//DTD PLIST 1.0//EN"
"http://www.apple.com/DTDs/PropertyList-1.0.dtd">
<plist version="1.0">
<dict>
        <key>com.apple.developer.ubiquity-container-identifiers</key>
        <array>

<string>$(TeamIdentifierPrefix).com.yourdomain.icloudapp</string>
        </array>
        <key>com.apple.developer.ubiquity-kvstore-identifier</key>

<string>$(TeamIdentifierPrefix).com.yourdomain.icloudapp</string>
</dict>
</plist>
```

265

Preparing an iOS 6 App to use iCloud Storage

Create this file using a text editor and save it as *<appname>.entitlements* (where <appname> is the name of your application), modifying the App ID accordingly for each entitlement request. Once saved, the file may be included into the corresponding Xcode project by opening the project and using the *File -> Add File* menu option or by dragging the file from a Finder window and dropping it onto the Xcode project navigator panel. The contents of the file may be viewed and modified from within Xcode at any time by selecting it in the Xcode project navigator panel so that it appears in the editing panel as illustrated in Figure 34-5:

Key	Type	Value
▼ com.apple.developer.ubiquity-container-	Array	(1 item)
Item 0	String	$(TeamIdentifierPrefix)com.payloadmedia.iCloudStore
com.apple.developer.ubiquity-kvstore-	String	$(TeamIdentifierPrefix)com.payloadmedia.iCloudStore
▼ keychain-access-groups	Array	(1 item)
Item 0	String	$(AppIdentifierPrefix)com.payloadmedia.iCloudStore

Figure 34-5

To modify a value simply double click on the corresponding field to enter edit mode.

34.8 Accessing Multiple Ubiquity Containers

The *ubiquity-container-identifiers* value is an array that may reference multiple iCloud containers. If an application requires access to more than one ubiquity container it will need to specifically reference the identifier of the required container. This is achieved by specifying the container identifier when constructing URL paths to documents within the iCloud storage. For example, the following code fragment defines a container identifier constant and then uses it to obtain the URL of the container in storage:

```
#define UBIQUITY_CONTAINER_URL @"ABCDEF12345.com.yourdomain.icloudapp"

ubiquityURL = [[filemgr
    URLForUbiquityContainerIdentifier:UBIQUITY_CONTAINER_URL]
    URLByAppendingPathComponent:@"Documents"];
```

If *nil* is passed through as an argument in place of the container identifier the method will simply return the URL of the first container in the *ubiquity-container-identifiers* array of the entitlements file:

```
ubiquityURL = [[filemgr
    URLForUbiquityContainerIdentifier:nil]
    URLByAppendingPathComponent:@"Documents"];
```

34.9 Ubiquity Container URLs

When documents are saved to the cloud they will be placed in sub folders of a folder on iCloud using the following path:

```
/private/var/mobile/Library/Mobile Documents/<ubiquity container id>/
```

34.10 Summary

iCloud brings cloud based storage and application data synchronization to iOS 6 based applications. Before an application can take advantage of iCloud it must first be provisioned with an iCloud enabled profile and built against an appropriately configured entitlements file.

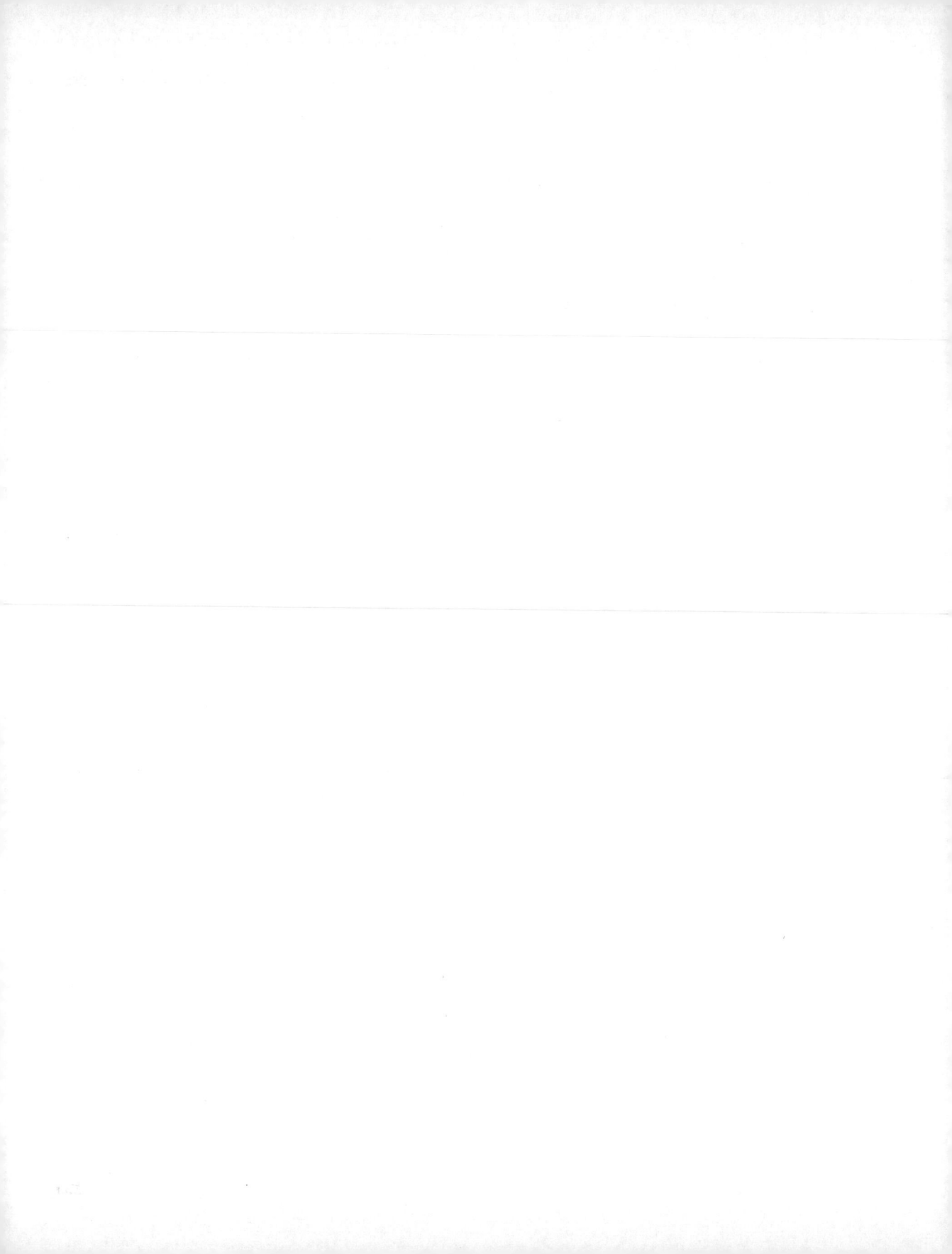

Chapter 35

35. Managing Files using the iOS 6 UIDocument Class

Use of iCloud to store files requires a basic understanding of the UIDocument class. Introduced as part of the iOS 5 SDK, the UIDocument class is the recommended mechanism for working with iCloud based file and document storage.

The objective of this chapter is to provide a brief overview of the UIDocument class before working through a simple example demonstrating the use of UIDocument to create and perform read and write operations on a document on the local device file system. Once these basics have been covered the next chapter will extend the example to store the document using the iCloud document storage service.

35.1 An Overview of the UIDocument Class

The iOS UIDocument class is designed to provide an easy to use interface for the creation and management of documents and content. Whilst primarily intended to ease the process of storing files using iCloud, UIDocument also provides additional benefits in terms of file handling on the local file system such as reading and writing data asynchronously on a background queue, handling of version conflicts on a file (a more likely possibility when using iCloud) and automatic document saving.

35.2 Subclassing the UIDocument Class

UIDocument is an *abstract class*, in that it cannot be directly instantiated from within code. Instead applications must create a subclass of UIDocument and, at a minimum, override two methods:

- **contentsForType:error:** - This method is called by the UIDocument subclass instance when data is to be written to the file or document. The method is responsible for gathering the data to be written and returning it in the form of an NSData or NSFileWrapper object.
- **loadFromContents:ofType:error:** - Called by the subclass instance when data is being read from the file or document. The method is passed the content that has been read from the file by the UIDocument subclass and is responsible for loading that data into the application's internal data model.

35.3 Conflict Resolution and Document States

Storage of documents using iCloud means that multiple instances of an application can potentially access the same stored document consecutively. This considerably increases the risk of a conflict occurring when application instances simultaneously make different changes to the same document. One option is to simply let the most recent save operation overwrite any changes made by the other application instances. A more user friendly alternative, however, is to implement conflict detection code in the application and present the user with the option to resolve the conflict. Such resolution options will be application specific but might include presenting the file differences and letting the user choose which one to save, or allowing the user to merge the conflicting file versions.

The current state of a UIDocument subclass object may be identified by accessing the object's *documentState* property. At any given time this property will be set to one of the following constants:

- **UIDocumentStateNormal** – The document is open and enabled for user editing.
- **UIDocumentStateClosed** – The document is currently closed. This state can also indicate an error in reading a document.
- **UIDocumentStateInConflict** – Conflicts have been detected for the document.
- **UIDocumentStateSavingError** – An error occurred when an attempt was made to save the document.
- **UIDocumentStateEditingDisabled** – The document is busy and is not currently safe for editing.

Clearly one option for detecting conflicts is to periodically check the *documentState* property for a UIDocumentStateInConflict value. That said, it only really makes sense to check for this state when changes have actually be made to the document. This can be achieved by registering an observer on the *UIDocumentStateChangedNotification* notification. When the notification is received that the document state has changed the code will need to check the *documentState* property for the presence of a conflict and act accordingly.

35.4 The UIDocument Example Application

The remainder of this chapter will focus on the creation of an application designed to demonstrate the use of the UIDocument class to read and write a document locally on an iOS 6 based iPhone device. Since the application requires an iCloud enabled provisioning profile it is essential that the steps outlined in the *previous* chapter of this book be performed to create a profile and install it into the Xcode development environment.

To create the project, begin by launching Xcode and create a new product named *iCloudStore* with a corresponding class prefix using the *Single View Application* template. On the project options page ensure that the *Company Identifier* matches that specified when the iCloud enabled provisioning profile for this project was created. Also make sure that the *Use Storyboards* and *Automatic Reference Counting* options are enabled before clicking the *Next* button and creating the new project in a suitable file system location.

35.5 Creating a UIDocument Subclass

As previously discussed, UIDocument is an abstract class that cannot be directly instantiated. It is necessary, therefore, to create a subclass and to implement some methods in that subclass before using the features that UIDocument provides. The first step in this project is to create the source files for the subclass so select the Xcode *File -> New -> File...* menu option and in the resulting panel select the *Objective-C class* template and click *Next*. On the options panel, set the *Subclass of* menu to *UIDocument,* name the class *MyDocument* and click *Next* to create the new class.

With the basic outline of the subclass created the next step is to begin implementing the user interface and the corresponding outlets and actions.

35.6 Designing the User Interface

The finished application is going to consist of a user interface comprising a UITextView and UIButton. The user will enter text into the text view and initiate the saving of that text to a file by touching the button.

Select *MainStoryboard.*storyboard file and display the Interface Builder Object Library (*View -> Utilities -> Show Object Library*). Drag and drop the Text View and Button objects into the view canvas, resizing the text view so that occupies only the upper area of the view. Double click on the button object and change the label text to "Save":

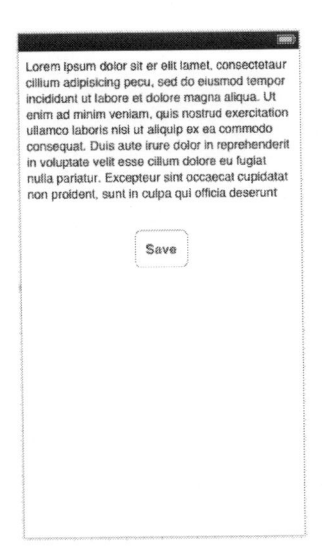

Figure 35-1

271

Remove the example Latin text from the text view object by selecting it in the view canvas and deleting the value from the *Text* property in the *Attribute Inspector* panel.

With the user interface designed it is now time to connect the action and outlet. Select the Text View object in the view canvas, display the Assistant Editor panel and verify that the editor is displaying the contents of the *iCloudStoreViewController.h* file. Ctrl-click on the Text View object and drag to a position just below the @interface line in the Assistant Editor. Release the line and in the resulting connection dialog establish an outlet connection named *textView*.

Finally, Ctrl-click on the button object and drag the line to the area immediately beneath the newly created outlet in the Assistant Editor panel. Release the line and, within the resulting connection dialog, establish an Action method on the *Touch Up Inside* event configured to call a method named *saveDocument*.

35.7 Implementing the Application Data Structure

So far we have created and partially implemented a UIDocument subclass named *MyDocument* and designed the user interface of the application together with corresponding actions and outlets. As previously discussed, the *MyDocument* class will require two methods that are responsible for interfacing between the *MyDocument* object instances the application's data structures. Before we can implement these methods, however, we first need to implement the application data structure. In the context of this application the data simply consists of the string entered by the user into the text view object. Given the simplicity of this example we will declare the data structure, such as it is, within the *MyDocument* class where it can be easily accessed by the *contentsForType* and *loadFromContents* methods. To implement the data structure, albeit a single data value, select the *MyDocument.h* file and add a declaration for an NSString object:

```
#import <UIKit/UIKit.h>

@interface MyDocument : UIDocument

@property (strong, nonatomic) NSString *userText;
@end
```

Now that the data model is defined it is now time to complete the *MyDocument* class implementation.

35.8 Implementing the contentsForType Method

The *MyDocument* class is a subclass of UIDocument. When an instance of MyDocument is created and the appropriate method is called on that instance to save the application's data to a file, the class makes a call to its *contentsForType* instance method. It is the job of this method to collect the data to be stored in the document and to pass it back to the MyDocument object instance in the form of an NSData object. The content of the NSData object will then be written to the document. Whilst this may sound complicated most of the work is done for us by the parent UIDocument class. All the method needs to do, in fact, is get the current value of the *userText* NSString object, put it into an NSData object and return it.

Select the *MyDocument.m* file and add the *contentsForType* method as follows:

```
-(id)contentsForType:(NSString *)typeName
           error:(NSError * __autoreleasing *)outError
{
    return [NSData dataWithBytes:[_userText UTF8String]
                          length:[_userText length]];
}
```

35.9 Implementing the loadFromContents Method

The *loadFromContents* instance method is called by an instance of MyDocument when the object is instructed to read the contents of a file. This method is passed an NSData object containing the content of the document and is responsible for updating the application's internal data structure accordingly. All this method needs to do, therefore, is convert the NSData object contents to a string and assign it to the *userText* object:

```
-(BOOL) loadFromContents:(id)contents
             ofType:(NSString *)typeName
             error:(NSError * __autoreleasing *)outError
{
    if ( [contents length] > 0) {
        _userText = [[NSString alloc]
                      initWithBytes:[contents bytes]
                      length:[contents length]
                      encoding:NSUTF8StringEncoding];
    } else {
        _userText = @"";
    }
    return YES;
}
```

The implementation of the MyDocument class is now complete and it is time to begin implementing the application functionality.

35.10 Loading the Document at App Launch

The ultimate goal of the application is to save any text in the text view to a document on the local file system of the device. When the application is launched it needs to check if the document exists and,

Managing Files using the iOS 6 UIDocument Class

if so, load the contents into the text view object. If, on the other hand, the document does not yet exist it will need to be created. As is usually the case, the best place to perform these tasks is the *viewDidLoad* method of the view controller.

Before implementing the code for the *viewDidLoad* method we first need to perform some preparatory work in the *iCloudStoreViewController.h* file. Firstly, since we will be creating instances of the MyDocument class within the view controller it will be necessary to import the *MyDocument.h* file. Secondly, both the *viewDidLoad* and *saveDocument* methods will need access to an NSURL object containing a reference to the document and also an instance of the *MyDocument* class, so these need to be declared in the view controller implementation file. With *iCloudStoreViewController.h* selected in the project navigator, modify the file as follows:

```
#import <UIKit/UIKit.h>
#import "MyDocument.h"

@interface iCloudStoreViewController : UIViewController

@property (strong, nonatomic) IBOutlet UITextView *textView;
@property (strong, nonatomic) NSURL *documentURL;
@property (strong, nonatomic) MyDocument *document;
-(IBAction) saveDocument;
@end
```

The first task for the *viewDidLoad* method is to identify the path to the application's *Documents* directory (a task outlined in *Working with Directories on iOS 6*) and construct a full path to the document which will be named *document.doc*. The method will then need to create an NSURL object based on the path to the document and use it to create an instance of the *MyDocument* class. The code to perform these tasks can be implemented as outlined in the following code fragment:

```
NSArray *dirPaths =
    NSSearchPathForDirectoriesInDomains(NSDocumentDirectory,
      NSUserDomainMask, YES);

  NSString *docsDir = dirPaths[0];
  NSString *dataFile =
    [docsDir stringByAppendingPathComponent:
      @"document.doc"];

  _documentURL = [NSURL fileURLWithPath:dataFile];
  _document = [[MyDocument alloc] initWithFileURL:_documentURL];
  _document.userText = @"";
```

Managing Files using the iOS 6 UIDocument Class

The next task for the method is to create an NSFileManager instance and use it to identify whether the file exists. In the event that it does, the *openWithCompletionHandler* method of the *MyDocument* instance object is called to open the document and load the contents (thereby automatically triggering a call to the *loadFromContents* method created earlier in the chapter).

The *openWithCompletionHandler* allows for a code block to be written to which is passed a Boolean value indicating the success or otherwise of the file opening and reading process. On a successful read operation this handler code simply needs to assign the value of the *userText* property of the *MyDocument* instance (which has been updated with the document contents by the *loadFromContents* method) to the text property of the *textView* object, thereby making it visible to the user.

In the event that the document does not yet exist, the *saveToURL* method of the *MyDocument* class will be called using the argument to create a new file:

```
NSFileManager *filemgr = [NSFileManager defaultManager];

if ([filemgr fileExistsAtPath: dataFile])
{
    [_document openWithCompletionHandler:
        ^(BOOL success) {
          if (success){
              NSLog(@"Opened");
              _textView.text = _document.userText;
          } else {
              NSLog(@"Not opened");
          }
      }];

} else {
      [_document saveToURL:_documentURL
          forSaveOperation: UIDocumentSaveForCreating
          completionHandler:^(BOOL success) {
              if (success){
                  NSLog(@"Created");
              } else {
                  NSLog(@"Not created");
              }
          }];
}
```

Note that for the purposes of debugging, NSLog calls have been made at key points in the process. These can be removed once the application is verified to be working correctly.

Managing Files using the iOS 6 UIDocument Class

Bringing the above code fragments together results in the following, fully implemented *viewDidLoad* method:

```
- (void)viewDidLoad
{
    [super viewDidLoad];

    NSArray *dirPaths =
    NSSearchPathForDirectoriesInDomains(NSDocumentDirectory,
        NSUserDomainMask, YES);

    NSString *docsDir = dirPaths[0];
    NSString *dataFile =
      [docsDir stringByAppendingPathComponent:
        @"document.doc"];

    _documentURL = [NSURL fileURLWithPath:dataFile];
    _document = [[MyDocument alloc] initWithFileURL:_documentURL];
    _document.userText = @"";
    NSFileManager *filemgr = [NSFileManager defaultManager];

    if ([filemgr fileExistsAtPath: dataFile])
    {
        [_document openWithCompletionHandler:
          ^(BOOL success) {
            if (success){
                NSLog(@"Opened");
                _textView.text = _document.userText;
            } else {
                NSLog(@"Not opened");
            }
        }];

    } else {
        [_document saveToURL:_documentURL
            forSaveOperation: UIDocumentSaveForCreating
           completionHandler:^(BOOL success) {
              if (success){
                  NSLog(@"Created");
              } else {
                  NSLog(@"Not created");
              }
        }];
    }
}
```

}

35.11 Saving Content to the Document

When the user touches the application's save button the content of the text view object needs to be saved to the document. An action method has already been connected to the user interface object for this purpose and it is now time to write the code for this method.

Since the *viewDidLoad* method has already identified the path to the document and initialized the *document* object, all that needs to be done is to call that object's *saveToURL* method using the *UIDocumentSaveForOverwriting* option. The *saveToURL* method will automatically call the *contentsForType* method implemented previously in this chapter. Prior to calling the method, therefore, it is important that the *userText* property of the *document* object be set to the current text of the *textView* object.

Bringing this all together results in the following implementation of the *saveDocument* method:

```
- (void)saveDocument:(id)sender
{
    _document.userText = _textView.text;

    [_document saveToURL:_documentURL
        forSaveOperation:UIDocumentSaveForOverwriting
       completionHandler:^(BOOL success) {
            if (success) {
                NSLog(@"Saved for overwriting");
            } else {
                NSLog(@"Not saved for overwriting");
            }
    }];
}
```

35.12 Testing the Application

All that remains is to test that the application works by clicking on the *Run* button. Upon execution, any text entered into the text view object should be saved to the *document.doc* file when the Save button is touched. Once some text has been saved, click on the *Stop* button located in the Xcode toolbar. On subsequently restarting the application the text view should be populated with the previously saved text.

35.13 Summary

Whilst the UIDocument class is the cornerstone of document storage using the iCloud service it is also of considerable use and advantage in terms of using the local file system storage of an iPhone

Managing Files using the iOS 6 UIDocument Class

device. As an abstract class, UIDocument must be subclassed and two mandatory methods implemented within the subclass in order to operate. This chapter worked through an example of using UIDocument to save and load content using a locally stored document. The next chapter will look at using UIDocument to perform cloud based document storage and retrieval.

Chapter 36

36. Using iCloud Storage in an iOS 6 iPhone Application

The two preceding chapters of this book were intended to convey the knowledge necessary to begin implementing iCloud based document storage in iOS 6 based iPhone applications. Having outlined the steps necessary to enable iCloud access in the chapter entitled *Preparing an iOS 6 App to use iCloud Storage*, and provided an overview of the UIDocument class in *Managing Files using the iOS 6 UIDocument Class*, the next step is to actually begin to store documents using the iCloud service.

Within this chapter the *iCloudStore* application created in the previous chapter will be re-purposed to store a document using iCloud storage instead of the local device based file system. The assumption is also made that the project has been enabled for iCloud storage following the steps outlined in *Preparing an iOS 6 App to use iCloud Storage*.

36.1 iCloud Usage Guidelines

Before implementing iCloud storage in an application there a few rules that must first be understood. Some of these are mandatory rules and some are simply recommendations made by Apple:

- Applications must be associated with a provisioning profile enabled for iCloud storage.
- The application projects must include a suitably configured entitlements file for iCloud storage.
- Applications should not make unnecessary use of iCloud storage. Once a user's initial free iCloud storage space is consumed by stored data the user will either need to delete files or purchase more space.
- Applications should, ideally, provide the user with the option to select which documents are to be stored in the cloud and which are to stored locally.
- When opening a *previously created* iCloud based document the application should never use an absolute path to the document. The application should instead search for the document by name in the application's iCloud storage area and then access it using the result of the search.

Using iCloud Storage in an iOS 6 iPhone Application

- Documents stored using iCloud should be placed in the application's *Documents* directory. This gives the user the ability to delete individual documents from the storage. Documents saved outside the *Document* folder can only be deleted in bulk.

36.2 Preparing the iCloudStore Application for iCloud Access

Much of the work performed in creating the local storage version of the *iCloudStore* application in the previous chapter will be reused in this example. The user interface, for example, remains unchanged and the implementation of the UIDocument subclass will not need to be modified. In fact, the only methods that need to be rewritten are the *saveDocument* and *viewDidLoad* methods of the view controller.

Load the iCloudStore project into Xcode and select the *iCloudStoreViewController.m* file. Locate the *saveDocument* method and remove the current code from within the method so that it reads as follows:

```
- (void)saveDocument
{
}
```

Next, locate the *viewDidLoad* method and modify it accordingly to match the following fragment:

```
- (void)viewDidLoad
{
    [super viewDidLoad];
}
```

36.3 Configuring the View Controller

Before writing any code there are a number of variables that need to be defined within the view controller's *iCloudStoreViewController.h* interface file in addition to those implemented in the previous chapter.

In addition to the URL of the local version of the document, it will also now be necessary to create a URL to the document location in the iCloud storage. When a document is stored on iCloud it is said to be *ubiquitous* since the document is accessible to the application regardless of the device on which it is running. The object used to store this URL will, therefore, be named *ubiquityURL*.

As previously stated, when opening a stored document, an application should search for the document rather than directly access it using a stored path. An iCloud document search is performed using an *NSMetaDataQuery* object which needs to be declared in the interface file for the view controller, in this instance using the name *metaDataQuery*. Note that declaring the object locally to the method in which it is used will result in the object being released by the automatic array counting service (ARC) before it has completed the search.

To implement these requirements, select the *iCloudStoreViewController.h* file in the Xcode project navigator panel and modify the file as follows:

```
#import <UIKit/UIKit.h>
#import "MyDocument.h"

@interface iCloudStoreViewController : UIViewController

@property (strong, nonatomic) IBOutlet UITextView *textView;
@property (strong, nonatomic) NSURL *documentURL;
@property (strong, nonatomic) MyDocument *document;
@property (strong, nonatomic) NSURL *ubiquityURL;
@property (strong, nonatomic) NSMetadataQuery *metadataQuery;
-(IBAction)saveDocument;
@end
```

36.4 Implementing the viewDidLoad Method

The purpose of the code in the view controller *viewDidLoad* method is to construct both the URL to the local version of the file (assigned to *documentURL*) and the URL for the ubiquitous version stored using iCloud (assigned to *ubiquityURL*). For *documentURL* it is first necessary to identify the location of the application's *Documents* directory, create the full path to the *document.doc* file and then initialize the NSURL object. If the *document.doc* file exists already it is removed:

```
NSArray *dirPaths =
    NSSearchPathForDirectoriesInDomains(NSDocumentDirectory,
    NSUserDomainMask, YES);
NSString *docsDir = dirPaths[0];
NSString *dataFile =
    [docsDir stringByAppendingPathComponent: @"document.doc"];

_documentURL = [NSURL fileURLWithPath:dataFile];

NSFileManager *filemgr = [NSFileManager defaultManager];
[filemgr removeItemAtURL:_documentURL error:nil];
```

The ubiquitous URL is constructed by calling the *URLForUbiquityContainerIdentifier:* method of the NSFileManager passing through *nil* as an argument to default to the first container listed in the entitlements file. Since it is recommended that documents be stored in the *Documents* sub-directory, this needs to be appended to the URL path:

Using iCloud Storage in an iOS 6 iPhone Application

```
_ubiquityURL = [[filemgr
    URLForUbiquityContainerIdentifier:nil]
    URLByAppendingPathComponent:@"Documents"];
```

By default, the iCloud storage area for the application will not already contain a *Documents* sub-directory so the next step is to check to see if the sub-directory already exists and, in the event that is does not, create it:

```
if ([filemgr fileExistsAtPath:[_ubiquityURL path]] == NO)
    [filemgr createDirectoryAtURL:_ubiquityURL
       withIntermediateDirectories:YES
       attributes:nil
       error:nil];
```

Having created the *Documents* directory if necessary, the next step is to append the document name (*document.doc*) to the end of the *ubuiquityURL* path:

```
_ubiquityURL =
            [_ubiquityURL URLByAppendingPathComponent:@"document.doc"];
```

The final task for the *viewDidLoad* method is to initiate a search in the application's iCloud storage area to find out if the *document.doc* file already exists and to act accordingly subject to the result of the search. The search is performed by calling the methods on an instance of the *NSMetaDataQuery* object. This involves creating the object, setting a predicate to indicate the files to search for and defining a ubiquitous search scope (in other words instructing the object to search iCloud storage). Once initiated, the search is performed on a separate thread and issues a notification when completed. For this reason, it is also necessary to configure an observer to be notified when the search is finished. The code to perform these tasks reads as follows:

```
_metadataQuery = [[NSMetadataQuery alloc] init];

[_metadataQuery setPredicate:[NSPredicate
    predicateWithFormat:@"%K like 'document.doc'",
    NSMetadataItemFSNameKey]];

[_metadataQuery setSearchScopes:[NSArray
      arrayWithObjects:NSMetadataQueryUbiquitousDocumentsScope,nil]];

[[NSNotificationCenter defaultCenter]
      addObserver:self
      selector:@selector(metadataQueryDidFinishGathering:)
      name: NSMetadataQueryDidFinishGatheringNotification
      object:_metadataQuery];
```

Using iCloud Storage in an iOS 6 iPhone Application

```
[_metadataQuery startQuery];
```

Once the *[metadataQuery startQuery]* method is called, the search will run and trigger the *metadataQueryDidFinishGathering:* method once the search is complete. The next step, therefore, is to implement the *metadataQueryDidFinishGathering:* method. Before doing so, however, note that the *viewDidLoad* method is now complete and the full implementation should read as follows:

```
- (void)viewDidLoad
{
    [super viewDidLoad];

    NSArray *dirPaths =
      NSSearchPathForDirectoriesInDomains(NSDocumentDirectory,
      NSUserDomainMask, YES);
    NSString *docsDir = dirPaths[0];
    NSString *dataFile =
      [docsDir stringByAppendingPathComponent: @"document.doc"];

    _documentURL = [NSURL fileURLWithPath:dataFile];

    NSFileManager *filemgr = [NSFileManager defaultManager];

    [filemgr removeItemAtURL:_documentURL error:nil];

    _ubiquityURL = [[filemgr
        URLForUbiquityContainerIdentifier:nil]
        URLByAppendingPathComponent:@"Documents"];

    if ([filemgr fileExistsAtPath:[_ubiquityURL path]] == NO)
        [filemgr createDirectoryAtURL:_ubiquityURL
            withIntermediateDirectories:YES
            attributes:nil
            error:nil];

    _ubiquityURL =
       [_ubiquityURL URLByAppendingPathComponent:@"document.doc"];

    // Search for document in iCloud storage
    _metadataQuery = [[NSMetadataQuery alloc] init];
    [_metadataQuery setPredicate:[NSPredicate
    predicateWithFormat:@"%K like 'document.doc'",
       NSMetadataItemFSNameKey]];
    [_metadataQuery setSearchScopes:[NSArray
       arrayWithObjects:NSMetadataQueryUbiquitousDocumentsScope,nil]];
```

283

```
    [[NSNotificationCenter defaultCenter]
        addObserver:self
        selector:@selector(metadataQueryDidFinishGathering:)
        name: NSMetadataQueryDidFinishGatheringNotification
        object:_metadataQuery];
    [_metadataQuery startQuery];
}
```

36.5 Implementing the metadataQueryDidFinishGathering: Method

When the meta data query was triggered in the *viewDidLoad* method to search for documents in the application's iCloud storage area, an observer was configured to call a method named *metadataQueryDidFinishGathering* when the initial search completed. The next logical step is to implement this method. The first task of the method is to identify the query object that caused this method to be called. This object must then be used to disable any further query updates (at this stage the document either exists or doesn't exist so there is nothing to be gained by receiving additional updates) and stop the search. It is also necessary to remove the observer that triggered the method call. Combined, these requirements result in the following code:

```
NSMetadataQuery *query = [notification object];
    [query disableUpdates];

[[NSNotificationCenter defaultCenter]
        removeObserver:self
        name:NSMetadataQueryDidFinishGatheringNotification
        object:query];

[query stopQuery];
```

Next, the *query* method of the query object needs to be called to extract an array of documents located during the search:

```
NSArray *results = [[NSArray alloc] initWithArray:[query results]];
```

A more complex application would, in all likelihood, need to implement a *for* loop to iterate through more than one document in the array. Given that the iCloudStore application searched for only one specific file name we can simply check the array element count and assume that if the count is 1 then the document already exists. In this case, the ubiquitous URL of the document from the query object needs to be assigned to our *ubiquityURL* member property and used to create an instance of our MyDocument class called *document*. The *openWithCompletionHandler:* method of the *document* object is then called to open the document in the cloud and read the contents. This will trigger a call to the *loadFromContents* method of the *document* object which, in turn, will assign the contents of the document to the *userText* property. Assuming the document read is successful the value of *userText* needs to be assigned to the *text* property of the text view object to make it visible to the user. Bringing this together results in the following code fragment:

```
if ([results count] == 1)
{
    // File exists in cloud so get URL
    _ubiquityURL = [results[0]
        valueForAttribute:NSMetadataItemURLKey];

    _document = [[MyDocument alloc]
            initWithFileURL:_ubiquityURL];
    [_document openWithCompletionHandler:
      ^(BOOL success) {
        if (success) {
            NSLog(@"Opened iCloud doc");
            _textView.text = _document.userText;
        } else {
            NSLog(@"Failed to open iCloud doc");
        }
    }];
} else {
}
```

In the event that the document does not yet exist in iCloud storage the code needs to create the document using the *saveToURL* method of the *document* object passing through the value of *ubiquityURL* as the destination path on iCloud:

-
-

```
} else {
    // File does not exist in cloud.
    _document = [[MyDocument alloc]
            initWithFileURL:_ubiquityURL];

    [_document saveToURL:_ubiquityURL
        forSaveOperation: UIDocumentSaveForCreating
        completionHandler:^(BOOL success) {
            if (success) {
                NSLog(@"Saved to cloud");
            } else {
                NSLog(@"Failed to save to cloud");
            }
```

Using iCloud Storage in an iOS 6 iPhone Application

```
    }];
}
```

The individual code fragments outlined above combine to implement the following *metadataQueryDidFinishGathering:* method:

```
- (void)metadataQueryDidFinishGathering:
(NSNotification *)notification {
  NSMetadataQuery *query = [notification object];
  [query disableUpdates];

    [[NSNotificationCenter defaultCenter]
        removeObserver:self
        name:NSMetadataQueryDidFinishGatheringNotification
        object:query];

    [query stopQuery];
    NSArray *results = [[NSArray alloc] initWithArray:[query results]];

    if ([results count] == 1)
    {
      // File exists in cloud so get URL
      _ubiquityURL = [results[0]
            valueForAttribute:NSMetadataItemURLKey];

      _document = [[MyDocument alloc]
            initWithFileURL:_ubiquityURL];
      [_document openWithCompletionHandler:
        ^(BOOL success) {
           if (success) {
              NSLog(@"Opened iCloud doc");
              _textView.text = _document.userText;
           } else {
              NSLog(@"Failed to open iCloud doc");
           }
      }];
    } else {
        // File does not exist in cloud.
        _document = [[MyDocument alloc]
            initWithFileURL:_ubiquityURL];

        [_document saveToURL:_ubiquityURL
           forSaveOperation: UIDocumentSaveForCreating
           completionHandler:^(BOOL success) {
```

286

```
            if (success) {
                NSLog(@"Saved to cloud");
            } else {
                NSLog(@"Failed to save to cloud");
            }
       }];
    }
}
```

36.6 Implementing the saveDocument Method

The final task before building and running the application is to implement the *saveDocument* method. This method simply needs to update the *userText* property of the *document* object with the text entered into the text view and then call the *saveToURL* method of the *document* object, passing through the *ubiquityURL* as the destination URL using the *UIDocumentSaveForOverwriting* option:

```
- (void)saveDocument:(id)sender
{
    _document.userText = _textView.text;
    [_document saveToURL:_ubiquityURL
        forSaveOperation:UIDocumentSaveForOverwriting
        completionHandler:^(BOOL success) {
            if (success) {
                NSLog(@"Saved to cloud for overwriting");
            } else {
                NSLog(@"Not saved to cloud for overwriting");
            }
        }];
}
```

All that remains now is to build and run the iCloudStore application on an iPhone device, but first some settings on the device need to be checked.

36.7 Enabling iCloud Document and Data Storage on an iPhone

Whether or not applications are permitted to use iCloud storage on an iPhone is controlled by the iCloud settings on that device. To review these settings, open the Settings application on the iPhone and select the *iCloud* category. Scroll down the list of various iCloud related options and verify that the *Documents & Data* option is set to *On*:

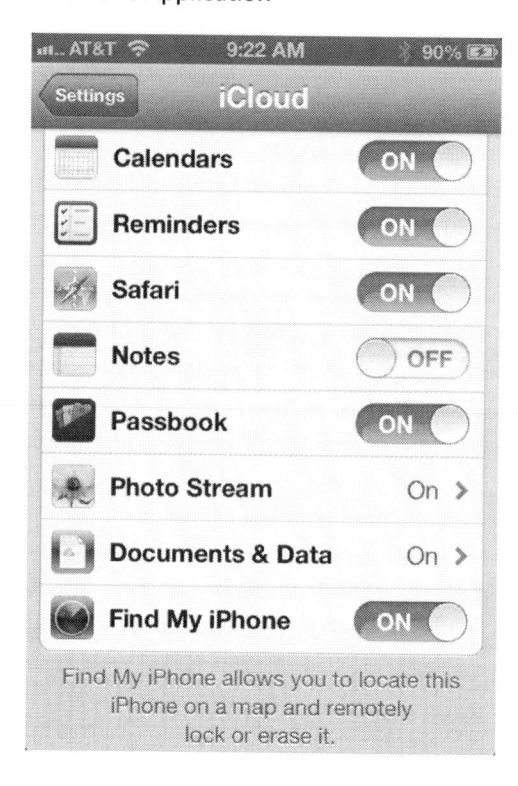

Figure 36-1

36.8 Running the iCloud Application

Test the iCloudStore app by connecting a suitably provisioned device to the development Mac OS X system, selecting it from the Xcode target menu and clicking on the *Run* button. Enter text into the text view and touch the *Save* button. In the Xcode toolbar click on *Stop* to exit the application followed by *Run* to re-launch the application. On the second launch the previously entered text will be read from the document in the cloud and displayed in the text view object.

36.9 Reviewing and Deleting iCloud Based Documents

The files currently stored in a user's iCloud account may be reviewed or deleted from the iPhone Settings app. To review the currently stored documents select the *iCloud* option from the main screen of the *Settings* app. On the *iCloud* screen, scroll to the bottom and select the *Storage & Backup* option. On the resulting screen, select *Manage Storage* followed by the name of the application for which stored documents are to be listed. A list of documents stored using iCloud for the selected application will then appear including the current file size:

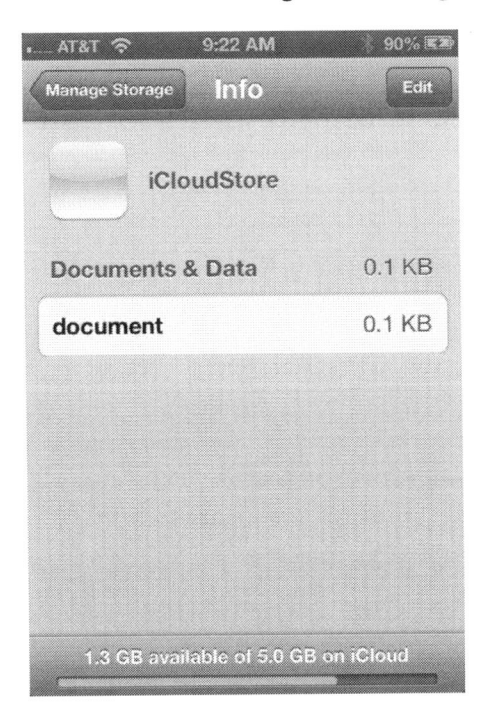

Figure 36-2

To delete the document, select the *Edit* button located in the toolbar. All listed documents may be deleted using the *Delete All* button, or deleted individually.

36.10 Making a Local File Ubiquitous

In addition to writing a file directly to iCloud storage as illustrated in this example application, it is also possible to transfer a pre-existing local file to iCloud storage, thereby making it ubiquitous. This can be achieved using the *setUbiquitous* method of the NSFileManager class. Assuming that *documentURL* references the path to the local copy of the file, and *ubiquityURL* the iCloud destination, a local file can be made ubiquitous using the following code:

```
NSFileManager *filemgr = [NSFileManager defaultManager];
NSError *error = nil;

if ([filemgr setUbiquitous:YES itemAtURL:_documentURL
     destinationURL:_ubiquityURL error:&error] == YES)
{
     NSLog(@"setUbiquitous OK");
}
else
     NSLog(@"setUbiquitous Failed error = %@", error);
```

36.11 Summary

The objective of this chapter was to work through the process of developing an application that stores a document using the iCloud service. Both techniques of directly creating a file in the iCloud storage, and making an existing locally created file ubiquitous were covered. In addition, some important guidelines that should be observed when using iCloud were outlined.

Chapter 37

37. Synchronizing iPhone iOS 6 Key-Value Data using iCloud

When considering the use of iCloud in an application it is important to note that the Apple ecosystem is not limited to the iPhone platform. In fact, it also encompasses the iPad and a range of Mac OS X based laptop and desktop computer systems, all of which have access to iCloud services. This increases the chance that a user will have the same app in one form or another on a number of different devices and platforms. Take, for the sake of an example, a hypothetical news magazine application. A user may have an instance of this application installed on both an iPhone and an iPad. If the user begins reading an article on the iPhone instance of the application and then switches to the same app on iPad at a later time, the iPad application should take the user to the position reached in the article on the iPhone so that the user can resume reading.

This kind of synchronization between applications is provided by the Key-Value data storage feature of iCloud. The goal of this chapter is to provide an overview of this service and work through a very simple example of the feature in action in an iPhone iOS 6 application.

37.1 An Overview of iCloud Key-Value Data Storage

The primary purpose of iCloud Key-Value data storage is to allow small amounts of data to be shared between instances of applications running on different devices, or even different applications on the same device. The data may be synchronized as long as it is encapsulated in either an NSString, NSDate, NSArray, NSData, Boolean, NSDictionary or NSNumber object.

iCloud data synchronization is achieved using the NSUbiquitousKeyValueStore class introduced as part of the iOS 5 SDK. Values are saved with a corresponding key using the setter method corresponding to the data type, the format for which is set*<datatype>:* where *<datatype>* is replaced by the type of data to be stored (e.g. the *setString:* method is used to save an NSString value). For example, the following code fragment creates an instance of an NSUbiquitousKeyValueStore object and then saves a string value using the key "MyString":

```
NSUbiquitousKeyValueStore *keyStore =
    [[NSUbiquitousKeyValueStore alloc] init];
[keyStore setString:@"Saved String" forKey:@"MyString"];
```

Synchronizing iPhone iOS 6 Key-Value Data using iCloud

Once key-value pairs have been saved locally they will not be synchronized with iCloud storage until a call is made to the *synchronize* method of the NSUbiquitousKeyValueStore method:

```
[keyStore synchronize];
```

It is important to note that a call to the synchronize method does not result in an immediate synchronization of the locally saved data with the iCloud store. iOS will, instead, perform the synchronization at what the Apple documentation refers to as "an appropriate later time".

A stored value may be retrieved by a call to the appropriate method corresponding to the data type to be retrieved (the format of which is *<datatype>*forKey:) and passing through the key as an argument. For example, the stored string in the above example may be retrieved as follows:

```
NSString *storedString = [keyStore stringForKey:@"MyString"];
```

37.2 Sharing Data Between Applications

As with iCloud document storage, key-value data storage requires the implementation of appropriate iCloud entitlements. In this case the application must have the *com.apple.developer.ubiquity-kvstore-identifier* entitlement key configured in the project's entitlements file. The value assigned to this key is used to identify which applications are able to share access to the same iCloud stored key-value data.

If, for example, the *ubiquity-kvstore-identifier* entitlement key for an application named *MyApp* is assigned a value of *ABCDE12345.com.mycompany.MyApp* (where ABCDEF12345 is developer's unique team or individual ID) then any other applications using the same entitlement value will also be able to access the same stored key-value data. This, by definition, will be any instance of the *MyApp* running on multiple devices, but applies equally to entirely different applications (for example *MyOtherApp*) if they also use the same entitlement value.

37.3 Data Storage Restrictions

iCloud key-value data storage is provided to meet the narrow requirement of performing essential synchronization between application instances, and the data storage limitations imposed by Apple clearly reflect this.

The amount of data that can be stored per key-value pair is 64Kb. The per-application key-value storage limit is 256 individual keys which, combined, must also not exceed 64Kb in total.

37.4 Conflict Resolution

In the event that two application instances make changes to the same key-value pair, the most recent change is given precedence.

37.5 Receiving Notification of Key-Value Changes

An application may register to be notified when stored values are changed by another application instance. This is achieved by setting up an observer on the *NSUbiquitousKeyValue-StoreDidChangeExternallyNotification* notification. This notification is triggered when a change is made to any key-value pair in a specified key value store and is passed an array of strings containing the keys that were changed together with an NSNumber indicating the reason for the change. In the event that the available space for the key-value storage has been exceeded this number will match the *NSUbiquitousKeyValueStoreQuotaViolationChange* constant value.

37.6 An iCloud Key-Value Data Storage Example

The remainder of this chapter is devoted to the creation of an application that uses iCloud key-value storage to store a key with a string value using iCloud. In addition to storing a key-value pair, the application will also configure an observer to receive notification when the value is changed by another application instance.

Begin the application creation process by launching Xcode and creating a new *Single View Application* project with the name and class prefix of *iCloudKeys* with Storyboard support and Automatic Reference Counting enabled.

37.7 Enabling the Application for iCloud Key Value Data Storage

A mandatory step in the development of the application is to configure the appropriate iCloud entitlement. This is achieved by selecting the application target at the top of the Xcode project navigator panel and selecting the *Summary* tab in the main panel. Scroll down the summary information until the entitlements section comes into view and turn on the *Entitlements*, *Enable iCloud* and *Key-Value Store* options:

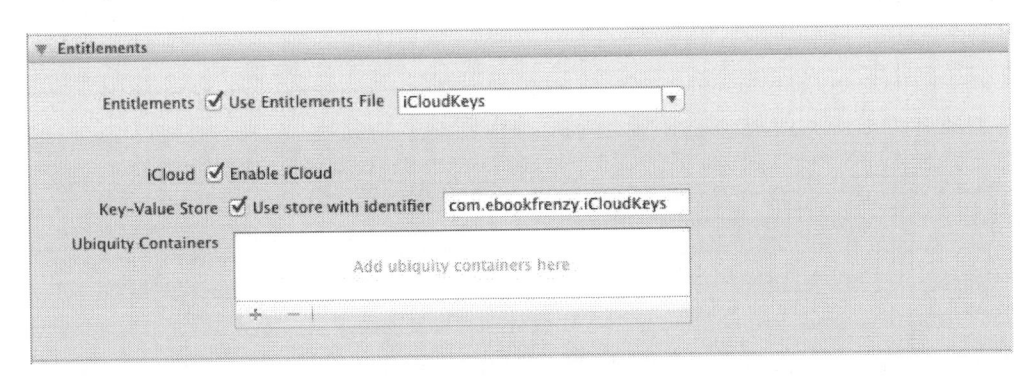

Figure 37-1

Once selected, Xcode will create an entitlements file for the project named *iCloudKeys.entitlements* containing the appropriate iCloud entitlements key-value pairs. Select the entitlements file from the

Synchronizing iPhone iOS 6 Key-Value Data using iCloud

project navigator and note the value assigned to the *ubiquity-kvstore-identity* key. By default this is typically comprised of your team or individual developer ID combined with the application's Bundle identifier. Any other applications that use the same value for the entitlement key will share access to the same iCloud based key-value data stored by this application.

37.8 Designing the User Interface

The application is going to consist of a text field into which a string may be entered by the user and a button which, when selected, will save the string to the application's iCloud key-value data store. Select the *MainStoryboard.storyboard* file, display the object library (*View -> Utilities -> Show Object Library*) and drag and drop the two objects into the view canvas. Double click on the button object and change the text to *Store Key*. The completed view should resemble Figure 37-2:

Figure 37-2

Select the text field object in the view canvas, display the Assistant Editor panel and verify that the editor is displaying the contents of the *iCloudKeysViewController.h* file. Ctrl-click on the text field object and drag to a position just below the @interface line in the Assistant Editor. Release the line and in the resulting connection dialog establish an outlet connection named *textField*.

Finally, Ctrl-click on the button object and drag the line to the area immediately beneath the newly created outlet in the Assistant Editor panel. Release the line and, within the resulting connection

37.9 Implementing the View Controller

In addition to the action and outlet references created above, an instance of the *NSUbiquitousKeyStore* class will be needed. Choose the *iCloudKeysViewController.h* file, therefore, and modify it as follows:

```
#import <UIKit/UIKit.h>

@interface iCloudKeysViewController : UIViewController
@property (strong, nonatomic) NSUbiquitousKeyValueStore *keyStore;
@property (strong, nonatomic) IBOutlet UITextField *textField;
- (IBAction)saveKey:(id)sender;
@end
```

37.10 Modifying the viewDidLoad Method

The next step is to modify the *viewDidLoad* method of the view controller. Select the *iCloudKeysViewController.m* implementation file, locate the *viewDidLoad* method and modify it so that it reads as follows:

```
#import "iCloudKeysViewController.h"

@interface iCloudKeysViewController ()

@end

@implementation iCloudKeysViewController

- (void)viewDidLoad
{
    [super viewDidLoad];

    _keyStore = [[NSUbiquitousKeyValueStore alloc] init];

    NSString *storedString = [_keyStore stringForKey:@"MyString"];

    if (storedString != nil){
        _textField.text = storedString;
    }

    [[NSNotificationCenter defaultCenter] addObserver:self
```

```
            selector: @selector(ubiquitousKeyValueStoreDidChange:)
            name:
NSUbiquitousKeyValueStoreDidChangeExternallyNotification
            object:_keyStore];
}
```

The method begins by allocating and initializing an instance of the NSUbiquitousKeyValueStore class and assigning it to the keyStore variable previously declared in the *iCloudKeysViewController.h* file. Next, the *stringForKey* method of the keyStore object is called to check if the *MyString* key is already in the key-value store. If the key exists, the string value is assigned to the *text* property of the text field object via the textField outlet.

Finally, the method sets up an observer to call the *ubiquitousKeyValueStoreDidChange:* method when the stored key value is changed by another application instance.

Having implemented the code in the *viewDidLoad* method the next step is to write the *ubiquitousKeyValueStoreDidChange:* method.

37.11 Implementing the Notification Method

Within the context of this example application the *ubiquitousKeyValueStoreDidChange:* method, which is triggered when another application instance modifies an iCloud stored key-value pair, is provided to notify the user of the change via an alert message and to update the text in the text field with the new string value. The code for this method, which needs to be added to the *iCloudKeysViewController.m* file is as follows:

```
-(void) ubiquitousKeyValueStoreDidChange: (NSNotification *)notification
{
    UIAlertView *alert = [[UIAlertView alloc]
                initWithTitle:@"Change detected"
                message:@"iCloud key-value store change detected"
                delegate:nil
                cancelButtonTitle:@"Ok"
                otherButtonTitles:nil, nil];
    [alert show];
    _textField.text = [_keyStore stringForKey:@"MyString"];
}
```

37.12 Implementing the saveData Method

The final coding task involves implementation of the *saveData:* action method. This method will be called when the user touches the button in the user interface and needs to be implemented in the *iCloudKeysViewController.m* file:

```
- (IBAction)saveKey:(id)sender {
    [_keyStore setString:_textField.text forKey:@"MyString"];
    [_keyStore synchronize];
}
```

The code for this method is quite simple. The *setString* method of the keyStore object is called, assigning the current text property of the user interface textField object to the "MyString" key. The synchronize method of the keyStore object is then called to ensure that the key-value pair is synchronized with the iCloud store.

37.13 **Testing the Application**

In order to adequately test the application it must first be installed on a physical device since iCloud functionality cannot be tested using the iOS Simulator. For details on installing applications on a device refer to the chapter entitled *Testing iOS 6 Apps on the iPhone – Developer Certificates and Provisioning Profiles*. Once the application is installed and running on the device, enter some text into the text field and touch the *Store Key* button. Stop the application from running by clicking on the *Stop* button in the Xcode toolbar then re-launch by clicking *Run*. When the application reloads, the text field should be primed with the saved value string.

In order to test the change notification functionality, install the application on a second device, and with the application running on both devices change the string on one device and save the key. After a short delay the second device will detect the change, display the alert and update the text field to the new value.

In the absence of a second device, simply create an identical second application with a different name but the same entitlement key value and install it on the same device. Launch the first application and leave it running the in background on the device. Launch the second application, change the value in the text field and click the *Store Key* button. Return the first application to the foreground and wait for the alert to appear:

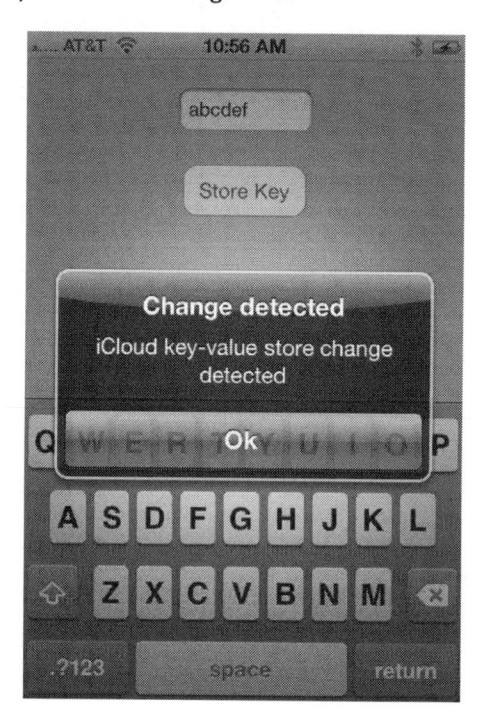

Synchronizing iPhone iOS 6 Key-Value Data using iCloud

Figure 37-3

Chapter 38

38. iOS 6 iPhone Data Persistence using Archiving

In the previous chapters of this book we have looked at some basic file and directory handling operations which can be performed within an iOS 6 iPhone application. In the chapter entitled *Working with iPhone Files on iOS 6* we looked at creating files and reading and writing data from within an iOS application before looking at iCloud based storage in subsequent chapters. In this chapter we will look at another form of data persistence on the iPhone using a more object oriented approach known as *archiving*.

38.1 An Overview of Archiving

iPhone iOS applications are inherently object oriented in so much as they are developed using Objective-C and consist of any number of objects designed to work together to provide the required functionality. As such, it is highly likely that any data created or used within an application will be held in memory encapsulated in an object. It is also equally likely that the data encapsulated in an object may need to be saved to the iPhone's file system so that it can be restored on future invocations of the application. One approach might be to write code that extracts each data element from an object and writes it to a file. Similarly, code would need to be written to read the data from the file, create an instance of the original object and then assign the data to that object accordingly. Whilst this can be achieved, it can quickly become complex and time consuming to implement.

An alternative is to use a mechanism called *archiving*. Archiving involves encoding objects into a format that is written to a file. Data may subsequently be decoded (or *unarchived*) and used to automatically rebuild the object. This concept is somewhat analogous to *serialization* as supported by languages such as Java.

A number of approaches to archiving are supported by the Foundation Framework. Arguably the most flexible option is that provided by the NSKeyedArchiver class. This class provides the ability to encode an object into the form of a *binary property list* that is written to file and may subsequently be decoded to recreate the object using the NSKeyedUnarchiver class.

An alternative option is to use the *writeToFile:anatomically* method available with a subset Foundation class. This mechanism writes the object data to file in the form of an *XML property list* file. This approach, however, is limited to NSArray, NSData, NSDate, NSDictionary, NSNumber and NSString based objects.

In the remainder of this chapter we will work through an example of archiving using the NSKeyedArchiver and NSKeyedUnarchiver classes.

38.2 The Archiving Example Application

The end product of this chapter is an application that prompts the user for a name, address and phone number. Once this data has been entered, pressing a button causes the contact data to be stored in an array object which is then archived to a binary property file. On a subsequent reload of the application this data is unarchived and used to recreate the array object. The restored data is then extracted from the array object and presented to the user.

Begin by launching Xcode and create a new iOS iPhone project named *Archive* using the *Single View Application* template with Storyboard support and Automatic Reference Counting enabled. Once the main Xcode project window appears populated with the template files, it is time to start developing the application.

38.3 Designing the User Interface

The user interface for our application is going to consist of three UILabels, three UITextFields and single UIButton. Select *MainStoryboard.storyboard* in the main Xcode project navigator and display the Object library panel (*View -> Utilities -> Show Object Library*) if it is not already visible. Drag, drop, resize, position and configure objects on the View window canvas until your design approximates that illustrated in Figure 38-1:

iOS 6 iPhone Data Persistence using Archiving

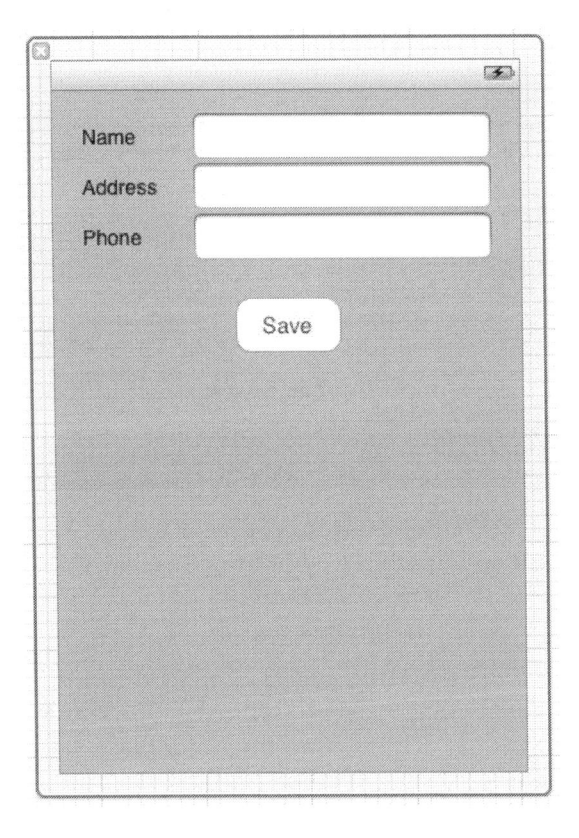

Figure 38-1

The next step is to establish the connections to our action and outlets.

Select the top most text field object in the view canvas, display the Assistant Editor panel and verify that the editor is displaying the contents of the *ArchiveViewController.h* file. Ctrl-click on the text field object again and drag to a position just below the @interface line in the Assistant Editor. Release the line and in the resulting connection dialog establish an outlet connection named *name*.

Repeat the above steps to establish outlet connections for the remaining text fields to properties named *address* and *phone* respectively.

Ctrl-click on the button object and drag the line to the area immediately beneath the newly created outlets in the Assistant Editor panel. Release the line and, within the resulting connection dialog, establish an Action method on the *Touch Up Inside* event configured to call a method named *saveData*.

Select the *ArchiveViewController.h* file and add an additional NSString property to store a reference to the path to the archive data file:

```
#import <UIKit/UIKit.h>
```

301

iOS 6 iPhone Data Persistence using Archiving

```
@interface ArchiveViewController : UIViewController

@property (strong, nonatomic) IBOutlet UITextField *name;
@property (strong, nonatomic) IBOutlet UITextField *address;
@property (strong, nonatomic) IBOutlet UITextField *phone;
@property (strong, nonatomic) NSString *dataFilePath;
- (IBAction) saveData;
@end
```

38.4 Checking for the Existence of the Archive File on Startup

Each time the application is launched by the user, the code will need to identify whether the archive data file exists from a previous session. In the event that it does exist, the application will need to read the contents to recreate the original array object from which the archive was created. Using this newly recreated array object, the array elements will then be extracted and used to populate the name, address and phone text fields.

The traditional location for placing such initialization code is in the *viewDidLoad* method of the view controller class. Within the project window, therefore, select the *ArchiveViewController.m* file and scroll down the contents of this file until you reach the *viewDidLoad* method. Having located the method, modify it as outlined in the following code fragment:

```
- (void)viewDidLoad {
    [super viewDidLoad];
    NSFileManager *filemgr;
    NSString *docsDir;
    NSArray *dirPaths;

    filemgr = [NSFileManager defaultManager];

    // Get the documents directory
    dirPaths = NSSearchPathForDirectoriesInDomains(
        NSDocumentDirectory, NSUserDomainMask, YES);

    docsDir = dirPaths[0];

    // Build the path to the data file
    _dataFilePath = [[NSString alloc] initWithString: [docsDir
            stringByAppendingPathComponent: @"data.archive"]];

    // Check if the file already exists
    if ([filemgr fileExistsAtPath: _dataFilePath])
    {
```

```
        NSMutableArray *dataArray;

        dataArray = [NSKeyedUnarchiver
         unarchiveObjectWithFile: _dataFilePath];

        _name.text = dataArray[0];
        _address.text = dataArray[1];
        _phone.text = dataArray[2];
    }
}
```

Within this method a number of variables are declared before creating an instance of the NSFileManager class.

A call is then made to the *NSSearchPathForDirectoriesInDomains* function and the path to the application's *Documents* directory extracted from the returned array object. This path is then used to construct the full pathname of the archive data file, which in turn is stored in the *dataFilePath* instance variable we previously added to the view controller class interface file.

Having identified the path to the archive data file, the file manager object is used to check for the existence of the file. If it exists, the file is "unarchived" into a new array object using the *unarchiveObjectWithFile* method of the NSKeyedUnarchiver class. The data is then extracted from the array and displayed in the corresponding text fields.

With this code implemented, select the *Run* toolbar button to compile and execute the application in the simulator. Assuming no problems are encountered, the next step is to implement the action method. If problems are encountered, check the details reported by Xcode and correct any syntax errors that may have been introduced into the code. Once the app has launched successfully, exit from the iOS Simulator and return to the main Xcode project window.

38.5 Archiving Object Data in the Action Method

The *Save* button in the user interface design is connected to the *saveData* method of the view controller class. Edit the *ArchiveViewController.m* file and modify the template action method as follows:

```
- (void) saveData: (id) sender
{
    NSMutableArray *contactArray;

    contactArray = [[NSMutableArray alloc] init];
    [contactArray addObject: _name.text];
    [contactArray addObject: _address.text];
```

```
            [contactArray addObject:_phone.text];
            [NSKeyedArchiver archiveRootObject:
                contactArray toFile:_dataFilePath];
}
```

When triggered, this method creates a new array and assigns the content of each text field to an element of that array. The array object is then archived to the predetermined data file using the *archiveRootObject* method of the NSKeyedArchiver class. The instance data of the array object is now saved to the archive ready to be loaded next time the application is executed.

38.6 Testing the Application

Save the code changes and build and run the application in the simulator environment. Enter a name, address and phone number into the respective text fields and press the save button. Stop the application by clicking the *Stop* button located in the Xcode toolbar and then relaunch the application by clicking *Run*. The application should re-appear with the text fields primed with the contact information saved during the previous session:

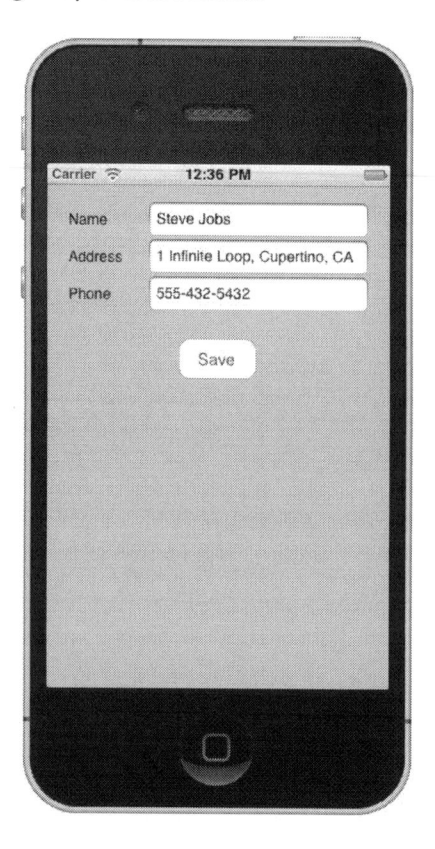

Figure 38-2

38.7 Summary

Whilst data can be written to files on the iPhone using a variety of mechanisms, archiving provides the ability to save the instance data of an object to file at a particular point and then restore the object to that state at any time in the future. This provides an object-oriented approach to data persistence on iOS iPhone based applications.

Chapter 39

39. iOS 6 iPhone Database Implementation using SQLite

Whilst the preceding chapters of this book have looked at data storage within the context of iOS 6 iPhone based applications, this coverage has been limited to using basic file and directory handling and object archiving. In many instances, by far the most effective data storage and retrieval strategy requires the use of some form of database management system.

In order to address this need, the iOS 6 SDK includes everything necessary to integrate SQLite based databases into iPhone applications. The goal of this chapter, therefore, is to provide an overview of how to use SQLite to perform basic database operations within your iPhone application. Once the basics have been covered, the next chapter (entitled *An Example SQLite based iOS 6 iPhone Application*) will work through the creation of an actual application that uses a SQLite database to store and retrieve data.

39.1 What is SQLite?

SQLite is an embedded, relational database management system (RDBMS). Most relational databases (Oracle and MySQL being prime examples) are standalone server processes that run independently, and in cooperation with, applications that require database access. SQLite is referred to as *embedded* because it is provided in the form of a library that is linked into applications. As such, there is no standalone database server running in the background. All database operations are handled internally within the application through calls to functions contained in the SQLite library.

The developers of SQLite have placed the technology into the public domain with the result that it is now a widely deployed database solution.

SQLite is written in the C programming language and therefore using SQLite on the iPhone involves direct calls to C functions and access to C data structures. In order to bridge the differences between Objective-C and the C based SQLite library it will be necessary, for example, to convert any NSString objects to UTF8 format before passing them through as arguments to these functions.

For additional information about SQLite refer to *http://www.sqlite.org*.

39.2 Structured Query Language (SQL)

Data is accessed in SQLite databases using a high level language known as Structured Query Language. This is usually abbreviated to SQL and pronounced *sequel*. SQL is a standard language used by most relational database management systems. SQLite conforms mostly to the SQL-92 standard.

Whilst some basic SQL statements will be used within this chapter, a detailed overview of SQL is beyond the scope of this book. There are, however, many other resources that provide a far better overview of SQL than we could ever hope to provide in a single chapter here.

39.3 Trying SQLite on MacOS X

For readers unfamiliar with databases in general and SQLite in particular, diving right into creating an iPhone application that uses SQLite may seem a little intimidating. Fortunately, MacOS X is shipped with SQLite pre-installed, including an interactive environment for issuing SQL commands from within a Terminal window. This is both a useful way to learn about SQLite and SQL, and also an invaluable tool for identifying problems with databases created by applications in the iOS simulator.

To launch an interactive SQLite session, open a Terminal window on your Mac OS X system, change directory to a suitable location and run the following command:

```
sqlite3 ./mydatbase.db
```

```
SQLite version 3.6.12
Enter ".help" for instructions
Enter SQL statements terminated with a ";"
sqlite>
```

At the *sqlite>* prompt, commands may be entered to perform tasks such as creating tables and inserting and retrieving data. For example, to create a new table in our database with fields to hold ID, name, address and phone number fields the following statement is required:

```
create table contacts (id integer primary key autoincrement, name text, address text, phone text);
```

Note that each row in a table must have a *primary key* that is unique to that row. In the above example we have designated the ID field as the primary key, declared it as being of type *integer* and asked SQLite to automatically increment the number each time a row is added. This is a common way to make sure that each row has a unique primary key. The remaining fields are each declared as being of type *text*.

To list the tables in the currently selected database use the *.tables* statement:

```
sqlite> .tables
```

contacts

To insert records into the table:

```
sqlite> insert into contacts (name, address, phone) values ("Bill
Smith", "123 Main Street, California", "123-555-2323");
sqlite> insert into contacts (name, address, phone) values ("Mike
Parks", "10 Upping Street, Idaho", "444-444-1212");
```

To retrieve all rows from a table:

```
sqlite> select * from contacts;
1|Bill Smith|123 Main Street, California|123-555-2323
2|Mike Parks|10 Upping Street, Idaho|444-444-1212
```

To extract a row that meets specific criteria:

```
sqlite> select * from contacts where name="Mike Parks";
2|Mike Parks|10 Upping Street, Idaho|444-444-1212
```

To exit from the sqlite3 interactive environment:

```
sqlite> .exit
```

When running an iPhone application in the iOS Simulator environment, any database files will be created on the file system of the computer on which the simulator is running. This has the advantage that you can navigate to the location of the database file, load it into the sqlite3 interactive tool and perform tasks on the data to identify possible problems occurring in the application code. If, for example, an application creates a database file named *contacts.db* in its documents directory, the file will be located on the host system in the following folder:

```
/Users/<user>/Library/Application Support/iPhone Simulator/<sdk
version>/Applications/<id>/Documents
```

Where *<user>* is the login name of the user running the iOS Simulator session, *<sdk version>* is the version of the iOS SDK used to build the application and *<id>* is the unique ID of the application.

39.4 Preparing an iPhone Application Project for SQLite Integration

By default, the Xcode environment does not assume that you will be including SQLite in your application. When developing SQLite based applications a few additional steps are required to ensure the code will compile when the application is built. Firstly, the project needs to be configured to include the *libsqlite3.dylib* dynamic library during the link phase of the build process. To achieve this select the target entry in the Xcode project navigator (the top entry with the product name) to display the summary information. Select the *Build Phases* tab to display the build information:

iOS 6 iPhone Database Implementation using SQLite

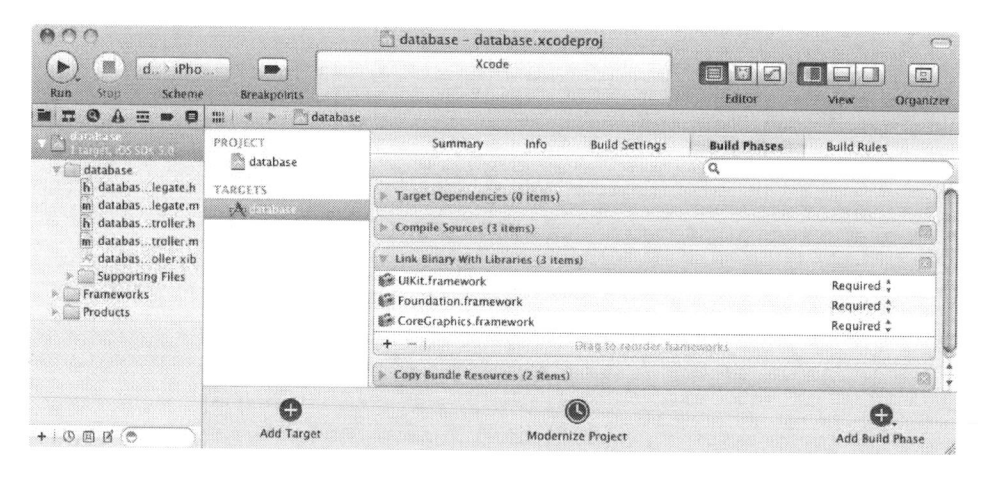

Figure 39-1

The *Link Binary with Libraries* section lists the libraries and frameworks already included in the project. To add another library or framework click on the '+' button to display the full list. From this list, select the required item (in this case *libsqlite3.dylib*) and click *Add*.

Secondly, the sqlite3.h include file must be imported into any files where references are made to SQLite definitions, declarations or functions. This file may be imported when needed as follows:

```
#import <sqlite3.h>
```

39.5 Key SQLite Functions

When implementing a database using SQLite it will be necessary to utilize a number of C functions contained within the *libsqlite3.dylib* library. A summary of the most commonly used functions is as follows:

- **sqlite3_open()** - Opens specified database file. If the database file does not already exist, it is created.
- **sqlite3_close()** - Closes a previously opened database file.
- **sqlite3_prepare_v2()** - Prepares a SQL statement ready for execution.
- **sqlite3_step()** - Executes a SQL statement previously prepared by the sqlite3_prepare_v2() function.
- **sqlite3_column_<type>()** - Returns a data field from the results of a SQL retrieval operation where *<type>* is replaced by the data type of the data to be extracted (text, blob, bytes, int, int16 etc).
- **sqlite3_finalize()** - Deletes a previously prepared SQL statement from memory.
- **sqlite3_exec()** - Combines the functionality of sqlite3_prepare_v2(), sqlite3_step() and sqlite3_finalize() into a single function call.

This, of course, represents only a small subset of the complete range of functions available with SQLite. A full list can be found at *http://www.sqlite.org/c3ref/funclist.html*.

39.6 Declaring a SQLite Database

Before any tasks can be performed on a database, it must first be declared. To do so it is necessary to declare a variable that points to an instance of a structure of type *sqlite3* (the *sqlite3* structure is defined in the *sqlite3.h* include file). For example:

```
sqlite3 *contactDB; //Declare a pointer to sqlite database structure
```

39.7 Opening or Creating a Database

Once declared, a database file may be opened using the *sqlite3_open()* function. If the specified database file does not already exist it is first created before being opened. The syntax for this function is as follows:

```
int sqlite3_open(const char *filename, sqlite3 **database);
```

In the above syntax, *filename* is the path to the database file in the form of a UTF-8 character string and *database* is the reference to the database structure. The result of the operation is returned as an int value. Various definitions for result values are defined in the include file such as SQLITE_OK for a successful operation.

For example, the code to open a database file named *contacts.db* in the Documents directory of an iPhone application might read as follows. Note that the code assumes an NSString variable named *databasePath* contains the path to the database file:

```
sqlite3 *contactDB; //Declare a pointer to sqlite database structure

const char *dbpath = [databasePath UTF8String]; // Convert NSString to UTF-8

if (sqlite3_open(dbpath, &contactDB) == SQLITE_OK)
{
        //Database opened successfully
} else {
        //Failed to open database
}
```

The key point to note in the above example is that the string contained in the NSString object was converted to a UTF-8 string before being passed to the function to open the database. This is a common activity that you will see performed frequently when working with SQLite in Objective-C.

311

39.8 Preparing and Executing a SQL Statement

SQL statements are prepared and stored in a structure of type *sqlite3_stmt* using the *sqlite3_prepare_v2()* function. For example:

```
sqlite3_stmt *statement;

NSString *querySQL = @"SELECT address, phone FROM contacts";

const char *query_stmt = [querySQL UTF8String];

if (sqlite3_prepare_v2(contactDB, query_stmt, -1,
        &statement, NULL) == SQLITE_OK)
{
        //Statement prepared successfully
} else {
        //Statement preparation failed
}
```

A prepared SQL statement may subsequently be executed using a call to the *sqlite3_step()* function, passing through the *sqlite3_stmt* variable as the sole argument:

```
sqlite3_step(statement);
sqlite3_finalize(statement);
```

Note that the *sqlite3_step()* function also returns a result value. The value returned, however, will depend on the nature of the statement being executed. For example, a successful insertion of data into a database table will return a SQLITE_OK result, whilst the successful retrieval of data will return SQLITE_ROW.

Alternatively, the same results may be achieved with a single call to the *sqlite3_exec()* function as illustrated in the following section.

39.9 Creating a Database Table

Database data is organized into *tables*. Before data can be stored into a database, therefore, a table must first be created. This is achieved using the SQL CREATE TABLE statement. The following code example illustrates the creation of a table named *contacts,* the preparation and execution of which is performed using the *sqlite3_exec()* function:

```
const char *sql_stmt = "CREATE TABLE IF NOT EXISTS CONTACTS (ID INTEGER PRIMARY KEY AUTOINCREMENT, NAME TEXT, ADDRESS TEXT, PHONE TEXT)";
```

```
if (sqlite3_exec(contactDB, sql_stmt, NULL, NULL, &errMsg) ==
SQLITE_OK)
{
           // SQL statement execution succeeded
}
```

39.10 Extracting Data from a Database Table

Those familiar with SQL will be aware that data is retrieved from databases using the SELECT statement. Depending on the criteria defined in the statement, it is typical for more than one data row to be returned. It is important, therefore, to learn how to retrieve data from a database using the SQLite C function calls.

As with previous examples, the SQL statement must first be prepared. In the following code excerpt, a SQL statement to extract the address and phone fields from all the rows of a database table named *contacts* is prepared:

```
sqlite3_stmt      *statement;

NSString *querySQL = @"SELECT address, phone FROM contacts";

const char *query_stmt = [querySQL UTF8String];

sqlite3_prepare_v2(contactDB, query_stmt, -1, &statement, NULL);
```

The statement subsequently needs to be executed. If a row of data matching the selection criteria is found in the database table, the *sqlite3_step()* function returns a SQLITE_ROW result. The data for the matching row is stored in the *sqlite3_stmt* structure and may be extracted using the *sqlite3_column_<type>()* function call, where *<type>* is replaced by the type of data being extracted from the corresponding field of data. Through the implementation of a while loop, the *sqlite3_step()* function can be called repeatedly to cycle through multiple matching rows of data until all the matches have been extracted. Note that the *sqlite_column_<type>()* function takes as its second argument the number of the column to be extracted. In the case of our example, column 0 contains the address and column 1 the phone number:

```
while (sqlite3_step(statement) == SQLITE_ROW)
{
        NSString *addressField =
               [[NSString alloc] initWithUTF8String:
                 (const char *) sqlite3_column_text(statement, 0)];

        NSString *phoneField =
               [[NSString alloc] initWithUTF8String:
```

```
                    (const char *) sqlite3_column_text(statement, 1)];

        // Code to do something with extracted data here

}
sqlite3_finalize(statement);
```

39.11 Closing a SQLite Database

When an application has finished working on a database it is important that the database be closed. This is achieved with a call to the *sqlite3_close()* function, passing through a pointer to the database to be closed:

```
sqlite3_close(contactDB);
```

39.12 Summary

In this chapter we have looked at the basics of implementing a database within an iPhone application using the embedded SQLite relational database management system. In the next chapter we will put this theory into practice and work through an example that creates a functional iPhone application that is designed to store data in a database.

Chapter 40

40. An Example SQLite based iOS 6 iPhone Application

In the chapter entitled *iOS 6 iPhone Database Implementation using SQLite* the basic concepts of integrating a SQLite based database into iOS 6 iPhone-based applications were discussed. In this chapter we will put this knowledge to use by creating a simple example application that demonstrates SQLite based database implementation and management on the iPhone.

40.1 About the Example SQLite iPhone Application

The focus of this chapter is the creation of a somewhat rudimentary iPhone iOS application that is designed to store contact information (names, addresses and telephone numbers) in a SQLite database. In addition to data storage, a feature will also be implemented to allow the user to search the database for the address and phone number of a specified contact name. Some knowledge of SQL and SQLite is assumed throughout the course of this tutorial. Those readers unfamiliar with these technologies in the context of iPhone application development are encouraged to first read the *previous chapter* before proceeding.

40.2 Creating and Preparing the SQLite Application Project

Begin by launching the Xcode environment and creating a new iOS iPhone *Single View Application* project with a name and class prefix of *Database* with Storyboard support and Automatic Reference Counting enabled.

Once the project has been created, the next step is to configure the project to include the SQLite dynamic library *(libsqlite3.dylib)* during the link phase of the build process. Failure to include this library will result in build errors.

To add this library, select the target entry in the Xcode project navigator (the top entry with the product name) to display the summary information panel. Select the *Build Phases* tab to display the build information. The *Link Binary with Libraries* section lists the libraries and frameworks already included in the project. To add another library or framework click on the '+' button to display the full list. From this list search for, and then select *libsqlite3.dylib* and click *Add*.

315

An Example SQLite based iOS 6 iPhone Application

40.3 Importing sqlite3.h and declaring the Database Reference

Before we can create a database we need to declare a variable pointer to a structure of type *sqlite3* that will act as the reference to our database. Since we will be working with the database in the view controller for our application the best place to declare this variable is in the *DatabaseViewController.h* file. Since we also need to import the *sqlite3.h* header file into any files where we make use of SQLite this is also an ideal place to include the file. Now is also a good time to declare an NSString property in which to store the path to the database. Within the main Xcode project navigator, select the *DatabaseViewController.h* file and modify it as follows:

```
#import <UIKit/UIKit.h>
#import <sqlite3.h>

@interface DatabaseViewController : UIViewController

@property (strong, nonatomic) NSString *databasePath;
@property (nonatomic) sqlite3 *contactDB;
@end
```

40.4 Designing the User Interface

The next step in developing our example SQLite iOS iPhone application involves the design of the user interface. Begin by selecting the *MainStoryboard.storyboard* file to edit the user interface and drag and drop components from the Object library (*View -> Utilities -> Object Library*) onto the view canvas and edit properties so that the layout appears as illustrated in Figure 40-1:

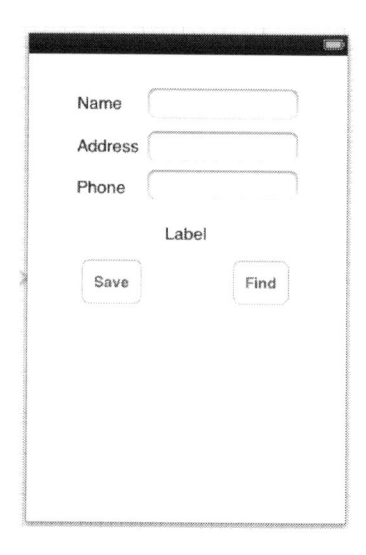

Figure 40-1

An Example SQLite based iOS 6 iPhone Application

Before proceeding, stretch the status label (located above the two buttons) so that it covers most of the width of the view. Finally, edit the label and remove the word "Label" so that it is blank.

Select the top most text field object in the view canvas, display the Assistant Editor panel and verify that the editor is displaying the contents of the *DatabaseViewController.h* file. Ctrl-click on the text field object again and drag to a position just below the @interface line in the Assistant Editor. Release the line and in the resulting connection dialog establish an outlet connection named *name*.

Repeat the above steps to establish outlet connections for the remaining text fields and the label object to properties named *address* and *phone* respectively and *status*.

Ctrl-click on the *Save* button object and drag the line to the area immediately beneath the newly created outlet in the Assistant Editor panel. Release the line and, within the resulting connection dialog, establish an Action method on the *Touch Up Inside* event configured to call a method named *saveData*. Repeat this step to create an action connection from the *Find* button to a method named *findContact*.

On completion of these steps, the *DatabaseViewController.h* file should read as follows:

```
#import <UIKit/UIKit.h>
#import <sqlite3.h>

@interface DatabaseViewController : UIViewController
@property (strong, nonatomic) IBOutlet UITextField *name;
@property (strong, nonatomic) IBOutlet UITextField *address;
@property (strong, nonatomic) IBOutlet UITextField *phone;
@property (strong, nonatomic) IBOutlet UILabel *status;

- (IBAction)saveData:(id)sender;
- (IBAction)findContact:(id)sender;

@property (strong, nonatomic) NSString *databasePath;
@property (nonatomic) sqlite3 *contactDB;
@end
```

40.5 Creating the Database and Table

When the application is launched it will need to check whether the database file already exists and, if not, create both the database file and a table within the database in which to store the contact information entered by the user. The code to perform this task can be placed in the *viewDidLoad* method of our view controller class. Select the *DatabaseViewController.m* file, scroll down to the *viewDidLoad* method and modify it as follows:

An Example SQLite based iOS 6 iPhone Application

```objc
- (void)viewDidLoad {
    [super viewDidLoad];
    NSString *docsDir;
    NSArray *dirPaths;

    // Get the documents directory
    dirPaths = NSSearchPathForDirectoriesInDomains(
        NSDocumentDirectory, NSUserDomainMask, YES);

    docsDir = dirPaths[0];

    // Build the path to the database file
    _databasePath = [[NSString alloc]
        initWithString: [docsDir stringByAppendingPathComponent:
        @"contacts.db"]];

    NSFileManager *filemgr = [NSFileManager defaultManager];

    if ([filemgr fileExistsAtPath: _databasePath ] == NO)
    {
        const char *dbpath = [_databasePath UTF8String];

        if (sqlite3_open(dbpath, &_contactDB) == SQLITE_OK)
        {
            char *errMsg;
            const char *sql_stmt =
            "CREATE TABLE IF NOT EXISTS CONTACTS (ID INTEGER PRIMARY KEY AUTOINCREMENT, NAME TEXT, ADDRESS TEXT, PHONE TEXT)";

            if (sqlite3_exec(_contactDB, sql_stmt, NULL, NULL, &errMsg) != SQLITE_OK)
            {
                _status.text = @"Failed to create table";
            }
            sqlite3_close(_contactDB);
        } else {
            _status.text = @"Failed to open/create database";
        }
    }
}
```

The code in the above method performs the following tasks:

318

- Identifies the application's Documents directory and constructs a path to the *contacts.db* database file.
- Creates an NSFileManager instance and subsequently uses it to detect if the database file already exists.
- If the file does not yet exist the code converts the path to a UTF-8 string and creates the database via a call to the SQLite *sqlite3_open()* function, passing through a reference to the *contactDB* variable declared previously in the interface file.
- Prepares a SQL statement to create the *contacts* table in the database.
- Reports the success or otherwise of the operation via the status label.
- Closes the database.

40.6 Implementing the Code to Save Data to the SQLite Database

The saving of contact data to the database is the responsibility of the *saveData* action method. This method will need to open the database file, extract the text from the three text fields and construct and execute a SQL INSERT statement to add this data as a record to the database. Having done this, the method will then need to close the database.

In addition, the code will need to clear the text fields ready for the next contact to be entered, and update the status label to reflect the success or failure of the operation.

In order to implement this behavior, therefore, we need to modify the template method created previously as follows:

```
- (void) saveData:(id)sender
{
    sqlite3_stmt    *statement;
    const char *dbpath = [_databasePath UTF8String];

    if (sqlite3_open(dbpath, &_contactDB) == SQLITE_OK)
    {

        NSString *insertSQL = [NSString stringWithFormat:
            @"INSERT INTO CONTACTS (name, address, phone) VALUES (\"%@\", \"%@\", \"%@\")",
            _name.text, _address.text, _phone.text];

        const char *insert_stmt = [insertSQL UTF8String];
        sqlite3_prepare_v2(_contactDB, insert_stmt,
            -1, &statement, NULL);
        if (sqlite3_step(statement) == SQLITE_DONE)
        {
```

```
                _status.text = @"Contact added";
                _name.text = @"";
                _address.text = @"";
                _phone.text = @"";
        } else {
                _status.text = @"Failed to add contact";
        }
        sqlite3_finalize(statement);
        sqlite3_close(_contactDB);
    }
}
```

The next step in our application development process is to implement the action for the find button.

40.7 Implementing Code to Extract Data from the SQLite Database

As previously indicated, the user will be able to extract the address and phone number for a contact by entering the name and touching the find button. To this end, the *Touch Up Inside* event of the find button has been connected to the *findContact* method, the code for which is outlined below:

```
- (void) findContact:(id)sender
{
    const char *dbpath = [_databasePath UTF8String];
    sqlite3_stmt    *statement;

    if (sqlite3_open(dbpath, &_contactDB) == SQLITE_OK)
    {
        NSString *querySQL = [NSString stringWithFormat:
            @"SELECT address, phone FROM contacts WHERE name=\"%@\"",
            _name.text];

        const char *query_stmt = [querySQL UTF8String];

        if (sqlite3_prepare_v2(_contactDB,
            query_stmt, -1, &statement, NULL) == SQLITE_OK)
        {
            if (sqlite3_step(statement) == SQLITE_ROW)
            {
                NSString *addressField = [[NSString alloc]
                    initWithUTF8String:
                    (const char *) sqlite3_column_text(
                        statement, 0)];
                _address.text = addressField;
```

```
                        NSString *phoneField = [[NSString alloc]
                            initWithUTF8String:(const char *)
                            sqlite3_column_text(statement, 1)];
                        _phone.text = phoneField;
                        _status.text = @"Match found";
                } else {
                        _status.text = @"Match not found";
                        _address.text = @"";
                        _phone.text = @"";
                }
                sqlite3_finalize(statement);
        }
        sqlite3_close(_contactDB);
    }
}
```

This code opens the database and constructs a SQL SELECT statement to extract any records in the database that match the name entered by the user into the name text field. The SQL statement is then executed. A return value of SQLITE_ROW indicates that at least one match has been located. In this case the first matching result data is extracted, assigned to NSString objects and displayed in the appropriate text fields. As an alternative, a while loop could have been constructed to display all matching results. For the purposes of keeping this example simple, however, we will display only the first match. The code then updates the status label to indicate whether a match was found and closes the database.

40.8 Building and Running the Application

The final step is to build and run the application. Click on the *Run* button located in the toolbar of the main Xcode project window. Assuming an absence of compilation errors, the application should load into the iOS Simulator environment. Enter details for a few contacts, pressing the *Save* button after each entry. Be sure to check the status label to ensure the data is being saved successfully. Finally, enter the name of one your contacts and click on the *Find* button. Assuming the name matches a previously entered record, the address and phone number for that contact should be displayed and the status label updated with the message "Match found":

An Example SQLite based iOS 6 iPhone Application

Figure 40-2

40.9 Summary

In this chapter we have looked at the basics of storing data on an iPhone using the SQLite database environment. For developers unfamiliar with SQL and reluctant to learn it, an alternative method for storing data in a database involves the use of the Core Data framework. This topic will be covered in detail in the next chapter entitled *Working with iOS 6 iPhone Databases using Core Data*.

Chapter 41

41. Working with iOS 6 iPhone Databases using Core Data

The preceding chapters covered the concepts of database storage using the SQLite database. In these chapters the assumption was made that the iPhone application code would directly manipulate the database using SQLite C API calls to construct and execute SQL statements. Whilst this is a perfectly good approach for working with SQLite in many cases, it does require knowledge of SQL and can lead to some complexity in terms of writing code and maintaining the database structure. This complexity is further compounded by the non-object-oriented nature of the SQLite C API functions. In recognition of these shortcomings, Apple introduced the *Core Data Framework*. Core Data is essentially a framework that places a wrapper around the SQLite database (and other storage environments) enabling the developer to work with data in terms of Objective-C objects without requiring any knowledge of the underlying database technology.

We will begin this chapter by defining some of the concepts that comprise the Core Data model before providing an overview of the steps involved in working with this framework. Once these topics have been covered, the next chapter will work through an *iOS 6 iPhone Core Data Tutorial*.

41.1 The Core Data Stack

Core Data consists of a number of framework objects that integrate to provide the data storage functionality. This stack can be visually represented as illustrated in Figure 41-1.

As we can see from Figure 41-1, the iOS iPhone based application sits on top of the stack and interacts with the managed data objects handled by the managed object context. Of particular significance in this diagram is the fact that although the lower levels in the stack perform a considerable amount of the work involved in providing Core Data functionality, the application code does not interact with them directly.

Working with iOS 6 iPhone Databases using Core Data

```
                    ┌─────────────────────────┐
                    │    iPhone Application   │
                    └─────────────────────────┘
           ┌──────────────────────────────────────┐
           │      Managed Object Context          │
           │         Managed Objects              │
           └──────────────────────────────────────┘
           ┌──────────────────────┐      ┌──────────────────────────┐
           │  Persistent Store    │ ───▶ │  Managed Object Model    │
           │    Coordinator       │      │   Entity Descriptions    │
           └──────────────────────┘      └──────────────────────────┘
           ┌──────────────────────┐
           │ Persistent Object Store │
           └──────────────────────┘
                    ↑    ↓
                ┌─────────┐
                │Data File│
                └─────────┘
```

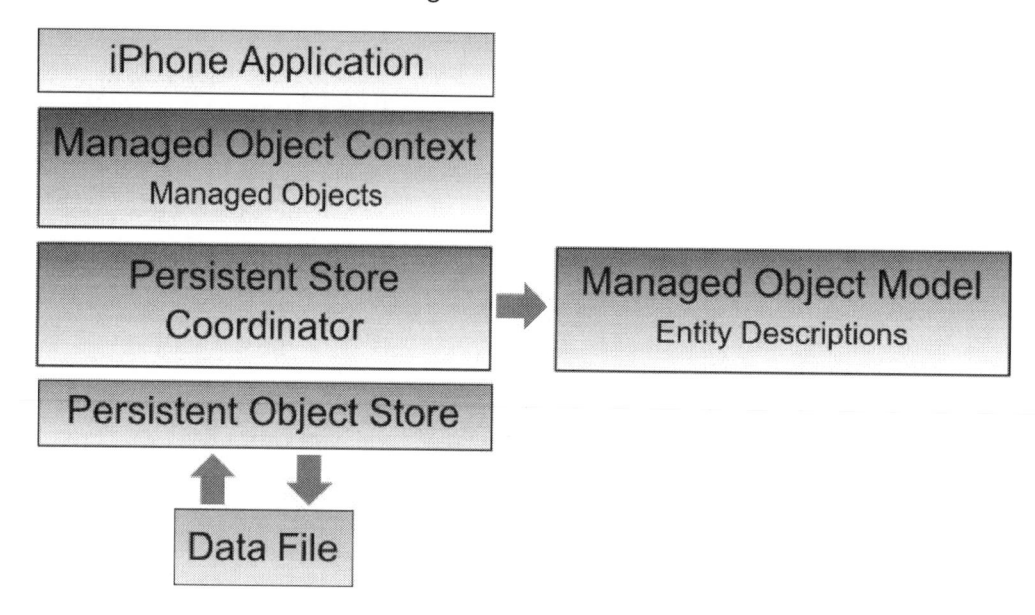

Figure 41-1

Before moving on to the more practical areas of working with Core Data it is important to spend some time explaining the elements that comprise the Core Data stack in a little more detail.

41.2 Managed Objects

Managed objects are the objects that are created by your application code to store data. A managed object may be thought of as a row or a record in a relational database table. For each new record to be added, a new managed object must be created to store the data. Similarly, retrieved data will be returned in the form of managed objects, one for each record matching the defined retrieval criteria. Managed objects are actually instances of the NSManagedObject class, or a subclass thereof. These objects are contained and maintained by the *managed object context*.

41.3 Managed Object Context

Core Data based applications never interact directly with the persistent store. Instead, the application code interacts with the managed objects contained in the managed object context layer of the Core Data stack. The context maintains the status of the objects in relation to the underlying data store and manages the relationships between managed objects defined by the *managed object model*. All interactions with the underlying database are held temporarily within the context until the context is instructed to save the changes, at which point the changes are passed down through the Core Data stack and written to the persistent store.

41.4 Managed Object Model

So far we have focused on the management of data objects but have not yet looked at how the data models are defined. This is the task of the *Managed Object Model* which defines a concept referred to as *entities*.

Much as a class description defines a blueprint for an object instance, entities define the data model for managed objects. In essence, an entity is analogous to the schema that defines a table in a relational database. As such, each entity has a set of attributes associated with it that define the data to be stored in managed objects derived from that entity. For example, a *Contacts* entity might contain *name*, *address* and *phone number* attributes.

In addition to attributes, entities can also contain *relationships, fetched properties* and *fetch requests*:

- **Relationships** – In the context of Core Data, relationships are the same as those in other relational database systems in that they refer to how one data object relates to another. Core Data relationships can be *one-to-one, one-to-many* or *many-to-many*.
- **Fetched property** – This provides an alternative to defining relationships. Fetched properties allow properties of one data object to be accessed from another data object as though a relationship had been defined between those entities. Fetched properties lack the flexibility of relationships and are referred to by Apple's Core Data documentation as "weak, one way relationships" best suited to "loosely coupled relationships".
- **Fetch request** – A predefined query that can be referenced to retrieve data objects based on defined predicates. For example, a fetch request can be configured into an entity to retrieve all contact objects where the name field matches "John Smith".

41.5 Persistent Store Coordinator

The *persistent store coordinator* is responsible for coordinating access to multiple *persistent object stores*. As an iPhone iOS developer you will never directly interact with the persistence store coordinator and, in fact, will very rarely need to develop an application that requires more than one persistent object store. When multiple stores are required, the coordinator presents these stores to the upper layers of the Core Data stack as a single store.

41.6 Persistent Object Store

The term *persistent object store* refers to the underlying storage environment in which data are stored when using Core Data. Core Data supports three disk-based and one memory-based persistent store. Disk based options consist of SQLite, XML and binary. By default, the iOS SDK will use SQLite as the persistent store. In practice, the type of store being used is transparent to you as

Working with iOS 6 iPhone Databases using Core Data

the developer. Regardless of your choice of persistent store, your code will make the same calls to the same Core Data APIs to manage the data objects required by your application.

41.7 Defining an Entity Description

Entity descriptions may be defined from within the Xcode environment. When a new project is created with the option to include Core Data, a template file will be created named *<projectname>.xcdatamodeld*. Selecting this file in the Xcode project navigator panel will load the model into the entity editing environment as illustrated in Figure 41-2:

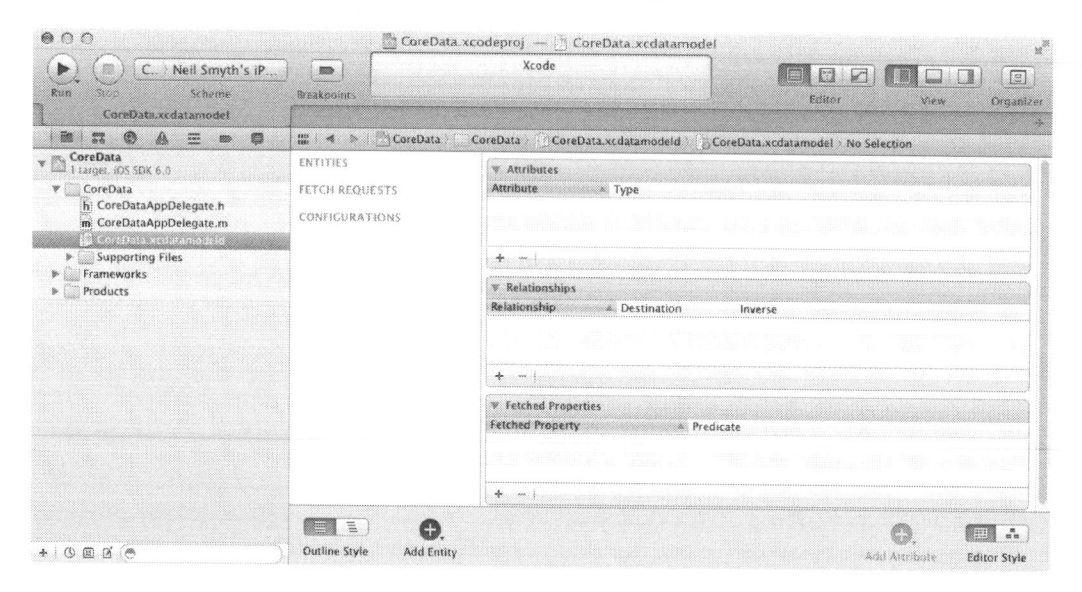

Figure 41-2

Create a new entity by clicking on the *Add Entity* button located in the bottom panel. The new entity will appear as a text box in the *Entities* list where a name may be typed.

To add attributes to the entity, click on the *Add Attribute* button located in the bottom panel. In the *Attributes* panel, name the attribute and specify the type and any other options that are required.

Repeat the above steps to add more attributes and additional entities.

The Xcode entity environment also allows relationships to be established between entities. Assume, for example, two entities named *Contacts* and *Sales*. In order to establish a relationship between the two tables select the *Contacts* entity and click on the + button beneath the *Relationships* panel. In the detail panel, name the relationship, specify the destination as the *Sales* entity and any other options that are required for the relationship. Once the relationship has been established it is, perhaps, best viewed graphically by selecting the *Table, Graph* option in the *Editor Style* control located in the bottom panel:

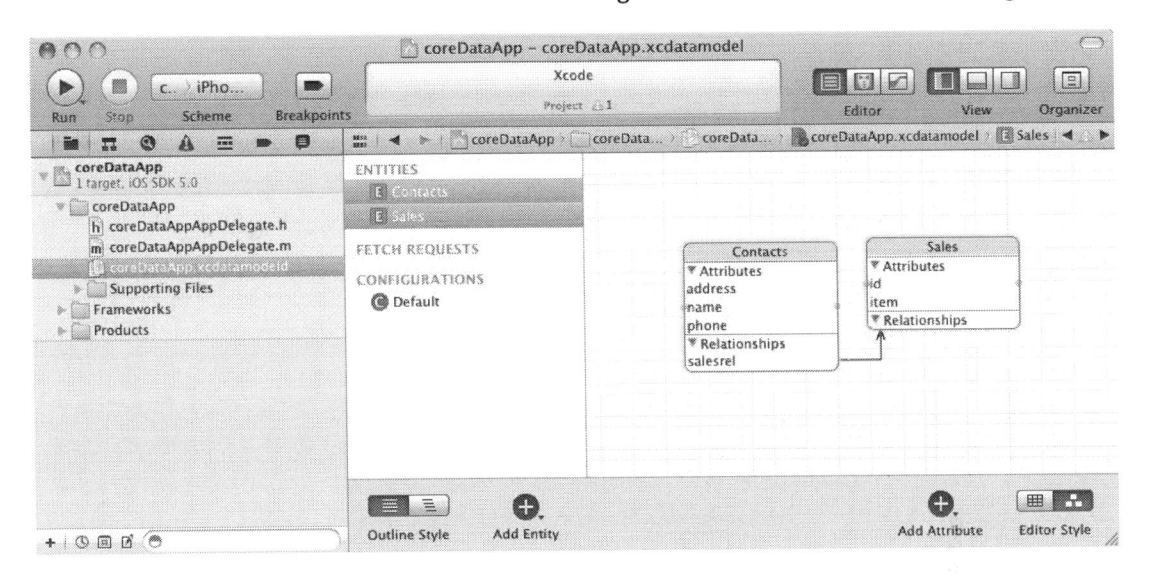

Working with iOS 6 iPhone Databases using Core Data

Figure 41-3

As demonstrated, Xcode makes the process of entity description creation fairly straightforward. Whilst a detailed overview of the process is beyond the scope of this book there are many other resources available that are dedicated to the subject.

41.8 Obtaining the Managed Object Context

Since many of the Core Data methods require the managed object context as an argument, the next step after defining entity descriptions often involves obtaining a reference to the context. This is achieved by first indentifying the application delegate and then calling the delegate object's *managedContextObject* method:

```
coreDataAppDelegate *appDelegate = [[UIApplication sharedApplication]
     delegate];
NSManagedObjectContext *context = [appDelegate managedObjectContext];
```

41.9 Getting an Entity Description

Before managed objects can be created and manipulated in code, the corresponding entity description must first be loaded. This is achieved by calling the *entityForName: inManagedObjectContext* method of the NSEntityDescription class, passing through the name of the required entity and the context as arguments and then making a *fetch request*. The following code fragment obtains the description for an entity with the name *Contacts*:

```
NSEntityDescription *entityDesc = [NSEntityDescription
     entityForName:@"Contacts" inManagedObjectContext:context];
NSFetchRequest *request = [[NSFetchRequest alloc] init];
```

327

```
[request setEntity:entityDesc];
```

41.10 Creating a Managed Object

Having obtained the managed context, a new managed object conforming to a specified entity description can be created as follows by referencing the context and entity description name:

```
NSManagedObject *newContact;
newContact = [NSEntityDescription
        insertNewObjectForEntityForName:@"Contacts"
        inManagedObjectContext:context];
NSError *error;
[context save:&error];
```

41.11 Getting and Setting the Attributes of a Managed Object

As previously discussed, entities and the managed objects from which they are instantiated contain data in the form of attributes. These attributes are stored in the objects using a *value-key coding* system, whereby the key is referenced in order to get or set the corresponding attribute. Assuming a managed object named *newContact* with attributes assigned the keys *name, address* and *phone* respectively, the values of these attributes may be set using the *setValue:forKey* method of the NSManagedObject instance:

```
[newContact setValue:@"John Smith" forKey:@"name"];
[newContact setValue:@"123 The Street" forKey:@"address"];
[newContact setValue:@"555-123-1234" forKey:@"phone"];
```

Conversely, the current value for a corresponding key may be accessed using the managed object's *valueForKey* method:

```
NSString *contactname = [newContact valueForKey:@"name"];
```

The above line of code extracts the current value for the *name* attribute of the *newContact* managed object and assigns it to a string object.

41.12 Fetching Managed Objects

Once managed objects are saved into the persistent object store it is highly likely that those objects and the data they contain will need to be retrieved. Objects are retrieved by executing a fetch request and are returned in the form of an NSArray object. The following code assumes that both the context and entity description have been obtained prior to making the fetch request:

```
NSFetchRequest *request = [[NSFetchRequest alloc] init];
[request setEntity:entityDesc];
NSError *error;
```

```
NSArray *matching_objects = [context executeFetchRequest:request
error:&error];
```

Upon execution, the *matching_objects* array will contain all the managed objects retrieved by the request.

41.13 Retrieving Managed Objects based on Criteria

The preceding example retrieved all of the managed objects from the persistent object store for a specified entity. More often than not only managed objects that match specified criteria are required during a retrieval operation. This is performed by defining a *predicate* that dictates criteria that a managed object must meet in order to be eligible for retrieval. For example, the following code implements a predicate in order to extract only those managed objects where the *name* attribute matches "John Smith":

```
NSFetchRequest *request = [[NSFetchRequest alloc] init];

[request setEntity:entityDesc];
NSPredicate *pred = [NSPredicate predicateWithFormat:@"(name = %@)",
"John Smith"];
[request setPredicate:pred];
NSError *error;
NSArray *matching_objects = [context executeFetchRequest:request
error:&error]; ;
```

41.14 Summary

The Core Data framework stack provides a flexible alternative to directly managing data using SQLite or other data storage mechanisms. By providing an object oriented abstraction layer on top of the data the task of managing data storage is made significantly easier for the iOS iPhone application developer. Now that the basics of Core Data have been covered the next chapter entitled *An iOS 6 iPhone Core Data Tutorial* will work through the creation of an example application.

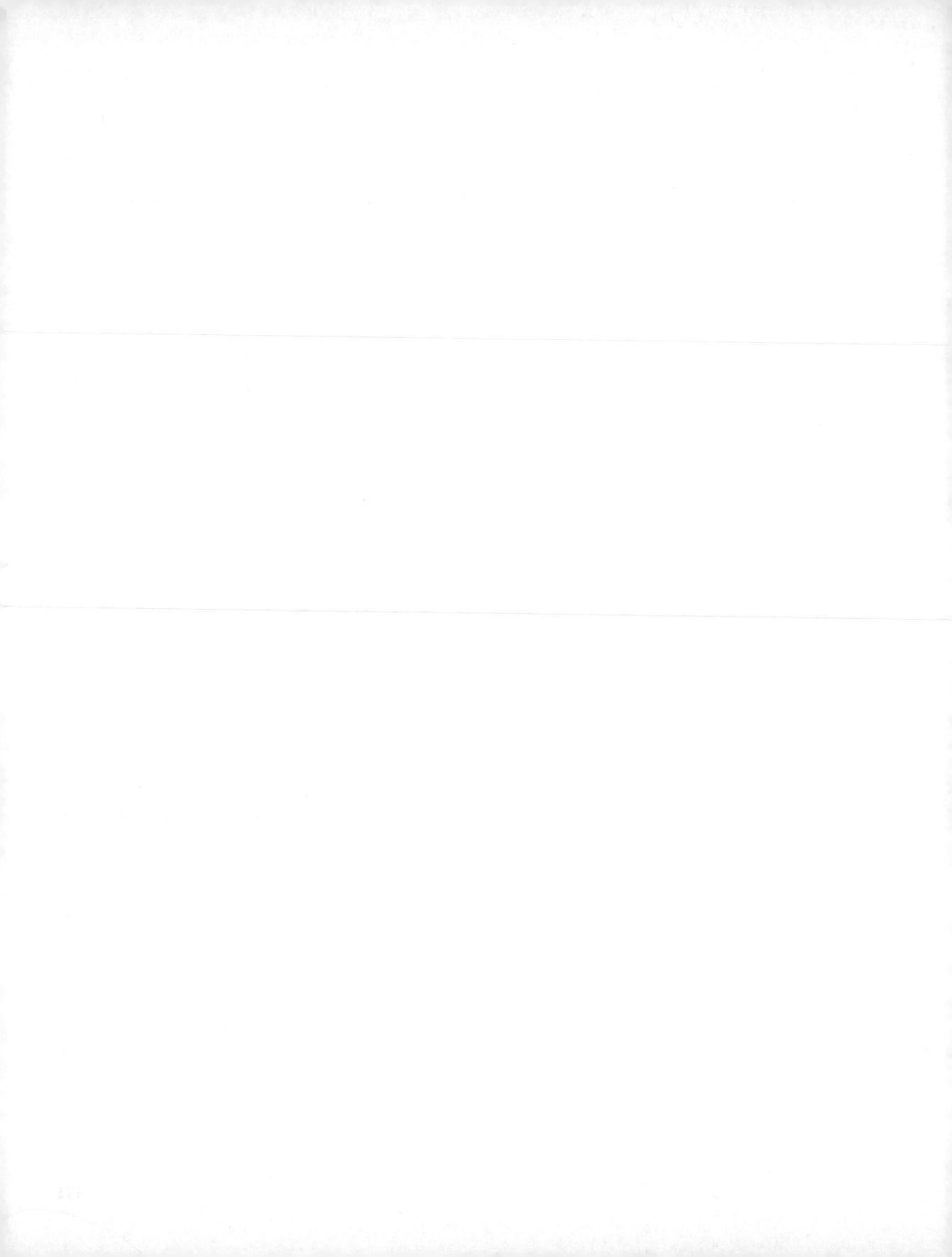

Chapter 42

42. An iOS 6 iPhone Core Data Tutorial

In the previous chapter, entitled *Working with iOS 6 iPhone Databases using Core Data*, an overview of the Core Data stack was provided, together with details of how to write code to implement data persistence using this infrastructure. In this chapter we will continue to look at Core Data in the form of a step by step tutorial that implements data persistence using Core Data in an iOS 6 iPhone application.

42.1 The iPhone Core Data Example Application

The application developed in this chapter will take the form of the same contact database application used in previous chapters, the objective being to allow the user to enter name, address and phone number information into a database and then search for specific contacts based on the contact's name.

42.2 Creating a Core Data based iPhone Application

As is often the case, we can rely on Xcode to do much of the preparatory work for us when developing an iPhone application that will use Core Data. Currently, however, only the Master-Detail Application, Utility Application and Empty Application project templates offer the option to automatically include support for Core Data.

To create the example application project, launch Xcode and select the option to create a new project. In the new project window, select the *Empty Application* option. In the next screen make sure that the *Devices* menu is set to *iPhone* and that the check boxes next to *Use Core Data* and *Use Automatic Reference Counting* are selected. In the *Product Name* and *Class Prefix* fields enter *CoreData* and click *Next* to select a location to store the project files. Xcode will create the new project and display the main project window. In addition to the usual files that are present when creating a new project, this time an additional file named *CoreData.xcdatamodeld* is also created. This is the file where the entity descriptions for our data model are going to be stored.

42.3 Creating the Entity Description

The entity description defines the model for our data, much in the way a schema defines the model of a database table. To create the entity for the Core Data application, select the *CoreData.xcdatamodeld* file to load the entity editor:

331

An iOS 6 iPhone Core Data Tutorial

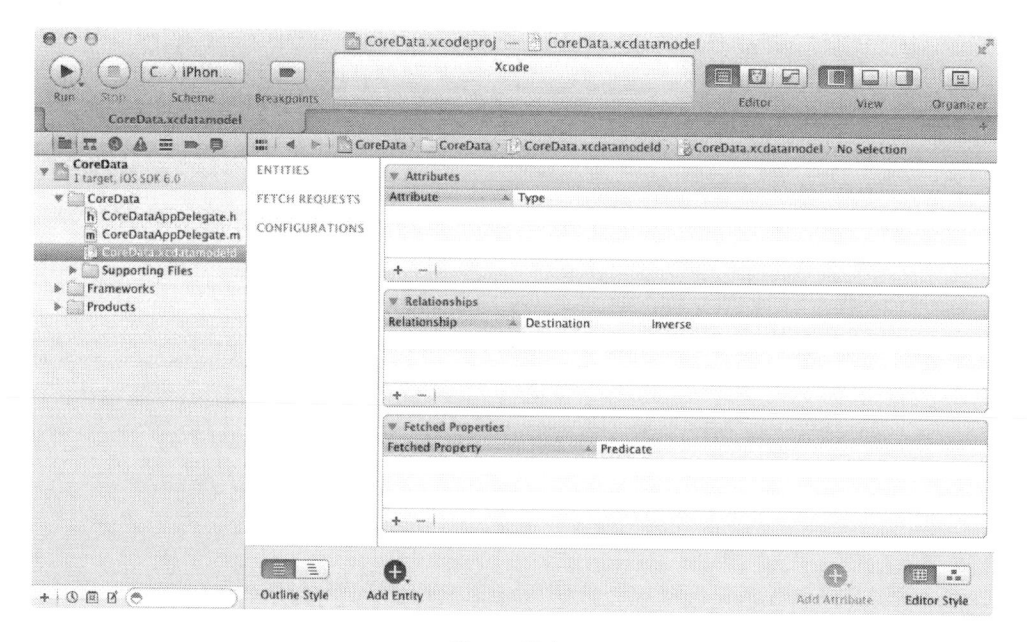

Figure 42-1

To create a new entity, click on the *Add Entity* button located in the bottom panel. In the text field that appears beneath the *Entities* heading name the entity *Contacts*. With the entity created, the next step is to add some attributes that represent the data that is to be stored. To do so, click on the *Add Attribute* button. In the *Attribute* pane, name the attribute *name* and set the Type to *String*. Repeat these steps to add two other String attributes named *address* and *phone* respectively:

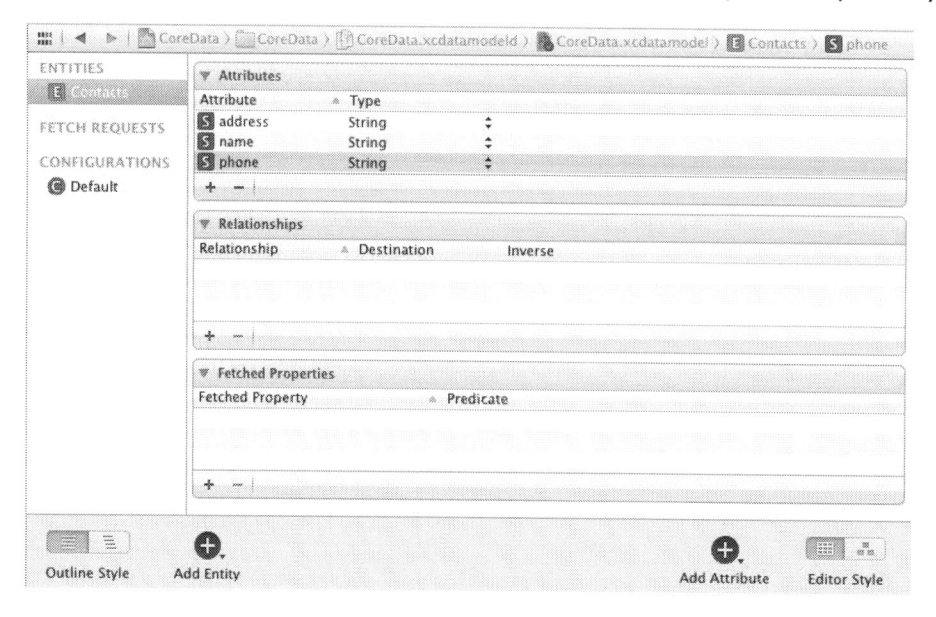

Figure 42-2

The entity is now defined and it is time to start writing code.

42.4 Adding a View Controller

In order to automatically add Core Data support to our application we had to choose the Empty Application project template option when we started Xcode. As such, we now need to create our own view controller.

Within the Xcode project navigator panel, Ctrl-click on the *CoreData* folder entry. From the popup menu, select *New File...* In the new file panel, select the iOS *Cocoa Touch Class* category followed by the *Objective-C class* icon and click *Next*. On the following options screen, make sure the *Subclass of* menu is set to *UIViewController* and name the class *CoreDataViewController*. Select the *With XIB for user interface* check box and make sure the *Targeted for iPad* option is off. Click *Next* and on the final panel click on *Create*.

Now that we have added the view controller class to the application we need to modify our app delegate to make this the root view controller. In the Xcode project navigator, select the *CoreDataAppDelegate.h* file and modify it to add a reference to our new view controller:

```objectivec
#import <UIKit/UIKit.h>
#import "CoreDataViewController.h"

@class CoreDataViewController;

@interface CoreDataAppDelegate : UIResponder <UIApplicationDelegate>

@property (strong, nonatomic) CoreDataViewController *viewController;
@property (strong, nonatomic) UIWindow *window;

@property (readonly, strong, nonatomic) NSManagedObjectContext *managedObjectContext;
@property (readonly, strong, nonatomic) NSManagedObjectModel *managedObjectModel;
@property (readonly, strong, nonatomic) NSPersistentStoreCoordinator *persistentStoreCoordinator;

- (void)saveContext;
- (NSURL *)applicationDocumentsDirectory;
@end
```

With an instance of the view controller declared in the interface file we now need to modify the *didFinishLaunchingWithOptions* method located in the *CoreDataAppDelegate.m* implementation file to initialize and allocate the CoreDataViewController instance and assign it as the application's root view controller so that it is visible to the user on application launch:

```objectivec
- (BOOL)application:(UIApplication *)application
didFinishLaunchingWithOptions:(NSDictionary *)launchOptions
{
```

An iOS 6 iPhone Core Data Tutorial

```
    self.window = [[UIWindow alloc] initWithFrame:[[UIScreen
mainScreen] bounds]];
    // Override point for customization after application launch.
    _viewController = [[CoreDataViewController alloc]
      initWithNibName:@"CoreDataViewController" bundle:nil];

    self.window.backgroundColor = [UIColor whiteColor];
    [self.window setRootViewController:_viewController];
    [self.window makeKeyAndVisible];
    return YES;
}
.
.
.
@end
```

42.5 Designing the User Interface

With the application delegate configured, now is a good time to design the user interface and establish the outlet and action connections. Select the *CoreDataViewController.xib* file to begin the design work. The user interface and corresponding connections used in this tutorial are the same as those in previous data persistence chapters. The completed view should, once again, appear as outlined in Figure 42-3:

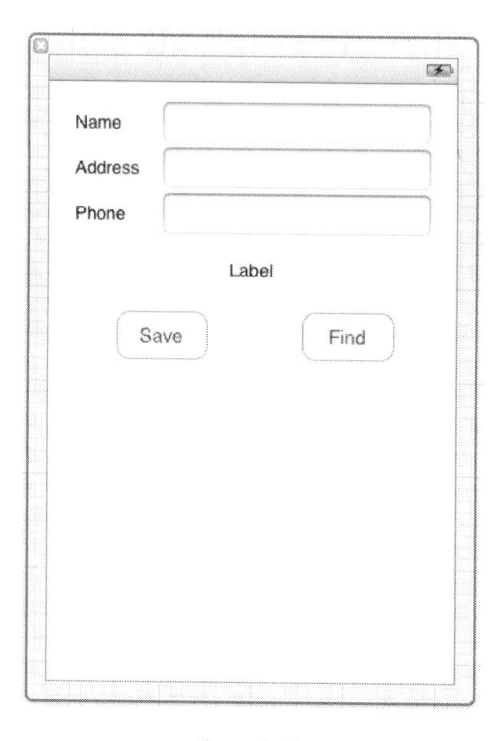

Figure 42-3

334

An iOS 6 iPhone Core Data Tutorial

Before proceeding, stretch the status label (located above the two buttons) so that it covers most of the width of the view. Finally, edit the label and remove the word "Label" so that it is blank.

Select the top most text field object in the view canvas, display the Assistant Editor panel and verify that the editor is displaying the contents of the *CoreDataViewController.h* file. Ctrl-click on the text field object again and drag to a position just below the @interface line in the Assistant Editor. Release the line and in the resulting connection dialog establish an outlet connection named *name*.

Repeat the above steps to establish outlet connections for the remaining text fields and the label object to properties named *address* and *phone* respectively and *status*.

Ctrl-click on the *Save* button object and drag the line to the area immediately beneath the newly created outlet in the Assistant Editor panel. Release the line and, within the resulting connection dialog, establish an Action method on the *Touch Up Inside* event configured to call a method named *saveData*. Repeat this step to create an action connection from the *Find* button to a method named *findContact*.

With the connections established, select the *CoreDataViewController.h* file and verify the settings are correct before modifying the file to import the *CoreDataAppDelegate.h* file which will be required by code added to the view controller later in the chapter:

```
#import <UIKit/UIKit.h>
#import "CoreDataAppDelegate.h"

@interface CoreDataViewController : UIViewController
@property (strong, nonatomic) IBOutlet UITextField *name;
@property (strong, nonatomic) IBOutlet UITextField *address;
@property (strong, nonatomic) IBOutlet UITextField *phone;
@property (strong, nonatomic) IBOutlet UILabel *status;
- (IBAction)saveData:(id)sender;
- (IBAction)findContact:(id)sender;
@end
```

42.6 Saving Data to the Persistent Store using Core Data

When the user touches the Save button the *saveData* method is called. It is within this method, therefore, that we must implement the code to obtain the managed object context and create and store managed objects containing the data entered by the user. Select the *CoreDataViewController.m* file, scroll down to the template *saveData* method and implement the code as follows:

```
- (IBAction)saveData:(id)sender {

    CoreDataAppDelegate *appDelegate =
        [[UIApplication sharedApplication] delegate];
```

335

```
    NSManagedObjectContext *context =
      [appDelegate managedObjectContext];
    NSManagedObject *newContact;
    newContact = [NSEntityDescription
        insertNewObjectForEntityForName:@"Contacts"
        inManagedObjectContext:context];
    [newContact setValue: _name.text forKey:@"name"];
    [newContact setValue: _address.text forKey:@"address"];
    [newContact setValue: _phone.text forKey:@"phone"];
    _name.text = @"";
    _address.text = @"";
    _phone.text = @"";
    NSError *error;
    [context save:&error];
    _status.text = @"Contact saved";

}
```

The above code identifies the application delegate instance and uses that object to identify the managed object context. This context is then used to create a new managed object using the Contacts entity description. The *setValue* method of the managed object is then called to set the name, address and phone attribute values of the managed object (which in turn are read from the text field user interface components). Finally, the context is instructed to save the changes to the persistent store with a call to the context's *save* method.

42.7 Retrieving Data from the Persistent Store using Core Data

In order to allow the user to search for a contact it is now necessary to implement the *findContact* action method. As with the save method, this method will need to identify the application delegate and managed object context. It will then need to obtain the entity description for the Contacts entity and then create a predicate to ensure that only objects with the name specified by the user are retrieved from the store. Matching objects are placed in an array from which the attributes for the first match are retrieved using the *valueForKey* method and displayed to the user. A full count of the matches is displayed in the status field.

The code to perform these tasks is as follows:

```
- (IBAction)findContact:(id)sender {
    CoreDataAppDelegate *appDelegate =
        [[UIApplication sharedApplication] delegate];

    NSManagedObjectContext *context =
        [appDelegate managedObjectContext];
```

```objc
NSEntityDescription *entityDesc =
    [NSEntityDescription entityForName:@"Contacts"
    inManagedObjectContext:context];

NSFetchRequest *request = [[NSFetchRequest alloc] init];
[request setEntity:entityDesc];

NSPredicate *pred =
    [NSPredicate predicateWithFormat:@"(name = %@)",
        _name.text];
[request setPredicate:pred];
NSManagedObject *matches = nil;

NSError *error;
NSArray *objects = [context executeFetchRequest:request
    error:&error];

if ([objects count] == 0) {
    _status.text = @"No matches";
} else {
    matches = objects[0];
    _address.text = [matches valueForKey:@"address"];
    _phone.text = [matches valueForKey:@"phone"];
    _status.text = [NSString stringWithFormat:
        @"%d matches found", [objects count]];
}
}
```

42.8 Building and Running the Example Application

The final step is to build and run the application. Click on the *Run* button located in the toolbar of the main Xcode project window. If errors are reported check the syntax of the code you have written, using the error message provided by Xcode as guidance. Once the application compiles it will launch and load into the iOS Simulator. Enter some test contacts (some with the same name). Having entered some test data, enter the name of the contact for which you created duplicate records and click the Find button. As shown in Figure 42-4, the address and phone number of the first matching record should appear together with an indication in the status field of the total number of matching objects that were retrieved:

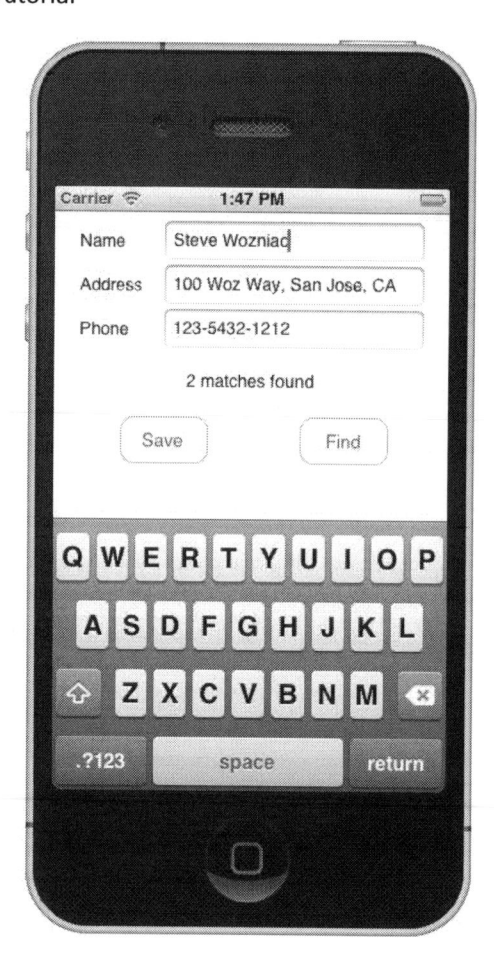

Figure 42-4

42.9 Summary

The Core Data framework provides an abstract, object oriented interface to database storage within iOS applications. As demonstrated in the example application created in this chapter, Core Data does not require any knowledge of the underlying database system and, combined with the visual entity creation features of Xcode, allows database storage to be implemented with relative ease.

Chapter 43

43. An Overview of iOS 6 iPhone Multitouch, Taps and Gestures

In terms of physical points of interaction between the device and the user, the iPhone provides three buttons, a switch and a touch screen. Without question, the user will spend far more time using the touch screen than any other aspect of the device. It is essential, therefore, that any application be able to handle gestures (touches, multitouches, taps, swipes and pinches etc) performed by the user's fingers on the touch screen.

Before writing code to handle these gestures, this chapter will spend some time talking about the responder chain in relation to touch screen events before delving a little deeper into the types of gestures an iPhone application is likely to encounter.

43.1 The Responder Chain

In the chapter entitled *Understanding iPhone iOS 6 Views, Windows and the View Hierarchy* we spent some time talking about the view hierarchy of an application's user interface and how that hierarchy also defined part of the application's *responder chain*. In order to fully understand the concepts behind the handling of touch screen gestures it is first necessary to spend a little more time learning about the responder chain.

When the user interacts with the touch screen of an iPhone the hardware detects the physical contact and notifies the operating system. The operating system subsequently creates an *event* associated with the interaction and passes it into the currently active application's *event queue* where it is subsequently picked up by the *event loop* and passed to the current *first responder* object; the first responder being the object with which the user was interacting when this event was triggered (for example a UIButton or UIView object). If the first responder has been programmed to handle the type of event received it does so (for example a button may have an action defined to call a particular method when it receives a touch event). Having handled the event, the responder then has the option of discarding that event, or passing it up to the *next responder* in the *response chain* (defined by the object's *nextResponder* property) for further processing, and so on up the chain. If the first responder is not able to handle the event it will also pass it to the next responder in the chain and so on until it either reaches a responder that handles the event or it reaches the end of the chain (the UIApplication object) where it will either be handled or discarded.

An Overview of iOS 6 iPhone Multitouch, Taps and Gestures

Take, for example, a UIView with a UIButton subview. If the user touches the screen over the button then the button, as first responder, will receive the event. If the button is unable to handle the event it will need to be passed up to the view object. If the view is also unable to handle the event it would then be passed to the view controller and so on.

When working with the responder chain, it is important to note that the passing of an event from one responder to the next responder in the chain does not happen automatically. If an event needs to be passed to the next responder, code must be written to make it happen.

43.2 Forwarding an Event to the Next Responder

An event may be passed on to the next responder in the response chain by calling the *nextResponder* method of the current responder, passing through the method that was triggered by the event and the event itself. Take, for example, a situation where the current responder object is unable to handle a *touchesBegan* event. In order to pass this to the next responder, the *touchesBegan* method of the current responder will need to make a call as follows:

```
- (void)touchesBegan:(NSSet *)touches 
withEvent:(UIEvent *)event {
    [self.nextResponder touchesBegan:touches withEvent:event];
}
```

43.3 Gestures

Gesture is an umbrella term used to encapsulate any single interaction between the touch screen and the user, starting at the point that the screen is touched (by one or more fingers) and the time that the last finger leaves the surface of the screen. *Swipes, pinches, stretches* and *flicks* are all forms of gesture.

43.4 Taps

A *tap*, as the name suggests, occurs when the user touches the screen with a single finger and then immediately lifts it from the screen. Taps can be single-taps or multiple-taps and the event will contain information about the number of times a user tapped on the screen.

43.5 Touches

A *touch* occurs when a finger establishes contact with the screen. When more than one finger touches the screen each finger registers as a touch up to a maximum of five fingers.

43.6 Touch Notification Methods

Touch screen events cause one of four methods on the first responder object to be called. The method that gets called for a specific event will depend on the nature of the interaction. In order to handle events, therefore, it is important to ensure that the appropriate methods from those outlined below are implemented within your responder chain. These methods will be used in the worked example contained in the *An Example iOS 6 iPhone Touch, Multitouch and Tap Application* and *Detecting iOS 6 iPhone Touch Screen Gesture Motions* chapters of this book.

43.6.1 touchesBegan method

The *touchesBegan* method is called when the user first touches the screen. Passed to this method are an argument called *touches* of type NSSet and the corresponding UIEvent object. The touches object contains a UITouch event for each finger in contact with the screen. The *tapCount* method of any of the UITouch events within the *touches* set can be called to identify the number of taps, if any, performed by the user. Similarly, the coordinates of an individual touch can be identified from the UITouch event either relative to the entire screen or within the local view itself.

43.6.2 touchesMoved method

The *touchesMoved* method is called when one or more fingers move across the screen. As fingers move across the screen this method gets called multiple times allowing the application to track the new coordinates and touch count at regular intervals. As with the *touchesBegan* method, this method is provided with an event object and an NSSet object containing UITouch events for each finger on the screen.

43.6.3 touchesEnded method

This method is called when the user lifts one or more fingers from the screen. As with the previous methods, *touchesEnded* is provided with the event and NSSet objects.

43.6.4 touchesCancelled method

When a gesture is interrupted due to a high level interrupt, such as the phone detecting an incoming call, the *touchesCancelled* method is called.

43.7 Summary

In order to fully appreciate the mechanisms for handling touch screen events within an iOS 6 iPhone application, it is first important to understand both the responder chain and the methods that are called on a responder depending on the type of interaction. We have covered these basics in this chapter. In the next chapter, entitled *An Example iOS 6 iPhone Touch, Multitouch and Tap Application* we will use these concepts to create an example application that demonstrates touch screen event handling.

Chapter 44

44. An Example iOS 6 iPhone Touch, Multitouch and Tap Application

Having covered the basic concepts behind the handling of iOS user interaction with an iPhone touch screen in the previous chapter, this chapter will work through a tutorial designed to highlight the handling of taps and touches. Topics covered in this chapter include the detection of single and multiple taps and touches, identifying whether a user single or double tapped the device display and extracting information about a touch or tap from the corresponding event object.

44.1 The Example iOS 6 iPhone Tap and Touch Application

The example application created in the course of this tutorial will consist of a view and some labels. The view object's view controller will implement a number of the touch screen event methods outlined in *An Overview of iOS 6 iPhone Multitouch, Taps and Gestures* and update the status labels to reflect the detected activity. The application will, for example, report the number of fingers touching the screen, the number of taps performed and the most recent touch event that was triggered. In the next chapter, entitled *Detecting iOS 6 iPhone Touch Screen Gesture Motions* we will look more closely at detecting the motion of touches.

44.2 Creating the Example iOS Touch Project

Begin by launching the Xcode development environment and selecting the option to create a new project. Select the iOS Application *Single View Application* template and the *iPhone* device option and name the project and class prefix *Touch* with Storyboard support and Automatic Reference Counting enabled. When the main Xcode project screen appears we are ready to start writing the code for our application.

44.3 Designing the User Interface

Load the storyboard by selecting the *MainStoryboard.storyboard* file. Using Interface Builder, modify the user interface by adding label components from the Object library (*View -> Utilities -> Show Object Library*) and modifying properties until the view appears as outlined in Figure 44-1.

When adding the labels to the right of the view, be sure to stretch them so that they reach to the right hand margin of the view area.

343

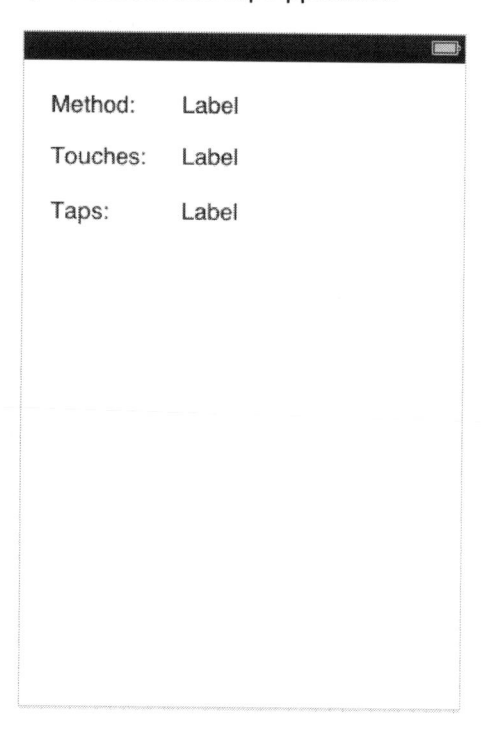

An Example iOS 6 iPhone Touch, Multitouch and Tap Application

Figure 44-1

Select label to the right of the "Method:" label, display the Assistant Editor panel and verify that the editor is displaying the contents of the *TouchViewController.h* file. Ctrl-click on the same label object and drag to a position just below the @interface line in the Assistant Editor. Release the line and in the resulting connection dialog establish an outlet connection named *methodStatus*.

Repeat the above steps to establish outlet connections for the remaining labels object to properties named *touchStatus* and *tapStatus*.

44.4 Enabling Multitouch on the View

By default, views are configured to respond to only single touches (in other words a single finger touching or tapping the screen at any one time). For the purposes of this example we plan to detect multiple touches. In order to enable this support it is necessary to change an attribute of the view object. To achieve this, click on the background of the *View* window, display the Attribute Inspector (*View -> Utilities -> Show Attribute Inspector*) and make sure that the *Multiple Touch* option is selected in the *Interaction* section at the bottom of the window:

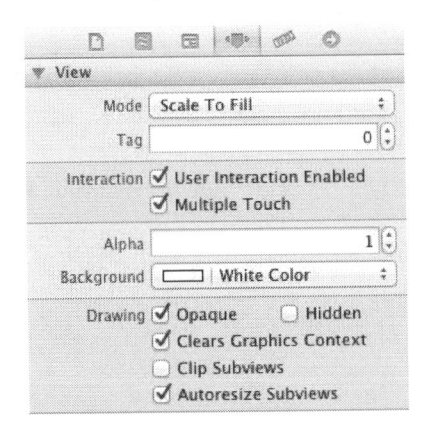

An Example iOS 6 iPhone Touch, Multitouch and Tap Application

Figure 44-2

44.5 Implementing the touchesBegan Method

When the user touches the screen, the *touchesBegan* method of the first responder is called. In order to capture these event types, we need to implement this method in our view controller. In the Xcode project navigator, select the *TouchViewController.m* file and add the *touchesBegan* method as follows:

```
- (void) touchesBegan:(NSSet *)touches 
withEvent:(UIEvent *)event {
    NSUInteger touchCount = [touches count];
    NSUInteger tapCount = [[touches anyObject] tapCount];
    _methodStatus.text = @"touchesBegan";
    _touchStatus.text = [NSString stringWithFormat:
        @"%d touches", touchCount];
    _tapStatus.text = [NSString stringWithFormat:
        @"%d taps", tapCount];
}
```

This method obtains a count of the number of touch objects contained in the *touches* set (essentially the number of fingers touching the screen) and assigns it to a variable. It then gets the tap count from one of the touch objects. The code then updates the *methodStatus* label to indicate that the *touchesBegan* method has been triggered, constructs a string indicating the number of touches and taps detected and displays the information on the *touchStatus* and *tapStatus* labels accordingly.

44.6 Implementing the touchesMoved Method

When the user moves one or more fingers currently in contact with the surface of the iPhone touch screen, the *touchesMoved* method is called repeatedly until the movement ceases. In order to capture these events it is necessary to implement the touchesMoved method in our view controller class:

An Example iOS 6 iPhone Touch, Multitouch and Tap Application

```
- (void) touchesMoved:(NSSet *)touches
withEvent:(UIEvent *)event {
    NSUInteger touchCount = [touches count];
    NSUInteger tapCount = [[touches anyObject] tapCount];
    _methodStatus.text = @"touchesMoved";
    _touchStatus.text = [NSString stringWithFormat:
       @"%d touches", touchCount];
    _tapStatus.text = [NSString stringWithFormat:
       @"%d taps", tapCount];
}
```

Once again we report the number of touches and taps detected and indicate to the user that this time the *touchesMoved* method is being triggered.

44.7 Implementing the touchesEnded Method

When the user removes a finger from the screen the *touchesEnded* method is called. We can, therefore, implement this method as follows:

```
- (void) touchesEnded:(NSSet *)touches
withEvent:(UIEvent *)event {
    NSUInteger touchCount = [touches count];
    NSUInteger tapCount = [[touches anyObject] tapCount];
    _methodStatus.text = @"touchesEnded";
    _touchStatus.text = [NSString stringWithFormat:
       @"%d touches", touchCount];
    _tapStatus.text = [NSString stringWithFormat:
       @"%d taps", tapCount];
}
```

44.8 Getting the Coordinates of a Touch

Although not part of this particular example, it is worth knowing that the coordinates of the location on the screen where a touch has been detected may be obtained in the form of a CGPoint structure by calling the *locationInView* method of the touch object. For example:

```
UITouch *touch = [touches anyObject];
CGPoint point = [touch locationInView:self.view];
```

The X and Y coordinates may subsequently be extracted from the CGPoint structure by accessing the corresponding elements:

```
CGFloat pointX = point.x;
CGFloat pointY = point.y;
```

An Example iOS 6 iPhone Touch, Multitouch and Tap Application

44.9 Building and Running the Touch Example Application

Build and run the application by clicking on the *Run* button located in the toolbar of the main Xcode project window. The application will run in the iOS Simulator where you should be able to click with the mouse pointer to simulate touches and taps. With each click, the status labels should update to reflect the interaction:

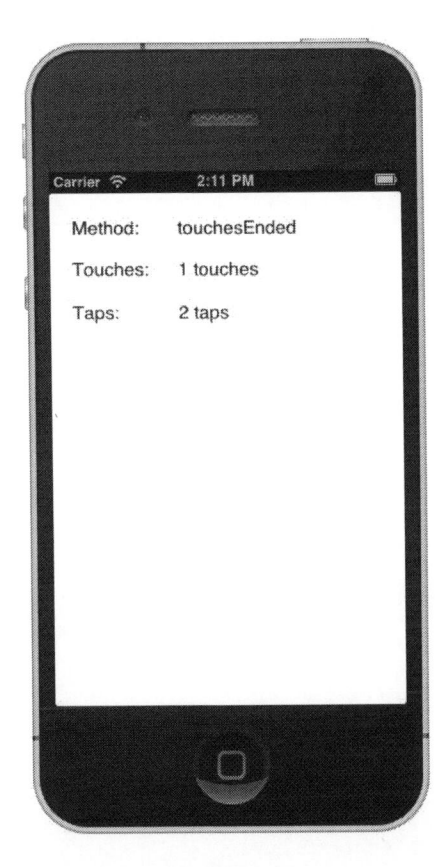

Figure 44-3

Of course, since a mouse only has one pointer it is not possible to trigger multiple touch events using the iOS Simulator environment. In fact, the only way to try out multitouch behavior in this application is to run it on a physical iPhone or iPod Touch device. For steps on how to achieve this, refer to the chapter entitled *Testing iOS 6 Apps on the iPhone – Developer Certificates and Provisioning Profiles*.

347

Chapter 45

45. Detecting iOS 6 iPhone Touch Screen Gesture Motions

The next area of iOS touch screen event handling that we will look at in this book involves the detection of gestures involving movement. As covered in a previous chapter, a *gesture* refers the activity that takes place in the time between a finger touching the screen and the finger then being lifted from the screen. In the chapter entitled *An Example iOS 6 iPhone Touch, Multitouch and Tap Application* we dealt with touches that did not involve any movement across the screen surface. We will now create an example that tracks the coordinates of a finger as it moves across the screen.

Note that the assumption is made throughout this chapter that the reader has already reviewed the *Overview of iOS 6 iPhone Multitouch, Taps and Gestures* chapter of this book.

45.1 The Example iOS 6 iPhone Gesture Application

This example application will detect when a single touch is made on the screen of the iPhone and then report the coordinates of that finger as it is moved across the screen surface.

45.2 Creating the Example Project

Start the Xcode environment and select the option to create a new project using the *Single View Application* template option for the iPhone and name the project and class prefix *TouchMotion* with Storyboard support and Automatic Reference Counting enabled.

45.3 Designing the Application User Interface

The application will display the X and Y coordinates of the touch and update these values in real-time as the finger moves across the screen. When the finger is lifted from the screen, the start and end coordinates of the gesture will then be displayed on two label objects in the user interface. Select the *MainStoryboard.storyboard* file and, using Interface Builder, create a user interface such that it resembles the layout in Figure 45-1:

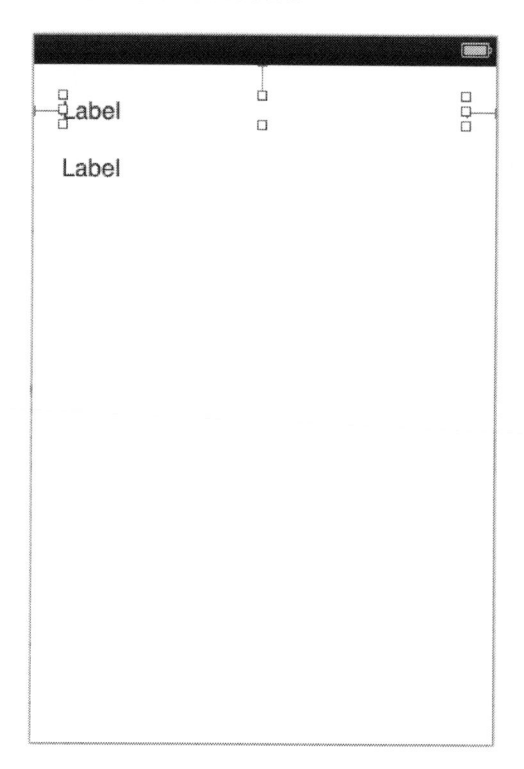

Detecting iOS 6 iPhone Touch Screen Gesture Motions

Figure 45-1

Be sure to stretch the labels so that they both extend to cover most of the width of the view.

Select the top label object in the view canvas, display the Assistant Editor panel and verify that the editor is displaying the contents of the *TouchMotionViewController.h* file. Ctrl-click on the same label object and drag to a position just below the @interface line in the Assistant Editor. Release the line and in the resulting connection dialog establish an outlet connection named *xCoord*. Repeat this step to establish an outlet connection to the second label object named *yCoord*.

Next, select the *TouchMotionViewController.h* file, verify that the outlets are correct, then declare a property in which to store coordinates of the start location on the screen:

```
#import <UIKit/UIKit.h>

@interface TouchMotionViewController : UIViewController
@property (strong, nonatomic) IBOutlet UILabel *xCoord;
@property (strong, nonatomic) IBOutlet UILabel *yCoord;
@property CGPoint startPoint;
@end
```

45.4 Implementing the touchesBegan Method

When the user first touches the screen the location coordinates need to be saved in the *startPoint* instance variable and the coordinates reported to the user. This can be achieved by implementing the *touchesBegan* method in the *TouchMotionViewController.m* file as follows:

```
- (void) touchesBegan:(NSSet *)touches
withEvent:(UIEvent *)event {
    UITouch *theTouch = [touches anyObject];
    _startPoint = [theTouch locationInView:self.view];
    CGFloat x = _startPoint.x;
    CGFloat y = _startPoint.y;
    _xCoord.text = [NSString stringWithFormat:@"x = %f", x];
    _yCoord.text = [NSString stringWithFormat:@"y = %f", y];
}
```

45.5 Implementing the touchesMoved Method

When the user's finger moves across the screen the *touchesMoved* event will be called repeatedly until the motion stops. By implementing the *touchesMoved* method in our view controller, therefore, we can detect the motion and display the revised coordinates to the user:

```
- (void) touchesMoved:(NSSet *)touches
withEvent:(UIEvent *)event {
    UITouch *theTouch = [touches anyObject];
    CGPoint touchLocation =
        [theTouch locationInView:self.view];
    CGFloat x = touchLocation.x;
    CGFloat y = touchLocation.y;
    _xCoord.text = [NSString stringWithFormat:@"x = %f", x];
    _yCoord.text = [NSString stringWithFormat:@"y = %f", y];
}
```

45.6 Implementing the touchesEnded Method

When the user's finger lifts from the screen the *touchesEnded* method of the first responder is called. The final task, therefore, is to implement this method in our view controller such that it displays the start and end points of the gesture:

```
- (void) touchesEnded:(NSSet *)touches
withEvent:(UIEvent *)event {
    UITouch *theTouch = [touches anyObject];
    CGPoint endPoint = [theTouch locationInView:self.view];
    _xCoord.text = [NSString stringWithFormat:
        @"start = %f, %f", _startPoint.x, _startPoint.y];
```

```
    _yCoord.text = [NSString stringWithFormat:
        @"end = %f, %f", endPoint.x, endPoint.y];
}
```

45.7 Building and Running the Gesture Example

Build and run the application using the *Run* button located in the toolbar of the main Xcode project window. When the application starts (either in the iOS Simulator or on a physical device) touch the screen and drag to a new location before lifting your finger from the screen (or mouse button in the case of the iOS Simulator). During the motion the current coordinates will update in real time. Once the gesture is complete the start and end locations of the movement will be displayed.

45.8 Summary

Simply by implementing the standard touch event methods the motion of a gesture can easily be tracked by an iPhone application. Much of an iPhone user's interaction with applications, however, involves some very specific gesture types such as swipes and pinches. To write code to correlate finger movement on the screen with a specific gesture type would be extremely complex. Fortunately, iOS 6 makes this task easy with the introduction of *gesture recognizers*. In the next chapter, entitled *Identifying iPhone Gestures using iOS 6 Gesture Recognizers*, we will look at this concept in more detail.

46. Identifying iPhone Gestures using iOS 6 Gesture Recognizers

In the chapter entitled *Detecting iOS 6 iPhone Touch Screen Gesture Motions* we looked at how to track the motion of contact with the iPhone screen. In practice, an application will need to respond to specific motions that take place during the course of a gesture. The swiping of a finger across the screen might, for example, be required slide a new view onto the display. Similarly, a pinching motion is typically used in iPhone applications to enlarge or reduce an image or view.

Prior to iOS 4, the identification of a gesture was the responsibility of the application developer and typically involved the creation of complex mathematical algorithms. In recognition of this complexity, and given the importance of gestures to user interaction with the iPhone, Apple introduced the UIGestureRecognizer class in iOS 4 thereby making the task of identifying the types of gestures a much easier task for the application developer.

The goal of this chapter, therefore, is to provide an overview of gesture recognition within the context of iOS 6 and the iPhone. The next chapter will work through *an iPhone iOS 6 Gesture Recognition Tutorial*.

46.1 The UIGestureRecognizer Class

The UIGestureRecognizer class is used as the basis for a collection of subclasses, each designed to detect a specific type of gesture. These subclasses are as follows:

- **UITapGestureRecognizer** – This class is designed to detect when a user taps on the screen of the device. Both single and multiple taps may be detected based on the configuration of the class instance.
- **UIPinchGestureRecognizer** – Detects when a pinching motion is made by the user on the screen. This motion is typically used to zoom in or out of a view or to change the size of a visual component.
- **UIPanGestureRecognizer** – Detects when a dragging or panning gesture is made by the user.
- **UISwipeGestureRecognizer** – Used to detect when the user makes a swiping gesture across the screen. Instances of this class may be configured to detect motion only in specific directions (left, right, up or down).

- **UIRotationGestureRecognizer** – Identifies when the user makes a rotation gesture (essentially two fingers in contact with the screen located opposite each other and moving in a circular motion).
- **UILongPressGestureRecognizer** – Used to identify when the user touches the screen with one or more fingers for a specified period of time (also referred to as "touch and hold").

These gesture recognizers must be attached to the view on which the gesture will be performed via a call to the view object's *addGestureRecognizer:* method. Recognizers must also be assigned an action method that is to be called when the specified gesture is detected. Gesture recognizers may subsequently be removed from a view via a call to the view's *removeGestureRecognizer:* method, passing through as an argument the recognizer to be removed.

46.2 Recognizer Action Messages

The iOS 6 gesture recognizers use the target-action model to notify the application of the detection of a specific gesture. When an instance of a gesture recognizer is created it is provided with the reference to the method to be called in the event that the corresponding gesture is detected.

46.3 Discrete and Continuous Gestures

Gestures fall into two distinct categories – *discrete* and *continuous*. A discrete gesture results in only a single call being made to the corresponding action method. Tap gestures (including multiple taps) are considered to be discrete because they only trigger the action method once. Gestures such as swipes, pans, rotations and pinches are deemed to be continuous in that they trigger a constant stream of calls to the corresponding action methods until the gesture ends.

46.4 Obtaining Data from a Gesture

Each gesture action method is passed as an argument a UIGestureRecognizer sender object which may be used to extract information about the gesture. For example, information about the scale factor and speed of a pinch gesture may be obtained by the action method. Similarly, the action method assigned to a rotation gesture recognizer may ascertain the amount of rotation performed by the user and the corresponding velocity.

46.5 Recognizing Tap Gestures

Tap gestures are detected using the UITapGestureRecognizer class. This must be allocated and initialized with an action selector referencing the method to be called when the gesture is detected. The number of taps that must be performed to constitute the full gesture may be defined by setting the *numberOfTapsRequired* property of the recognizer instance. The following code, for example, will result in a call to the *tapsDetected* method when two consecutive taps are detected on the corresponding view:

```
UITapGestureRecognizer *doubleTap =
        [[UITapGestureRecognizer alloc]
          initWithTarget:self
          action:@selector(tapDetected:)];
doubleTap.numberOfTapsRequired = 2;
[self.view addGestureRecognizer:doubleTap];
```

A template method for the action method for this and other gesture recognizers is as follows:

```
- (IBAction)tapDetected:(UIGestureRecognizer *)sender {
        // Code to respond to gesture here
}
```

46.6 Recognizing Pinch Gestures

Pinch gestures are detected using the UIPinchGestureRecognizer class. For example:

```
UIPinchGestureRecognizer *pinchRecognizer =
     [[UIPinchGestureRecognizer alloc]
       initWithTarget:self
       action:@selector(pinchDetected:)];
[self.view addGestureRecognizer:pinchRecognizer];
```

46.7 Detecting Rotation Gestures

Rotation gestures are recognized by the UIRotationGestureRecognizer, the sample code for which is as follows:

```
UIRotationGestureRecognizer *rotationRecognizer =
     [[UIRotationGestureRecognizer alloc]
       initWithTarget:self
       action:@selector(rotationDetected:)];
[self.view addGestureRecognizer:rotationRecognizer];
```

46.8 Recognizing Pan and Dragging Gestures

Pan and dragging gestures are detected using the UIPanGestureRecognizer class. Pan gestures are essentially any *continuous* gesture. For example, the random meandering of a finger across the screen will generally be considered by the recognizer as a pan or drag operation:

```
UIRotationGestureRecognizer *panRecognizer =
     [[UIPanGestureRecognizer alloc]
       initWithTarget:self
       action:@selector(panDetected:)];
[self.view addGestureRecognizer:panRecognizer];
```

Identifying iPhone Gestures using iOS 6 Gesture Recognizers

If both swipe and pan recognizers are attached to the same view it is likely that most swipes will be recognized as pans. Caution should be taken, therefore, when mixing these two gesture recognizers on the same view.

46.9 Recognizing Swipe Gestures

Swipe gestures are detected using the UISwipeGestureRecognizer class. All swipes, or just those in a specific direction, may be detected by assigning one of the following constants to the *direction* property of the class:

- UISwipeGestureRecognizerDirectionRight
- UISwipeGestureRecognizerDirectionLeft
- UISwipeGestureRecognizerDirectionUp
- USwipeIGestureRecognizerDirectionDown

If no direction is specified the default is to detect rightward swipes. The following code configures a UISwipeGestureRecognizer instance to detect upward swipes:

```
UISwipeGestureRecognizer *swipeRecognizer =
    [[UISwipeGestureRecognizer alloc]
    initWithTarget:self
    action:@selector(swipeDetected:)];
swipeRecognizer.direction = UISwipeGestureRecognizerDirectionUp;
[self.view addGestureRecognizer:swipeRecognizer];;
```

46.10 Recognizing Long Touch (Touch and Hold) Gestures

Long touches are detected using the UILongPressGestureRecognizer class. The requirements for the gesture may be specified in terms of touch duration, number of touches, number of taps and allowable movement during the touch. These requirements are specified by the *minimumPressDuration*, *numberOfTouchesRequired*, *numberOfTapsRequired* and *allowableMovement* properties of the class respectively. The following code fragment configures the recognizer to detect long presses of 3 seconds or more involving one finger. The default allowable movement is not set and therefore defaults to 10 pixels:

```
UILongPressGestureRecognizer *longPressRecognizer =
    [[UILongPressGestureRecognizer alloc]
    initWithTarget:self
    action:@selector(longPressDetected:)];
longPressRecognizer.minimumPressDuration = 3;
longPressRecognizer.numberOfTouchesRequired = 1;
[self.view addGestureRecognizer:longPressRecognizer];
```

46.11 Summary

In this chapter we have provided an overview of gesture recognizers and provided some examples of how to detect the various types of gesture typically used by iPhone users. In the *next chapter* we will work step-by-step through a tutorial designed to show these theories in practice.

Chapter 47

47. An iPhone iOS 6 Gesture Recognition Tutorial

Having covered the theory of gesture recognition on the iPhone in the chapter entitled *Identifying iPhone Gestures using iOS 6 Gesture Recognizers*, the purpose of this chapter is to work through an example application intended to demonstrate the use of the various UIGestureRecognizer subclasses.

The application created in this chapter will configure recognizers to detect a number of different gestures on the iPhone display and update a status label with information about each recognized gesture.

47.1 Creating the Gesture Recognition Project

Begin by invoking Xcode and creating a new iOS iPhone application project using the *Single View Application* template and name the project and class prefix *Recognizer* with Storyboard and the Automatic Reference Counting options enabled.

47.2 Designing the User Interface

The only visual component that will be present on our UIView object will be the label used to notify the user of the type of gesture detected. Since the text displayed on this label will need to be updated from within the application code it will need to be connected to an outlet. In addition, the view controller will also contain five gesture recognizer objects to detect pinches, taps, rotations, swipes and long presses. When triggered, these objects will need to call action methods in order to update the label with a notification to the user that the corresponding gesture has been detected.

Select the *MainStoryboard.storyboard* file and drag a Label object from the Object Library panel to the center of the view. Once positioned, stretch the label horizontally to the outer edges of the view until the blue dotted lines representing the recommended margins appear and then modify the label properties to center the label text.

Select the label object in the view canvas, display the Assistant Editor panel and verify that the editor is displaying the contents of the *RecognizerViewController.h* file. Ctrl-click on the same label object

An iPhone iOS 6 Gesture Recognition Tutorial

and drag to a position just below the @interface line in the Assistant Editor. Release the line and in the resulting connection dialog establish an outlet connection named *statusLabel*.

Next, the non-visual gesture recognizer objects need to be added to the design. Scroll down the list of objects in the Object Library panel until the *Tap Gesture Recognizer* object comes into view. Drag and drop the object onto the View in the design area (if the object is dropped outside the view, the connection between the recognizer and the view on which the gestures are going to be performed will not be established). Repeat these steps to add Pinch, Rotation, Swipe and Long Press Gesture Recognizer objects to the design. Note that document outline panel has updated to reflect the presence of the gesture recognizer objects as illustrated in Figure 47-1:

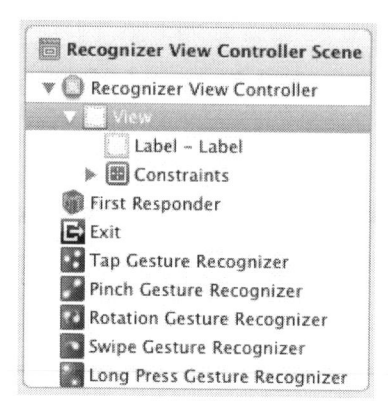

Figure 47-1

Within the document outline panel, select the Tap Gesture Recognizer instance and display the Attributes Inspector (*View -> Utilities -> Show Attributes Inspector*). Within the attributes panel, change the *Taps* value to 2 so that only double taps are detected.

Similarly, select the Long Press Recognizer object and change the *Press Duration* attribute to 3 seconds.

Having added and configured the gesture recognizers, the next step is to connect each recognizer to its corresponding action method.

Display the Assistant Editor and verify that it is displaying the content of *RecognizerViewController.h*. Ctrl-click on the *Tap Gesture Recognizer* object in the document outline panel and drag the line to the area immediately beneath the newly created outlet in the Assistant Editor panel. Release the line and, within the resulting connection dialog, establish an Action method configured to call a method named *tapDetected* with the *id* value set to *UITapGestureRecognizer* as illustrated in Figure 47-2:

An iPhone iOS 6 Gesture Recognition Tutorial

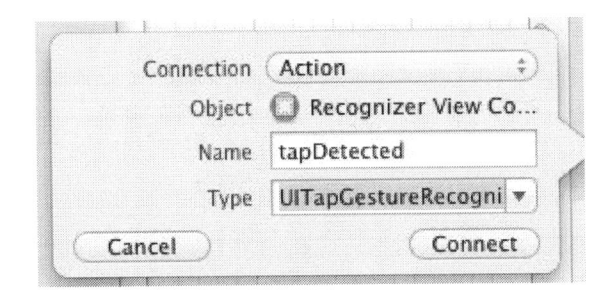

Figure 47-2

Repeat these steps to establish action connections for the pinch, rotation, swipe and long press gesture recognizers to methods named *pinchDetected*, *rotationDetected*, *swipeDetected* and *longPressDetected* respectively, taking care to select the corresponding id value for each action.

On completion of the above steps, the *RecognizerViewController.h* should read as follows:

```objectivec
#import <UIKit/UIKit.h>

@interface RecognizerViewController : UIViewController
@property (strong, nonatomic) IBOutlet UILabel *statusLabel;
- (IBAction)tapDetected:(UITapGestureRecognizer *)sender;
- (IBAction)rotationDetected:(UIRotationGestureRecognizer *)sender;
- (IBAction)pinchDetected:(UIPinchGestureRecognizer *)sender;
- (IBAction)swipeDetected:(UISwipeGestureRecognizer *)sender;
- (IBAction)longPressDetected:(UILongPressGestureRecognizer *)sender;

@end
```

47.3 Implementing the Action Methods

Having configured the gesture recognizers, the next step is to write the action methods that will be called by each recognizer when the corresponding gesture is detected. The methods stubs created by Xcode reside in the *RecognizerViewController.m* file and will update the status label with information about the detected gesture:

```objectivec
- (IBAction)longPressDetected:(UIGestureRecognizer *)sender {
    _statusLabel.text = @"Long Press";
}

- (IBAction)swipeDetected:(UIGestureRecognizer *)sender {
    _statusLabel.text = @"Right Swipe";
}

- (IBAction)tapDetected:(UIGestureRecognizer *)sender {
```

An iPhone iOS 6 Gesture Recognition Tutorial

```
    _statusLabel.text = @"Double Tap";
}

- (IBAction)pinchDetected:(UIGestureRecognizer *)sender {

    CGFloat scale = 
       [(UIPinchGestureRecognizer *)sender scale];
    CGFloat velocity =
       [(UIPinchGestureRecognizer *)sender velocity];

    NSString *resultString = [[NSString alloc] initWithFormat:
        @"Pinch - scale = %f, velocity = %f",
        scale, velocity];
    _statusLabel.text = resultString;
}

- (IBAction)rotationDetected:(UIGestureRecognizer *)sender {
    CGFloat radians =
         [(UIRotationGestureRecognizer *)sender rotation];
    CGFloat velocity =
         [(UIRotationGestureRecognizer *)sender velocity];

    NSString *resultString = [[NSString alloc] initWithFormat:
            @"Rotation - Radians = %f, velocity = %f",
            radians, velocity];
    _statusLabel.text = resultString;
}
```

47.4 Testing the Gesture Recognition Application

The final step is to build and run the application. In order to fully test the pinching and rotation recognition it will be necessary to run the application on a physical device (since it is not possible to emulate two simultaneous touches within the iOS Simulator environment). Assuming a provisioned device is attached (see *Testing iOS 6 Apps on the iPhone – Developer Certificates and Provisioning Profiles* for more details) simply click on the Xcode *Run* button. Once the application loads on the device, perform the appropriate gestures on the display and watch the status label update accordingly.

Chapter 48

48. An Overview of iOS 6 Collection View and Flow Layout

The Collection View and Flow Layout have been introduced as part of iOS 6 and combine to provide a new, flexible, and some might say long overdue, way to present content to the user. This is essentially achieved by providing a mechanism by which data driven content can be displayed in cells and the arrangement, appearance and behavior of those cells configured to meet a variety of different layout and organizational needs.

Before the introduction of Collection Views and Flow Layout, the closest iOS came to providing organized data presentation involved the use of the Table View. Whilst still a powerful user interface design option, the Table View was intended to fill a very specific need and, as such, has some limitations in terms of flexibility. Table View, for example, displays data in cells arranged in a single column layout. Collections views, on the other hand, provide a high degree of flexibility, allowing cells to be organized in just about any configuration imaginable, including grids, stacks, tiles and circular arrangements.

The goal of this chapter is to present an overview of the key elements that make up collection views prior to working through a step by step tutorial in the next chapter, entitled *An iPhone iOS 6 Storyboard-based Collection View Tutorial*.

48.1 An Overview of Collection Views

In the chapter entitled *Using Xcode Storyboards to Build Dynamic TableViews with Prototype Table View Cells*, a Table View layout was used to display a list of cars and corresponding images (Figure 48-1).

An Overview of iOS 6 Collection View and Flow Layout

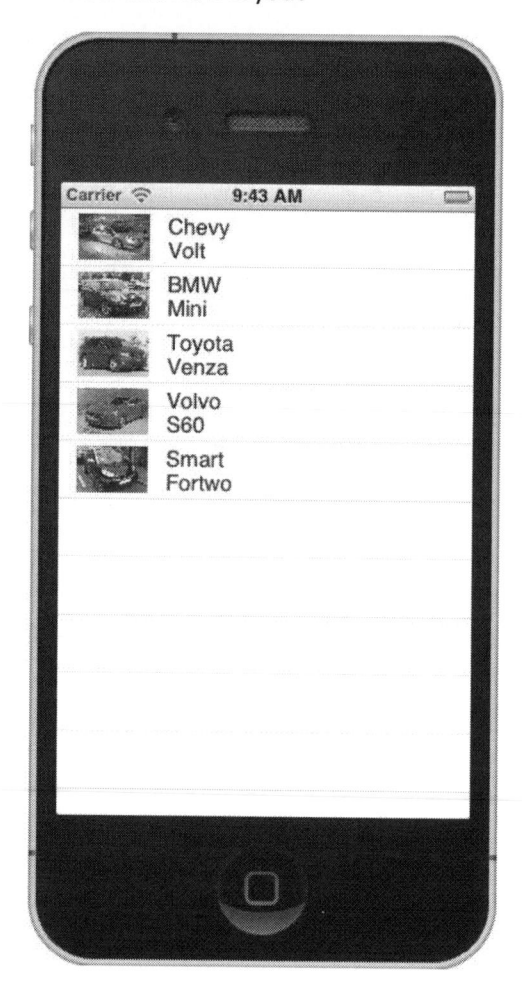

Figure 48-1

The fact is that whilst this presented the necessary information, the Table View provided very little in the way of customization options. Had the user interface been designed using a collection view, a much more visually appealing user interface could have been implemented. Figure 48-2, for example, illustrates how some of the car images associated with the earlier table view example could have been organized using a collection view configuration.

Figure 48-2

Whilst not entirely obvious from the previous screenshot, the collection view is actually scrollable, allowing the user to swipe left or right to view other car images. It is also important to note that this example is just the default behavior of a collection view with a flow layout. Customization options far beyond this are possible using collection views.

At an abstract level, a collection view consists of four key elements consisting of *cells*, *supplementary views*, *decoration views* and a *layout object*. A cell is a representation of an item of data to be displayed (for example an image or a set of text based data).

As with the Table View, a collection view may be divided into multiple sections. Supplementary views are objects that provide additional information about a section in a collection view. These are somewhat similar to section headers and footers in table views but are more general purpose and provide a greater level of flexibility in terms of positioning and content.

An Overview of iOS 6 Collection View and Flow Layout

Decoration views can be used to provide a decorative background for the collection view which scrolls along with the content. The classic example of a decoration view in Apple's own demonstrations involves constructing the image of a bookshelf behind a collection view containing photo images. It is important to note that the standard Flow Layout class does not support decoration views.

In practical terms, a collection view consists of multiple class instances, each of which will be described in more detail in the remainder of this chapter.

48.2 The UICollectionView Class

The UICollectionView class is responsible for managing the data items that are to be displayed to the user. The collection view instance needs a data source object from which to obtain the data items to be displayed, together with a delegate object to handle user interaction with the collection. These objects must implement the UICollectionViewDataSource and UICollectionViewDelegate protocols respectively.

Perhaps the most important requirement for the UICollectionView class is a layout object to control the layout and organization of the cells. By default, the UICollectionViewFlowLayout class is used by instances of the UICollectionView class. In the event that the flow layout does not provide the necessary behavior, this class may also be subclassed and extended to provide additional functionality. Perhaps the most impressive fact, however, is that an entirely new layout class may be created by subclassing UICollectionViewLayout and implementing application specific layout capabilities within that class. The custom layout is then essentially "plugged in" to the UICollectionView instance where it will dictate the layout of the data cells as it has been designed to do.

The UICollectionView class also includes a wide range of methods that can be used to perform such tasks as to add, remove, move, modify and select items.

48.3 The UICollectionViewCell Class

As the name suggests, the UICollectionViewCell class is responsible for displaying whatever data is provided to the UICollectionView instance by the data source with one cell corresponding to one data item. In terms of architecture, this class consists of two background views and one content view. The two background views may be used to provide a visual cue to the user when the corresponding cell is selected or highlighted. The content view contains the objects necessary to display the data to the user and can consist of any combination of valid UIKit classes. When adding subviews to a cell it is imperative that those objects be added to the *contentView* and not the background views, otherwise the objects will not be visible to the user.

An Overview of iOS 6 Collection View and Flow Layout

There is a clear separation between layout and the contents of a cell. The cell only knows what to display, the sizing and positioning of the cell within the wider context of the collection view is controlled by the layout object assigned to the collection view.

Instances of UICollectionViewCell class are not typically instantiated directly in code. Instead, the class is registered as the cell class for a collection view and is then created internally as needed. Collection views are scrollable and, consequently, at any one time only a subset of the cells in a collection are visible. This enables the system to reuse cell objects that are currently scrolled outside of the viewable area of the screen and only create new ones when necessary. This is achieved using a queuing mechanism and results in improved performance, particularly when dealing with larger data sets.

48.4 The UICollectionReusableView Class

The base class from which the UICellCollectionView class is derived, this class is most typically subclassed in application code to create supplementary views.

48.5 The UICollectionViewFlowLayout Class

The UICollectionViewFlowLayout class is the default layout class for collection views and is designed to layout cells in a grid-like manner.

This class requires a delegate object that conforms to the UICollectionViewDelegateFlowLayout protocol which is typically the collection view's UICollectionViewDelegate object.

By default, flow is implemented in a manner similar to that of "line wrapping" in a text editor. When one row of cells is full, the cells flow onto the next row and so on until all cells capable of fitting into the currently visible display region are visible. The flow layout class supports both horizontal and vertical scrolling configurable via the *scrollDirection* property. In addition, properties such as the spacing between lines of cells in the grid and cells in a row may be configured, together with default sizes for cells and supplementary views (unless overridden via methods implemented in the delegate object).

48.6 The UICollectionViewLayoutAttributes Class

Each item in a collection view, be it a cell or a supplementary view, has associated with it a set of attributes. The UICollectionViewLayoutAttributes class serves as an object into which these attributes can be stored and transferred between objects. A Flow Layout object will, for example, be asked by the collection view object to return the attributes for a cell at a given index in a collection view via a call to the *layoutAttributesForItemAtIndexPath:* method. This method, in turn, returns those attributes encapsulated in a UICollectionViewLayoutAttributes object. Similarly, such object instances can be used to apply new attributes to a collection view element. The attributes stored by the UICollectionViewLayoutAttributes class are as follows (keeping in mind that this class may be subclassed and extended to allow the storage of other values):

- **alpha** – the transparency of the item.
- **center** – the location of the center of the item.
- **frame** – the CGRect frame in which the item is displayed.
- **hidden** – whether or not the item is currently visible.
- **indexPath** – the index path location of the item in the collection view.
- **representedElementCategory** – The type of item for which the attributes apply (i.e. for a cell, supplementary or decoration view).
- **size** – the size of the item.
- **transform3D** – the current transform of the item. Attribute can be used to perform tasks such as rotating or scaling the item.
- **zIndex** – controls the position of the item in the z axis (in other words whether or not it is on top of or below other overlapping items).

48.7 The UICollectionViewDataSource Protocol

The UICollectionViewDataSource protocol needs to be implemented by the class responsible for supplying the collection view with the pre-configured cells and supplementary views to be displayed to the user. This basically consists of a number of methods that define information such how many items of data are to be displayed, how the data is divided into different sections and, most importantly, supplies the collection view with the cell objects to be displayed.

Mandatory methods in the protocol are as follows:

- **collectionView:numberOfItemsInSection:** - Returns the number of items to be displayed in the specified section of the collection view.
- **collectionView:cellForItemAtIndexPath:** - This method is called by the collection view when it is ready to display a cell at the specified index path location in the collection view. It is required to return a cell object configured appropriately for the referenced index.

Optional methods in the protocol are as follows:

- **numberOfSectionsInCollectionView:** - Indicates to the collection view the number of sections into which the collection view is to be divided.
- **collectionView:viewForSupplementaryElementOfKind:atIndexPath:** - Called by the collection view to request a supplementary view of the specified kind. Returns an appropriately configured object to be displayed. In terms of the UICollectionViewFlowLayout class, the layout will request a supplementary view for either a header (UICollectionElementKindSectionHeader) or footer (UICollectionElementKindSectionFooter).

48.8 The UICollectionViewDelegate Protocol

The UICollectionViewDelegate protocol defines a set of optional methods which, if implemented, will be called when certain events take place within the corresponding collection. These methods relate primarily to handling user interaction with the collection view elements (such as selecting a specific cell). Some of the key methods in this protocol include:

- **collectionView:shouldSelectItemAtIndexPath:** - Returns a boolean value indicating whether the specified item is selectable by the user.
- **collectionView:didSelectItemAtIndexPath:** - Called by the collection view when the specified item has been selected by the user.
- **collectionView:shouldDeselectItemAtIndexPath:** - Returns a boolean value to indicate whether the specified item may be deselected by the user.
- **collectionView:didDeselectItemAtIndexPath:** - Called by the collection view when the specified item has been selected by the user.
- **collectionView:shouldHighlightItemAtIndexPath:** - Returns a boolean value indicating whether the specified item should be highlighted as a pre-cursor to possible selection by the user.
- **collectionView:didHighlightItemAtIndexPath:** - Called by the collection view when the specified item has been highlighted.
- **collectionView:didUnhighlightItemAtIndexPath:** - Called by the collection view when the specified item has been un-highlighted.
- **collectionView:didEndDisplayingCell:forItemAtIndexPath:** - Called by the collection view when the specified cell has been removed from the collection view.
- **collectionView:didEndDisplayingSupplementaryView:forElementOfKind:atIndexPath:** - Called by the collection view when the specified supplementary view has been removed from the collection view.

48.9 The UICollectionViewDelegateFlowLayout Protocol

The UICollectionViewFlowLayout class has a number of properties that can be set to globally set default characteristics for items within a collection view (for example section inset, item spacing, line spacing, inter-cell spacing, supplementary view header and footer sizing etc). Alternatively, these values may be overridden on a per-cell and per-section basis by implementing the following delegate methods in a class which conforms to the UICollectionViewDelegateFlowLayout protocol. In most cases, this will be the same class as that implementing the UICollectionViewDelegate protocol. Note that in each case, the method is passed a reference either to the cell or section for which information is required:

- **collectionView:layout:sizeForItemAtIndexPath:** - Required to return to the flow layout object the size attributes for the item at the specified index path.

An Overview of iOS 6 Collection View and Flow Layout

- **collectionView:layout:insetForSectionAtIndex:** - Required to return the inset value for the specified collection view section.
- **collectionView:layout:minimumLineSpacingForSectionAtIndex:** - Required to return the inset value for the specified collection view section.
- **collectionView:layout:minimumInteritemSpacingForSectionAtIndex:** - Required to return the interim spacing between cells in a row for the specified collection view section.
- **collectionView:layout:referenceSizeForHeaderInSection:** - Required to return the size for the header supplementary view for specified collection view section. Note that if a size is not specified, the view will not appear.
- **collectionView:layout:referenceSizeForFooterInSection:** - Required to return the size for the footer supplementary view for specified collection view section. Note that if a size is not specified, the view will not appear.

48.10 Cell and View Reuse

As previously discussed, the code for a typical application using a collection view will not directly create instances of either the cell or supplementary view classes. The reasoning behind this becomes evident when performance and memory requirements are taken into consideration. Consider, for example, a collection view that is required to display 1000 photo images. It can be assumed with a reasonable degree of certainty that only a small percentage of cells will be visible to the user at any one time. If the application were permitted to create each of the 1000 cells in advance the device would very quickly run into memory limitations.

Instead, the application begins by registering with the collection view the class to be used for cell objects, along with a *reuse identifier*. If the cell class was written in code, the registration is performed using the *registerClass:* method of UICollectionView. For example:

```
[self.myCollectionView registerClass:[MyCollectionViewCell class]
forCellWithReuseIdentifier:@"MYCELL"];
```

In the event that the cell is contained within an Interface Builder NIB file, the *registerNib:* method is used instead.

The same concept applies to supplementary views which must also be registered with the collection view using either the *registerClass:forSupplementaryViewOfKind:* and *registerNib:forSupplementaryViewOfKind:* methods.

Perhaps the most important point to remember from this chapter is that if the cell or supplementary views are created using prototypes within a storyboard it is not necessary to register the class in code and, in fact, doing so will prevent the cell or view from appearing when the application runs.

An Overview of iOS 6 Collection View and Flow Layout

As the collection view initializes, it calls the *cellForItemAtIndexPath:* method of the datasource class passing through the index path for which a cell object is required. This method will then call the *dequeueReusableCellWithReuseIdentifier:* method of the collection view, passing through both the index path and the reuse ID assigned to the cell class when it was registered, to find out if there is a reusable cell object in the queue that can be used for this new cell. Since this is the initialization phase and no cells have been deemed eligible for reuse, the method will create a new cell and return it. Once all the visible cells have been created the collection view will stop asking for more cells. The code for the *cellForItemAtIndexPath:* will typically read as follows (though the code to customize the cell before returning it will be implementation specific):

```
-(UICollectionViewCell *)collectionView:(UICollectionView
*)collectionView cellForItemAtIndexPath:(NSIndexPath *)indexPath
{
    CollectionViewCell *myCell =
        [collectionView
            dequeueReusableCellWithReuseIdentifier:@"MYCELL"
            forIndexPath:indexPath];

    UIImage *image;

    if ([indexPath row] % 2)
            image = [UIImage imageNamed:@"volvo_s60_small.jpg"];
    else
        image = [UIImage imageNamed:@"chevy_volt.jpg"];

    myCell.myImage.image = image;

    return myCell;
}
```

As the user scrolls through the collection view, some cells will move out of the visible frame. When this happens, the collection view places them on the reuse queue. As cells are moving out of view, new ones are likely to be coming into view. For each cell moving into the view area, the collection view will call *cellForItemAtIndexPath:*. This time, however, when a call to *dequeueReusableCellWithReuseIdentifier:* is made, it is most likely that an existing cell object will be returned from the reuse queue, thereby avoiding the necessity to create a new object.

These same reuse concepts apply equally to supplementary views, with the exception that the collection view will call the *viewForSupplementaryElementOfKind:* method of the data source when seeking a view object which must, in turn, call *dequeueReusableSupplementaryViewOfKind:*.

48.11 Summary

Collection view and the flow layout were introduced into iOS 6 to provide a flexible approach to displaying data items to the user. The key objectives of collection views are flexibility and performance.

This chapter has outlined the overall concepts behind collection views and flow layout before looking in some detail at the different classes that can be brought together to implement collection views in iOS 6 applications. Finally, the chapter provided an explanation of cell and supplementary view object reuse.

The next chapter will work through the creation of an example application that utilizes collection views to present a gallery of images to the user.

Chapter 49

49. An iPhone iOS 6 Storyboard-based Collection View Tutorial

The primary goal of this chapter is to demonstrate, in a tutorial format, the steps involved in implementing a collection view based application user interface and, in doing so, serve to reenforce the collection view concepts outlined in the previous chapter. By far the most productive way to implement collection views (and the approach used in this tutorial) is to take advantage of the Storyboard feature of Xcode and, in particular, the collection view cell and supplementary view prototyping options of Interface Builder.

49.1 Creating the Collection View Example Project

Launch Xcode and create a new project by selecting the options to create a new iPhone iOS application based on the *Single View Application* template. Enter *CollectionDemo* as the product name and class prefix, set the device to *iPhone* and select the *Use Storyboards* and *Use Automatic Reference Counting* options if they are not already selected.

49.2 Removing the Template View Controller

Based on the template selection made when the project was set up, Xcode has created a generic UIViewController based subclass for the application. For the purposes of this tutorial, however, this needs to be replaced with a UICollectionViewController subclass. Begin, therefore, by selecting the *CollectionDemoViewController.m* and *CollectionDemoViewController.h* files in the project navigator and pressing the keyboard delete key. When prompted, click the button to move the files to trash.

Next, select the *MainStoryboard.storyboard* file and, in the storyboard canvas, select the view controller so that it is highlighted in blue (click either on the toolbar beneath the view or the status bar containing the battery indicator to select the view controller as opposed to the view) and hit the keyboard delete key to remove the controller.

An iPhone iOS 6 Storyboard-based Collection View Tutorial

49.3 Adding a Collection View Controller to the Storyboard

The first element that needs to be added to the project is a UICollectionViewController subclass. To add this, select the Xcode *File -> New -> File...* menu option. In the resulting panel, select *iOS Cocoa Touch* from the left hand panel, followed by *Objective-C class* in the main panel before clicking *Next*.

On the subsequent screen, name the new class *MyCollectionViewController* and from the *Subclass of* drop down menu choose *UICollectionViewController*. Verify that the options to create an XIB file and to target the iPad are off before clicking *Next*. Choose a location for the files and then click *Create*.

The project now has two new files named *MyCollectionViewController.m* and *MyCollectionViewController.h* that represent a new class named *MyCollectionViewController* which is itself a subclass of *UICollectionViewController*.

The next step is to add a UICollectionViewController instance to the storyboard and then associate it with the newly created class. Select the *MainStoryboard.storyboard* file and drag and drop a Collection View Controller object from the Object Library panel onto the storyboard canvas as illustrated in Figure 49-1.

Note that the UICollectionViewController added to the storyboard has also brought with it a UICollectionView instance (indicated by the black background) and a prototype cell (represented by the white square located in the top left hand corner of the collection view).

An iPhone iOS 6 Storyboard-based Collection View Tutorial

Figure 49-1

With the new view controller selected in the storyboard, display the Identity Inspector either by selecting the toolbar item in the Utilities panel or via the *View -> Utilities -> Show Identity Inspector* menu option and change the *Class* setting (Figure 49-2) from the generic UICollectionViewController class to the newly added *MyCollectionViewController* class.

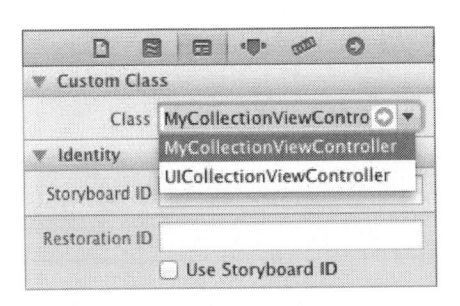

Figure 49-2

49.4 Adding the Collection View Cell Class to the Project

With a subclass of UICollectionViewController added to the project, a new class must now be added which subclasses UICollectionViewCell.

Once again, select the Xcode *File -> New -> File...* menu option. In the resulting panel, select *iOS Cocoa Touch* from the left hand panel, followed by *Objective-C class* in the main panel before clicking *Next*.

375

An iPhone iOS 6 Storyboard-based Collection View Tutorial

On the subsequent screen, name the new class *MyCollectionViewCell* and from the *Subclass of* drop down menu choose *UICollectionViewCell*. Click *Next*, choose a location for the files and then click *Create*.

Return to the *MainStoryboard.storyboard* file and select the white square in the collection view. This is the prototype cell for the collection view and needs to be assigned a reuse identifier and be associated with the new class. With the cell selected, open the Identity Inspector panel and change the Class to *MyCollectionViewCell*. Remaining in the Utilities panel, display the Attributes Inspector (Figure 49-3) and enter *MyCell* as the reuse identifier.

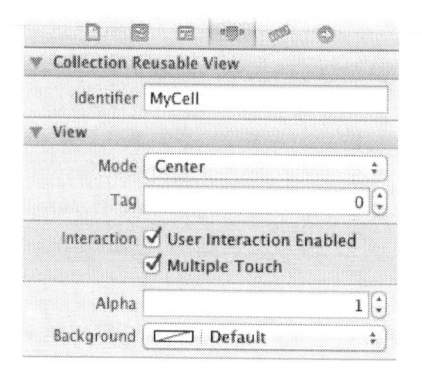

Figure 49-3

49.5 Designing the Cell Prototype

With the basic collection view classes implemented and associated with the storyboard objects, it is now time to design the cell. This is, quite simply, a matter of dragging and dropping items from the object library onto the prototype cell in the storyboard view. Additionally the size of the cell may be modified by selecting it and using the resulting resize handles. The exact design of the cell is entirely dependent on what is to be displayed. For the purposes of this example, however, each cell is simply going to display an image.

Begin by resizing the cell to a slightly larger size, locating the Image View object in the Object Library panel and dragging and dropping it into the prototype cell as shown in Figure 49-4.

An iPhone iOS 6 Storyboard-based Collection View Tutorial

Figure 49-4

Since it will be necessary to assign an image when a cell is configured, an outlet to the Image View will be needed. Display the Assistant Editor, make sure it is listing the code for the *MyCollectionViewCell.h* file then Ctrl-click and drag from the Image View object to a position immediately beneath the @interface line. Release the line and, in the resulting connection panel, establish an outlet connection named *imageView*. On completion of the connection, select *MyCollectionViewCell.h* in the project navigator and verify that it reads as follows:

```
#import <UIKit/UIKit.h>

@interface MyCollectionViewCell : UICollectionViewCell
@property (strong, nonatomic) IBOutlet UIImageView *imageView;

@end
```

With the connection established, the prototype cell implementation is complete.

49.6 Implementing the Data Model

The data model for this example application is going to consist of a set of images, each of which will be displayed in a cell within the collection view. The first step in creating this model is to load the images into the project. A Zip file containing the images can be downloaded from the following link:

```
http://www.ebookfrenzy.com/code/carImagesSmall.zip
```

377

An iPhone iOS 6 Storyboard-based Collection View Tutorial

Once downloaded, unzip the archive and drag and drop the 12 image files onto the *Supporting Files* section of the Xcode project navigator panel.

Next, select the *MyCollectionViewController.h* file and declare an array into which will be stored the image file names:

```
#import <UIKit/UIKit.h>

@interface MyCollectionViewController : UICollectionViewController

@property (strong, nonatomic) NSMutableArray *carImages;
@end
```

Finally, edit the *MyCollectionViewController.m* file and modify the *viewDidLoad* method to initialize the array with the names of the car image files:

```
- (void)viewDidLoad
{
    [super viewDidLoad];
    _carImages = [@[@"chevy_small.jpg",
                    @"mini_small.jpg",
                    @"rover_small.jpg",
                    @"smart_small.jpg",
                    @"highlander_small.jpg",
                    @"venza_small.jpg",
                    @"volvo_small.jpg",
                    @"vw_small.jpg",
                    @"ford_small.jpg",
                    @"nissan_small.jpg",
                    @"honda_small.jpg",
                    @"jeep_small.jpg"] mutableCopy];
}
```

Note that we are using Modern Objective-C syntax to initialize the array. As outlined in the chapter entitled *The Basics of Modern Objective-C*, this approach returns a non-mutable array by default. Later in the chapter we will be implementing code to remove items from the array, so need to call the *mutableCopy* method of the array to make sure we can modify the array later.

49.7 Implementing the Data Source

As outlined in the chapter entitled *An Overview of iOS 6 Collection Views and Flow Layout*, a collection view needs a data source and a delegate in order to provide all the functionality it is capable of providing. By default, Xcode has designated the *MyCollectionViewController* class as both the delegate and data source for the UICollectionView in the user interface. To verify this, select the

An iPhone iOS 6 Storyboard-based Collection View Tutorial

black background of the collection view controller in the storyboard to select the UICollectionView subclass instance and display the Connections Inspector (select the far right item in at the top of the Utilities panel or use the *View -> Utilities -> Show Connection Inspector* menu option). Assuming that the connections have been made, the *Outlets* section of the panel will be configured as shown in Figure 49-5.

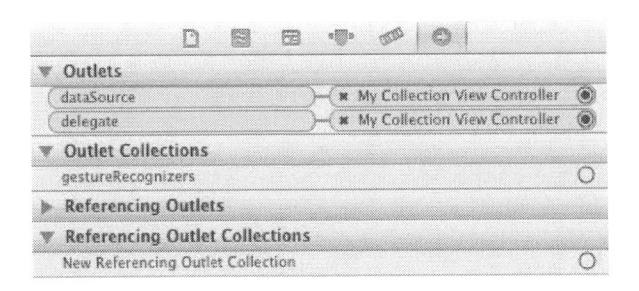

Figure 49-5

The next step is to declare which protocols the MyCollectionViewController class is going to implement. Since the class will also need to work with the MyCollectionViewCell class, now is also a good opportunity to import the header file for this class. Select the *MyCollectionViewController.h* file and modify it so that it reads as outlined in the following listing:

```
#import <UIKit/UIKit.h>
#import "MyCollectionViewCell.h"

@interface MyCollectionViewController : UICollectionViewController
<UICollectionViewDataSource, UICollectionViewDelegate>

@property (strong, nonatomic) NSMutableArray *carImages;
@end
```

A number of data source methods will now be implemented to conform with the UICollectionViewDataSource protocol. The first lets the collection view know how many sections are to be displayed. For the purposes of this example there is only going to be one section, so select the *MyCollectionViewController.m* file and implement the *numberOfSectionsInCollectionView:* method to return a value of 1.

```
#pragma mark -
#pragma mark UICollectionViewDataSource

-(NSInteger)numberOfSectionsInCollectionView:
       (UICollectionView *)collectionView
{
    return 1;
```

379

An iPhone iOS 6 Storyboard-based Collection View Tutorial

}

The next method is called by the collection view to identify the number of items that are to be displayed in each section. In this case, the sole collection view section will be required to display a cell for each element in the *carImages* array:

```
-(NSInteger)collectionView:(UICollectionView *)collectionView
      numberOfItemsInSection:(NSInteger)section
{
    return _carImages.count;
}
```

The *cellForItemAtIndexPath:* method will be called by the collection view in order to obtain cells configured based on the indexPath value passed to the method. This method will request a cell object from the reuse queue and then set the image on the Image View object which was configured in the cell prototype earlier in this chapter, using the index path row as the index into the *carImages* array:

```
-(UICollectionViewCell *)collectionView:(UICollectionView *)collectionView
cellForItemAtIndexPath:(NSIndexPath *)indexPath
{
    MyCollectionViewCell *myCell = [collectionView
          dequeueReusableCellWithReuseIdentifier:@"MyCell"
          forIndexPath:indexPath];

    UIImage *image;
    int row = [indexPath row];

    image = [UIImage imageNamed:_carImages[row]];

    myCell.imageView.image = image;

    return myCell;
}
```

49.8 Testing the Application

Compile and run the application, either on a physical iPhone device or using the iOS Simulator. Once loaded, the collection view will appear as illustrated in Figure 49-6. Clearly, each cell has been displayed at a fixed size causing the images to be compressed to fit into the containing cell. In order to improve the visual experience, some work is clearly still needed.

An iPhone iOS 6 Storyboard-based Collection View Tutorial

Figure 49-6

49.9 Setting Sizes for Cell Items

When the prototype cell was designed, it was set to a specific size. Unless additional steps are taken, each cell within the collection view will appear at that size. This means that images are not displayed at their original size. In actual fact, all of the car images differ in size from each other. What is needed is a way to set the size of each cell based on the size of the content it is required to display (in this instance the dimensions of the corresponding image). As outlined in the previous chapter, if a method named *sizeForItemAtIndexPath:* is implemented in the UICollectionViewFlowLayoutDelegate protocol class (which by default is the same class as the UICollectionViewDelegate delegate), it will be called for each cell to request size information. Clearly, by implementing this method it will be possible to have each image displayed at its own size. Remaining in *MyCollectionViewController.m*, implement this method to identify the size of the current image and return the result to the collection view:

```
#pragma mark -
#pragma mark UICollectionViewFlowLayoutDelegate

-(CGSize)collectionView:(UICollectionView *)collectionView
layout:(UICollectionViewLayout *)collectionViewLayout
sizeForItemAtIndexPath:(NSIndexPath *)indexPath
```

An iPhone iOS 6 Storyboard-based Collection View Tutorial

```
{
    UIImage *image;
    int row = [indexPath row];

    image = [UIImage imageNamed:_carImages[row]];

    return image.size;
}
```

Run the application once again and note that, as shown in Figure 49-7, the images are now displayed at their original sizes.

Figure 49-7

49.10 Changing Scroll Direction

As currently configured, the flow layout object assigned to the collection view is in vertical scrolling mode. As a demonstration of both one of the delegate methods for handling user interaction and the effects of horizontal scrolling, the example will now be extended to switch to horizontal scrolling when any cell in the view is selected.

When making changes to the flow layout assigned to a collection view, it is not possible to directly change properties on the layout object. Instead, and as illustrated in the following code, a new layout object must be created, configured and then set as the current layout object for the collection view. Within the *MyCollectionViewController.m* file, implement the *didSelectItemAtIndexPath:* delegate method as follows:

```
#pragma mark -
#pragma mark UICollectionViewDelegate

-(void)collectionView:(UICollectionView *)collectionView
didSelectItemAtIndexPath:(NSIndexPath *)indexPath
{
    UICollectionViewFlowLayout *myLayout =
        [[UICollectionViewFlowLayout alloc]init];

    myLayout.scrollDirection =
UICollectionViewScrollDirectionHorizontal;
    [self.collectionView setCollectionViewLayout:myLayout
animated:YES];
}
```

Compile and run the application and select an image once the collection view appears. Notice how the layout smoothly animates the transition from vertical to horizontal scrolling.

Note also that the layout adjusts automatically when the orientation of the device is rotated. Figure 49-8, for example shows the collection view in landscape orientation with horizontal scrolling enabled.

Figure 49-8

49.11 **Implementing a Supplementary View**

The next task in this tutorial is to demonstrate the implementation of supplementary views in the form of a header for the car image gallery. The first step is to ask Interface Builder to add a prototype

An iPhone iOS 6 Storyboard-based Collection View Tutorial

header supplementary view to the UICollectionView. To do this, select the *MainStoryboard.storyboard* file and click on the black background of the collection view controller canvas representing the UICollectionView object. Display the Attributes Inspector in the Utilities panel, locate the *Accessories* section listed under *Collection View* and set the *Section Header* check box as illustrated in Figure 49-9.

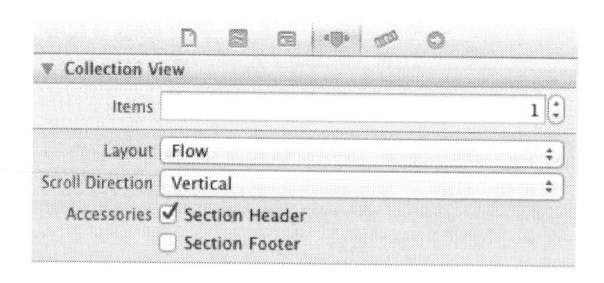

Figure 49-9

Once the header section has been enabled, a header prototype object will have been added to the storyboard view canvas. As with the prototype cell, this header can be configured using any combination of view objects from the Object Library panel. For this example, drag a Label object onto the prototype header and position it so the horizontal and vertical center auto layout lines appear. By default, labels have a black foreground so the text in the label will not be visible until a different color is selected. With the label still selected, move to the Attribute Inspector and change the Color property to white. Once completed, the layout should now resemble that of Figure 49-10.

Figure 49-10

An iPhone iOS 6 Storyboard-based Collection View Tutorial

With a header prototype added to the storyboard, a new class needs to be added to the project to serve as the class for the header. Select *File -> New -> File...* and add a new Objective-C Class named *MySupplementaryView* subclassed from UICollectionReusableView. Select the header in the storyboard and, using the Identity Inspector, change the class from UICollectionReusableView to MySupplementaryView.

As with cells, supplementary views are reused, so select the Attributes Inspector in the Utilities panel and enter *MyHeader* as the reuse identifier.

The text displayed on the header will be set within a data source method of the view controller. As such, an outlet to the label will be needed. Display the Assistant Editor and make sure that it is displaying the code for *MySupplementaryView.h*. If a different file is displayed, click on the Manual entries or the Tuxedo image located across the top of the Assistant Editor panel and select *Manual -> CollectionDemo -> MySupplementaryView.h*:

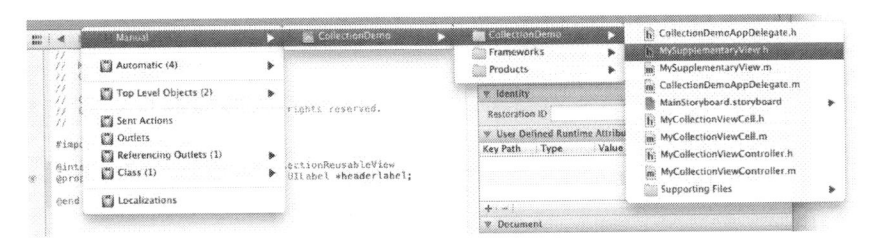

Figure 49-11

Once *MySupplementaryView.h* is displayed in the Assistant Editor, establish an outlet connection from the label in the header and name it *headerLabel*. On completion of the connection, the content of the file should read as follows:

```
#import <UIKit/UIKit.h>

@interface MySupplementaryView : UICollectionReusableView
@property (strong, nonatomic) IBOutlet UILabel *headerLabel;

@end
```

49.12 Implementing the Supplementary View Protocol Methods

In order for the supplementary header view to work, a data source method needs to be implemented. When the collection view is ready to display a supplementary view it will call the *viewForSupplementaryElementOfKind:* method of the data source and expect, in return, a configured object ready to be displayed. Passed through as an argument to this method is a value indicating whether this is a header or footer which can be checked by the code to return the appropriate object. Note also that supplementary views also use a dequeuing mechanism similar to cells. For this

385

example, implement the *viewForSupplementaryElementOfKind:* as follows in the *MyCollectionViewController.m* file:

```
-(UICollectionReusableView *)collectionView:(UICollectionView
*)collectionView viewForSupplementaryElementOfKind:(NSString *)kind
atIndexPath:(NSIndexPath *)indexPath
{
    MySupplementaryView *header = nil;

    if ([kind isEqual:UICollectionElementKindSectionHeader])
    {
        header = [collectionView
dequeueReusableSupplementaryViewOfKind:kind
            withReuseIdentifier:@"MyHeader"
            forIndexPath:indexPath];

        header.headerLabel.text = @"Car Image Gallery";
    }
    return header;
}
```

Next, select the *MyCollectionViewController.h* file and import the header file for the new *MySupplementaryView* class:

```
#import <UIKit/UIKit.h>
#import "MyCollectionViewCell.h"
#import "MySupplementaryView.h"

@interface MyCollectionViewController : UICollectionViewController
<UICollectionViewDataSource, UICollectionViewDelegate>
@property (strong, nonatomic) NSMutableArray *carImages;
@end
```

Compile and run the application once again (Figure 49-12) and note that the header supplementary view is now visible in the collection view.

Figure 49-12

49.13 Deleting Collection View Items

The last task in this tutorial is to implement functionality to allow items to be removed from the data model and the collection view. This is a two step process, the first step being the removal of the item from the data model (in this instance the *carItems* array). Having removed the item from the data model, the next step is to remove it from the collection view. This is achieved by passing through an array of index path objects for the items to be removed to the *deleteItemsAtIndexPaths:* method of the collection view object. For the purposes of this example, we will re-purpose the *didSelectItemAtIndexPath:* delegate method so that instead of changing the scroll direction it now causes the selected item to be deleted. Select the *MyCollectionViewController.m* file, locate the *didSelectItemAtIndexPath:* method and modify it so that it reads as outlined in the following listing:

```
-(void)collectionView:(UICollectionView *)collectionView
didSelectItemAtIndexPath:(NSIndexPath *)indexPath
{
    int row = [indexPath row];

    [_carImages removeObjectAtIndex:row];

    NSArray *deletions = @[indexPath];

    [self.collectionView deleteItemsAtIndexPaths:deletions];
}
```

Compile and run the application one final time and note that items are deleted from the collection view as they are selected. Note also how the collection view animates the re-arrangement of the remaining cells to fill the gap left as a result of a deletion.

49.14 Summary

The previous chapter (*An Overview of iOS 6 Collection Views and Flow Layout*) covered a considerable amount of ground in terms of the theory behind collection views in iOS 6. This chapter has put much of this theory into practice through the implementation of an example application that uses a collection view to display a gallery of images.

Chapter 50

50. Subclassing and Extending the iOS 6 Collection View Flow Layout

In this, the final chapter on the subject of collection views in iOS 6, the UICollectionViewFlowLayout class will be extended to provide custom layout behavior for the *CollectionDemo* application created in the previous chapter.

As previously described, whilst the collection view is responsible for displaying data elements in the form of cells, it is the layout object that controls how those cells are to be arranged and positioned on the screen. One of the most powerful features of collection views is the ability to switch out one layout object for another in order to change both the way in which cells are presented to the user, and the way in which that layout responds to user interaction.

In the event that the UICollectionViewFlowLayout class does not provide the necessary behavior for an application, therefore, it can be replaced with a custom layout object that does. By far the easiest way to achieve this is to subclass UICollectionViewFlowLayout class and extend it to provide the desired layout behavior.

50.1 About the Example Layout Class

This chapter will work step-by-step through the process of creating a new collection view layout class by subclassing and extending UICollectionViewFlowLayout. The purpose of the new layout class will be to allow the user to move and stretch cells in the collection view by pinching and dragging cells. As such, the example, will also demonstrate the use of gesture recognizers with collection views.

Begin by launching Xcode and loading the *CollectionDemo* project created in the previous chapter.

50.2 Subclassing the UICollectionViewFlowLayout Class

The first step is it to create a new class that is itself a subclass of UICollectionViewFlowLayout. Begin, therefore, by selecting the *File -> New -> File...* menu option in Xcode and in the resulting panel, create a new Cocoa Touch Objective-C class named *MyFlowLayout* that subclasses from UICollectionViewFlowLayout.

50.3 Extending the New Layout Class

The new layout class is now created and ready to be extended to add the new functionality. Since the new layout class is going to allow cells to be dragged around and resized by the user, it will need some properties to store a reference to the cell being manipulated, the scale value by which the cell is being resized and, finally, the current location of the cell on the screen. With these requirements in mind, select the *MyFlowLayout.h* file and modify it as follows:

```
#import <UIKit/UIKit.h>

@interface MyFlowLayout : UICollectionViewFlowLayout
@property (strong, nonatomic) NSIndexPath *currentCellPath;
@property (nonatomic) CGPoint currentCellCenter;
@property (nonatomic) CGFloat currentCellScale;

@end
```

When the scale and center properties are changed, it will be necessary to invalidate the layout so that the collection view is updated and the cell redrawn at the new size and location on the screen. To ensure that this happens, *setter* methods need to be implemented in the *MyFlowLayout.m* file for the center and scale properties that invalidate the layout in addition to storing the new property values:

```
#import "MyFlowLayout.h"

@implementation MyFlowLayout

-(void) setCurrentCellScale: (CGFloat) scale;
{
    _currentCellScale = scale;
    [self invalidateLayout];
}

- (void) setCurrentCellCenter: (CGPoint) origin
{
    _currentCellCenter = origin;
    [self invalidateLayout];
}
@end
```

50.4 Implementing the layoutAttributesForItemAtIndexPath: Method

The collection view object makes calls to a datasource delegate object to obtain cells to be displayed within the collection, passing though an index path object to identify the cell that is required. When

Subclassing and Extending the iOS 6 Collection View Flow Layout

a cell is returned by the datasource, the collection view object then calls the layout object and expects in return a set of layout attributes in the form of a UICollectionViewLayoutAttributes object for that cell indicating how and where it is to be displayed on the screen.

The method of the layout object called by the collection view will be one of either *layoutAttributesForItemAtIndexPath:* or *layoutAttributesForElementsInRect:*. The former method is passed the index path to the specific cell for which layout attributes are required. It is the job of this method to calculate these attributes based on internal logic and return the attributes object to the collection view.

The *layoutAttributesForElementsInRect:* method, on the other hand, is passed a CGRect object representing a rectangular region of the device display and expects, in return, an array of attribute objects for all cells that fall within the designated region.

In order to modify the behavior of the flow layout subclass, these methods need to be overridden to apply the necessary layout attribute changes to the cell items.

The first method to be implemented in this example is the *layoutAttributesForItemAtIndexPath:* method which should be implemented in the *MyFlowLayout.m* file as follows:

```
-(UICollectionViewLayoutAttributes
*)layoutAttributesForItemAtIndexPath:(NSIndexPath *)indexPath
{
    // Get the current attributes for the item at the indexPath
    UICollectionViewLayoutAttributes *attributes =
        [super layoutAttributesForItemAtIndexPath:indexPath];

    // Modify them to match the pinch values
    [self modifyLayoutAttributes:attributes];

    // return them to collection view
    return attributes;
}
```

Before the attributes for the requested cell can be modified, the method needs to know what those attributes would be for an unmodified UICollectionViewFlowLayout instance. Since this class is a subclass of UICollectionViewFlowLayout, we can obtain this information, as performed in the above method, via a call to the *layoutAttributesForItemAtIndexPath:* method of the superclass:

```
UICollectionViewLayoutAttributes *attributes =
        [super layoutAttributesForItemAtIndexPath:indexPath];
```

Subclassing and Extending the iOS 6 Collection View Flow Layout

Having ascertained what the attributes would normally be, the method then calls a custom method named *modifyLayoutAttributes:* and then returns the modified attributes to the collection view. It will be the task of the *modifyLayoutAttributes:* method (which will be implemented later) to apply the resize and movement effects to the attributes of the cell over which the pinch gesture is taking place.

50.5 Implementing the layoutAttributesForElementsInRect: Method

The *layoutAttributesForElementsInRect:* method will need to perform a similar task to the previous method in terms of getting the attributes values for cells in the designated display region from the superclass, calling the *modifyLayoutAttributes:* method and returning the results to the collection view object:

```
-(NSArray*)layoutAttributesForElementsInRect:(CGRect)rect
{
    // Get all the attributes for the elements in the specified frame
    NSArray *allAttributesInRect = [super
         layoutAttributesForElementsInRect:rect];

    for (UICollectionViewLayoutAttributes *cellAttributes in allAttributesInRect)
    {
        // Modify the attributes for the cells in the frame rect
        [self modifyLayoutAttributes:cellAttributes];
    }
    return allAttributesInRect;
}
```

50.6 Implementing the modifyLayoutAttributes: Method

By far the most interesting method to be implemented is the *modifyLayoutAttributes:* method. This is where the layout attributes for the cell the user is currently manipulating on the screen are modified. This method should now be implemented as outlined in the following listing:

```
-(void)modifyLayoutAttributes:(UICollectionViewLayoutAttributes
*)layoutAttributes
{
    // If the indexPath matches the one we have stored
    if ([layoutAttributes.indexPath isEqual:_currentCellPath])
    {
        // Assign the new layout attributes
        layoutAttributes.transform3D =
            CATransform3DMakeScale(_currentCellScale, _currentCellScale,
1.0);
```

```
            layoutAttributes.center = _currentCellCenter;
            layoutAttributes.zIndex = 1;
    }
}
```

In completing the example application, a pinch gesture recognizer will be attached to the collection view object and configured to set the currentCellPath, currentCellScale and currentCellCenter values of the layout object in real-time as the user pinches and moves a cell. As is evident from the above code, use is made of these settings during the attribute modification process.

Since this method will be called for each cell in the collection, it is important that the attribute modifications only be applied to the cell the user is currently moving and pinching. This cell is stored in the currentCellPath property as updated by the gesture recognizer:

```
if ([layoutAttributes.indexPath isEqual:_currentCellPath])
```

If the cell matches that referenced by the currentCellPath property, the attributes are transformed via a call to the *CATransform3DMakeScale* function of the QuartzCore Framework, using the currentCellScale property value which is updated by the gesture recognizer during a pinching motion:

```
layoutAttributes.transform3D =
CATransform3DMakeScale(_currentCellScale, _currentCellScale, 1.0);
```

Finally, the center location of the cell is set to the currentCellCenter property value and the zIndex property set to 1 so that the cell appears on top of overlapping collection view contents.

The implementation of a custom collection layout is now complete. All that remains is to implement the gesture recognizer in the application code so that the flow layout knows which cell is being pinched and moved, and by how much.

50.7 Adding the New Layout and Pinch Gesture Recognizer

In order to detect pinch gestures, a pinch gesture recognizer needs to be added to the collection view object. Code also needs to be added to replace the default layout object with our new custom flow layout object. This, in turn, will require that the *MyFlowLayout.h* file be imported into the *MyCollectionViewController.h* file as follows:

```
#import <UIKit/UIKit.h>
#import "MyCollectionViewCell.h"
#import "MySupplementaryView.h"
#import "MyFlowLayout.h"


@interface MyCollectionViewController : UICollectionViewController
```

Subclassing and Extending the iOS 6 Collection View Flow Layout

```
<UICollectionViewDataSource, UICollectionViewDelegate>
@property (strong, nonatomic) NSMutableArray *carImages;
@end
```

Next, select the *MyCollectionViewController.m* file and modify the *viewDidLoad:* method to change the layout to our new layout class and to add a pinch gesture recognizer configured to call a method named *handlePinch:*:

```
- (void)viewDidLoad
{
    [super viewDidLoad];

    MyFlowLayout *myLayout = [[MyFlowLayout alloc]init];

    [self.collectionView setCollectionViewLayout:myLayout
animated:YES];

    UIGestureRecognizer *pinchRecognizer =
        [[UIPinchGestureRecognizer alloc] initWithTarget:self
        action:@selector(handlePinch:)];

    [self.collectionView addGestureRecognizer:pinchRecognizer];

    _carImages = [@[@"chevy_small.jpg",
                    @"mini_small.jpg",
                    @"rover_small.jpg",
                    @"smart_small.jpg",
                    @"highlander_small.jpg",
                    @"venza_small.jpg",
                    @"volvo_small.jpg",
                    @"vw_small.jpg",
                    @"ford_small.jpg",
                    @"nissan_small.jpg",
                    @"honda_small.jpg",
                    @"jeep_small.jpg"] mutableCopy];
}
```

50.8 Implementing the Pinch Recognizer

Remaining within the *MyCollectionViewController.m* file, the last coding related task before testing the application is to write the pinch handler method, the code for which reads as follows:

```
- (IBAction)handlePinch:(UIPinchGestureRecognizer *)sender {
```

```objc
    // Get a reference to the flow layout

    MyFlowLayout *layout =
            (MyFlowLayout *)self.collectionView.collectionViewLayout;

    // If this is the start of the gesture
    if (sender.state == UIGestureRecognizerStateBegan)
    {
        // Get the initial location of the pinch?
        CGPoint initialPinchPoint =
            [sender locationInView:self.collectionView];

        //Convert pinch location into a specific cell
        NSIndexPath *pinchedCellPath =
            [self.collectionView
 indexPathForItemAtPoint:initialPinchPoint];

        // Store the indexPath to cell
        layout.currentCellPath = pinchedCellPath;
    }
    else if (sender.state == UIGestureRecognizerStateChanged)
    {
        // Store the new center location of the selected cell
        layout.currentCellCenter =
            [sender locationInView:self.collectionView];
        // Store the scale value
        layout.currentCellScale = sender.scale;
    }
    else
    {
        [self.collectionView performBatchUpdates:^{
            layout.currentCellPath = nil;
            layout.currentCellScale = 1.0;
        } completion:nil];
    }
}
```

The method begins by getting a reference to the layout object associated with the collection view:

```objc
MyFlowLayout *layout =
        (MyFlowLayout *)self.collectionView.collectionViewLayout;
```

Next, it checks to find out if the gesture has just started. If so, the method will need to identify the cell over which the gesture is taking place. This is achieved by identifying the initial location of the

Subclassing and Extending the iOS 6 Collection View Flow Layout

gesture and then passing that location through to the *indexPathForItemAtPoint:* method of the collection view object. The resulting indexPath is then stored in the currentCellPath property of the layout object where it can be accessed by the *modifyLayoutAttributes:* method previously implemented in the MyFlowLayout class:

```
if (sender.state == UIGestureRecognizerStateBegan)
{
    // Get the initial location of the pinch?
    CGPoint initialPinchPoint =
        [sender locationInView:self.collectionView];

    //Convert pinch location into a specific cell
    NSIndexPath *pinchedCellPath =
        [self.collectionView
indexPathForItemAtPoint:initialPinchPoint];

    // Store the indexPath to cell
    layout.currentCellPath = pinchedCellPath;
}
```

In the event that the gesture is in progress, the current scale and location of the gesture need to be stored in the layout object:

```
else if (sender.state == UIGestureRecognizerStateChanged)
{
    // Store the new center location of the selected cell
    layout.currentCellCenter = [sender
            locationInView:self.collectionView];
    // Store the scale value
    layout.currentCellScale = sender.scale;
}
```

Finally, if the gesture has just ended, the scale needs to be returned to 1 and the currentCellPath property reset to *nil*:

```
else
{
    [self.collectionView performBatchUpdates:^{
        layout.currentCellPath = nil;
        layout.currentCellScale = 1.0;
    } completion:nil];
}
```

This task is performed as a batch update so that the changes take place in a single animated update.

50.9 Avoiding Image Clipping

When the user pinches on a cell in the collection view and stretches the cell, the image contained therein will stretch with it. In order to avoid the enlarged image from being clipped by the containing cell when the gesture ends, a property on the MyCollectionViewCell class needs to be modified.

Within Xcode, select the *MainStoryboard.storyboard* file and select the *My Collection View Cell* entry in the Document Outline panel to the left of the storyboard canvas. Display the Attribute Inspector and, in the *Drawing* section of the panel, unset the checkbox next to *Clip Subviews*.

50.10 Adding the QuartzCore Framework to the Project

The function used to transform the scale of the selected cell in the *modifyLayoutAttributes* method of the MyFlowLayout class actually resides in the QuartzCore Framework library. Before the application will compile and link, therefore, this framework needs to be added to the project build phases. Within the project navigator panel, select the *CollectionDemo* target at the top of the list and in the main panel select the *Build Phases* tab. In the *Link Binary with Libraries* category, click on the + button and in the resulting list of libraries search for and add the *QuartzCore.framework* library.

50.11 Testing the Application

With a suitably provisioned iPhone device attached to the development system, run the application. Once running, use pinching motions on the display to resize an image in cell, noting that the cell can be moved during the gesture. On ending the gesture, the cell will spring back to the original location but continue to display the image at the larger or smaller size. Figure 50-1 shows the collection view after a number of images have been resized.

It is important to note that the changes to the collection view layout in this example are purely visual and do not resulting changes to the size of the images in the data model. As such, modified images will return to the original size when scrolled out of the frame of view.

Subclassing and Extending the iOS 6 Collection View Flow Layout

Figure 50-1

50.12 Summary

Whilst the UICollectionViewFlowLayout class provides considerable flexibility in terms of controlling the way in which data is presented to the user, additional functionality can be added by subclassing and extending this class. In most cases the changes simply involve overriding two methods and modifying the layout attributes within those methods to implement the required layout behavior.

This chapter has worked though the implementation of a custom layout class that extends UICollectionViewFlowLayout to allow the user to move and resize the images contained in collection view cells. The chapter also looked at the use of gesture recognizers within the context of collection views.

Chapter 51

51. Drawing iOS 6 iPhone 2D Graphics with Quartz

The ability to draw two dimensional graphics on the iPhone is provided as part of the Core Graphics Framework in the form of the Quartz 2D API. The iOS implementation of Quartz on the iPhone is the same implementation as that provided with Mac OS X and provides a set of C functions designed to enable the drawing of 2D graphics in the form of images, lines and shapes together with range of fill patterns and gradients.

In this chapter we will provide an overview of Quartz 2D. The next chapter, entitled *An iOS 6 iPhone Graphics Drawing Tutorial using Quartz 2D*, provides a step-by-step tutorial designed to teach the basics of two dimensional drawing on the iPhone.

51.1 Introducing Core Graphics and Quartz 2D

Quartz 2D is a two dimensional graphics drawing engine that makes up the bulk of the UIKit Core Graphics Framework. It is a C based application programming interface (API) and as such is utilized primarily through calls to a range of C functions. Quartz 2D drawing typically takes place on a UIView object (or, more precisely a subclass thereof). Drawings are defined in terms of the paths that a line must follow and rectangular areas into which shapes (rectangles, ellipses etc) must fit.

51.2 The drawRect Method

The first time a view is displayed, and each time part of that view needs to be redrawn as a result of another event, the *drawRect* method of the view is called. Drawing is achieved, therefore, by subclassing the UIView class, implementing the *drawRect* method and placing within that method the Quartz 2D API calls to draw the graphics.

In instances where the *drawRect* method is not automatically called, a redraw may be forced via a call to the *setNeedsDisplay* or *setNeedsDisplayInRect* methods.

51.3 Points, Coordinates and Pixels

The Quartz 2D API functions work on the basis of *points*. These are essentially the x and y coordinates of a two dimensional coordinate system on the device screen with 0, 0 representing the top left hand corner of the display. These coordinates are stored in the form of CGFloat variables.

An additional C structure named CGPoint is used to contain both the x and y coordinates to specify a point on the display. Similarly, the CGSize structure stores two CGFloat values designating the width and height of an element on the screen.

Further, the position and dimension of a rectangle can be defined using the CGRect structure which contains a CGPoint (the location) and CGSize (the dimension) of a rectangular area.

Of key importance when working with points and dimensions is that these values do not correspond directly to screen pixels. In other words there is not a one to one correlation between pixels and points. Instead the underlying framework decides, based on a *scale factor*, where a point should appear and at what size, relative to the resolution of the display on which the drawing is taking place. This enables the same code to work on both higher and lower resolution screens (for example an iPhone 3GS screen and an iPhone 4 retina display) without the programmer having to worry about it.

For more precise drawing requirements, iOS version 4 and later allows the *scale factor* for the current screen to be obtained from UIScreen, UIView, UIImage, and CALayer classes allowing the correlation between pixels and points to be calculated for greater drawing precision. For iOS 3 or older the scale factor is always returned as 1.0.

51.4 The Graphics Context

Almost without exception, all Quartz API function calls require that the *graphics context* be passed as an argument. Each view has its own context which is responsible for performing the requested drawing tasks and subsequently rendering those drawings onto the corresponding view. The graphics context can be obtained with a call to the *UIGraphicsGetCurrentContext()* function which returns a result of type *CGContextRef*:

```
CGContextRef graphics_context = UIGraphicsGetCurrentContext();
```

51.5 Working with Colors in Quartz 2D

The Core Graphics CGColorRef data type is used to store colors when drawing with Quartz. This data type holds information about the *colorspace* of the color (RGBA, CMYK or gray scale) together with a set of component values that specify both the color and the transparency of that color. For example, the color red with no transparency would be defined with the RGBA components 1.0, 0.0, 0.0, 1.0.

Drawing iOS 6 iPhone 2D Graphics with Quartz

A *colorspace* can be created via a Quartz API function call. For example, to create an RGB colorspace:

```
CGColorSpaceRef colorspace = CGColorSpaceCreateDeviceRGB();
```

If the function fails to create a colorspace, it will return a NULL value. In the case of a successful creation, the colorspace must be released when no longer required via a call to the *CGColorSpaceRelease()* function:

```
CGColorSpaceRelease(colorspace);
```

Gray scale and CMYK color spaces may similarly be created using the *CGColorSpaceCreateDeviceGray()* and *CGColorSpaceCreateDeviceCMYK()* functions respectively.

Once the colorspace has been created, the next task is to define the components. The following declaration defines a set of RGBA components for a semi-transparent blue color:

```
CGFloat components[] = {0.0, 0.0, 1.0, 0.5};
```

With both the colorspace and the components defined, the CGColorRef structure can be created:

```
CGColorRef color = CGColorCreate(colorspace, components);
```

The color may then be used to draw using the Quartz 2D drawing API functions. When no longer required the color must be released:

```
CGColorRelease (color);
```

Another useful method for creating colors involves the UIKit UIColor class. Whilst this class cannot be used directly with the Quartz function since it an Objective-C class, it is possible to extract a color in CGColorRef format from the UIColor class by referencing the CGColor property.

The advantage offered by UIColor, in addition to being object oriented, is that it includes a range of convenience methods that can be used to create colors. For example, the following code uses the UIColor class to create the color red, and then accesses the CGColor property for use as an argument to *CGCreateSetStrokeColorWithColor()* C function:

```
CGContextSetStrokeColorWithColor(context, [UIColor redColor].CGColor);
```

The color selection and transparency can be further refined using this technique simply by specifying additional components in conjunction with the UIColor *colorWith<color>* methods. For example:

```
[UIColor colorWithRed:1.0 green:0.3f blue:0.8f alpha:0.5f];
```

As we can see, the use of UIColor avoids the necessity to create colorspaces and components when working with colors. Refer to the Apple documentation for more details of the range of methods provided by the UIColor class.

51.6 **Summary**

This chapter has covered some of the basic principles behind the drawing of two dimensional graphics on the iPhone using the Quartz 2D API. Topics covered included obtaining the graphics context, implementing the *drawRect* method and the handling of colors and transparency. In *An iOS 6 iPhone Graphics Drawing Tutorial using Quartz 2D*, this theory will be put into practice with examples of how to draw a variety of shapes and images on an iPhone screen.

Chapter 52

52. An iOS 6 iPhone Graphics Tutorial using Quartz 2D and Core Image

As previously discussed in *Drawing iOS 6 iPhone 2D Graphics with Quartz*, the Quartz 2D API is the primary mechanism by which 2D drawing operations are performed within iOS 6 iPhone applications. Having provided an overview of Quartz 2D as it pertains to iOS development for the iPhone in that chapter, the focus of this chapter is to provide a tutorial that provides examples of how 2D drawing is performed. If you are new to Quartz 2D and have not yet read *Drawing iOS 6 iPhone 2D Graphics with Quartz* it is recommended that you do so now before embarking on this tutorial.

52.1 The iOS iPhone Drawing Example Application

The application created in this tutorial will contain a subclassed UIView component within which the *drawRect* method will be overridden and used to perform a variety of 2D drawing operations.

52.2 Creating the New Project

Create the new project by launching the Xcode development environment and selecting the option to create a new project. When prompted to select a template for the application, choose the *Single View Application* option and name the project and class prefix *Draw2D* with Storyboard support and Automatic Reference Counting enabled.

52.3 Creating the UIView Subclass

In order to draw graphics on the view it is necessary create a subclass of the UIView object and override the *drawRect* method. In the project navigator panel located on the left hand side of the main Xcode window Ctrl-click on the *Draw2D* folder entry and select *New File...* from the resulting menu. In the *New File* window, select the *Objective-C class* icon and click *Next*. On the subsequent options screen, change the *Subclass of:* menu to *UIView* and the class name to *Draw2D*. Click Next and on the final screen click on the *Create* button.

An iOS 6 iPhone Graphics Tutorial using Quartz 2D and Core Image

Select the *MainStoryboard.storyboard* file and select the UIView component in either the view controller canvas or the document outline panel. Display the Identity Inspector (*View -> Utilities -> Show Identity Inspector*) and change the *Class* setting from *UIView* to our new class named *Draw2D*:

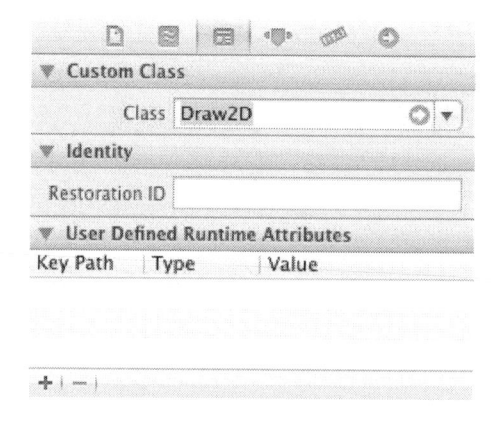

Figure 52-1

52.4 Locating the drawRect Method in the UIView Subclass

Now that we have subclassed our application's UIView the next step is to implement the *drawRect* method in this subclass. Fortunately Xcode has already created a template of this method for us. To locate this method, select the *Draw2D.m* file in the project navigator panel of the main Xcode project window and scroll down the file contents in the edit pane until the *drawRect* method comes into view (it should be located immediately beneath the *initWithFrame* method). Having located the method in the file, remove the comment markers (/* and */) within which it is currently encapsulated:

```
#import "Draw2D.h"

@implementation Draw2D

- (id)initWithFrame:(CGRect)frame
{
    self = [super initWithFrame:frame];
    if (self) {
        // Initialization code
    }
    return self;
}

// Only override drawRect: if you perform custom drawing.
// An empty implementation adversely affects performance during animation.
```

404

```
- (void)drawRect:(CGRect)rect
{
    // Drawing code
}
.
.
@end
```

In the remainder of this tutorial we will modify the code in the *drawRect* method to perform a variety of different drawing operations.

52.5 Drawing a Line

In order to draw a line on an iPhone screen using Quartz 2D we first need to obtain the graphics context for the view:

```
CGContextRef context = UIGraphicsGetCurrentContext();
```

Once the context has been obtained, the width of the line we plan to draw needs to be specified:

```
CGContextSetLineWidth(context, 2.0);
```

Next, we need to create a color reference. We can do this by specifying the RGBA components of the required color (in this case opaque blue):

```
CGFloat components[] = {0.0, 0.0, 1.0, 1.0};
CGColorRef color = CGColorCreate(colorspace, components);
```

Using the color reference and the context we can now specify that the color is to be used when drawing the line:

```
CGContextSetStrokeColorWithColor(context, color);
```

The next step is to move to the start point of the line that is going to be drawn:

```
CGContextMoveToPoint(context, 0, 0);
```

The above line of code indicates that the start point for the line is the top left hand corner of the device display. We now need to specify the end point of the line, in this case 300, 400:

```
CGContextAddLineToPoint(context, 300, 400);
```

Having defined the line width, color and path, we are ready to draw the line and release the colorspace and color reference objects:

```
CGContextStrokePath(context);
CGColorSpaceRelease(colorspace);
```

An iOS 6 iPhone Graphics Tutorial using Quartz 2D and Core Image

```
CGColorRelease(color);
```

Bringing this all together gives us a *drawRect* method that reads as follows:

```
- (void)drawRect:(CGRect)rect {
    CGContextRef context = UIGraphicsGetCurrentContext();
    CGContextSetLineWidth(context, 5.0);
    CGColorSpaceRef colorspace = CGColorSpaceCreateDeviceRGB();
    CGFloat components[] = {0.0, 0.0, 1.0, 1.0};
    CGColorRef color = CGColorCreate(colorspace, components);
    CGContextSetStrokeColorWithColor(context, color);
    CGContextMoveToPoint(context, 0, 0);
    CGContextAddLineToPoint(context, 300, 400);
    CGContextStrokePath(context);
    CGColorSpaceRelease(colorspace);
    CGColorRelease(color);
}
```

When compiled and run, the application should display as illustrated in Figure 52-2:

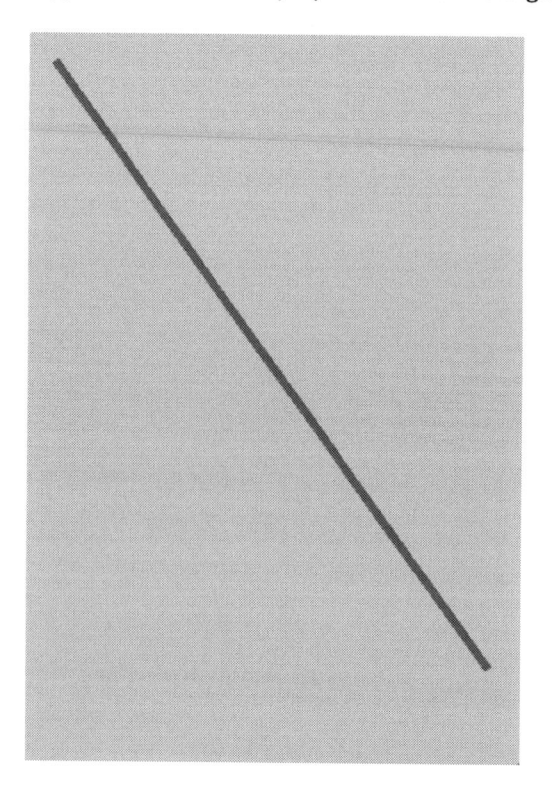

Figure 52-2

An iOS 6 iPhone Graphics Tutorial using Quartz 2D and Core Image

Note that in the above example we manually created the colorspace and color reference. As described in *Drawing iOS 6 iPhone 2D Graphics with Quartz* colors can also be created using the UIColor class. For example, the same result as outlined above can be achieved with fewer lines of code as follows:

```
- (void)drawRect:(CGRect)rect {
    CGContextRef context = UIGraphicsGetCurrentContext();
    CGContextSetLineWidth(context, 2.0);
    CGContextSetStrokeColorWithColor(context, [UIColor
        blueColor].CGColor);
    CGContextMoveToPoint(context, 0, 0);
    CGContextAddLineToPoint(context, 300, 400);
    CGContextStrokePath(context);
}
```

52.6 Drawing Paths

As you may have noticed, in the above example we draw a single line by essentially defining the path between two points. Defining a path that comprises multiple points allows us to draw using a sequence of straight lines all connected to each other using repeated calls to the *CGContextAddLineToPoint()* function. Non-straight lines may also be added to a shape using calls to, for example, the *CGContextAddArc()* function.

The following code, for example, draws a diamond shape:

```
- (void)drawRect:(CGRect)rect {
    CGContextRef context = UIGraphicsGetCurrentContext();
    CGContextSetLineWidth(context, 4.0);
    CGContextSetStrokeColorWithColor(context,
        [UIColor blueColor].CGColor);
    CGContextMoveToPoint(context, 100, 100);
    CGContextAddLineToPoint(context, 150, 150);
    CGContextAddLineToPoint(context, 100, 200);
    CGContextAddLineToPoint(context, 50, 150);
    CGContextAddLineToPoint(context, 100, 100);
    CGContextStrokePath(context);
}
```

When executed, the above code should produce output that appears shown in Figure 52-3:

407

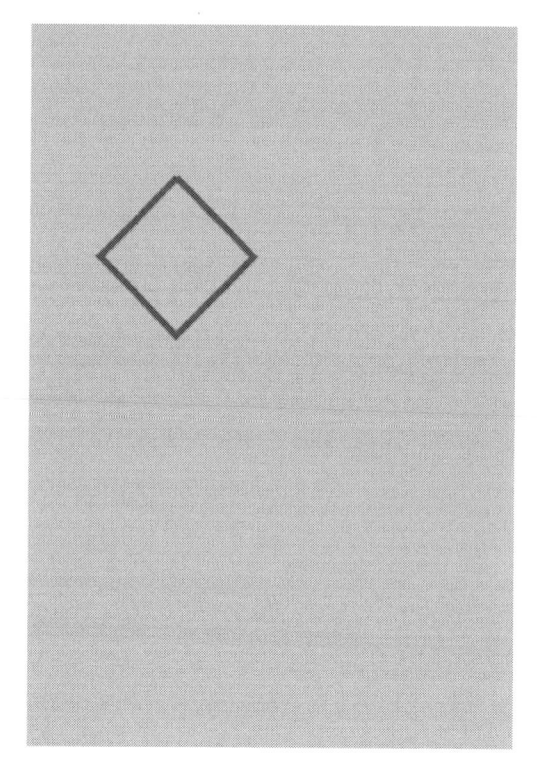

Figure 52-3

52.7 Drawing a Rectangle

Rectangles are drawn in much the same way as any other path is drawn, with the exception that the path is defined by specifying the x and y co-ordinates of the top left hand corner of the rectangle together with the rectangle's height and width. These dimensions are stored in a CGRect structure and passed through as an argument to the *CGContextAddRect* function:

```
- (void)drawRect:(CGRect)rect {
    CGContextRef context = UIGraphicsGetCurrentContext();
    CGContextSetLineWidth(context, 4.0);
    CGContextSetStrokeColorWithColor(context,
       [UIColor blueColor].CGColor);
    CGRect rectangle = CGRectMake(60,170,200,80);
    CGContextAddRect(context, rectangle);
    CGContextStrokePath(context);
}
```

The above code will result in the following display when compiled and executed:

An iOS 6 iPhone Graphics Tutorial using Quartz 2D and Core Image

Figure 52-4

52.8 Drawing an Ellipse or Circle

Circles and ellipses are drawn by defining the rectangular area into which the shape must fit and then calling the *CGContextAddEllipseInRect()* function:

```
- (void)drawRect:(CGRect)rect {
    CGContextRef context = UIGraphicsGetCurrentContext();
    CGContextSetLineWidth(context, 4.0);
    CGContextSetStrokeColorWithColor(context,
      [UIColor blueColor].CGColor);
    CGRect rectangle = CGRectMake(60,170,200,80);
    CGContextAddEllipseInRect(context, rectangle);
    CGContextStrokePath(context);
}
```

When compiled, the above code will produce the following graphics:

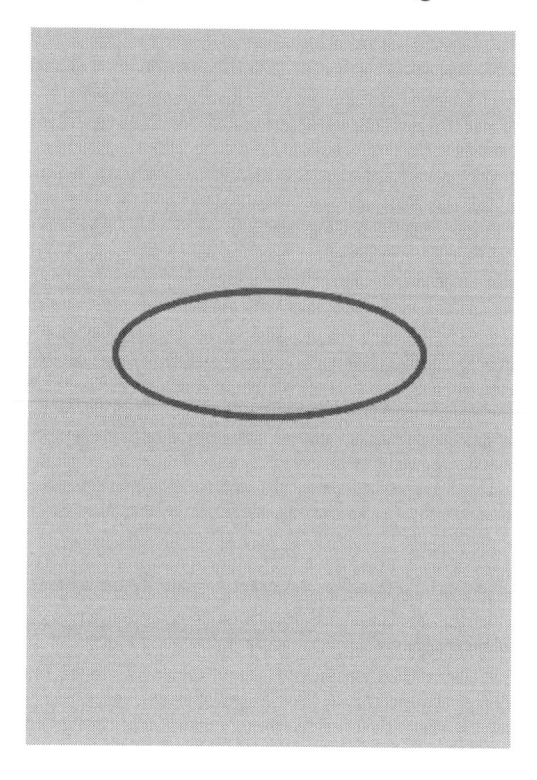

Figure 52-5

In order to draw a circle simply define a rectangle with equal length sides (a square in other words).

52.9 Filling a Path with a Color

A path may be filled with a color using a variety of Quartz 2D API functions. Rectangular and elliptical paths may be filled using the *CGContextFillRect()* and *CGContextFillEllipse()* functions respectively. Similarly, a path may be filled using the *CGContextFillPath()* function. Prior to executing a fill operation, the fill color must be specified using the *CGContextSet-FillColorWithColor()* function.

The following example defines a path and then fills it with the color red:

```
- (void)drawRect:(CGRect)rect {
    CGContextRef context = UIGraphicsGetCurrentContext();
    CGContextMoveToPoint(context, 100, 100);
    CGContextAddLineToPoint(context, 150, 150);
    CGContextAddLineToPoint(context, 100, 200);
    CGContextAddLineToPoint(context, 50, 150);
    CGContextAddLineToPoint(context, 100, 100);
    CGContextSetFillColorWithColor(context,
        [UIColor redColor].CGColor);
    CGContextFillPath(context);
```

An iOS 6 iPhone Graphics Tutorial using Quartz 2D and Core Image

}

The above code produces the following graphics on the device or simulator display when executed:

Figure 52-6

The following code draws a rectangle with a blue border and then once again fills the rectangular space with red:

```
- (void)drawRect:(CGRect)rect {
    CGContextRef context = UIGraphicsGetCurrentContext();
    CGContextSetLineWidth(context, 4.0);
    CGContextSetStrokeColorWithColor(context,
        [UIColor blueColor].CGColor);
    CGRect rectangle = CGRectMake(60,170,200,80);
    CGContextAddRect(context, rectangle);
    CGContextStrokePath(context);
    CGContextSetFillColorWithColor(context,
        [UIColor redColor].CGColor);
    CGContextFillRect(context, rectangle);
}
```

When added to the example application, the resulting display should appear as follows:

Figure 52-7

52.10 Drawing an Arc

An arc may be drawn by specifying two tangent points and a radius using the *CGContextAddArcToPoint()* function, for example:

```
- (void)drawRect:(CGRect)rect {
    CGContextRef context = UIGraphicsGetCurrentContext();
    CGContextSetLineWidth(context, 4.0);
    CGContextSetStrokeColorWithColor(context,
        [UIColor blueColor].CGColor);
    CGContextMoveToPoint(context, 100, 100);
    CGContextAddArcToPoint(context, 100,200, 300,200, 100);
    CGContextStrokePath(context);
}
```

The above code will result in the following graphics output:

Figure 52-8

52.11 Drawing a Cubic Bézier Curve

A cubic Bézier curve may be drawn by moving to a start point and then passing two control points and an end point through to the *CGContextAddCurveToPoint()* function:

```
- (void)drawRect:(CGRect)rect {
    CGContextRef context = UIGraphicsGetCurrentContext();
    CGContextSetLineWidth(context, 4.0);
    CGContextSetStrokeColorWithColor(context,
        [UIColor blueColor].CGColor);
    CGContextMoveToPoint(context, 10, 10);
    CGContextAddCurveToPoint(context, 0, 50, 300, 250, 300, 400);
    CGContextStrokePath(context);
}
```

The above code will cause the curve illustrated in Figure 52-9 to be drawn when compiled and executed in our example application:

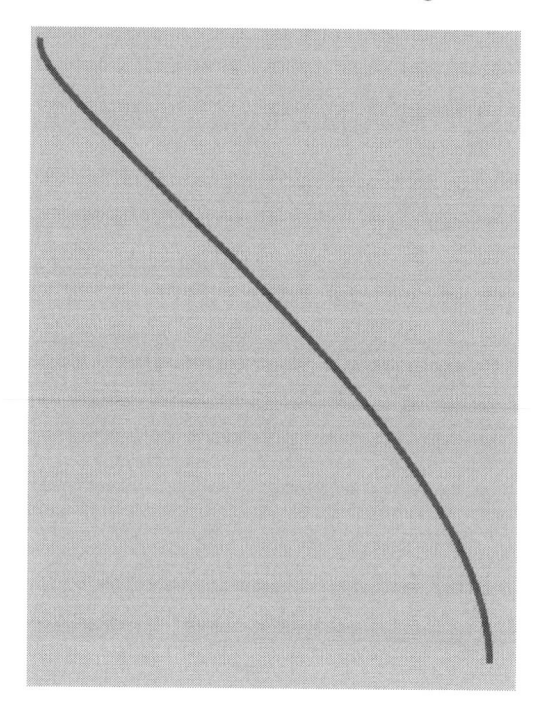

An iOS 6 iPhone Graphics Tutorial using Quartz 2D and Core Image

Figure 52-9

52.12 Drawing a Quadratic Bézier Curve

A quadratic Bézier curve is drawn using the *CGContextAddQuadCurveToPoint()* function, providing a control and end point as arguments having first moved to the start point:

```
- (void)drawRect:(CGRect)rect {
    CGContextRef context = UIGraphicsGetCurrentContext();
    CGContextSetLineWidth(context, 4.0);
    CGContextSetStrokeColorWithColor(context,
        [UIColor blueColor].CGColor);
    CGContextMoveToPoint(context, 10, 200);
    CGContextAddQuadCurveToPoint(context, 150, 10, 300, 200);
    CGContextStrokePath(context);
}
```

The above code, when executed, will display a curve that appears as illustrated in the following figure:

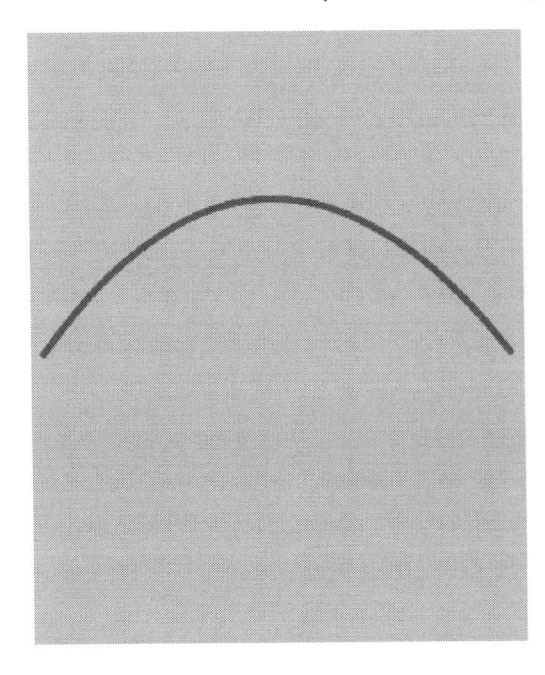

Figure 52-10

52.13 Dashed Line Drawing

So far in this chapter we have performed all our drawing with a solid line. Quartz also provides support for drawing dashed lines. This is achieved via the Quartz *CGContextSetLineDash()* function which takes as its arguments the following:

- **context** – The graphics context of the view on which the drawing is to take place
- **phase** - A floating point value that specifies how far into the dash pattern the line starts
- **lengths** – An array containing values for the lengths of the painted and unpainted sections of the line. For example an array containing 5 and 6 would cycle through 5 painted unit spaces followed 6 unpainted unit spaces.
- **count** – A count of the number of items in the lengths array

For example, a [2,6,4,2] lengths array applied to a curve drawing of line thickness 5.0 will appear as follows:

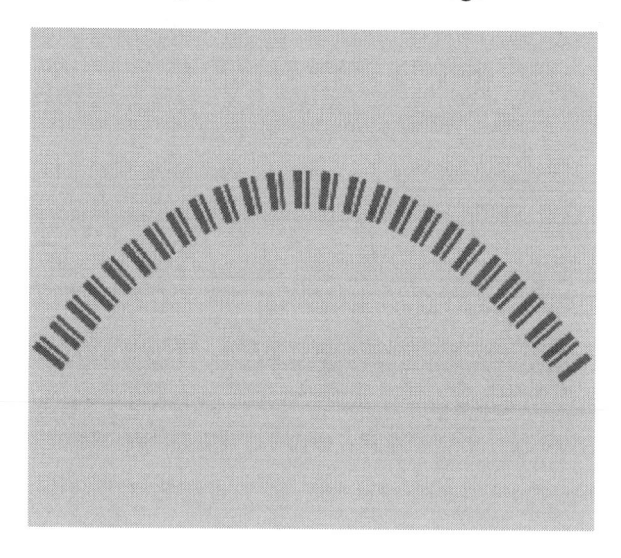

An iOS 6 iPhone Graphics Tutorial using Quartz 2D and Core Image

Figure 52-11

The corresponding drawRect code that drew the above line reads as follows:

```
- (void)drawRect:(CGRect)rect {
    CGContextRef context = UIGraphicsGetCurrentContext();
    CGContextSetLineWidth(context, 20.0);
    CGContextSetStrokeColorWithColor(context,
        [UIColor blueColor].CGColor);
    CGFloat dashArray[] = {2,6,4,2};
    CGContextSetLineDash(context, 3, dashArray, 4);
    CGContextMoveToPoint(context, 10, 200);
    CGContextAddQuadCurveToPoint(context, 150, 10, 300, 200);
    CGContextStrokePath(context);
}
```

52.14 Drawing an Image into a Graphics Context

An image may be drawn into a graphics context either by specifying the coordinates of the top left hand corner of the image (in which case the image will appear full size) or resized so that it fits into a specified rectangular area. Before we can display an image in our example application, however, that image must first be added to the project resources.

Begin by locating the desired image using the Finder and then drag and drop that image onto the *Supporting Files* category of the project navigator panel of the Xcode main project window.

The following example drawRect method code displays the image full size located at 0, 0:

```
- (void)drawRect:(CGRect)rect {
```

```
UIImage *myImage = [UIImage imageNamed:@"pumpkin.jpg"];
CGPoint imagePoint = CGPointMake(0, 0);
[myImage drawAtPoint:imagePoint];
}
```

As is evident when the application is run, the size of the image far exceeds the available screen size:

Figure 52-12

Using the *drawInRect* method of the UIImage object, however, we can scale the image to fit better on the screen. In this instance it is useful to identify the screen size since this changes depending on the device on which the application is running. This can be achieved using the *mainScreen* and *bounds* methods of the UIScreen class. The *mainScreen* method returns another UIScreen object representing the device display. Calling the *bounds* method of that object returns the dimensions of the display in the form of a CGRect object:

```
- (void)drawRect:(CGRect)rect {
    UIImage *myImage = [UIImage imageNamed:@"pumpkin.jpg"];
    CGRect imageRect =[[UIScreen mainScreen] bounds];
    [myImage drawInRect:imageRect];
}
```

This time, the entire image fits comfortably on the screen:

An iOS 6 iPhone Graphics Tutorial using Quartz 2D and Core Image

Figure 52-13

52.15 Image Filtering with the Core Image Framework

Having covered the concept of displaying images within an iPhone application, now is a good time to provide a basic overview of the Core Image Framework.

Core Image was introduced with iOS 5 and provides a mechanism for filtering and manipulating still images and videos. Included with Core Image is a wide range of different filters together with the ability to build custom filters to meet specific requirements. Examples of filters that may be applied include cropping, color effects, blurring, warping, transformations and gradients. A full listing of filters is available in Apple's *Core Image Filter Reference* document which is located in the iOS Developer portal.

A CIImage object is typically initialized with a reference to the image to be manipulated. A CIFilter object is then created and configured with the type of filtering to be performed, together with any input parameters required by that filter. The CIFilter object is then instructed to perform the operation and the modified image is subsequently returned in the form of a CIImage object. The application's CIContext reference may then be used to render the image for display to the user.

By way of an example of Core Image in action we will modify the *drawRect* method of our Draw2D example application to render the previously displayed image in a sepia tone using the CISepiaTone filter. The first step, however, is to add the CoreImage framework to the project. This is achieved by

An iOS 6 iPhone Graphics Tutorial using Quartz 2D and Core Image

selecting the *Draw2D* target at the top of the project navigator and then selecting the *Build Phases* tab in the main panel. Unfold the *Link Binary with Libraries* section of the panel, click on the + button and locate and add the *CoreImage.framework* library from the resulting list.

Having added the framework, select the *Draw2D.m* file and modify *drawRect* as follows:

```
- (void)drawRect:(CGRect)rect
{
    // Drawing code
    UIImage *myimage = [UIImage imageNamed:@"pumpkin.jpg"];
    CIImage *cimage = [[CIImage alloc] initWithImage:myimage];

    CIFilter *sepiaFilter = [CIFilter filterWithName:@"CISepiaTone"];
    [sepiaFilter setDefaults];
    [sepiaFilter setValue:cimage forKey:@"inputImage"];
    [sepiaFilter setValue:[NSNumber numberWithFloat:0.8f]
        forKey:@"inputIntensity"];

    CIImage *image = [sepiaFilter outputImage];
    CIContext *context = [CIContext contextWithOptions: nil];
    CGImageRef cgImage = [context createCGImage:
            image fromRect: image.extent];
    UIImage *resultUIImage = [UIImage imageWithCGImage: cgImage];

    CGRect imageRect =[[UIScreen mainScreen] bounds];
    [resultUIImage drawInRect:imageRect];
}
```

The method begins by loading the image .jpg file used in the previous section of this chapter. Since Core Image works on CIImage objects it is then necessary to convert the UIImage to a CIImage. Next a new CIFilter object is created and initialized with the CISepiaTone filter. The filter is then set to the default settings before being configured with the input image (in this case our *cimage* object) and the value of intensity of the filter (0.8).

With the filter object configured, its *outputFile* method is called to perform the manipulation and the resulting modified image assigned to a new CImage object. The CIContext reference for the application is then obtained and used to convert the CImage object to a CGImageRef object. This, in turn, is converted to a UIImage object which is then displayed to the user using the object's *drawInRect* method. When compiled and run the image will appear in a sepia tone.

52.16 Summary

By subclassing the UIView class and overriding the *drawRect* method a variety of 2D graphics drawing functions may be performed on the view canvas. In this chapter we have explored some of

An iOS 6 iPhone Graphics Tutorial using Quartz 2D and Core Image

the graphics drawing capabilities of Quartz 2D to draw a variety of line types and paths and to present images on the iPhone screen.

Introduced in iOS 5, the Core Image framework is designed specifically for the filtering and manipulation of images and video. In this chapter we have provided a brief overview of Core Image and worked through a simple example that applied a sepia tone filter to an image.

Chapter 53

53. Basic iOS 6 iPhone Animation using Core Animation

The majority of the visual effects used throughout the iOS 6 user interface on the iPhone are performed using *Core Animation*. Core Animation provides a simple mechanism for implementing basic animation within an iPhone application. If you need a user interface element to gently fade in or out of view, slide smoothly across the screen or gracefully resize or rotate before the user's eyes, these effects can be achieved using Core Animation in just a few lines of code.

In this chapter we will provide an overview of the basics of Core Animation and work through a simple example. While much can be achieved with Core Animation, however, it should be noted that if you plan to develop a graphics intensive 3D style application then it is more likely that OpenGL ES will need to be used, a subject area to which numerous books are dedicated.

53.1 UIView Core Animation Blocks

The concept of Core Animation involves the implementation of so-called *animation blocks*. Animation blocks are used to mark the beginning and end of a sequence of changes to the appearance of a UIView and its corresponding subviews. Once the end of the block is reached, the animation is committed and the changes are performed over a specified duration. For the sake of example, consider a UIView object that contains a UIButton connected to an outlet named *theButton*. The application requires that the button gradually fade from view over a period of 3 seconds. This can be achieved by making the button transparent through the use of the *alpha* property:

```
theButton.alpha = 0;
```

Simply setting the alpha property to 0, however, causes the button to immediately become transparent. In order to make it fade out of sight gradually we need to place this line of code in an animation block. The start of an animation block is represented by a call to the *beginAnimations* class method of the UIView class:

```
[UIView beginAnimations:nil context:nil];
```

Basic iOS 6 iPhone Animation using Core Animation

The end of the animation block triggers the animation sequence through a call to the *commitAnimations* method:

```
[UIView commitAnimations];
```

A variety of properties may also be defined within the animation block. For example, the duration of the animation (in our hypothetical example this needs to be 3 seconds) can be declared by a call to the *setAnimationDuration* class method:

```
[UIView setAnimationDuration:3];
```

Bringing this all together gives us a code sequence to gradually fade out a button object over a period of 3 seconds:

```
[UIView beginAnimations:nil context:nil];
[UIView setAnimationDuration:3];
theButton.alpha = 0;
[UIView commitAnimations];
```

53.2 Understanding Animation Curves

In addition to specifying the duration of an animation sequence, the linearity of the animation timeline may also be defined by calling the UIView *setAnimationCurve* class method. This setting controls whether the animation is performed at a constant speed, whether it starts out slow and speeds up and so on. There are currently four possible animation curve settings:

- **UIViewAnimationCurveLinear** – The animation is performed at constant speed for the specified duration.
- **UIViewAnimationCurveEaseOut** – The animation starts out fast and slows as the end of the sequence approaches
- **UIViewAnimationCurveEaseIn** – The animation sequence starts out slow and speeds up as the end approaches.
- **UIViewAnimationCurveEaseInOut** – The animation starts slow, speeds up and then slows down again.

53.3 Receiving Notification of Animation Completion

Once an animation sequence has been committed and is underway it may be necessary to receive notification when the animation is completed so that the application code can, for example, trigger another animation sequence. The UIView *setAnimationDidStopSelector* class method allows a method to be specified that will be called when the animation sequence is completed. For example, the following code fragment declares that the method named *animationFinished* is to be called at the end of the animation sequence:

```
[UIView setAnimationDidStopSelector:
    @selector(animationFinished:finished:context:)];
```

The *animationFinished* method would subsequently be declared as follows:

```
-(void)animationFinished:(NSString *)animationID
finished:(NSNumber *)finished
context:(void *)context
{
       // Code to be executed on completion of animation sequence
}
```

53.4 Performing Affine Transformations

Transformations allow changes to be made to the coordinate system of a screen area. This essentially allows the programmer to rotate, resize and translate a UIView object. A call is made to one of a number transformation functions and the result assigned to the *transform* property of the UIView object.

For example, to change the scale of a UIView object named *myView* by a factor of 2 in both height and width:

```
myView.transform = CGAffineTransformMakeScale(2, 2);
```

Similarly, the UIView object may be rotated using the *CGAffineTransformMakeRotation* which takes as an argument the angle (in radians) by which the view is to be rotated. The following code, for example, rotates a view by 90 degrees:

```
myView.transform = CGAffineTransformMakeRotation( 90 * M_PI / 180);
```

The key point to keep in mind with transformations is that they become animated effects when performed within an animation block. The transformations evolve over the duration of the animation and follow the specified animation curve in terms of timing.

53.5 Combining Transformations

Two transformations may be combined to create a single transformation effect via a call to the *CGAffineTransformConcat()* function. This function takes as arguments the two transformation objects that are to be combined. The result may then be assigned to the transform property of the UIView object to be transformed. The following code fragment, for example, both scales and rotates a UIView object named *myView*:

```
CGAffineTransform scaleTrans =
     CGAffineTransformMakeScale(2, 2);
CGAffineTransform rotateTrans =
```

```
        CGAffineTransformMakeRotation(angle * M_PI / 180);
myView.transform = CGAffineTransformConcat(scaleTrans, rotateTrans);
```

Affine transformations offer an extremely powerful and flexible mechanism for creating animations and it is just not possible to do justice to these capabilities in a single chapter. In order to learn more about affine transformations, a good starting place is the *Transforms* chapter of Apple's *Quartz 2D Programming Guide*.

53.6 Creating the Animation Example Application

The remainder of this chapter is dedicated to the creation of an iPhone application intended to demonstrate the use of Core Animation. The end result is a simple application on which a blue square appears. When the user touches a location on the screen the box moves to that location. Through the use of affine transformations, the box will rotate 180 degrees as it moves to the new location whilst also changing in size.

Begin by launching Xcode and creating a new Single View Application with both product and class prefix named *Animate* and the Storyboard and Automatic Reference Counting options enabled.

53.7 Implementing the Interface File

For the purposes of this application we will need a UIView to represent the blue square and variables to contain the rotation angle and scale factor by which the square will be transformed. These need to be declared in the *AnimateViewController.h* file as follows:

```
#import <UIKit/UIKit.h>

@interface AnimateViewController : UIViewController

@property (nonatomic) float scaleFactor;
@property (nonatomic) float angle;
@property (strong, nonatomic) UIView *boxView;
@end
```

53.8 Drawing in the UIView

Having declared the UIView reference, we now need to initialize an instance object and draw a blue square located at a specific location on the screen. We also need to initialize our *scaleFactor* and *angle* variables and add *boxView* as a subview of the application's main view object. These tasks only need to be performed once when the application first starts up so a good option is to override *loadView:* method in the *AnimateViewController.m* file:

```
- (void)loadView {
    [super loadView];
```

```
    _scaleFactor = 2;
    _angle = 180;
    CGRect frameRect = CGRectMake(10, 10, 45, 45);
    _boxView = [[UIView alloc] initWithFrame:frameRect];
    _boxView.backgroundColor = [UIColor blueColor];
    [self.view addSubview:_boxView];
}
```

53.9 Detecting Screen Touches and Performing the Animation

When the user touches the screen the blue box needs to move from its current location to the location of the touch. During this motion, the box will rotate 180 degrees and change in size. The detection of screen touches was covered in detail in *An Overview of iOS 6 iPhone Multitouch, Taps and Gestures*. For the purposes of this example we want to initiate the animation at the point that the user's finger is lifted from the screen so we need to implement the *touchesEnded* method in the *animateViewController.m* file:

```
-(void)touchesEnded:(NSSet *)touches withEvent:(UIEvent *)event
{
    UITouch *touch = [touches anyObject];
    CGPoint location = [touch locationInView:self.view];
    [UIView beginAnimations:nil context:nil];
    [UIView setAnimationDelegate:self];
    [UIView setAnimationDuration:2];
    [UIView setAnimationCurve:UIViewAnimationCurveEaseInOut];
    CGAffineTransform scaleTrans =
       CGAffineTransformMakeScale(_scaleFactor, _scaleFactor);
    CGAffineTransform rotateTrans =
       CGAffineTransformMakeRotation(_angle * M_PI / 180);
    _boxView.transform = CGAffineTransformConcat(scaleTrans, rotateTrans);
    _angle = (_angle == 180 ? 360 : 180);
    _scaleFactor = (_scaleFactor == 2 ? 1 : 2);
    _boxView.center = location;
    [UIView commitAnimations];
}
```

Before compiling and running the application we need to take some time to describe the actions performed in the above method. First, the method gets the UITouch object from the *touches* argument and the *locationInView* method of this object is called to identify the location on the screen where the touch took place:

```
UITouch *touch = [touches anyObject];
CGPoint location = [touch locationInView:self.view];
```

Basic iOS 6 iPhone Animation using Core Animation

The animation block is then started and the current class declared as the delegate. The duration of the animation is set to 2 seconds and curve set to ease in/ease out:

```
[UIView beginAnimations:nil context:nil];
[UIView setAnimationDelegate:self];
[UIView setAnimationDuration:2];
[UIView setAnimationCurve:UIViewAnimationCurveEaseInOut];
```

Two transformations are then generated for the view, one to scale the size of the view and one to rotate it 180 degrees. These transformations are then combined into a single transformation and applied to the UIView object:

```
CGAffineTransform scaleTrans =
    CGAffineTransformMakeScale(_scaleFactor, _scaleFactor);
CGAffineTransform rotateTrans =
    CGAffineTransformMakeRotation(_angle * M_PI / 180);
_boxView.transform = CGAffineTransformConcat(scaleTrans, rotateTrans);
```

Ternary operators are then used to switch the scale and rotation angle variables ready for the next touch. In other words, after rotating 180 degrees on the first touch the view will need to be rotated to 360 degrees on the next animation. Similarly, once the box has been scaled by a factor of 2 it needs to scale back to its original size on the next animation:

```
_angle = (_angle == 180 ? 360 : 180);
_scaleFactor = (_scaleFactor == 2 ? 1 : 2);
```

Finally, the location of the view is moved to the point on the screen where the touch occurred before the animation is committed:

```
_boxView.center = location;
[UIView commitAnimations];
```

Once the *touchesEnded* method has been implemented it is time to try out the application.

53.10 Building and Running the Animation Application

Once the all the code changes have been made and saved, click on the *Run* button in the Xcode toolbar. Once the application has compiled it will load into the iOS Simulator (refer to *Testing iOS 6 Apps on the iPhone – Developer Certificates and Provisioning Profiles* for steps on how to run the application on an iPhone device).

When the application loads the blue square should appear near the top left hand corner of the screen. Click (or touch if running on a device) the screen and watch the box glide and rotate to the new location, the size of the box changing as it moves:

Figure 53-1

53.11 Summary

Core Animation provides an easy to implement interface to animation within iOS 6 iPhone applications. From the simplest of tasks such as gracefully fading out a user interface element to basic animation and transformations, Core Animation provides a variety of techniques for enhancing user interfaces. This chapter covered the basics of Core Animation before working step-by-step through an example to demonstrate the implementation of motion, rotation and scaling animation.

Chapter 54

54. Integrating iAds into an iOS 6 iPhone App

In the first 11 months of business, Apple's iTunes App Store reached 1 billion downloads. This actually turned out to be something of a slow start, and in the following year and a half the total number of downloads grew to 10 billion. Clearly this spectacular market growth would not have been possible without the availability of hundreds of thousands of high quality applications available to iPhone users in the App Store. Whilst some of these apps may have been developed by those with altruistic motives, it is most likely that the majority of the companies and individuals that invested the time and effort in creating apps did so in order to make money.

In terms of revenue generation options, the iTunes App Store eco-system provides a number of options. Perhaps the most obvious source of revenue for app developers involves charging the user an upfront fee for the application. Another option involves a concept referred to as "in-app purchase" whereby a user buys something from within the installed and running application. This typically takes the form of virtual goods (a packet of seeds in farming simulation or a faster car in a racing game) or premium content such as access to specific articles in a news application. Yet another option involves the inclusion of advertisements in the application. It is, of course, also common to generate revenue from a mixture of these three options.

The subject of this chapter involves the use of advertising, specifically using Apple's iAds system to incorporate adverts into an iOS 6 based iPhone application.

54.1 iOS iPhone Advertising Options

In the early days of the iOS application market, the dominant advertising network was provided by a company called AdMob. AdMob provided an SDK that enabled developers to incorporate AdMob sourced adverts into their iOS applications. In the early days AdMob came under some criticism for the quality of the ads that were served (which mostly took the form of ads for other iPhone applications). Eyeing AdMob's dominance with envy and concern, both Apple and Google began negotiations to purchase the mobile advertising company. After lengthy discussions, very few details of which were ever made public, AdMob was acquired by Google.

Having lost out on the AdMob acquisition, Apple quickly moved to purchase another mobile advertising network named Quattro Wireless. Part of the attraction of Quattro Wireless was the fact that the company handled mobile advertising for a number of major companies enabling Apple to target premium advertising with iAds. Apple eventually closed down the Quattro Wireless advertising network and used it as the basis for the iAds program which is now built into the iOS SDK ready for any developer to generate advertising revenue from premium quality adverts.

54.2 iAds Advertisement Formats

The iAds platform supports two sizes of banner ad and, with the introduction of the iOS 4.3 SDK, a full screen ad format called an *interstitial*.

The banner ads are intended to typically appear either at the top or bottom of the display and are provided in two formats so that ads may be displayed when the device is either in portrait or landscape orientation. iAds banner based advertising is incorporated into iOS iPhone applications through the ADBannerView class.

iAds interstitial adverts occupy the full device display and are primarily intended to be displayed when a user transitions from one screen to another within an application. Interstitial ads are incorporated into applications using the ADInterstitialView class.

54.3 Basic Rules for the Display of iAds

Apple provides the iAds framework as part of the iOS SDK and will serve ads to your application from an inventory of advertisers allowing you to keep 60% of the revenue.

Whilst implementation of iAds is relatively straightforward, there are some responsibilities that must be met by the application developer. In the first instance, the inclusion of an iAd advert on a particular screen of an iOS application does not guarantee that Apple will have an advert available to be displayed from the iAds network inventory. If no ad is available, the area of the screen occupied by the iAd object will remain blank. It is essential, therefore, that the application only displays an advert when the ad creative has been successfully downloaded onto the device.

As previously mentioned, iAd creative are available in formats suitable for display in both portrait and landscape orientations. If your application is capable of handling device rotation, it is important that the code supporting the display of iAds be able to switch the advert orientation to match that of the device.

Finally, once an ad appears in an application the user may choose to interact with it. This may, amongst other things, involve watching a movie clip, launching Safari to visit the advertiser's web site or the display of an interactive view. It is entirely possible, therefore, that a user's interaction with an iAds advert may result in your application being placed into the background or visually obscured for the duration of the interaction.

Given these requirements and possibilities it is important that the application code keep track of when an ad is displayed and the events that may unfold as a result of a user interacting with that ad. Fortunately this can easily be achieved by implementing a number of delegate methods defined in the ADBannerViewDelegate protocol as outlined later in this chapter.

54.4 Creating an Example iAds iPhone Application

In the remainder of this chapter we will work step by step through the creation of a simple iOS 6 iPhone application that includes an iAd banner view advertisement. Begin this tutorial by launching Xcode and creating a new iOS iPhone application project named *iAdApp* using the *Single View Application* template with the Storyboard and Automatic Reference Counting options enabled.

The ultimate goal of this example is to create an application consisting of a table view and an iAd banner view. The banner will be configured to only appear when an ad is successfully downloaded from the iAds server and will change format to match the orientation of the device.

54.5 Adding the iAds Framework to the Xcode Project

Once the new project has been created, the first step is to make sure the iAds framework is included in the project. Failure to add this framework will result in compilation and linking errors when building the application.

To add the iAds framework, select the *iAdApp* target located at the top of the project navigator panel. In the center pane, select the *Build Phases* tab and unfold the *Link Binary With Libraries* panel. Click on the '+' button to display a list of existing frameworks, locate and select *iAd.framework* and click the *Add* button. The iAd.framework will now appear in the frameworks list along with the other frameworks already included in the project.

54.6 Configuring the View Controller

The next step is to declare an instance of the ADBannerView class within the view controller and import the *<iAd/iAd.h>* header file. These steps are performed in the *iAdAppViewController.h* interface file and the necessary changes are outlined below:

```
#import <UIKit/UIKit.h>
#import <iAd/iAd.h>

@interface iAdAppViewController : UIViewController
    <ADBannerViewDelegate>
```

431

Integrating iAds into an iOS 6 iPhone App

```
@property (strong, nonatomic) ADBannerView *bannerView;
@end
```

In the above code we have also added a line that reads <ADBannerViewDelegate>. This indicates to the compiler that within the view controller we will be implementing the delegate methods for the banner view protocol.

54.7 Designing the User Interface

The next step is to design the user interface which will consist of a single table view object. Select the *MainStoryboard.storyboard* file, display the Object library (*View -> Utilities -> Show Object Library*) and drag and drop a UITableView object into the View window as illustrated in Figure 54-1:

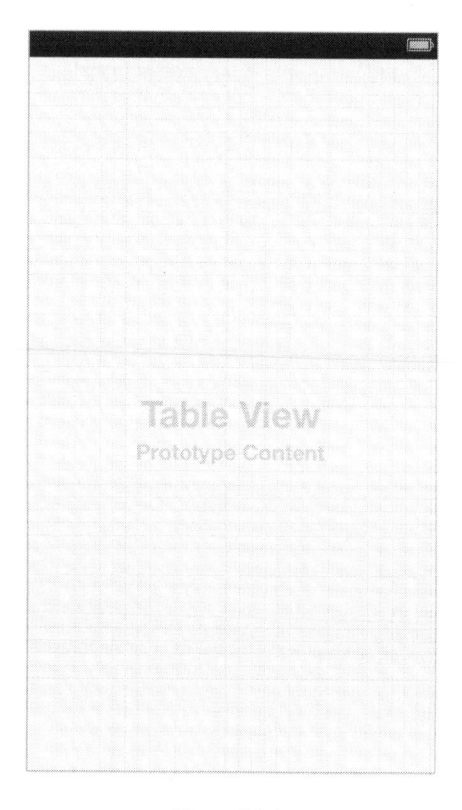

Figure 54-1

Select the table view object in the view canvas, display the Assistant Editor panel and verify that the editor is displaying the contents of the *iAdAppViewController.h* file. Ctrl-click on the table view object and drag to a position just below the @interface line in the Assistant Editor. Release the line and in the resulting connection dialog establish an outlet connection named *tableView*.

Integrating iAds into an iOS 6 iPhone App

54.8 Creating the Banner Ad

For the purposes of this example we will create an instance of the ADBannerView in the *viewDidLoad:* method of the view controller. Select the *iAdAppViewController.m* implementation file, locate the method and modify it as follows:

```
- (void)viewDidLoad {
    [super viewDidLoad];
    _bannerView = [[ADBannerView alloc]
           initWithFrame:CGRectZero];

    _bannerView.delegate = self;
}
```

Within the body of the *viewDidLoad* method the code creates a new ADBannerView instance and assigns it to our bannerView variable. Finally, the view controller is declared as being the banner view's delegate.

54.9 Displaying the Ad

If we were to compile and run our application now, no ad would be visible because we have not, as yet, taken any steps to display it. As previously mentioned, an ad should not be displayed to the user until the ad creative has been successfully downloaded from the iAds server. On successful download of an ad, the *bannerViewDidLoadAd* delegate method is called. By implementing this delegate method in our view controller, therefore, we can make sure the ad is displayed only when an ad is ready. Within the *iAdAppViewController.m* file, implement this method as follows:

```
- (void)bannerViewDidLoadAd:(ADBannerView *)banner
{
    _tableView.tableHeaderView = _bannerView;
}
```

All that this method needs to do is assign the bannerView ad object as the header of our tableView component in the user interface.

Build and run the application in the iOS Simulator to verify that the code works:

Integrating iAds into an iOS 6 iPhone App

Figure 54-2

In the real world, there will be situations where an ad is not available to be displayed to the user. This might be because Apple does not have a suitable ad available in its inventory, or simply because the device does not have an internet connection and cannot connect the Apple ad server. It is important, therefore, to test that the application gracefully handles such situations. In recognition of this fact, iOS provides a mechanism for simulating the absence of ad inventory (otherwise known as the ad fill rate) while testing an application. These settings are accessible via the *Developer* section of the Settings app on the device. Settings are available to adjust the ad refresh rate and also, as illustrated in the following figure, the fill rate.

In the event that the ad does not appear, keep in mind that it can take a while for the Ad to arrive from the server. If no ad appears after about a minute, open the Console window application (located in the *Applications/Utilities* folder of your Mac OS X system) and check for error messages. The most likely error is that an ad was not available from the iAds inventory and that the application is behaving as intended. Alternatively, it may be worth accessing the Developer settings on the device and changing the fill rate to 100%.

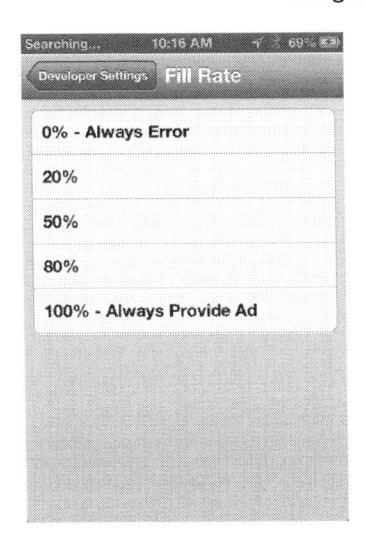

Figure 54-3

54.10 Implementing the Delegate Methods

In order to fully implement the ADBannerViewDelegate protocol there are a few more methods that should be implemented within the view controller. What these methods actually do will depend on the requirements of the application and in some cases it may not even be necessary for these methods to do anything. We have already implemented one of these methods in the form of the *bannerViewDidLoadAd* method. The other delegate methods are as follows:

54.10.1 bannerViewActionShouldBegin

This method is triggered when the user touches the iAds banner in your application. If the *willLeave* argument passed through to the method is *YES* then your application will be placed into the background while the user is taken elsewhere to interact with or view the ad. If the argument is *NO* then the ad will be superimposed over your running application in which case the code in this method may optionally suspend the screen output until the user returns.

```
- (BOOL)bannerViewActionShouldBegin:
(ADBannerView *)banner
willLeaveApplication:(BOOL)willLeave
{
    return YES;
}
```

If the ad places the application into the background, the application will be resumed automatically once the action is completed.

54.10.2 bannerViewActionDidFinish

This method is called when the ad view removes the ad content currently obscuring the application interface. If the application was paused during the ad view session this method can be used to resume activity:

```
- (void)bannerViewActionDidFinish:(ADBannerView *)banner
{
}
```

54.10.3 bannerView:didFailToReceiveAdWithError

This method is triggered when an advertisement could not be loaded from the iAds system (perhaps due to a network connectivity issue). If you have already taken steps to only display an ad when it has successfully loaded it is not typically necessary to implement the code for this method.

```
- (void)bannerView:(ADBannerView *)banner
didFailToReceiveAdWithError:(NSError *)error
{
}
```

54.10.4 bannerViewWillLoadAd

Introduced as part of the iOS 5 SDK, this method is triggered when the banner confirms that an advertisement is available but before the ad is downloaded to the device and is ready for presentation to the user.

```
- (void)bannerViewDidLoadAd:(ADBannerView *)banner
{
    _tableView.tableHeaderView = _bannerView;
}
```

54.11 Summary

There are a variety of methods for generating revenue from an iPhone application. Perhaps one of the more obvious solutions, aside from charging an upfront fee for the application, is to integrate advertising into the user interface. The iAds framework provides an easy to use mechanism for the integration of advertisements sourced from Apple's iAds inventory. This chapter has covered the basics of the iAds framework and worked through the creation of an example iPhone application.

Chapter 55

55. An Overview of iOS 6 iPhone Multitasking

Multitasking refers to the ability of an operating system to run more than one application concurrently. The introduction of iOS version 4.0 was met with much fanfare relating to the fact that the operating system now supported multitasking. In actual fact, iOS has always been able to support multitasking and many of the applications bundled with the device (such as the Mail, Phone and Music apps) have been leveraging the multitasking abilities of iOS since the very first iPhone shipped. What was, in fact, significant about iOS 4 was that some (though not all) of the multitasking capabilities of the operating system were now being made available to us as third party application developers. These capabilities are, unsurprisingly, still available in iOS 6.

Multitasking in iOS, within the context of third part application development at least, is not without some restrictions however. The goal of this chapter, therefore, is to provide an overview of the capabilities, limitations and implementation of multitasking in iOS 6 running on the iPhone.

55.1 Understanding iOS Application States

At any given time an iOS application can be in one of a number of different states. Applications in the *not running* state have either yet to be launched by the user or were previously launched but have been terminated either by the user or the operating system.

An application is in the *foreground* state when it is the current application displayed to the user. At any one time only one application can be in the foreground state. Applications in the foreground can be in one of two sub-states, namely *active* or *not active*.

When in the *not active* state, the application is running in the foreground but is not actively receiving or handling any events (for example because the system is awaiting a user response to an event such as an incoming phone call or because the screen lock has been activated).

An *active* application, on the other hand, is running in the *foreground* and currently receiving events (perhaps due to interaction with the user or via the network).

An application is considered to be in the *background* state when it is no longer the *foreground* application. Applications in this state are still executing code either because they have requested additional background execution time to complete a task or because they have requested permission to remain running in the background and, in so doing, have met the criteria (discussed later in the chapter) to do so. An application typically enters the background when the user launches another application, or brings another background application into the foreground. With iOS 4.0 or later it is also possible to launch an application directly into the background.

Applications enter the *suspended* state when they have been moved to the background and are no longer executing code. The application is still stored in memory preserving its state at the point of suspension but is neither using any CPU cycles nor is it placing additional load on the battery. This state of suspended animation allows the application to be quickly moved into the foreground and execution resumed at the request of the user thereby providing near instantaneous application switching. Suspended applications may be terminated at any time at the discretion of the operating system (typically in order to free up memory resources) so it is essential that applications save any status information to non-volatile storage prior to entering the suspended state.

55.2 A Brief Overview of the Multitasking Application Lifecycle

The lifecycle of an iPhone iOS 6 application primarily involves a series of transitions between the various states outlined in the preceding section. At each stage of the lifecycle, calls are made to specific methods in the application's delegate so that the application can take appropriate action where necessary.

When an application is launched it transitions from *not running* to either the *active* or *background* state. Once the application has loaded the *didFinishLaunchingWithOptions* delegate method is called. If the newly launched application is entering *foreground* mode the *applicationDidBecomeActive* method is then called. If, on the other hand the application is moving directly to the background state (either by design or by necessity), then the *applicationDidEnterBackground* delegate method is triggered.

When a foreground application enters the background the application transitions to the *inactive* state, triggering a call to the application delegate's *applicationWillResignActive* method. This in turn is followed by a transition to *background* status which is accompanied by a call to the *applicationDidEnterBackground* method.

If the application has not indicated that it is eligible to continue running in the background the application is given 5 seconds to complete any tasks before returning from the *applicationDidEnterBackground* method. If these tasks cannot be performed in the time given they may be performed by making a call to the *beginBackgroundTaskWithExpirationHandler* method followed by a call to the *endBackgroundTask* method when the task is complete. Failure to return from the *applicationDidEnterBackground* method within the allocated time will result in the application being terminated.

An Overview of iOS 6 iPhone Multitasking

When an application is moved from the background to the foreground, the *applicationWillEnterForeground* method is triggered, followed by a call to *applicationDidBecomeActive*.

Finally, when an application is about to be terminated (either by the user or the system) the application delegate's *applicationWillTerminate* method is called.

55.3 Disabling Multitasking for an iOS Application

Multitasking support is the default for all applications developed in Xcode using the iOS 4.0 SDK or later. In situations where an application is required to exit rather than enter background mode a configuration setting is required in the application's *Info.plist* file. To achieve this, load the project associated with the app into Xcode and select the Info.plist file from the *Supporting Files* section of the project navigator panel.

In order to disable multitasking, the *Application does not run in background* key must be added to the file with the value of *YES*. If this key is not already listed in the file, select the bottom most item in the list and click on the + button to add a new key. At this point a drop down menu will appear containing a list of available keys. Scroll down the list to locate and select the *Application does not run in background* key as illustrated in Figure 55-1:

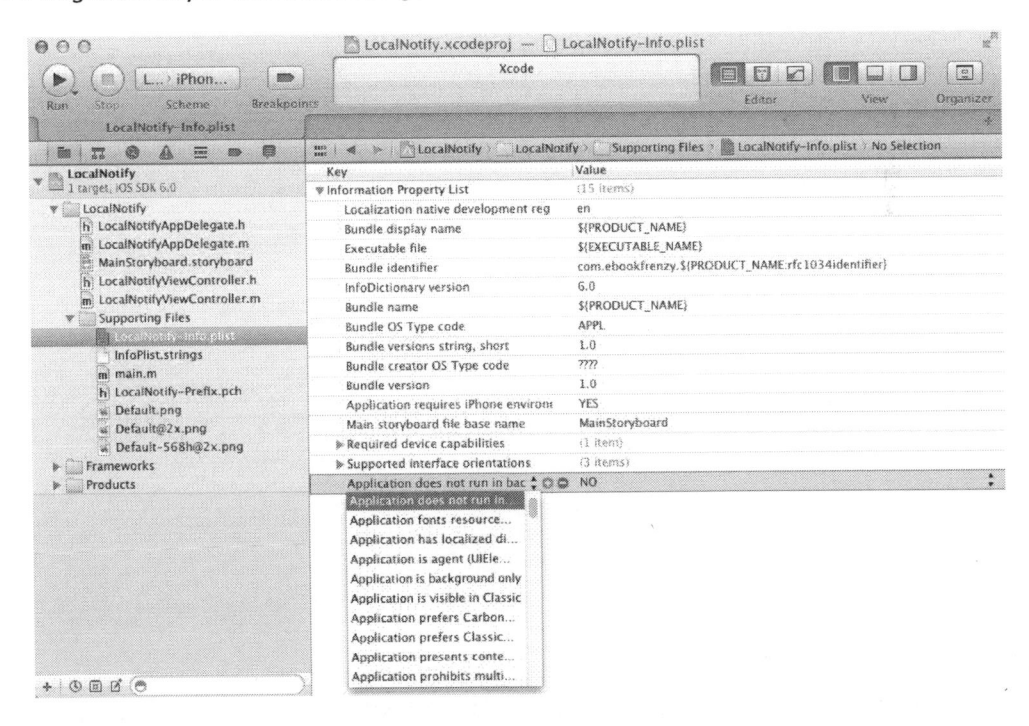

Figure 55-1

Once selected, set the value located in the *Value* column to YES:

439

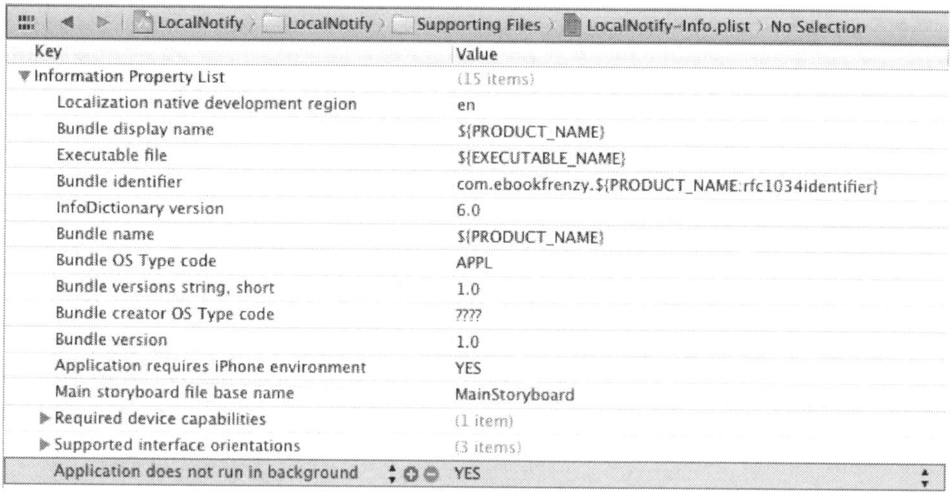

An Overview of iOS 6 iPhone Multitasking

Figure 55-2

55.4 Checking for Multitasking Support

Multitasking is only supported on the iPhone 3GS and later devices running iOS 4.0 or newer. In the case of devices where multitasking is not supported, applications are simply terminated rather than being placed in the background.

If you are developing an application that relies on multitasking it is recommended that defensive code be implemented to check for multitasking support so that application behavior can be modified to compensate for the missing functionality. This can be achieved using the following code fragment:

```
-(bool)multitaskingAvailable
{
   UIDevice* device = [UIDevice currentDevice];
   backgroundIsSupported = NO;
   if ([device respondsToSelector:
       @selector(isMultitaskingSupported)])
         backgroundISSupported = device.multitaskingSupported;
   return backgroundIsSupported;
}
```

When the above method is called it returns either YES or NO depending on whether or not multitasking is supported on the device.

55.5 Supported Forms of Background Execution

So far we have looked primarily at the types of applications for which a suspended background state is acceptable to the user. Apple, however, recognizes three categories in which application

An Overview of iOS 6 iPhone Multitasking

suspension would be detrimental to the user experience, these being *audio, location updates* and *voice over IP (VOIP)*.

The background execution modes supported by an application are configured in the application's *Info.plist* file using the *UIBackgroundModes* key and the *audio, location* and *voip* values. The value for the key is actually an array allowing an application to register for more than one of the three background execution modes. To configure this setting select the Info.plist file and add the *Required background modes* key and required value items. The following figure, for example, illustrates an Info.plist file configured to allow background execution for audio and location updates:

Key	Value
▼ Information Property List	(15 items)
Localization native development region	en
Bundle display name	${PRODUCT_NAME}
Executable file	${EXECUTABLE_NAME}
Bundle identifier	com.ebookfrenzy.${PRODUCT_NAME:rfc1034identifier}
InfoDictionary version	6.0
Bundle name	${PRODUCT_NAME}
Bundle OS Type code	APPL
Bundle versions string, short	1.0
Bundle creator OS Type code	????
Bundle version	1.0
Application requires iPhone environment	YES
Main storyboard file base name	MainStoryboard
▶ Required device capabilities	(1 item)
▶ Supported interface orientations	(3 items)
▼ Required background modes	(2 items)
Item 0	App plays audio
Item 1	App registers for location updates

Figure 55-3

In the case of audio background execution, the audio iOS frameworks responsible for playing sound automatically prevent the application from being suspended whilst in the background. Location based background execution is slightly different in that the application is woken up at required intervals by the operating system in order to handle location related events. For background tracking of location information Apple strongly recommends the use of the *significant location changes* setting (whereby the application is only notified when the device has moved a significant distance) in order to extend battery life.

Finally, the background operation of VOIP based applications can be configured such that the system monitors network sockets for incoming voice calls and wakes the application up from suspension only when traffic is detected.

441

55.6 The Rules of Background Execution

Apple recommends that a number of rules be observed when running an application in background execution mode:

- Only perform the minimum tasks when the application is in background mode. For example, if the application is playing audio content, the application should only perform the tasks necessary to maintaining the audio stream. All other tasks should be placed on hold until the application is returned to the foreground.
- Do not perform updates to the user interface of the application. Since the application is in the background the user cannot see the user interface. There is nothing, therefore, to be gained (except for unnecessarily using CPU cycles and draining the battery) by continuing to update the UI.
- Do not perform OpenGL ES calls. Doing so will cause your application to be terminated.
- Always save the state and data information for the application when notification is received that it is entering the background. Even when suspended, an application may be terminated by the system in order to free up resources.
- Stop using shared resources such as the address book or calendar when the background notification is received to avoid termination.
- Attempt to release any memory used by the application that can safely be released without impacting the application's subsequent return to the foreground. The more memory a suspended application is holding on to the more likely it is to be terminated should the system need to free up resources.
- Cancel Bonjour related services.

55.7 Scheduling Local Notifications

Suspended applications and those running in one of the three background execution modes do not, by definition, have access to the display of the iPhone device. In recognition of the fact that background applications may still need to display alert messages to users, Apple introduced the *Local Notifications* feature in iOS 4. Unlike the *Push Notifications* functionality available in previous versions of iOS, local notifications allow alerts to be triggered from within the local application without the need to rely on a remote server.

A local notification may be triggered at any time by an executing background application. Suspended applications must, however, schedule the notification to be delivered at a future time as part of the clean up process contained within the *applicationDidEnterBackground* method. A step-by-step example of how to schedule a local notification within an application entering suspended mode is covered in the chapter entitled *Scheduling iOS 6 iPhone Local Notifications*.

Chapter 56

56. Scheduling iOS 6 iPhone Local Notifications

Local Notifications were introduced with iOS 4.0 and provide a mechanism for an application to schedule an alert to notify the user about an event. These notifications take the form of an alert box or notification panel containing a message accompanied by a sound and the vibration of the iPhone device.

The primary purpose of local notifications is to provide a mechanism for a suspended or background application to gain the attention of the user. For example, an audio streaming app might need to notify the user of the loss of network connection or a calendar based application an approaching appointment. Local notifications are similar to the *push notification* system introduced with iOS 3.0 with the primary difference that notifications are scheduled locally by the application and so do not require the involvement of a remote server.

The goal of this chapter is to build upon the groundwork established in *An Overview of iOS 6 iPhone Multitasking* by developing a simple iPhone application that, when placed into the background by the user, schedules a local notification event for a future time.

56.1 Creating the Local Notification iPhone App Project

The first step in demonstrating the use of local notifications is to create a new Xcode project. Begin by launching Xcode and selecting the options to create a new iPhone iOS project using the *Single View Application* template. When prompted to do so name the product and class prefix *LocalNotify* and verify that the Automatic Reference Counting and Storyboard options are enabled.

56.2 Locating the Application Delegate Method

The goal of this exercise is to configure a local notification to be triggered 10 seconds after our application enters the background (for additional information on background and suspended applications refer to *An Overview of iOS 6 iPhone Multitasking*). When an application is placed in the background, the application delegate's *applicationDidEnterBackground* method is triggered. It is within this method, therefore, that the code to schedule the local notification must be placed. In the case of this example, a template method can be found in the *LocalNotifyAppDelegate.m* file. Within

443

Scheduling iOS 6 iPhone Local Notifications

the main Xcode project navigator panel, select this file and scroll down until the method comes into view:

```
- (void)applicationDidEnterBackground:(UIApplication *)application {
    /*
     Use this method to release shared resources, save user data,
 invalidate timers, and store enough application state information to
 restore your application to its current state in case it is terminated
 later.
     If your application supports background execution, called instead
 of applicationWillTerminate: when the user quits.
     */
}
```

56.3 Adding a Sound File to the Project

When a local notification is triggered, the option is available to play a sound to gain the user's attention. If such an audio alert is required the corresponding sound file must be added to the application project resources. If no sound file is specified, the default is for the notification to be silent (though the iPhone device will still vibrate).

For the purposes of this exercise, we will use a public domain sound clip file which may be downloaded using the following URL:

http://www.ebookfrenzy.com/code/bell_tree.mp3

Once downloaded, drag this file and drop it onto the *Supporting Files* category located in the Xcode project navigator panel and click the *Finish* button in the resulting panel. The audio file should now be included in the list of resources for the project ready to be accessed by the application code.

56.4 Scheduling the Local Notification

Local notifications require the use of the UILocalNotification class combined with an NSDate object configured with the date and time that the notification is to be triggered. Properties may also be set to specify the text to be displayed to the user, an optional repeat interval and a message to be displayed to the user in the alert box. With these requirements in the mind, the following code creates an NSDate object based on the current date and time plus 10 seconds. This date object is then used to schedule a notification with no repeats, a text message and the sound from the audio file:

```
- (void)applicationDidEnterBackground:(UIApplication *)application
{
    NSDate *alertTime = [[NSDate date]
            dateByAddingTimeInterval:10];
```

Scheduling iOS 6 iPhone Local Notifications

```
    UIApplication* app = [UIApplication sharedApplication];
    UILocalNotification* notifyAlarm = [[UILocalNotification alloc]
            init];
    if (notifyAlarm)
    {
        notifyAlarm.fireDate = alertTime;
        notifyAlarm.timeZone = [NSTimeZone defaultTimeZone];
        notifyAlarm.repeatInterval = 0;
        notifyAlarm.soundName = @"bell_tree.mp3";
        notifyAlarm.alertBody = @"Staff meeting in 30 minutes";
        [app scheduleLocalNotification:notifyAlarm];
    }
}
```

56.5 Testing the Application

To test the application click on the *Run* tool bar button located in the Xcode project window. After compiling and linking the application, it will load and run in the iOS Simulator. Once the application has loaded into the iPhone simulator, click on the device home button to place the app into background mode. After 10 seconds have elapsed the notification should appear accompanied by the sound from the audio file as illustrated in Figure 56-1.

Figure 56-1

445

56.6 Cancelling Scheduled Notifications

Previously scheduled notifications may be cancelled by obtaining a list of outstanding notifications. These notifications are provided in the form of an NSArray object, the contents of which may be used to cancel individual notifications using the *cancelLocalNotification* method. All currently scheduled notifications may also be cancelled using the *cancelAllLocalNotifications* method as outlined in the following code fragment:

```
UIApplication* app = [UIApplication sharedApplication];
NSArray*    oldNotifications = [app scheduledLocalNotifications];

if ([oldNotifications count] > 0)
    [app cancelAllLocalNotifications];
```

56.7 Immediate Triggering of a Local Notification

In addition to the cancellation of a local notification, previously scheduled notifications may be triggered to present immediately to the user irrespective of the fireDate property setting. For example, the following code identifies the list of currently scheduled notifications and then triggers the first notification in the array for immediate presentation:

```
NSArray *notifications = [app scheduledLocalNotifications];
if ([notifications count] > 0)
    [app presentLocalNotificationNow:notifications[0]];
```

Note that notifications presented using the *presentLocalNotificationNow* method will still trigger again when the specified fireDate is reached unless they are specifically cancelled.

56.8 Summary

Local notifications were introduced in iOS 4.0 alongside multitasking support as a way for iOS applications placed in the background or in a suspended state to notify the user of an event. In this chapter we have worked through an example of scheduling a local notification for a future time when an application receives notification that it is transitioning to the background state. Also covered were the steps necessary to cancel pending notifications and to trigger the immediate presentation of a notification regardless of the scheduled delivery time.

Chapter 57

57. An Overview of iOS 6 Application State Preservation and Restoration

Application state preservation and restoration is all about presenting the user with application continuity in terms of appearance and behavior. This is, in part, already provided through support for applications to run in the background. Users have come to expect to be able to switch from one app to another and, on returning to the original app, to find it in the exact state it was in before the switch took place. Unless the application developer took specific steps to save and restore state, however, this continuity did not extend between sessions that involve the application stopping and restarting (usually as a result of the operating system killing a background application to free resources). For most applications available today, such a scenario results in the application starting at the home screen with no consideration being given to the previous state of the application.

Apple feels strongly that the continuity of a user's interaction with an application should extend between the application stopping and restarting. In recognition of this fact, iOS 6 introduces a set of new features to the UIKit framework intended to make it easier for developers to save and restore application state.

The topic of this chapter is to introduce the concepts of application state preservation and restoration in iOS 6 and outline the steps that are involved in implementing this behavior.

57.1 The Preservation and Restoration Process

The UIKit preservation and restoration system provides a mechanism by which an application is able to save and restore the state of specific view controllers and views between different application invocations. UIKit achieves this by defining a flexible structure to which the application must conform in terms of providing information on what is to be saved, and implementing methods that are called by UIKit at certain points during the preservation and restoration process.

During the application design process, the developer must decide which view controllers and views that comprise the application need to have state preserved to ensure continuity for the user. Each item for which state is to be saved must then be assigned a *restoration identifier*. Those views and view controllers without a restoration ID will not, by default, be included in the saved state. It should

An Overview of iOS 6 Application State Preservation and Restoration

also be noted that if a view controller does not have a restoration ID, none that controller's child views or view controllers will be saved, irrespective of whether or not those sub-views have a restoration ID.

Each time a running application is placed into the background, UIKit will ask the application whether or not it requires state preservation. In the event that the application requires the state to be saved, UIKit will traverse the view controller hierarchy of the application and save the state of each object that has a restoration ID. As it does this, it will call a method on each eligible object in order to provide that object with an opportunity to encode and return additional data to be included in the saved state. Once the state information has been gathered, it is saved to a file on the local file system of the device.

When the application is next launched (as opposed to being brought out of the background and into the foreground) UIKit will look for a saved state file for the application. In the event that it finds one, it will ask the application if state restoration is required. If the application responds affirmatively, UIKit will use the saved state to guide the application through the process of re-creating the views and view controllers to the previous state. As will be seen later in this chapter, the exact sequence of events for this restoration will depend on the nature of the application, but essentially involves UIKit making calls to specific methods (primarily on the application delegate) asking for the objects to be recreated. Once the view controller and view objects have been recreated, UIKit calls methods on those objects passing through any additional data that was saved during the preservation process.

57.2 Opting In to Preservation and Restoration

By default, UIKit does not attempt to save and restore the state of an application. An application must, instead, "opt-in". This is achieved by implementing methods in the application delegate which return a boolean value to indicate whether or not preservation and restoration are required. The following methods, for example, indicate to UIKit that both state restoration and preservation are required:

```
-(BOOL)application:(UIApplication *)application
shouldRestoreApplicationState:(NSCoder *)coder
{
        return YES;
}

-(BOOL)application:(UIApplication *)application
shouldSaveApplicationState:(NSCoder *)coder
{
        return YES;
}
```

57.3 Assigning Restoration Identifiers

When UIKit walks the view controller hierarchy of an application to preserve state, only those objects with a restoration ID will be saved.

Restoration IDs can be assigned to objects either in code or from within Interface Builder. The restoration ID can be any valid string and may be assigned in code via the *restorationID* property of the UIView and UIViewController classes. For example:

```
myViewController.restorationIdentifier = @"myFirstView";
```

When using Interface Builder, the restoration ID may be assigned by selecting the object and entering the ID into the *Restoration ID* field located in the *Identity* section of the Identity Inspector as illustrated in Figure 57-1.

In the case of storyboards, the restoration ID can be set to use the storyboard ID if one has already been assigned.

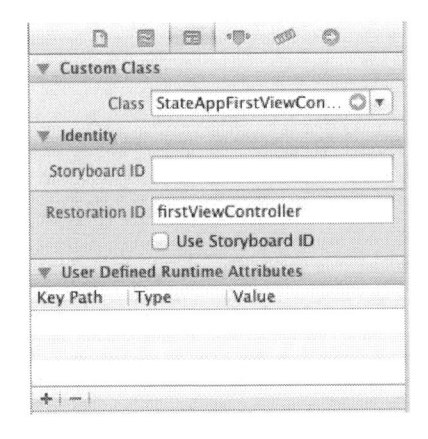

Figure 57-1

When assigning restoration IDs in Interface Builder, it is important to distinguish between views and view controllers. Clicking on the white background of view in a storyboard, for example, will select the UIView object, not the view controller. Clicking on the black status bar containing the battery life indicator will, on the other hand, select the view controller. As a general rule, wherever possible, state preservation should be implemented by saving and restoring the state of the view controller which, in turn, will be responsible for restoring the state of any child view objects. Directly saving and restoring the state of individual view objects in a user interface layout should only be performed when preservation requirements cannot be met using the view controller state.

57.4 Default Preservation Features of UIKit

Once state preservation has been enabled and restoration identifiers assigned appropriately, it is worth being aware that UIKit will preserve certain state information by default and without the need to write any additional code. By default, the following state information is saved and restored automatically for view controllers:

- Currently presented view controller
- Currently selected tab
- State of navigation stacks

In the case of views, the following is preserved by default:

- Current scroll position
- Currently selected cell in a table view
- Current state of an image view (zoom, pan, etc)
- Web history (including scroll position and zoom level)

Additional state preservation will, as will be outlined in the remainder of this chapter, require some coding.

57.5 Saving and Restoring Additional State Information

So far we have ascertained that UIKit will store information about which view controllers and views are to be saved based on whether or not those objects have a restoration ID. In many cases, each object will have additional information that it needs to save in order to restore the application exactly as the user left it. This might, for example, relate to a specific item the user has selected, or some text that has been entered into a Text View but not yet been committed to the application's data model. Fortunately, UIKit has a way to handle this.

Once UIKit discovers, for example, that the state of a specific view controller is to be saved, it will check to see if a method named *encodeRestorableStateWIthCoder:* has been implemented in that object's class. If the method has been implemented, UIKit will call that method, passing through a reference to an NSCoder object. It is then the responsibility of that method to store any additional state data that needs to be preserved into that NSCoder object before returning. UIKit will then save that NSCoder object along with the rest of the application's state.

When UIKit restores the view controller object on a subsequent launch of the application, it will call the *decodeRestorableStateWithCoder:* method of that object, passing through the NSCoder object containing the previously stored state data. The method is then responsible for decoding the object and using the data contained therein to restore the view to the previous state. The following code

An Overview of iOS 6 Application State Preservation and Restoration

listing shows an example implementation of these two methods for a view controller class intended to save any text that has been entered by the user but not yet saved to the applications data model:

```
-(void)encodeRestorableStateWithCoder:(NSCoder *)coder
{
    [coder encodeObject:_myTextView.text forKey:@"UnsavedText"];
    [super decodeRestorableStateWithCoder:coder];
}

-(void)decodeRestorableStateWithCoder:(NSCoder *)coder
{
    _myTextView.text = [coder decodeObjectForKey:@"UnsavedText"];
    [super encodeRestorableStateWithCoder:coder];
}
```

Note that it is important to call the corresponding method in the superclass before returning from the above methods.

57.6 Understanding the Restoration Process

Although UIKit handles the task of remembering which view controllers are to be restored, the actual recreation of those objects is the responsibility of the application code. Restoration can either be performed within the application delegate class, or by implementing a *restoration class* for the view controller.

Restoration classes are useful for restoring view controllers that are not stored in a storyboard file. When attempting to restore a specific view controller, UIKit will first check whether or not a restoration class exists for that controller. If one exists, UIKit instantiates it and calls its *viewControllerWithRestorationIdentifierPath:* method and expects the method to create the corresponding view controller object and return it. If the method returns a nil value, however, UIKit assumes the view controller is not to be restored.

In order for a class to qualify as restoration class is must implement the *UIViewControllerRestoration* protocol. Typically, a view controller not stored in a storyboard file will implement this protocol and act as its own restoration class.

When an application is started and UIKit finds a file containing a preserved state, UIKit makes a call to the *application:willFinishLaunchingWithOptions:* method of the application delegate class. This will be followed by repeated calls to an application delegate method named *viewControllerWithRestorationIdentifierPath:*. This method will be called once for each saved view controller for which a restoration class cannot be found. Passed through as an argument to this method is an array identifying the *restoration path* explicitly referencing the view controller which is to be recreated.

451

An Overview of iOS 6 Application State Preservation and Restoration

This restoration path is essentially made up from the restoration IDs of the elements in the view controller hierarchy, starting with the root controller and walking down the tree to the view controller UIKit is looking for. Consider, for example, the view hierarchy illustrated in Figure 57-2 where each tree node is labeled using the restoration ID of the corresponding view or view controller object.

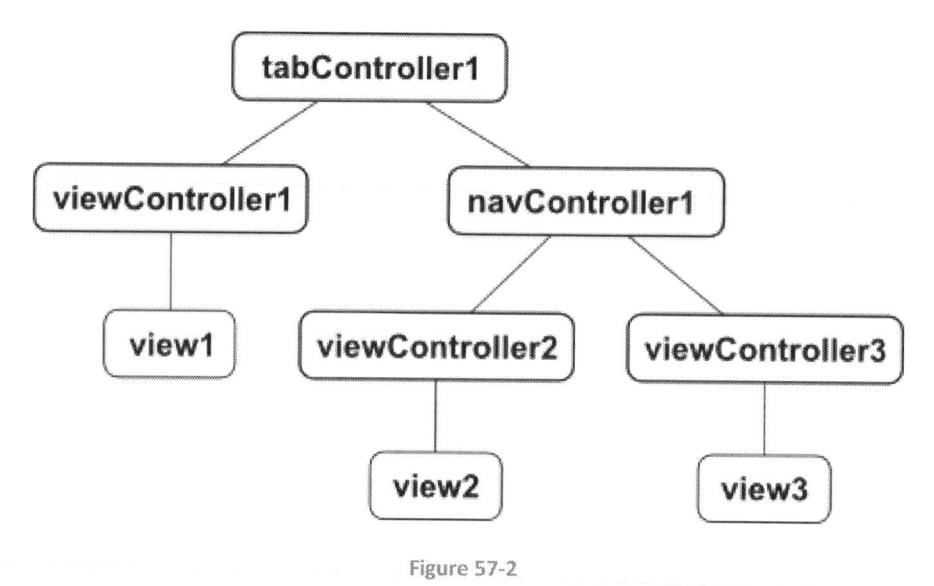

Figure 57-2

In the event that UIKit needs viewController2 to be recreated, the restoration path passed to the application delegate would be:

`tabController1 / navController1 / viewController2`

The application delegate method now has two choices. Either it can recreate the view controller object and return it to UIKit or it can return a *nil* value. To recreate a view controller, the application delegate can either instantiate the appropriate view controller class and return it or, if the view controller is stored in a storyboard file, load it and create it from there.

If the *viewControllerWithRestorationIdentifierPath:* returns a nil value, UIKit will continue looking for the view controller object. UIKit will first check to make sure the view controller object has not already been created as part of the application's initialization process. Failing that, if the view controller resides in a storyboard file, UIKit will find it *implicitly* and load and recreate it automatically.

57.7 Saving General Application State

So far in this chapter we have focused exclusively on saving the state of the user interface in terms of views and view controllers. There will also be situations where other data may be relevant to the state of the application but not directly associated with the user interface elements. In order to

An Overview of iOS 6 Application State Preservation and Restoration

address this need, the following two methods may be implemented within the application delegate class:

- application:willEncodeRestorableStateWithCoder
- application:didEncodeRestorableStateWithCoder

The former method is called by UIKit at the start of the preservation process and is passed a reference to an NSCoder object into which state data may be stored. The *application:didEncodeRestorableStateWithCoder:* method, on the other hand, is called when UIKit has completed the restoration process and is passed the NSCoder object into which general state data was previously stored.

57.8 Summary

A key part of providing an optimal user experience is to ensure that continuity of application appearance and behavior is maintained between one application launch instance and the next. Prior to iOS 6, this involved writing custom code to save and restore state. iOS 6, however, introduces new features in the UIKit Framework designed specifically to ease the implementation of state preservation and restoration in iOS applications. In this chapter, the basic concepts of state preservation have been covered. The next chapter, entitled *An iOS 6 iPhone State Preservation and Restoration Tutorial*, will work through a practical demonstration of how these concepts are implemented in an application.

Chapter 58

58. An iOS 6 iPhone State Preservation and Restoration Tutorial

In the previous chapter, a significant amount of information was conveyed relating to using the new features of UIKit in iOS 6 to preserve and restore application state when an application currently placed into the background is terminated by the operating system and needs to be restarted.

The knowledge covered in the previous chapter will now be re-enforced through the creation of an example application that demonstrates exactly how to implement state preservation and restoration in iOS 6.

58.1 Creating the Example Application

Begin by launching Xcode and selecting the options to create a new iPhone iOS application based on the *Tabbed Application* template. Enter *StateApp* as the product name and class prefix, set the device to *iPhone* and select the *Use Storyboards* and *Use Automatic Reference Counting* options if they are not already enabled.

58.2 Trying the Application without State Preservation

The Tabbed Application template has provided enough functionality to experience some of the default effects of state preservation and restoration. First, run the application without opting in to state preservation. To so do, simply select a target of either the iOS Simulator or a physical iPhone device in the Xcode toolbar and click on the Run button. When the application has loaded, select the *Second* tab so that the *Second View* is visible before pressing the round home button at the bottom of the device to place the application into the background.

The easiest way to test state preservation is to simulate the application being terminated by the operating system whilst in the background. To achieve this, simply click on the *Stop* button in the Xcode toolbar. Once the application has stopped running, launch it a second time by clicking on the Run button. When the application launches, the *First* tab will be selected instead of the *Second* tab. Clearly no application state has been preserved between application launches. This is because the application has not "opted-in" to state preservation and restoration.

455

58.3 Opting-in to State Preservation

Before any kind of state preservation and restoration will become effective, the application must first opt in to the system. Within the project navigator panel, select the application delegate implementation source file (*StateAppAppDelegate.m*) and modify it to add the two methods required to opt in to both the saving and restoration of application state:

```
-(BOOL)application:(UIApplication *)application
shouldRestoreApplicationState:(NSCoder *)coder
{
    return YES;
}

-(BOOL)application:(UIApplication *)application
shouldSaveApplicationState:(NSCoder *)coder
{
    return YES;
}
```

With the above code changes implemented, once again run the application and perform the previous test to verify that the application is restored to the *Second* tab. Yet again, the application will re-launch with the *First* tab selected. This is because, although the application opted in to state preservation, restoration IDs have not been assigned. As far as UIKit is concerned, therefore, no state needed to be preserved.

58.4 Setting Restoration Identifiers

So far the application storyboard consists of a Tab Bar Controller, two view controllers and a view for each controller (each of which in turn currently contains labels added by Xcode when the Tabbed Application template was selected). In order for any kind of application state to be saved, restoration IDs must be assigned to appropriate objects. The rules of state preservation dictate that any view or view controller object, and its direct ancestors up to and including the root view controller must have a restoration ID in order to be included in the state save file. In the case of this application, restoration IDs need to be added to the Tab Controller and the two view controllers. Since the view controllers will be responsible for the state of the views, these views do not need restoration IDs.

Select the *MainStoryboard.storyboard* file in the project navigator panel and locate the Tab Bar Controller in the storyboard canvas. Display the Identity Inspector and enter *tabController1* into the *Restoration ID* field as illustrated in Figure 58-1:

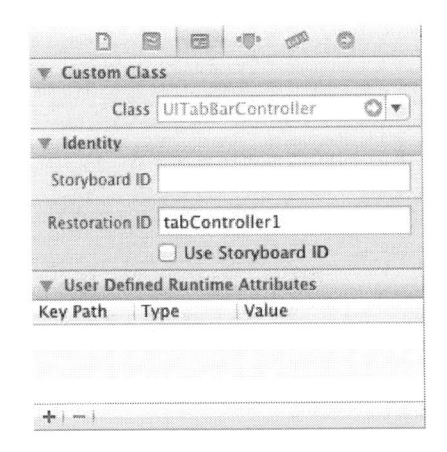

Figure 58-1

Repeat these steps to assign restoration IDs of *viewController1* and *viewController2* to the first and second view controllers respectively. When doing so, make sure that it is the view controllers, and not the view objects, that are being selected by clicking on the black status bar at the top of the view containing the battery status indicator and not the white background of the view.

With the restoration IDs assigned, run the application and select the *Second* tab. Put the application into the background and then stop and restart the application. This time the application will re-launch and restore the second view as the current view. The default state saving features of UIKit in iOS 6 are now working and more advanced examples of state preservation can be explored.

58.5 Encoding and Decoding View Controller State

The next phase of this tutorial will extend the example application to demonstrate encoding and decoding the state of a view controller. In order to do so, however, some design changes will need to be made to the second view controller.

With the *MainStoryboard.storyboard* file still selected, locate the second view controller and select and delete the labels currently present in the layout. With a blank view object to work with, drag and drop a Text View object onto the layout. Using the resize handles, reduce the height of the Text View so that it is approximately a quarter of the height of the containing view. Next, add a button, change the label to "Press Me" and position it beneath the Text View as illustrated in Figure 58-2.

An iOS 6 iPhone State Preservation and Restoration Tutorial

Figure 58-2

Select the Text View object, display the Attribute Inspector and delete the sample Latin text from the *Text* property.

Select the Text View object, display the Assistant Editor and click and drag from the Text View object to the space beneath the @interface line. Release the line and in the resulting panel, establish a new outlet connection named *myTextView*. Close the Assistant Editor.

Build and run the application and, once running, select the second tab and then select and enter some text into the Text View object. Place the application into the background and stop the application using the Xcode *Stop* button. Click on run to launch the application again. Whilst the selection of the second tab has been preserved, the text entered into the Text View has been lost.

In order to preserve the text entered by the user, it will be necessary to implement the *encodeRestorableStateWithCoder:* and *decodeRestorableStateWithCoder:* methods in the parent view controller of the Text View (in this case *StateAppSecondViewController*).

Select the *StateAppSecondViewController.m* file and add the encoding methods as follows:

```
-(void)encodeRestorableStateWithCoder:(NSCoder *)coder
{
```

```
    [coder encodeObject:_myTextView.text forKey:@"UnsavedText"];
    [super encodeRestorableStateWithCoder:coder];
}
```

This code is actually very straightforward. The method is called by UIKit while the state of the view controller is being saved and is passed an NSCoder object. The *encodeObject:* method of the coder (methods exist for other types of data as documented in Apple documentation for the NSCoder class) is then used to encode the text that is currently held in the myTextView object using a key that will be used to decode the data later. The superclass method is then called and the method returns.

The corresponding decode method also needs to be added:

```
-(void)decodeRestorableStateWithCoder:(NSCoder *)coder
{
    _myTextView.text = [coder decodeObjectForKey:@"UnsavedText"];
    [super decodeRestorableStateWithCoder:coder];

}
```

This method simply does the reverse of the encode method. It is called by UIKit during the view controller restoration process and passed the NSCoder object containing the saved data. The method decodes the text using the previously assigned key and assigns it to the Text View.

Compile and run the application once again, enter some text into the Text View object. Place the application into the background before stopping and restarting the application. The previously entered text should now be restored and any work entered by the user but not saved has not been lost between application invocations, a key objective of iOS state preservation.

58.6 Adding a Navigation Controller to the Storyboard

Up until this point in the tutorial all view controllers have resided within a storyboard file. As such, UIKit has been able to implicitly find and load the controllers at run time. The tutorial has so far, therefore, failed to demonstrate the use of a restoration class to restore a view controller that was created in code as opposed to being stored in a storyboard file. The remainder of this chapter will focus on just such a scenario.

Within the storyboard, select the Second view controller and insert a navigation controller using the *Editor -> Embed In -> Navigation Controller* menu option. Once added, the storyboard should match that illustrated in Figure 58-3.

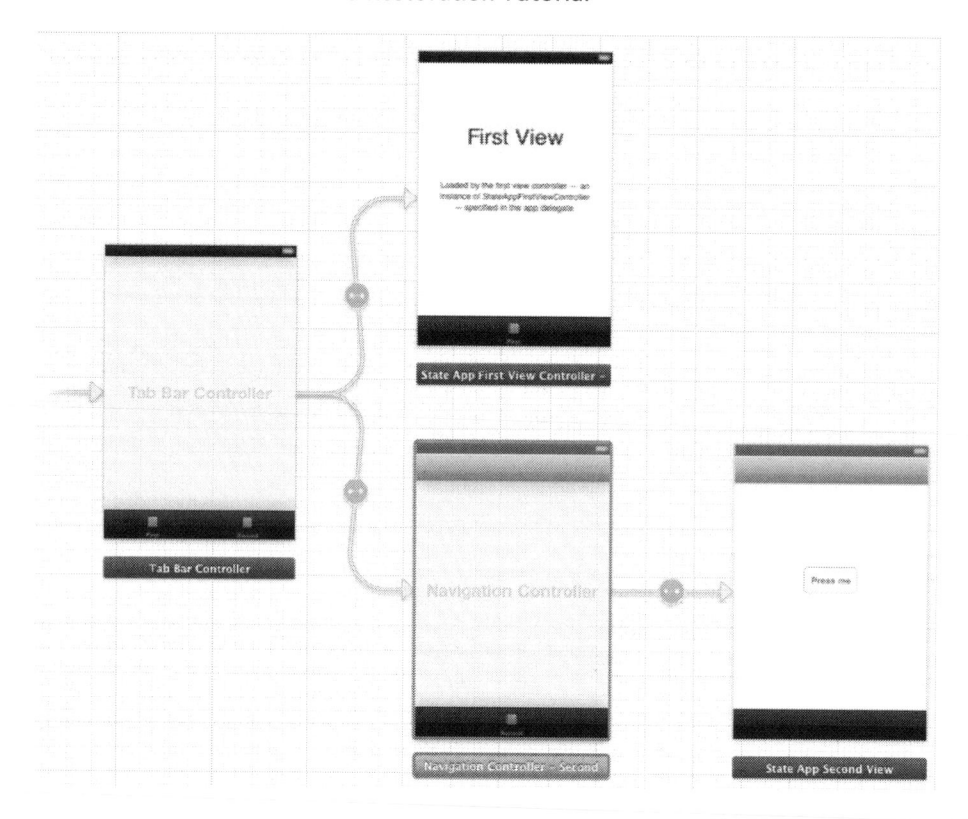

An iOS 6 iPhone State Preservation and Restoration Tutorial

Figure 58-3

Select the navigation controller in the storyboard canvas, display the Identity Inspector and set the restoration ID to *navController1*. Next, select the Second view controller, display the Assistant Editor and Ctrl-click from the Button object in the second view to a location just beneath the *myTextView* outlet in the Assistant Editor panel before releasing the line. In the resulting panel, change the Connection type to *Action* and specify *displayVC3* as the method name. It is within this action method that the third view controller will be instantiated and pushed onto the navigation controller stack so that it becomes visible to the user. At this point the *StateAppSecondViewController.h* interface file should read as follows:

```
#import <UIKit/UIKit.h>

@interface StateAppSecondViewController : UIViewController
@property (strong, nonatomic) IBOutlet UITextView *myTextView;
- (IBAction)displayVC3:(id)sender;
@end
```

58.7 Adding the Third View Controller

When the "Press Me" button in the second view is touched by the user, a third view controller needs to be instantiated and presented to the user using the navigation controller. This new view controller class first needs to be created. Since the objective here is to demonstrate the use of a restoration class, the view will be created in code and not in the storyboard file. Begin, therefore, by selecting the *File -> New -> File…* menu option and in the resulting panel select *Objective-C class* from the list of templates before clicking on the *Next* button.

On the next screen, name the class *StateAppThirdViewController* and configure it to be subclass of UIViewController. Ensure that the *With XIB for user interface* option is selected and click *Next* followed by *Create*.

Select the newly created *StateAppThirdViewController.xib* file to load it into Interface Builder and add a label that indicates this is the view for the third view controller (Figure 58-4):

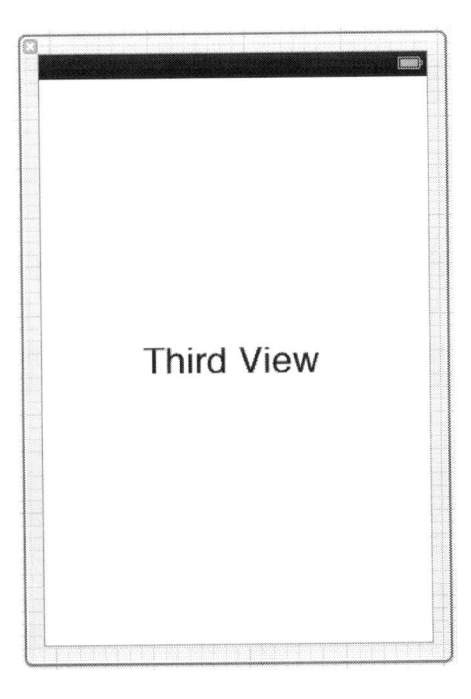

Figure 58-4

The next step is to write some code in the second view controller to create an instance of the StateAppThirdViewController class and to push it onto the navigation controller stack when the "Press Me" button is touched.

An iOS 6 iPhone State Preservation and Restoration Tutorial

Select the *StateAppSecondViewController.h* file and modify it to import the interface file for the StateAppThirdViewController class and to declare a property for the corresponding view controller object when it is created:

```
#import <UIKit/UIKit.h>
#import "StateAppThirdViewController.h"

@interface StateAppSecondViewController : UIViewController
@property (strong, nonatomic) IBOutlet UITextView *myTextView;
@property (strong, nonatomic) UIViewController *thirdViewController;

- (IBAction)displayVC3:(id)sender;

@end
```

Select the *StateAppSecondViewController.m* file and modify the *viewDidLoad:* method to create a new instance of the third view controller class and the *displayVC3:* action method to push the view controller onto the navigation stack so that it is appears to the user when the button is touched:

```
- (void)viewDidLoad
{
    [super viewDidLoad];
    // Do any additional setup after loading the view, typically from a nib.
    _thirdViewController = [[StateAppThirdViewController alloc]
            initWithNibName:@"StateAppThirdViewController"
            bundle:nil];
}
.
.
.
- (IBAction)displayVC3:(id)sender {
    [self.navigationController
            pushViewController:_thirdViewController animated:YES];
}
```

Finally, the code in the StateAppThirdViewController class needs to be modified so that instances of the class are assigned a restoration ID. Select the *StateAppThirdViewController.m* file and add a line to the *viewDidLoad:* method:

```
- (void)viewDidLoad
{
    [super viewDidLoad];
    // Do any additional setup after loading the view from its nib.
```

```
    self.restorationIdentifier = @"thirdViewController";
}
```

Build and run the application, navigate to the third view controller in the user interface and then perform the usual background/kill/run cycle. Note that the application returned to the second view controller screen and not the third view controller. Because the third view controller was created in code, UIKit is unable to find a way to recreate it when the application state is restored. This is where it becomes necessary to implement and register a restoration class for the StateAppThirdViewController class.

58.8 Creating the Restoration Class

There are three very simple rules for implementing a restoration class. Firstly, the class must implement the *<UIViewControllerRestoration>* protocol. Secondly, in doing so, it must implement the *viewControllerWithRestorationIdentifierPath:* class method which, in turn, must return an instance of the view controller for which it is acting as the restoration class. Lastly, the restoration class must be assigned to the *restorationClass* property of the view controller it is designed to restore.

In this instance, the StateAppThirdViewController class is going to act as its own restoration class. Select the *StateAppThirdViewController.h* file, therefore, and modify it to declare that the class now implements the view controller restoration protocol:

```
#import <UIKit/UIKit.h>

@interface StateAppThirdViewController : UIViewController
<UIViewControllerRestoration>
@end
```

Next, implement the *viewControllerWithRestorationIdentifierPath:* class method in the *StateAppThirdViewController.m* file:

```
+(UIViewController
*)viewControllerWithRestorationIdentifierPath:(NSArray
*)identifierComponents coder:(NSCoder *)coder
{
    UIViewController * myViewController =
            [[StateAppThirdViewController alloc]
              initWithNibName:@"StateAppThirdViewController"
              bundle:nil];

    return myViewController;
}
```

An iOS 6 iPhone State Preservation and Restoration Tutorial

All this class method does is create a new instance of the StateAppThirdViewController class initialized with the user interface XIB file and returns it to UIKit.

The last task is to the make sure the restoration class is assigned to the view controller. This is achieved by adding a single line to the *viewDidLoad:* method, referencing *self* since the class is acting as its own restoration class:

```
- (void)viewDidLoad
{
    [super viewDidLoad];
    // Do any additional setup after loading the view from its nib.
    self.restorationIdentifier = @"thirdViewController";
    self.restorationClass = [self class];
}
```

Compile and run the application, navigate to the third view controller and background, stop and rerun the application. On the second run, the application should now be restored to the view of the third view controller, a clear sign that the restoration class worked.

58.9 Summary

The objective of this chapter has been to work through the creation of an example application designed to demonstrate the practical implementation of state preservation and restoration using the new features of the UIKit Framework in the iOS 6 SDK.

Chapter 59

59. Integrating Maps into iPhone iOS 6 Applications using MKMapItem

If there is one single fact about Apple that we can state with any degree of certainty, it is that the company is fanatical about retaining control of its own destiny. One glaring omission in this overriding corporate strategy has been the reliance on a competitor (in the form of Google) for mapping data in iOS. This dependency officially ends with iOS 6 through the introduction of Apple Maps.

Apple Maps officially replaces the Google-based map data of previous iOS releases with data provided primarily by a company named TomTom (but also including technology from other companies, including some acquired by Apple for this purpose). Headquartered in the Netherlands, TomTom specializes in mapping and GPS systems. Of particular significance, however, is that TomTom (unlike Google) does not make smartphones, nor does it develop an operating system that competes with iOS, making it a more acceptable partner for Apple.

Political issues aside, there are also technological advantages to the change. Of particular significance is the fact that Google maps were assembled from collections of static images. This led to fuzzy images when zooming in and out and a lack of precision when declaring map regions. The new maps in iOS 6 are dynamically rendered, vector-based images making them both scalable and more precise.

As part of the iOS 6 revamp of mapping, the SDK also introduces a new class in the form of MKMapItem, designed solely for the purpose of easing the integration of maps and turn-by-turn directions into iOS applications.

For more advanced mapping requirements, the iOS 6 SDK still includes the original classes of the MapKit framework, details of which will be covered in later chapters.

59.1 MKMapItem and MKPlacemark Classes

The purpose of the MKMapItem class is to make it easy for applications to launch maps without having to write significant amounts of code. MKMapItem works in conjunction with the MKPlacemark class, instances of which are passed to MKMapItem to define the locations that are to be displayed in the resulting map. A range of options are also provided with MKMapItem to configure both the appearance of maps and the nature of turn-by-turn directions that are to be displayed (i.e. whether directions are to be for driving or walking).

59.2 An Introduction to Forward and Reverse Geocoding

It is difficult to talk about mapping, in particular when dealing with the MKPlacemark class, without first venturing into the topic of geocoding. Geocoding can best be described as the process of converting a textual based geographical location (such as a street address) into geographical coordinates expressed in terms of longitude and latitude.

Within the context of iOS 6 development, geocoding may be performed by making use of the CLGeocoder class which is used to convert a text based address string into a CLLocation object containing the coordinates corresponding to the address. The following code, for example, converts the street address of the Empire State Building in New York to longitude and latitude coordinates:

```
[geocoder geocodeAddressString:@"350 5th Avenue New York, NY"
        completionHandler:^(NSArray *placemarks, NSError *error) {

            if (error) {
                NSLog(@"Geocode failed with error: %@", error);
                return;
            }

            if (placemarks && placemarks.count > 0)
            {
                CLPlacemark *placemark = placemarks[0];
                CLLocation *location = placemark.location;
                CLLocationCoordinate2D coords =
                        location.coordinate;

                NSLog(@"Latitude = %f, Longitude = %f",
                        coords.latitude, coords.longitude);
            }
        }
];
```

The code simply calls the *geocodeAddressString:* method of a CLGeocoder instance, passing through a string object containing the street address and a completion handler to be called when the translation is complete. Passed as arguments to the handler are an array of CLPlacemark objects (one for each match for the address) together with an Error object which may be used to identify the reason for any failures.

For the purposes of this example the assumption is made that only one location matched the address string provided. The location information is then extracted from the CLPlacemark object at location 0 in the array and the coordinates displayed on the console.

The above code is an example of *forward-geocoding* in that coordinates are calculating based on a text address description. *Reverse-geocoding*, as the name suggests, involves the translation of geographical coordinates into a human readable address string. Consider, for example, the following code:

```
CLGeocoder *geocoder = [[CLGeocoder alloc] init];

CLLocation *newLocation = [[CLLocation alloc]
                initWithLatitude:40.74835
                longitude:-73.984911];

[geocoder reverseGeocodeLocation:newLocation
        completionHandler:^(NSArray *placemarks,
                        NSError *error) {

        if (error) {
            NSLog(@"Geocode failed with error: %@", error);
            return;
        }

        if (placemarks && placemarks.count > 0)
        {
            CLPlacemark *placemark = placemarks[0];

            NSDictionary *addressDictionary =
                        placemark.addressDictionary;

            NSString *address = [addressDictionary
            objectForKey:
                    (NSString *)kABPersonAddressStreetKey];
            NSString *city = [addressDictionary
                objectForKey:
                    (NSString *)kABPersonAddressCityKey];
            NSString *state = [addressDictionary
                objectForKey:
                    (NSString *)kABPersonAddressStateKey];
            NSString *zip = [addressDictionary
                objectForKey:
                    (NSString *)kABPersonAddressZIPKey];
```

```
            NSLog(@"%@ %@ %@ %@", address,city, state, zip);
    }
}];
```

In this case, a CLLocation object is initialized with longitude and latitude coordinates and then passed through to the *reverseGeocodeLocation:* method of a CLGeocoder object. The method passes through to the completion handler an array of matching addresses in the form of CLPlacemark objects. Each object contains an NSDictionary object which, in turn, contains the address information for the matching location. Once again, the code assumes a single match is contained in the array and uses the dictionary keys to access and display the address, city, state, zip and country values. The address dictionary keys follow the standard defined in the *Address Property* section of the iOS SDK Address Book Person reference.

When executed, the above code results in output which reads:

338 5th Avenue New York, New York 10001, United States

It should be noted that the geocoding is not actually performed on the iPhone device, but rather on a server to which the device connects when a translation is required and the results subsequently returned when the translation is complete. As such, geocoding can only take place when the iPhone has an active internet connection.

59.3 Creating MKPlacemark Instances

Each location that is to be represented when a map is displayed using the MKMapItem class must be represented by an MKPlacemark object. When MKPlacemark objects are created, they must be initialized with the geographical coordinates of the location together with an NSDictionary object containing the address property information. Continuing the example for the Empire State Building in New York, an MKPlacemark object would be created as follows:

```
CLLocationCoordinate2D coords =
      CLLocationCoordinate2DMake(40.74835, -73.984911);

    NSDictionary *address = @{
        (NSString *)kABPersonAddressStreetKey: @"350 5th Avenue",
        (NSString *)kABPersonAddressCityKey: @"New York",
        (NSString *)kABPersonAddressStateKey: @"NY",
        (NSString *)kABPersonAddressZIPKey: @"10118",
        (NSString *)kABPersonAddressCountryCodeKey: @"US"
    };

    MKPlacemark *place = [[MKPlacemark alloc]
```

```
        initWithCoordinate:coords addressDictionary:address];
```

Whilst it is possible to initialize an MKPlacemark object passing through a *nil* value for the address dictionary, this will result in the map appearing, albeit with the correct location marked, but it will be tagged as "Unknown" instead of listing the address. The coordinates are, however, mandatory when creating an MKPlacemark object. In the event that the application knows the text address but not the coordinates of a location, geocoding will need to be used to obtain the coordinates prior to creating the MKPlacemark instance.

59.4 Working with MKMapItem

Given the tasks that it is able to perform, the MKMapItem class is actually extremely simple to use. In its simplest form, it can be initialized via a call to the *initWithPlacemark:* method, passing through a single MKPlacemark object as an argument, for example:

```
MKMapItem *mapItem = [[MKMapItem alloc]
        initWithPlacemark:myplacemark];
```

Once initialized, the *openInMapsWithLaunchOptions:* method will open the map positioned at the designated location with an appropriate marker as illustrated in Figure 59-1:

```
[mapItem openInMapsWithLaunchOptions:nil];
```

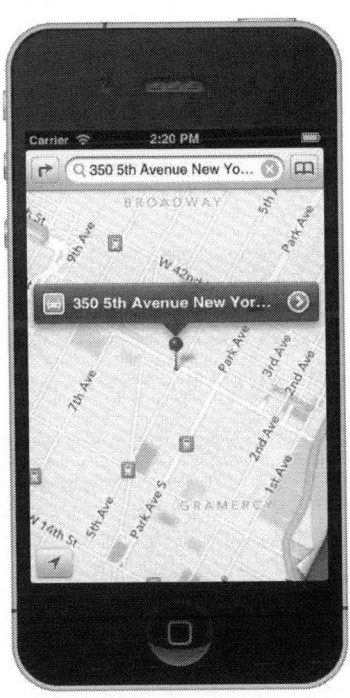

Figure 59-1

Similarly, the map may be initialized to display the current location of the user's device via a call to the *mapItemForCurrentLocation:* method:

```
MPMapItem *item = [MKMapItem mapItemForCurrentLocation];
```

Multiple locations may be tagged on the map by placing two or more MKMapItem objects in an array and then passing that array through to the *openMapsWithItems:* class method of the MKMapItem class. For example:

```
NSArray *mapItem = @[mapItem1, mapItem2, mapItem3];

[MKMapItem openMapsWithItems:mapItems launchOptions:nil];
```

59.5 MKMapItem Options and Enabling Turn-by-Turn Directions

In the example code fragments presented in the preceding sections, a *nil* value was passed through as the options argument to the MKMapItem methods. In actual fact, there are a number of configuration options that are available for use when opening a map. These values need to be set up within an NSDictionary object using a set of pre-defined keys and values:

- **MKLaunchOptionsDirectionsModeKey** – Controls whether turn-by-turn directions are to be provided with the map. In the event that only one placemarker is present, directions from the current location to the placemarker will be provided. The mode for the directions should be one of either *MKLaunchOptionsDirectionsModeDriving* or *MKLaunchOptionsDirectionsModeWalking*.
- **MKLaunchOptionsMapTypeKey** – Indicates whether the map should display satellite, hybrid or standard map images.
- **MKLaunchOptionsMapCenterKey** – Corresponds to a CLLocationCoordinate2D structure value containing the coordinates of the location on which the map is to be centered.
- **MKLaunchOptionsMapSpanKey** – An MKCoordinateSpan structure value designating the region that the map should display when launched.
- **MKLaunchOptionsShowsTrafficKey** – A Boolean value indicating whether or not traffic information should be superimposed over the map when it is launched.

The following code, for example, opens a map in satellite mode with traffic data displayed and includes turn-by-turn driving directions between two map items, the result of which is illustrated in Figure 59-2:

```
NSArray *mapItem = @[mapItem1, mapItem2];

NSDictionary *options = @{
 MKLaunchOptionsDirectionsModeKey:
      MKLaunchOptionsDirectionsModeDriving,
 MKLaunchOptionsMapTypeKey:
```

```
        [NSNumber numberWithInteger:MKMapTypeSatellite],
           MKLaunchOptionsShowsTrafficKey:@YES
};

[MKMapItem openMapsWithItems:mapItems launchOptions:options];
```

Figure 59-2

59.6 Adding Item Details to an MKMapItem

When a location is marked on a map, the address is displayed together with a blue arrow which, when selected, displays an information card for that location. Figure 59-3 shows the location marker for the Empire State Building alongside the information card displayed when that location marker is selected:

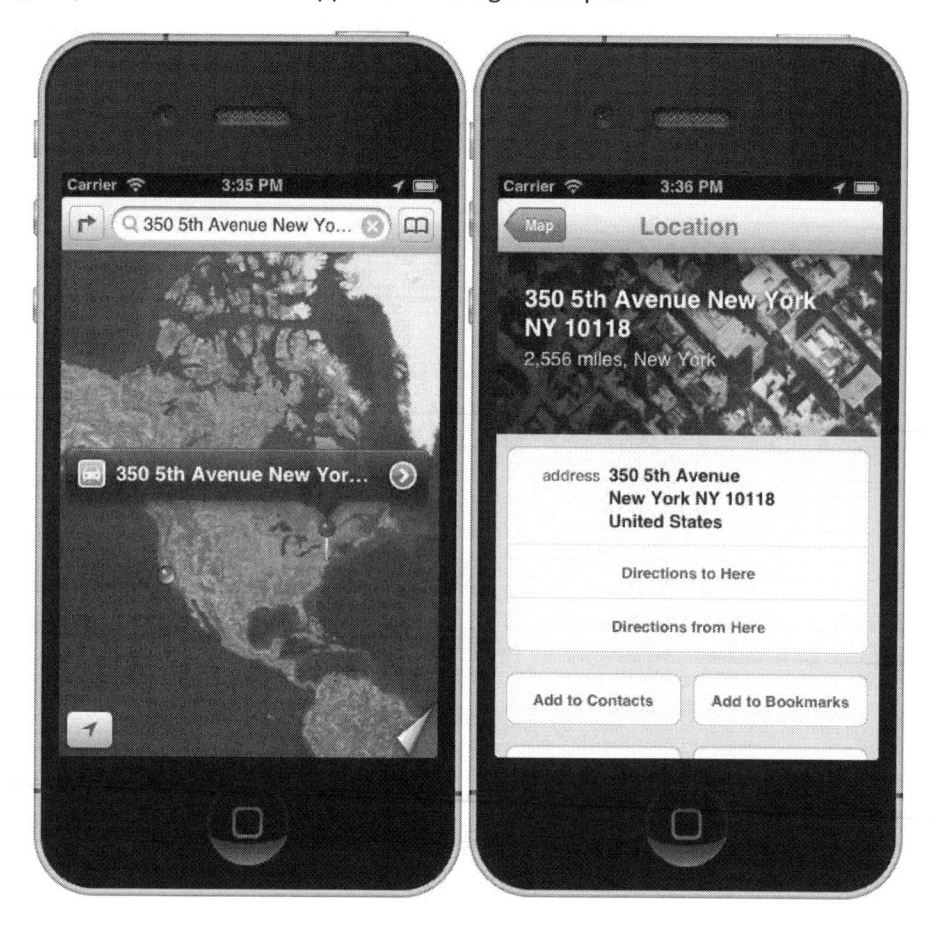

Integrating Maps into iPhone iOS 6 Applications using MKMapItem

Figure 59-3

The MKMapItem class allows additional information to be added to a location through the *name*, *phoneNumber* and *url* properties. The following code, for example, adds these properties to the map item for the Empire State Building:

```
mapItem.name = @"Empire State Building";
mapItem.phoneNumber = @"+12127363100";
mapItem.url = [NSURL URLWithString:@"http://www.esbnyc.com/"];

[mapItem openInMapsWithLaunchOptions:options];
```

When the code is executed, the map place marker displays the location name instead of the address and the information card includes the phone number and URL:

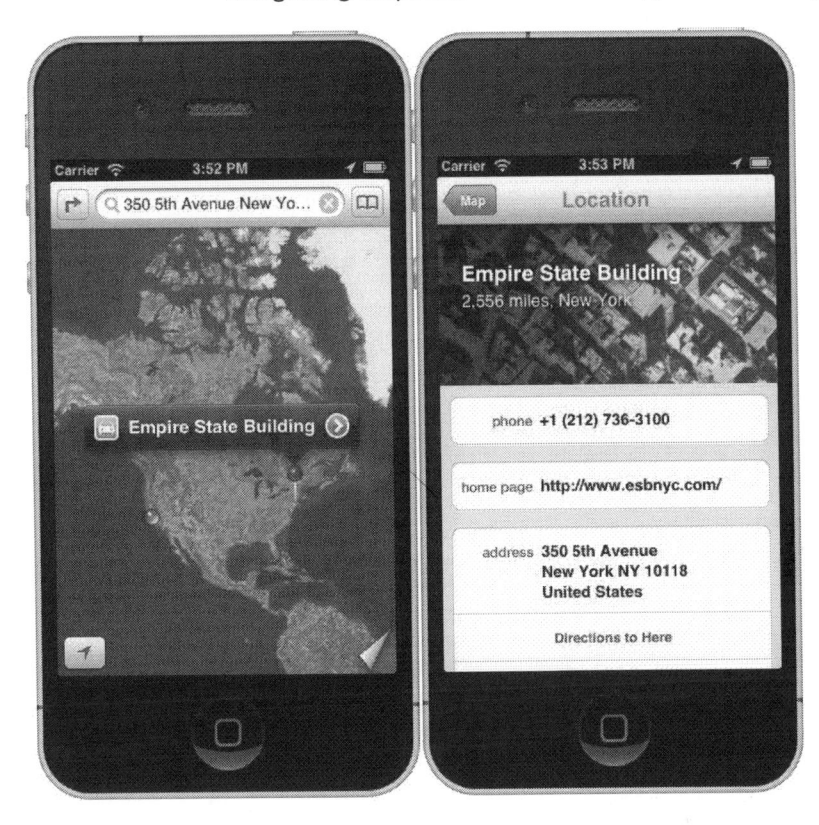

Figure 59-4

59.7 Summary

iOS 6 replaces Google Maps with maps provided by TomTom. Unlike Google Maps, which were assembled from static images, the new Apple Maps are dynamically rendered resulting in clear and smooth zooming and more precise region selections. iOS 6 also introduced the MKMapItem class, the purpose of which is to make it easy for iOS application developers to launch maps and provide turn-by-turn directions with the minimum amount of code.

Within this chapter, the basics of geocoding and the MKPlacemark and MKMapItem classes have been covered. The next chapter, entitled *An Example iOS 6 iPhone MKMapItem Application*, will work through the creation of an example application that utilizes the knowledge covered in this chapter.

Chapter 60

60. An Example iOS 6 iPhone MKMapItem Application

The objective of this chapter is to work through the creation of an example iOS 6 iPhone application which makes use of reverse geocoding together with the MKPlacemark and MKMapItem classes. The application will consist of a screen into which the user will be required to enter destination address information. When a button is selected by the user, a map will be launched containing turn-by-turn directions from the user's current location to the specified destination.

60.1 Creating the MapItem Project

Launch Xcode and create a new project by selecting the options to create a new iPhone iOS application based on the *Single View Application* template. Enter *MapItem* as the product name and class prefix, set the device menu to *iPhone* and select the *Use Storyboards* and *Use Automatic Reference Counting* options if they are not already selected.

60.2 Designing the User Interface

The user interface will consist of four Text Field objects into which the destination address will be entered, together with a Button to launch the map. Select the *MainStoryboard.storyboard* file in the project navigator panel and, using the Object Library palette, design the user interface layout such that it resembles that of Figure 60-1:

An Example iOS 6 iPhone MKMapItem Application

Figure 60-1

If you reside in a country that is not divided into States and Zip code regions, feel free to adjust the user interface accordingly.

The next step is to connect the outlets for the text views and declare an action for the button. Select the *Street address* Text Field object and display the Assistant Editor using *View -> Assistant Editor -> Show Assistant Editor* menu option or the center button of the row of Editor toolbar buttons in the top right hand corner of the main Xcode window.

Ctrl-click on the *Street address* Text Field object and drag the resulting line to the area immediately beneath the @interface directive in the Assistant Editor panel. Upon releasing the line, the configuration panel will appear. Configure the connection as an *Outlet* named *address* and click on the *Connect* button. Repeat these steps for the *City*, *State* and *Zip* text fields, connecting them to outlets named *city, state* and *zip* respectively.

Ctrl-click on the *Get Directions* button and drag the resulting line to a position beneath the new outlets declared in the Assistant Editor. In the resulting configuration panel, change the *Connection* type to *Action* and name the method *getDirections*. On completion, the *MapItemViewController.h* file should read as follows:

```
#import <UIKit/UIKit.h>

@interface MapItemViewController : UIViewController
@property (strong, nonatomic) IBOutlet UITextField *address;
```

```
@property (strong, nonatomic) IBOutlet UITextField *city;
@property (strong, nonatomic) IBOutlet UITextField *state;
@property (strong, nonatomic) IBOutlet UITextField *zip;
- (IBAction)getDirections:(id)sender;
@end
```

60.3 Converting the Destination using Forward Geocoding

When the user touches the button in the user interface, the *getDirections:* method will be able to extract the address information from the text fields. The objective will be to create an MKPlacemark object to contain this location. As outlined in *Integrating Maps into iPhone iOS 6 Application using MKMapItem*, an MKPlacemark instance requires the longitude and latitude of an address before it can be instantiated. The first step in the *getDirections:* method is to perform a forward geocode translation of the address. Before doing so, however, it is necessary to declare a property in the *MapItemViewController.h* file in which to store these coordinates once they have been calculated. This will, in turn, require that the *<CoreLocation/CoreLocation.h>* file be imported. Now is also an opportune time to import the *<MapKit/MapKit.h>* and *<AddressBook/AddressBook.h>* files, both of which will be required later in the chapter:

```
#import <UIKit/UIKit.h>
#import <CoreLocation/CoreLocation.h>
#import <MapKit/MapKit.h>
#import <AddressBook/AddressBook.h>

@interface MapItemViewController : UIViewController
@property (strong, nonatomic) IBOutlet UITextField *address;
@property (strong, nonatomic) IBOutlet UITextField *city;
@property (strong, nonatomic) IBOutlet UITextField *state;
@property (strong, nonatomic) IBOutlet UITextField *zip;
- (IBAction)getDirections:(id)sender;
@property CLLocationCoordinate2D coords;
@end
```

Next, select the *MapItemViewController.m* file, locate the *getDirections:* method stub and modify it to convert the address string to geographical coordinates:

```
- (IBAction)getDirections:(id)sender {
    CLGeocoder *geocoder = [[CLGeocoder alloc] init];

    NSString *addressString = [NSString stringWithFormat:
                               @"%@ %@ %@ %@",
                               _address.text,
                               _city.text,
                               _state.text,
```

An Example iOS 6 iPhone MKMapItem Application

```
                            _zip.text];

    [geocoder geocodeAddressString:addressString
        completionHandler:^(NSArray *placemarks, NSError *error) {

            if (error) {
                NSLog(@"Geocode failed with error: %@", error);
                return;
            }

            if (placemarks && placemarks.count > 0)
            {
                CLPlacemark *placemark = placemarks[0];

                CLLocation *location = placemark.location;
                _coords = location.coordinate;
                _coords = location.coordinate;

                [self showMap];
            }
       }];
}
```

The steps used to perform the geocoding translation mirror those outlined in *Integrating Maps into iPhone iOS 6 Application using MKMapItem* with one difference in that a method named *showMap:* is called in the event that a successful translation took place. All that remains, therefore, is to implement this method.

60.4 Launching the Map

With the address string and coordinates obtained, the final task is to implement the *showMap:* method. This method will create a new MKPlacemark instance for the destination address, configure options for the map to request driving directions and then launch the map. Since the map will be launched with a single map item, it will default to providing directions from the current location. With the *MapItemViewController.m* file still selected, add the code for the *showMap:* method so that it reads as follows:

```
-(void) showMap
{
    NSDictionary *address = @{
        (NSString *)kABPersonAddressStreetKey: _address.text,
        (NSString *)kABPersonAddressCityKey: _city.text,
        (NSString *)kABPersonAddressStateKey: _state.text,
```

```
        (NSString *)kABPersonAddressZIPKey: _zip.text
    };

    MKPlacemark *place = [[MKPlacemark alloc]
            initWithCoordinate:_coords
            addressDictionary:address];

    MKMapItem *mapItem =
        [[MKMapItem alloc]initWithPlacemark:place];

    NSDictionary *options = @{
        MKLaunchOptionsDirectionsModeKey:
            MKLaunchOptionsDirectionsModeDriving
    };

    [mapItem openInMapsWithLaunchOptions:options];
}
```

The method simply creates an NSDictionary containing the AddressBook keys and values for the destination address and then creates an MKPlacemark instance using the address dictionary and the coordinates from the forward-geocoding operation. A new MKMapItem object is created using the placemarker object before another dictionary is created and configured to request driving directions. Finally, the map is launched.

60.5 Adding Build Libraries

Before the application can be successfully compiled, some libraries need to be added to the build phases. Within the project navigator panel, select the *MapItem* target at the top of the list and in the main panel select the *Build Phases* tab. In the *Link Binary with Libraries* category, click on the + button and in the resulting list of libraries search for, select and add the *CoreLocation.framework* library. Repeat this step to also add the *MapKit.framework* and *AddressBook.framework* libraries.

60.6 Building and Running the Application

Within the Xcode toolbar, click on the Run button to compile and run the application, either on a physical iPhone device or the iOS Simulator. Once loaded, enter an address into the text fields before touching the *Get Directions* button. The map should subsequently appear together with route between your current location and the destination address. Note that if the app is running in the simulator, the current location will likely default to Apple's headquarters in California.

An Example iOS 6 iPhone MKMapItem Application

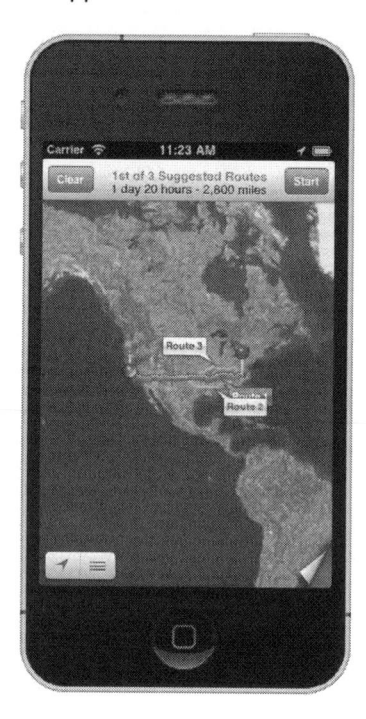

Figure 60-2

60.7 Summary

The goal of this chapter has been to work through the creation of a simple application designed to use a combination of geocoding and the MKPlacemark and MKMapItem classes. The example application created in this chapter has demonstrated the ease with which maps and directions can be integrated into iOS 6 applications for the iPhone.

Chapter 61

61. Getting iPhone Location Information using the iOS 6 Core Location Framework

The iPhone is able to employ a number of different techniques for obtaining information about the current geographical location of the device. These mechanisms include GPS, cell tower triangulation and finally (and least accurately), by using the IP address of available Wi-Fi connections. The mechanism that is used by iOS to detect location information is, however, largely transparent to the application developer and the system will automatically use the most accurate solution available at any given time. In fact, all that is needed to integrate location based information into an iOS 6 iPhone application is an understanding of how to use the Core Location Framework which, incidentally, is the subject of this chapter.

Once the basics of location tracking with Core Location have been covered in this chapter, the next chapter will provide detailed steps on how to create *an Example iOS 6 iPhone Location Application*.

61.1 The Basics of Core Location

The key classes contained within the Core Location framework are CLLocationManager and CLLocation. An instance of the CLLocationManager class is created within the application and a property set to indicate the level of location accuracy that is required by the application. The location manager is then instructed to start tracking location information:

```
CLLocationManager *locationMgr =
     [[CLLocationManager alloc] init];
locationMgr.desiredAccuracy = kCLLocationAccuracyBest;
locationMgr.delegate = self;

[locationMgr startUpdatingLocation];
```

With each location update, an application delegate method named *didUpdateToLocation* is called by the location manager and passed information about the current location. The above code also, therefore, assigns the current class as the location manager's delegate.

61.2 Configuring the Desired Location Accuracy

The level of accuracy to which location information is to be tracked is specified via the *desiredAccuracy* property of the CLLocationManager object. It is important to keep in mind when configuring this property that the greater the level of accuracy selected the greater the drain on the device battery. An application should, therefore, never request a greater level of accuracy than is actually needed.

A number of predefined constant values are available for use when configuring this property:

- **kCLLocationAccuracyBestForNavigation** – Uses the highest possible level of accuracy augmented by additional sensor data. This accuracy level is intended solely for use when the device is connected to an external power supply.
- **kCLLocationAccuracyBest** – The highest recommended level of accuracy for devices running on battery power.
- **kCLLocationAccuracyNearestTenMeters** - Accurate to within 10 meters.
- **kCLLocationAccuracyHundredMeters** – Accurate to within 100 meters.
- **kCLLocationAccuracyKilometer** – Accurate to within one kilometer.
- **kCLLocationAccuracyThreeKilometers** – Accurate to within three kilometers.

61.3 Configuring the Distance Filter

The default configuration for the location manager is to report updates whenever any changes are detected in the location of the device. The *distanceFilter* property of the location manager allows applications to specify the amount of distance the device location must change before an update is triggered. If, for example, the distance filter is set to 1000 meters the application will only receive a location update when the device travels 1000 meters or more from the location of the last update. For example, to specify a distance filter of 1500 meters:

```
locationMgr.distanceFilter = 1500.0f;
```

The distance filter may be cancelled, thereby returning to the default setting, using the kCLDistanceFilterNone constant:

```
locationMgr.distanceFilter = kCLDistanceFilterNone;
```

61.4 The Location Manager Delegate

Location manager updates and errors result in calls to two delegate methods defined within the CLLocationManagerDelegate protocol. Templates for the two delegate methods that must be implemented to comply with this protocol are as follows:

```
#pragma mark -
```

```
#pragma mark CLLocationManagerDelegate

-(void)locationManager:(CLLocationManager *)manager
    didUpdateToLocation:(CLLocation *)newLocation
    fromLocation:(CLLocation *)oldLocation
{
       // Handle location updates
}

-(void)locationManager:(CLLocationManager *)manager
didFailWithError:(NSError *)error
{
       // Handle error
}
```

61.5 Obtaining Location Information from CLLocation Objects

Location information is passed through to the *didUpdateLocation* delegate method in the form of CLLocation objects. A CLLocation object encapsulates the following data:

- Latitude
- Longitude
- Horizontal Accuracy
- Altitude
- Altitude Accuracy

61.5.1 Longitude and Latitude

Longitude and latitude values are stored as type CLLocationDegrees and may be obtained from a CLLocation object as follows:

```
CLLocationDegrees currentLatitude = location.coordinate.latitude;
CLLocationDegrees currentLongitude = location.coordinates.longitude;
```

61.5.2 Accuracy

Horizontal and vertical accuracy are stored in meters as CLLocationDistance values and may be accessed as follows:

```
CLLocation verticalAccuracy = location.verticalAccuracy;
CLLocation horizontalAccurcy = location.horizontalAccuracy;
```

61.5.3 Altitude

The altitude value is stored in meters as a type CLLocationDistance value and may be accessed from a CLLocation object as follows:

```
CLLocation altitude = location.altitude;
```

61.6 Calculating Distances

The distance between two CLLocation points may be calculated by calling the *distanceFromLocation* method of the end location and passing through the start location as an argument. For example, the following code calculates the distance between the points specified by *newLocation* and *oldLocation*:

```
CLLocationDistance distance = [newLocation
distanceFromLocation:oldLocation];
```

61.7 Location Information and Multitasking

Location based iPhone applications are one of the three categories of application that are permitted to continue executing when placed into the background (for a detailed description of multitasking refer to *An Overview of iOS 6 iPhone Multitasking*). If location updates are required when the application is in the background state it is strongly recommended that the desired accuracy setting be reduced within the *applicationDidEnterBackground* method by making a call to the *startMonitoringSignificantLocationChanges* method of the location manager object. This will ensure that the application is only notified of significant changes to the location of the device thereby reducing the load on the battery.

61.8 Summary

This chapter has provided an overview of the use of the iOS Core Location Framework to obtain location information within an iPhone application. This theory will be put into practice in the next chapter entitled *An Example iOS 6 iPhone Location Application*.

Chapter 62

62. An Example iOS 6 iPhone Location Application

Having covered the basics of location management in iOS 6 iPhone applications in the previous chapter it is now time to put theory into practice and work step-by-step through an example application. The objective of this chapter is to create a simple iOS application that tracks the latitude, longitude and altitude of an iPhone. In addition the level of location accuracy will be reported, together with the distance between a selected location and the current location of the device.

62.1 Creating the Example iOS 6 iPhone Location Project

The first step, as always, is to launch the Xcode environment and start a new project to contain the location application. Once Xcode is running, select the *File -> New -> Project...* menu option and configure a new iOS iPhone application named *Location* with a matching class prefix using the *Single View Application* template with Storyboards and Automatic Reference Counting enabled.

62.2 Adding the Core Location Framework to the Project

In order to access the location features of the iPhone the Core Location Framework must be included into the project. This can be achieved by selecting the product target entry from the project navigator panel (the top item named *Location*) and clicking on the *Build Phases* tab in the main panel. In the *Link Binary with Libraries* section click on the '+' button, select the *CoreLocation.framework* entry from the resulting panel and click on the *Add* button.

62.3 Designing the User Interface

The user interface for this example location app is going consist of a number of labels and a button that will be connected to an action method. Initiate the user interface design process by selecting the *MainStoryboard.storyboard* file. Once the view has loaded into the Interface Builder editing environment, create a user interface that resembles as closely as possible the view illustrated in Figure 62-1:

An Example iOS 6 iPhone Location Application

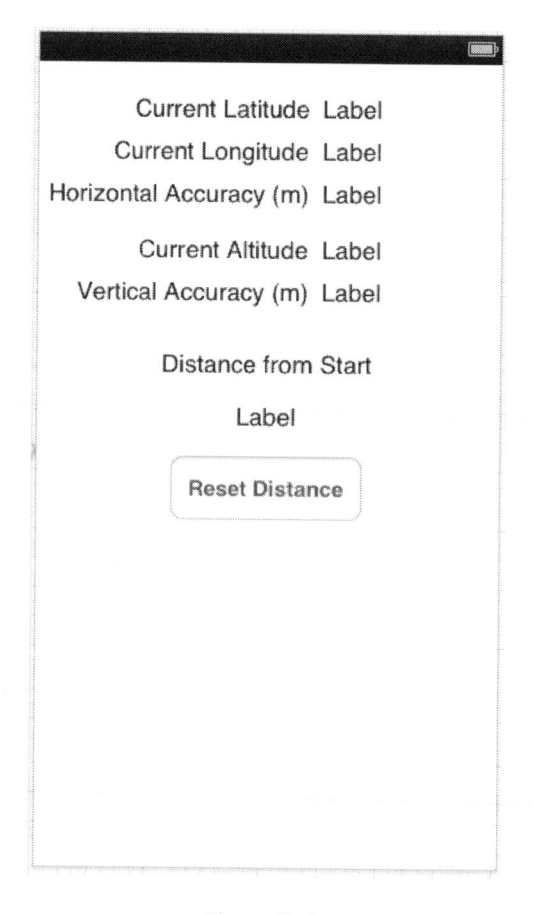

Figure 62-1

In the case of the five labels in the right hand column which will display location and accuracy data, make sure that the labels are stretched to the right until the blue margin guideline appears. The data will be displayed to multiple levels of decimal points requiring space beyond the default size of the label.

Select the label object to the right of the "Current Latitude" label in the view canvas, display the Assistant Editor panel and verify that the editor is displaying the contents of the *LocationViewController.h* file. Ctrl-click on the same Label object and drag to a position just below the @interface line in the Assistant Editor. Release the line and in the resulting connection dialog establish an outlet connection named *latitude*. Repeat these steps for the remaining labels, connecting then to properties named *longitude, horizontalAccuracy, altitude, verticalAccuracy* and *distance* respectively.

The final step of the user interface design process is to connect the button object to an action method. Ctrl-click on the button object and drag the line to the area immediately beneath the newly created outlets in the Assistant Editor panel. Release the line and, within the resulting connection

An Example iOS 6 iPhone Location Application

dialog, establish an Action method on the *Touch Up Inside* event configured to call a method named *resetDistance*.

Select the *LocationViewController.h* file, verify that the outlets are configured correctly and add a property in which to store the start location coordinates and the location manager object. Now is also an opportune time to import the <CoreLocation/CoreLocation.h> header file and to declare the class as implementing the CLLocationManagerDelegate protocol:

```
#import <UIKit/UIKit.h>
#import <CoreLocation/CoreLocation.h>

@interface LocationViewController : UIViewController
    <CLLocationManagerDelegate>

@property (strong, nonatomic) IBOutlet UILabel *latitude;
@property (strong, nonatomic) IBOutlet UILabel *longitude;
@property (strong, nonatomic) IBOutlet UILabel *horizontalAccuracy;
@property (strong, nonatomic) IBOutlet UILabel *altitude;
@property (strong, nonatomic) IBOutlet UILabel *verticalAccuracy;
@property (strong, nonatomic) IBOutlet UILabel *distance;

@property (strong, nonatomic) CLLocationManager *locationManager;
@property (strong, nonatomic) CLLocation *startLocation;
- (IBAction)resetDistance:(id)sender;
@end
```

62.4 Creating the CLLocationManager Object

The next task is to implement the code to create an instance of the CLLocationManager class. Since this needs to occur when the view loads, an ideal location is in the view controller's *viewDidLoad* method in the *LocationViewController.m* file:

```
- (void)viewDidLoad {
    [super viewDidLoad];
    _locationManager = [[CLLocationManager alloc] init];
    _locationManager.desiredAccuracy = kCLLocationAccuracyBest;
    _locationManager.delegate = self;
    [_locationManager startUpdatingLocation];
    _startLocation = nil;
}
```

The above code creates a new CLLocationManager object instance and configures it to use the "best accuracy" setting. It then declares itself as the application delegate for the object. The location manager object is then instructed to begin updating location information via a call to the

An Example iOS 6 iPhone Location Application

startUpdatingLocation method. Since location tracking has just begun at this point, the *startLocation* object is also set to nil.

62.5 Implementing the Action Method

The button object in the user interface is connected to the *resetDistance* action method so the next task is to implement that action. All this method needs to do is set the *startlocation* object to nil:

```
-(void)resetDistance:(id)sender
{
        _startLocation = nil;
}
```

62.6 Implementing the Application Delegate Methods

When the location manager detects a location change, it calls the *didUpdateToLocation* delegate method. Since the view controller was declared as the delegate for the location manager in the *viewDidLoad* method, it is necessary to now implement this method in the *LocationViewController.m* file:

```
#pragma mark -
#pragma mark CLLocationManagerDelegate

-(void)locationManager:(CLLocationManager *)manager
   didUpdateToLocation:(CLLocation *)newLocation
          fromLocation:(CLLocation *)oldLocation
{
    NSString *currentLatitude = [[NSString alloc]
              initWithFormat:@"%+.6f",
              newLocation.coordinate.latitude];
    _latitude.text = currentLatitude;

    NSString *currentLongitude = [[NSString alloc]
          initWithFormat:@"%+.6f",
          newLocation.coordinate.longitude];
    _longitude.text = currentLongitude;

    NSString *currentHorizontalAccuracy =
            [[NSString alloc]
             initWithFormat:@"%+.6f",
             newLocation.horizontalAccuracy];
    _horizontalAccuracy.text = currentHorizontalAccuracy;

    NSString *currentAltitude = [[NSString alloc]
```

```
            initWithFormat:@"%+.6f",
            newLocation.altitude];
    _altitude.text = currentAltitude;

    NSString *currentVerticalAccuracy =
            [[NSString alloc]
            initWithFormat:@"%+.6f",
            newLocation.verticalAccuracy];
    _verticalAccuracy.text = currentVerticalAccuracy;

    if (_startLocation == nil)
            _startLocation = newLocation;

    CLLocationDistance distanceBetween = [newLocation
            distanceFromLocation:_startLocation];

    NSString *tripString = [[NSString alloc]
            initWithFormat:@"%f",
            distanceBetween];
    _distance.text = tripString;
}
```

Despite the apparent length of the method it actually performs some very simple tasks. To begin with, it extracts location and accuracy information from the *newLocation* CLLocation object passed through to the method as an argument. In each case, it creates an NSString object containing the extracted value and displays it on the corresponding user interface label.

If this is the first time that the method has been called either since the application was launched or the user pressed the *Reset Distance* button, the *locationDistance* object is set to the current location. The *distanceFromLocation* method of the *newLocation* object is then called, passing though the *locationDistance* object as an argument in order to calculate the distance between the two points. The result is then displayed on the distance label in the user interface.

The *didFailWithError* delegate method is called when an error is encountered by the location manager instance. This method should also, therefore, be implemented:

```
-(void)locationManager:(CLLocationManager *)manager
didFailWithError:(NSError *)error
{
}
```

The action taken within this method is largely up to the application developer. The method, might, for example, simply display an alert to notify the user of the error.

62.7 Building and Running the iPhone Location Application

Click on the *Run* button located in the Xcode project window toolbar. Once the application has compiled and linked it will launch into the iOS Simulator. Before location information can be gathered, the user is prompted to grant permission. Once permission is granted, the application will begin tracking location information. By default, the iOS Simulator will be configured to have no current location causing the labels to remain unchanged. In order to simulate a location, select the iOS Simulator *Debug -> Location* menu option and select either one of the pre-defined locations or journeys (such as City Bicycle Ride), or *Custom Location...* to enter a specific latitude and longitude. The following figure shows the application running in the iOS Simulator after the *Apple* location has been selected from the menu:

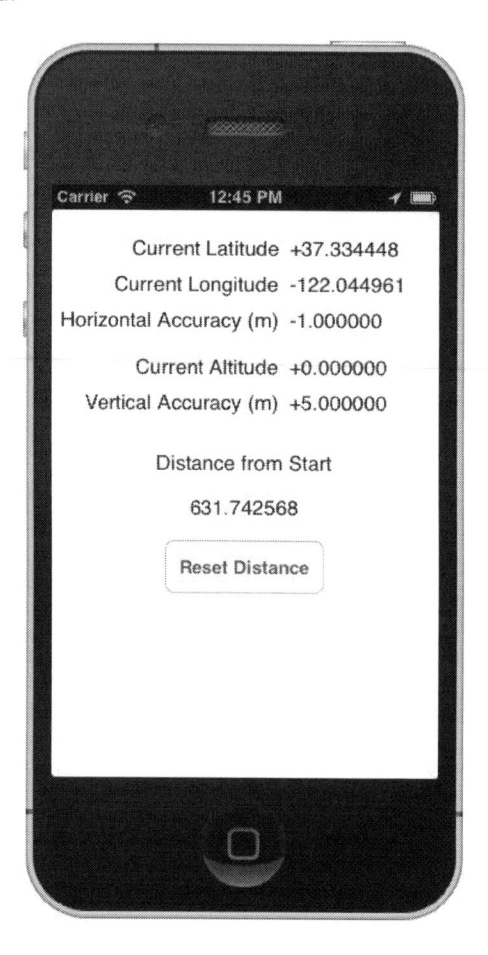

Figure 62-2

To experience the full functionality of the application it will be necessary to install it on a physical iPhone device, a process that is outlined in the chapter entitled *Testing iOS 6 Apps on the iPhone –*

An Example iOS 6 iPhone Location Application

Developer Certificates and Provisioning Profiles. Once the application is running on an iPhone the location data will update as you change location with the device.

One final point to note is that the distance data relates to the distance between two points, not the distance travelled. For example, if the device accompanies the user on a 10 mile trip that returns to the start location the distance will be displayed as 0 (since the start and end points are the same).

Chapter 63

63. Working with Maps on the iPhone with MapKit and the MKMapView Class

In the preceding chapters we spent some time looking at handling raw geographical location information in the form of longitude, latitude and altitude data. The next step is to learn about the presentation of location information to the user in the form of maps and satellite images. The goal of this chapter, therefore, is provide an overview of the steps necessary to present the iPhone iOS 6 application user with location, map and satellite imagery using the MapKit framework and, in particular, the MKMapView class.

63.1 About the MapKit Framework

The MapKit Framework is based on the Apple Maps data and APIs and provides iPhone developers with a simple mechanism for integrating detailed and interactive mapping capabilities into any application.

The core element of the MapKit framework from the point of view of the app developer is the MKMapView class. This class is a subclass of UIView and provides a canvas onto which map and satellite information may be presented to the user. Information may be presented in map, satellite or hybrid (whereby the map is superimposed onto the satellite image) form. The displayed geographical region may be changed manually by the user via a process of pinching stretching and panning gestures, or programmatically from within the application code via methods calls and property manipulation on the MkMapView instance. The current location of the device may also be displayed and tracked on the map view.

The MapKit framework also includes support for adding annotations to a map. This takes the form of a pin or custom image, title and subview that may be used to mark specific locations on a map.

Implementation of the MKMapViewDelegate protocol allows an application to receive notifications of events relating to the map view such as a change in either the location of the user or region of the map displayed or the failure of the device to identify the user's current location or to download map data.

63.2 Understanding Map Regions

The area of the map that is currently displayed to the user is referred to as the *region*. This is defined in terms of a *center location* (declared by longitude and latitude) and span of the surrounding area to be displayed. Adjusting the span has the effect of zooming in and out of the map relative to the specified center location. The region's span may be specified using either distance (in meters) or coordinate based degrees. When using degrees, one degree of latitude is equivalent to 111 km. Latitude, however, varies depending on the longitudinal distance from the equator. Given this complexity, the map view tutorial in this chapter will declare the span in terms of distance.

63.3 About the iPhone MKMapView Tutorial

The objective of this tutorial is to develop an iPhone application designed to display a map with a marker indicating the user's current location. Buttons located in a navigation bar are provided to allow the user to zoom in on the current location and to toggle between map and satellite views. Through the implementation of the MKMapViewDelegate protocol the map will update as the user's location changes so that the current location marker is always the center point of the displayed map region. Finally, a basic annotation will be implemented to mark a specific location on the map with a pin and title.

63.4 Creating the iPhone Map Tutorial

Begin by launching Xcode and creating a new iOS iPhone project named *MapSample* using the *Single View Application* template with Storyboards and Automatic Reference Counting enabled.

63.5 Adding the MapKit Framework to the Xcode Project

Since we will be making use of the MapKit framework during this tutorial the first step is to add the framework to the project. To achieve this, select the *Build Phases* tab on the *MapSample* summary panel and unfold the *Link Binary with Libraries* section. Click on the '+' button, locate the *MapKit.framework* entry from the resulting list and click *Add*.

63.6 Creating the MKMapView Instance and Toolbar

The next step is to create an instance of the MKMapView class we will be using in our application and to add a toolbar instance to the user interface. Begin by selecting the *MainStoryboard.storyboard* and dragging a Tool Bar from the Object Library, placing it at the bottom of the view canvas. Next, drag and drop a Map View object onto the canvas and resize and position it so that it takes up the remaining space in the view above the toolbar. By default the Interface Builder tool will have added a single UIBarButtonItem to the new toolbar. For the purposes of this example, however, two buttons will be required so drag and drop a second Bar Button Item from the Object Library panel onto the toolbar. Finally, double click on the toolbar button items and change the text to "Zoom" and "Type" respectively:

Working with Maps on the iPhone with MapKit and the MKMapView Class

Figure 63-1

Select the MKMapView object in the view canvas, display the Assistant Editor panel and verify that the editor is displaying the contents of the *MapSampleViewController.h* file. Ctrl-click on the MKMapView object and drag to a position just below the @interface line in the Assistant Editor. Release the line and in the resulting connection dialog establish an outlet connection named *mapView*.

Click on the "Zoom" button to select it (note that in order to select a toolbar button item it may be necessary to click on it twice since the first click selects the toolbar parent). With the button item selected, Ctrl-click on the button object and drag the line to the area immediately beneath the newly created outlet in the Assistant Editor panel. Release the line and, within the resulting connection dialog, establish an Action method on the *Touch Up Inside* event configured to call a method named *zoomIn*. Repeat this step to connect the "Type" button to a method named *changeMapType*.

Select the *MapSampleViewController.h* file from the project navigator panel and verify that the outlets and actions have been set up correctly. Also take this opportunity to import <MapKit/MapKit.h> file and to declare the class as implementing the <MKMapViewDelegate> protocol:

```
#import <UIKit/UIKit.h>
#import <MapKit/MapKit.h>

@interface MapSampleViewController : UIViewController
    <MKMapViewDelegate>
```

Working with Maps on the iPhone with MapKit and the MKMapView Class

```
@property (strong, nonatomic) IBOutlet MKMapView *mapView;
- (IBAction)zoomIn:(id)sender;
- (IBAction)changeMapType:(id)sender;
@end
```

Perform a test run of the application's progress so far by clicking on the *Run* button in the Xcode toolbar. The application should run in the iOS simulator as illustrated in Figure 63-2:

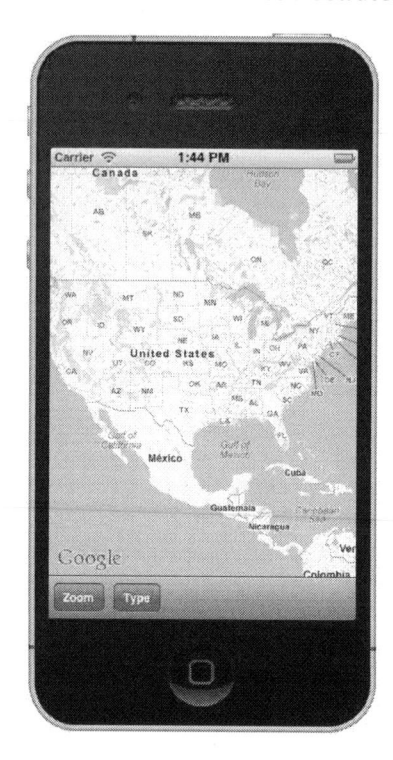

Figure 63-2

63.7 Configuring the Map View

By default the Map View does not indicate the user's current location. By setting the *showsUserLocation* property of the MKMapView class the map is instructed to display a representation of the current location on the map in the form of a blue translucent ball. In order to set this property, select the *MapSampleViewController.m* file and locate and modify *viewDidLoad:* method as follows:

```
- (void)viewDidLoad
{
    [super viewDidLoad];
    _mapView.showsUserLocation = YES;
```

63.8 Changing the MapView Region

When the Zoom button is tapped by the user the map view region needs to be changed so that the user's current location is set as the center location and the region span needs to be changed to 50 meters (analogous to zooming in to the map region). The code to implement this belongs in the *zoomIn* method which now needs to be implemented in the *mapSampleViewController.m* file:

```
- (IBAction)zoomIn:(id)sender {
    MKUserLocation *userLocation = _mapView.userLocation;
    MKCoordinateRegion region =
        MKCoordinateRegionMakeWithDistance (
            userLocation.location.coordinate, 50, 50);
    [_mapView setRegion:region animated:NO];
}
```

This method performs some very simple operations in order to achieve the desired effect in the mapView object. Firstly, the user's current location is ascertained by accessing the *userLocation* property of the map view object. This is stored in the form of an MKUserLocation object which, in turn, contains the coordinates of the user. Next, the *MKCoordinateRegionMakeWithDistance* function is called in order to generate an MKCoordinateRegion object consisting of the user's location coordinates and a span that stretches 50 meters both to the North and South of the current location. Finally, this region object is passed through to the *setRegion* method of the mapView object.

Now that the Zoom functionality has been implemented it is time to configure the map type switching feature of the application.

63.9 Changing the Map Type

The map type of a map view is controlled by the object's *mapType* property. Supported values for this property are MKMapTypeStandard, MKMapTypeSatellite and MKMapTypeHybrid. For the purposes of this example application the map will switch between standard and satellite modes. Within the *MapSampleViewController.m* file modify the *changeMapType* action method connected to the Type button as follows:

```
- (IBAction)changeMapType:(id)sender {
    if (_mapView.mapType == MKMapTypeStandard)
        _mapView.mapType = MKMapTypeSatellite;
    else
        _mapView.mapType = MKMapTypeStandard;
}
```

This very simple method simply toggles between the two map types when the button is tapped by the user.

63.10 Testing the iPhone MapView Application

Now that more functionality has been implemented, it is a good time to build and run the application again so click on the Xcode *Run* button to load the application into the iOS iPhone Simulator. Once the application has loaded, a blue dot should appear over Northern California. Since the application is running in the simulator environment the location information is simulated to match the coordinates of Apple's headquarters in Cupertino, CA. Select the Type button to display the satellite view and then zoom in to get a better look at the company's buildings:

Figure 63-3

To get real location information, load the application onto an iPhone device (details of which can be found in the *Testing iOS 6 Apps on the iPhone – Developer Certificates and Provisioning Profiles* chapter of this book).

63.11 Updating the Map View based on User Movement

Assuming that you installed the application on a physical iPhone device and went somewhere with the device in your possession you may have noticed that the map did not update as your location changed and that the blue dot marking your current location eventually went off the screen (also assuming, of course, that you had zoomed in).

In order to configure the application so that the map automatically tracks the movements of the user, the first step is to make sure the application is notified when the location changes. At the start of this tutorial the view controller was declared as conforming to the MKMapViewDelegate delegate protocol. One of the methods that comprise this protocol is the *didUpdateUserLocation* method. When implemented, this method is called by the map view object whenever the location of the device changes. We must, therefore, first specify that the MapSampleViewContoller class is the delegate for the mapView object, which can be performed by adding the following line to the *viewDidLoad* method located in the *MapSampleViewController.m* file:

```
_mapView.delegate = self;
```

The next task involves the implementation of the *didUpdateUserLocation* method in the *MapSampleViewController.m* file:

```
- (void)mapView:(MKMapView *)mapView
didUpdateUserLocation:
(MKUserLocation *)userLocation
{
    _mapView.centerCoordinate =
         userLocation.location.coordinate;
}
```

The delegate method is passed as an argument an MKUserLocation object containing the current location coordinates of the user. This value is simply assigned to the center coordinate property of the mapView object such that the current location remains at the center of the region. When the application is now installed and run on a device the current location will no longer move outside the displayed region as the device location changes. To experience this effect within the simulator, simply select the *Debug -> Location -> City Run* menu option and then select the Zoom button in the user interface.

63.12 Adding Basic Annotations to a Map View

The last task in this tutorial is to add an annotation at a specific location on the map view. For the purposes of this example, we will add a standard annotation (represented by default by a red pin) at the coordinates of Microsoft's headquarters in Redmond, Washington. Although this is a very simple example it is important to keep in mind that annotations may also be used to perform more advanced tasks such as displaying custom images and multiple annotations on a single map.

The annotation in this example will also display a title and subtitle when selected by the user. In order to create a basic annotation it is necessary to create a CLLocationCoordinate2D object containing the coordinates at which the annotation is to appear. An MKPointAnnotation object is then created and assigned the coordinate object, title and subtitle strings. Finally the *addAnnotation*

Working with Maps on the iPhone with MapKit and the MKMapView Class

method of the map view object is called to add the annotation to the map. The code fragment for these steps is as follows:

```
CLLocationCoordinate2D annotationCoord;

annotationCoord.latitude = 47.640071;
annotationCoord.longitude = -122.129598;

MKPointAnnotation *annotationPoint = [[MKPointAnnotation alloc] init];
annotationPoint.coordinate = annotationCoord;
annotationPoint.title = @"Microsoft";
annotationPoint.subtitle = @"Microsoft's headquarters";
[_mapView addAnnotation:annotationPoint];
```

Add this code to the end of the *viewDidLoad* method and build and run the application. The map should now appear with a red pin located at the designated location. Tapping the pin will display the title and subtitle:

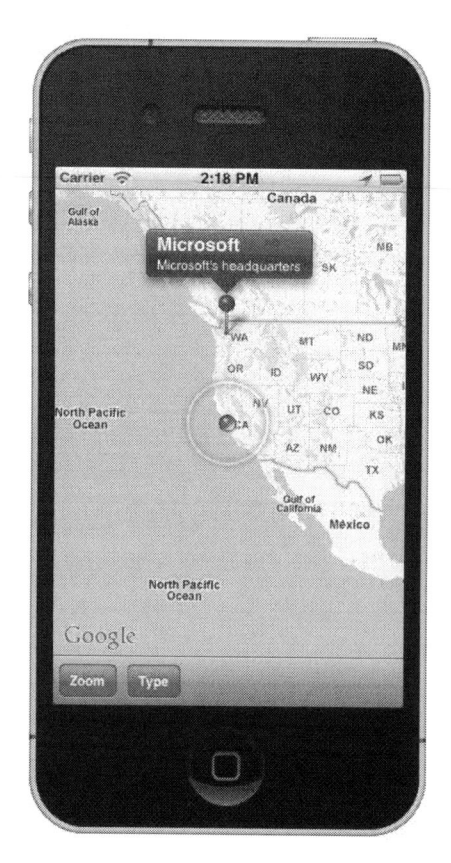

Figure 63-4

Chapter 64

64. Using iOS 6 Event Kit to Create Date and Location Based Reminders

iOS 5 introduced the Reminders application, the purpose of which was to allow users to specify events about which they wished to be reminded. Reminders can be specified for a specific date and time, or even to be triggered when the user either arrives at or leaves a specified location. You might, for example, use the Reminders app to remind you to buy milk on your way home when your iPhone detects that you are leaving your office.

With the introduction of iOS 6, it is now possible to create and manage reminders from within your own applications using the Event Kit Framework.

This chapter will cover some of the basics of calendars and reminders before working step-by-step through the creation of an example application that demonstrates the creation of both date and location based reminders.

64.1 An Overview of the Event Kit Framework

The Event Kit Framework consists of a range of classes designed specifically to provide access to the calendar database and to facilitate the management of events, reminders and alarms. In terms of integrating reminders into an iOS application, these classes are EKCalendar, EKEventStore, EKReminder and EKAlarm.

The EKEventStore class provides an interface between applications and the underlying calendar database. The calendar database can, in turn, contain multiple calendars (for example the user may have a work calendar and a personal calendar configured). Each calendar in a database is represented in code in the form of an EKCalendar object.

Within each calendar there are events and reminders, each of which is managed in code using the EKEvent and EKReminder classes respectively.

Finally, the EKAlarm class is used to configure alarms to alert the user at a specified point in the future.

501

64.2 The EKEventStore Class

In order to work with reminders in an iOS application, an instance of the EKEventStore class must be created. It is important to note that there is system overhead in requesting access to the calendar database so the call to initialize an EKEventStore object should ideally only be performed once within an application. In some situations, the system will prompt the user to allow the application access to the calendar. As such, the EKEventStore object should only be initialized immediately prior to the point in the code where calendar access is required. A reference to this event store object should then be retained and used for future calendar interaction throughout the lifespan of the application.

An EKEventStore object must request access to the calendar at the point that it is initialized. This request must specify whether access is required for calendar events (EKEntityTypeEvent) or reminders (EKEntityTypeReminder). Whether or not access is granted will depend on the current privacy settings for the application in the Privacy section of the device Settings app. Privacy settings are available for both Calendar and Reminders access. When an application seeks access for the first time, the user will be prompted by the system to allow the application to access either the calendar events or reminders. If the user declines access, the application will need to handle this gracefully. This is achieved via the completion handler of the *requestAccessToEntityType:* method of the EKEventStore class. The following code excerpt, for example, seeks access to reminders in the calendar database and reports an error in the console log in the event that access was declined:

```
[_eventStore requestAccessToEntityType:EKEntityTypeReminder
            completion:^(BOOL granted, NSError *error) {
                if (!granted)
                    NSLog(@"Access to store not granted");
}];
```

Once access has been accepted or denied by the user, the privacy setting for that application can be viewed and changed within the Privacy section of the Settings application. Figure 64-1, for example, shows that the access for an application named ReminderApp to Reminders on the system is currently disabled.

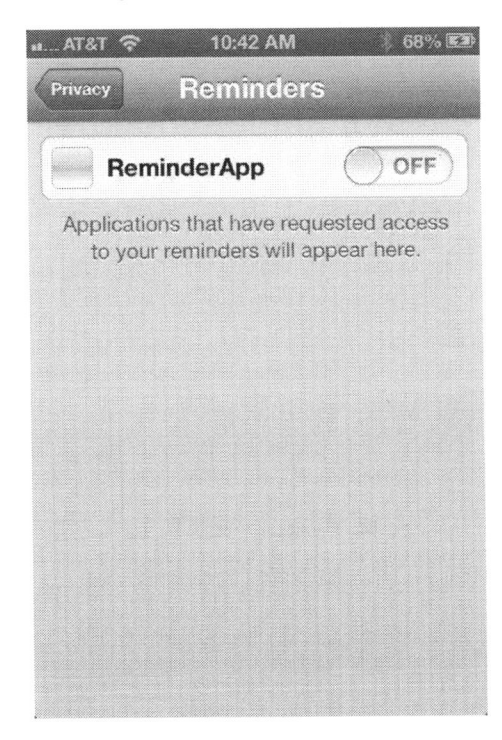

Using iOS 6 Event Kit to Create Date and Location Based Reminders

Figure 64-1

In addition, it is worth noting that the message used by the system to request access to the calendar database can be configured by adding an entry to the Info.plist file for the project. By default a message similar to that illustrated in Figure 64-2 will be displayed.

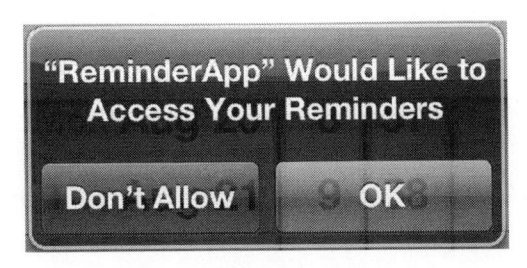

Figure 64-2

By editing the Info.plist file, for example, and adding a "Privacy – Reminders Usage Description" key and value, the message may be augmented to provide the user with additional information as to why access is required. Once defined, the custom message will appear when access is requested from the user:

Using iOS 6 Event Kit to Create Date and Location Based Reminders

Figure 64-3

64.3 Accessing Calendars in the Database

As previously stated, the calendar database on an iOS device can contain multiple calendars, both for the events calendar and for reminders. An array of available calendars can be obtained via a call to the *calendarsForEntityType:* method of the event store object, specifying as an argument whether event or reminder calendars are required. The following code outputs a list, by title, of the reminder calendars configured on the device. Note that each calendar entry in the array is represented by an EKCalendar object:

```
NSArray *calendars = [_eventStore
        calendarsForEntityType:EKEntityTypeReminder];

for (EKCalendar *calendar in calendars)
{
    NSLog(@"Calendar = %@", calendar.title);
}
```

The Event Kit framework has the concept of a default calendar for the addition of new reminders and events. This default calendar may be configured by the user within the Settings app on the device (*Settings -> Reminders* and *Settings -> Mail, Contacts, Calendars*). These are represented in code by the *defaultCalendarForNewReminders* and *defaultCalendarForNewEvents* constants. Whilst some applications may need to let the user choose which calendar to use, these defaults can be useful when selection is not necessary.

64.4 Accessing Current Reminders

The reminders currently configured in a database calendar may be accessed using a variety of methods depending on the scope of the search to be performed. The reminders may be filtered to include only those that match a given predicate. Matching results are returned in the form of an array of EKReminder objects. The following code excerpt outputs a list of all reminders from all calendars in the database:

```
NSArray *calendars = [_eventStore
```

```
        calendarsForEntityType:EKEntityTypeReminder];

for (EKCalendar *calendar in calendars)
{
    NSLog(@"Calendar = %@", calendar.title);
}
```

In addition to the *calendarsForEntityType:* method, predicates may also be generated using the following additional methods of the EKEventStore class:

- **predicateForIncompleteRemindersWithDueDateStarting** - Searches for incomplete reminders specified between optional start and end dates.
- **predicateForCompletedRemindersWithCompletionDateStarting:** - Searches for completed reminders between optional start and end dates.

64.5 Creating Reminders

New reminders are added to the calendar by creating new instances of the EKReminder class, configuring the object according to the requirements of the reminder and then adding it to the event store.

The following example code creates a reminder and adds it to the default calendar for new reminder entries:

```
EKReminder *reminder = [EKReminder
reminderWithEventStore:self.eventStore];

reminder.title = @"Go to the store and buy milk";

reminder.calendar = [_eventStore defaultCalendarForNewReminders];

NSError *error = nil;

[_eventStore saveReminder:reminder commit:YES error:&error];
```

The above code creates a new EKReminder object and, in so doing, associates it with the event store before setting the title of the reminder. Next, the reminder is configured so that it will be added to the user's default reminder calendar before being saved to the event store.

Reminders can be general as in the above example or, as will be demonstrated in the following tutorial, configured to be triggered at a specific date and time, or when the user arrives at or departs from a physical geographical location (a concept known as *geofencing*).

505

Using iOS 6 Event Kit to Create Date and Location Based Reminders

64.6 Creating Alarms

The EKAlarm class can be used to add an alarm to the reminder. Alarms can be specified either using a specific date and time (via a call to *alarmWithAbsoluteDate:* and passing through an NSDate object) or using a relative time interval (via a call to *alarmWithRelativeOffset:* passing through an NSTimeInterval value).

Once an EKAlarm object has been created and configured it must be added to the EKReminder object with which the alarm is to be associated. When the specified time arrives, the user will be notified of the reminder with sound, vibration and a notification panel.

64.7 Creating the Example Project

Begin by launching Xcode and selecting the options to create a new iPhone iOS application based on the *Tabbed Application* template. Enter *ReminderApp* as the product name and class prefix, set the device to *iPhone* and select the *Use Storyboards* and *Use Automatic Reference Counting* options if they are not already selected.

In the remainder of this chapter, an application will be constructed designed to allow the user to add reminders based on either date/time or location factors.

64.8 Designing the User Interface for the Date/Time Based Reminder Screen

Upon reviewing the *MainStoryboard.storyboard* file, it is clear that Xcode has created a template-based tabbed application consisting of Tab Bar Controller and two Views, each of which has its own view controller. For the purposes of this example, the first view will be used to implement a screen whereby the user can create a new date and time based reminder. Within the Storyboard canvas, therefore, locate the Reminder App First View screen and remove the current labels that were added by Xcode. With a clean view, add a Text Field, Date Picker and Button object to the view canvas. Once added, position and configure the user interface layout so that it resembles that of Figure 64-4:

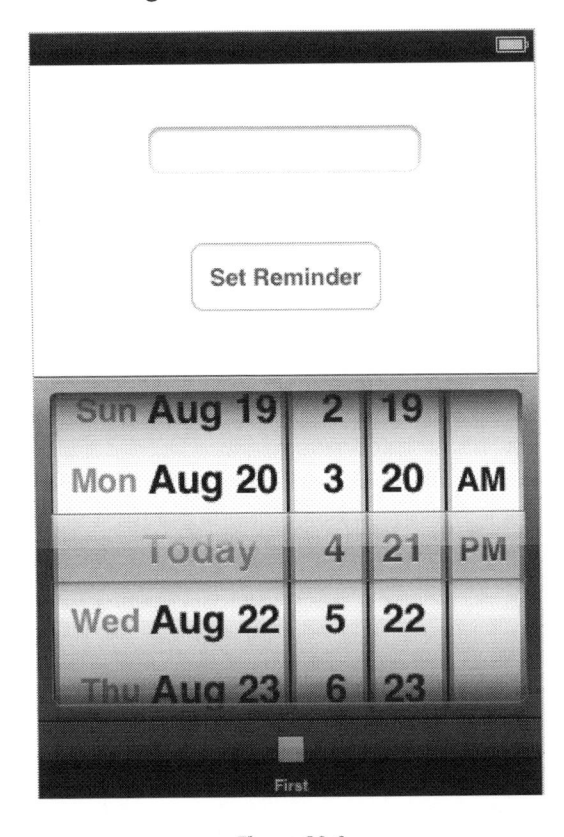

Using iOS 6 Event Kit to Create Date and Location Based Reminders

Figure 64-4

Select the Text Field object and display the Assistant Editor using *View -> Assistant Editor -> Show Assistant Editor* menu option, making sure that it is displaying the content of the *ReminderAppFirstViewController.h* file. If it is not, click on the file name in the bar at the top of the Assistant Editor panel and select the file from the drop down menu (Figure 64-5):

Figure 64-5

Using iOS 6 Event Kit to Create Date and Location Based Reminders

Ctrl-click on the Text Field object in the view and drag the resulting line to the area immediately beneath the @interface directive in the Assistant Editor panel. Upon releasing the line, the configuration panel will appear. Configure the connection as an *Outlet* named *reminderText* and click on the *Connect* button. Repeat this step to add an outlet connection to the Date Picker object named *myDatePicker*.

Finally, Ctrl-click on the Button object, drag the line to the Assistant Editor and release it beneath the last outlet connection added. In the resulting connection panel, change the connection type to *Action* and name the action *setReminder*.

64.9 Implementing the Reminder Code

With the user interface view designed, the next step is to implement the code in the view controller for the first view to access the event store and set up the reminder. We will need a place to store the event store object once it has been requested and, as previously discussed, it is recommended that access to the event store be requested only once. As such we will need a location to store the reference once it has been obtained, so select the *ReminderAppFirstViewController.m* file and add an additional property. This is also an opportune time to import the EventKit framework headers:

```
#import <UIKit/UIKit.h>
#import <EventKit/EventKit.h>

@interface ReminderAppFirstViewController : UIViewController

@property (strong, nonatomic) EKEventStore *eventStore;

@property (strong, nonatomic) IBOutlet UIDatePicker *myDatePicker;
@property (strong, nonatomic) IBOutlet UITextField *reminderText;
- (IBAction)setReminder:(id)sender;
@end
```

Within the project navigator, select the *ReminderAppFirstViewController.m* file, locate the *setReminder:* template stub and add the following code:

```
- (IBAction)setReminder:(id)sender {

    if (_eventStore == nil)
    {
        _eventStore = [[EKEventStore alloc]init];

        [_eventStore requestAccessToEntityType:EKEntityTypeReminder
completion:^(BOOL granted, NSError *error) {
```

```
            if (!granted)
                NSLog(@"Access to store not granted");
        }];
    }

    if (_eventStore != nil)
        [self createReminder];
}
```

The code added to the method verifies that access to the event store has not already been obtained and, in the event that it has not, requests access to the reminder calendars. If access is denied a message is reported to the console. In the event that access is granted, a second method named *createReminder:* is called. With *ReminderAppFirstViewController.m* still in the editing panel, implement this method:

```
-(void)createReminder
{
    EKReminder *reminder = [EKReminder
            reminderWithEventStore:self.eventStore];

    reminder.title = _reminderText.text;

    reminder.calendar = [_eventStore defaultCalendarForNewReminders];

    NSDate *date = [_myDatePicker date];

    EKAlarm *alarm = [EKAlarm alarmWithAbsoluteDate:date];

    [reminder addAlarm:alarm];

    NSError *error = nil;

    [_eventStore saveReminder:reminder commit:YES error:&error];

    if (error)
        NSLog(@"error = %@", error);

}
```

The *createReminder:* method creates a new EKReminder object associated with the event store and sets the title property to the content of the Text Field object in the user interface. The code elects the default calendar as the target for the reminder and then creates an EKAlarm object primed with the date value selected by the user in the Date Picker object. The alarm is then added to the reminder which, in turn, is saved in the event store. Errors are output to the console for debugging purposes.

64.10 Hiding the Keyboard

Before moving on to the next part of the tutorial, some code will now need to be added to the application so that the keyboard is withdrawn when the user touches the view background.

Select the *MainStoryboard.storyboard* file and click on the background of the view. Display the Identity Inspector (*View -> Utilities -> Show Identity Inspector*) and change the object's class from UIView to UIControl. Display the Assistant Editor, Ctrl-click on the view background and drag to a position beneath the *setReminder:* action in the Assistant Editor and declare an action connection named *hideKeyboard* for the *Touch Down* event.

Within the *ReminderAppFirstViewController.m* file, implement the code in the *hideKeyboard:* stub method:

```
- (IBAction)hideKeyboard:(id)sender {
    [_reminderText resignFirstResponder];
}
```

With the time and date based reminder phase of the application completed, the next step is to implement the location based reminder functionality.

64.11 Designing Location-based Reminder Screen

The tab controller created on our behalf by Xcode contains a second view that will be used for the location based reminder creation. The goal of this view will be to allow the user to specify a reminder and alarm that will be triggered when the user moves away from the geographical location at which the reminder was created.

Begin by selecting the *MainStoryboard.storyboard* file and locating the second view. Remove the template labels added by Xcode and design a new user interface using a Button and a Text Field as illustrated in Figure 64-6.

Using the Assistant Editor (taking care to ensure that that editor displays the code for the *ReminderAppSecondViewController.h* file not the file for the first view controller), establish an outlet connection for the Text Field named *locationText*. Next, establish an Action connection from the button to a method named *setLocationReminder*.

Figure 64-6

Finally, add an event store property to the *ReminderAppSecondViewController.h* file and import the Event Kit header:

```
#import <UIKit/UIKit.h>
#import <EventKit/EventKit.h>

@interface ReminderAppSecondViewController : UIViewController

@property (strong, nonatomic) EKEventStore *eventStore;
@property (strong, nonatomic) IBOutlet UITextField *locationText;
- (IBAction)setLocationReminder:(id)sender;
@end
```

64.12 Creating a Location-based Reminder

The code for accessing the event store is the same as that for the date/time example. Note that in practice the two view controllers could share the event store, but for now we will work with two store objects within the application. Since the application will need to get the user's current location,

Using iOS 6 Event Kit to Create Date and Location Based Reminders

the <CoreLocation/CoreLocation.h> file will need to be imported. The code will require the use of CLLocationManager so a property for the manager instance will also be needed, as will a declaration that the view controller now implements the CLLocationManagerDelegate protocol:

```
#import <UIKit/UIKit.h>
#import <EventKit/EventKit.h>
#import <CoreLocation/CoreLocation.h>

@interface ReminderAppSecondViewController : UIViewController
<CLLocationManagerDelegate>

@property (strong, nonatomic) EKEventStore *eventStore;
@property (strong, nonatomic) CLLocationManager *manager;
@property (strong, nonatomic) IBOutlet UITextField *locationText;
- (IBAction)setLocationReminder:(id)sender;

@end
```

All that remains is to implement the code to access the event store and create the alert and reminder. Select the *ReminderAppSecondViewController.m* file and modify the *setLocationReminder:* method:

```
-(void)setLocationReminder:(id)sender
{
    if (_eventStore == nil)
    {
        _eventStore = [[EKEventStore alloc]init];

        [_eventStore requestAccessToEntityType:EKEntityTypeReminder
completion:^(BOOL granted, NSError *error) {

            if (!granted)
                NSLog(@"Access to store not granted");
        }];
    }

    if (_eventStore)
    {
        _manager = [[CLLocationManager alloc]init];
        _manager.delegate = self;
        _manager.distanceFilter = kCLDistanceFilterNone;
        _manager.desiredAccuracy = kCLLocationAccuracyBest;

        [_manager startUpdatingLocation];
```

Using iOS 6 Event Kit to Create Date and Location Based Reminders

		}
}

As with the previous example, access to the event store is requested. This time, however, a CLLocationManager instance is created and started up. This will result in a call to the *didUpdateLocations:* delegate method where the code to obtain the current location and to create the alarm and reminder will need to be implemented:

```objc
#pragma mark -
#pragma mark CLLocationManagerDelegate

-(void)locationManager:(CLLocationManager *)manager
        didUpdateLocations:(NSArray *)locations
{
    [_manager stopUpdatingLocation];

    EKReminder *reminder = [EKReminder
            reminderWithEventStore:_eventStore];

    reminder.title = _locationText.text;

    reminder.calendar = [_eventStore defaultCalendarForNewReminders];

    EKStructuredLocation *location = [EKStructuredLocation
            locationWithTitle:@"Current Location"];

    location.geoLocation = [locations lastObject];

    EKAlarm *alarm = [[EKAlarm alloc]init];

    alarm.structuredLocation = location;

    alarm.proximity = EKAlarmProximityLeave;

    [reminder addAlarm:alarm];

    NSError *error = nil;

    [_eventStore saveReminder:reminder commit:YES error:&error];

    if (error)
        NSLog(@"Failed to set reminder: %@", error);
}
```

Using iOS 6 Event Kit to Create Date and Location Based Reminders

Since this code introduces some new concepts a more detailed breakdown is probably warranted. To begin with, the code stops the location manager from sending further updates.

```
[_manager stopUpdatingLocation];
```

Next, a new EKReminder instance is created and initialized with the text entered by the user into the Text Field.

```
EKReminder *reminder = [EKReminder
        reminderWithEventStore:_eventStore];

reminder.title = _locationText.text;
```

The default calendar is selected to store the reminder and then an EKStructuredLocation instance created with a location title of "Current Location". This is the title by which the location will be listed in the Reminders app. The most recent location from the location update is extracted from the end of the locations array (see chapter *Getting iPhone Location Information using the iOS 6 Core Location Framework* for more details on location awareness) and the coordinates assigned to the EKStructuredLocation object.

```
reminder.calendar = [_eventStore defaultCalendarForNewReminders];

EKStructuredLocation *location = [EKStructuredLocation
        locationWithTitle:@"Current Location"];

location.geoLocation = [locations lastObject];
```

The location is then added to a newly created alarm instance which is subsequently configured to be triggered when the user moves away from the location proximity:

```
EKAlarm *alarm = [[EKAlarm alloc]init];
alarm.structuredLocation = location;
alarm.proximity = EKAlarmProximityLeave;
```

Finally, the fully configured reminder is saved to the event store.

```
NSError *error = nil;

[_eventStore saveReminder:reminder commit:YES error:&error];

if (error)
     NSLog(@"Failed to set reminder: %@", error);
```

64.13 Adding the Core Location and Event Kit Frameworks

Whilst the coding is complete, an attempt to compile the application at this point will result in undefined symbols because the Core Location and Event Kit Frameworks have not yet been added to the project. Within the project navigator panel, select the *ReminderApp* target at the top of the list and in the main panel select the *Build Phases* tab. In the *Link Binary with Libraries* category, click on the + button and in the resulting list of libraries search for and add the *CoreLocation.framework* library. Repeat this step for *EventKit.framework*.

64.14 Testing the Application

Since the application will rely on a default calendar having been designated for reminders, the first step is to make sure this has been configured. Launch the Settings application, scroll down to and then select *Reminders*, and make sure that a calendar has been assigned to the *Default List*.

Compile and run the application on a physical iPhone device (reminders do not currently work on the iOS Simulator). Select a time a few minutes into the future, and enter some text onto the first screen before touching the Set Reminder button. Put the app into the background and launch the built-in Reminder app where the new reminder should be listed in the default reminder list. When the designated time arrives the alarm should trigger, displaying the text entered by the user.

Using the tab bar, switch to the second screen, enter a message and touch the "When I Leave Here" button. Once again, switch to the built in Reminders app, locate the new reminder and select it. Listed amongst the reminder settings will be an option entitled "Current Location" with the "When I Leave" option selected as shown in Figure 64-7:

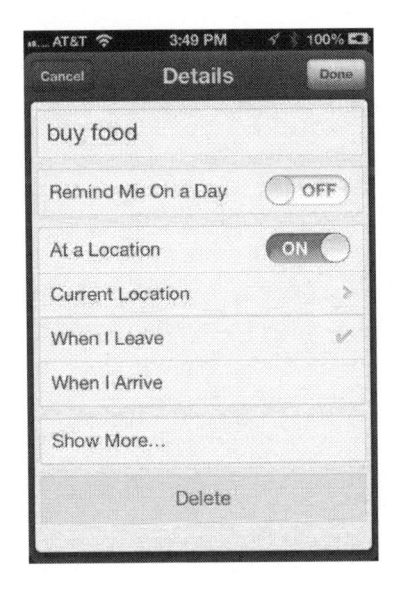

Figure 64-7

Using iOS 6 Event Kit to Create Date and Location Based Reminders

When you next leave your current location the alarm should trigger.

64.15 Summary

The Event Kit Framework provides a platform for building reminders into iOS application. Reminders can be triggered based on either a date and time or change of geographical location. This chapter has provided an overview of Event Kit based reminders before working through the creation of an example application.

Chapter 65

65. Accessing the iPhone Camera and Photo Library

The iOS 6 SDK provides access to both the iPhone camera device and photo library through the UIImagePickerController class. This allows videos and photographs to be taken from within an iPhone application and for existing photos and videos to be presented to the user for selection.

This chapter will cover the basics and some of the theory behind the use of the UIImagePickerController class before working through the step by step creation of an example application in *An Example iOS 6 iPhone Camera Application*.

65.1 The iOS 6 UIImagePickerController Class

The ultimate purpose of the UIImagePickerController class is to provide applications with either an image or video. It achieves this task by providing the user with access to the camera, camera roll and photo libraries on the device. In the case of the camera, the user is able to either take a photo or record a video depending on the capabilities of the device and the application's configuration of the UIImagePickerController object. In terms of camera roll and library access, the object provides the application with the existing image or video selected by the user. The controller also allows new photos and videos created within the application to be saved to the library.

65.2 Creating and Configuring a UIImagePickerController Instance

In order to use the UIImagePickerController, an instance of the class must first be created. In addition, properties of the instance need to be configured to control the source for the images or videos (camera, camera roll or library). Further, the types of media that are acceptable to the application must also be defined (photos, videos or both). Another configuration option defines whether the user has the option to edit a photo once it has been taken and before it is passed to the application.

The source of the media is defined by setting the *sourceType* property of the UIImagePickerController object to one of the three supported types:

- UIImagePickerControllerSourceTypeCamera

Accessing the iPhone Camera and Photo Library

- UIImagePickerControllerSourceTypeSavedPhotosAlbum
- UIImagePickerControllerSourceTypePhotoLibrary

The types of media acceptable to the application are defined by setting the *mediaTypes* property, an NSArray object that can be configured to support both video and images. The KUTTypeImage and KUTTypeMovie definitions contained in the *<MobileCoreServices/MobileCoreServices.h>* include file can be used as values when configuring this property.

Whether or not the user is permitted to perform editing before the image is passed on to the application is controlled via the *allowsEditing* boolean property.

The following code creates a UIImagePickerController instance and configures it for camera use with movie and image support and editing allowed. It then displays the controller and releases the controller object:

```
UIImagePickerController *imagePicker =
  [[UIImagePickerController alloc] init];

imagePicker.delegate = self;

imagePicker.sourceType =
         UIImagePickerControllerSourceTypeCamera;

imagePicker.mediaTypes = @[(NSString *) kUTTypeImage,
                           (NSString *) kUTTypeMovie];

imagePicker.allowsEditing = YES;
[self presentViewController:imagePicker
            animated:YES completion:nil];
```

It should be noted that the above code also configured the current class as the delegate for the UIImagePickerController instance. This is actually a key part of how the class works and is covered in the next section.

65.3 Configuring the UIImagePickerController Delegate

When the user is presented with the UIImagePickerController object user interface the application essentially hands control to that object. That being the case, the controller needs some way to notify the application that the user has taken a photo, recorded a video or made a library selection. It does this by calling delegate methods. The class that instantiates a UIImagePickerController instance should, therefore, declare itself as the object's delegate, conform to the UIImagePickerControllerDelegate and UINavigationControllerDelegate protocols and implement the *didFinishPickingMediaWithInfo* and *imagePickerControllerDidCancel* methods. When the user has

Accessing the iPhone Camera and Photo Library

selected or created media, the *didFinishPickingMediaWithInfo* method is called and passed an NSDictionary object containing the media and associated data. In the event that the user cancels the operation the *imagePickerControllerDidCancel* method is called. In both cases it is the responsibility of the delegate method to dismiss the view controller:

```
-(void)imagePickerController:
(UIImagePickerController *)picker
didFinishPickingMediaWithInfo:(NSDictionary *)info
{
     // Code here to work with media
     [self dismissViewControllerAnimated:YES completion:nil];
}

-(void)imagePickerControllerDidCancel:
(UIImagePickerController *)picker
{
     [self dismissViewControllerAnimated:YES completion:nil];
}
```

The *info* argument passed to the *didFinishPickingMediaWithInfo* method is an NSDictionary object containing the data relating to the image or video created or selected by the user. The first step is typically to identify the type of media:

```
NSString *mediaType = info[UIImagePickerControllerMediaType];

if ([mediaType isEqualToString:(NSString *)kUTTypeImage])
{
       // Media is an image
}
else if ([mediaType isEqualToString:(NSString *)kUTTypeMovie])
{
       // Media is a video
}
```

The original, unedited image selected or photographed by the user may be obtained from the *info* dictionary as follows:

```
UIImage *image = info[UIImagePickerControllerOriginalImage];
```

Assuming that editing was enabled on the image picker controller object, the edited version of image may be accessed via the *UImagePickerControllerEditedImage* dictionary key:

```
UIImage *image = info[UIImagePickerControllerEditedImage];
```

If the media is a video, the URL of the recorded media may be accessed as follows:

519

```
NSURL *url = info[UIImagePickerControllerMediaURL];
```

Once the image or video URL has been obtained the application can optionally save the media to the library and either display the image to the user or play the video using the MPMoviePlayer class as outlined in the chapter entitled *Video Playback from within an iOS 6 iPhone Application*.

65.4 Detecting Device Capabilities

Not all iOS devices provide the same functionality. iPhone models prior to the 3GS model, for example, do not support the recording of video. Some iPod Touch models do not have a camera so neither the camera, nor camera roll are available via the image picker controller. These differences in functionality make it important to detect the capabilities of a device when using the UIImagePickerController class. Fortunately, this may easily be achieved by a call to the *isSourceTypeAvailable* class method of the UIImagePickerController. For example, to detect the presence of a camera:

```
if ([UIImagePickerController isSourceTypeAvailable:
        UIImagePickerControllerSourceTypeCamera])
{
     // code here
}
```

Similarly, to test for access to the camera roll:

```
if ([UIImagePickerController isSourceTypeAvailable:
    UIImagePickerControllerSourceTypeSavedPhotosAlbum])
{
     // code here
}
```

Finally, to check for support for photo libraries:

```
if ([UIImagePickerController isSourceTypeAvailable:
    UIImagePickerControllerSourceTypePhotoLibrary])
{
     // code here
}
```

65.5 Saving Movies and Images

Once a video or photo created by the user using the camera is handed off to the application it is then the responsibility of the application code to save that media into the library. Photos and videos may be saved via calls to the *UIImageWriteToSavedPhotosAlbum* and *UISaveVideoAtPathToSavedPhotosAlbum* methods respectively. These methods use a *target-action* mechanism whereby the save action is initiated and the application continues to run. When the action is complete a specified method is called to notify the application of the success or otherwise of the operation.

To save an image:

```
UIImageWriteToSavedPhotosAlbum(image, self,
    @selector(image:finishedSavingWithError:contextInfo:),
    nil);
```

To save a video:

```
if (UIVideoAtPathIsCompatibleWithSavedPhotosAlbum(videoPath))
{
    UISaveVideoAtPathToSavedPhotosAlbum(videoPath,
        self,
        @selector(video:finishedSavingWithError:contextInfo:),
        nil);
}
```

Last, but by no means least, is the *finishedSavingWithError* method which will be called when the action is either complete or failed due to an error:

```
-(void)image:(UIImage *)image
finishedSavingWithError:(NSError *)
error contextInfo:(void *)contextInfo
{
    if (error) {
        UIAlertView *alert = [[UIAlertView alloc]
            initWithTitle: @"Save failed"
            message: @"Failed to save image/video"
            delegate: nil
            cancelButtonTitle:@"OK"
            otherButtonTitles:nil];
        [alert show];
    }
}
```

65.6 Summary

In this chapter we have provided an overview of the UIImagePickerController and looked at how this class can be used either to allow a user to take a picture or record video from within an iPhone application or select media from the device photo libraries. Now that the theory has been covered, the next chapter entitled *An Example iOS 6 iPhone Camera Application* will work through the development of an example application designed to implement the theory covered in this chapter.

521

Chapter 66

66. An Example iOS 6 iPhone Camera Application

In the chapter entitled *Accessing the iPhone Camera and Photo Library* we looked in some detail at the steps necessary to provide access to the iPhone camera and photo libraries in an iOS 6 application. The purpose of this chapter is to build on this knowledge by working through an example iPhone application designed to access the device's camera and photo libraries.

66.1 An Overview of the Application

The application user interface for this example will consist of an image view and a toolbar containing two buttons. When touched by the user, the first button will display the camera to the user and allow a photograph to be taken which will subsequently be displayed in the image view. The second button will provide access to the camera roll where the user may select an existing photo image. In the case of a new image taken with the camera, this will be saved to the camera roll.

Since we will be covering the playback of video in the next chapter (*Video Playback from within an iOS 6 iPhone Application*) the camera roll and camera will be restricted to still images in this example. The addition of video support to this application is left as an exercise for the reader.

66.2 Creating the Camera Project

Begin the project by launching Xcode and creating a new iPhone iOS application project named *Camera* using the *Single View Application* template with the Storyboard and Automatic Reference Counting options enabled.

66.3 Adding Framework Support

The application developed in this chapter relies on the MobileCoreServices framework. This framework must be added to the project by selecting the product target entry from the project navigator panel (the top item named *Camera*) and clicking on the *Build Phases* tab in the main panel. In the *Link Binary with Libraries* section click on the '+' button, select the *MobileCoreServices.framework* entry from the resulting panel and click on the *Add* button.

66.4 Designing the User Interface

The next step in this tutorial is to design the user interface. This is a very simple user interface consisting of an image view, a toolbar and two bar buttons items. Select the

523

An Example iOS 6 iPhone Camera Application

MainStoryboard.storyboard file and drag and drop components from the Library window (*View -> Utilities -> Show Object Library*) onto the view. Position and size the components and set the text on the bar button items so that the user interface resembles Figure 66-1.

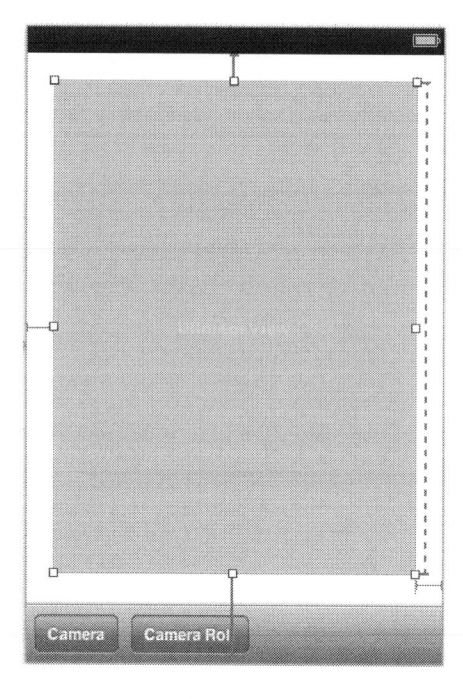

Figure 66-1

In terms of auto layout constraints, note that the priority of the height constraint on the image view has been reduced (represented by the dotted line) so that the image view will resize depending on the screen size of the iOS device on which the application is running. A vertical space constraint has also been placed on the bottom of the image view to the superview. Finally, the bottom edge of the toolbar has been constrained with a vertical space of zero with the bottom edge of the superview.

With the image view object selected, display the Attributes Inspector and change the *Mode* setting listed under *View* to *Aspect Fill*. This will ensure that the aspect ratio of the images displayed does not get distorted in the image view.

Next, display the Size Inspector and change the *Vertical Content Hugging* priority of the image view to 1000. This will prevent the image view from growing vertically and obscuring the toolbar when displaying large images.

Select the image view object in the view canvas, display the Assistant Editor panel and verify that the editor is displaying the contents of the *CameraViewController.h* file. Ctrl-click on the image view object and drag to a position just below the @interface line in the Assistant Editor. Release the line, and in the resulting connection dialog, establish an outlet connection named *imageView*.

With the Assistant Editor visible, establish action connections for the two buttons to methods named *useCamera* and *useCameraRoll* respectively (keeping mind that it may be necessary to click twice on each button to select it since the first click will typically select the toolbar parent object).

Finally, select the *CameraViewController.h* file and modify it further to add import and delegate protocol declarations together with a boolean property declaration that will be required later in the chapter:

```
#import <UIKit/UIKit.h>
#import <MobileCoreServices/MobileCoreServices.h>

@interface CameraViewController : UIViewController
<UIImagePickerControllerDelegate,
        UINavigationControllerDelegate>

@property BOOL newMedia;
@property (strong, nonatomic) IBOutlet UIImageView *imageView;
- (IBAction)useCamera:(id)sender;
- (IBAction)useCameraRoll:(id)sender;
@end
```

66.5 Implementing the Action Methods

The *useCamera* and *useCameraRoll* action methods now need to be implemented. The *useCamera* method first needs to check that the device on which the application is running has a camera. It then needs to create a UIImagePickerController instance, assign the cameraViewController as the delegate for the object and define the media source as the camera. Since we do not plan on handling videos the supported media types property is set to images only. Finally, the camera interface will be displayed. The last task is to set the *newMedia* flag to YES to indicate that the image is new and is not an existing image from the camera roll. Bringing all these requirements together gives us the following *useCamera* method:

```
- (void) useCamera:(id)sender
{
    if ([UIImagePickerController isSourceTypeAvailable:
            UIImagePickerControllerSourceTypeCamera])
    {
        UIImagePickerController *imagePicker =
            [[UIImagePickerController alloc] init];
        imagePicker.delegate = self;
        imagePicker.sourceType =
            UIImagePickerControllerSourceTypeCamera;
        imagePicker.mediaTypes = @[(NSString *) kUTTypeImage];
        imagePicker.allowsEditing = NO;
```

An Example iOS 6 iPhone Camera Application

```
            [self presentViewController:imagePicker
                animated:YES completion:nil];
            _newMedia = YES;
        }
    }
    .
    .
@end
```

The *useCameraRoll* method is remarkably similar to the previous method with the exception that the source of the image is declared to be UIImagePickerControllerSourceTypePhotoLibrary and the *newMedia* flag is set to NO (since the photo is already in the library we don't need to save it again):

```
- (void) useCameraRoll:(id)sender
{
    if ([UIImagePickerController isSourceTypeAvailable:
            UIImagePickerControllerSourceTypeSavedPhotosAlbum])
    {
        UIImagePickerController *imagePicker =
            [[UIImagePickerController alloc] init];
        imagePicker.delegate = self;
        imagePicker.sourceType =
            UIImagePickerControllerSourceTypePhotoLibrary;
         imagePicker.mediaTypes = @[(NSString *) kUTTypeImage];
        imagePicker.allowsEditing = NO;
        [self presentViewController:imagePicker
            animated:YES completion:nil];
        _newMedia = NO;
    }
}
```

66.6 Writing the Delegate Methods

As described in *Accessing the iPhone Camera and Photo Library*, in order to fully implement an instance of the image picker controller delegate protocol it is necessary to implement some delegate methods. The most important method is *didFinishPickingMediaWithInfo* which is called when the user has finished taking or selecting an image. The code for this method in our example reads as follows:

```
#pragma mark -
#pragma mark UIImagePickerControllerDelegate

-(void)imagePickerController:(UIImagePickerController *)picker
didFinishPickingMediaWithInfo:(NSDictionary *)info
{
```

An Example iOS 6 iPhone Camera Application

```objc
    NSString *mediaType = info[UIImagePickerControllerMediaType];

    [self dismissViewControllerAnimated:YES completion:nil];

    if ([mediaType isEqualToString:(NSString *)kUTTypeImage]) {
        UIImage *image = info[UIImagePickerControllerOriginalImage];

        _imageView.image = image;
        if (_newMedia)
            UIImageWriteToSavedPhotosAlbum(image,
                self,
                @selector(image:finishedSavingWithError:contextInfo:),
                nil);
    }
    else if ([mediaType isEqualToString:(NSString *)kUTTypeMovie])
    {
            // Code here to support video if enabled
    }
}

-(void)image:(UIImage *)image
finishedSavingWithError:(NSError *)error
contextInfo:(void *)contextInfo
{
    if (error) {
        UIAlertView *alert = [[UIAlertView alloc]
            initWithTitle: @"Save failed"
            message: @"Failed to save image"
            delegate: nil
            cancelButtonTitle:@"OK"
            otherButtonTitles:nil];
        [alert show];
    }
}
```

The code in this delegate method dismisses the image picker view and identifies the type of media passed from the image picker controller. If it is an image it is displayed on the view image object of the user interface. If this is a new image it is saved to the camera roll. The *finishedSavingWithError* method is configured to be called when the save operation is complete. If an error occurred it is reported to the user via an alert box.

An Example iOS 6 iPhone Camera Application

It is also necessary to implement the *imagePickerControllerDidCancel* delegate method which is called if the user cancels the image picker session without taking a picture or making an image selection. In most cases all this method needs to do is dismiss the image picker:

```
-(void)imagePickerControllerDidCancel:(UIImagePickerController *)picker
{
    [self dismissViewControllerAnimated:YES completion:nil];
}
```

66.7 Building and Running the Application

In order to experience the full functionality of this application it will be necessary to install it on a physical iPhone or iPod Touch device with a camera. Steps on performing this are covered in *Testing iOS 6 Apps on the iPhone – Developer Certificates and Provisioning Profiles*.

Assuming certificates and provisioning are configured, click on the *Run* button to launch the application. Once application loads, select the *Camera* button to launch the camera interface.

Figure 66-2

Once the picture has been taken and selected for use in the application, it will appear in the image view object of our application user interface.

An Example iOS 6 iPhone Camera Application

Selecting the *Camera Roll* button will provide access to the camera roll and photo stream on the device where an image selection can be made:

Figure 66-3

529

Chapter 67

67. Video Playback from within an iOS 6 iPhone Application

Whilst the iPhone 3GS model introduced support for recording videos using the built in camera, all iPhone models and iOS versions have included support for video playback. Video playback support in iOS 6 is provided by the MPMoviePlayerController class.

This chapter presents an overview of the MPMoviePlayerController class followed by a step by step example of the use of this class to play a movie within an iOS 6 iPhone application.

67.1 An Overview of the MPMoviePlayerController Class

The sole purpose of the MPMoviePlayerController is to play video content. It is initialized with the URL of the media to be played (either a path to a local movie file on the device or the URL of network based media). The movie player view is added as a subview of the current view, configured using a variety of properties and then displayed to the user. The playback window can run in a full screen mode, or embedded in an existing view.

By default, the movie player includes a number of controls that enable the user to manage the playback experience. The exact controls displayed to the user may be configured by setting the movie player's *controlStyle* property. Playback may also be controlled from the application code by implementing the methods defined in the MPMediaPlayback protocol.

The MPMoviePlayerController class also employs the *target-action* model for notifying the application of events such as the movie starting, finishing, being paused, entering and leaving full screen mode etc.

67.2 Supported Video Formats

The MPMoviePlayerController class supports the playback of movies of type .mov, .mp4, .mpv and .3gp. In terms of compression, the class supports H.264 Baseline Profile Level 3.0 and MPEG-4 Part 2 video.

531

67.3 The iPhone Movie Player Example Application

The objective of the remainder of this chapter is to create a simple application that will play back a video when a button is pressed. The video will be streamed over the internet from a movie file located on a web server.

Begin by launching Xcode and creating a new iOS iPhone application project based on the *Single View Application* template, naming the product and class prefix *Movie* when prompted to do so, making sure that the *Use Storyboards* and *Use Automatic Reference Counting* options are enabled.

67.4 Adding the MediaPlayer Framework to the Project

The MPMoviePlayerController class is contained within the *MediaPlayer* framework. This framework must, therefore, be included in any projects that make use of this class. This can be achieved by selecting the product target entry from the project navigator panel (the top item named *Movie*) and clicking on the *Build Phases* tab in the main panel. In the *Link Binary with Libraries* section click on the '+' button, select the *MediaPlayer.framework* entry from the resulting panel and click on the *Add* button.

67.5 Designing the User Interface

Select the *MainStoryboard.storyboard* file and display the Object library (*View -> Utilities -> Object Library*). Drag a single Button instance to the view window and change the text on the button to "Play Movie".

Display the Assistant Editor, Ctrl-click on the button object and drag the line to the area immediately beneath the @interface line in the Assistant Editor panel. Release the line and, within the resulting connection dialog, establish an Action method on the *Touch Up Inside* event configured to call a method named *playMovie*.

67.6 Declaring the MoviePlayer Instance

Before proceeding, it is imperative that the *<MediaPlayer/MediaPlayer.h>* file be imported to avoid a catalog of unresolved references when the application is compiled. A reference to an instance of the MPMoviePlayerController class is also going to required. Select the *MovieViewController.h* file, therefore, and modify it as follows:

```
#import <UIKit/UIKit.h>
#import <MediaPlayer/MediaPlayer.h>

@interface MovieViewController : UIViewController

@property (strong, nonatomic) MPMoviePlayerController *moviePlayer;
```

```
- (IBAction)playMovie:(id)sender;
@end
```

67.7 Implementing the Action Method

The next step is to write the code for the action method so that video playback is initiated when the button is touched by the user. The stub method for the *playMovie* action has been created in *MovieViewController.m* and should be modified as follows.

```
-(void)playMovie:(id)sender
{
    NSURL *url = [NSURL URLWithString:
        @"http://www.ebookfrenzy.com/ios_book/movie/movie.mov"];

    _moviePlayer =  [[MPMoviePlayerController alloc]
                initWithContentURL:url];

    [[NSNotificationCenter defaultCenter] addObserver:self
                selector:@selector(moviePlayBackDidFinish:)
                name:MPMoviePlayerPlaybackDidFinishNotification
                object:_moviePlayer];

    _moviePlayer.controlStyle = MPMovieControlStyleDefault;
    _moviePlayer.shouldAutoplay = YES;
    [self.view addSubview:_moviePlayer.view];
    [_moviePlayer setFullscreen:YES animated:YES];
}
```

The above method constructs an NSURL object using the URL of a web based video file. This is then used in the creation of a new instance of the MPMoviePlayerController class. A notification is then configured such that the *moviePlaybackDidFinish* method is called when the playback finishes. Next, properties are set to ensure that the standard movie controls are available to the user and that the movie automatically starts playing once it is ready. Finally the movie player object is added as a subview to the current view and displayed to the user in full screen mode.

67.8 The Target-Action Notification Method

The *playButton* action method declared that when the movie has finished playing, the movie player object is to call a method named *moviePlaybackDidFinish*. It is the responsibility of this method to cancel the notification and remove the movie player interface from display. Edit the *MovieViewController.m* file and add this method as follows:

```
- (void) moviePlayBackDidFinish:(NSNotification*)notification {
    MPMoviePlayerController *player = [notification object];
```

```
    [[NSNotificationCenter defaultCenter]
        removeObserver:self
        name:MPMoviePlayerPlaybackDidFinishNotification
        object:player];

    if ([player
        respondsToSelector:@selector(setFullscreen:animated:)])
    {
        [player.view removeFromSuperview];
    }
}
```

67.9 Build and Run the Application

With the design and coding phases complete, all that remains is to build and run the application. Click on the *Run* button located in the toolbar of the main Xcode project window. Assuming that no errors occur, the application should launch within the iOS Simulator or device. Note that in addition to the application code, the *movie.mov* file added as a resource to the project also needs to be loaded. If a large video file was used it may take some time before the application starts up. Once loaded, touching the *Play Movie* button should launch the movie player in full screen mode and playback should automatically begin:

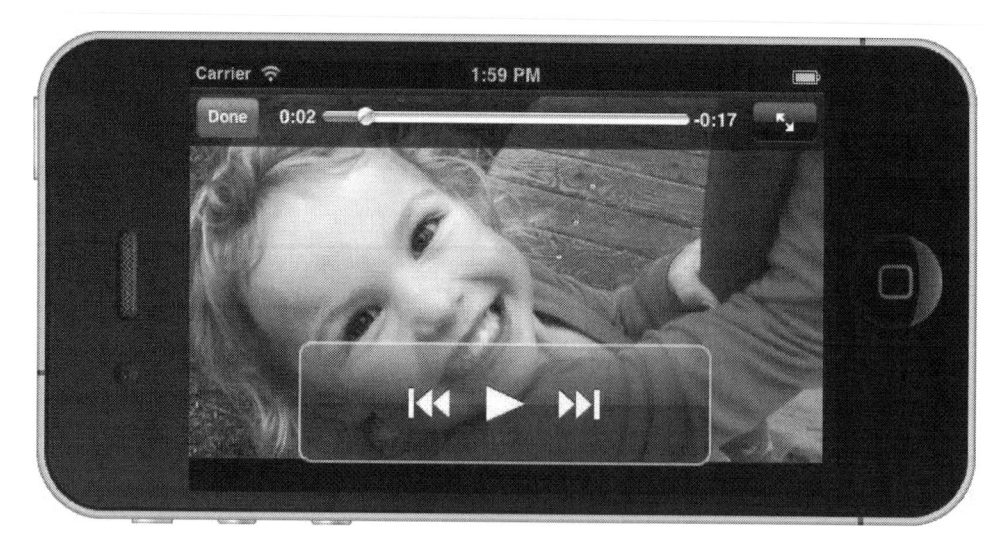

Figure 67-1

Chapter 68

68. Playing Audio on an iPhone using AVAudioPlayer

The iOS 6 SDK provides a number of mechanisms for implementing audio playback from within an iPhone application. The easiest technique from the perspective of the application developer is to use the AVAudioPlayer class which is part of the AV Foundation Framework.

The goal of this chapter is to provide an overview of audio playback using the AVAudioPlayer class. Once the basics have been covered, a tutorial is worked through step by step. The topic of recording audio from within an iPhone application is covered in the next chapter entitled *Recording Audio on an iPhone with AVAudioRecorder*.

68.1 Supported Audio Formats

The AV Foundation framework supports the playback of a variety of different audio formats and codecs including both software and hardware based decoding. Codecs and formats currently supported are as follows:

- AAC (MPEG-4 Advanced Audio Coding)
- ALAC (Apple Lossless)
- AMR (Adaptive Multi-rate)
- HE-AAC (MPEG-4 High Efficiency AAC)
- iLBC (internet Low Bit Rate Codec)
- Linear PCM (uncompressed, linear pulse code modulation)
- MP3 (MPEG-1 audio layer 3)
- µ-law and a-law

If an audio file is to be included as part of the resource bundle for an application it may be converted to a supported audio format prior to inclusion in the application project using the Mac OS X *afconvert* command-line tool. For details on how to use this tool, run the following command in a Terminal window:

```
afconvert -h
```

68.2 Receiving Playback Notifications

An application receives notifications from an AVAudioPlayer instance by declaring itself as the object's delegate and implementing some or all the following AVAudioPlayerDelegate protocol methods:

- **audioPlayerDidFinishPlaying:** – Called when the audio playback finishes. An argument passed through to the method indicates whether the playback completed successfully or failed due to an error.
- **audioPlayerDecodeErrorDidOccur:** - Called when a decoding error is encountered by the AVAudioPlayer object during audio playback. An error object containing information about the nature of the problem is passed through to this method as an argument.
- **audioPlayerBeginInterruption:** – Called when audio playback has been interrupted by a system event such as an incoming phone call. Playback is automatically paused and the current audio session deactivated.
- **audioPlayerEndInterruption:** - Called after an interruption ends. The current audio session is automatically activated and playback may be resumed by calling the *play* method of the corresponding AVAudioPlayer instance.

68.3 Controlling and Monitoring Playback

Once an AVAudioPlayer instance has been created the playback of audio may be controlled and monitored programmatically via the methods and properties of that instance. For example, the self explanatory *play*, *pause* and *stop* methods may be used to control playback. Similarly, the *volume* property may be used to adjust the volume level of the audio playback whilst the *playing* property may be accessed to identify whether or not the AVAudioPlayer object is currently playing audio.

In addition, playback may be delayed to begin at a later time using the *playAtTime* instance method which takes as an argument the number of seconds (as an NSTimeInterval value) to delay before beginning playback.

The length of the current audio playback may be obtained via the *duration* property whilst the current point in the playback is stored in the *currentTime* property.

Playback may also be programmed to loop back and repeatedly play a specified number of times using the *numberofLoops* property.

68.4 Creating the iPhone Audio Example Application

The remainder of this chapter will work through the creation of a simple iPhone iOS 6 application which plays an audio file. The user interface of the application will consist of play and stop buttons to control playback and a slider to adjust the playback volume level.

Playing Audio on an iPhone using AVAudioPlayer

Begin by launching Xcode and creating a new iPhone iOS *Single View Application* named *Audio* with a matching class prefix when prompted to do so, making sure that the *Use Storyboards* and *Use Automatic Reference Counting* options are enabled.

68.5 Adding the AVFoundation Framework

Since the iOS 6 AVAudioPlayer class is part of the AV Foundation framework, it will be necessary to add the framework to the project. This can be achieved by selecting the product target entry from the project navigator panel (the top item named *Audio*) and clicking on the *Build Phases* tab in the main panel. In the *Link Binary with Libraries* section click on the '+' button, select the *AVFoundation.framework* entry from the resulting panel and click on the *Add* button.

68.6 Adding an Audio File to the Project Resources

In order to experience audio playback it will be necessary to add an audio file to the project resources. For this purpose, any supported audio format file will be suitable. Having identified a suitable audio file, drag and drop it into the *Supporting Files* category of the project navigator panel of the main Xcode window. For the purposes of this tutorial we will be using an MP3 file named *Moderato.mp3* which may be downloaded from the following URL:

http://www.ebookfrenzy.com/code/Moderato.mp3.zip

Having downloaded and unzipped the file, locate it in a Finder window and drag and drop it onto the *Supporting Files* section of the Xcode project navigator panel.

68.7 Designing the User Interface

The application user interface is going to comprise two buttons labeled "Play" and "Stop" and a slider to allow the volume of playback to be adjusted. Select the MainStoryboard.storyboard file, display the Object Library (*View -> Utilities -> Show Object Library*), drag and drop components from the Library onto the View window and modify properties so that the interface appears as illustrated in Figure 68-1:

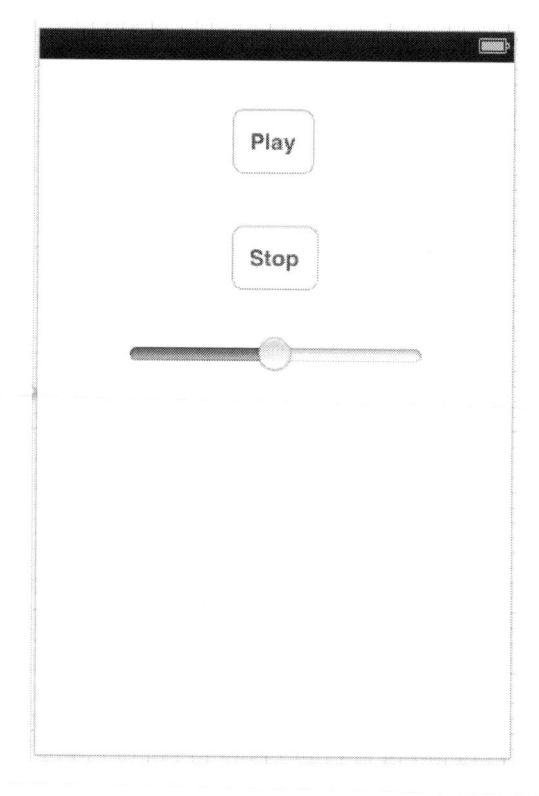

Playing Audio on an iPhone using AVAudioPlayer

Figure 68-1

Select the slider object in the view canvas, display the Assistant Editor panel and verify that the editor is displaying the contents of the *AudioViewController.h* file. Ctrl-click on the slider object and drag to a position just below the @interface line in the Assistant Editor. Release the line and in the resulting connection dialog establish an outlet connection named *volumeControl*.

Ctrl-click on the "Play" button object and drag the line to the area immediately beneath the newly created outlet in the Assistant Editor panel. Release the line and, within the resulting connection dialog, establish an Action method on the *Touch Up Inside* event configured to call a method named *playAudio*. Repeat these steps to establish an action on the "Stop" button to a method named *stopAudio*.

Ctrl-click on the slider object and drag the line to the area immediately beneath the newly created actions in the Assistant Editor panel. Release the line and, within the resulting connection dialog, establish an Action method on the *Value Changed* event configured to call a method named *adjustVolume*.

Select the *AudioViewController.h* file in project navigator panel and add an import directive and delegate declaration, together with a property to store AVAudioPlayer instance as follows:

538

Playing Audio on an iPhone using AVAudioPlayer

```
#import <UIKit/UIKit.h>
#import <AVFoundation/AVFoundation.h>

@interface AudioViewController : UIViewController
    <AVAudioPlayerDelegate>

@property (strong, nonatomic) AVAudioPlayer *audioPlayer;
@property (strong, nonatomic) IBOutlet UISlider *volumeControl;
- (IBAction)adjustVolume:(id)sender;
- (IBAction)playAudio:(id)sender;
- (IBAction)stopAudio:(id)sender;
@end
```

68.8 Implementing the Action Methods

The next step in our iPhone audio player tutorial is to implement the action methods for the two buttons and the slider. Select the *AudioViewController.m* file, locate and implement these methods as outlined in the following code fragment:

```
- (IBAction)adjustVolume:(id)sender {
    if (_audioPlayer != nil)
    {
        _audioPlayer.volume = _volumeControl.value;
    }
}

- (IBAction)playAudio:(id)sender {
    [_audioPlayer play];
}

- (IBAction)stopAudio:(id)sender {
    [_audioPlayer stop];
}
```

68.9 Creating and Initializing the AVAudioPlayer Object

Now that we have an audio file to play and appropriate action methods written, the next step is to create an AVAudioPlayer instance and initialize it with a reference to the audio file. Since we only need to initialize the object once when the application launches a good place to write this code is in the *viewDidLoad* method of the *AudioViewController.m* file:

```
- (void)viewDidLoad {
    [super viewDidLoad];
    NSURL *url = [NSURL fileURLWithPath:[[NSBundle mainBundle]
```

Playing Audio on an iPhone using AVAudioPlayer

```
                pathForResource:@"Moderato"
                ofType:@"mp3"]];

    NSError *error;
    _audioPlayer = [[AVAudioPlayer alloc] 
                        initWithContentsOfURL:url 
                        error:&error];
    if (error)
    {
        NSLog(@"Error in audioPlayer: %@",
                [error localizedDescription]);
    } else {
        _audioPlayer.delegate = self;
        [_audioPlayer prepareToPlay];
    }
}
```

In the above code we create an NSURL reference using the filename and type of the audio file added to the project resources. Keep in mind that this will need to be modified to reflect the audio file used in your own project.

Next, an AVAudioPlayer instance is created using the URL of the audio file. Assuming no errors were detected, the current class is designated as the delegate for the audio player object. Finally, a call is made to the audioPlayer object's *prepareToPlay* method. This performs initial buffering tasks so that there is no buffering delay when the play button is subsequently selected by the user.

68.10 Implementing the AVAudioPlayerDelegate Protocol Methods

As previously discussed, by declaring our view controller as the delegate for our AVAudioPlayer instance our application will be able to receive notifications relating to the playback. Templates of these methods are as follows and may be placed in the *AudioViewController.m* file as follows:

```
-(void)audioPlayerDidFinishPlaying:
(AVAudioPlayer *)player successfully:(BOOL)flag
{
}
-(void)audioPlayerDecodeErrorDidOccur:
(AVAudioPlayer *)player error:(NSError *)error
{
}
-(void)audioPlayerBeginInterruption:(AVAudioPlayer *)player
{
}
-(void)audioPlayerEndInterruption:(AVAudioPlayer *)player
```

```
{
}
```

For the purposes of this tutorial it is not necessary to implement any code for these methods and they are provided solely for completeness.

68.11 Building and Running the Application

Once all the requisite changes have been made and saved, test the application in the iOS simulator or a physical device by clicking on the *Run* button located in the Xcode toolbar. Once the application appears, click on the Play button to begin playback. Adjust the volume using the slider and stop playback using the Stop button. If the playback is not audible on an iPhone device, make sure that the switch on the side of the device is not set to silent mode.

Chapter 69

69. Recording Audio on an iPhone with AVAudioRecorder

In addition to audio playback, the iOS AV Foundation framework provides the ability to record sound on the iPhone using the AVAudioRecorder class. This chapter will work step-by-step through a tutorial demonstrating the use of the AVAudioRecorder class to record audio.

69.1 An Overview of the iPhone AVAudioRecorder Tutorial

The goal of this chapter is to create an iOS 6 iPhone application that will record and playback audio. It will do so by creating an instance of the AVAudioRecorder class and configuring it with a file to contain the audio and a range of settings dictating the quality and format of the audio. Playback of the recorded audio file will be performed using the AVAudioPlayer class which was covered in detail in the chapter entitled *Playing Audio on an iPhone using AVAudioPlayer*.

Audio recording and playback will be controlled by buttons in the user interface that are connected to action methods which, in turn, will make appropriate calls to the instance methods of the AVAudioRecorder and AVAudioPlayer objects respectively.

The view controller of the example application will also implement the AVAudioRecorderDelegate and AVAudioPlayerDelegate protocols and a number of corresponding delegate methods in order to receive notification of events relating to playback and recording.

69.2 Creating the Recorder Project

Begin by launching Xcode and creating a new iPhone iOS single view-based application named *Record* with a corresponding class prefix with Storyboards and Automatic Reference Counting enabled.

Since the iOS 6 AVAudioRecorder class is part of the AV Foundation framework it will be necessary to add the framework to the project. This can be achieved by selecting the product target entry from the project navigator panel (the top item named *Record*) and clicking on the *Build Phases* tab in the main panel. In the *Link Binary with Libraries* section click on the '+' button, select the *AVFoundation.framework* entry from the resulting panel and click on the *Add* button.

Recording Audio on an iPhone with AVAudioRecorder

69.3 Designing the User Interface

Select the *MainStoryboard.storyboard* file and, once loaded, drag Button objects from the Object Library window (*View -> Utilities -> Object Library*) and position them on the View window. Once placed in the view, modify the text on each button so that the user interface appears as illustrated in Figure 69-1:

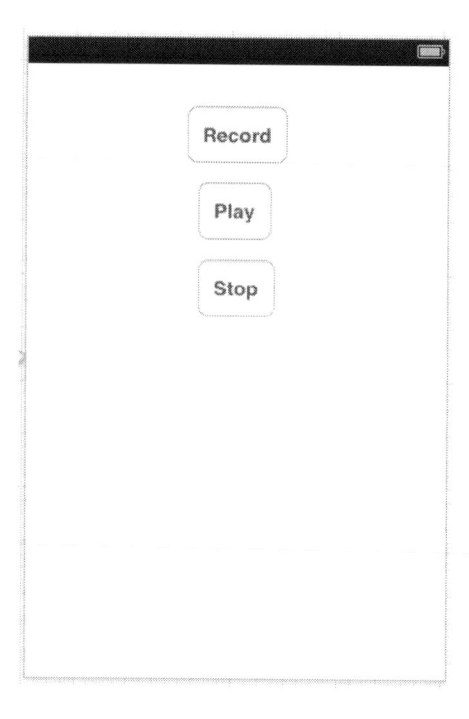

Figure 69-1

Select the "Record" button object in the view canvas, display the Assistant Editor panel and verify that the editor is displaying the contents of the *RecordViewController.h* file. Ctrl-click on the Record button object and drag to a position just below the @interface line in the Assistant Editor. Release the line and, in the resulting connection dialog, establish an outlet connection named *recordButton*. Repeat these steps to establish outlet connections for the "Play" and "Stop" buttons named *playButton* and *stopButton* respectively.

Continuing to use the Assistant Editor, establish Action connections from the three buttons to methods named *recordAudio*, *playAudio* and *stop*.

Select the *RecordViewController.h* file and modify it to import <AVFoundation/AVFoundation.h>, declare adherence to delegate protocols and add properties to store references to AVAudioRecorder and AVAudioPlayer instances:

```
#import <UIKit/UIKit.h>
```

```
#import <AVFoundation/AVFoundation.h>

@interface RecordViewController : UIViewController
    <AVAudioRecorderDelegate, AVAudioPlayerDelegate>

@property (strong, nonatomic) AVAudioRecorder *audioRecorder;
@property (strong, nonatomic) AVAudioPlayer *audioPlayer;
@property (strong, nonatomic) IBOutlet UIButton *recordButton;
@property (strong, nonatomic) IBOutlet UIButton *playButton;
@property (strong, nonatomic) IBOutlet UIButton *stopButton;
- (IBAction)recordAudio:(id)sender;
- (IBAction)playAudio:(id)sender;
- (IBAction)stop:(id)sender;

@end
```

69.4 Creating the AVAudioRecorder Instance

When the application is first launched, an instance of the AVAudioRecorder class needs to be created. This will be initialized with the URL of a file into which the recorded audio is to be saved. Also passed as an argument to the initialization method is an NSDictionary object indicating the settings for the recording such as bit rate, sample rate and audio quality. A full description of the settings available may be found in the appropriate *Apple iOS reference materials*.

As is often the case, a good location to initialize the AVAudioRecorder instance is the *viewDidLoad* method of the view controller located in the *RecordViewController.m* file. Select the file in the project navigator, locate this method and modify it so that it reads as follows:

```
- (void)viewDidLoad {
    [super viewDidLoad];
    _playButton.enabled = NO;
    _stopButton.enabled = NO;

    NSArray *dirPaths;
    NSString *docsDir;

    dirPaths = NSSearchPathForDirectoriesInDomains(
        NSDocumentDirectory, NSUserDomainMask, YES);
    docsDir = dirPaths[0];

    NSString *soundFilePath = [docsDir
        stringByAppendingPathComponent:@"sound.caf"];

    NSURL *soundFileURL = [NSURL fileURLWithPath:soundFilePath];
```

```
        NSDictionary *recordSettings = [NSDictionary
                dictionaryWithObjectsAndKeys:
                [NSNumber numberWithInt:AVAudioQualityMin],
                AVEncoderAudioQualityKey,
                [NSNumber numberWithInt:16],
                AVEncoderBitRateKey,
                [NSNumber numberWithInt: 2],
                AVNumberOfChannelsKey,
                [NSNumber numberWithFloat:44100.0],
                AVSampleRateKey,
                nil];

    NSError *error = nil;

    _audioRecorder = [[AVAudioRecorder alloc]
                    initWithURL:soundFileURL
                    settings:recordSettings
                    error:&error];

    if (error)
    {
            NSLog(@"error: %@", [error localizedDescription]);
    } else {
            [_audioRecorder prepareToRecord];
    }
}
```

Since no audio has yet been recorded, the above method disables the play and stop buttons. It then identifies the application's documents directory and constructs a URL to a file in that location named *sound.caf*. An NSDictionary object is then created containing the recording quality settings before an instance of the AVAudioRecorder class is created. Assuming no errors are encountered, the audioRecorder instance is prepared to begin recording when requested to do so by the user.

69.5 Implementing the Action Methods

The next step is to implement the action methods connected to the three button objects. Select the *RecordViewController.m* file and modify it as outlined in the following code excerpt:

```
- (IBAction)recordAudio:(id)sender {
    if (!_audioRecorder.recording)
    {
            _playButton.enabled = NO;
            _stopButton.enabled = YES;
```

```objc
        [_audioRecorder record];
    }
}

- (IBAction)playAudio:(id)sender {
    if (!_audioRecorder.recording)
    {
        _stopButton.enabled = YES;
        _recordButton.enabled = NO;

        NSError *error;

        _audioPlayer = [[AVAudioPlayer alloc]
        initWithContentsOfURL:_audioRecorder.url
        error:&error];

        _audioPlayer.delegate = self;

        if (error)
                NSLog(@"Error: %@",
                [error localizedDescription]);
        else
                [_audioPlayer play];
    }
}

- (IBAction)stop:(id)sender {
    _stopButton.enabled = NO;
    _playButton.enabled = YES;
    _recordButton.enabled = YES;

    if (_audioRecorder.recording)
    {
            [_audioRecorder stop];
    } else if (_audioPlayer.playing) {
            [_audioPlayer stop];
    }
}
```

Each of the above methods performs the step necessary to enable and disable appropriate buttons in the user interface and to interact with the AVAudioRecorder and AVAudioPlayer object instances to record or play back audio.

69.6 Implementing the Delegate Methods

In order to receive notification about the success or otherwise of recording or playback it is necessary to implement some delegate methods. For the purposes of this tutorial we will need to implement the methods to indicate errors have occurred and also when playback finished. Once again, edit the *recordViewController.m* file and add these methods as follows:

```
-(void)audioPlayerDidFinishPlaying:
(AVAudioPlayer *)player successfully:(BOOL)flag
{
        _recordButton.enabled = YES;
        _stopButton.enabled = NO;
}

-(void)audioPlayerDecodeErrorDidOccur:
(AVAudioPlayer *)player
error:(NSError *)error
{
        NSLog(@"Decode Error occurred");
}

-(void)audioRecorderDidFinishRecording:
(AVAudioRecorder *)recorder
successfully:(BOOL)flag
{
}

-(void)audioRecorderEncodeErrorDidOccur:
(AVAudioRecorder *)recorder
error:(NSError *)error
{
        NSLog(@"Encode Error occurred");
}
```

69.7 Testing the Application

Follow the steps outlined in *Testing iOS 6 Apps on the iPhone – Developer Certificates and Provisioning Profiles* to configure the application for installation on an iPhone device. Configure Xcode to install the application on the connected iPhone device and build and run the application by clicking on the *Run* button in the main toolbar. Once loaded onto the device, touch the Record button and record some sound. Touch the Stop button when the recording is completed and use the Play button to play back the audio.

Chapter 70

70. Integrating Twitter and Facebook into iPhone iOS 6 Applications

Social networking services are, for better or for worse, becoming an increasingly prominent aspect of our daily lives. Apple began to provide support for integrating social elements into iOS apps with the introduction of Twitter support in iOS 5. With iOS 6, this support has now been extended to cover Facebook and Sina Weibo.

Within this chapter, the basics of Twitter and Facebook integration will be covered.

70.1 The iOS 6 UIActivityViewController class

Integration of social networks into iOS 6 applications is performed through the use of either the UIActivityViewController class, or the classes of the new Social Framework of the iOS 6 SDK. At the time of writing, social networks supported by these classes consist of Facebook, Twitter and Sina Weibo, though it is probable that more will follow in future SDK releases.

For general purpose social network integration, the UIActivityViewController class is the recommended path. When using this class, the user is presented with a screen providing a choice of social network services to which a message may be posted (together with options to print or post via the built-in Mail or Message apps). Once the user of the application has selected a target service, the class then presents the user with a message preview panel where the message may be reviewed and modified prior to being sent. Once the message has been posted, the class handles all aspects of connecting to the user's chosen social network and subsequently posting the update to that service.

70.2 The Social Framework

The iOS 6 Social Framework contains two classes designed to provide more flexible and general purpose mechanisms for social network integration.

The SLComposeViewController class, unlike the UIActivityViewController class, allows a post to be targeted to a specific social network service within the application code, without requiring the user to make a selection from those services available. The target service is simply specified at the point that an instance of the class is created within the application code. The user is then presented with a preview sheet appropriate to the specified service.

The SLRequest class of the Social Framework, on the other hand, is provided for developers with specific needs in terms of social network integration and who are familiar with, or prepared to learn, the corresponding social network APIs. In essence, the SLRequest class allows iOS applications to interact directly with social network APIs through HTTP based requests.

70.3 iOS 6 Accounts Framework

The purpose of the Accounts Framework is to provide access to device based system accounts from within iOS applications. The term *system accounts* is somewhat misleading since, in the case of the first release of iOS 6 at least, this is limited solely to Facebook, Twitter and Sina Weibo accounts, though this will likely be extended to other platforms in future iOS releases. Using the Accounts framework, code can be written to access, create and validate social network accounts stored on iOS 6 based devices.

The iOS 6 operating system running on iPhone and iPad devices is able to store multiple Twitter accounts but only one Facebook account at a time. These are accessible both from the device *Settings* application in addition to using the Accounts Framework within application code.

To manually view and configure Twitter accounts on a device, select the *Settings* application and choose the *Twitter* option. As illustrated in Figure 70-1, any pre-configured Twitter accounts will be listed together with a button providing the option to add a new Twitter account and switches providing control over which applications may be granted permission to access those Twitter accounts:

Integrating Twitter and Facebook into iPhone iOS 6 Applications

Figure 70-1

The current Facebook account settings on the device may, similarly, be viewed and modified by selecting the Facebook option of the main screen of the Settings application. Options are also provided on the Facebook settings panel to control which applications have access to the Facebook account, and to modify or delete the currently configured Facebook account.

When using the SLRequest class to construct API requests, it will be necessary to use the Accounts framework to identify and request permission to use the corresponding social network accounts in an application. When using the UIActivityViewController or SLComposeViewController classes, however, the account handling is performed automatically by the class. The remainder of this chapter will focus on the UIActivityViewController and SLComposeViewController classes. The SLRequest class will be covered in detail in the chapter entitled *iPhone iOS 6 Facebook and Twitter Integration Tutorial using SLRequest*.

70.4 Using the UIActivityViewController Class

The UIActivityViewController class is instantiated within an application at the point at which a posting is ready to be made to a social network. Once the user takes an action to post an update

Integrating Twitter and Facebook into iPhone iOS 6 Applications

from within an application, the screen shown in Figure 70-2 will appear listing the options that are available:

Figure 70-2

Once a destination social network has been selected, the preview sheet for the chosen service (Figure 70-3 shows the sheet for a Facebook posting) will appear primed with the content of the update to be sent consisting of text and any optional image attachments. Having reviewed and, optionally, modified the post, user may then send the message.

Figure 70-3

In the event that the user has not yet configured an account for the selected social network in the Settings application, a dialog will appear providing the option to either set up an account or cancel the post.

The assumption is generally made that at the point an instance of UIActivityViewController is created, the application will already have gathered together the text and images that are to be included in the post. These items need to be placed into an NSArray object and passed to the controller before it is presented to the user. The following code excerpt, for example, instantiates a UIActivityViewController instance primed with text and an image to be included in the post and presents it to the user:

```
NSString *postText = @"My first Facebook post from iOS 6";
UIImage *postImage = [UIImage imageNamed:@"myImage.png"];

    NSArray *activityItems = @[postText, postImage];

    UIActivityViewController *activityController =
         [[UIActivityViewController alloc]
             initWithActivityItems:activityItems
             applicationActivities:nil];
```

```
[self presentViewController:activityController
         animated:YES completion:nil];
```

70.5 Using the SLComposeViewController Class

In order to use the SLComposeViewController class, a number of steps should be performed in sequence. Firstly, the application may optionally check to verify whether a message can be sent to the specified social network service. This essentially equates to checking if a valid social network account has been configured on the device and is achieved using the *isAvailableForServiceType:* class method, passing through as an argument the type of service required from the following options:

- SLServiceTypeFacebook
- SLServiceTypeTwitter
- SLServiceTypeSinaWeibo

The following code, for example, verifies that the Twitter service is available to the application:

```
if ([SLComposeViewController
isAvailableForServiceType:SLServiceTypeTwitter])
{
        // Device is able to send a Twitter message
}
```

This method call is optional and, in the event that an account for the specified social network has yet to be set up, the composer will simply take the user to the device's *Settings* application where a Twitter account may be configured.

The next step is to create an instance of the SLComposeViewController class and supply an optional completion handler to be called when the composer screen is either cancelled by the user or used to send a message. Next, a range of methods may be called on the instance to initialize the object with the content of the message, including the initial text of the message, an image attachment and a URL:

- **setInitialText:** - Sets the initial text of the message on the SLComposeViewController instance.
- **addImage:** - Adds image files as attachments to the message.
- **addURL:** - Adds a URL to the message. The method automatically handles the URL shortening.

Each of the above methods returns a Boolean result indicating whether the addition of content was successful.

Finally, when the message is ready to be presented to the user, the SLComposeViewController object is presented modally by calling the *presentViewController:* method of the parent view controller.

The following code excerpt demonstrates the steps to create, configure and present a typical SLComposeViewController instance for posting to Facebook:

```
SLComposeViewController *composeController = [SLComposeViewController
        composeViewControllerForServiceType:SLServiceTypeFacebook];

[composeController setInitialText:@"Just found this great website"];
[composeController addImage:postImage.image];
[composeController addURL: [NSURL URLWithString:
        @"http://www.ebookfrenzy.com"]];

[self presentViewController:composeController
        animated:YES completion:nil];
```

Once called, this method will present the composer view to the user primed with any text, image and URL contents pre-configured via the method calls. Once displayed, the user has the option to modify the text of the message, cancel the message, add location data or send the message. If a completion handler has been configured it will be called and passed a value indicating the action that was taken by the user within the composer view. Possible values are:

- **SLComposeViewControllerResultCancelled** – The user cancelled the composition session by touching the *Cancel* button.
- **SLComposeViewControllerResultDone** – The user sent the composed message by touching the *Send* button.

70.6 Summary

iOS 6 introduced both the UIActivityViewController class and Social Framework, both of which may be used to integrate Twitter, Facebook and Sina Weibo functionality into iOS 6 applications.

For general purpose requirements, both the UIActivityViewController and the SLComposeViewController classes provide an easy to implement path to social network integration. For more complex requirements, however, the SLRequest class may be used in conjunction with the Accounts framework to access social network accounts and construct and submit HTTP requests to supported social network APIs. This chapter provided an overview of the UIActivityViewController and SLComposeViewController classes and outlined the steps necessary to deploy them in applications. The next chapter, entitled *An iPhone iOS 6 Facebook Integration Tutorial using UIActivityViewController* will work through the development of an example application using the UIActivityViewController class to implement Facebook integration into an iOS 6 based iPhone app. The concepts behind the SLRequest class will be covered in *iPhone iOS 6 Facebook and Twitter Integration Tutorial using SLRequest*.

Chapter 71

71. An iPhone iOS 6 Facebook Integration Tutorial using UIActivityViewController

With the basics of the iOS 6 Social Framework and UIActivityViewController class covered in the previous chapter, the goal of this chapter will be to create an example application designed to demonstrate the UIActivityViewController class in action. The end result will be an application designed to post status updates to the iPhone user's Facebook page, including text and an image.

71.1 Creating the Facebook Social App

Begin by launching Xcode and selecting the options to create a new iPhone iOS application based on the *Single View Application* template. Enter *SocialApp* as the product name and class prefix, set the device to *iPhone* and select the *Use Storyboards* and *Use Automatic Reference Counting* options if they are not already selected.

71.2 Designing the User Interface

Navigate to the *MainStoryboard.storyboard* file in the project navigator panel and select it to load it into to the editing panel. Click on the background of the view object and change the background color to a light shade of grey using the Attribute Inspector panel.

Drag, position and configure a Text View, Image View and two Buttons on the view canvas so that the user interface reflects that illustrated in Figure 71-1:

An iPhone iOS 6 Facebook Integration Tutorial using UIActivityViewController

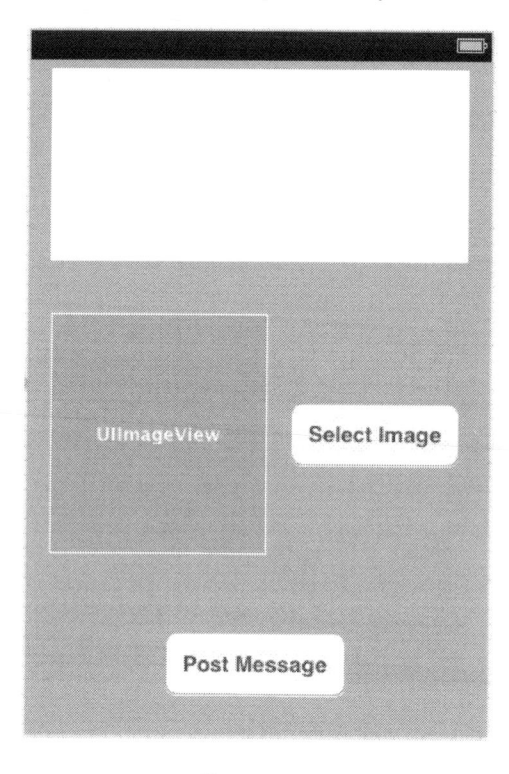

Figure 71-1

Note that the sample Latin text has been removed from the text view object (select the object, display the Attribute Inspector and delete the contents assigned to the *Text* property).

Select the Image View object, display the Attributes Inspector and change the *Mode* setting to *Aspect Fit*. This will ensure that the aspect ratio of the image is preserved when displayed in the image view.

71.3 Creating Outlets and Actions

In order to create the outlets and actions for the application we will, as always, make use of the Assistant Editor. First, select the Text View object and then display the editor using *View -> Assistant Editor -> Show Assistant Editor* menu option. Alternatively, it may also be displayed by selecting the center button (the one containing an image of a bow tie and tuxedo) of the row of Editor toolbar buttons in the top right hand corner of the main Xcode window.

Ctrl-click on the Text View object in the view and drag the resulting line to the area immediately beneath the @interface directive in the Assistant Editor panel. Upon releasing the line, the configuration panel will appear. Configure the connection as an *Outlet* named *postText* and click on the *Connect* button. Repeat the above steps to add an outlet for the Image View object named *postImage*.

An iPhone iOS 6 Facebook Integration Tutorial using UIActivityViewController

The application will require three actions. One for each of the button objects and one for the background view that will be used to hide the keyboard when the user has finished entering text. Ctrl-click on the *Select Image* button and drag the resulting line to a position beneath the new outlets previously declared in the Assistant Editor. In the resulting configuration panel, change the *Connection* type to *Action* and name the method *selectImage*. Repeat this step to add an action for the *Post Message* button, this time naming the action *sendPost*.

In order to assign an action to the View object, it will need to be changed so that it is a subclass of UIControl. Click on the background of the view, display the Identity Inspector (*View -> Utilities -> Show Identity Inspector*) and change the object's class from UIView to UIControl. Having changed the class, Ctrl-click on the view background and drag to a position beneath the other actions in the Assistant Editor panel and declare an action connection named *hideKeyboard* for the *Touch Down* event.

Once the connections have been established, select the *SocialAppViewController.h* file and further modify it to configure the class to act as an image picker delegate and to add some imports that will be required later in the tutorial:

```
#import <UIKit/UIKit.h>
#import <Social/Social.h>
#import <MobileCoreServices/MobileCoreServices.h>

@interface SocialAppViewController : UIViewController
<UIImagePickerControllerDelegate, UINavigationControllerDelegate>

@property (strong, nonatomic) IBOutlet UITextView *postText;
@property (strong, nonatomic) IBOutlet UIImageView *postImage;
- (IBAction)selectImage:(id)sender;
- (IBAction)sendPost:(id)sender;
- (IBAction)hideKeyboard:(id)sender;

@end
```

71.4 Implementing the selectImage and Delegate Methods

The purpose of the *selectImage* action method is to provide the user with access to photos on the device and allow one to be selected for inclusion in the Facebook post. With these requirements in mind, select the *SocialAppViewController.m* file, locate the *selectImage* stub added by the Assistant editor and modify it as follows:

```
- (IBAction)selectImage:(id)sender {
    if ([UIImagePickerController isSourceTypeAvailable:
        UIImagePickerControllerSourceTypeSavedPhotosAlbum])
```

An iPhone iOS 6 Facebook Integration Tutorial using UIActivityViewController

```objc
{
    UIImagePickerController *imagePicker =
    [[UIImagePickerController alloc] init];
    imagePicker.delegate = self;
    imagePicker.sourceType =
    UIImagePickerControllerSourceTypePhotoLibrary;
    imagePicker.mediaTypes = @[(NSString *) kUTTypeImage];
    imagePicker.allowsEditing = NO;
    [self presentViewController:imagePicker
        animated:YES completion:nil];
}
}
```

Next, add the other image picker delegate methods so that the picker is dismissed when the user has made a selection:

```objc
#pragma mark -
#pragma mark UIImagePickerControllerDelegate

-(void)imagePickerController:(UIImagePickerController *)picker
didFinishPickingMediaWithInfo:(NSDictionary *)info
{
    NSString *mediaType = info[UIImagePickerControllerMediaType];
    [self dismissViewControllerAnimated:YES completion:nil];
    if ([mediaType isEqualToString:(NSString *)kUTTypeImage]) {
        UIImage *image =
                info[UIImagePickerControllerOriginalImage];

        _postImage.image = image;
    }
}

-(void)imagePickerControllerDidCancel:(UIImagePickerController *)picker
{
    [self dismissViewControllerAnimated:YES completion:nil];
}
```

71.5 Hiding the Keyboard

When the user touches the view object in the background of the user interface, we need the keyboard to be removed from view. This will require that code be implemented in the *hideKeyboard* action method stub:

```objc
- (IBAction)hideKeyboard:(id)sender {
```

```
    [_postText resignFirstResponder];
}
```

71.6 Posting the Message to Facebook

All that remains is to implement the code to instantiate a UIActivityViewController instance, prime it with the text and image entered by the user and then post the message to the user's Facebook page. These tasks are to be performed within the *sendPost* action method. Within the *SocialAppViewController*.m file, locate the stub for this method and modify it as follows:

```
- (IBAction)sendPost:(id)sender {
    NSArray *activityItems;

    if (_postImage.image != nil) {
        activityItems = @[_postText.text, _postImage.image];
    } else {
        activityItems = @[_postText.text];
    }

    UIActivityViewController *activityController =
                [[UIActivityViewController alloc]
                initWithActivityItems:activityItems
                applicationActivities:nil];

    [self presentViewController:activityController
                animated:YES completion:nil];
}
```

The code simply creates an array of items to be included in the post (in this case the text entered by the user and an image in the event that one was selected), creates a UIActivityViewController instance initialized with that array and presents the controller to the user.

71.7 Adding the Social Framework to the Build Phases

Whilst the coding is complete, an attempt to compile the application at this point will result in undefined symbols because the Social Framework and Mobile Core Services libraries have not yet been added to the project. Within the project navigator panel, therefore, select the *SocialApp* target at the top of the list and in the main panel select the *Build Phases* tab. In the *Link Binary with Libraries* category, click on the + button and in the resulting list of libraries select and add the *Social.framework* library. Repeat this step to also add the *MobileCoreServices.framework* library to the project.

An iPhone iOS 6 Facebook Integration Tutorial using UIActivityViewController

71.8 Running the Social Application

With the coding now complete, click on the Run button in the Xcode toolbar to launch the application either on an iPhone device or using the Simulator environment. When the application appears, enter some text into the text area and select an image from the device (note that when using the simulator no images will be available). Touch the *Post Message* button to display the target selection screen shown in Figure 71-2:

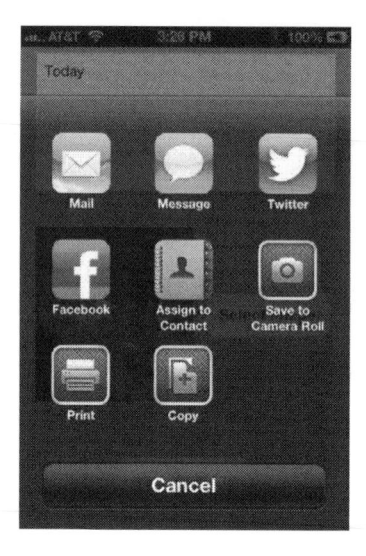

Figure 71-2

Select the Facebook button to display the preview sheet (Figure 71-3) and then, assuming no changes to the post need to be made, touch the *Post* button to send the message to your Facebook page.

An iPhone iOS 6 Facebook Integration Tutorial using UIActivityViewController

Figure 71-3

71.9 Summary

This chapter has worked through the creation of an example application that uses the UIActivityViewController class to post updates to the user's Facebook page. The next chapter will look in more detail at using both the Accounts and Social Frameworks to implement social network integration using the SLRequest class.

563

Chapter 72

72. iPhone iOS 6 Facebook and Twitter Integration using SLRequest

Whilst the UIActivityViewController and SLComposeViewController classes provide a quick and easy way to integrate social network interaction to iOS applications, these classes lack the flexibility that might be required to implement more advanced integration. Perhaps the most significant shortcoming of these classes is the fact that they implement one-way communication with social networks. In other words, they can be used to post information to a social network, but do not provide a way to receive information, such as the entries in the timeline of a Twitter or Facebook account.

In recognition of this fact, Apple introduced the SLRequest class as part of the Social Framework included with iOS 6. Using the SLRequest class, in conjunction with the Accounts framework, it is possible to construct HTTP based requests and send them to the application programming interfaces (APIs) of Twitter, Facebook and Sina Weibo and receive data in response. This, in essence, allows an iOS application to perform just about any task allowed by the API of the respective social network service.

This chapter will provide an overview of the way in which the SLRequest class and the Accounts framework interact to provide social media integration. Once these basics have been covered, the next chapter will work through the implementation of an example application that uses SLRequest to query the entries in a Twitter timeline.

72.1 Using SLRequest and the Account Framework

Both the SLRequest class and the Accounts framework are required in order to interact with the API of a social network. Implementation follows a standard sequence of events which can be summarized as follows:

1. The application requests access to one of the user's social network accounts as configured in the Settings app. This is achieved via a call to the *requestAccessToAccountsWithType:* method of the ACAccountStore class, passing through as an argument the type of social network for which access is being requested together with a range of options depending on the target service.

2. An SLRequest instance is created and initialized with the URL required by the service for interaction, the HTTP request type to be used (GET, POST etc) and any additional parameters required by the API of the service.

3. The *account object* created in step 1 above is assigned to the *account* property of the SLRequest object created in step 2.

4. The request is sent to the target social network service via a call to the *performRequestWithHandler:* method of the SLRequest object. The results from the request are passed to the handler code together with an Error object containing information about the reason for any failure.

72.2 Twitter Integration using SLRequest

Integration with the Twitter API begins with gaining access to an account, and is based on the assumption that at least one Twitter account has been configured via the Settings app on the device. Since iOS 6 supports different social networks, the request must also include the type of social network for which access is being requested. This, in turn, is represented by an appropriately configured ACAccountType object.

The following code, for example, seeks access to the Twitter accounts configured on the device:

```
ACAccountStore *account = [[ACAccountStore alloc] init];
ACAccountType *accountType = [account
accountTypeWithAccountTypeIdentifier:
            ACAccountTypeIdentifierTwitter];

[account requestAccessToAccountsWithType:accountType
            options:nil
            completion:^(BOOL granted, NSError *error)
{
        if (granted == YES)
        {
                // Get account and communicate with Twitter API
        }
}];
}
```

In the event that access is granted, an array of Twitter accounts on the device can be obtained via a subsequent call to the *accountsWithAccountType:* method of the account object used for the request. The required account may then be extracted from the array of accounts for use in constructing an SLRequest object. The following code accesses the array of accounts, selects the last account entry and assigns it to *twitterAccount*:

iPhone iOS 6 Facebook and Twitter Integration using SLRequest

```
ACAccountStore *account = [[ACAccountStore alloc] init];
ACAccountType *accountType = [account
accountTypeWithAccountTypeIdentifier:
            ACAccountTypeIdentifierTwitter];

[account requestAccessToAccountsWithType:accountType options:nil
        completion:^(BOOL granted, NSError *error)
{
    if (granted == YES)
    {
        NSArray *arrayOfAccounts = [account
                accountsWithAccountType:accountType];

        if ([arrayOfAccounts count] > 0)
        {
            ACAccount *twitterAccount =
                [arrayOfAccounts lastObject];
        }
    }];
}
```

The next task is to request an SLRequest object for Twitter access. This is achieved via a call to the *requestForServiceType:* class method of the SLRequest class, passing through the following values:

- The type of social network service for which the SLRequest will be used (in this case SLServiceTypeTwitter)
- The HTTP request method type (SLRequestMethodPOST, SLRequestMethodGET or SLRequestMethodDELETE)
- The URL required by the social network API for interaction
- An NSDictionary object containing any parameters required by the social network API to complete the transaction.

The following code changes request an SLRequest instance configured for sending a Twitter update containing the text "My first Twitter post from iOS 6":

```
ACAccountStore *account = [[ACAccountStore alloc] init];
ACAccountType *accountType = [account
accountTypeWithAccountTypeIdentifier:
            ACAccountTypeIdentifierTwitter];

[account requestAccessToAccountsWithType:accountType options:nil
        completion:^(BOOL granted, NSError *error)
{
```

567

```objc
        if (granted == YES)
        {
            NSArray *arrayOfAccounts = [account
                    accountsWithAccountType:accountType];

            if ([arrayOfAccounts count] > 0)
            {
               ACAccount *twitterAccount =
                    [arrayOfAccounts lastObject];

                NSDictionary *message = @{@"status": @"My First Twitter post from iOS 6"};

                NSURL *requestURL = [NSURL
           URLWithString:@"http://api.twitter.com/1/statuses/update.json"];

                SLRequest *postRequest = [SLRequest
                    requestForServiceType:SLServiceTypeTwitter
                    requestMethod:SLRequestMethodPOST
                    URL:requestURL parameters:message];
            }
     }];
}
```

Finally, the account object needs to be assigned to the SLRequest object, and the request posted to the Twitter API:

```objc
ACAccountStore *account = [[ACAccountStore alloc] init];
ACAccountType *accountType = [account
accountTypeWithAccountTypeIdentifier:
            ACAccountTypeIdentifierTwitter];

[account requestAccessToAccountsWithType:accountType options:nil
            completion:^(BOOL granted, NSError *error)
{
    if (granted == YES)
    {
        NSArray *arrayOfAccounts = [account
                accountsWithAccountType:accountType];

        if ([arrayOfAccounts count] > 0)
        {
           ACAccount *twitterAccount =
                [arrayOfAccounts lastObject];
```

```
            NSDictionary *message = @{@"status": @"My First Twitter
post from iOS6"};

            NSURL *requestURL = [NSURL
URLWithString:@"http://api.twitter.com/1/statuses/update.json"];

            SLRequest *postRequest = [SLRequest
                requestForServiceType:SLServiceTypeTwitter
                    requestMethod:SLRequestMethodPOST
                    URL:requestURL parameters:message];

            postRequest.account = twitterAccount;

            [postRequest
                performRequestWithHandler:^(NSData *responseData,
                NSHTTPURLResponse *urlResponse, NSError *error)
            {
                NSLog(@"Twitter HTTP response: %i",
                    [urlResponse statusCode]);
            }];
        }
    }
}];
```

For the purposes of this example, the handler for the *performRequestWithHandler:* method simply outputs the HTTP response code for the request to the console.

The above coding example demonstrates the steps involved in posting an update to a Twitter account using SLRequest. In the next chapter, an example application will be created that requests entries from the timeline of a Twitter account and displays those results in the TableView object.

For more information about the Twitter API, refer to the online documentation at:

https://dev.twitter.com/docs

72.3 Facebook Integration using SLRequest

To all intents and purposes, the steps to integrate with Facebook are the same as those for accessing Twitter with one or two significant differences. Firstly, any iOS application requiring access to the Facebook API must first be registered in the Facebook developer portal (*http://developers.facebook.com*). Registration includes providing the iOS bundle ID of the application (as defined when the application was created in Xcode). Once registered, the app will be assigned a Facebook App ID which must be referenced when seeking account access.

iPhone iOS 6 Facebook and Twitter Integration using SLRequest

Additionally, the application may also declare the access permissions it requires whilst interacting with the API. A full list of permission options is available in the Facebook developer documentation online at:

https://developers.facebook.com/docs/authentication/permissions/.

These permissions are declared using the ACFacebookPermission key. When defining permissions, the ACFacebookAudienceKey value must also be declared and set to one of the following values:

- ACFacebookAudienceEveryone
- ACFacebookAudienceFriends
- ACFacebookAudienceOnlyMe.

The following code demonstrates the steps involved in posting a message to the user's Facebook page:

```
ACAccountStore *accountStore = [[ACAccountStore alloc] init];

ACAccountType *facebookAccountType = [self.accountStore
    accountTypeWithAccountTypeIdentifier:
        ACAccountTypeIdentifierFacebook];

// Specify App ID and permissions
NSDictionary *options = @{
    ACFacebookAppIdKey: @"012345678912345",
    ACFacebookPermissionsKey: @[@"publish_stream",
                                @"publish_actions"],
    ACFacebookAudeinceKey: ACFacebookAudienceFriends
};

[accountStore requestAccessToAccountsWithType:facebookAccountType
    options:options completion:^(BOOL granted, NSError *e) {
        if (granted) {
            NSArray *accounts = [self.accountStore
                accountsWithAccountType:facebookAccountType];
            facebookAccount = [accounts lastObject];
        }
        else
        {
            // Handle Failure
        }
}];
```

iPhone iOS 6 Facebook and Twitter Integration using SLRequest

```
NSDictionary *parameters = @{@"message": @"My first iOS 6 Facebook posting "};

NSURL *feedURL = [NSURL
URLWithString:@"https://graph.facebook.com/me/feed"];

SLRequest *feedRequest = [SLRequest
        requestForServiceType:SLServiceTypeFacebook
        requestMethod:SLRequestMethodPOST
        URL:feedURL
        parameters:parameters];

    feedRequest.account = self.facebookAccount;

    [feedRequest
        performRequestWithHandler:^(NSData *responseData,
        NSHTTPURLResponse *urlResponse, NSError *error)
    {
        // Handle response
    }];
```

When incorporated into an iOS 6 application, the above code will cause a message to be posted to the user's Facebook account which reads "My first iOS 6 Facebook posting".

Additional information on the Facebook API can be found online at https://developers.facebook.com/docs.

72.4 Summary

Whilst the SLComposeViewController and UIActivityViewController classes provide an easy path to social network integration, they lack the flexibility and two-way communication needed by many applications. In order to gain greater flexibility in terms of integration, iOS 6 introduced the SLRequest class.

The goal of this chapter has been to provide a low level overview of the way in which the Accounts framework and iOS 6 SLRequest class can be used together to access and interact with Twitter and Facebook accounts using the service APIs of those social networks.

Chapter 73

73. An iOS 6 iPhone Twitter Integration Tutorial using SLRequest

Having covered much of the theory of using the Accounts framework and SLRequest class to integrate social networks into iOS 6 iPhone applications in the previous chapter, this chapter will put this theory into practice by creating an application to request and display the entries in the timeline of a Twitter account.

73.1 Creating the TwitterApp Project

Begin by launching Xcode and selecting the options to create a new iPhone iOS application based on the *Single View Application* template. Enter *TwitterApp* as the product name and class prefix, set the device to *iPhone* and select the *Use Storyboards* and *Use Automatic Reference Counting* options if they are not already selected.

73.2 Designing the User Interface

Navigate to the *MainStoryboard.storyboard* file in the project navigator panel and select it to load it into to the editing panel. From the Object Library panel, drag and drop a Table View component onto the view canvas and position it so that fills the entire view space as shown in Figure 73-1.

Select the Table View object and display the Assistant Editor using *View -> Assistant Editor -> Show Assistant Editor* menu option. Ctrl-click on the Table View object in the view and drag the resulting line to the area immediately beneath the @interface directive in the Assistant Editor panel. Upon releasing the line, the connection panel will appear. Configure the connection as an *Outlet* named *tweetTableView* and click on the *Connect* button.

An iOS 6 iPhone Twitter Integration Tutorial using SLRequest

Figure 73-1

With the Table View still selected, display the Connections Inspector (*View -> Utilities -> Show Connections Inspector*). Click on the circle to the right of the *dataSource* outlet and drag the line to the *Twitter App View Controller* entry in the *Twitter App View Controller Scene* in the document outline panel as illustrated in Figure 73-2:

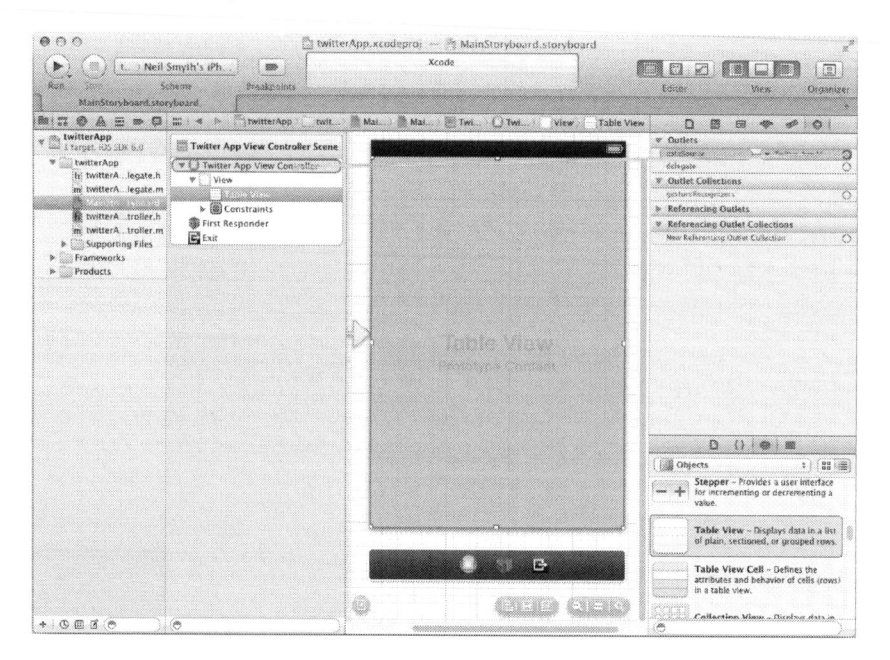

Figure 73-2

Repeat the steps to establish the same connection for the *delegate* outlet.

An iOS 6 iPhone Twitter Integration Tutorial using SLRequest

73.3 Modifying the Interface File

Before writing code to talk to the Twitter API, some additional files need to be imported to avoid undefined symbols when we start working with the Accounts and SLRequest classes. In addition, an array is going to be needed to act as the data source for the application which will ultimately contain the tweets that are returned by the Twitter API. The compiler also needs to be notified that this class is acting as both the data source and delegate for the Table View.

Select the *TwitterAppViewController.h* file and modify it as follows:

```objc
#import <UIKit/UIKit.h>
#import <Accounts/Accounts.h>
#import <Social/Social.h>

@interface TwitterAppViewController : UIViewController
<UITableViewDataSource, UITableViewDelegate>

@property (strong, nonatomic) IBOutlet UITableView *tweetTableView;
@property (strong, nonatomic) NSArray *dataSource;
@end
```

73.4 Accessing the Twitter API

The code to access the Twitter account and extract the posts from the account timeline will reside in a method named *getTimeLine:* located in the *TwitterAppViewController.m* file. Select this file and modify it to add the code for this new method:

```objc
- (void)getTimeLine {
    ACAccountStore *account = [[ACAccountStore alloc] init];
    ACAccountType *accountType = [account
accountTypeWithAccountTypeIdentifier:ACAccountTypeIdentifierTwitter];

    [account requestAccessToAccountsWithType:accountType
      options:nil completion:^(BOOL granted, NSError *error)
    {
        if (granted == YES)
        {
            NSArray *arrayOfAccounts = [account
                    accountsWithAccountType:accountType];

            if ([arrayOfAccounts count] > 0)
            {
                ACAccount *twitterAccount =
```

An iOS 6 iPhone Twitter Integration Tutorial using SLRequest

```objc
                [arrayOfAccounts lastObject];

            NSURL *requestURL = [NSURL 
URLWithString:@"http://api.twitter.com/1/statuses/home_timeline.json"];

            NSMutableDictionary *parameters = 
                [[NSMutableDictionary alloc] init];
            [parameters setObject:@"20" forKey:@"count"];
            [parameters setObject:@"1" 
forKey:@"include_entities"];

            SLRequest *postRequest = [SLRequest 
                requestForServiceType:SLServiceTypeTwitter
                requestMethod:SLRequestMethodGET
                URL:requestURL parameters:parameters];

            postRequest.account = twitterAccount;

            [postRequest performRequestWithHandler:
                ^(NSData *responseData, NSHTTPURLResponse 
                *urlResponse, NSError *error)
                {
                    self.dataSource = [NSJSONSerialization 
                        JSONObjectWithData:responseData
                        options:NSJSONReadingMutableLeaves 
                        error:&error];

                    if (self.dataSource.count != 0) {
                        dispatch_async(dispatch_get_main_queue(), ^{
                            [self.tweetTableView reloadData];
                        });
                    }
                }];
            }
        } else {
            // Handle failure to get account access
        }
    }];
}
```

Much of the code in this method will be familiar from the previous chapter. There are, however, some notable exceptions. Firstly, the URL used in the request is intended to return the entries in the time line of the user's Twitter account:

```
NSURL *requestURL = [NSURL
URLWithString:@"http://api.twitter.com/1/statuses/home_timeline.json"];
```

The URL specified requires additional parameters specifying how much data is to be returned. In this case the request is limited to the 20 most recent posts and configured to include the tweet entities:

```
NSMutableDictionary *parameters =
                [[NSMutableDictionary alloc] init];
            [parameters setObject:@"20" forKey:@"count"];
            [parameters setObject:@"1"
forKey:@"include_entities"];
```

The SLRequest object is primed to use the *SLRequestMethodGET* HTTP method. This is appropriate since this time we are *getting*, as opposed to *posting*, data:

```
SLRequest *postRequest = [SLRequest
                requestForServiceType:SLServiceTypeTwitter
                requestMethod:SLRequestMethodGET
                URL:requestURL parameters:parameters];
```

Finally, the handler code for the *postRequest:* method call now accesses the returned NSData object. The NSJSONSerialization class is then used to parse and serialize the data returned and assign it to the dataSource NSArray object. The Table View object is then told to reload the data it is displaying, causing it to re-read the data in the dataSource array and display it to the user. An important point to note here is that iOS performs the Twitter API request in a different thread from the main thread of the application. Threads are the cornerstone of any multitasking operating system and can be thought of as mini-processes running within a main process, the purpose of which is to enable at least the appearance of parallel execution paths within applications.

Since user interface updates take place in the main thread of the application, code has been added to ensure that the Table View reload call is made in the main thread as opposed to the thread used for the post request:

```
[postRequest performRequestWithHandler:
            ^(NSData *responseData, NSHTTPURLResponse
            *urlResponse, NSError *error)
        {
            self.dataSource = [NSJSONSerialization
                JSONObjectWithData:responseData
                options:NSJSONReadingMutableLeaves
                error:&error];

            if (self.dataSource.count != 0) {
                dispatch_async(dispatch_get_main_queue(), ^{
```

An iOS 6 iPhone Twitter Integration Tutorial using SLRequest

```
                [self.tweetTableView reloadData];
            });
        }
    }];
```

All that remains is to implement the delegate methods for the Table View so that the tweets are displayed to the user.

73.5 Calling the getTimeLine Method

Having implemented the *getTimeLine* method we need to make sure it gets called when the application is launched. This involves the addition of a single line of code to the *viewDidLoad:* method located in the *TwitterAppViewController.m* file:

```
- (void)viewDidLoad
{
    [super viewDidLoad];
    [self getTimeLine];
}
```

73.6 The Table View Delegate Methods

At a minimum, the delegate for a Table View must implement the *numberOfRowsInSection:* and *cellForRowAtIndexPath:* delegate methods. In terms of this example application, the former simply needs to return the number of items in the dataSource array. Remaining within the *TwitterAppViewController.m* file, therefore, implement this method as follows:

```
#pragma mark -
#pragma mark UITableViewDataSource

- (NSInteger)tableView:(UITableView *)tableView
numberOfRowsInSection:(NSInteger)section {
    return _dataSource.count;
}
```

The *cellForRowAtIndexPath:* method, on the other hand, needs to extract the text of the tweet corresponding to the current table row from the dataSource array and assign it to the table cell. Since each tweet is stored in the array in the form of an NSDictionary object, the tweet object first needs to be extracted and then the entry matching the "text" key in the dictionary used to access the text:

```
- (UITableViewCell *)tableView:(UITableView *)tableView
cellForRowAtIndexPath:(NSIndexPath *)indexPath {
```

```
    static NSString *CellIdentifier = @"Cell";

    UITableViewCell *cell = [self.tweetTableView
            dequeueReusableCellWithIdentifier:CellIdentifier];

    if (cell == nil) {
        cell = [[UITableViewCell alloc]
                initWithStyle:UITableViewCellStyleDefault
                reuseIdentifier:CellIdentifier];
    }

    NSDictionary *tweet = _dataSource[[indexPath row]];

    cell.textLabel.text = tweet[@"text"];
    return cell;
}
```

73.7 Adding the Account and Social Frameworks to the Build Phases

Within the project navigator panel, select the *TwitterApp* target at the top of the list and in the main panel select the *Build Phases* tab. In the *Link Binary with Libraries* category, click on the + button and in the resulting list of libraries, search for and add the *Social.framework* library. Repeat this step to also add the *Accounts.framework* library.

73.8 Building and Running the Application

Click on the Run button located in the Xcode toolbar and wait for the application to launch either on a physical iPhone device or the iOS Simulator. Assuming a Twitter account has been configured, the application will display the 20 most recent tweets posted to that account.

An iOS 6 iPhone Twitter Integration Tutorial using SLRequest

Figure 73-3

73.9 Summary

In addition to posting entries, the SLRequest class can used to retrieve information from supported social networks. In this chapter, a list of tweets posted to a Twitter account have been requested using the SLRequest class and displayed to the user within a Table View. The example also introduced the use of the NSJSONSerialization class to serialize the data returned from a Twitter API request.

Chapter 74

74. Making Store Purchases with the SKStoreProductViewController Class

For quite some time, the iOS SDK has included the Store Kit Framework, the purpose of which is to enable applications to implement what are referred to as "in-app purchases". This typically provides a mechanism for application developers to charge users for additional items and services over and above the initial purchase price of the application. Typical examples include purchasing access to higher levels in a game or a monthly subscription to premium content.

The Store Kit Framework has also traditionally provided the ability to enable users to purchase items from Apple's iTunes, App and iBook stores. Prior to the introduction of iOS6, the Store Kit Framework took the user out of the current application and into the iTunes application to initiate and complete an iTunes Store purchase. iOS 6, however, introduces a new view controller class (SKStoreProductViewController) which presents the store product directly within the application using a pre-configured view.

This chapter will provide an overview of the SKStoreProductViewController class before working through an example implementation of this class in an iPhone application.

74.1 The SKStoreProductViewController Class

The SKStoreProductViewController class makes it possible to integrate purchasing from Apple's iTunes, App and iBooks stores directly into iOS 6 applications with minimal coding work. The developer of a music review application, might, for example want to provide the user with the option to purchase an album from iTunes after reading a review in the application. The developer of multiple applications may want to encourage users of one of those applications to purchase related applications.

All that is required to implement the SKStoreProductViewController functionality is to initialize an instance of the class with an item ID for the product to be purchased from the store and then to load the product details. Once product details have been loaded, the view controller is presented to the user.

Making Store Purchases with the SKStoreProductViewController Class

Product item IDs can be obtained a number of ways. For specific items, the ID can be obtained by locating the product in iTunes and Ctrl-clicking (or right-clicking on Windows) on the product image. In the resulting menu, select the option to copy the URL. Paste the URL into a text editor and extract the ID from the end. The ID from the following URL, for example, is 527049179.

```
http://itunes.apple.com/us/movie/the-pirates!-band-of-
misfits/id527049179
```

Alternatively, searches may be performed on a variety of criteria using the Apple Search API, details of which can be found at the following URL:

http://www.apple.com/itunes/affiliates/resources/documentation/itunes-store-web-service-search-api.html.

When the user has finished in the store view, a delegate method is called to notify the application, at which point the store view controller can be dismissed.

The remainder of this chapter will work through the creation of a simple example application to demonstrate the use and implementation of the SKStoreProductViewController class.

74.2 Creating the Example Project

The example application created in this chapter will consist of a single button which, when touched, will display the store kit view controller primed with a specified product.

Launch Xcode and create a new project by selecting the options to create a new iPhone iOS application based on the *Single View Application* template. Enter *StoreKitDemo* as the product name and class prefix, set the device to *iPhone* and select the *Use Storyboards* and *Use Automatic Reference Counting* options if they are not already selected.

74.3 Creating the User Interface

Within the project navigator panel, select the *MainStoryboard.storyboard* file and drag and drop a Button from the Object Library to the center of the view. Double click on the button text and change it to "Buy Now" so that the layout matches Figure 74-1.

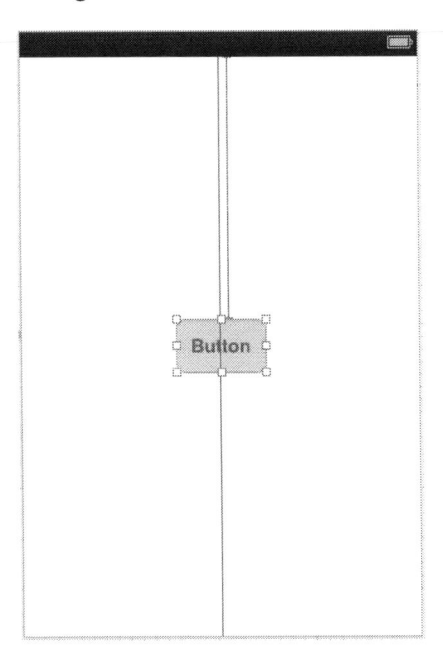

Figure 74-1

Display the Assistant Editor and make sure it is showing the code for the *StoreKitDemoViewController.h* file. Select the button in the view and then Ctrl-click on it and drag the resulting line to a location just beneath the @interface line in the Assistant Editor panel. Release the line and in the resulting panel change the connection type to *Action* and name the method *showStoreView*. Click on the *Connect* button and close the Assistant Editor panel.

74.4 Displaying the Store Kit Product View Controller

When the user touches the *Buy Now* button, the SKStoreProductViewController instance needs to be created, configured and displayed. Before writing this code, however, it will be necessary to declare the StoreKitDemoViewController class as implementing the <SKStoreProductViewControllerDelegate> protocol. The <StoreKit/StoreKit.h> file also needs to be imported. Both of these tasks need to be performed in the *StoreKitDemoViewController.h* file which should be modified to read as follows:

```
#import <UIKit/UIKit.h>
#import <StoreKit/StoreKit.h>

@interface StoreKitDemoViewController : UIViewController
<SKStoreProductViewControllerDelegate>

- (IBAction)showStoreView:(id)sender;
@end
```

Making Store Purchases with the SKStoreProductViewController Class

Within the *StoreKitDemoViewController.m* file, locate the stub *showStoreView* method and implement the code as outlined in the following listing:

```
- (IBAction)showStoreView:(id)sender {

        SKStoreProductViewController *storeViewController =
            [[SKStoreProductViewController alloc] init];

        storeViewController.delegate = self;

        NSDictionary *parameters =
            @{SKStoreProductParameterITunesItemIdentifier:
                [NSNumber numberWithInteger:333700869]};

        [storeViewController loadProductWithParameters:parameters
            completionBlock:^(BOOL result, NSError *error) {
            if (result)
                [self presentViewController:storeViewController
                                animated:YES
                                completion:nil];
        }];

}
```

The code begins by creating and initializing a new SKStoreProductViewController instance:

```
SKStoreProductViewController *storeViewController =
                [[SKStoreProductViewController alloc] init];
```

Next, the view controller class assigns itself as the delegate for the storeViewController instance:

```
storeViewController.delegate = self;
```

An NSDictionary instance is then created and initialized with a key of *SKStoreProductParameterITunesItemIdentifier* associated with an NSNumber value representing a product in a Store (in this case an album in the iTunes store).

```
NSDictionary *parameters =
            @{SKStoreProductParameterITunesItemIdentifier:
                [NSNumber numberWithInteger:333700869]};
```

Finally, the product is loaded into the view controller and, in event that the load was successful, the view controller is presented to the user:

```
[storeViewController loadProductWithParameters:parameters
```

584

```
            completionBlock:^(BOOL result, NSError *error) {
          if (result)
              [self presentViewController:storeViewController
                              animated:YES
                            completion:nil];
}];
```

74.5 Implementing the Delegate Method

All that remains is to implement the delegate method that will be called when the user has either completed or cancelled the product purchase. Since the StoreKitDemoViewController class was designated as the delegate for the SKStoreProductViewController instance, the method needs to be implemented in the *StoreKitDemoViewController.m* file:

```
#pragma mark -
#pragma mark SKStoreProductViewControllerDelegate

-(void)productViewControllerDidFinish:(SKStoreProductViewController
*)viewController
{
    [viewController dismissViewControllerAnimated:YES completion:nil];
}
```

For the purposes of this example, all the method needs to do is to tell the view controller to dismiss itself.

74.6 Adding the Store Kit Framework to the Build Phases

Within the project navigator panel, select the *StoreKitDemo* target at the top of the list and in the main panel select the *Build Phases* tab. In the *Link Binary with Libraries* category, click on the + button and in the resulting list of libraries search for and add the *StoreKit.framework* library.

74.7 Testing the Application

Build and run the application either on a physical iPhone device or using the iOS Simulator. Touch the button and wait until the store kit product view controller appears as illustrated in Figure 74-2. Note that there may be a short delay while the store kit contacts the iTunes store to request and download the product information.

Touching the *Cancel* button should trigger the delegate, dismissing the view controller and returning the user to the original view controller screen containing the button.

Making Store Purchases with the SKStoreProductViewController Class

Figure 74-2

Edit the code for the *showStoreView:* method and modify the item ID from 333700869 (an iTunes Store product) with 435744790 (an iBook Store product). Re-run the application and note that the view controller class has changed layout automatically to accommodate a book product (Figure 74-3).

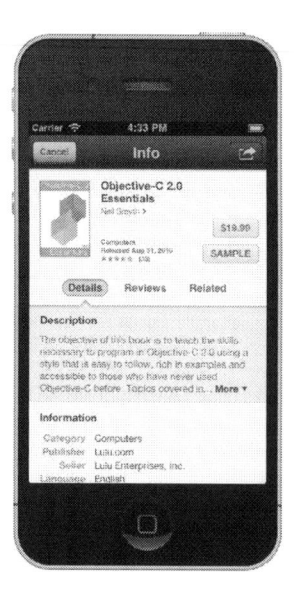

Figure 74-3

The class, will, of course, adapt similarly when passed the ID of an app or movie.

74.8 Summary

The SKStoreProductViewController class is new to iOS 6 and provides an easy and visually appealing interface for allowing Apple-based store purchases such as movies, books, music and apps to be made directly from within an iOS application. As demonstrated, this functionality can be added to an application with a minimal amount of code.

Chapter 75

75. Building In-App Purchasing into iPhone iOS 6 Applications

The previous chapter explored the mechanism for allowing users to purchase items from Apple's iTunes, App and iBooks stores from within an application. A far more common requirement for application developers, however, is the need to generate revenue by charging users to unlock additional functionality or to gain access to some form of premium content. This is a concept referred to as "In-App Purchase" (IAP) and is made possible by a collection of classes within the Store Kit Framework combined with settings configured using the iTunes Connect web portal.

Whilst in-app purchasing has been available for a while, iOS 6 now introduces the option to host content associated with purchases on Apple's own servers.

75.1 In-App Purchase Options

In-app purchase allows digital or virtual items to be purchased from within applications. These typically take the form of additional content (such as an eBook or digital magazine edition), access to more advanced levels in a game or the ability to buy virtual goods or property (such as crop seeds in a farming game).

Purchases fall into the categories of *consumable* (the item must be purchased each time it is required by the user such as virtual currency in a game), *non-consumable* (only needs to be purchased once by the user such as content access) and *subscription* based.

In the case of subscription based purchases, these can be *non-renewing* (item remains active for a specified amount of time), *auto-renewing* (the subscription is renewed automatically at specified intervals until cancelled by the user) or *free subscription* based (allowing free access to content for Newsstand based applications).

Non-consumable and auto-renewable purchases should be configured such that they can be restored, at the request of the user, on any of the user's iOS devices.

The item purchased by the user can either be *built-in* or *server* based. The term "built-in" refers to content or functionality that is already present in the application, but currently locked in some way.

589

Once the purchase has been made, the functionality is unlocked. Server based purchases involve downloading of the item from a remote server. This might, for example, be a new background image for a game or a file containing additional content.

Prior to iOS 6, it was the responsibility of the application developer to set up, configure and maintain a server system for server based in-app purchases. With the introduction of iOS 6, however, the downloadable content can be hosted either on the developer's own server or placed on an Apple hosted server (a concept referred to as *App Store hosted content*).

75.2 Uploading App Store Hosted Content

In the event that a purchase involves the download of additional content hosted on the App Store, this content must first be uploaded. The files containing the content are placed in a structured folder. The root level of the folder must contain a *ContentInfo.plist* XML file that contains two keys:

- **ContentVersion** – The version number of the content.
- **IAPProductIdentifier** – The product identifier of the product with which the content is associated

The actual content files must be placed in a subfolder named *Contents*.

In practice, much of the work involved in packaging and uploading content can be performed using either Xcode or the Application Loader tool as outlined in the chapter entitled *Configuring and Creating Hosted Content for iOS 6 In-App Purchases*.

75.3 Configuring In-App Purchase Items

The application developer is responsible for defining the products that are available for purchase. This involves assigning product identifiers, descriptions and pricing to each item and is performed using iTunes Connect.

75.4 Sending a Product Request

When the user needs to purchase one or more items, the application uses the Store Kit Framework to send a product request. The request is packaged in the form of an SKProductRequest object configured with product identifiers of one or more items to be purchased. The application should also check whether or not the user has used the Settings app to disable in-app purchases on the device before initiating the purchase:

```
if ([SKPaymentQueue canMakePayments])
{
    SKProductsRequest *request = [[SKProductsRequest alloc]
        initWithProductIdentifiers:
```

```
        [NSSet setWithObject:@"com.ebookfrenzy.consumable1"]];

    request.delegate = self;

    [request start];
}
else
{
    // Tell user that In-App Purchase is disabled in Settings
}
```

When the App Store has located and returned the product information, the Store Kit Framework calls the application's *didReceiveResponse:* delegate method passing it an object of type SKProductsResponse. This object contains an SKProduct object for each product that matched the request, along with a list of any product items for which a match could not be found in the store. If, on the other hand, the Store Kit was unable to contact the App Store, the *didFailWithError:* delegate method will be called to notify the application:

```
-(void)productsRequest:(SKProductsRequest *)request
didReceiveResponse:(SKProductsResponse *)response
{
    NSArray *products = response.products;

    for (SKProduct *product in products)
    {
        // Display the a "buy product" screen containing details
        // from product object
    }

    products = response.invalidProductIdentifiers;

    for (SKProduct *product in products)
    {
        // Handle invalid product IDs if required
    }
}
```

Each SKProduct object will contain product information (name, description and price) and a Boolean property indicating whether the product has associated with it downloadable content hosted on the App Store.

There is no SKStoreProductViewController equivalent for in-app purchasing. It is the responsibility of the application, therefore, to create and display a view where the user can review the product details (which should be extracted from the SKProduct object rather than hard coded into the application code) and initiate or cancel the purchase.

75.5 Accessing the Payment Queue

In order to process the purchase in the event that the user decides to buy the product, it will be necessary for the application to place requests on the application's *payment queue*. The SKPaymentQueue instance is not an object that is created by the application, but rather an existing object on which the application makes method calls. One such method call must be made in order to assign a *transaction observer object* to the queue:

```
- (void)viewDidLoad
{
    [super viewDidLoad];
    [[SKPaymentQueue defaultQueue] addTransactionObserver:self];
}
```

Since the payment queue continues to process requests independently of the application (and even in the event that the application exits) it is recommended that access to the payment queue and transaction observer object assignment takes place when the application is first launched. This will ensure that the application will be notified immediately of any payment transactions that were completed after the application last exited.

75.6 The Transaction Observer Object

The transaction observer object assigned to the payment queue can be an instance of any class within the application that implements the SKPaymentTransactionObserver protocol. Compliance with the protocol involves, at a minimum, implementing the *updatedTransactions:* method. If the application is required to download App Store hosted content, the *updatedDownloads:* method also needs to be implemented.

In the event that downloads are to be performed, the *updatedDownloads:* method will be called at regular intervals, providing status updates on the download progress.

75.7 Initiating the Purchase

In order to process the purchase, the application creates a payment request in the form of an SKPayment object containing the matching SKProduct object for the item (this is usually just a case of using the object passed through to the *productsRequest:* method). The payment request is then placed into the SKPaymentQueue which is then responsible for communicating with the App Store to process the purchase.

```
SKPayment *payment = [SKPayment paymentWithProduct:product];
```

```
[[SKPaymentQueue defaultQueue] addPayment:payment];
```

75.8 The Transaction Process

The payment queue will call the *updatedTransactions:* method on the observer object when the purchase is complete, passing through as an argument an array of SKPaymentTransaction objects (one for each item purchased). The method will need to check the *transactionState* property of each transaction object to verify the success or otherwise of the payment and, in the event of a successful transaction, either download or unlock the purchased content or feature.

Each SKPaymentTransaction objection contains a *downloads* property. This is an array containing an entry for each content package hosted on the App Store server that needs to be downloaded as part of the purchase. In the event that the purchase requires content downloads, these downloads can be initiated via a call to the *startDownloads:* method of the SKPaymentQueue instance.

```
-(void)paymentQueue:(SKPaymentQueue *)queue
updatedTransactions:(NSArray *)transactions
{
    for (SKPaymentTransaction *transaction in transactions)
    {
        switch (transaction.transactionState) {
            case SKPaymentTransactionStatePurchased:
                if (transaction.downloads)
                {
                    [[SKPaymentQueue defaultQueue]
                        startDownloads:transaction.downloads];
                } else {
                    // Unlock feature or content here before
                    // finishing transaction
                    [[SKPaymentQueue defaultQueue]
                        finishTransaction:transaction];
                }
                break;

            case SKPaymentTransactionStateFailed:
                [[SKPaymentQueue defaultQueue]
                        finishTransaction:transaction];
                break;

            default:
                break;
        }
    }
}
```

Building In-App Purchasing into iPhone iOS 6 Applications

Once started, the system will perform any necessary downloads in the background. As the download progresses, the *updatedDownloads:* method of the observer object will be called at regular intervals. Each time the method is called, it will be passed an array of SKDownload objects (one for each download currently in progress) containing information such as download progress, estimated time to completion and state.

Download state can be one of a number of values including active, waiting, finished, failed, paused or cancelled. When the download is completed, the file URL of the downloaded file is accessible via the *contentURL* property of the SKDownload object. At this point, the file is in temporary cache so should be moved to a permanent location (such as the Documents directory).

```
-(void)paymentQueue:(SKPaymentQueue *)queue updatedDownloads:(NSArray 
*)downloads
{
    for (SKDownload *download in downloads)
    {
        switch (download.downloadState) {
            case SKDownloadStateActive:
                NSLog(@"Download progress = %f",
                      download.progress);
                NSLog(@"Download time = %f",
                      download.timeRemaining);
                break;
            case SKDownloadStateFinished:
                // Download is complete. Content file URL is at
                // path referenced by download.contentURL. Move
                // it somewhere safe, unpack it and give the user
                // access to it
                 break;
            default:
                break;
        }
    }
}
```

Finally, for each transaction returned by the payment queue, and after the purchased feature or content access has been granted to the user, the application must call the queue's *finishTransaction:* method in order to complete the transaction. In the case of content downloads, any downloaded files must be moved from temporary cache to a safe location before this method call is made.

The hosted content package is downloaded in the form of a Zip file which may then be unpacked using one of a variety of freely available source code packages for iOS. One such package is SSZipArchive, details of which can be found at:

https://github.com/samsoffes/ssziparchive

75.9 Transaction Restoration Process

As previously mentioned, purchases that fall into the categories of non-consumable or auto-renewable subscription should be made available on any other iOS devices on which the user has installed the corresponding application. This can be achieved using the transaction restoration feature of the Store Kit Framework.

In order to restore transactions, the application makes a call to the *restoreCompletedTransactions:* method of the payment queue. The queue will then contact the App Store and return to the application (via the observer object) an array of SKPaymentTransaction objects for any previous purchases. Each object will contain a copy of the original transaction object which is accessible via the *originalTransaction* property. This may then be used to reactivate the purchase within the application and, if appropriate, download any associated content files hosted on the App Store.

It is important to be aware that restoration should not be performed automatically at application launch time. This should, instead, be implemented by providing the user with an option within the application to restore previous purchases.

75.10 Testing In-App Purchases

Clearly it would be less than ideal if the only way to test in-app purchasing was to spend real money to purchase the items. Fortunately, Apple provides what it calls a "sandbox" environment via which purchasing can be tested without spending any money.

By default, applications signed with a development certificate will automatically connect to the sandbox when purchases are made.

In order for the sandbox to be operable, it is necessary to create a test user using iTunes Connect and set up the products that are to be made available for in-app purchase.

75.11 Summary

In-app purchases present the application developer with additional sources of revenue by charging the user for content or to unlock additional features from within an application. In-app purchases can be consumable, non-consumable or subscription-based.

The item purchased by the user can be built-in, in that the functionality is unlocked internally within the application, or server based, whereby content is downloaded from a server. In terms of server based purchases, iOS 6 now provides the option to host the content on Apple's own servers.

Chapter 76

76. Preparing an iOS 6 Application for In-App Purchases

The previous chapter provided an overview of the mechanism by which an in-app purchasing can be implemented within iOS applications. The next few chapters will take this knowledge and put it into practice by working through the creation of an example application containing locked content that can only be accessed by the user after making an in-app purchase.

An important part of supporting in-app purchases occurs before any code is written and is the topic this chapter. These steps involve the creation of an App ID with in-app purchases enabled, configuration of code signing within Xcode and the use of iTunes Connect to create a test user, application and in-app purchase item. Once these steps have been outlined, the next chapter, entitled *An iPhone iOS 6 In-App Purchase Tutorial*, will focus on the application development process.

76.1 About the Example Application

The example application created in this chapter will simulate the requirements of a fictitious, multi-level game whereby the user is provided with access to level 1 when the game is first installed, but must make an in-app purchase to unlock access to a second level.

For ease of testing, the in-app purchase must be performed each time the application runs. In a real world situation, however, a purchase of this type would be considered to be a non-consumable purchase and the application would need to check at startup whether the purchase had been made and unlock the premium level appropriately.

76.2 Creating the App ID

In order to use in-app purchases, an application must be associated with an *explicit* App ID rather than a wildcard ID. For example, *com.ebookfrenzy.MyApp* is a valid App ID for in-app purchase, whilst *com.ebookfrenzy.** is not. In addition, the App ID must have In-App Purchase support enabled (this is the default setting for newly created explicit App IDs).

Create a new App ID specifically for the purposes of this example application by logging into your developer account on the Apple Developer portal (http://developer.apple.com) and selecting the iOS

597

Preparing an iOS 6 Application for In-App Purchases

Provisioning Portal. Within the Provisioning Portal, click on *App IDs* from the list in the left hand panel, followed by the *New App ID* button.

In the *Create App ID* panel, enter *InAppDemo* into the description field, select either your Team ID or a bundle seed ID and then input an appropriate Bundle Identifier (such as com.example.InAppPurchase).

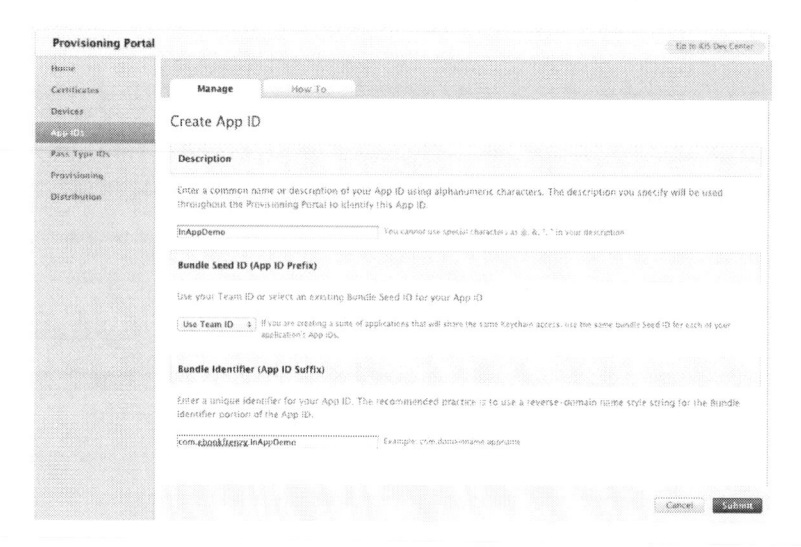

Figure 76-1

Once the appropriate settings have been entered, click on the *Submit* button to create the new App ID. On the App IDs page of the portal, locate the newly created ID (Figure 76-2) and review the settings to verify that In-App Purchase has been enabled for both production and development execution. In the event that In-App Purchase is listed as *Configurable*, click on the *Configure* link to enable support.

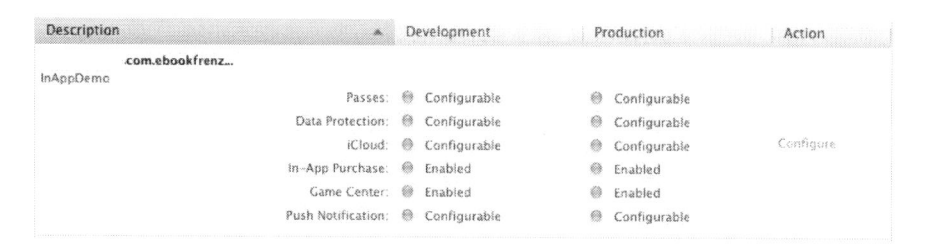

Figure 76-2

76.3 Creating the Provisioning Profile

With the App ID created, the next step is to create a provisioning profile for the application. Remaining within the Provisioning portal, select *Provisioning* from the left hand panel and click on the *New Profile* button. Enter *InAppDemo* as the profile name, select the appropriate certificates and

Preparing an iOS 6 Application for In-App Purchases

change the App ID to the new app id created in the previous section. Finally, set the check box next to each device on which the application is required to run during testing before clicking on the *Submit* button.

Upon returning to the list of provisioning profiles, the new profile will be listed as *Pending*. Use the browser refresh button to reload the page, at which point the profile should be listed as *Active*.

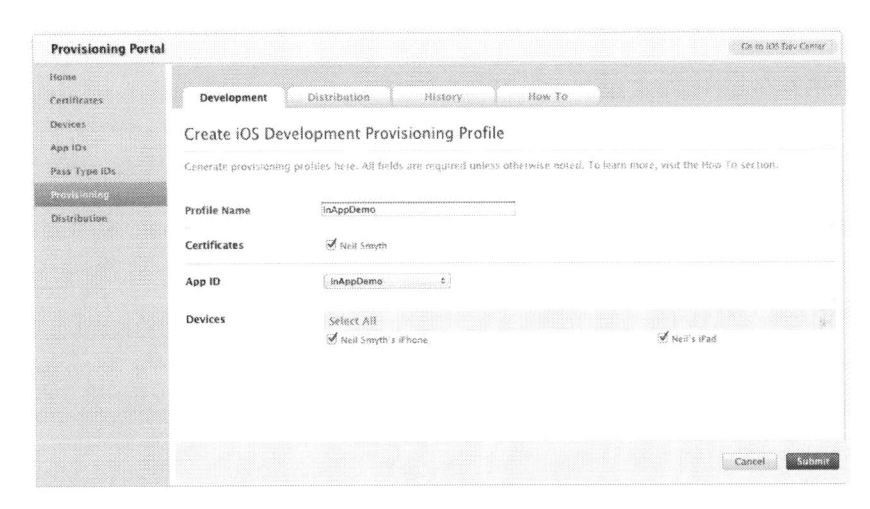

Figure 76-3

76.4 Creating the Xcode Project

Launch Xcode and create a new project based on the *Single View Application* template. Enter *InAppDemo* as the product name and class prefix. Check the *Bundle Identifier* field. This *must* match the identifier specified for the App ID created earlier in this chapter. If it does not match, in-app purchasing will fail.

Finally, make sure that Automatic Reference Counting and Storyboard support are enabled before proceeding with the project creation process.

76.5 Installing the Provisioning Profile

Before further steps are taken, it is vital that the previously created developer provisioning profile be downloaded and installed both on the development system and the target iPhone device. Attach the iPhone device to the development system and, within Xcode, display the *Organizer* by clicking on the button on the far right of the Xcode toolbar. Within the organizer, select the *Devices* tab followed by the *Provisioning Profiles* item in the left hand panel.

Click on *Refresh* located in the bottom right hand corner of the Organizer window and enter your developer program credentials if prompted to do so. Once the refresh is complete, the new *InAppDemo* profile should now be listed.

599

Preparing an iOS 6 Application for In-App Purchases

To install the profile onto the iPhone device, drag the profile and drop it onto the *Provisioning Profiles* entry beneath the device in the left hand panel. Click on the Provisioning Profiles entry beneath the device and verify that the *InAppDemo* profile is now listed.

76.6 Configuring Code Signing

When the application is compiled, it must be signed with the InAppDemo profile. To achieve this, click on the *InAppDemo* target located at the top of the project navigator panel on the left side of the main Xcode window. Within the main panel, select the *Build Settings* tab and scroll down to the *Code Signing* section.

Within the code signing section, locate the *Any iOS SDK* entry listed under *Debug* and click on the developer profile in the right hand column. This will cause a menu of available developer bundles to appear (Figure 76-4). From this menu, select the *InAppDemo* bundle.

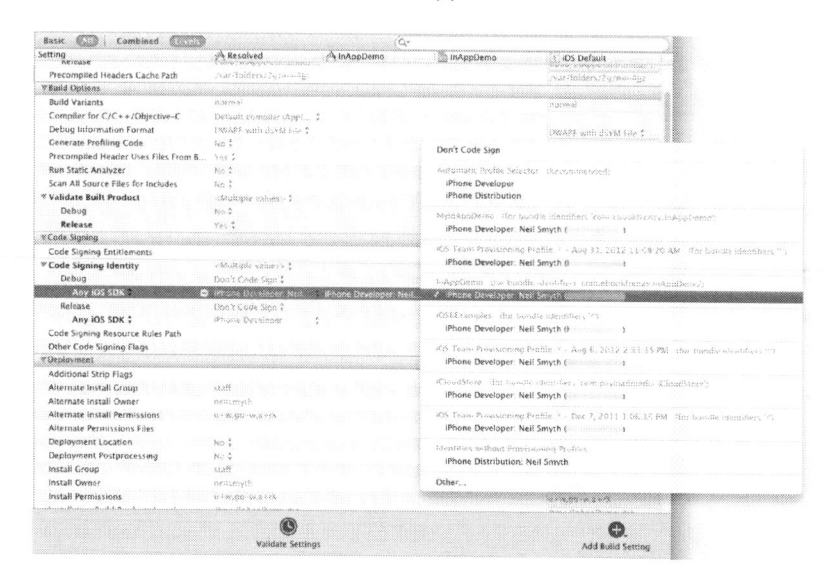

Figure 76-4

76.7 Configuring the Application in iTunes Connect

Enrollment in the Apple Developer program automatically results in the creation of an iTunes Connect account using the same login credentials. iTunes Connect is a web portal where developers enter tax and payment information, input details about applications and track the status of those applications in terms of sales and revenues.

Access iTunes Connect by navigating to *http://itunesconnect.apple.com* in a web browser and entering your Apple Developer program login and password details.

First time users should click on the *Contracts, Taxes and Banking* link and work through the various tasks to accept Apple's terms and conditions and to input appropriate tax and banking information for the receipt of sales revenue. Failure to complete these steps in advance may prevent in-app purchases from working.

In order to test in-app purchases using the sandbox feature, it is first necessary to create a test user account. These are the account details that will be entered on the device when testing in-app purchases. Within iTunes Connect, click on the *Manage Users* link, then *Add New User* followed by the *Test User* option. When prompted, enter the credentials for the test user, taking care not to try to use an email address already associated with an active iTunes account.

Once the administrative tasks are complete, select the *Manage Your Applications* option followed by *Add New App.* Provide an App Name (this must be a name that has not been used by another developer so may involve some trial and error) and a SKU Number (which can be any sequence of characters involving letters, numbers, hyphens, underscores and periods). From the Bundle ID menu, select the *InAppDemo* bundle created previously.

On the subsequent screens, configure information relating to pricing, availability, content and images before saving the new application configuration.

76.8 Creating an In-App Purchase Item

With the application configured, the next step is to add an in-app purchase item to it. Within iTunes Connect, select *Manage Your Applications*. A new screen will appear including any apps previously configured, including the new *InAppDemo* app. Click on the application in the list to navigate to the *App Information* screen as illustrated in Figure 76-5.

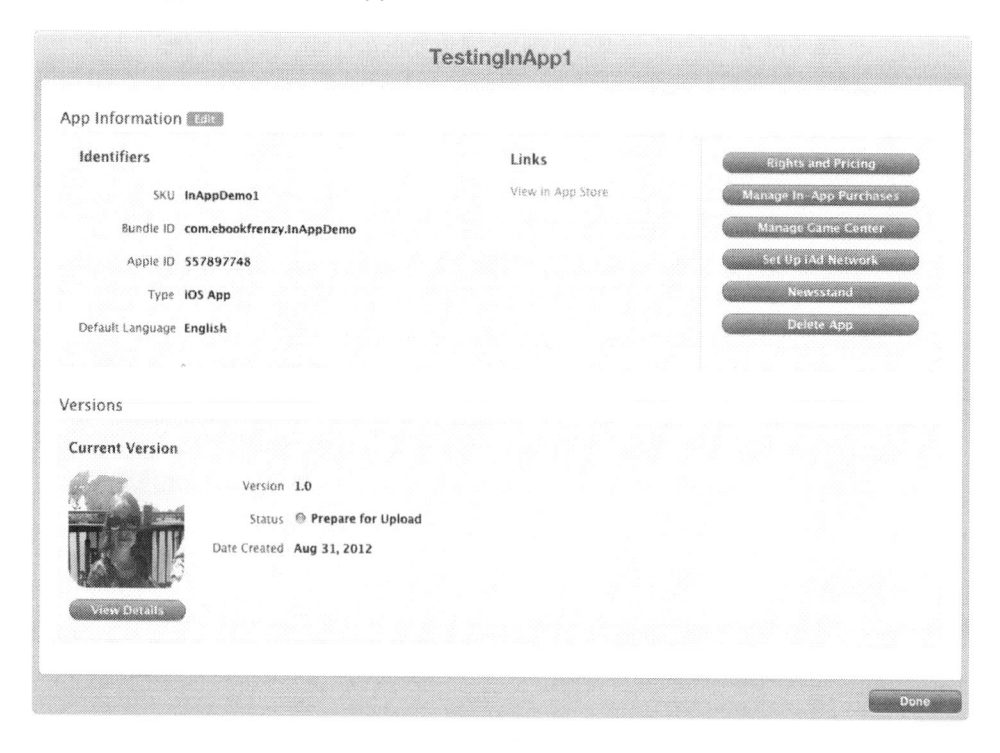

Preparing an iOS 6 Application for In-App Purchases

Figure 76-5

To configure an in-app purchase item, click on the *Manage In-App Purchases* button and, in the resulting screen, select the *Create New* button. From the list of in-app purchase types, select the *Non-consumable* option to move to the *In-App Summary* screen where the following information will be required:

- **Reference Name** – The name by which the item will be listed in iTunes Connect and in sales reports.
- **Product ID** – The unique product ID for the item. This is usually constructing using the bundle identifier of the application with which the purchase is associated. For the purposes of this example set the product ID to *com.ebookfrenzy.nonconsumable1*.
- **Price and Availability** – The price of the item and whether the item is available for sale. For this tutorial, set the *Price Tier* to 1 and *Cleared for Sale* to *Yes*.
- **In-App Purchase Details** – For each language the application is required to support, enter a Display Name and a Description for the item. Whatever you enter here will appear in the application later when the user is prompted to make an in-app purchase.
- **Hosting Content with Apple** – Indicates whether or not content will be hosted on Apple's servers for this purchase. For this example no content will be stored.

Once the settings have been configured, click on the *Save* button. Upon returning to the in-app purchases list, the new purchase item should be listed as *Waiting for Screenshot* and we are ready to start developing the application in the next chapter.

76.9 Summary

Before any code is written for the application, a number of important steps must first be performed in order to support in-app purchases. These include creating an appropriately configured App ID and configuring code signing of the application. The iTunes Connect portal is then used to create a test account for testing of purchases, an entry in the App Store for the application and to declare and create items for the user to purchase. All of these steps are important and, if not completed accurately, can lead to problems occurring in the purchasing process.

77. An iPhone iOS 6 In-App Purchase Tutorial

This chapter assumes that the steps outlined in the previous chapter (*Preparing an iOS 6 Application for In-App Purchases*) have been followed and implemented carefully. This chapter will continue the development of the *InAppDemo* project to demonstrate the application side of in-app purchasing.

77.1 The Application User Interface

When completed, the application will consist of three views (Figure 77-1). The goal is for the Level 2 view to be inaccessible from the Level 1 view until the user has made an in-app purchase using the product purchase view:

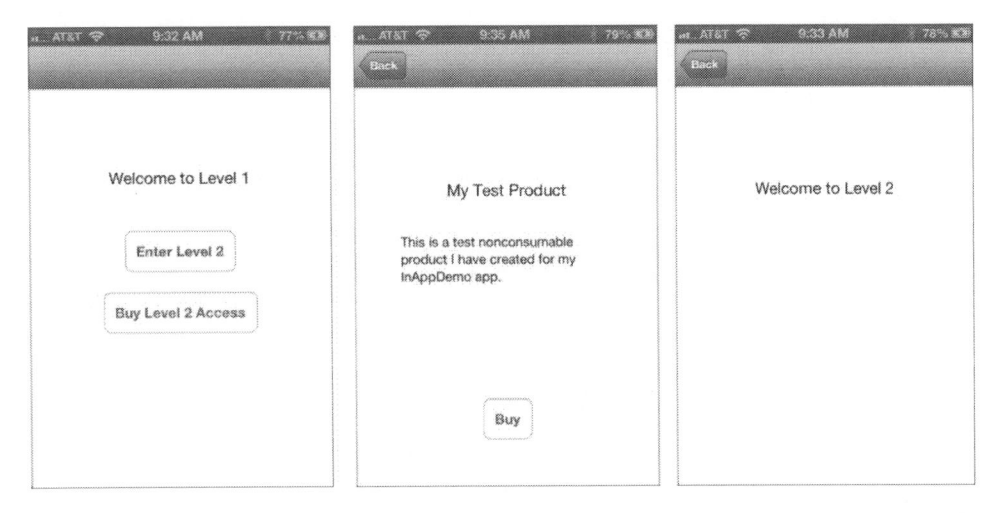

Figure 77-1

605

've# An iPhone iOS 6 In-App Purchase Tutorial

77.2 Designing the Storyboard

Load the *InAppDemo* project into Xcode, select the *MainStoryboard.storyboard* file, select the In App Demo View Controller scene and choose the *Editor -> Embed In -> Navigation Controller* menu option to add a navigation controller to the storyboard.

Next, design the user interface for the Level 1 screen as illustrated in the far left view of Figure 77-1. Using the Assistant Editor, establish an *Action* connection from the "Buy Level 2 Access" button to an action method named *purchaseItem:*. Also establish an *Outlet* connection for the "Enter Level 2" button named *level2Button*.

On completion of these steps, the *InAppDemoViewController.h* file should read as follows:

```
#import <UIKit/UIKit.h>
#import <StoreKit/StoreKit.h>

@interface InAppDemoViewController : UIViewController
- (IBAction)purchaseItem:(id)sender;
@property (strong, nonatomic) IBOutlet UIButton *level2Button;
@end
```

Add another scene to the storyboard by dragging and dropping a View Controller object from the Object Library onto the canvas. Add a label to the view of the new scene and change the label's text to "Welcome to Level 2".

Establish a segue from the "Enter Level 2" button to the Level 2 scene by Ctrl clicking and dragging from the button to the new scene. Release the line and select *push* from the resulting menu.

Finally, select the "Enter Level 2" button, display the Attribute Inspector and turn off the *Enabled* checkbox in the *Control* section. This will ensure that the button is disabled until the user has purchased access to level 2.

The completed storyboard should appear as shown in Figure 77-2.

An iPhone iOS 6 In-App Purchase Tutorial

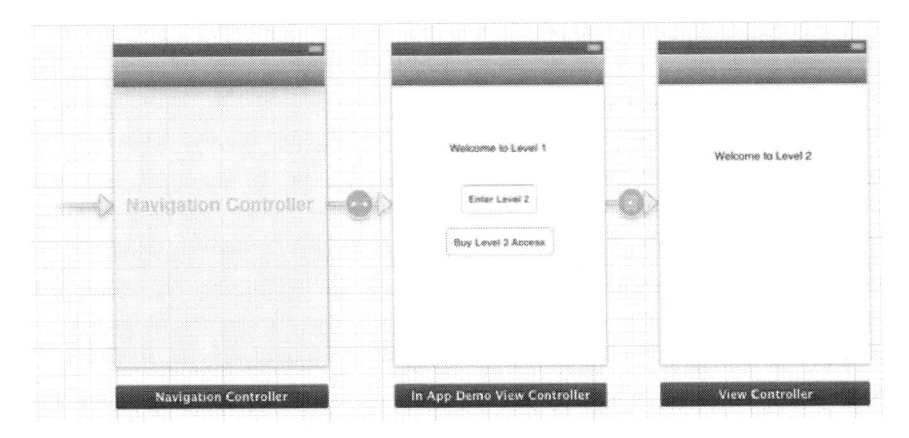

Figure 77-2

77.3 Creating the Purchase View Controller

Select *File -> New -> File...* and create a new Objective-C class named *PurchaseViewController* subclassed from UIViewController with the *With XIB for user interface* option selected. Select the *PurchaseViewController.xib* file and design the layout to match that shown in Figure 77-3, using Label, Text View and Button objects.

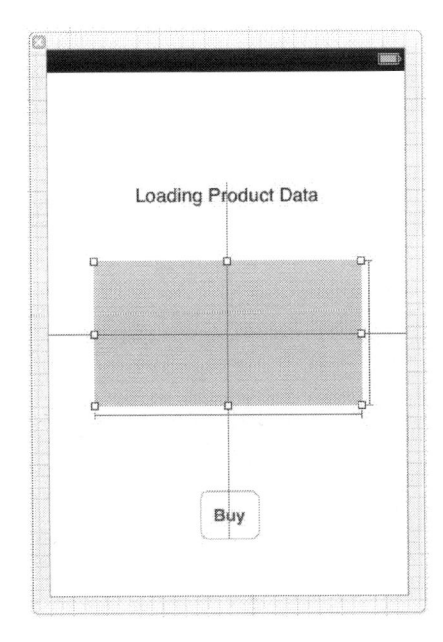

Figure 77-3

Using the Assistant Editor, establish *outlets* for the label, text view and button named *productTitle*, *productDescription* and *buyButton* respectively.

Next, establish an Action connection from the Buy button to a method named *buyProduct*.

An iPhone iOS 6 In-App Purchase Tutorial

Locate and select the *PurchaseViewController.h* file, verify the outlets and action are correctly implemented, then add additional properties and declarations that will be needed later in the chapter:

```
#import <UIKit/UIKit.h>
#import <StoreKit/StoreKit.h>

@interface PurchaseViewController : UIViewController
<SKPaymentTransactionObserver, SKProductsRequestDelegate>

@property (strong, nonatomic) SKProduct *product;
@property (strong, nonatomic) NSString *productID;
@property (strong, nonatomic) IBOutlet UILabel *productTitle;
@property (strong, nonatomic) IBOutlet UIButton *buyButton;
@property (strong, nonatomic) IBOutlet UITextView *productDescription;
- (IBAction)buyProduct:(id)sender;
-(void)getProductInfo:(UIViewController *)viewController;
@end
```

Since the class will use the Store Kit Framework, the *<StoreKit/StoreKit.h>* file has also been imported. The class is also going to act as the transaction observer and products request delegate so this fact is declared. Properties have been added to allow the class to keep track of the product ID and SKProduct object. Finally, a method named *getProductInfo:* which will be implemented later in the chapter has been declared.

77.4 Completing the InAppDemoViewController Class

In order to complete the InAppDemoViewController class implementation, select the *InAppDemoViewController.h* file and modify it to import *<StoreKit/StoreKit.h>* and *PurchaseViewController.h*. Also, declare a method named *enableLevel2:* and add a property to store a reference to an instance of the PurchaseViewController class.

```
#import <UIKit/UIKit.h>
#import <StoreKit/StoreKit.h>
#import "PurchaseViewController.h"

@interface InAppDemoViewController : UIViewController

- (IBAction)purchaseItem:(id)sender;
@property (strong, nonatomic) IBOutlet UIButton *level2Button;
@property (strong, nonatomic) PurchaseViewController *purchaseController;
-(void)enableLevel2;
```

An iPhone iOS 6 In-App Purchase Tutorial

@end

Open the *InAppDemoViewController.m* file and modify the *viewDidLoad:* method to create an instance of the PurchaseViewController class and to designate it as the transaction observer for the payment queue:

```objc
- (void)viewDidLoad
{
    [super viewDidLoad];

    _purchaseController = [[PurchaseViewController alloc]init];

    [[SKPaymentQueue defaultQueue]
        addTransactionObserver:_purchaseController];
}
```

When the "Buy Level 2 Access" button is selected, the *purchaseItem:* method is configured to be called. Locate the stub of this method and modify it as follows:

```objc
- (IBAction)purchaseItem:(id)sender {

    _purchaseController.productID =
            @"com.ebookfrenzy.nonconsumable1";

    [self.navigationController
            pushViewController:_purchaseController animated:YES];

    [_purchaseController getProductInfo: self];
}
```

Note that the product ID must match that defined for the in-app purchase item created using iTunes Connect in the previous chapter.

Finally, implement the *enableLevel2* method which will be called to enable the Level 2 access button once the purchase is complete:

```objc
-(void)enableLevel2
{
    _level2Button.enabled = YES;
}
```

The InAppDemoViewController class is now complete.

609

An iPhone iOS 6 In-App Purchase Tutorial

77.5 Completing the PurchaseViewController Class

The first steps in completing the PurchaseViewController class are to locally import the *InAppDemoViewController.h* file and use the class extension mechanism in the implementation file to declare a property that is private to the *PurchaseViewController.m* file in which to store a reference to the In App Demo View Controller object. Select *PurchaseViewController.m* in the project navigator, therefore, and modify it as follows:

```
#import "PurchaseViewController.h"
#import "InAppDemoViewController.h"

@interface PurchaseViewController ()
@property (strong, nonatomic) InAppDemoViewController
*homeViewController;
@end

@implementation PurchaseViewController
.
.
.
@end
```

Until the product information has been obtained, the buy button should be disabled so modify the *viewDidLoad:* method accordingly:

```
- (void)viewDidLoad
{
    [super viewDidLoad];
    _buyButton.enabled = NO;
}
```

When the user decides to purchase Level 2 access, the *getProductInfo:* method of the PurchaseViewController instance will be called by the InAppDemoViewController instance. Passed as an argument to this method will be a reference to the InAppDemoViewController instance which needs to be saved in the previously declared *homeViewController* property. It will then be the job of the *getProductInfo:* method to contact the App Store and get product information for the specified ID. The code for this belongs in *PurchaseViewController.m* and reads as follows:

```
-(void)getProductInfo: (InAppDemoViewController *) viewController
{
    _homeViewController = viewController;

    if ([SKPaymentQueue canMakePayments])
    {
        SKProductsRequest *request = [[SKProductsRequest alloc]
```

```
                    initWithProductIdentifiers:
                    [NSSet setWithObject:self.productID]];
    request.delegate = self;

    [request start];
    }
    else
        _productDescription.text =
            @"Please enable In App Purchase in Settings";
}
```

The request for product information will result in a call to the *didReceiveResponse:* delegate method which should be implemented as follows:

```
#pragma mark -
#pragma mark SKProductsRequestDelegate

-(void)productsRequest:(SKProductsRequest *)request
didReceiveResponse:(SKProductsResponse *)response
{

    NSArray *products = response.products;

    if (products.count != 0)
    {
        _product = products[0];
        _buyButton.enabled = YES;
        _productTitle.text = _product.localizedTitle;
        _productDescription.text = _product.localizedDescription;
    } else {
        _productTitle.text = @"Product not found";
    }

    products = response.invalidProductIdentifiers;

    for (SKProduct *product in products)
    {
        NSLog(@"Product not found: %@", product);
    }
}
```

Note that the above code displays the product information to the user and enables the Buy button. This is configured to call the *buyProduct:* method, the stub for which now needs to be completed:

An iPhone iOS 6 In-App Purchase Tutorial

```objc
- (IBAction)buyProduct:(id)sender {
    SKPayment *payment = [SKPayment paymentWithProduct:_product];
    [[SKPaymentQueue defaultQueue] addPayment:payment];
}
```

This code will initiate the purchasing process and cause calls to be made to the *updatedTransactions:* method of the transaction observer object. Since the PurchaseViewController instance was declared as the transaction observer, this method needs to be implemented in *PurchaseViewController.m*:

```objc
#pragma mark -
#pragma mark SKPaymentTransactionObserver

-(void)paymentQueue:(SKPaymentQueue *)queue
updatedTransactions:(NSArray *)transactions
{
    for (SKPaymentTransaction *transaction in transactions)
    {
        switch (transaction.transactionState) {
            case SKPaymentTransactionStatePurchased:
                [self unlockFeature];
                [[SKPaymentQueue defaultQueue]
                    finishTransaction:transaction];
                break;

            case SKPaymentTransactionStateFailed:
                NSLog(@"Transaction Failed");
                [[SKPaymentQueue defaultQueue]
                    finishTransaction:transaction];
                break;

            default:
                break;
        }
    }
}
```

Regardless of the success or otherwise of the purchase, the code finishes the transaction. In the event of a successful purchase, however, the *unlockFeature:* method will be called, and should now be implemented in *PurchaseViewController.m* as follows:

```objc
-(void)unlockFeature
{
    _buyButton.enabled = NO;
    [_buyButton setTitle:@"Purchased"
```

```
            forState:UIControlStateDisabled];
    [_homeViewController enableLevel2];
}
```

This method simply disables the Buy button, changes the text on the button to "Purchased" and calls the *enableLevel2:* method of the InAppDemoViewController instance, the reference to which was passed as an argument to the *getProductInfo:* method and stored in the private homeViewController property.

77.6 Adding the StoreKit Framework to the Build

Within the project navigator panel, select the *InAppDemo* target at the top of the list and in the main panel select the *Build Phases* tab. In the *Link Binary with Libraries* category, click on the + button and in the resulting list of libraries search for and add the *StoreKit.framework* library.

77.7 Testing the Application

Connect an iPhone device to the development system (in-app purchasing cannot be tested in the iOS Simulator environment). In the Settings application on the device, choose the iTunes & App Store option, select your usual account and choose *Sign Out* from the popup dialog.

Run the application and note that the "Enter Level 2" button is initially disabled. Touch the "Purchase Level 2 Access" button and, after a short delay, note that the product information appears on the purchase screen. Select the Buy button and wait for the purchase confirmation dialog to appear (Figure 77-4). Note that the dialog includes text which reads "[Environment: Sandbox]" to indicate that the sandbox is being used and that this is not a real purchase.

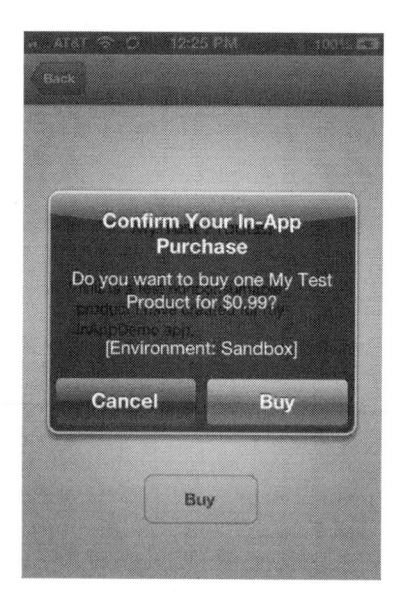

Figure 77-4

Confirm the purchase and, when prompted to do so, enter the test account details configured in the previous chapter. When the purchase is complete the Buy button will change to "Purchased" and Level 2 should now be accessible.

77.8 Troubleshooting

By just about any standard, in-app purchasing is a multistep process and, as with any multistep process, implementation of in-app purchases can be susceptible to errors.

In the event that the example application does not work there are few areas that are worthwhile checking:

- Verify that the application bundle ID matches the one used to create the provisioning profile and the app entry in iTunes.
- Make sure that the matching developer profile is being used to sign the application
- Check that the product ID used in code matches the ID assigned to the in-app purchase item in iTunes Connect.
- Verify that the item was configured as being available for purchase in iTunes Connect.
- Make sure that Tax and Banking details are entered and correct in iTunes Connect.
- Try deleting the application from the device and re-installing it.

77.9 Summary

This chapter has taken the steps to complete a demonstration of in-app purchasing from within an iPhone iOS 6 application and provided some guidance in terms of troubleshooting tips in the event that in-app purchasing does not work.

Chapter 78

78. Configuring and Creating App Store Hosted Content for iOS 6 In-App Purchases

As discussed in *Building In-App Purchasing into iPhone iOS 6 Applications*, iOS 6 provides the option to host the content associated with a server based in-app purchase on Apple's own App Store servers. This service is provided by Apple to application developers at no additional cost. Prior to iOS 6, it was the responsibility of the developer to set up and configure a server based system for server based in-app purchases.

The steps involved in implementing hosted content downloads from within application code were covered in the *Building In-App Purchasing into iPhone iOS 6 Applications* chapter. One area that has yet to be covered in detail, and the main focus of this chapter, involves the mechanism for creating the hosted content package and uploading it to the App Store server.

78.1 Configuring an Application for In-App Purchase Hosted Content

Before a hosted content package is created and uploaded, the corresponding application and in-app purchase product item must be configured in iTunes Connect. Assuming that the application is registered, select the application under the *Manage Your Applications* link and, within the App Information screen, click on the *Manage In-App Purchases* button.

Click on the *Create New* button on the In-App Purchases screen and select the type of purchase to be configured (for hosted content this is most likely to be non-consumable). Enter a reference name for the product (this will be used to list the product in iTunes Connect and within sales reports) and the product ID that will be used when referencing this product in the application code. Mark the product as cleared for sale, set a pricing tier and then specify a product title and description for at least one language.

Finally, set the *Hosting Content with Apple* option to *Yes* before saving the new product to the App Store. Once saved, the purchase will be listed by iTunes Connect as "Waiting for Upload".

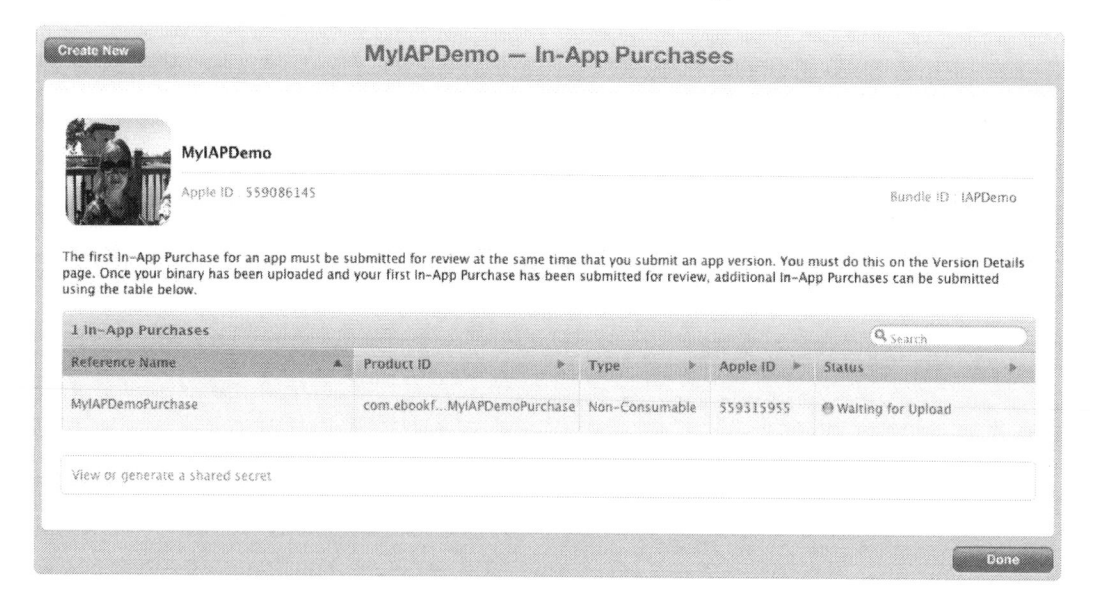

Figure 78-1

78.2 The Anatomy of an In-App Purchase Hosted Content Package

An in-app purchase hosted content package consists of a structured folder, the root level of which must contain a *ContentInfo.plist* file which, in turn, contains two keys:

- **ContentVersion** – The version number of the content.
- **IAPProductIdentifier** – The product identifier of the product with which the content is associated.

The folder must also contain a sub-folder named *Contents* in which resides the content files associated with the in-app purchase. App Store hosted content packages are limited to 2GB in size and must not contain executable code or content that violates any of Apple's guidelines.

78.3 Creating an In-App Purchase Hosted Content Package

The easiest way to create a hosted content package is to use Xcode. To do so, launch Xcode and create a new project. When prompted to select a template for the new project, select the *Other* entry listed under *iOS* in the left hand panel of the template screen and, in the main panel, select *In-App Purchase Content* as demonstrated in Figure 78-2:

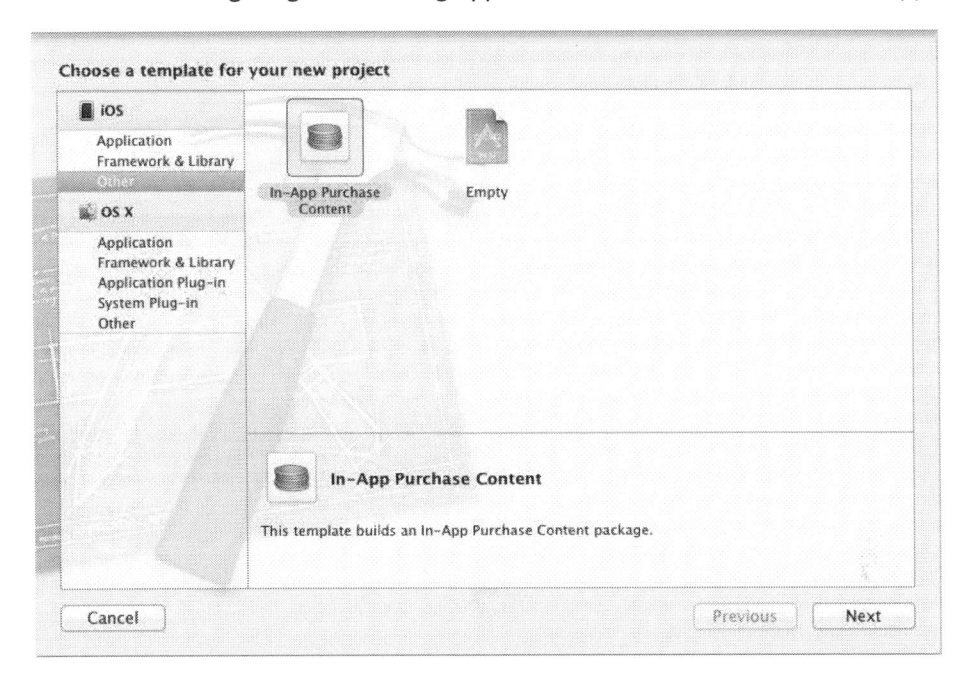

Figure 78-2

Click *Next*, and on the subsequent screen enter a name for the content package which matches the product ID of the purchase item as declared in iTunes Connect. Click *Next* and choose a location for the project before clicking on the *Create* button

Within the main Xcode screen, unfold the *Supporting Files* section of the project navigator panel and select the *ContentInfo.plist* file. Review the contents of the file and note that the version is set to 1.0 by default. Since this is the first version of the content this can be left unchanged. If the content is modified at any point in the future this version number should be incremented accordingly.

Using a Finder window, locate the content files that are to be hosted on the App Store and drag and drop them onto the *Supporting Files* header in the Xcode project navigator panel and click *Finish* on the resulting panel.

78.4 Archiving the Hosted Content Package

With the content configured, the next step is to create the hosted content package file. This is achieved by selecting the Xcode *Product -> Archive* menu option. Once the package has been created, display the Organizer window and select the *Archives* tab as shown in Figure 78-3:

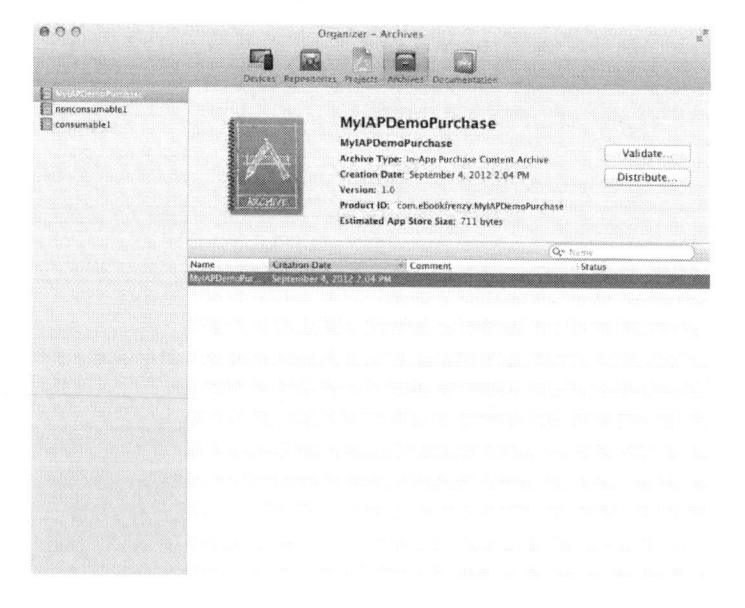

Figure 78-3

78.5 Validating the Hosted Content Package

Before the package is uploaded to Apple's servers, it should first be validated to ensure it does not contain ineligible content. To perform the verification, click on the *Validate...* button in the Organizer window and enter your Apple developer program credentials to verify that the content meets Apple's format guidelines. Xcode will then ask that the application and in-app purchase product for which the content is to be associated be selected from two drop down menus as illustrated in Figure 78-4.

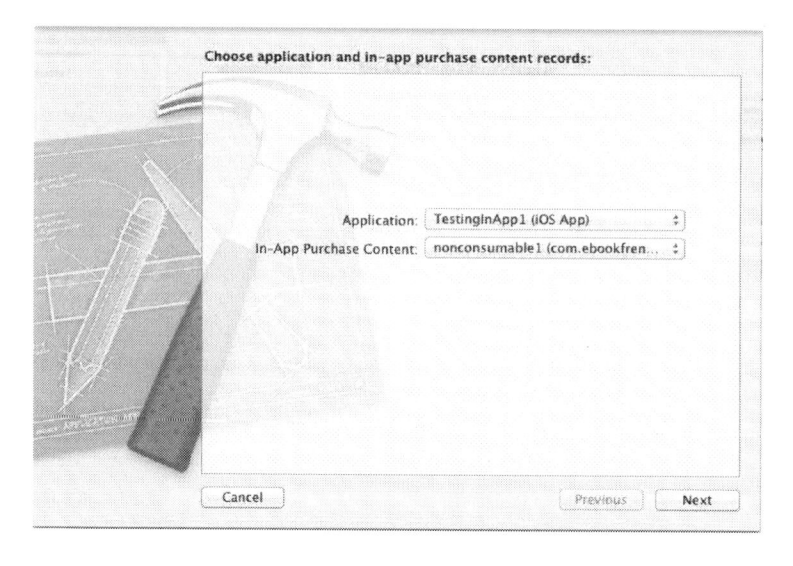

Figure 78-4

With the correct Application and In-App Purchase Content items selected, click *Next* to initiate the validation process. If the validation succeeds, the package is ready for upload. In the event that the validation fails, read the error description and make corrections to the content files accordingly.

78.6 Uploading the Hosted Content Package

Assuming validation was successful, click on the *Distribute...* button in the Organizer window and select the option to *Submit in-app purchase content*. Once again, enter your developer program credentials and select both the application and product ID to complete the upload process.

As an alternative to submitting the content within Xcode, select the option to *Export Package*, and then use the Application Loader tool to upload it to iTunes Connect.

Once the upload is complete, the hosted content package will be listed in iTunes Connect (Figure 78-5).

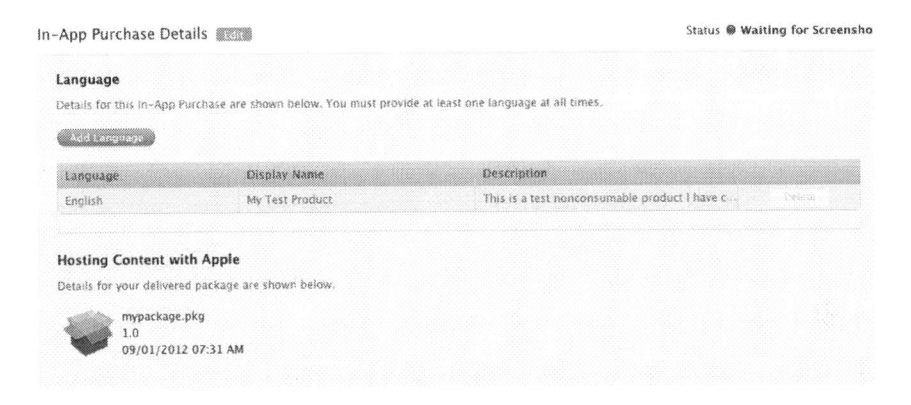

Figure 78-5

The content is now available for download as part of an in-app purchase using the steps outlined in *Building In-App Purchasing into iPhone iOS 6 Applications*.

78.7 Summary

In-app purchases can potentially include additional content that needs to be downloaded to the user's device as part of the purchase process. Prior to the introduction of iOS 6, the hosting of this content on a remote server was the responsibility of the application developer, including the associated security infrastructure to validate purchases prior to download.

iOS 6, however, introduced the ability to upload content packages for hosting on Apple's App Store servers. The steps to initiate in-app purchase downloads from the App Store were covered in the chapter entitled *Building In-App Purchasing into iPhone iOS 6 Applications*. This chapter has walked

Configuring and Creating App Store Hosted Content for iOS 6 In-App Purchases

through the steps involved in creating an App Store in-app hosted package and uploading it to the App Store.

Chapter 79

79. Preparing and Submitting an Application to the App Store

Having developed an iOS 6 iPhone application the final step is to submit it to Apple's App Store. Preparing and submitting an application is a multistep process details of which will be covered in this chapter.

79.1 Generating an iOS Distribution Certificate Signing Request

The first step in the application preparation process involves the creation of your iOS Distribution Certificate. This is achieved by first generating a *Certificate Signing Request* using the Mac OS X *Keychain Access* tool. Locate this tool by opening a Finder window, entering *Keychain Access* into the search box and selecting the *File Name* filter.

Once located and launched, perform the following steps to generate the CSR:

1. Select the *Keychain Access -> Preferences...* menu option and in the preferences panel select *Certificates* and verify that both the *Online Certificate Status Protocol (OCSP)* and *Certificate Revocation List (CRL)* are set to *Off*.

2. Select the *Keychain Access -> Certificate Assistant -> Request a Certificate from a Certificate Authority...* menu option. In the resulting dialog enter your email address and organization name as they appear in your iOS Developer program account. Leave the *CA Email Address* field blank and select the *Saved to disk* and *Let me specify key pair information* options before clicking *Continue*. Name the file appropriately and save it to a suitable location.

3. On the *Key Pair Information* screen, make sure that the *Key Size* is set to 2048 bits and that the *RSA* algorithm is selected before clicking *Continue*.

79.2 Submitting the Certificate Signing Request

The Certificate Signing Request created in the preceding section must now be submitted to the Apple developer provisioning portal for approval. The steps to achieve this are as follows:

623

Preparing and Submitting an Application to the App Store

1. Open a browser window, navigate to http://developer.apple.com and select the *Member Center* link. Once logged in, select the *iOS Provisioning Portal* link and click on the *Certificates* link located in the left hand panel. From within the Certificates screen click on the *Distribution* tab.

2. Click on the *Request Certificate* button and on the resulting *Create iOS Distribution Certificate* screen click on the *Choose File* button, selecting the previously created certificate signing request in the file selection panel. Once the file has been selected click on the *Submit* button.

3. After submission, the certificate will be listed as *Pending Issuance*. Use the browser refresh button to reload the page, at which point the certificate should be ready to download.

79.3 Installing the Distribution Certificate

Click on the *Download* button located next to the certificate and save the file to the local system. The file will be saved as *distribution_identity.cer*. Double clicking on the file will load it into the *Keychain Access* tool where it will be listed under *Certificates*.

79.4 Generating an App Store Distribution Provisioning Profile

Applications destined for the App Store must be re-built using a *Distribution Provisioning Profile* before they can be submitted. The steps to achieve this are as follows:

1. In the developer Provisioning Portal select the *Provisioning* link in the left hand panel and choose the *Distribution* tab in resulting screen.

2. Click on the *New Profile* button and select *App Store* from the *Distribution Method* options and provide a suitably descriptive name for the profile.

3. From the *App ID* menu select the ID corresponding to the application that is to be submitted to the App Store before clicking the *Submit* button. On the resulting screen the profile will be listed as *Pending*. Refresh the browser page and click on the *Download* button to save the profile to the local system.

4. Drag and drop the downloaded profile onto either the Xcode or iTunes icon in the dock to install it on the system.

79.5 Adding an Icon to the Application

Before rebuilding the application for distribution it is important to ensure that a launch icon has been added to the application. This is the icon that is used to represent your application on the home screen of the user's device. Two versions of this image must be provided in PNG format, one 57x57 pixel image for use on standard iPhone displays and another 114x114 pixel image for devices with a retina display.

Preparing and Submitting an Application to the App Store

Once these images are ready, launch Xcode and open the project for the application. Select the application target located at the top of the project navigator panel and scroll down the *Summary* page until the *App Icons* section comes into view. Locate the images in a Finder window and drag and drop them onto the corresponding *No image specified* place holders:

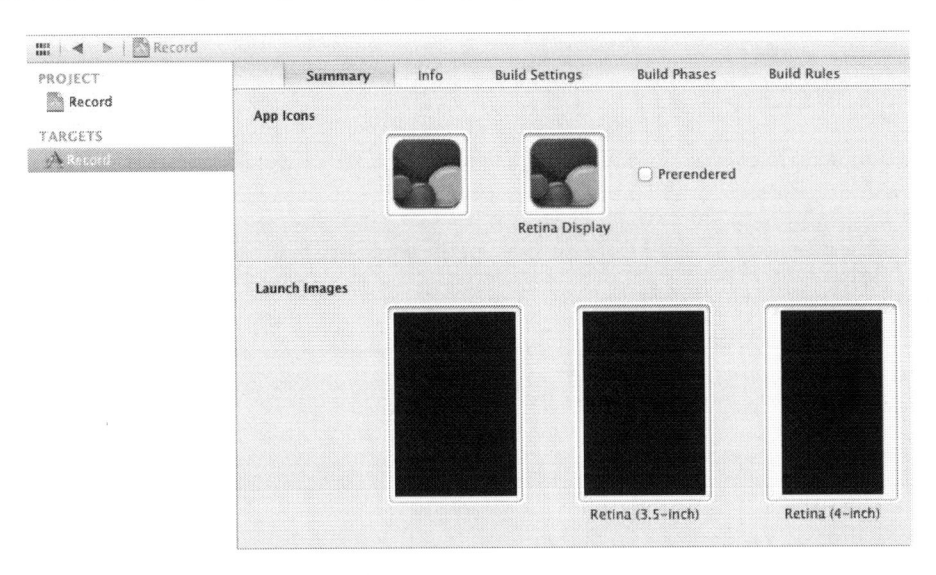

Figure 79-1

Similar steps may also be taken to upload splash images that will appear on the screen as the application loads by specifying *Launch Images*. Launch images are also required to be in PNG format and in 320x480 and 640x960 sizes.

79.6 Archiving the Application for Distribution

The application must now be rebuilt using the previously installed distribution profile. This involves using the *Archive* scheme for the project. In the toolbar of the main Xcode window is a drop down menu that displays the name of the application and the target on which the application will run when compiled. To view available schemes click on the application name and select *Manage Schemes...* from the menu as illustrated in Figure 79-2:

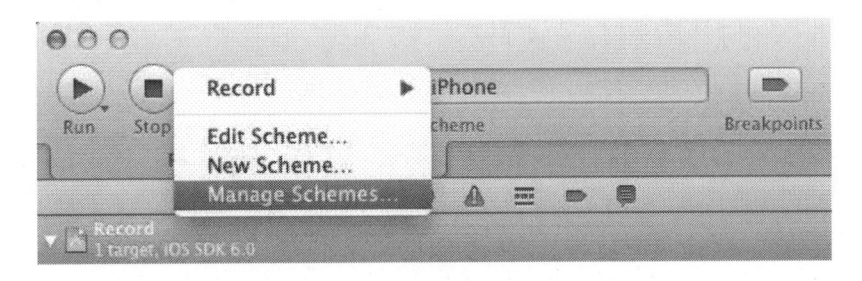

Figure 79-2

625

Preparing and Submitting an Application to the App Store

When the schemes panel appears, select the application from the list and click on the *Edit...* button to display the current list of schemes:

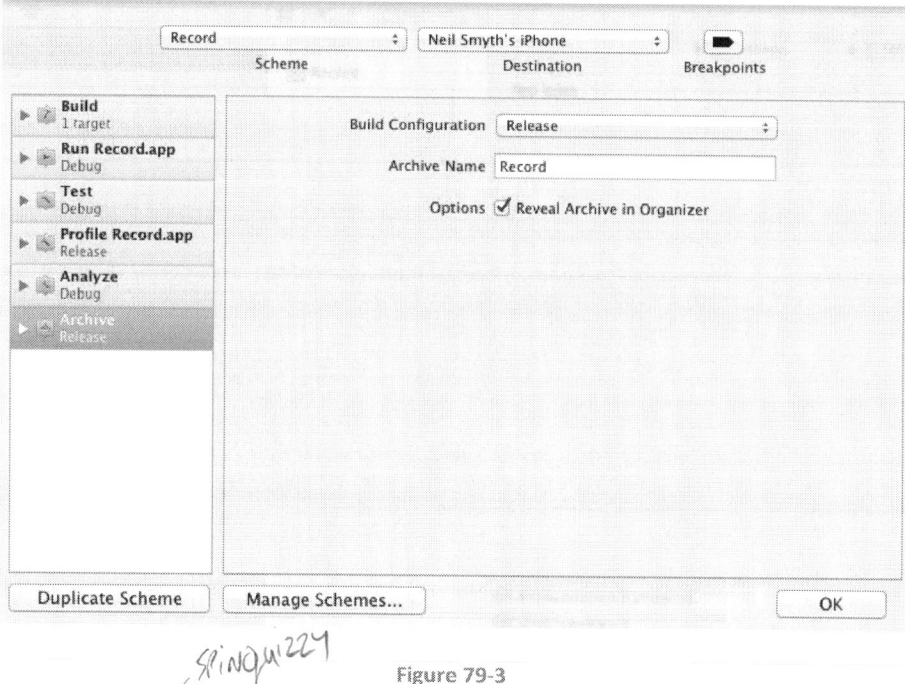

Figure 79-3

Select the *Archive* option located in the left hand panel as illustrated in Figure 79-3 and make a note of the *Archive Name* setting. Also verify that *Release* build configuration is selected and that the *Reveal Archive in Organizer* option is set before clicking on *OK*.

Next, select the application target name from the top of the project navigator, select *Build Settings* in the main panel and scroll down to the *Code Signing* section. Under the *Release* settings make sure that your desired iOS SDK target is selected and that the *Distribution* certificate is also selected. The following figure illustrates the *Release* build configured to use any SDK and to use the distribution certificate:

Figure 79-4

Preparing and Submitting an Application to the App Store

With the certificate selected and the correct build settings defined, select the Xcode *Product -> Archive* menu option. Xcode will proceed to archive the application ready for submission. Once the process is complete the archive will be displayed in the Organizer window:

Figure 79-5

79.7 Configuring the Application in iTunes Connect

Before an application can be submitted to the App Store for review it must first be configured in iTunes Connect. Enrollment in the Apple Developer program automatically results in the creation of an iTunes Connect account using the same login credentials. iTunes Connect is a portal where developers enter tax and payment information, input details about applications and track the status of those applications in terms of sales and revenues.

Access iTunes Connect by navigating to *http://itunesconnect.apple.com* in a web browser and entering your Apple Developer program login and password details.

First time users should click on the *Contracts, Taxes and Banking* link and work through the various tasks to accept Apple's terms and conditions and to input appropriate tax and banking information for the receipt of sales revenue.

Once the administrative tasks are complete, select the *Manage Your Applications* link and click on the *Add New App* button to enter information about the application. Begin by entering a name for the application and SKU of your own creation. Also select the bundle seed that matches the

Preparing and Submitting an Application to the App Store

application that has been prepared for upload in Xcode. Next, choose pricing information and specify an availability date before clicking on the *Continue* button. The remainder of the application configuration process involves specifying items such the version name, application description and ratings and then uploading images and screen shots.

Once the application information has been specified and saved a summary screen will appear similar to the one illustrated in Figure 79-6:

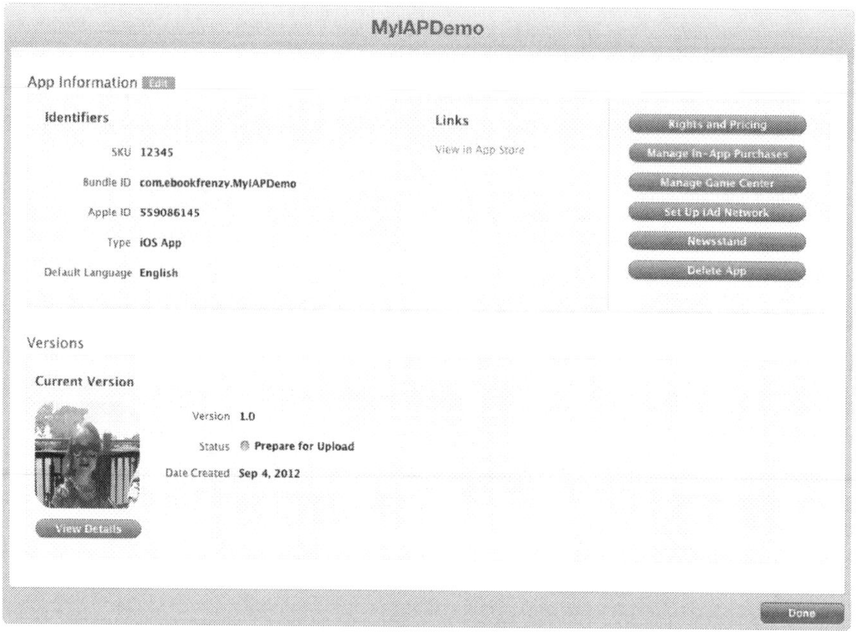

Figure 79-6

Click on the *View Details* button located beneath the application image and review the information for accuracy. Assuming that the information is correct click on the *Ready to Upload Binary* button, answer the question about cryptography and then click *Save*. The status of the application will now be listed as *Waiting for Upload* and you will receive an email message from Apple also notifying you of this fact.

79.8 Validating and Submitting the Application

To validate the application click, return to the Archives page of the Xcode Organizer Window, make sure the application archive is selected and click on the *Validate...* button. Enter your iOS Developer program login credentials when prompted to do so.

Xcode will connect to the iTunes Connect service and perform a validation check on the archived application. Assuming no validation errors were detected a screen similar to Figure 79-7 will appear:

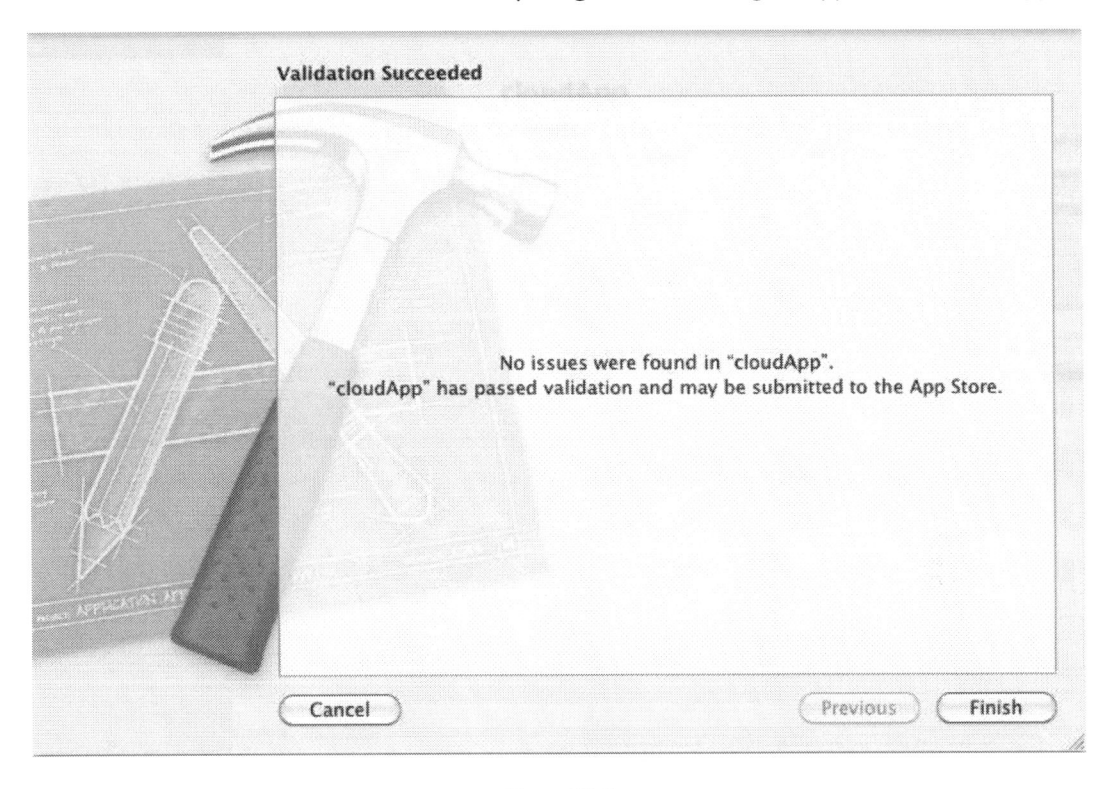

Figure 79-7

Click on the *Finish* button to dismiss the panel. The application is now ready to be uploaded for App Store review.

Make sure the application archive is still selected and click on the *Distribute...* button. Enter your developer program login credentials when prompted, select the application from the menu and proceed through the uploading process.

Once the upload is complete the application will automatically be submitted to Apple for review. Once the review is complete an email will arrive stating whether the application has been accepted or not. In the event that the application has been rejected, reasons for the rejection will be stated and the application may be resubmitted once these issues have been addressed.

Index

!

! · 52

&

&& · 52

@

@implementation · 60
@interface · 58

^

^ · 52

|

|| · 52

A

ACAccountType · 566
Accelerate Framework · 34
Account Framework · 565
Accounts Framework · 29, 550
Address Book Framework · 32
Address Book UI Framework · 28
Affine Transformations · 423
Alarms
    creating · 506
Alignment Rects · 115
AND · 52
Animation · 421
    example · 424
Animation Blocks · 421
Animation Curves · 422
App ID
    associating with app · 45
    creation · 43
    wildcard · 44
App Store
    creating archive · 625
    provisioning profile · 624
    submission · 623
ARC · 61
Archiving · 299
    example · 300
Assets Library Framework · 30
Attributes Inspector · 19
Audio · 535
Audio Formats · 535
Audio Support · 31
Auto Layout
    addConstraint: · 141
    Alignment Rects · 115
    Auto Resizing Translation · 142
    Automatic Constraints · 123
    Compression Resistance · 115
    constraintsWithVisualFormat · 155
    Content Hugging · 115
    Creating Constraints in Code · 139
    Cross Hierarchy Constraints · 147
    cross-view hierarchy constraints · 114
    Editing Constraints · 125
    Enabling and Disabling · 119

Index

Intrinsic Content Size · 115
introduction · 113
Removing Constraints · 145
user constraints · 123
Visual Format Language · 116, 153
Auto Resizing Translation · 142
Automatic Constraints · 123
Automatic Reference Counting · 61
autosizing · 114
AV Foundation framework · 31
AVAudioPlayer · 543
AVAudioRecorder · 543
AVFoundation Framework · 537

B

binary operators · 51
break statement · 55
Build Phases · 17
Build Rules · 17
Build Settings · 17
Bundle Identifier · 44, 46

C

Camera
    tutorial · 523
Camera and Photo Library · 517
Certificate Assistant · 40
Certificate Revocation List · 38
Certificate Signing Request · 40
CFNetwork Framework · 32
CGImageRef · 419
CIContext · 418
CIFilter · 418
CIImage · 418
Class
    renaming · 171
Class Methods · 59
CLGeocoder · 466
CLLocation · 466, 481
CLLocationManager · 481
CLPlacemark · 467
Cocoa Touch · 26

Collection View
    Cell and View Reuse · 370
    cellForItemAtIndexPath · 380
    data model · 377
    data source · 378
    deleting items · 387
    dequeueReusableCellWithReuseIdentifier · 371
    Designing cell prototype · 376
    didSelectItemAtIndexPath · 383
    gusture recognizers · 393
    Overview · 363
    prototype cell · 375
    scroll direction · 382
    sizeForItemAtIndexPath · 381
    Supplementary View · 383
    Tutorial · 373
company identifier · 16
Component Properties · 20
Compression Resistance · 115
Connections Inspector · 19
Constraints · 114
    Outlets · 148
    Removing · 145
constraintsWithVisualFormat · 155
container controller · 213
Container Views · 111
Content Hugging · 115
Controls · 111
Core Animation · 421
Core Audio Frameworks · 31
Core Data · 323
    Entity Description · 326
    Managed Object Context · 324
    Managed Object Model · 325
    Managed Objects · 324
    Persistent Object Store · 325
    Persistent Store Coordinator · 325
    stack · 323
    tutorial · 331
Core Data Framework · 32
Core Foundation Framework · 32
Core Graphics · 399
Core Graphics Framework · 30
Core Image Framework · 30, 418
Core Location
    basics of · 481

Index

Core Location Framework · 33
Core Media Framework · 32
Core Midi Framework · 31
Core OS Layer · 34
Core Services Layer · 32
Core Telephony Framework · 32
Core Text Framework · 29
Core Video Framework · 29
CRL · 38
cross-view hierarchy constraints · 114
CSR · 37, 40
Current Working Directory · 241

D

data encapsulation · 58
Default Property Synthesis · 73
Delegation · 81
dequeueReusableCellWithIdentifier · 193
design patterns · 79
Developer Program · 5
Development Certificate
    creation · 40
    installation · 41
Development Certificate Signing Request · 37
didFinishLaunchingWithOptions · 81, 333
Directory
    attributes of · 245
    changing · 242
    contents of · 245
    creating · 243
    deleting · 244
display
    dimension of · 417
Display Views · 111
Distribution Certificate Signing Request · 623
Documents Directory · 239
    locating · 241
dot notation · 63

E

EKAlarm · 506
EKCalendar · 504
EKEntityTypeEvent · 502
EKEntityTypeReminder · 502
EKEventStore · 502
Empty Application · 15
Event forwarding · 340
Event Kit Framework · 501
Event Kit UI Framework · 29
EventKit Framework · 33
External Accessory Framework · 34

F

Facebook
    integration · 549
false · 52
File
    access permissions · 248
    comparing · 248
    copying · 249
    deleting · 249
    existence of · 247
    offsets and seeking · 251
    reading and writing · 250
    reading data · 252
    renaming and moving · 249
    symbolic link · 250
    truncation · 253
    writing data · 253
File Inspector · 19
File's Owner · 90
first responder · 96, 97
Flow Layout
    extending · 389
font setting · 21
Forward Geocoding · 477
Foundation Framework · 33

G

Game Kit Framework · 28
Geocoding · 466, 477
geofencing · 505
Gesture
    identification · 353

633

Index

tutorial · 349
Gesture Recognition · 359
Gestures · 340
GLKit Framework · 31
Graphics Context · 400

I

iAd Framework · 29
iAds
    formats · 430
    guidelines · 430
    overview · 429
    tutorial · 431
IBAction · 80, 87
IBOutlet · 81, 87
iCloud
    application preparation · 262
    conflict resolution · 270
    document storage · 279
    enabled App ID · 262
    enabling on iPhone · 287
    entitlements · 264
    guidelines · 279
    key-value change notifications · 293
    key-value conflict resolution · 292
    key-value data storage · 291
    key-value storage restrictions · 292
    overview · 261
    provisioning profile · 263
    reviewing and deleting documents · 288
    searching · 280
    storage services · 261
    UBIQUITY_CONTAINER_URL · 267
Identity Inspector · 19
if statement · 53
Image I/O Framework · 29
In-App Purchase
    App Store Hosted Content · 590, 617
    code signing · 600
    hosted content package · 618
    options · 589
    Provisioning Profile · 598
In-App Purchase Item
    creation · 601

In-App Purchasing · 589
instance variables · 58
Interface Builder · 18
    simulated metrics · 121
Intrinsic Content Size · 115
iOS 5
    architecture · 25
iOS 5 SDK
    installation · 9
    system requirements · 9
iOS Developer Program · 5
iPhone
    app installation · 47
    enabling for development · 45
iTunes Connect · 627

K

key pair information · 38
keyboard
    hiding · 95
Keychain Access tool · 37, 41

L

libsqlite3.dylib · 315
LibSystem · 34
Local Notifications · 443
Location Accuracy · 482
Location Information · 481

M

main() routine · 67
Map Kit Framework · 28
Map Regions · 493
Map View Annotations · 499
MapKit Framework · 493
Master-Detail Application · 15
Media Player Framework · 31
Message UI Framework · 28
Method Ordering · 75
MKMapItem · 465

Index

example app · 475
options · 470
turn-by-turn directions · 470
MKMapView · 493
tutorial · 494
MKPlacemark · 465
creating · 468
Mobile Core Services Framework · 33
Model View Controller (MVC) · 79
Modern Objective-C · 73
MPMoviePlayerController · 531, 532
Multitasking · 437
application lifecycle · 438
Application States · 437
checking for support · 440
enabling and disabling · 439
Multitouch
enabling · 344
MVC · 79

N

navigation controller · 197
stack · 197
NewsstandKit Framework · 31
NIB file · 17
NSArray Literals · 76
NSData · 240
NSDictionary · 225
NSDictionary Literals · 77
NSDocumentDirectory · 241
NSFileHandle · 240
creating · 251
working with files · 251
NSFileManager · 240
creating · 247
defaultManager · 247
reading and writing files · 250
NSJSONSerialization · 577
NSKeyedArchiver · 300
NSKeyedUnarchiver · 300
NSLayoutConstraint · 116
NSMetaDataQuery · 280
NSNumber Literals · 75
NSSearchPathForDirectoriesInDomains · 241

NSString · 89

O

object copying · 66
Object library · 20
Objective-C · 49
class implementation · 60
class interface · 57
data types and variables · 49
do ... while · 55
expressions · 50
flow control · 53
for loop · 55
object oriented programming · 57
Open Audio Library · 31
Open GL Game · 15
OpenGL ES framework · 30
OR · 52
Organizer · 42
outlet
connecting · 92

P

Page-based Application · 15
Pathnames · 240
Picker components · 229
prepareForSegue
passing data · 202
Project Navigator · 17
Provisioning Portal · 40, 41
Provisioning Profile
creation · 44
installation · 44
Push Notification Service · 28

Q

Quartz 2D API · 399
Quartz Core Framework · 30
Quick Look Framework · 34

635

Index

R

Recording Audio · 543
Registered Apple Developer · 5
Reminders · 501
 accessing · 504
 creating · 505
 location based · 511
resignFirstResponder · 97
responder chain · 110, 339
restoration class · 451
Reverse Geocoding · 466
root controller · 170
Rounded Rect Button · 85

S

screen
 dimension of · 417
Security Framework · 34
Segue
 unwind · 165
Sent Events · 92
serialization · 299
setUbiquitous · 289
simulated metrics · 121
Sina Weibo · 550
Single View Application · 15
Size Inspector · 19
SKDownload · 594
SKPaymentQueue · 592
SKPaymentTransaction · 593
SKPaymentTransactionObserver · 592
SKProductRequest · 590
SKProductsResponse · 591
SKStoreProductViewController · 581
SLComposeViewController · 551, 554
SLRequest · 551, 565
 Facebook integration · 569
 Twitter integration · 573
 Twitter Integration · 566
Social Framework · 549
SQLite · 307
 application preparation · 309
 closing database · 314
 data extraction · 313
 database creation · 311
 example application · 315
 functions · 310
 on Mac OS X · 308
 overview · 307
 statement preparation and execution · 312
 table creation · 312
SQLite library · 33
State Preservation · 447
 opting in · 448
 Restoration Class · 463
 restoration identifiers · 449
 restoration path · 452
 shouldRestoreApplicationState · 456
 shouldSaveApplicationState · 456
State Restoration · 447
Store Kit Framework · 33, 581
Storyboard
 add navigation controller · 199
 add table view controller · 186
 Add view controller · 173
 add view controller relationship · 173
 change table view content type · 206
 design scene · 174
 design table view cell prototype · 188
 dynamic table view example · 185
 file · 157
 Insert Tab Bar Controller · 171
 prepareForSegue on table view cell · 202
 programming segues · 166
 scenes · 159
 segues · 161
 static table view · 205
 static vs. dynamic table views · 179
 Tab Bar · 169
 Tab Bar example · 170
 table view navigation · 197
 table view ovewrview · 179
 table view segue · 199
 unwind segue · 165
Structured Query Language · 308
Subclassing · 81
subview · 108
superview · 108

System Configuration Framework · 34

T

Tabbed Application · 15
Table View · 179
    cell styles · 181
    styles · 180
Taps · 340
Target-Action · 80
Temporary Directory · 242
Touch
    coordinates of · 346
Touch Up Inside · 92
Touches · 340
touchesBegan · 341
touchesCancelled · 341
touchesEnded · 341
touchesMoved · 341
true · 52
Twitter
    integration · 549
Twitter Framework · 29

U

UDID · 42
UIActionSheet · 111
UIActivityViewController · 551
UIActivityViewController · 549
UIActivityViewController · 557
UIAlertView · 111
UIApplication · 81
UIButton · 107
UICollectionView · 366
    cells · 365
    decoration views · 365
    dequeueReusableCellWithReuseIdentifier · 371
    registerClass · 370
    supplimentary views · 365
UICollectionViewCell · 366
UICollectionViewDataSource Protocol · 368
UICollectionViewDelegate Protocol · 369
UICollectionViewDelegateFlowLayout Protocol · 369

UICollectionViewFlowLayout · 367
    extending · 389
    layoutAttributesForItemAtIndexPath · 390
UICollectionViewFLowLayout
    layoutAttributesForElementsInRect · 392
UICollectionViewLayoutAttributes · 367
UIControl · 98, 111
UIDatePicker · 229
    example · 230
UIDocument · 269
    contentsForType · 269
    documentState · 270
    example · 270
    loadFromContents · 269
    overview · 269
    subclassing · 271
UIGestureRecognizer · 353
UIImagePickerController · 517
UIKit Framework · 27
UILabel · 89
UINavigationBar · 197
UINavigationController · 170
UIPageViewController · 213
    double sided · 215
    example · 217
    initialization · 224
    navigation orientation · 214
    spine location · 214
UIPickerView · 229
    data source · 233
    delegate · 233
    example · 233
UIScreen · 417
UIScrollView · 111
UITabBar · 169
UITabBarController · 170
UITableView · 111, 197
UITableViewCell · 179
UITextField · 89, 107
UITextView · 111
UIToolbar · 111
UIViewController · 81, 86
UIWebView · 111, 218
UIWindow · 107
Unique Device identifier · 42
user constraints · 123

637

Index

Utility Application · 15

V

Video Formats · 531
Video Playback · 531
View Controller State
   encoding and decoding · 457
view hierarchies · 107
views · 107
Visual Format Language · 116, 153
   constraintsWithVisualFormat · 155

W

windows · 107
WWDR intermediate certificate · 40

X

Xcode
   create project · 14
Xcode 4
   installation · 9
Xcode 4.5
   system requirements · 9
XIB file · 18
XOR · 52

Printed in Great Britain
by Amazon.co.uk, Ltd.,
Marston Gate.